New South Wales
& the ACT

a Lonely Planet Australia guide

Jon Murray

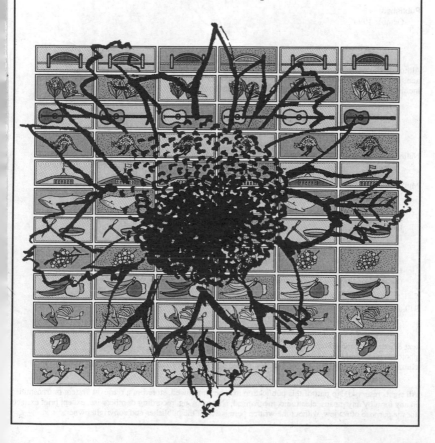

New South Wales & the ACT

1st edition

Published by
Lonely Planet Publications
Head Office: PO Box 617, Hawthorn, Vic 3122, Australia
Branches: 155 Filbert St, Suite 251, Oakland, CA 94607, USA
10 Barley Mow Passage, Chiswick, London W4 4PH, UK
71 bis rue du Cardinal Lemoine, 75005 Paris, France

Printed by
Colorcraft Ltd, Hong Kong

Photographs by
Mark Armstrong (MA), Mark Fraser (MF), Richard I'Anson (RI), Jon Murray (JM),
Richard Nebesky (RN), Bruce Pollack Publicity (BP), Paul Steel (PS)

Front cover: Australian characters outside Silverton Hotel, NSW
(Dianna Calder – Scoopix Photo Library)

Published
October 1994

National Library of Australia Cataloguing in Publication Data

Murray, Jon
New South Wales & the ACT – a travel survival kit.

1st ed.
Includes index.
ISBN 0 86442 223 7.

1. New South Wales – Guidebooks. 2. Australian Capital Territory – Guidebooks.
I. Title. II. Title: New South Wales and the Australian Capital Territory.
(Series: Lonely Planet travel survival kit).

919.4404

text & maps © Lonely Planet 1994
photos © photographers as indicated 1994
climate charts compiled from information supplied by Patrick J Tyson, © Patrick J Tyson, 1994

Magpies The black-and-white magpie (no relation to the European bird of the same name) has a distinctive and beautiful warbling call. Magpies can be aggressively territorial when nesting (around September). Being 'swooped' by a magpie is an unnerving experience as it dives at you silently from behind.

Reptiles

Snakes There are many species of snake in NSW all protected. Many are poisonous, some deadly, but very few are at all aggressive and they'll usually get out of your way before you even realise that they are there. See the Dangers and Annoyances section of the Facts for the Visitor chapter for ways of avoiding being bitten and what to do in the unlikely event that you are.

Lizards There is a wide variety of lizards, from tiny skinks to prehistoric-looking goannas which can grow up to 2.5 metres long, although most species you'll meet in NSW are much smaller. Goannas can run very fast and when threatened will use those big claws to climb the nearest tree – or perhaps the nearest leg!

Bluetongue lizards, slow-moving and stumpy, are children's favourites and are sometimes kept as pets. Their even slower and stumpier relations, shinglebacks, are common in the outback.

Introduced Species

The Acclimatisation Society was a bunch of do-gooders in the Victorian era who devoted themselves to 'improving' the countries of the British Empire by introducing plants and animals. On the whole, their work was a disastrous blunder.

Exotic animals thriving in NSW include rabbits, cats (big, bad feral versions of the domestic moggie), pigs (now bristly black razorbacks with long tusks) and goats. In the alps and towards the Queensland border you might see wild horses, mean brutes which travel in bad-tempered packs. All these have been disastrous for the native animals, as predators and as competitors for food and water.

Probably the biggest change to the ecosystem has been caused by another exotic animal: the sheep. To make room for sheep there was wholesale clearing of the bush, and the plains were planted with exotic grasses. Many small marsupials became extinct when their habitats changed, and major reasons for the incarceration and massacre of Aborigines were that they hunted sheep and resisted the theft of their land by graziers.

Disruption of Aboriginal land-management meant that there was no longer regular burning of the bush and plains, causing less-frequent but disastrous bushfires which fed on the accumulated growth, and a change in an ecosystem which depended on regular low-intensity fires for germination.

Sheep were the first hoofed animals to tread NSW's light, fine topsoil, and in a remarkably short time they had trodden it into a hard-packed mass which could not support many species of native flora and was vulnerable to erosion.

National Parks

There are more than 70 national parks in NSW, covering nearly four million hectares and protecting environments as diverse as

Kingfisher

the peaks of the Snowy Mountains, the subtropical rainforest of the Border Ranges and the vast arid plains of the outback. Many of the parks are World Heritage Areas of exceptional beauty and significance. Some parks include designated wilderness areas which offer outstanding remote-area walking.

The National Parks & Wildlife Service (usually called just National Parks) does a good job, and many national parks have visitor centres where you can learn about the area, as well as campsites and often walking tracks. Where there isn't a visitor centre, visit the nearest National Parks office for information. Bush camping (ie, heading off into the bush and camping where you please) is allowed in many national parks, but not all – check before you go.

The National Parks head office in Sydney has an information line (☎ (02) 584 6333) during office hours, although there are often long delays and the information is pretty general. For information on specific parks, it's better to call the ranger or district office.

There is, at least theoretically, an entrance fee to all national parks: about $7.50 per car for most and $12 *per day* for Kosciusko National Park. Camping fees are about $5, often less for bush camping.

There's a $50 annual pass which gives free entry (but not free camping) to all parks except Kosciusko. It probably isn't worth buying unless you plan a systematic coverage (not a bad idea, as there are some magnificent parks), but the $60 pass which includes Kosciusko is definitely worthwhile if you plan to visit Kosciusko plus a few other parks.

National Parks is also responsible for some other reserves. State Recreation Areas are set aside for recreation activities. They often contain bushland, but the quality of the forest might not be as good as in national parks. Many are centred on lakes or large dams where watersports are popular and they can be crowded in summer. There is often commercial accommodation (usually a caravan park), and bush camping is usually not permitted. There are exceptions to this, however.

Nature Reserves are generally smaller reserves, usually with day-use facilities, protecting specific ecosystems.

Historic sites protect areas of historical significance, such as the ghost town of Hill End near Bathurst and Aboriginal rock-art sites.

State Forests

State forests are timber reserves, most of which are are systematically logged. They cover around three million hectares and can be beautiful, although logging often means that the bush is young and of poor quality. Bush camping (free) is allowed in most state forests, but so are trail bikes, 4WDs, pets...

GOVERNMENT

Australia has a federal system of government, with elements of both the US and Westminster systems. The various state governments have no control over areas of national importance such as defence, foreign affairs and income tax, and they are dependent on the federal government for a lot of their funding. The High Court can overrule a state's Supreme Court. Apart from this, state governments are pretty much autonomous Westminster-style governments, with premiers occupying positions equivalent to that of prime minister. There are upper and lower houses in most states, both elected.

Australia's head of state is the governor general, and each state has a governor. Governors are technically the British monarch's representatives, although they are appointed by the various Australian governments.

Political Parties

There are three main parties. The Liberal Party isn't especially liberal – it's the party of the conservatives and stands for free enterprise, law and order, 'family values' and the like. The Liberals' most trenchant supporters have traditionally been British-oriented people blessed with 'old money', but this group is dwindling, and growing popular support for a republic has left the party in a quandary. The Liberals have held power in

NSW since 1988 and the current premier is John Fahey.

The Liberal's minority partner is the National Party, once the Country Party. The 'Nats' stand fair and square behind the man on the land (and his little woman) and are dead-set against dole-bludging and all that socialism stuff, but they are also damn sure that they want more government subsidies for agriculture... Issues raised at a recent National Party conference included the right to bear arms (as if there weren't already enough bullet-holes in country road-signs) and the worrying number of single mothers – they could cause inbreeding!

The Labor Party has been in existence for over 100 years and grew out of the great shearers' strikes last century. Socialist in a wishy-washy way and given to shooting itself in the foot, Labor has surprised everyone by holding onto federal government since 1983. The most recent Labor premier of NSW was the hapless Barry Unsworth who inherited the mantle from the charismatic Neville Wran.

The NSW state parliament includes several independents, including the entertaining Fred Nile, leader of the Festival of Light. Fred and his hard-core Christian cronies are against just about everything, and Sydney's Gay & Lesbian Mardi Gras really gets their blood boiling.

The ACT now has self-government (it used to be run by the federal government), although the scale of its activities is closer to that of a city council than a state.

ECONOMY

Australia is a relatively affluent industrialised nation, but much of its wealth still comes from agriculture and mining. NSW fits this pattern, with coal exports being the greatest earner of foreign exchange, followed by wool, iron and steel, cotton, and meat. Most of Australia's foreign trade is conducted in this state. As in the rest of Australia (and the rest of the world, seemingly), tourism is gaining in importance.

The main industry in the ACT is bureaucracy, although there's now a growing private sector.

POPULATION & PEOPLE

The population of NSW is approaching six million, over a third of Australia's total population. With well over four million people living within 100 km or so of Sydney, the rest of the state is sparsely populated. More than half the state has a population density of less than two people per square km.

The ACT's population is around 282,000, with almost everyone living in Canberra.

Like the rest of Australia, NSW has a very diverse population. Mass migration since WW II has profoundly changed Australia, and the success of multi-cultural policies is demonstrated by the remarkable lack of tension between ethnic groups, regardless of what their ancestors are doing to each other back home. There are occasional incidents such as brawls between soccer fans supporting different ethnically-based clubs, but the only real trouble has come from racist Australians of Western-European descent, and that doesn't amount to much beyond the loony ravings of White supremacist groups. Although there is occasional violence against people of non-European descent, there is nothing remotely like the racial tensions of Britain or Germany.

Approximately 20% of people in NSW were born in other countries and many more are children of people born in other countries.

If you come to Australia in search of a real Australian, you will find one quite easily – they are not known to be a shy breed. He or she may be a Lebanese cafe-owner, an English used-car salesperson, an Aboriginal musician, a Malaysian architect or a Greek greengrocer.

Aborigines

About 70,000 people in NSW considered themselves to be Aborigines or Torres Strait Islanders in the 1991 census.

Anglos

Although many Australians have British

ancestors, nearly all regard themselves as Australians, not British. The days of a privileged class regarding Britain as 'home' are long gone. While there have always been cultural similarities between the two countries, Australians have also felt a keen sense of separateness which could not be extinguished by the rhetoric of empire.

Non-Anglos

The 19th-century gold rushes brought the first wave of non-British immigrants to Australia. One group of long standing has been the Chinese, although racist policies saw them keep a fairly low profile until after WW II when the great waves of immigration began and prejudices waned.

After WW II, many Jewish survivors of the Holocaust came to Australia, along with many other European refugees. Subsequent large-scale immigration has drawn people from Italy, Greece, Turkey, Lebanon, Yugoslavia, the Pacific and, most recently, from South-East Asia and especially Vietnam. Many people from Hong Kong are just beginning to arrive in Australia, and significant minorities from many other countries also live here.

Although more recent immigrants tend to stay in the larger cities, you'll find non-Anglo-Celtic people all over the state. A country-town cliché used to be the Greek cafe; now there is hardly a town that doesn't have a Vietnamese restaurant. Where there are orchards or vineyards, chances are you'll find people of Italian descent, often Australians of many generations' standing. But as soon as you cross the Great Divide you're entering Anglo-Celtic country.

Note that Asia means the countries of the 'far east' to most Australians; people from the Indian subcontinent, the 'near east' and the 'middle east' are not commonly considered to be Asian. (Eurocentric terms are still often used, although the term 'our northern neighbours' is replacing 'far east'.)

ARTS & CULTURE
Aboriginal Arts & Culture

Many non-Aboriginal perceptions of Ab-

original cultures are just wrong. For example 'going walkabout' was not the shiftless, irresponsible wandering that non-Aborigines have portrayed it as. Very complex systems of trade, seasonal food gathering and religious duties meant that peoples travelled regularly, and social and economic ties between widely separated groups were maintained by regular meetings, developed over hundreds of centuries.

This lack of understanding is in part due to the fact that the initial, disastrous contact between Whites and Blacks was often undertaken by avaricious settlers who were hell-bent on grabbing land without regard for the British laws, much less the rights of the Aborigines. Not only were these Whites likely to act inhumanely but they were not interested in recording information about the cultures they were destroying.

Non-Aboriginals who oppose what they call 'the guilt industry' trot out the maxim that you can't judge historical events by today's standards, but even by 19th-century standards the treatment of Aborigines was

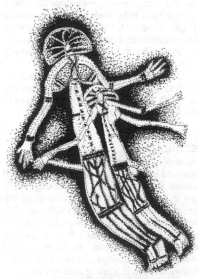

Aboriginal rock-painting

Top: Old building, Milparinka, far west (JM)
Middle: Dying country town, Riverina (JM)
Bottom: Old ferries, Darling Harbour, Sydney (JM)

Top: Family of emus, far west (JM)
Middle: Blue Mountains, near Sydney (JM)
Bottom: Winter morning, Hawkesbury River, near Sydney (JM)

very bad. And many of these abuses continued well into the 20th century.

Whites who were interested in other cultures, or were at least prepared to see Blacks as people rather than vermin, didn't arrive in most areas until Aboriginal cultures had been severely disrupted by disease and the loss of land. That's why northern Australia, which was settled by Europeans relatively recently, remains the stronghold of traditional cultures.

For a long time even enlightened Whites saw Aborigines as a pathetic, childlike race which was doomed to extinction. White appreciation of the richness and complexity of Aboriginal cultures is a recent phenomenon and came too late to save the cultures of many peoples in the areas which were settled early. However, much remains and even in NSW, the first area to be settled, Aborigines retain their links with the past.

Places in NSW where you can see concrete remains of traditional culture include rock-art sites in the Sydney area, (such as Ku-Ring-Gai Chase National Park), the Goulburn River National Park in the Hunter Valley, the Grenfell Historic Site near Cobar and Mootwingee National Park near Broken Hill. At Brewarrina there are the remains of large-scale stone fish-traps. On the far north coast, for example near Tweed Heads, there are *bora* rings, large ceremonial grounds, and all along the coast there are middens, piles of shells accumulated after centuries of shellfish feasts. Mungo National Park, south-east of Broken Hill, is a treasure-house of human history.

The NSW Central Mapping Authority produces an interesting map, *Aboriginal New South Wales*, which shows which peoples lived where at the time of European settlement and gives a rough idea as to the distribution of the various sites.

Today Most Aborigines in NSW live an urban life in towns, yet they remain distinctively Aboriginal. In Sydney the Tranby Aboriginal College is run by and for Aborigines and the suburb of Redfern has a large and vital Koori population. (Many Aborigines in south-eastern Australia describe themselves as Kooris). Right across the state you'll find Koori communities whose voices are at last beginning to be heard in the political process.

Assimilation policies have been discredited, but there are moves by many Koori communities to participate in the Australian economy on their own terms. Small industries producing Aboriginal-designed fashions are appearing, and in a few places in NSW (such as Bega and Forster-Tuncurry) Aboriginal-run tours will show you the country from the Koori perspective. One community near Glen Innes plans to open a fast-food joint selling bush tucker!

Probably the greatest contribution to non-Aboriginal understanding of contemporary Aboriginal culture has been made by rock musicians such as Yothu Yindi and Archie Roach. Not only do they play good music but they are uncompromisingly Aboriginal in outlook. That a song demanding a treaty between White and Black Australia could become a chart-topping dance hit would have been unthinkable just a decade ago.

Mainstream Arts & Culture

Australians' self-image as a resourceful, self-reliant people at home in the bush has never been strictly correct. That's not to say that the hardy pioneers, the lusty shearers, the tough bullockies with hearts of gold and the 'lithe, laughing girls, as handy with a horse as a teacup' didn't exist. They did, but they were objects of bemused admiration for the majority, who lived in towns. 'True blue' Aussie values, such as egalitarianism and willingness to give anyone a 'fair go', are still strong, but in today's multicultural society the narrowness and intolerance that went with them are vanishing. There are still plenty of rednecks out there, though.

It is an offence against the normal social practice of this community and we should do everything in our power to stop it.

**Small-town councillor on learning that
someone was behaving differently**

The popular myths about hard-riding, hard-

Traditional Aboriginal Culture
The Aborigines have a rich and complex culture, which flourished in Australia for over 40,000 years prior to the arrival of Europeans.

Society & Lifestyle Aborigines were traditionally tribal people living in extended family groups, or bands. Each band had a defined territory, within which were a number of spiritually significant places, known as sacred sites. It was the responsibility of the clan, or particular members of it, to maintain and protect the site in the correct way so that the ancestral beings were not offended and would continue to look after the clan. Traditional punishments for those who fell down in these responsibilities were often severe, as their actions could affect the whole clan's wellbeing – food and water shortages, natural disasters and mysterious illnesses could all be attributed to disgruntled or offended ancestral beings.

Many Aboriginal communities were semi-nomadic, while others were sedentary, one of the deciding factors being the availability of food. Where food and water were readily available, the people tended to remain in a limited area. When they did wander, however, it was to visit sacred places to carry out rituals, or perhaps take advantage of seasonal foods available elsewhere. The traditional role of the men was that of hunter, tool-maker and custodian of male law; the women reared the children, and gathered and prepared food. There was also female law and ritual which the women would be responsible for.

Environmental Awareness Wisdom and skills obtained over millennia enabled Aborigines to use their environment to the maximum. An intimate knowledge of the behaviour of animals and the correct time to harvest the many plants they utilised ensured that food shortages were rare. They never hunted an animal species or harvested a plant species to the point where it was threatened with extinction. Like other hunter-gatherer peoples of the world, the Aborigines were true ecologists.

Although Aborigines in northern Australia had been in regular contact with the farming peoples of Indonesia for at least 1000 years, the farming of crops and domestication of livestock held no appeal. The only major modification of the landscape practised by the Aborigines was the selective burning of undergrowth in forests and dead grass on the plains. This encouraged new growth, which in turn attracted game animals to the area. It also prevented the build-up of combustible

---

drinking Australians obscure the fact that there has always been a strong streak of free-thinking. Henry Lawson is well-known for his idealisation of mateship in the bush, but fewer people remember that his mother, Louisa, began publishing a feminist magazine, *The Dawn*, in 1888.

I suppose I'm stronger and taller than most women. And why shouldn't a woman be tall and strong? I feel sorry for some of the women that come to see me sometimes – they look so weak and helpless – as if they expected me to pick 'em up and pull 'em to pieces and put 'em together again. I try to speak softly to them but sometimes I can't help letting out...
Louisa Lawson

Cinema
The Australian film industry began as early as 1896, a year after the Lumière brothers opened the world's first cinema in Paris.

Maurice Sestier, one of the Lumières' photographers, came to Australia and made the first films in the streets of Sydney.

Cinema historians regard an Australian film, *Soldiers of the Cross*, as the world's first 'real' movie. It was first screened in 1901, cost £600 to make and was shown throughout America in 1902. A flourishing industry developed and over 250 silent feature films were made before the 1930s, when the talkies and Hollywood took over.

In the 1930s, film companies such as Cinesound sprang up. Cinesound made 17 features between 1931 and 1940, many based on Australian history or literature. *Forty Thousand Horsemen*, directed by Cinesound's great film-maker Charles Chauvel, was a highlight of this era of locally made and financed films which ended in 1959, the year of Chauvel's death.

material in the forests, making hunting easier and reducing the possibility of major bushfires. Dingoes were domesticated to assist in the hunt and to guard the camp from intruders.

Technology & Trade Similar technology – for example the throwing-stick (boomerang) and spear – was used throughout the continent, but techniques were adapted to the environment and the species being hunted. In the wetlands of northern Australia, fish-traps hundreds of metres long were built from bamboo and cord to catch fish at the end of the wet season. In the area now known as Victoria, permanent stone weirs many km long were used to trap migrating eels, while in the tablelands of Queensland finely woven nets were used to snare herds of wallabies and kangaroos.

Various goods found their way along the long trade-routes which criss-crossed the continent. Many of the items traded, such as certain types of stone or shell, were rare and had great ritual significance. Boomerangs and ochre were other important trade items. Along the trading networks large numbers of people would often meet for 'exchange ceremonies', where not only goods but also songs and dance styles were passed on. Near Brewarrina in the north-west of NSW you can still see ingenious stone fish-traps which caught fish to feed the huge gatherings there.

Cultural Life The simplicity of the Aborigines' technology is in contrast with the sophistication of their cultural life. Religion, history, law and art are integrated in complex ceremonies which depict the activities of the ancestral beings, and prescribe codes of behaviour and responsibilities for looking after the land and all living things. The link between the Aborigines and the ancestral beings is totems, and each person has his or her own totem, or Dreaming. These totems take many forms, such as caterpillars, snakes, fish and magpies. Songs explain how the landscape contains these powerful creator ancestors, who can still exert either a benign or a malevolent influence. They also tell of the best places and times to hunt and where to find water in drought years, and specify kinship relations and correct marriage partners.

Ceremonies are still performed in many parts of Australia. Many of the sacred sites are believed to be dangerous, and entry to them is prohibited under traditional Aboriginal law. These restrictions may seem to be based on superstition, but in many cases they have a pragmatic origin. For example, one site in northern Australia was believed to cause sores to break out all over the body of anyone visiting the area. Subsequently, the area was found to have a dangerously high level of radiation from naturally occurring radon gas. ■

Before the introduction of government subsidies in 1969, the Australian film industry found it difficult to compete with US and British interests. The New Wave era of the 1970s, a renaissance of Australian cinema, produced films like *Picnic at Hanging Rock*, *Sunday Too Far Away*, *Caddie* and *The Devil's Playground*, which appealed to large local and international audiences. Since the '70s, Australian actors and directors like Mel Gibson, Judy Davis, Greta Scacchi, Paul Hogan, Bruce Beresford, Peter Weir, Gillian Armstrong and Fred Schepesi have gained international recognition. Films such as *Gallipoli*, *The Year of Living Dangerously*, *Mad Max*, *Malcolm*, *Crocodile Dundee*, *Proof*, *The Man from Snowy River*, *The Year My Voice Broke* and most recently *Strictly Ballroom* have entertained and impressed audiences worldwide.

Painting

It's interesting to see what the first European landscape painters made of Australia. The colours seem wrong and the features they chose to depict aren't what we see as 'typically Australian'. But then, I was born here. Perhaps to a first-time visitor these paintings seem appropriate. Visit the Art Gallery of NSW in Sydney and see for yourself.

In the 1880s, artists were discovering, surprisingly belatedly, that the Australian landscape had its own moods and that the quality of light in Sydney was radically different to that in Europe. Major Australian artists, such as Arther Streeton and Tom Roberts, came to Sydney. Their paintings have virtually defined all subsequent reactions to the harbour and its surrounding bushlands. Similarly, Grace Cossington-Smith's paintings of the Harbour Bridge under construction in the 1930s also created enduring images of the city. In the 1940s, artists such as Sidney Nolan and Arthur Boyd again broke the mould, producing works which both reflected and helped define the country. The best known modern Sydney artist was Brett Whiteley, who died in 1992. As is so often the case in this fashion-conscious city, Whiteley's star status and lifestyle were as much a part of his popular success as the quality of his work – which was very high.

Sydney's annual Archibald Prize for portraiture usually manages to produce controversy, sometime resulting in court cases. The head of the Art Gallery of NSW was sued in 1993 for describing a painting hanging in the gallery as 'Yuk'!

Less academic but vigorous and distinctively Australian, the Brushmen of the Bush of Broken Hill, such as Pro Hart and Jack Absalom, produce naive works that are well worth seeing. Broken Hill, a mining town, has somewhat surprisingly become a major art centre.

Sydney has a huge range of interesting galleries, and in the larger country towns there are some very good regional galleries which often have important collections of local works and interesting visiting exhibitions. Many of these are well worth looking out for.

Literature

While Tom Roberts and his mates were developing a distinctive art style, there were a number of writers doing similar things with the written word.

Two of the first distinctively Australian writers to achieve popular acclaim were Henry Lawson (1867-1922) and A B ('Banjo') Paterson (1864-1941).

Paterson's generally cheerful poems and short stories (the film *The Man from Snowy River* is based on his poem) have to some extent been hijacked by the nostalgia industry, but they are worth reading if only to understand the myths being pushed by advertising agencies. Think of him as a distant relation of Kipling and you'll be on the right track.

Lawson is a different matter. A gloomy alcoholic for much of his life, he nevertheless wrote some extremely funny short stories, such as *The Loaded Dog*, as well as bitter reflections on the Australian way of life, such as *The Drover's Wife*. His poetry tends to be mawkish but it remains popular. A handy compilation of Lawson's work is *The Picador Henry Lawson* edited by Geoffrey Dutton (Picador Australia, paperback, about $25).

Less well-known, Joseph Furphy wrote only one book, but one that is arguably among the best ever written in Australia. *Such is Life* is on the surface a rambling and very funny series of bush yarns, but it is surprisingly modern in its construction and attitude.

Miles Franklin (1879–1954) made a decision early in her life to become a writer rather than a traditional wife and mother. Her best-known book, *My Brilliant Career*, was also her first. It was written at the turn of the century when the author was only 20, and brought her both widespread fame and criticism. She endowed an annual award for an Australian novel; today the Miles Franklin Award is the most prestigious in the country.

Another well-known writer of this century is Eleanor Dark, who in the 1940s wrote the historical trilogy *The Timeless Land*, *Storm of Time* and *No Barrier*. These covered the period 1788–1914, and were highly unusual at the time for the sympathetic treatment they gave to the Aboriginal culture.

The works of Nobel Prize-winner Patrick White are some of the best to come out of Australia. His better-known books include *Voss* (1957), *The Riders in the Chariot* and *The Eye of the Storm* (1973).

Other contemporary writers of note include Peter Carey, who has won both the Miles Franklin Award (for *Bliss* in 1981) and the Booker Prize (for *Oscar & Lucinda* in 1988); Thomas Keneally, who has won two Miles Franklin Awards and one Booker Prize and is well-known for his novels, such as *The Chant of Jimmy Blacksmith* and *Schindler's*

Ark (the film *Schindler's List* is based on it); Elizabeth Jolley, a novelist and short-story writer with a keen eye for the eccentric; and Thea Astley. David Ireland's *The Glass Canoe* is an excellent novel which explores urban life in general and pub culture in particular.

Less serious but offering an insight into the seamier side of Sydney is the work of crime-writer Peter Corris. Crime-writing has become something of a boom-genre and several other authors, such as Marele Day, have crime novels set in Sydney.

Architecture

Although NSW has some fine Georgian architecture, mainly in and around Sydney, the Victorian era has left the larger legacy. Any country town worth its salt has an impressive town hall complete with Corinthian columns. Older courthouses are also in neo-Renaissance style, with domes and colonnaded porticos, but those built around the turn of the century have a distinctive, heavy look to them.

Lands Department buildings are always worth looking out for (some are now state government offices). They are quite different from the more imposing public buildings, being often made of wood with nice touches such as shutters and fanciful fretwork. They seem to be the only large buildings which have attempted to beat the hot climate by cunning rather than sheer bulk.

Railway stations, post offices and banks are also often worth seeing.

The only private buildings to rival these shrines of government and business are pubs, but they make a pretty good fist of it. Although many country pubs are past their prime (the ubiquitous clubs have stolen their customers), many are still spectacularly grand buildings, and all dedicated to the thirst of workers.

Buried in most urban subconciousnesses is a myth about grand old homesteads commanding the plains, their broad verandahs dripping with iron lace. Unfortunately, it *is* a myth. The average farm might contain a roughly-built barn that was once the first

homestead, a wooden cottage falling into disrepair or housing the retired patriarch, and a modern brick-veneer house which is home to his son (yep; not many daughters get to inherit the family farm), the current farmer. There are exceptions in the districts settled early, but not many.

Around the turn of the century, Australia developed its own style of domestic architecture. Houses of the Federation style, as it is known, were built to make life in a hot climate comfortable, unlike the previous Victorian-era houses which were basically boxes with verandahs tacked on.

Modern Australian architecture struggles to maintain a distinctive style, with overseas trends dominating large projects and the lowest-common-denominator applied most to suburban housing. The most interesting 'modern' buildings are often recycled Victorian structures. There are some exceptions, such as the Convention Centre at Darling Harbour, designed by Philip Cox, and a few beachside homes dotted along the north coast. The museum in Kempsey is a little gem, designed by Glenn Murcutt.

The Historic Houses Trust of NSW (☎ (02) 692 8366) in Sydney at 61 Darghan St, Glebe, publishes a useful booklet, *Identifying Australian Houses*. It covers only Georgian, Victorian and Federation styles and doesn't go into a lot of detail, but it is worth having if you are interested in placing

Old and new architecture

buildings in their historical context. It costs about $3 per copy.

See the ACT chapter for the distinctive architecture of Canberra.

Music

In NSW you can hear everything from world-class opera to grungy pub bands. As with the other arts, most Australian music derives from foreign forms but often has a distinctive local twist.

Australian folk music is a mixture of English, Irish and Scottish roots, in much the same way that American folk music is. Bush bands, playing fast-paced and high-spirited folk music for dancing, can be anything from performers trotting out standards such as *Click Go the Shears* to serious musicians who happen to like a rollicking time. Fiddles and banjos feature, plus the indigenous 'lagerphone', a percussion instrument made from a great many beer-bottle tops nailed to a stick and shaken or banged on the ground. If you have a chance to go to a bush dance, take it! Aboriginal music is a strong influence on contemporary folk music. The Bush Music Festival in Glen Innes is a good place to sample a range of folk music.

Country music, of the American variety, is very popular west of the Divide, and Tamworth's big festival is the place to be if you want to wear fancy shirts and big hats. Some people say that country music is developing an Australian slant, but I can't really see it myself – just singing about Mudgee rather than Memphis doesn't really count.

The rock music scene is pretty interesting and although Sydney isn't such a breeding-ground of innovative groups as Melbourne is (introspection isn't a popular Sydney pastime), anyone who's anyone will play in Sydney eventually. See the Entertainment section in the Sydney chapter for some venues.

Out of the Mainstream

Although good ol' Aussie culture seems pretty all-pervasive, there is a lot of cultural diversity out there. For a start, there are the immigrants who maintain their cultures – the Queen's Birthday, Greek Easter and Chinese New Year are some of the events which are recognised by the wider community.

Gay & Lesbian Culture Gay and Lesbian culture is so strong, especially in Sydney, that it is almost mainstream. Sydney's Oxford St was proclaimed a Gay & Lesbian Precinct in 1993, and the Gay & Lesbian Mardi Gras is the most colourful event on the Sydney social calendar.

However, there's still a strong streak of homophobia among Dinkum Aussies, and violence against homosexuals is not unknown.

Publications such as the *g'day guide*, about $18, list places specifically catering to travelling gays and lesbians.

Alternative Lifestyles Probably the first Australians to seek an alternative lifestyle were the group who sailed for Patagonia in 1893 to establish Utopia. 'Back to the land' movements began in the late '60s around the Nimbin area and continue quite strongly today. State legislation legalised hamlet development in the '70s and throughout the Great Dividing Range there are communities whose lifestyles bear little relation to mainstream Australia's. Some even have their own barter systems, and it's a sign of how widespread this is that the Taxation Department is looking into ways of getting its piece of those non-currency transactions.

RELIGION

A shrinking majority of people in NSW are at least nominally Christian. Most Protestant churches have merged to become the Uniting Church, although the Church of England has remained separate. The Catholic Church is popular (about 30% of Christians are Catholics), with the original Irish adherents boosted by the large numbers of Mediterranean immigrants.

Non-Christian minorities abound, the main ones being Buddhist, Jewish and Muslim.

LANGUAGE

Any visitor from abroad who thinks Australian (that's 'Strine') is simply a weird variant of English/American will soon have a few surprises. For a start, many Australians don't even speak Australian – they speak Italian, Lebanese, Turkish, Greek or Vietnamese. English is the official and dominant language, but it's estimated that over 15% of people in NSW use a different language at home.

There is a slight regional variation in the Australian accent, while the difference between city and country speech is mainly a matter of speed. Some of the most famed Aussie words are hardly heard at all – 'mates' are more common than 'cobbers'. If you want to pass for a native, try speaking slightly nasally, shortening any word of more than two syllables and then adding a vowel to the end of it, making anything you can into a diminutive (even the Hell's Angels can become mere 'bikies') and peppering your speech with as many expletives as possible. The list that follows may help.

Glossary of Australian words

arvo – afternoon

avagoyermug – traditional rallying call, especially at cricket matches

award wage – minimum pay rate

back o' Bourke – back of beyond, middle of nowhere

bail up – hold up, rob, earbash

barbie – barbecue

barking up the wrong tree – labouring under a misapprehension

barrack – cheer on team at sporting event, support (as in 'who do you barrack for?')

battler – hard trier, struggler

beaut, beauty, bewdie – great, fantastic

big mobs – a large amount, heaps

bikies – motorcyclists

billabong – water hole in dried-up riverbed, more correctly an ox-bow bend

billy – tin container used to boil tea in the bush

bitumen road – surfaced road

black stump – where the 'back o' Bourke' begins

bloke – man

blowies – blowflies

bludger – lazy person, one who won't work

blue – argument or fight (as in 'have a blue')

bluey – swag, or nickname for a red-haired person

bonzer – great, ripper

boomer – very big, a particularly large male kangaroo

boomerang – a curved flat wooden instrument used by Aborigines for hunting

booze bus – police van used for random breath-testing for alcohol

bottle shop – liquor shop

Buckley's – no chance at all

bunyip – Australia's yeti or bigfoot

burl – have a try (as in 'give it a burl')

bush – country, anywhere away from the city

bushbash – to force your way through pathless bush

bushranger – Australia's equivalent of the outlaws of the American Wild West (some goodies, some baddies)

bush tucker – native foods, usually in the outback

BYO – Bring Your Own (booze to a restaurant, meat to a barbecue, etc)

camp oven – large, cast-iron pot with lid, used for cooking on an open fire

caniva... – please may I have a...

cask – wine box (a great Australian invention)

chook – chicken

chuck a U-ey – do a U-turn

cobber – mate (archaic)

cocky – small-scale farmer

come good – turn out all right

compo – compensation such as workers' compensation

counter meal, countery – pub meal

cozzie – swimming costume (togs, trunks)

crook – ill, badly made, substandard

cut lunch – sandwiches

dag, daggy – dirty lump of wool at back end of a sheep, also an affectionate or mildly abusive term for a socially inept person *daks* – trousers

damper – bush loaf made from flour and water and cooked in a camp oven

deli – delicatessen, milk bar in South Australia

didgeridoo – cylindrical wooden musical instrument played by Aboriginal men

dill – idiot

dinkum, fair dinkum – honest, genuine

dinky-di – the real thing

divvy van – police divisional van

dob in – to tell on someone

donk – car or boat engine

don't come the raw prawn – don't try and fool me

drongo – worthless person

dunny – outdoor lavatory

earbash – talk nonstop

esky – large insulated box for keeping beer etc cold

fair go! – give us a break

fair crack of the whip! – fair go!

flake – shark meat, used in fish & chips

fossick – hunt for gems or semiprecious stones

galah – noisy parrot, thus noisy idiot

game – brave (as in 'game as Ned Kelly')

gander – look (as in 'have a gander')

garbo – person who collects your garbage

gibber – Aboriginal word for stony desert

gizza... – please give me a...

give it away – give up

g'day – good day, traditional Australian greeting

good on ya – well done

grazier – large-scale sheep or cattle farmer

grog – general term for alcohol

grouse – very good

hoon – idiot, hooligan, yahoo

how are ya? – standard greeting (expected answer: 'good, thanks, how are *you*?')

icy-pole – frozen lolly water or ice cream on a stick

jackaroo – young male trainee on a station (farm)

jillaroo – young female trainee on a station

jocks – men's underpants

journo – journalist

a kangaroo short in the top paddock – 'not all there'; a bit silly, mad

knock – criticise, deride

knocker – one who knocks

lair – layabout, ruffian

lairising – acting like a lair

lamington – square of sponge cake covered in chocolate icing and coconut

larrikin – a bit like a lair

lay-by – put a deposit on an article so the shop will hold it for you

lollies – sweets, candy

lurk – a scheme

manchester – household linen

mate – general term of familiarity, whether you know the person or not

middy – 285 ml beer glass

milk bar – general store

mozzies – mosquitoes

no hoper – hopeless case

northern summer – summer in the northern hemisphere

no worries – she'll be right, that's OK

nulla-nulla – a wooden club, used by Aborigines

ocker – an uncultivated or boorish Australian

off-sider – assistant or partner

outback – remote part of the bush, back o' Bourke

paddock – field

pastoralist – large-scale grazier

pavlova – meringue and cream dessert, named after Anna Pavlova

perve – to gaze with lust

pineapple (rough end of) – stick (sharp end of)

piss – beer

pissed – drunk

pissed off – annoyed

piss turn – boozy party
piss-weak – no good; gutless
Pom – English person
pokies – poker machines
postie – mailperson
push – group or gang of people, such as
  shearers

ratbag – friendly term of abuse
ratshit – lousy
rapt – delighted, enraptured
reckon! – you bet!, absolutely!
rego – registration, as in 'car rego'
ridgy-didge – original, genuine
ripper – good (also 'little ripper')
root – have sexual intercourse
rooted – tired
ropable – very bad-tempered or angry
rubbish (ie *to rubbish*) – deride, tease

Salvo – member of the Salvation Army
sanger – sandwich
scallops – fried potato cakes in NSW; shellfish elsewhere
schooner – large beer glass
sealed road – surfaced road
sea wasp – deadly box jellyfish
semi-trailer – articulated truck
session – lengthy period of heavy drinking
sheila – woman
shellacking – comprehensive defeat
she'll be right – no worries
shoot through – leave in a hurry
shout – buy round of drinks (as in 'it's your
  shout')
sickie – day off work ill (or malingering)
smoko – tea break
snag – sausage
squatter – pioneer farmer who occupied land
  as a tenant of the government
squattocracy – Australian 'old money' folk,
  who made it by being first on the scene
  and grabbing the land
station – large farm
stickybeak – nosy person
strides – daks
stubby – small bottle of beer
sunbake – sunbathe (well, the sun's hot in
  Australia)
surfies – surfing fanatics

swag – canvas-covered bed-roll used in the
  outback; also a large amount

take the piss – send up, tease
tall poppies – achievers (knockers like to cut
  them down)
tea – evening meal
thingo – thing, whatchamacallit, hooza
  meebob, doo velacki, thingamejig
tinny – can of beer
too right! – absolutely!
trucky – truck driver
true blue – dinkum
tucker – food
two-pot screamer – person unable to hold
  their drink
two-up – traditional heads/tails gambling
  game

uni – university
ute – utility, pickup truck

wag (ie *to wag*) – to skip school or work
walkabout – lengthy walk away from it all
wallaby track (on the) – to wander from
  place to place seeking work (archaic)
weatherboard – wooden house
wharfie – docker
whinge – complain, moan
wowser – spoilsport, puritan
wobbly – disturbing, unpredictable behaviour (as in throw a wobbly)
woomera – stick used by Aborigines for
  throwing spears

yabbie – small freshwater crayfish
yahoo – noisy and unruly person
yakka – work (from an Aboriginal language)
yobbo – uncouth, aggressive person
yonks – ages; a long time
yous – the plural of 'you'. English needs a
  second-person plural, and 'yous' supplies
  it beautifully. However, because of snob-
  bery you won't hear anyone with any pre-
  tension to education using the word. If you
  think that Australia is an egalitarian
  society, try using 'yous' in an upmarket
  situation!

Aboriginal Language

It's an old joke that while Australians can say 'g'day' in any number of European languages, you're unlikely to meet a White Australian who can say it in an Aboriginal language.

At the time of European settlement there were around 250 separate Australian languages spoken by the 600 to 700 Aboriginal 'tribes', and some were as distinct from each other as English and Chinese. Often three or four adjacent tribes would speak what amounted to dialects of the same language, but another adjacent tribe might speak a completely different language.

It is believed that all these languages evolved from a single language family as the Aborigines gradually moved out over the entire continent and split into new groups. There are a number of words that occur right across the continent, such as *jina* (foot) and *mala* (hand), and similarities also exist in the often complex grammatical structures.

The number of Aboriginal languages has been drastically reduced. At least eight separate languages were spoken in Tasmania alone, but none of these was recorded before the native speakers either died or were killed. Only around 30 languages are today spoken on a regular basis and taught to children.

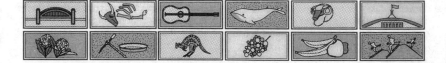

Facts for the Visitor

VISAS & EMBASSIES

Once upon a time, Australia was fairly free and easy about allowing visitors in, particularly if they were from the UK or Canada. These days, only New Zealanders get any sort of preferential treatment, and even they need at least a passport. Everybody else has to have a visa.

Visa application forms are available from Australian diplomatic missions overseas and some travel agents. There are several different types of visas, depending on the reason for your visit.

Australian Embassies

Australian consular offices overseas include:

Canada
    Suite 710, 50 O'Connor St, Ottawa K1P 6L2 (☎ (613) 236 0841); also Toronto and Vancouver
China
    15 Dongzhimenwai Dajie, San Li Tun, Beijing (☎ (1) 532 2331)
Denmark
    Kristianagade 21, 2100 Copenhagen (☎ 3126 2244)
France
    4 Rue Jean Rey, Paris, 15hme (☎ (1) 40 59 33 00)
Germany
    Godesberger Allee 107, 5300 Bonn 1 (☎ (0228) 81030); also in Frankfurt and Berlin
Greece
    37 Dimitriou Soutsou, Ambelokpi, Athens 11512 (☎ (01) 644 7303)
Hong Kong
    Harbour Centre, 24th floor, 25 Harbour Rd, Wanchai, Hong Kong Island (☎ (5) 73 1881)
India
    Australian Compound, No 1/50-G Shantipath, Chanakyapuri, New Delhi 110021 (☎ 60 1336); also in Bombay
Indonesia
    Jalan Thamrin 15, Gambir, Jakarta (☎ (21) 323109); also in Denpasar
Ireland
    Fitzwilton House, Wilton Terrace, Dublin 2 (☎ (01) 76 1517)
Italy
    Via Alessandria 215, Rome 00198 (☎ (06) 832 721); also in Milan

Japan
    2-1-14 Mita, Minato-ku, Tokyo (☎ (3) 5232 4111); also in Osaka
Malaysia
    6 Jalan Yap Kwan Seng, Kuala Lumpur 50450 (☎ (03) 242 3122)
Netherlands
    Camegielaan 12, 2517 KH The Hague (☎ (070) 310 8200)
New Zealand
    72-78 Hobson St, Thorndon, Wellington (☎ (4) 73 6411); also in Auckland
Papua New Guinea
    Independence Drive, Waigani, Port Moresby (☎ 25 9333)
Philippines
    Bank of Philippine Islands Building, Paseo de Roxas, Makati, Manila (☎ 817 7911)
Singapore
    25 Napier Rd, Singapore 10 (☎ 737 9311)
Sweden
    Sergels Torg 12, Stockholm C (☎ (08) 613 2900)
Switzerland
    29 Alpenstrasse, Berne (☎ (031) 43 0143); also in Geneva
Thailand
    37 South Sathorn Rd, Bangkok 10120 (☎ (2) 287 2680)
UK
    Australia House, The Strand, London WC2B 4LA (☎ (071) 379 4334); also in Edinburgh and Manchester
USA
    1601 Massachusetts Ave NW, Washington DC, 20036 (☎ (202) 797 3000); also in Los Angeles, Chicago, Honolulu, Houston, New York and San Francisco

Tourist Visas

Tourist visas are generally valid for a stay of up to six months within a 12-month period. If you intend staying less than three months, the visa is free; otherwise there is a $30 fee.

When you apply for a visa, you need to present your passport and a passport photo, as well as signing an undertaking that you have an onward or return ticket and 'sufficient funds' – the latter is obviously open to interpretation. Like those of any country, Australian visas seem to cause their hassles, although the authorities do seem to be more uniform in their approach these days.

Working Visas
Young visitors from Britain, Ireland, Canada, Holland and Japan may be eligible for a 'working holiday' visa. 'Young' is fairly loosely interpreted as around 18 to 26 years, and 'working holiday' means up to 12 months, but the emphasis is supposed to be on casual employment rather than full-time, so you are only supposed to work for three months. Officially this visa can only be applied for in your home country, but some travellers report that the rule can be bent.

Visa Extensions
The maximum stay is one year, including extensions.

Visa extensions are made through Department of Immigration & Ethnic Affairs offices in Australia and, as the process takes some time, it's best to apply about a month before your visa expires. There is an application fee – either $50 or $100 depending on the extension length – and even if they turn down your application they can still keep your money! Some offices are very thorough, requiring things like bank statements and interviews. Extending visas is a notoriously slow process, so allow plenty of time.

There's an office of the Department of Immigration & Ethnic Affairs in Sydney which handles visa extensions. It's at 88 Cumberland St, the Rocks (☎ (02) 258 4555). There are other offices in Sydney and in Canberra, Newcastle and Wollongong.

Foreign Embassies & Consulates
Canberra is home to most foreign embassies, but many countries maintain consulates in Sydney as well – see the Sydney and ACT chapters for addresses.

CUSTOMS
When entering Australia you can bring most articles in free of duty, provided that Customs is satisfied they are for personal use and that you'll be taking them with you when you leave. There's also the usual duty-free per-person quota of one litre of alcohol, 250 cigarettes and dutiable goods up to the value of A$400.

There are two other areas of concern. Number one is, of course, drugs. Customs has a positive mania about the stuff and can be extremely efficient when it comes to finding it. Unless you have a real desire to investigate prison conditions, do not bring any in with you.

Problem two is animal and plant quarantine: the authorities are naturally keen to prevent weeds, pests and diseases getting into the country. You can't import any animal or vegetable matter that might be a risk to Australia's agriculture, and that includes food items such as salami and fresh fruit and vegetables, and animal matter – maybe even the skin on that drum you bought in India. You can arrange to have wood and animal products fumigated, but it's at your expense and takes time.

Australia also prohibits the importation of products from endangered species. It's a long list, but basically you won't be able to bring in ivory or other elephant products, big-cat skins or many turtle products. And why would you want to?

When you leave, don't take any protected flora or fauna with you. Australia's unique birds and animals fetch big bucks from overseas collectors, and Customs comes down hard on animal smugglers. Penalties include jail sentences and huge fines.

MONEY
The unit of currency is the Australian dollar, which is divided into 100 cents. There are $100, $50, $20, $10 and $5 notes and $2, $1, 50c, 20c, 10c and 5c coins. It's easy to confuse the new plastic $5 and $10 notes, which look much more alike than did the old paper ones (which you still sometimes see). The 2c and 1c coins have been taken out of circulation, although prices can still be set in odd cents. Shops round prices up (or down) to the nearest 5c on your *total* bill, not on individual items.

It's nearly 30 years since decimal currency replaced pounds, shillings and pence, but no slang terms have appeared, other than the American 'buck' for dollar. The 'old money' had plenty of slang terms and older people might still refer to 'bob' (shilling, replaced by the 10c coin) or 'quid' (pound, once equivalent to $2).

There are no notable restrictions on importing or exporting currency or travellers' cheques, except that you may not take out more than A$5000 in cash without prior approval.

Exchange Rates

The Australian dollar swings quite a lot on the foreign exchange markets, generally fetching between US70c and US65c, so it's always worth checking the rates before changing a big wad of money. Approximate exchange values are:

Canadian dollars	C$1	=	A$1.02
Deutsche marks	DM1	=	A$0.85
Dutch guilders	Dfl1	=	A$0.75
Hong Kong dollars	HK$10	=	A$1.82
Japanese yen	¥100	=	A$1.37
New Zealand dollars	NZ$1	=	A$0.81
Pounds sterling	UK£1	=	A$2.10
Singapore dollars	S$1	=	A$0.90
US dollars	US$1	=	A$1.40

Changing Money

There are money-changing services at Sydney's Kingsford-Smith Airport and at quite a few other places around the city, including Circular Quay, but their rates are generally not as good as you'll get in a bank. The Westpac bank has a branch at the airport.

Travellers' Cheques

American Express, Thomas Cook and other well-known brands of travellers' cheques can be changed at most banks in the state. A passport will usually be adequate for identification; it would be sensible to carry a driver's licence, credit cards or a plane ticket in case of problems.

If your cheques are in A$ most banks do not charge a fee, although some individual branches do. Foreign currency travellers' cheques attract a fee, sometimes hefty and

sometimes varying between branches of the same bank. The Commonwealth Bank tends to charge the lowest fees.

Australia Post issues its own version of travellers' cheques, called travellers' money orders. These cost $1 each, which is more than the usual 1% commission on travellers' cheques unless you buy the $100 size. With so many post offices where you can cash them they might be handy, although they can't be used outside Australia. Replacing lost or stolen money orders could be slow.

Credit Cards

Visa and MasterCard are widely accepted. American Express and to a lesser extent Diners Club are also common, but don't expect every country motel to take every card. Cash advances from credit cards are available over the counter and from many automatic teller machines (ATMs), depending on the card.

A credit card makes renting a car much simpler; they're looked upon with much greater favour than nasty old cash, and many agencies simply won't rent you a vehicle if you don't have a card.

Local Bank Accounts

Opening a bank account is the simplest way to keep your money safe and you'll even earn a little interest (which will be automatically taxed at 10%).

For the first six weeks after you arrive in Australia you can open a bank account using only your passport as ID, but after that you will need to supply a lot of other ID, such as a birth certificate. This can be a major hassle.

Westpac (which was the Bank of NSW, the first bank in Australia, before a corporate facelift) has branches all over the state and throughout Australia. The Commonwealth Bank has fewer branches but it is government-owned and all post offices are agencies for the bank. You can use either a passbook (if it has a blacklight signature) or a card at post offices.

Other major banks include the National, the ANZ and, in NSW, the State Bank of NSW.

Passbook accounts can be opened at any branch. You usually have to return to the same branch to close the account when the time comes to leave Australia, but that isn't a hassle unless you care about the last dollar.

If you want a card account you'll have to wait about a week, and many banks (including Westpac) will only mail the card to an address; you can't go into the bank and pick it up.

Card accounts are handy because you can get after-hours cash at ATMs, but you won't necessarily find these in small towns. With a passbook account you're restricted to banking hours, but you don't have to worry about forgetting your personal identification number (PIN). It's a major hassle if you do, as they have to issue you a whole new card. There is a limit on how much you can withdraw each day from your card account. This varies from bank to bank but is usually $400 to $500 per day.

Many businesses, such as service stations, supermarkets and convenience stores, are linked into the EFTPOS system (Electronic Funds Transfer at Point Of Sale), which allows you to use your card to pay for services or purchases direct, and sometimes to withdraw cash as well. Cards (either credit cards or bank-account cards) can be used to make local, STD and international phone calls in some public telephones.

Costs

Prices in Australia have remained fairly stable over the past few years, but now that the economy is coming out of a recession there might be some 'catch-up' price-hikes in the near future.

Compared to the USA, Canada and European countries, Australia is cheaper in some ways and more expensive in others. Most manufactured goods tend to be more expensive, but food is both high in quality and low in cost.

Accommodation is also very reasonably priced. In virtually every town where backpackers are likely to stay there'll be a backpackers' hostel with dorm beds for around $12, or a caravan park with on-site vans for around $25 for two people. An average-to-good motel room costs around $45/55 (more in Sydney), with plenty of cheaper places and a lot of regional variation – you'll pay a lot more on the coast in summer, for example.

Transport isn't especially expensive in terms of dollars per km, but the distances are long so the fares are high.

Tipping

The tipping disease is rampant in Sydney (about 10% is reasonable), but elsewhere you aren't expected to tip, except perhaps in the most upmarket places. Once upon a time, egalitarian Australians saw tipping as slightly offensive; it seemed to suggest that a person didn't have the integrity to perform their job well unless there was the prospect of a monetary reward in addition to their wages. Those days are gone.

WHEN TO GO

At any time of year you'll find warm weather and clear skies somewhere in NSW. Generally speaking, however, the winter months of June, July and August are cool and sometimes dreary through much of the state. Winter is the best time to visit the outback and the only time you'll be able to ski.

Summer in Sydney can be sticky and unpleasant, although that's what all those beaches are for, and the major Sydney festivals are held during this time. Summer is also Sydney's peak season for visitors, so there are few accommodation bargains then. Autumn is probably Sydney's best season.

For more information see the Climate section in the Facts About NSW chapter.

The other major consideration is school holidays. Families take to the road (and air) en masse at these times, many places (especially at beach resorts) are booked out, prices rise considerably and things generally get a bit crazy. The main holiday period is from mid-December to late January; the other two-week periods are roughly early to mid-April, late June to mid-July, and late September to early October. Easter is another busy time.

WHAT TO BRING

Bring at least one warm jumper (pullover, sweater) or jacket, even if visiting during the summer, to cope with air-con or a cool spell. Sydney's rainfall tends to come in drenching downpours, so wet-weather gear can be very handy.

Australia gets a lot of UV radiation through a hole in the ozone layer, and you'll find that safe sun is as important a public health issue as safe sex. Sunhat, sunglasses and a sunscreen are essential, and lathering zinc cream onto your nose is a socially acceptable way to be safe.

If you're intending to bushwalk, bring good, strong and comfortable walking boots. The ubiquitous rubber sandals, known as thongs (easily bought here on arrival), are fine for the beach or a barbecue, but not for sightseeing or bushwalking.

Generally, Australians are casual dressers, but in Sydney's more expensive hotels and restaurants, men will be required to wear jackets and ties.

TOURIST OFFICES
Local Tourist Offices

The government-run NSW Travel Centre has a range of publications, some with quite detailed information on prices and deals on accommodation and packages. However, places featured have to pay for the space, so many aren't listed. It's always worth checking out the Travel Centre's accommodation deals, as they often have bargains at middle and top-end places, especially in Sydney.

Interstate Tourist Offices

There are NSW Travel Centres in other state capitals:

Adelaide
    45 King William St
    (☎ (08) 231 3167, 1800 882 818 toll-free)
Brisbane
    40 Queen St
    (☎ (07) 229 8833, 1800 177 490 toll-free)
Melbourne
    38 Bourke St
    (☎ (03) 670 7461, 1800 133 528 toll-free)

A step down from the government tourist offices are the local or regional tourist offices. Almost every major town (and many minor ones) maintains a tourist office with local information not readily available from the larger state offices.

If a town is too small to have a tourist office, it's small enough for everyone living there to have an encyclopedic knowledge of the local area, which they'll be more than happy to share with you.

Overseas Reps

The Australian Tourist Commission (ATC) is the government body which informs potential visitors about the country. ATC offices have a useful free booklet called *Travellers' Guide to Australia* that is a good introduction to the country, its geography, flora, fauna, transport, accommodation, food and so on. They also have a useful free map. This literature is intended for distribution overseas only; if you want copies, get them before you come to Australia. Addresses of the ATC offices for literature requests are:

Australia
    80 William St, Woolloomooloo, Sydney, NSW 2011 (☎ (02) 360 1111)
Germany
    Neue Mainzerstrasse 22, D6000 Frankfurt/Main 1 (☎ (069) 274 0060)
Hong Kong
    Suite 6, 10th Floor, Central Plaza, 18 Harbour Rd, Wanchai (☎ 802 7700)
Japan
    8th floor, Sankaido Building, 9-13, Akasaka 1-chome, Minato-ku, Tokyo 107 (☎ (03) 3582 2191); 4th floor, Yuki Building, 3-3-9 Hiranomachi, Chuo-Ku, Osaka 541 (☎ (06) 229 3601)
New Zealand
    Level 13, 44-48 Emily Place, Auckland 1 (☎ (09) 379 9594)
Singapore
    Suite 1703, United Square, 101 Thomson Rd, Singapore 1130 (☎ 255 4555)
UK
    Gemini House, 10-18 Putney Hill, London SW15 (☎ (071) 780 2227)
USA
    Suite 1200, 2121 Avenue of the Stars, Los Angeles, CA 90067 (☎ (213) 552 1988); 31st floor, 489 Fifth Ave, New York, NY 10017 (☎ (212) 687 6300)

USEFUL ORGANISATIONS
Conservation & the Environment
Australian Conservation Foundation

This is the largest of many non-government organisations that are concerned with protecting the environment. Their Sydney offices include 18 Argyle St in the Rocks (☎ (02) 247 1497).

Wilderness Society

Also a large non-government organisation, but more directly focussed on protection of wilderness and the creation of wilderness areas. There are Wilderness Society Shops where you can buy books, T-shirts, posters, badges etc.

Environment Centres

In many towns you'll find environment centres, run by volunteers and concerned with local issues. It's always worth dropping in as the people are friendly and can be a good source of information, both about the natural environment of the area and on local events such as markets and fund-raising dances.

Australian Trust for Conservation Volunteers

The Australian Trust for Conservation Volunteers (☎ (02) 228 6461), 3rd floor, 22-33 Bridge St, Sydney, runs a large number of conservation projects around the country and provides transport, food and accommodation for volunteers. You might find yourself helping with a legless lizard survey, removing woody weeds or just building a fence. Remember that not all conservation projects are in romantic bushland settings; some are on the edge of pretty ordinary towns, but on the other hand you might find yourself in a spectacularly remote location.

Most projects are either for a weekend or a week, and all food, transport and accommodation are supplied in return for a contribution to help cover costs. Most travellers who take part in ATCV join a Banksia Package, which lasts six weeks and includes six different projects. The cost is $650 and further weeks can be added for $105. You can organise a stint with the Trust from overseas, on a package with Travel Active at 3 Orwell St in Sydney's Kings Cross (☎ (02) 357 4477).

Animal Rescue

You see a lot of native animals killed by the roadside. They have no road sense at all. You might find injured animals, especially young marsupials which often survive road trauma that kills their mothers, hidden in the pouch. Essentially, baby animals separated from their mothers will be cold (so wrap them up), stressed (disturb them as little as possible) and dehydrated (but don't give them cow's milk).

Wildlife Information & Rescue (WIRES) is a voluntary organisation which cares for native animals. There are WIRES branches in many places, but for the current contact numbers phone the Sydney head office (☎ (02) 975 1633, 1800 641 188 toll-free). Alternatively, a vet will know of local animal welfare organisations.

Automobile Associations

Australia has a national automobile association, the Australian Automobile Association, but this exists mainly as an umbrella organisation for the various state associations. The day-to-day operations are all handled by the state organisations which provide emergency breakdown service, literature, excellent maps and detailed guides to accommodation.

The NRMA (National Roads & Motorists Association) is the NSW motoring association and has reciprocal arrangements with the other state associations and with some similar organisations overseas. Bring proof of membership with you. The NRMA's head office (☎ (02) 260 9222) is at 151 Clarence St, Sydney 2000. There are other offices around the state and most towns have a garage affiliated with the NRMA. As well as helping out with major breakdowns, these are very handy if your car is making funny noises and you want a quick opinion on what the trouble might be.

WWOOF

WWOOF (Willing Workers on Organic Farms) is a relatively new organisation in

Australia, although it is well established in other countries. The idea is that you do a few hours' work each day on a farm in return for bed and board. Some places have a minimum stay of a couple of days, but many will take you for just a night. Some will let you stay for months if they like the look of you, and you can become involved with some interesting large-scale projects.

Becoming a WWOOFer is a great way to meet interesting people and to travel cheaply. There are about 200 WWOOF associates in Australia, mostly in Victoria, NSW and Queensland.

As the name says, the farms are supposed to be organic, but that isn't always so. Some places aren't even farms – you might help out at a pottery or do the books at a seed wholesaler. There are even a few straight commercial farms which tend to exploit WWOOFers as cheap harvest labour, although these are rare. Whether they have a farm or just a vegie patch, most participants in the scheme are concerned to some extent with alternative lifestyles.

To join WWOOF send $15 (A$20 from overseas) to WWOOF, W Tree, Buchan, Vic 3885 (☎ (051) 55 0218) and they'll send you a membership number and a booklet listing WWOOF places all over Australia.

Disabled Travellers

The office of ACROD, the National Industries for Disability Services (☎ (06) 282 4333), produces information sheets for disabled travellers, including lists of state-level organisations, specialist travel agents, wheelchair and equipment hire and access guides. They can also sometimes help with specific queries. They would be grateful if enquirers could send at least the cost of postage. They can be contacted at PO Box 60, Curtin, ACT 2605.

The Disability Information & Referral Centre (☎ (02) 369 3594) in Sydney might also be able to help.

BUSINESS HOURS & HOLIDAYS

Business hours are usually from 9 am to 5 pm, Monday to Friday. Banking hours are shorter, usually from 9.30 am to 4 pm.

Shops open between about 8.30 or 9 am and 5 or 5.30 pm and on Saturday morning. Larger towns will have at least one night a week when the shops stay open until 9 pm. Shopping hours are becoming more flexible, although there still isn't a great deal happening on Sundays. 24-hour convenience stores are common in Sydney and the other cities. On the major highways you'll come across 24-hour service stations, often with cafes attached.

Pub hours are much less restricted than they once were and some have 24-hour licenses, but most open at 10 am and close sometime around 11 pm or midnight, later on weekends.

Public holidays in NSW and the ACT are:

New Year's Day	– 1 January
Australia Day	– 26 January
Trades & Labour Day (ACT only)	– 1 March
Easter (Good Friday & Easter Monday)	– March/April
Anzac Day	– 25 April
Queen's Birthday	– June (2nd Monday)
Bank Holiday (NSW only)	– Early August
Labour Day	– October (1st Monday)
Christmas Day	– 25 December
Boxing Day	– 26 December

Most public holidays become long weekends, and if a fixed-date holiday such as New Year's Day falls on a weekend, the following Monday will usually be a holiday. Some country towns have holidays for local festivals, such as show day.

FESTIVALS & EVENTS

January

Australia Day – this national holiday, commemorating the arrival of the First Fleet in 1788, is observed on the first Monday after 26 January, although there are moves to celebrate Australia Day on the day it falls

February

Royal Canberra Show – held in late February

February/March

Gay & Lesbian Mardi Gras – the most colourful event on the Sydney social calendar, culminating in a spectacular parade down Oxford St.

March
> *Hunter Valley Vintage Festival* – wine enthusiasts flock to the Hunter Valley for wine tasting, and grape picking and treading contests.

March to April
> *Canberra Festival* – held over 10 days in mid-March, ending with a public holiday.
> *National Folk Festival* – held in late March in Canberra.

April
> *Anzac Day* – a national public holiday, on 25 April, commemorating the landing of Anzac troops at Gallipoli in 1915. Memorial marches by the returned soldiers of both world wars and the veterans of Korea and Vietnam are held all over the country.

June
> *Ski season opens* – Snowy Mountains

September
> *Mudgee Wine Festival*

October
> *Tooheys Bathurst 1000* – motor-racing enthusiasts flock to Bathurst for the annual 1000 km, touring-car race on the superb Mt Panorama circuit.

November
> *Melbourne Cup* – on the first Tuesday in November, Australia's premier horse-race is run in Melbourne. The whole country shuts down for three minutes or so while the race is run. Many country towns schedule racing events to coincide with it.

December to January
> These are the busiest summer months, with Christmas, school holidays, lots of beach activities, rock and jazz festivals, international sporting events including tennis and cricket, a whole host of outdoor activities and lots of parties.

See the Festivals & Events sections of the Sydney and Canberra chapters for information on celebrations in those cities. Most other communities have festivals and events, some well worth seeing. You'll find details in the various sections of this guide. There are also some regular events to look out for while you're travelling around.

Agricultural Shows

For a taste of rural life you should visit an agricultural show. Sydney's Royal Easter Show is by far the biggest, but it's a case of the city being given a glimpse of the country. For a look at country people kicking up their heels in their own element you need to visit a country show. There are plenty of them.

Field Days

Without the side-show-alley attractions of the agricultural shows, field days are aimed at farmers. Apart from the opportunity to see at close hand the big toys and the latest developments in agri-business, there are also sheepdog trials and other events of more general interest. The biggest field days are listed below, but other centres also hold them.

Ag-Quip Field Days	– Tamworth, mid-August; Gunnedah, August
Henty Machinery Field Days	– Henty, third week in September
Australian National Field Days	– range, mid-November

There are also small farm field days, with less emphasis on the big machinery and offering more chance of meeting alternative lifestylers. One of the most popular small farm field days is held at Mudgee in mid-July.

Livestock Sales

Just about every large country town west of the Great Divide (and some east) has saleyards, and the local paper will tell the date of

---

At the Livestock Sales

The graziers wear their best: the standard uniform for men is an Akubra hat (the good one, not the old one), moleskin trousers, boots and a sportscoat; women might be dressed similarly, or in their church-going gear. The sale offers a chance to catch up on district gossip, and tea is drunk amidst the Landcruisers, utes and Fairlanes parked in the shade. Later there might be a few beers at the pub.

Over at the yards, the dogs are working hard, responding to shrill whistles or, if something is going awry, furious yelling. The cattle bellow, the sheep set up a cacophony of baas and clattering hooves, semis growl in and out with loads of livestock and there might be a couple of drovers on horseback, cracking whips around a swirling mob of cattle. Up on the boardwalk, the auctioneer's quickfire patter is interspersed with lusty shouts from the bidders, and his clerk knows all the buyers by name. And that all-pervading smell? Big bucks. ■

the next sales. It's well worth attending one for an undiluted look at rural Australia.

Music Festivals

The relaxed Australian Bush Music Festival in the friendly town of Glen Innes (New England), held over the Labour Day long weekend in October, is a great introduction to rural life. The much bigger and glitzier Tamworth Australian Country Music Festival held over the Australia Day weekend in January is also a fun time – but close your eyes and you could be in Nashville. Various folk music clubs have annual festivals, and the Marijuana Harvest Ball is occasionally held in Nimbin towards the end of Autumn.

Surf Lifesaving Carnivals

The volunteer surf lifesaver is one of Australia's icons, but despite the macho image about a third of lifesavers are female and the proportion is growing. Each summer, surf carnivals are held all along the coast where you can see the lifesavers in action. Check at a local surf lifesaving club for dates or contact the Surf Lifesaving Association of NSW (☎ (02) 663 4298).

POST & TELECOMMUNICATIONS
Postal Rates

Australia's postal services are relatively efficient but not too cheap. It costs 45c to send a standard letter or postcard within Australia, while aerogrammes cost 70c.

Airmail letters/postcards cost 75/70c to New Zealand, Singapore and Malaysia; 95/90c to Hong Kong and India; $1.05/95c to the USA and Canada; and $1.20/$1 to Europe and the UK.

Sending Mail

It isn't worth thinking about sending international letters by anything but airmail. Don't forget to stick a blue airmail sticker on your postcards, otherwise they may take longer to get home than you do.

Post offices are open from 9 am to 5 pm Monday to Friday, but you can often get stamps from agencies such as newsagencies or from Australia Post shops, found in large cities, on Saturday mornings.

Receiving Mail

All post offices will hold mail for visitors. You can also have mail sent to you at American Express offices in big cities if you have an Amex card or Amex travellers' cheques.

Shipping Agents

If you want to send home a lot of stuff, the post is exorbitantly expensive. Shipping agents usually charge by volume (not weight) for sea-freight, and this can be relatively inexpensive. Sydney agents include Austpac (☎ (02) 742 5253) at 7 Pilcher St in South Stratfield. A tea-chest (supplied free) collected from your address in Sydney and delivered to a London address costs about $200, or only $100 if you pick it up in London (Staples Corner). A second tea-chest costs only $45 and there are various other deals. They can deliver to any UK address, and they freight to other countries. Sea-freight to the UK takes six to eight weeks.

Telephone

Australia has taken the first steps towards privatising its telecommunications system, with the government-owned Telecom now in competition with privately-owned Optus for long-distance (STD – Subscriber Trunk Dialling) and international (IDD – International Direct Dialling) calls. All public phones (payphones) are still operated by Telecom, but if you have access to a private phone it's worth checking out the special deals offered by the rivals.

No matter where you are, you can just dial the number without worrying about which carrier handles the call, but if you especially want a specific carrier you'll have to consult a local directory to see which is that area's designated carrier. If it isn't the company you want you'll have to dial a special access code. This whole messy process was still being worked out at the time of writing.

Local phone calls cost 30c (25c from private phones) for unlimited time.

It's also possible to make long-distance

New Telephone Numbers

Australia is running out of telephone numbers! In response to this problem, the Australian Telecommunications Authority (AUSTEL) began to implement a new numbering plan in June 1994. Every number in Australia will gain an extra one or two digits, so that all telephone numbers will have eight digits. In metropolitan Sydney, a '9' will be added to the front of every seven-digit number.

Most of the changes in Sydney will take place in July 1996, although all numbers formerly beginning with 99 (Mona Vale area) changed in July 1994 and all numbers beginning with 9 (north shore suburbs) will change in July 1995.

AUSTEL is also merging the country's 54 area codes into four codes covering larger areas. When the changes are implemented, all of NSW and the ACT will have an 02 area code. Regional numbers which are currently six digits will have the last two numbers of their current area code attached to their number to make an eight-digit number. Their new area code will be 02. For example, (047) 31 3000 will become (02) 47 31 3000.

There will be a six-month period when both the old and new numbers will be accessible, followed by a further three-month period when a recorded message will refer callers back to the White Pages' information section.

The change will not affect the cost of calls.

You can call AUSTEL's information hotline for further information (☎ 1800 888 888), or look in the White Pages directory for a complete update.

All telephone numbers given in this book are the pre-change numbers. ■

and international calls from virtually any public phone. Many public phones accept Telecom Phonecards, which are very convenient. The cards come in $5, $10, $20 and $50 denominations and are available from retail outlets such as newsagents and pharmacies. Phone cards are *not* usually available from post offices (which are nevertheless the places where you'll always find phones that take phone cards), an idiotic result of the telephone and postal services being told to go their separate ways. Otherwise, have plenty of 10c, 20c, 50c and $1 coins.

Some public phones are set up to take bank cash-cards or credit cards. The minimum charge for a call on one of these phones is $1.20. Most larger towns have one of these phones outside the post office.

As well as Telecom's phone booths there are often payphones in shops, hotels, bars, etc. Some of these privately-operated payphones might not offer international calls, and some may charge more than the standard rates.

Many businesses and some government departments operate a toll-free service (prefix 1800) so, no matter where you are ringing from around the country, it's only the cost of a local call, or free from a public phone. Phone numbers with the prefix 018, 015 or 041 are mobile or car phones. Many companies, such as the airlines, have six-digit numbers beginning with 13, and these are charged at the rate of a local call. Often they'll be Australia-wide numbers, but sometimes they apply only to specific districts. Unfortunately there's no way of telling without actually ringing the number.

Other odd numbers you may come across are nine-digit numbers starting with 0055. These calls, usually recorded information services and the like, are provided by private companies, and your call is charged in multiples of 25c (30c from public phones) at a rate selected by the provider (Premium 70c per minute, Value 55c per minute, Budget 35c per minute).

The rates for STD calls can drop dramatically with special deals, but generally fall into one of three price brackets, listed here in ascending order of cost:

Economy – from 6 pm Saturday to 8 am Monday;
            10 pm to 8 am every night
Night   – from 6 to 10 pm Monday to Friday
Day   – from 8 am to 6 pm Monday to Saturday

From most phones you can also make international calls. All you do is dial 0011 for overseas, the country code (44 for Britain, 1 for the USA or Canada, 64 for New Zealand), the city code (71 or 81 for London, 212 for New York, etc), and then the telephone number.

A standard call to the USA or Britain costs $2.50 a minute ($2 off-peak); New Zealand is $2.10 a minute ($1.40 off-peak). Off-peak times, if available, vary depending on the destination – see the front of any telephone book for more details. Sundays are often the cheapest day to ring. Keep an eye on the papers for ads announcing special deals for international calls.

Country Direct is a service which gives direct access to operators in 32 other countries. You can then make collect or credit-card calls. For a full list of the countries available, check any local telephone book. Some of them include:

Canada	– ☎ 0014 881 150
Germany	– ☎ 0014 881 490
Japan	– ☎ 0014 881 810
New Zealand	– ☎ 0014 881 640
UK	– ☎ 0014 881 440

Some useful numbers include:

Emergency (free call)
  ☎ 000 from any phone in the country
Directory assistance (free call)
  ☎ 013 for a number in the area you are in;
  ☎ 0175 for a number elsewhere in Australia;
  ☎ 0103 for an overseas number
Reverse Charges – Domestic
  ☎ 0176 from a payphone;
  ☎ 011 from a private phone
Reverse Charges – International
  ☎ 0107 from a payphone;
  ☎ 0101 from a private phone

Telegrams (Cables)

Local telegrams are no longer available (but faxes do the same job), but you can send an international telegram at a flat rate of $7.50 plus 60c per word, including the address. Delivery is by the country's normal postal system (so it's usually next day), but in countries where the post office can arrange

courier delivery, you can pay an extra $16 for same-day delivery. It's almost always cheaper to send a fax.

Fax

All post offices (but few agencies) send faxes. If you send a fax to another fax machine it costs $4, which is also the rate for sending a fax to a postal address. The fax is sent to the local post office and delivered in the normal mail service, usually the next day. You can send a same-day fax to a postal address if you get it in by 1 pm ($12), and there's a two-hour courier delivery service open until 4 pm ($20). These rates apply to the first page of any fax. Subsequent pages cost $1, no matter which service you use.

Overseas faxes, either to a fax machine or delivered in the local mail service, cost $10 for the first page and $5 for following pages.

If you are sending a fax to a fax machine it's worth seeing if any businesses offer a fax service, as they can be cheaper than the Post Office.

TIME

NSW uses Eastern Standard Time (as do Queensland, Victoria and Tasmania), which is 10 hours ahead of UTC (Greenwich Mean Time).

Other time-zones in Australia are Central Time (half an hour behind Eastern Standard Time and used in South Australia and the Northern Territory) and Western Time (two hours behind Eastern Standard Time and used in Western Australia). Note that Broken Hill, in the far west of NSW, uses Central Time.

At noon in Sydney it's 2 am in London, 3 am in Rome, 9 am in Bangkok, 2 pm in Auckland, 6 pm the previous day in Los Angeles and 9 pm the previous day in New York.

From the last Sunday in October to the first Sunday in March, NSW is on Eastern Summer Time, one hour ahead of standard time. This does not apply in Queensland, which is on Eastern Standard Time all year.

The astronomically-minded might like to know that Eastern Standard Time is based on the line of longitude 150° East – that is, when you're somewhere on this line, the sun really is at its highest at noon. There are plans to build a 40-metre sundial somewhere along the meridian, probably at Bermagui on the south coast.

ELECTRICITY

Voltage is 220-240 V and the plugs are three-pin, but not the same as British three-pin plugs. Some of the more expensive hotels have 110 V outlets for electric shavers. Adaptors can be found in good hardware shops and some chemists and travel agents.

WEIGHTS & MEASURES

Australia uses the metric system. See the back of this book for conversion tables. In country areas you'll still hear people using imperial units and when you're receiving directions it's a good idea to make sure that they are talking about km, not miles.

BOOKS

If you want a souvenir of Australia, try one of the numerous coffee-table books like *A Day in the Life of Australia*. At the Wilderness Society shops in Sydney and elsewhere and at Government Printing Office shops in Sydney and Canberra you'll find a good range of wildlife posters, calendars and books.

Aborigines

The Australian Aborigines by Kenneth Maddock is a good cultural summary. The award-winning *Triumph of the Nomads* by Geoffrey Blainey is also good. For accounts of what's happened to the original Australians since Whites arrived, read *Aboriginal Australians* by Richard Broome. *A Change of Ownership*, by Mildred Kirk, covers similar ground to Broome's book, but does so more concisely, focusing on the land-rights movement.

The Other Side of the Frontier, by Henry Reynolds, uses historical records to give a vivid account of an Aboriginal view of the arrival and takeover of Australia by Europeans. His *With the White People* identifies the essential Aboriginal contributions to the survival of the early White settlers. *My Place*, Sally Morgan's prize-winning autobiography, traces her discovery of her Aboriginal heritage. *The Fringe Dwellers*, by Nene Gare, describes just what it's like to be an Aborigine growing up in a White-dominated society.

Don't Take Your Love to Town by Ruby Langford and *My People* by Oodgeroo Noonuccal (formerly Kath Walker) are also recommended reading for people interested in Aborigines' experience.

History

For a good introduction to Australian history, read *A Short History of Australia* by the late Manning Clark, a much-loved Aussie historian. A single-volume condensation of Clark's definitive (and controversial) six-volume history of Australia is also available.

The Fatal Shore, Robert Hughes's best-selling account of the convict era, is also a very good read.

Finding Australia, by Russel Ward, traces the early days from the first Aboriginal arrivals up to 1821. His *Concise History of Australia* (1992, University of Queensland Press) is another quick introduction.

The Exploration of Australia, by Michael Cannon, is a coffee-table book in size, presentation and price, but it's a fascinating reference book about the gradual European uncovering of the continent. An intriguing combination of history and nature study is Eric Rolls' excellent *A Million Wild Acres* (1981, Penguin Books paperback, about $17). It tells the story of the Pilliga Scrub in north-western NSW, but in the context of the state's history and largely from the point of view of the farmers and timber-cutters who pioneered White settlement.

Fiction

You don't need to worry about bringing a few good novels from home for your trip to Australia, as there's plenty of excellent recent Australian literature – see the Arts section of the Facts About NSW chapter for some suggestions.

Travel Guides

Burnum Burnum's Aboriginal Australia is subtitled 'a traveller's guide'. If you want to explore Australia from the Aboriginal point of view, this large and lavish hardback is the book for you.

See the Activities section for guides to specific sports and activities.

The NRMA publishes star-rated accommodation guides to caravan parks and motel-style accommodation, available free to members, and to members of other states' motoring organisations. Non-members pay about $10. They don't list most pubs and you'll miss the simpler, cheaper places if you rely on these, but they are handy to keep in the glove-box.

The Australian Bed & Breakfast Book (Moonshine Press, paperback, about $13) lists B&B places across the country.

The information in Lonely Planet's *Sydney city guide* is similar to the information in this guidebook but if you're reading this guide in a bookshop and plan to visit only Sydney, have a look at the city guide. It's that handy pocket-sized book on the other shelf. There are plenty of other guides to Sydney, most targeting particular interests – see the Sydney chapter.

For travel elsewhere in Australia, Lonely Planet publishes *Australia – a travel survival kit*, *Victoria*, *Melbourne city guide*, *Outback Australia* and *Islands of Australia's Great Barrier Reef*. Other state guides are forthcoming.

Lonely Planet guides to Australia & Sydney

Children's Books

Two classics for younger children which are essential reading are Norman Lindsay's *The Magic Pudding* and May Gibbs' *Snugglepot & Cuddlepie*. Lindsay's home, now open as a museum, is near Springwood in the Blue Mountains. There are displays relating to *The Magic Pudding*, although more space is devoted to his sculpture and painting, much of which is cheerfully erotic. Nutcote, May Gibbs' house in North Sydney, has recently been saved from developers and will be opened as a museum.

Flora & Fauna

Identifying the state's strange and beautiful plants and trees is rewarding but difficult. Handy guides include the *Field Guide to Native Plants of Australia* (Bay Books), *Key Guide to Australian Trees* (Reed) and *Key Guide to Australian Wildflowers* (Reed). These will help, but the range of flora is so wide that becoming familiar with it all takes years.

Guides to fauna include *Key Guide to Australian Mammals* (Reed).

National Parks

Gregory's National Parks of NSW (paperback, about $20) is a handy guide to the state's national parks and the more popular of the nature reserves, state recreation areas and historic sites. It is sold in many National Parks offices as well as bookshops.

MAPS

You can get by with the maps in this book supplemented with a roadmap of the state, but if you're planning to bushwalk, cycle or explore minor roads you need more detailed maps.

The Department of Conservation & Land Management (C&LM) is the main publisher of maps in the state, with a wide range of topographic maps and also some informative maps designed for tourists, focussing on popular areas and individual national parks. Their series of 1:25,000 maps cover most of the Great Divide and are essential for bushwalking. C&LM's head office is in

Sydney, at 23-33 Bridge St (☎ (02) 228 6111); their main mapping office is at the Land Information Centre in Bathurst (☎ (063) 32 8200). You can make telephone orders with a credit card. The Land Information Centre used to be called the Central Mapping Authority (CMA), and some of their maps are still known as CMA maps.

The Australian Surveying & Land Information Group (AUSLIG) is the national mapping authority and also has credit-card phone sales. Contact AUSLIG, Department of Administrative Services, PO Box 2, Belconnen, ACT 2616 (☎ (06) 201 4300).

Shops selling outdoor equipment and some of the larger tourist information centres often carry topographic maps.

If you're planning to do a lot of driving you should take along the NRMA's series of roadmaps which show just about every road and track in the state. They are accurate and surprisingly up-to-date in their descriptions of road conditions. Take a general roadmap of the whole state as well (the NRMA has one of these, too) because the detailed maps show so many alternative routes that it can be difficult to work out which is the most direct. Any NRMA office (and some associated garages) will have the maps to its area and probably the whole set as well. They are free to members, and to members of motoring organisations in other states.

The NRMA maps are detailed enough for cyclists, but they don't show topography. If you want to avoid steep hills you'll need to investigate C&LM's range of topographic maps.

MEDIA
Newspapers & Magazines

The *Sydney Morning Herald* is probably the best newspaper in the country. It's a serious broadsheet but it captures some of Sydney's larrikinism as well. The other Sydney paper is the *Telegraph Mirror*, a tabloid but much tamer than other products of the Rupert Murdoch stables.

The *Australian*, another Murdoch paper, is a conservative daily and Australia's only national newspaper. It often has interesting reading, especially the weekend edition.

Quite a number of newspapers are published throughout rural NSW, although many appear only weekly. These are essential reading for local events.

The *Bulletin* is a venerable weekly newsmagazine which was first published last century, when it almost single-handedly created and popularised Australian political and cultural identity. It was so widely read that Henry Lawson, in describing a typical country hamlet in outback NSW, felt compelled to add, along with the pub, the store and the railway station, 'a sundowner sitting listlessly on a bench on the verandah, reading the *Bulletin*'. It has moved steadily to the right of the political spectrum since then, but it's still worth reading to get an idea of what conservative Australia thinks.

There are many papers, usually weeklies, produced by and for the various ethnic groups, some in English.

Widely available international papers include the *International Herald Tribune*, the *European* and the *Guardian Weekly*. *Time* produces an Australian edition, and the *Bulletin* carries a condensed version of *Newsweek*.

Radio

The Australian Broadcasting Corporation (ABC) is government-funded, commercial-free and by far the largest broadcaster in the country. There are two main services, Radio National, which can be heard just about everywhere (sometimes on AM and sometimes via FM relays), and lighter regional services, generally only available around major centres. Fine Music is the ABC's classical music station and Triple J is its rock station; neither is available everywhere.

Outside Sydney, which has more than 20 radio stations, you'll usually be able to pick up one or more of the ABC stations, a local commercial station or two and often a local public station which will broadcast a lot of announcements about interesting local events in addition to a pretty diverse range of music and news. You might also be able to tune into the SBS foreign-language programmes.

Some of the ABC's programmes are well worth finding. Australia All Over (early Sunday morning) has a big rural audience and concentrates on everyday life in a True Blue context. An urban, baby-boomer version of this is the Coodabeen Champions (Sunday evening) which has managed to remain amusing for years, mainly because it isn't slick and nothing is taken terribly seriously.

Music Deli on Saturday night has a fascinating range of new and old music made by Australia's various ethnic groups (including the Anglo-Celtics). You'll often hear traditional Aboriginal music and collaborations with contemporary composers.

The Coming Out Show (Saturday from 5 pm, repeated Thursday evening) discusses women's issues.

The morning AM and evening PM programmes are the best radio news services.

In summer, huge slabs of the ABC's airtime are taken up with broadcasts of international cricket matches, and in the winter Australia's overseas test matches are often broadcast, especially the Ashes series from England. The regional ABC stations broadcast horseracing from around the country on Saturday afternoons.

TV

There are five main TV networks in NSW: the government-funded ABC (Australian Broadcasting Corporation) and SBS (Special Broadcasting Service), and the three commercial networks, channels 10, 9 and 7. The ABC and at least one commercial station can be received almost everywhere in the state, but SBS is only available in Sydney (and the other state capital cities) and a few other large centres such as Broken Hill and Orange.

The commercial channels are just like commercial channels anywhere, with a diet of sport, soap operas, lightweight news and sensationalised current affairs, plus plenty of sit-coms (mainly American).

The ABC, which was consistently last in the ratings until SBS came along, produces some excellent current affairs and documentaries as well as showing a lot of sport, slightly heavier news and sit-coms (mainly British). The ABC also has a knack of making good comedy and drama programmes which receive critical acclaim and low ratings.

SBS caters to Australia's non-English-speaking population, but as well as Spanish soap operas, 'how to use a telephone'-type educational programmes and the like, it also screens some of the best programmes on TV. There is an excellent news service at 6.30 pm nightly (in English), serious current affairs and interesting documentaries. It's on SBS that you'll see the best films (with English subtitles when necessary), eclectic 'video hits' shows and some very adventurous television. With a tiny but quite sophisticated audience, SBS demonstrates how cowardly the other broadcasters are.

FILM & PHOTOGRAPHY

If you come to Australia via Hong Kong or Singapore it's worth buying film there, but otherwise Australian film prices are not too far out of line with those of the rest of the Western world. Including developing, 36-exposure Kodachrome 64 or Fujichrome 100 slide films cost from around $25, but with a little shopping around you can find it for around $20 – even less if you buy it in quantity.

The more popular print films are sold everywhere, but the availability of slide film is a bit hit-and-miss outside Sydney.

There are plenty of camera shops, and standards of camera service are high. Developing standards are also high (or as high as they can be with automatic processing machines), with many places offering one-hour developing of print film.

Remember that film is susceptible to heat, so protect your film, keeping it cool and having it processed as soon as possible. Dust and humidity also affect film, unexposed or exposed.

The best results are gained early in the morning and late in the afternoon, especially in summer when the glare from the noonday sun washes out colours.

As in any country, politeness goes a long way when taking photographs: ask before taking pictures of people. Note that most Aborigines are not keen on being treated as exhibits in a theme park.

HEALTH

Unless you have visited an infected country in the past 14 days (aircraft refuelling stops do not count), no vaccinations are required for entry.

Medical care in Australia is first-class and only moderately expensive. A typical visit to the doctor costs around $35. Health insurance cover is available in Australia, but there is usually a waiting period after you sign up before any claims can be made.

Although there is universal health care in Australia (for Australians and citizens of nations which have reciprocal rights), there is a minimum of bureaucracy and you can choose your own doctor. Seeing a doctor is just a matter of finding one nearby – check the Yellow Pages under Medical Practitioners. Most hospitals are public hospitals and the best health professionals work in them.

Visitors from the UK, New Zealand, Malta, Italy, Sweden and the Netherlands have reciprocal health rights in Australia. Register at any Medicare office.

If you have an immediate health problem, contact the casualty section at the nearest public hospital; in an emergency call an ambulance (☎ 000).

Travel Insurance

It's a good idea to buy some travel insurance that covers accidents, illness and loss of baggage. Make sure the policy includes health care and medication in the countries you plan to visit; covers 'dangerous' activities such as diving, abseiling etc if they're on your agenda; and includes a flight home for you and anyone you're travelling with, should your condition warrant it.

Medical Kit

It's always a good idea to travel with a basic medical kit even when your destination is a country like Australia where first-aid supplies are readily available. Don't forget any medication you're already taking, and contraceptives if necessary.

Health Precautions

You need to be aware of the intensity of the sun in Australia. Those ultraviolet rays can burn you to a crisp even on an overcast day. Australia has the highest incidence of skin cancer in the world, so cover up and wear plenty of sunscreen. The sun is at its most fierce between 11 am and 3 pm, so be especially careful at these times.

The contraceptive pill is available on prescription only, so a visit to a doctor is necessary. Doctors are listed in the Yellow Pages under 'Medical Practitioners'.

Salbutamol inhalers (Ventolin) are available without prescription, but you have to give your name and address to the chemist.

Condoms are available from chemists, convenience stores and vending machines in public toilets of universities and some pubs.

WOMEN TRAVELLERS

NSW is generally a safe place for women travellers, although you should avoid walking alone in Sydney late at night. Sexual harassment is uncommon, although the Aussie male culture does have its sexist elements. Don't tolerate any harassment or discrimination.

DANGERS & ANNOYANCES
Theft

NSW is a relatively safe place to visit, but it's better to play it safe and take reasonable precautions, especially in Sydney. Don't leave hotel rooms or cars unlocked, and don't leave your money, wallets, purses or cameras unattended or in full view through car windows, for instance.

If you are unlucky enough to have something stolen, immediately report all details to the nearest police station. If your credit cards, cash card or travellers' cheques have been taken, notify your bank or the relevant company immediately (most have 24-hour 'lost or stolen' numbers listed under 'Banks' or 'Credit Card Organisations' in the Yellow Pages).

Swimming

It seems unnecessary to mention it, but don't ever go swimming if you have been drinking alcohol. Swimming after a heavy meal is also unwise.

Ocean Beaches The surf lifesaving clubs that line the beaches right along the coast aren't there for show – many people are rescued from the surf each year.

To signal that you are in trouble in the water, *raise your arm* and keep it raised while treading water or floating. If you have been sensible enough to swim at a patrolled beach (indicated by flags), help will come quickly.

Dumpers, waves that break in shallow water, can cause spinal injuries, but most people who are rescued have been caught in rips. A rip is the 'river' by which water from the surf makes its way back to the sea. Finding yourself swept out in a rip can be terrifying, but keep your head. All you have to do is stay afloat and raise your arm. Most rips lose their momentum quickly, so you won't disappear over the horizon.

If you want to rescue yourself from a rip, wait until you seem to have slowed, then swim parallel to the shore for about 30 metres. By then you should be out of the rip and can swim back to shore. Never try to swim back to shore against a rip.

You can expect to find rips near river and lake mouths, especially after rain, but they occur anywhere.

Rivers & Lakes Most rivers and lakes are murky affairs. Watch out for dead trees and the like which can tangle you up, and never jump or dive in if you can't see the bottom.

Sharks & Other Ocean-going Nasties

Shark attacks are extremely rare. You are much more likely to be involved in a car accident on the way to the beach than to be attacked by a shark when you get there.

Some major beaches, especially around Sydney, have shark-netting. The nets usually don't actually stop sharks from approaching the beach – they run out from the shore to deter sharks from cruising along the beaches and checking out the menu. The more popular beaches also have shark-spotting planes at peak times.

There are various poisonous marine animals, such as stone fish (with poison spines) and deadly blue-ringed octopuses (they're small and hang out in rock pools). Basically, if you don't know what it is, don't touch it.

Snakes & Spiders

All snakes are protected. Some are deadly, but very few are aggressive. The noise you make walking through the bush is enough to scare away most snakes, but wearing proper shoes and long socks isn't a bad idea if you're walking through thick grass. Most people who are bitten have done something silly, like stepping over a log without checking what's sunbaking on the other side, putting their hands in holes or being careless collecting firewood. Remember that snakes might still be moving around at night in summer, perhaps soaking up some of the warmth from a rock or the road.

If someone is bitten, fetch help quickly, as anti-venenes are available. It helps if you know what sort of snake it was, but never

Redback spider

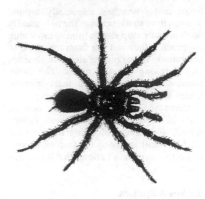

Funnel-web spider

attempt to catch the snake if you risk being bitten. The victim must not go blundering around after the snake; keeping still is much more important than identifying the snake.

The old first aid of applying a tourniquet and sucking the puncture-site is definitely out. Snake bites can be survived if you apply a very tight bandage over the whole of the bitten limb and ensure that the victim keeps as still and calm as possible. The idea is to slow the poison's entry into the system to a point where the body can handle it. Never try to walk a victim to help.

There are a couple of spiders to watch out for: the redback, a small spider related to the black widow; and the funnel-web, an ugly, aggressive brute which lives in holes in the ground (after rain they might be flooded out and go wandering). Both can be fatal, especially to children. Treat a funnel-web bite like a snake bite; put ice on a redback bite and get help quickly.

Insects

Flies The swarms of bushflies that descend on you in outback areas are unbelievably annoying, but other than driving you demented they do no harm. If you're walking you might want to take a tip from the swaggies and string some corks (traditionally, but anything will do) from the brim of your hat to save you spending your whole day waving

flies from your face. Or you could just use insect repellent. Flies vanish at sunset, but that's when the mosquitoes come out...

Mosquitoes Mozzies can be a problem. Fortunately, none of them are malaria carriers although every few years there are localised outbreaks of mosquito-borne fevers.

Ticks The common bush-tick (found in the forest and scrub country along the eastern coast of Australia) can be dangerous if left lodged in the skin, as the toxin the tick excretes can cause paralysis and sometimes death. Check your body for lumps every night if you're walking in tick-infested areas. The tick should be removed by dousing it with methylated spirits or kerosene and levering it out, but make sure you remove it intact. Remember to check children and dogs for ticks after a walk in the bush.

Cockroaches Sydney and some of the more humid coastal areas suffer from cockies. No, not the birds – cockroaches. Sydneysiders seem to get by with a mixture of tolerance and all-out chemical warfare, but if you haven't encountered a giant cockroach before, you're in for a surprise.

Animals
In the unlikely event that you should corner a red kangaroo, it might grasp you with its forelegs while booting you in the stomach with those huge rear legs. Wild boars are shy and cunning, so you'll rarely see them, but be aware that a wounded or cornered boar will charge, and those long, sharp tusks will make a mess of you.

Bushfire
In dry, hot weather, bushfires can raze thousands of hectares of eucalypt forests, with the volatile haze of eucalyptus oil exploding into a wall of flames 40 metres high. If a firestorm develops, the inferno can devour the bush faster than you can drive away from it.

Be *extremely* careful of fire when camping in summer. The catastrophic bushfires which devastated the Great Divide in 1994 were almost all started by people, accidentally or deliberately.

Apart from a real risk of dying in the fire, you can be hit with huge fines and even jail sentences if you light a fire on a day of Total Fire Ban. This includes stoves fuelled by gas or liquid. *Never* throw a cigarette butt out of a car. Australians don't like 'dobbing' people to the police, but they happily make exceptions of people who light fires on days of Total Fire Ban.

If there is a fire in the area, you should leave early. Most deaths in bushfires occur in the panic of last-minute evacuations.

If you're caught in a fire you must shelter from the intense radiant heat. It melts glass in seconds! Put a wall or just a dampened woollen jumper between you and the flames. In a crisis, stay in your car and park in as clear a space as you can find. Lie on the floor under the dashboard, covering yourself with a woollen blanket if possible. The fire front often passes quickly and it can be safer to head back into the burnt area than to run or drive away from the fire. Watch out for falling trees.

Bushwalkers should take local advice before setting out. On a Total Fire Ban Day, don't go – delay your trip until the weather has changed. There's a recorded message service (☎ 11 540) giving current fire restrictions. If you're out in the bush and you see smoke, even at a great distance, take it seriously. Go to the nearest open space, downhill if possible. A forested ridge is the most dangerous place to be. Bushfires move very quickly and change direction with the wind.

WORK

If you have a 12-month 'working holiday' visa, you can officially only work for three out of those 12 months. Working on a regular tourist visa is strictly *verboten*. To receive wages you must have a Tax File Number, issued by the Taxation Department. Forms are available from post offices and you'll need to show your passport and visa.

With unemployment high, it is much more difficult to find casual work than it once was, and you shouldn't count on getting a job to pay for your ticket home, for instance. However, many travellers seem to find some work. The best prospects for casual work include bar work, waiting on tables or washing dishes, nanny work, fruit picking and collecting for charities. People with office skills can often find temp work in Sydney. There are plenty of Commonwealth Employment Service (CES) offices, and the staff generally have a good idea of what is

---

The Fires of '94

In early 1994 more than 100 huge fires broke out in the Great Divide and raged for nearly a fortnight. High temperatures, low humidity and strong winds produced cataclysmic conditions, and when fires began to explode along Sydney's green corridors, to within km of the city centre, an unprecedented disaster seemed imminent.

Thanks to the heroic efforts of 20,000 volunteer firefighters from brigades around the country, the toll of property and human life was remarkably low. Lessons had been learned in the Ash Wednesday fires in Victoria and South Australia a decade earlier, which killed 80 people and destroyed thousands of homes.

However, with more than 800,000 hectares of national parks and state forests burnt out, the ecological effects are more deep-seated and serious. Although Australian flora and fauna are used to fires, the fires of '94 were so extensive that it is feared that some species may not recover because most bushland is now surrounded by towns or farmland which can't provide new stocks of plants and animals.

Fires on this scale might not recur for many years, but almost every summer there are big fires somewhere in the state's forests. They are largely ignored by the media (as were the '94 fires outside the populated areas) because they don't offer juicy shots of grief and destruction, but they are just as dangerous. ■

available where. Try the classified section of the daily papers under Situations Vacant. Hostels often have information about work.

Harvests are the main source of casual work in rural areas. The CES produces a booklet detailing harvest times and locations, but you should use this as a general guide only – call the local CES office to confirm the dates and availability of work before heading off into the sticks.

Grape harvests in the Hunter Valley and around Griffith begin around mid-February and last through March. Other fruit is picked around Griffith from November to March. The apple harvest near Orange and Batlow begins in early March. Cherry picking around Young begins in late spring. Hot work on the cotton harvest is sometimes available near Moree and Bourke in early summer. See the various sections in this book for more information.

With persistence and a bit of luck you might find a farm or station willing to give you board and lodging (and perhaps some pocket money) in return for work. This won't make you rich but it's one of the better ways to experience the country. If you don't have any contacts, the only way is to turn up in person and see what's doing. Expect a lot of knock-backs.

See the earlier Useful Organisations section for information on voluntary conservation work and the work-for-board WWOOFing organisation.

EMERGENCY

In a life-threatening situation, dial 000. This call is free from any phone and the operator will connect you with the police, ambulance or fire brigade. To dial any of these services direct, check the inside front cover of any local telephone book.

For other telephone crisis and personal counselling services (such as sexual assault, poisons information, or alcohol and drug problems), check the Community pages of the local telephone book.

Medical Emergencies

In an emergency, call an ambulance (☎ 000)

or go to the casualty ward of the nearest public hospital. Foreigners (except those from countries which have reciprocal health agreements with Australia) are charged at least $160 for a visit to casualty, although, unlike in some other countries, you will be treated before they see the colour of your money – they bill your home address.

ACTIVITIES

There are plenty of activities that you can take part in while travelling around the state. NSW has a flourishing skiing industry – a fact that takes a number of travellers by surprise. Bushwalking is cheap and you can do it anywhere. There are many fantastic walks in the various national parks. If you're interested in surfing you will find great beaches and surf, and there's good diving along the coast. You can go horseriding just about everywhere, from the high country to the outback plains. You can cycle all around NSW; for the athletic there are long, challenging routes and for the not so masochistic there are plenty of great day-trips.

Wildwise (☎ (02) 360 2099, 1800 655 325 toll-free), PO Box 299 Darlinghurst, NSW 2010, runs a wide range of adventure trips for women of all ages and backgrounds. As well as longer trips there are 'how to' weekends costing about $200 and teaching the basics of anything from rock climbing to surfing.

Bushwalking

Opportunities for bushwalking abound in NSW, with a huge variety of standards, lengths and terrains. Almost every national park either has walking trails or offers wilderness walking. Near Sydney there are popular walks in the Blue Mountains and Royal National Park, with the wilderness areas of Wollemi National Park not far away.

Longer routes include the three-day Six Foot Track to the Jenolan Caves and the 140 km Ensign Barralier track from Katoomba to Mittagong. The Great North Walk from Sydney to Newcastle can be walked in sections or as a two-week trek. The Great North Walk Kit (about $10) is available from various bushwalking suppliers and National Parks outlets, with more detailed tracknotes in *The Great North Walk* by McDougall & Shearer-Herlot (Kangaroo Press, about $13). The Hume & Hovell Walking Track from Yass to near Albury follows the route of two early explorers and passes through some beautiful high country. It can be walked in sections or as a trek of up to 25 days. C&LM publishes a guide to the track by Harry Hill ($19.95).

The best way to find out about walking areas is to contact a bushwalking club – contact the NSW Confederation of Bushwalking Clubs at GPO Box 2090, Sydney 2001 or check the Yellow Pages under 'Clubs – Bushwalking' for the current contact number. Outdoor stockists such as Paddy Pallin and Mountain Designs are also good sources of information. If you want to walk without the bother of carrying a pack, contact an outfit such as Great Australian Walks (☎ (02) 555 7580).

Lonely Planet's *Bushwalking in Australia* describes 23 walks of different lengths and difficulty in various parts of the country, including some in NSW.

Bicycling

There are possibilities for some great rides in NSW, from the endless western plains to the Snowy Mountains in summer. See the Getting Around chapter for information on long-distance cycling.

The Blue Mountains – A Guide For Cyclists by Jim Smith (paperback, $15) is pricey for its size but has been recommended for its detail. The adventurous could try *Cycle the Bush* by Sven Klinge (paperback, Hill of Content, $20), which details 100 rides in NSW for mountain-bikers. Several experienced cyclists who have tried these rides report that they are excellent, but many people will find them much more difficult than the very fit author did. On some rides recommended equipment includes a length of rope to lower your bike down cliffs!

If you're having trouble finding these titles, try contacting the Bicycle Institute of

NSW (☎ (02) 212 5628), GPO Box 272, Sydney 2001.

Whitewater Rafting

There are some excellent thrills to be had shooting down rapids in a raft. See the Coffs Harbour section of the North Coast chapter for a couple of operators, and the South-East and ACT chapters for others.

Canoeing & Kayaking

Many of the state's waterways are suitable for canoeing, with adventurous runs on the short, swift rivers flowing to the coast from the Great Divide, and long, lazy treks on the meandering inland rivers.

The Canoe Association of NSW (☎ 660 4597) can help you with general canoeing queries and can point you towards clubs and hire places. The also have a recorded message (☎ (00555 0889) telling you the river heights throughout the state.

You can rent sea kayaks in Sydney and on the south coast.

Hang-Gliding & Paragliding

Hang-gliding is popular near Wollongong and Byron Bay, and you can take tandem flights. Paragliding outfits can be found at many beach resorts.

Horseriding & Trekking

Opportunities for horseriding abound, from hour-long jaunts to overnight (or longer) treks. Popular areas for organised horse treks include New England and the North-West.

Rock Climbing & Abseiling

The sheer cliffs of the Blue Mountains are very popular for climbing and abseiling and a number of places in Katoomba run beginners' courses.

Skiing

Some excellent skiing is available in the Snowy Mountains. See the South-East chapter for more information.

Swimming

A visit to NSW will involve swimming at a

surf beach sooner or later – there are just so many! – but there are also many lakes and rivers where you can cool off. Also, most towns have an Olympic-sized pool.

Surfing

I could not help concluding that this man felt the most supreme pleasure while he was driven in so fast and so smoothly by the sea.
Captain Cook on seeing a Tahitian surfer in 1777

With 1900 km of coastline, much of it surf beaches, it makes sense to get out there and surf. That isn't as easy as it sounds, though, and boogie-boarding or body-surfing is as far as most visitors get. You can learn to surf in Coffs Harbour and Byron Bay, and a new outfit, Surf Camps of Australia (☎ (065) 66 0395)) is opening in Crescent Head.

Tracks magazine provides good insights into Aussie surfing, and *Surfing Australia's East Coast* by Aussie surf-star Nat Young is a slim, cheap, comprehensive guide to the best breaks. He's also written the *Surfing &*

Sailing on the coast

Sailboard Guide to Australia, which covers the whole country. Surfing enthusiasts can also look for the expensive coffee-table book *Atlas of Australian Surfing*, by Mark Warren.

Highlights

Sydney has enough highlights of its own to keep you occupied for some time, and the nearby national parks (Royal, Ku-Ring-Gai Chase and Blue Mountains) offer great escapes, as do the wineries in the nearby Hunter Valley. However, if you're prepared to venture further afield there are many more places worth visiting.

The whole coastline is a string of wonderful beaches, and a visit to Byron Bay is a must. While you're there, check out the alternative lifestyles of the hinterland.

With such diversity of landscapes, it's hard to say which of the national parks are the best. You can choose between the alpine forests of Kosciusko, the rainforests of Border Ranges, the eerie outback expanses of Mungo or Sturt, the jagged peaks of Warrumbungle, the lush bush and idyllic beaches of Murramarang – or one of the other 60 or so parks!

Canberra is an intriguing place with plenty of attractions, but then so is Broken Hill, a city in the outback. Smaller towns are also intriguing, such as the near ghost-town of Hill End, prosperous old towns like Mudgee, the outback mining settlements of Lightning Ridge and White Cliffs, sleepy riverside centres like Deniliquin, the planned towns of the Murrumbidgee Irrigation Area, fishing ports like Eden, the timber towns of Bombala and Wauchope, outback hamlets like Mt Hope or Ivanhoe...

There's no shortage of adventure activities either: sailing on Sydney Harbour, abseiling in the Blue Mountains, surfing at Coffs Harbour, cattle-droving on horseback in the north-west, whitewater rafting in New England, bushwalking through the Great Divide, tandem hang-gliding on the north coast, or just dropping a line in a river and waiting for a 50-kg Murray cod to take the bait.

Almost any road running from the coast up the escarpment of the Great Divide climbs through superb forests and offers dramatic views. Two of my favourites are the road between Batemans Bay and Canberra and the long but rewarding trip from Gloucester to Scone, skirting Barrington Tops National Park. The steep climb from Bellingen to Dorrigo is also spectacular, as is the drive from Grafton to Glen Innes... In complete contrast, the lonely outback roads in the far west offer unlimited horizons, huge skies and a surprising amount of wildlife. ■

Top: Old building, South Grafton, north coast (JM)
Middle: Cattle station farmer, far west (PS)
Bottom: Road train on the North Bourke Bridge, far west (JM)

Top: Tilba Tilba, south coast (JM)
Middle: Hill End, central west (JM)
Bottom: Bridge on the Colo River, near Sydney (JM)

Shooting

Not a recommended activity, but a popular one. A lot of native wildlife (protected or not) is killed by shooters, and there aren't many rural road-signs which haven't been peppered with bullets.

However, NSW does have an enormous problem with feral animals. As well as the direct harm they cause native species, pigs, goats and rabbits are a significant cause of erosion and land degradation, one of Australia's major problems. It has been suggested that the Australian army would be best employed shooting feral goats and pigs, and only the most committed vegetarian could argue that killing these pests is immoral.

The bushie's ethos is popularly supposed to include the dictum 'if it moves, shoot it; if it doesn't, cut it down'. There's an uncomfortable amount of truth in this, and a brochure advertising shooting holidays on an outback property hinted at a new development: the customers were warned that they must not shoot live trees!

ACCOMMODATION

NSW is very well equipped with youth hostels, backpackers' hostels and caravan parks. A typical town of a few thousand people will have a basic motel at around $40/45 for singles/doubles, an old hotel with rooms (shared bathrooms) at $25/30 or less, and a caravan park – probably with tent-sites for around $10 and on-site vans or cabins for $25 to $30 for two. If the town is on anything like a main road or is bigger, it'll probably have several of each.

If there's a group of you, the rates for three or four people in a room are always worth checking. Often there are larger 'family' rooms or units with two bedrooms.

Camping

Camping in the bush is for many people one of the highlights of a visit to Australia.

If you're using a tent as your main accommodation you'll find that almost every town in the state has a caravan park. If you want to get around Australia on the cheap, then camping is the cheapest way of all, with nightly costs for two at around $10 (double that in some beachside resorts in summer).

One drawback of caravan parks is that they are, as the name says, intended more for caravans (house trailers for any North Americans out there) than for camping, but most will have a lawn area set aside for tents. Apart from bathrooms and laundries, there are few communal facilities. Caravan parks are generally on the edge of town, which means they can be a long way from the centre of big towns.

Many caravan parks also have on-site vans which you can rent for the night. These give you the comfort of a caravan without the inconvenience of actually towing one of the damned things. On-site cabins are also widely available, and these are more like a small self-contained unit. They usually have one bedroom, or at least an area which can be screened off from the rest of the unit – just the thing if you have small kids. Cabins also have the advantage of having their own bathroom and toilet, although this is sometimes an optional extra. They are also much less cramped than caravans, and the price difference is not always that great – say $25 to $30 for an on-site van, $30 to $40 for a cabin.

Hostels

YHA If you've sampled YHAs in other countries, you're in for a pleasant surprise in Australia. YHAs here don't impose chores and they don't kick you out during the day – all except a few of the smallest hostels have 24-hour access. The rules at YHA hostels are no stricter than those at any well-run backpacker hostel and they are reliably clean, friendly and helpful. There are no fly-by-night YHAs.

Hostels are great places for meeting people and great travellers' centres, and in many busier hostels the foreign visitors will outnumber the Australians.

Charges are usually about $12 a night in a dorm and about $15 or so per person in the increasing number of twin rooms. You must have a regulation sheet sleeping-bag or bed linen – for hygiene reasons a regular sleeping bag will not do. If you don't have sheets they can be rented at many hostels (usually for $3), but it's cheaper, after a few nights' stay, to have your own. YHA offices and some larger hostels sell the official YHA sheet bag.

Accommodation can usually be booked directly with the manager or through the YHA Membership & Travel Centre (☎ 261 1111) at 422 Kent St in Sydney. The YHA handbook tells all.

You have to be a member to stay at YHA hostels, although these are outnumbered by associate YHAs which take anyone but give discounts to members. Membership costs $24 per year, plus a $16 joining fee for Australians – overseas visitors don't pay the joining fee. There are also some good 'try before you buy' deals available. Members can pre-buy packs of accommodation vouchers which can work out at $11 a night. These packs are available only from YHA travel centres and some of the larger hostels – Glebe (Sydney), Canberra, Katoomba, Port Macquarie and Nowra/Bomaderry.

The YHA has built up an impressive Australia-wide list of discounts on everything from meals to hiking gear, and you could recoup your membership fees with a single bus-pass purchase.

Other Backpacker Hostels In recent years the number of backpackers' hostels has increased dramatically. The standards of these hostels vary enormously: some are rundown inner-city hotels where the owners have tried to fill empty rooms; unless renovations have been done, these places are generally pretty gloomy and depressing. A few are former motels, so each unit, typically with four to six beds, will have fridge, TV and bathroom. Still others are purpose-built as backpackers' hostels; these are usually the best places in terms of facilities, although sometimes they are simply too big.

In Sydney especially, backpackers are often employed to do the day-to-day running of hostels and usually it's not too long before standards start to slip. The best places are often the smaller hostels where the owner is also the manager.

Prices at backpackers' hostels are generally in line with YHA hostels, typically $10 to $12, sometimes more in Sydney and Byron Bay.

There's at least one organisation (VIP) which you can join to receive a discount card (valid for 12 months) and a list of participating hostels, for a modest fee (typically $15). This is hardly a great inducement to join, but you do also receive useful discounts on other services, such as bus passes, so they may be worth considering.

You won't find backpacker hostels in the more out-of-the-way places, as they aren't philanthropic like the YHA. In NSW they are nearly all on the lucrative backpacker trail up the coast.

Colleges
Many university colleges in Sydney offer inexpensive accommodation during vacations. See the Sydney chapter for more information.

Guesthouses & B&Bs
These are the fastest growing segment of the accommodation market. New places are opening all the time, and they include everything from converted barns and stables, renovated and rambling old guesthouses, upmarket country homes and simple bedrooms in family homes. Some of these places are listed in this book, but for a greater selection contact an organisation such as Homestay International (☎ (02) 948 8384; fax 949 7690), PO Box 324, Manly 2095, or Bed & Breakfast Australia (☎ (02)498 5344), PO Box 408, Gordon 2075. The average price for the double rooms on their books is about $85 or $110 for a farmstay (which includes transport to/from railway stations or bus-stops, all meals and activities). Phone (☎ 498 5344) to book and pay by credit card. You'll find many other B&Bs with prices starting at about $40 a double. Some of these places don't accept credit cards or cheques, so find out before you arrive.

Farmstays
Farmstays are another growth area. Right

across the state you will find properties offering accommodation, and sometimes a programme of farm activities. Some are just B&Bs in farmhouses, others are cottages which happen to be on farms. Expect to pay around $300 for a week in a self-contained cottage and from about $70 (sometimes less) to about $180 per person per night for full board and activities.

Some farmstays are listed in this guide, but for a more complete list contact NSW Farm & Country Holidays (☎ (02) 436 4757), PO Box 772, Crows Nest 2065. They have a brochure and can make credit-card bookings. Packages which can be booked from overseas are arranged by Australian Farmhost Holidays Pty Ltd, PO Box 65, Culcairn 2660 (☎ (060) 29 8621, Neville Lowe). Many overseas travel agents can make direct bookings with this organisation.

See the earlier Useful Organisations section for information on voluntary conservation work and also the work-for-board WWOOFing organisation.

Pubs

Outside of Sydney and a very few big towns, hotel accommodation means pub accommodation. Although the grandest buildings in country towns are often the pubs, the standard of accommodation rarely lives up to the architecture. Many pubs would prefer not to offer accommodation, but the licensing laws require them to do so.

Pub rooms are usually clean but pretty basic, with not much more than a bed, a wardrobe and sometimes a wash-basin. The bathroom is almost always shared. Despite the lack of luxury, it's worth considering staying in pubs rather than motels. Apart from the saving in cost (around $15/25 is average for basic pub accommodation), staying at 'the pub' means that you have an entree to the town's social life. Rather than watching networked TV all night in a motel room, you're likely to spend some time in the bar and, as you'll already be known to the bar-person, you won't have trouble meeting people. The smaller the town, the friendlier the pub will be.

The two essentials in choosing a pub room are to get one which isn't directly above the noisy bar (not a problem if you plan to be in the bar until closing time), and to check that the bed is in reasonable condition.

A big plus with pubs is that the breakfasts (sometimes included in the tariff, but increasingly it's an extra charge) can be quite enormous.

Motels

If you want a more modern place than a pub, with your own bathroom and other facilities, then you're moving into the motel bracket. Prices vary, and with motels (unlike hotels), singles are often not much cheaper than doubles. The reason is quite simple – in the old hotels many of the rooms really are singles, relics of the days when single men travelled the country looking for work. In motels, the rooms are almost always doubles. You'll sometimes find motel rooms for less than $35, and in most places will have no trouble finding something for under $50. Sydney and Canberra are the exceptions.

Hotels

As well as pubs, the other end of the hotel spectrum is well represented, in Sydney and Canberra at least. There are many excellent four and five-star hotels and quite a few lesser places where standards vary widely. Outside the capitals, quality accommodation is offered by the more expensive motels or beach resorts.

Serviced Apartments

Pretty much restricted to Sydney and Canberra, serviced apartments offer hotel-style convenience (the apartment is cleaned for you and there's a reception desk downstairs) with cooking facilities and a bit more room to move than a hotel room. They are becoming increasingly popular in the upper price brackets, with the cheaper ones very attractive for families travelling on a budget. See the Sydney and ACT chapters for more information.

Holiday Flats

Holiday flats, found mainly in beachside towns, are geared to family holidays, so they fill up at peak times and often have minimum rental periods of a week. Outside peak times you might be able to let one by the night. Standards and prices vary enormously, but if you have a group they can be very affordable and might even be cheaper than hostels outside peak season.

Houseboats

The Hawksbury River near Sydney, Port Stephens and the nearby Myall Lakes, the Clarence River and the Murray River are some of the waterways where you can hire houseboats. Houseboat hire rates are second only to those of ski lodges in complexity, but basically if you have a few people (say three or four) and hire midweek outside of peak times, the cost can be comparable to motels.

FOOD

Fresh, high quality ingredients make eating in NSW a pleasure. The state grows everything from tropical fruit to cold-climate vegetables and is even a major producer of rice. The beef and lamb are among the best in the world and the Pacific Ocean supplies superb seafood.

Add to this the huge variety of ethnic cuisines and you have the recipe for some memorable meals.

An Australian cuisine seems to be developing (at last), with 'modern Australian' becoming a recognisable style. It's something like an amalgamation of Mediterranean, South-East Asian and Californian styles, with a look and taste that's distinctively Australian. Sydney, with its multitude of excellent eateries for all budgets, is a foodie's paradise. Canberra is catching up fast, and in any of the larger towns, especially on the coast, there is a range of eating places.

This good news is relatively recent; it isn't so long since meat-and-three-veg was all anyone ever ate, and in country areas you might find that steak-and-plenty-of-it is still the main item on the menu. In some small,

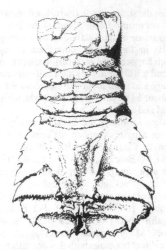

Balmain bug (it's local seafood)

remote country towns you might still be served canned vegetables.

Shopping for Food

A wide range of produce is sold in supermarkets and (perhaps fresher) in neighbourhood shops. Prices are low. Some seasonal variation in prices and availability does occur, but with produce shipped in from all over Australia you can almost always find what you want at a reasonable price.

There are many excellent delis selling cheeses, processed meats and a wide range of delights such as pickled octopus or six varieties of olives. They often have very tempting pastries, salads and other takeaways as well. It's difficult to go into a deli without seeing something that you simply *must* have.

For more basic supplies, there are corner stores or milk bars stocking staples such as milk, bread, tinned food and maybe some fresh fruit and vegetables.

These days, even the old-fashioned butcher shops sell delicious pre-marinated, pre-seasoned, pre-portioned meats which you can cook with a minimum of fuss. Bakeries also stock a much wider range of products than they once did, although in small towns you'll still find some bakeries where lamingtons, cream buns, eclairs and elaborate wedding cakes fill up the window displays.

In coastal towns, see if there's a fishing co-op selling seafood straight off the boat.

Takeaway Food

Australia's original takeaway food, the meat pie, is sold everywhere. While there are a few state-wide brands, most towns have a baker who makes pies. They can be pretty good.

Other fast food also abounds, and if you can't do without mass-produced, over-packaged junkfood served by adolescents in uniform there are plenty of outlets. However, you're much better off seeing what the local takeaway shop has on offer. (But avoid takeaways where the food is pre-cooked.) Even in country towns it's becoming quite common for takeaway shops to have a selection of salads.

English visitors will barely recognise fish & chips here. For a start, they're fried in vegetable oil, not lard, and the flavour and texture have more than a passing resemblance to fish and potatoes. Hamburgers from local takeaways are usually good. If you're a little hungrier, try a steak sandwich. In country towns your plain steak sandwich comes piled with salad (including an obligatory slab of canned beetroot, for some reason) and you'd better be hungry before you say 'gizza steak sandwich with the lot,

thanks mate'. Note that the items called potato cakes in other states are called scallops (as in scalloped potatoes) in NSW.

As well as the fish & chip or hamburger shop (interchangeable terms, usually), you can get takeaway sandwiches, rolls, etc at delis, milk bars (corner stores) and some bakeries. Many towns have Vietnamese (or Chinese) takeaways, or at least restaurants where you can buy takeaways.

Pub & Club Food

For a sit-down meal in a country town, head for the pub, where you can almost always buy counter meals. These were once eaten at the bar, but nowadays there are usually tables. The quantities are usually large (I was once confronted with a steak so big that the three veg had to come on a second plate) and prices are low (I paid $6.50), unless the pub serves meals in the dining room and calls it a bistro. The menu is usually restricted to roasts, steaks, sausages, mixed grills and the like, although seafood and pasta dishes are becoming more common. There are usually set times for counter meals, say noon to 1.30 or 2 pm for lunch and 6 to 8 pm for dinner (or tea, as it's known).

Just about every town in the state has a club, usually called something like the Returned Servicemen's Club, which thrives on profits from poker machines and has an inexpensive dining room or bistro. Visitors are welcome, although there might be some basic dress restrictions (no thongs, no T-shirts, for example).

Cooking Yabbies

There are several farms in NSW where you can catch yabbies, and just about every creek and dam in the Riverina will yield them, but how do you cook them? Here is a recipe, from Premier Yabbies (near Culcairn):

Cool the yabbies in iced water and bring a large pot of water to the boil.
Add a lemon cut into quarters and half a cup of brown sugar.
Put the yabbies into the boiling water, up to 10 at a time.
Return the water to the boil and wait for the yabbies to float to the top (about three minutes). Remove, rinse and drain the yabbies.
Now you have to shell and clean them, a knack that's best acquired with practice. It's similar to cleaning prawns: remove the shell and tail, then strip out the vein and the digestive tract. ■

Cafes & Restaurants

In Sydney, Canberra and the other large centres you'll find plenty of cafes and restaurants offering a myriad of cuisines and ambiences, but in country towns you might be restricted to an old-style cafe (often just a takeaway shop with tables) and a Chinese restaurant.

If there are more than a couple of Chinese places you'll often find that they are in hot competition and offer good deals, such as three dishes for $5, especially at lunchtime. Don't expect great cuisine in country-town Chinese restaurants, though – the owners have learned that country people often judge food by the size of the serving.

Country motels sometimes have dining rooms but you're often paying restaurant prices for pub food. Order the least complicated dish on the menu.

This scenario is changing, and any place with the hint of a tourist industry, especially along the coast, is likely to have some good places to eat.

DRINKS

Nonalcoholic Drinks

In the non-alcoholic department, Australians knock back Coke and flavoured milk like there's no tomorrow and also have some excellent mineral water brands. Coffee enthusiasts will be relieved to find excellent coffee served all over Sydney. De-caf hasn't made much of an impression and is rarely offered in cafes or restaurants.

Alcohol

Beer Australian beer will be fairly familiar to North Americans; it's similar to what's known as lager in the UK. It may taste like lemonade to the European real-ale addict, but it packs quite a punch. It is invariably chilled before drinking.

Once, buying a beer was simple. You decided whether you wanted 'new' or 'old' (a heavier lager) and asked for a 'middy' (285 ml/10 oz glass) or a 'schooner' (450 ml/16 oz glass) and the barperson filled one for you. No questions asked. Nowadays you have to stand there dithering between many fairly similar brands of lager and decide whether you want light or full-strength beer.

Toohey's is the largest brewer in the state, with Resches maintaining a market, especially in rural areas. The Carlton brewery, an interloper from Victoria, has made big inroads especially with their Victoria Bitter (VB or Vic). Carlton also brews Fosters, perhaps the best-known of Australia's beer brands, but you don't see it very often in NSW.

Small 'boutique' brewers have also been making a comeback and you'll find one-off brands such as Redback, Dogbolter and Eumundi. They're more expensive than the big commercial brands but definitely worth a try. Guinness is occasionally found on draught, usually in Irish pubs.

A word of warning to visitors: Australian beer has a higher alcohol content than British or American beers. Standard beer is generally around 4.9% alcohol, although most breweries now produce light beers, with an alcohol content of between 2% and 3.5%. Toohey's Blue is a popular light beer.

Wine If you don't fancy the beer, then turn to wines. European wine experts now realise just how good Australian wines can be – exporting wine is a multi-million dollar business. Wines need not be expensive. You're entering the 'pretty good' bracket if you pay over $10 for a bottle and very drinkable wines can be found for much less. Tyrrell's Long Flat reds and whites are Hunter wines with international reputations, retailing for well under $10 a bottle.

It takes a little while to become familiar with Australian wineries and their styles, but it's an effort worth making. Apart from browsing through bottle-shops, the best way to sample a lot of styles is to visit wineries. New wineries are opening all over the state, but the main areas are the Hunter Valley and the smaller Mudgee area. Most wineries welcome visitors for tastings, although they also expect you to actually buy something if, for example, you taste every Chardonnay that that vineyard has ever produced.

You'll find some restaurants advertising

that they're BYO. The initials stand for 'Bring Your Own' and it means that they're not licensed to sell alcohol but you are permitted to bring your own with you. This is a real boon to wine-loving but budget-minded travellers, because you can bring your own bottle of wine from the local bottle shop or from that winery you visited last week and not pay any mark-up. There might be a small 'corkage' charge (typically 60c to $1 per person) if you bring your own.

ENTERTAINMENT
Cinema
Although the cinema business took a huge knock from the meteoric rise in the home-video market (Australians love electronic gizmos and have the highest per capita ownership of videos in the world), it has bounced back as people rediscover the joys of the big screen.

In the big cities there are commercial cinema chains, such as Village, Hoyts and Greater Union, and their cinemas are usually found in centres which will have anything from two to 10 screens in the one complex. Smaller towns have just the one cinema and many of these are almost museum pieces in themselves. Seeing a new-release mainstream film is expensive, around $12 ($7.50 for children under 15), maybe less in country areas. City cinemas often have one day a week when the price is lower.

In Sydney and Canberra you'll find art-house and independent cinemas and these places generally screen either films that aren't made for mass consumption or specialise purely in re-runs of classics and cult movies.

Spectator Sports
If you're an armchair – or wooden bench – sports fan, NSW has plenty to offer. Many of the following sports are best seen in Sydney – see the Entertainment section in that chapter for details.

Football At least four types of football are played in NSW, each type being called

'football' by its aficionados. The season runs from about March to September.

Rugby is the main game in NSW and it's rugby league, the 13-a-side working-class version, that attracts the crowds. Rugby union, the 15-a-side game for amateurs, was less popular until Australia won the World Cup in 1991.

Soccer is a bit of a poor cousin: it's widely played on an amateur basis, but the national league is only semi-professional and attracts a small following. It's slowly gaining popularity, thanks in part to the success of the national team. At the local level, there are ethnically based teams representing a wide range of national origins.

Aussie Rules, an indigenous game based on elements of Gaelic football, has gained a toe-hold in Sydney and is played in Canberra and the southern Riverina.

Cricket In Sydney you'll find the Sydney Cricket Ground, one of the great shrines of cricket, and on summer Saturday afternoons all over the state hard-fought games are played. This is definitely not village-green stuff.

Other Basketball is growing in popularity as a spectator sport and there is a national league. There's also yacht racing, some good tennis and golf, and the Australian round of the World 500cc Motorcycle Grand Prix is held annually in April. Just about every other sport you care to think of is played somewhere in the state.

Gambling
Hardly a town in the state is without a horse racing track or a Totalisator Agency Board (TAB) betting office. You can bet on the horses, the trots (harness racing) and the dogs (greyhound racing). Sydneysiders can also bet on some yacht races. For poker machines, all you have to do is step into one of the ubiquitous clubs.

Oddly, despite a national propensity for placing bets, gambling is strictly controlled and only a very few forms of it are legal. Political corruption scandals in NSW often revolve around people being paid to keep the police away from illegal casinos. Two-up (betting on the fall of two coins) is right up there with koalas and vegemite as far as True Blue values are concerned, but until recently you couldn't legally play it (on Anzac Day a blind eye is traditionally turned to diggers playing two-up). There is now a legal two-up 'school' in Broken Hill which claims to have retained the atmosphere of the old-style game, and sanitised versions are played in casinos around the country (Canberra has a casino and NSW will soon have one).

THINGS TO BUY
Aboriginal Art
Top of the list of real Australian purchases would have to be Aboriginal art.

Aboriginal art is a traditional and symbolic art form. In ancient times, the main forms of art were body painting, cave painting and rock engraving, and it's only recently that Aboriginal artists have begun painting in more portable formats and using Western art materials like canvas and acrylic paints.

These works have quickly gained wide appreciation. The paintings depict traditional Dreamtime stories and ceremonial designs, and each design has a particular spiritual significance. These works capture

the essence of the Australian outback, and make a wonderful reminder of a trip to Australia.

Prices of the best works are way out of reach for the average traveller, but among the cheaper artworks on sale are prints, baskets, small carvings, and some very beautiful screen-printed T-shirts produced by Aboriginal craft co-operatives – and a larger number of commercial rip-offs. It's worth shopping around and paying a few dollars more for the real thing.

Much of the Aboriginal art available in NSW, especially the traditional styles, comes from other areas of Australia and is sold in Sydney galleries. If you're travelling up the north coast, call in at Gurrigai Aboriginal Arts & Crafts at the New Italy site, off the Pacific Highway between Maclean and Ballina.

Australiana
The term 'Australiana' is a euphemism for souvenirs. These are the things you buy as gifts for the folks back home or to remember your visit by, and are supposedly representative of Australia and Aussie culture. Some of the more popular items are:

Stuffed toys, especially koalas and kangaroos; wool products such as hand-knitted jumpers; sheepskin products; Akubra bush hats and straw sunhats; T-shirts, windcheaters and towels printed with Australian symbols or typical slogans like 'No flies on me, mate!'; Australia-shaped egg-flippers; koala keyrings; jewellery made from opals and pewter, often in the shape of native animals or flora; boomerangs (most of which are decorative rather than of the returning variety); painted didgeridoos; local glassware and ceramics; and high-kitsch items like ceramic flying pigs or koalas.

The seeds of many of Australia's native plants are on sale all over the place. Try growing kangaroo paws back home, if your own country will allow them in.

For those last-minute gifts, drop into a deli. Australian wines are well known overseas, but why not try honey (leatherwood honey is one of a number of powerful local varieties) or macadamia nuts? We have also

Aboriginal artefacts

heard rumours of tinned witchetty grubs, honey ants and other bush tucker.

Aussie Clothing

While you're here, fit yourself out in some local clothes – made in Australia for Australian conditions. Start off with some Bonds undies and a singlet, a pair of Holeproof Explorer socks and Blundstone or Rossi boots. Then there's anything from the R M Williams line (boots, moleskin trousers, shirts), some Yakka or King Gee workwear, a shearer's top or bush shirt, a greasy-wool jumper, a Bluey (a coarse woollen worker's coat), a Driza-bone (an oilskin riding coat) – and top it off with an Akubra hat.

Or there are all sorts of sheepskin products, from car-seat covers to 'ugg boots'. A high-quality sheepskin to put in a child's pushchair – or to sit on yourself! – can cost as little as $50.

Australia also produces some of the world's best surfing equipment and clothing, and clothing companies like 100% Mambo produce some mind-bogglingly off-the-wall designs.

Outdoor Gear

With Australians among the world's keenest travellers, Sydney's outdoor and adventure shops carry an excellent range of both Australian-made and imported gear. In many cases, the locally made products are of equivalent quality to (and cheaper than) the imports. Paddy Pallin, Mountain Designs and Kathmandu are among the local firms.

Opals

The opal is Australia's national gemstone, and opals and opal jewellery are popular souvenirs. They are beautiful stones, but buy wisely and shop around – quality and prices can vary widely from place to place. See the Lightning Ridge section of the North-West chapter for information on the various types of opals.

Antiques

A large proportion of antique furniture on the Australian market is imported from Europe, especially England. Instead, look for early Australian colonial furniture made from cedar or huon pine; Australian silver jewellery; ceramics – either early factory pieces or studio pieces (especially anything by the Boyd family); glassware such as Carnival glass; and Australiana collectables and bric-a-brac such as old signs, tins, bottles etc.

If you're serious about buying antiques, *Carter's Price Guide to Antiques in Australia* is an excellent price reference which is updated annually.

Crafts

You'll find many shops and galleries displaying crafts by local artists, as well as goods from almost every region of the world. The local craft scene is especially strong in the fields of ceramics, jewellery, stained glass and leathercraft. To see some of the best before you start travelling around the state, call in at Craftspace in the Rocks, in Sydney.

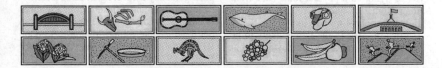

Getting There & Away

AIR

Almost all visitors to Australia arrive by air, and most arrive at Sydney's Kingsford-Smith Airport.

Australia is a long way from almost everywhere else, and air fares can be expensive. Australia's current international popularity adds another problem – flights are often heavily booked. If you want to fly to Australia at a particularly popular time of year (the middle of summer – around Christmas – is notoriously difficult) or on a particularly popular route (like Hong Kong-Sydney or Singapore-Sydney), then plan well ahead.

There are a number of deals to ease the pain of ticket prices.

Discount Tickets

Buying airline tickets these days is like shopping for a car or a camera – five different travel agents will quote you five different prices. Rule number one if you're looking for a cheap ticket is to go to an agent, not directly to the airline. The airline can usually only quote you the regular fare, but an agent can offer all sorts of special deals, particularly on competitive routes.

Ideally an airline would like to fly all its flights with every seat in use and every passenger paying the highest fare possible. Fortunately, life usually isn't like that and airlines would rather have a half-price passenger than an empty seat. When faced with too many seats, they will either let agents sell them at cut prices, or occasionally make one-off special offers on particular routes – watch the travel ads in the press.

What's available and what it costs depends on what time of year it is, what route you're flying and who you're flying with. If you're flying on a popular route (like from Hong Kong) or one where the choice of flights is very limited (like from South America or Africa), the fare is likely to be higher or there may be nothing available but the official fare.

Similarly the dirt-cheap fares are likely to be less conveniently scheduled, and to go by less convenient routes or with less popular airlines.

Things to consider when choosing a ticket are its validity (you don't want to buy a return ticket that's only valid for two weeks) and the number of stopovers you want. As a rule of thumb, the cheaper the ticket the fewer stopovers you'll be allowed. Also think about how much of a hassle it will be if you have to change planes on the way to Australia. Sometimes paying a bit more for a ticket is worth it to avoid sitting around a foreign departure lounge for hours on end.

Round-The-World Tickets

Round-the-World tickets have become very popular and many will take you through Australia. The airline RTW tickets are often real bargains and, since Australia is pretty much at the other side of the world from Europe or North America, it can work out no more expensive, or even cheaper, to keep going in the same direction right round the world rather than U-turn when you return.

The official airline RTW tickets are usually put together by a combination of two airlines and permit you to fly anywhere you want on their route systems so long as you do not backtrack. Other restrictions are that you (usually) must book the first sector in advance, and cancellation penalties then apply. There may be restrictions on how many stops you are permitted, and usually the tickets are valid from 90 days up to a year. Typical prices for these South Pacific RTW tickets are around £816 or US$1900.

An alternative type of RTW ticket is one put together by a travel agent using a combination of discounted tickets from a number of airlines. A UK agent like Trailfinders can put together interesting London-to-London RTW combinations including Australia for £750 to £930.

Circle Pacific Tickets

Circle Pacific fares are a similar idea to RTW tickets, using a combination of airlines to circle the Pacific – combining Australia, New Zealand, North America and Asia. Examples would be Qantas-Northwest, Canadian Airlines International-Cathay Pacific, and so on. As with RTW tickets, there are advance purchase restrictions and limits to how many stopovers you can take. Typically, fares range between US$1750 and US$2180. A possible Circle Pacific route is Los Angeles/Hawaii/Auckland/Sydney/Singapore/Bangkok/Hong Kong/Tokyo/Los Angeles.

To/From the UK

The cheapest tickets in London are from the numerous 'bucket shops' (discount ticket agencies) which advertise in magazines and papers like *Time Out*, *City Limits*, *Southern Cross* and *TNT*. The magazine *Business Traveller* also has a great deal of good advice on airfare bargains. Most bucket shops are trustworthy and reliable, but the occasional sharp operator appears – *Time Out* and *Business Traveller* give some useful advice on precautions to take.

Trailfinders (☎ (071) 938 3366) at 46 Earls Court Rd, London W8 and STA Travel (☎ (071) 581 4132) at 74 Old Brompton Rd, London SW7 and 117 Euston Rd, London NW1 (☎ (071) 465 0484) are good, reliable agents for cheap tickets.

The cheapest London to Sydney bucket-shop tickets are about £310 one-way or £572 return. Such prices are usually only available if you leave London in the low season – March to June. In September and mid-December fares go up about 30%, while for the rest of the year they are somewhere in between.

From Australia you can expect to pay around A$1200 one-way and A$1800 return to London and other European capitals, with stops in Asia on the way.

To/From North America

There are a variety of connections across the Pacific from Los Angeles, San Francisco and Vancouver to Australia, including direct flights, flights via New Zealand, island-hopping routes or more circuitous Pacific rim routes via nations in Asia. Qantas, Air New Zealand and United all fly USA/Australia, while Qantas, Air New Zealand and Canadian Airlines International all fly Canada/Australia.

If flying via Hawaii, it might pay to fly with Qantas or Air New Zealand. If you fly with a US airline, you might find that the west coast to Hawaii sector is treated as a domestic flight (this means that you have to pay for drinks and headsets, goodies that are free on international sectors).

An interesting option from the east coast is the Northwest Airlines flight via Japan.

To find good fares to Australia, check the travel ads in the Sunday travel sections of papers like the *Los Angeles Times, San Francisco Chronicle-Examiner, New York Times* or *Toronto Globe & Mail*. The straightforward return excursion fare from the USA west coast is around US$1090, depending on the season, but plenty of deals are available. Return fares from the USA east coast range from US$1185 to US$2100. You can typically get a one-way ticket from US$800 (west coast) or US$1050 (east coast). In the USA, good agents for discounted tickets are the two student travel operators, Council Travel and STA Travel, both of which have lots of offices around the country. Canadian west-coast fares out of Vancouver will be similar to the US west coast. From Toronto, fares go from around C$1650 return.

Air France has an interesting island-hopping route between the US west coast and Australia, which includes the French colonies of New Caledonia and French Polynesia (Tahiti etc). The Air France flight is often discounted and its multiple Pacific stopover possibilities make it very popular with travellers. Los Angeles to Sydney on Air France costs about US$830 one way and US$1000 return. Polynesian Airlines has a similar route (Los Angeles-Sydney via Hawaii and Apia in Western Samoa) which costs between US$800 and US$1000 return. If Pacific island-hopping is your aim, check out the airlines of Pacific island nations, some of which have good deals on indirect routings. Qantas can give you Fiji or Tahiti along the way, Air New Zealand can offer both and the Cook Islands as well. See the Circle Pacific section for more details.

One-way/return fares available from Australia include: San Francisco A$1000/1650, New York A$1150/2000 and Vancouver $1150/1800.

To/From New Zealand

Air New Zealand and Qantas operate a network of trans-Tasman flights linking Auckland, Wellington and Christchurch in New Zealand with most major Australian gateway cities. You can fly directly between a lot of places in New Zealand and a lot of places in Australia.

From New Zealand to Sydney you're looking at around NZ$520 one-way and NZ$650 return. There is a lot of competition on this route, so there is bound to be some discounting going on.

To/From Asia

Ticket discounting is widespread in Asia, particularly in Singapore, Hong Kong, Bangkok and Penang. There are a lot of fly-by-nights in the Asian ticketing scene, so a little care is required. Also, the Asian routes fill up fast. Flights between Hong Kong and Australia are notoriously heavily booked, while flights to or from Bangkok and Singapore are often part of the longer Europe to Australia route, so they are also sometimes very full. Plan ahead. For much more information on South-East Asian travel and on to Australia see Lonely Planet's *South-East Asia on a shoestring*.

Typical one-way fares to Sydney from Asia include from Hong Kong for around HK$4400 or from Singapore for around S$540.

You can also pick up some interesting tickets in Asia to include Australia on the way across the Pacific. Air France were first in this market, but Qantas and Air New Zealand are also offering discounted trans-Pacific tickets. On the Air France ticket you

can stop over in Jakarta, Sydney, Noumea, Auckland and Tahiti.

From Australia, return fares from the east coast to Singapore, Kuala Lumpur and Bangkok range from $700 to $900, and to Hong Kong from $900 to $1300.

To/From Africa & South America

There is only a handful of direct flights each week between Africa and Australia, and then only between Perth and Harare (Zimbabwe) or Johannesburg (South Africa). A cheaper alternative from East Africa is to fly from Nairobi to India or Pakistan and on to South-East Asia, and then to connect from there to Australia.

Sydney to Harare costs about $2000 return; to Johannesburg it's from about $1600 return.

Two routes now operate between South America and Australia. The long-running Chile connection involves a Lan Chile flight Santiago/Easter Island/Tahiti, from where you fly Qantas or another airline to Australia. Alternatively, there is a route which skirts the Antarctic circle, flying Buenos Aires/Auckland/Sydney; this is operated by Aerolineas Argentinas.

Sydney to Santiago or Buenos Aires costs about $2000 return.

Arriving & Departing

Australia's dramatic increase in visitor arrivals has caused some severe bottlenecks at the entry points, particularly at Sydney where the airport is often operating at more than full capacity and delays on arrival or departure are frequent. Even when you're on the ground it can take ages to get through Immigration and Customs.

First-time travellers to Australia may be alarmed to find themselves being sprayed with insecticide by the airline stewards. It happens to everyone.

There's a departure tax of $25 which is payable by everyone leaving Australia. You can pre-pay the departure tax either at a post office (maybe it's a good idea to get it over with while you still have the cash) or at the airport.

Domestic Flights

The major domestic carriers are Ansett (☎ 13 1300), which also flies a few international routes, and Qantas (☎ 13 1313), which is also the international flag-carrier. Both fly between Sydney and all the other capital cities, and both have subsidiaries (Eastern Australia is part of Qantas, Ansett Express is part of Ansett) which fly smaller planes on shorter inter-and intra-state routes.

You don't have to reconfirm domestic flights on Ansett and Qantas, but you should phone on the day of your flight to check the details. For Ansett, call 13 1515; for Qantas, call 13 1223.

Because Qantas flies both international and domestic routes, flights leave from both the international and domestic terminals. Flights with flight numbers from QF001 to QF399 operate from international terminals; flight numbers QF400 and above from domestic terminals.

All airports and domestic flights are non-smoking.

Fares Few people pay full fare on domestic travel, as the airlines offer a wide range of discounts. These come and go and there are regular 'spot specials', so keep your eyes open. Because discounting is so unpredictable, we quote full economy fares in this book.

Full-time university or other higher education students get 25% off the regular economy fare on production of student ID or an ISIC card, but you can usually find fares discounted by more than that.

Note that there are no longer stand-by fares, but there are discount fares which allow same-day travel on certain flights, usually those which are uncomfortably early or late.

The cheapest fares are advance purchase deals. Some advance purchase fares offer up to 33% off one-way fares and up to 50% or more off return fares. You have to book one to three weeks ahead, and you often have to stay away for at least one Saturday night (for some reason). There are restrictions on changing flights and you can lose up to 100%

of the ticket price if you cancel, although you can buy health-related cancellation insurance.

International travellers (Australians and foreigners) can get a 25% to 40% discount on Qantas or Ansett domestic flights simply by presenting their international ticket (any airline, one-way or return) when booking. It seems there is no limit to the number of domestic flights you can take, but there might be time limits, say 60 days after you arrive in Australia. Note that the discount applies only to the full economy fare, and so in many cases it will be cheaper to take advantage of other discounts offered.

Air Passes With so much discounting these days, air passes do not represent the value they once did, although pre-buying a pass does save you the hassle of hunting around for special deals. Both Ansett and Qantas offer two types of passes, one which you have to buy before you arrive in Australia and one which you can buy after you arrive. The passes which are sold overseas are supposed to be for non-Australians only, but it might be possible to get around this. You'll probably save more money if you buy a pass overseas, with the downside of lack of flexibility in your itinerary.

Rules and prices for air passes change fairly frequently, so you should talk to a knowledgeable travel agent to find out what's currently available. You might have to be persistent, as it isn't unusual for airline booking staff to be unfamiliar with the passes on offer.

Qantas has two versions of the Australia Explorer Pass, available overseas only. One is for travel between major towns and cities, and the other is for longer-haul domestic destinations, such as Perth, northern Queensland and Alice Springs. Contact a Qantas office or representative for more information.

The Qantas pass which is sold within Australia is called the Backpackers Pass. You have to be a member of one of the hostel organisations (YHA, VIP, ITC and perhaps others) or have a Greyhound Pioneer Australia bus pass.

Ansett's Kangaroo Airpass can be bought in Australia and it gives you two options – 6000 km with two or three stopovers for $949 ($729 for children), or 10,000 km with three to seven stopovers for $1499 ($1149 for children). Restrictions include a minimum travel time (10 nights) and a maximum (45 nights). One of the stops must be at a non-capital-city destination and be for at least four nights. All sectors must be booked when you purchase the ticket, although these can be changed without penalty unless the ticket needs rewriting, in which case there's a $50 charge. Refunds are available before travel commences but not after you start using the ticket.

On a 6000-km airpass you could, for example, fly Sydney/Alice Springs/Cairns/Brisbane/Sydney. That gives you three stops, and two of them are in non-capital cities. The regular fare for that circuit would be $1498, but with current discounts it's only $1076, so you save $127 but have the restrictions. A one-way route might be Adelaide/Melbourne/Sydney/Alice Springs/Perth. There are three stops, one of which is a non-capital city. Regular cost for that route would be $1465, but with discounts it's $1016, so the saving is only $67.

Ansett also has passes available only to foreign visitors. Currently, the Visit Australia Pass must be bought and booked overseas, but you can alter your bookings and buy extra coupons after arrival. Four coupons (each giving a day's travel in the one direction) cost about $650, or $750 if you include Perth, and each additional coupon costs about $160, $210 if it includes Perth.

Warning

Prices for international travel are volatile, routes are introduced and cancelled, schedules change, rules are amended, special deals come and go, borders open and close. Airlines and governments seem to take a perverse pleasure in making price structures and regulations as complicated as possible, and you should check directly with the airline or travel agent to make sure you understand how a fare (and ticket you may buy) works.

In addition, the travel industry is highly competitive and there are many lurks and perks. The upshot of this is that you should get opinions, quotes and advice from as many airlines and travel agents as possible before you part with your hard-earned cash. The details given in this chapter should be regarded only as pointers and cannot be any substitute for your own careful, up-to-date research.

LAND

Interstate travel can mean a major journey. The nearest state capital to Sydney is Melbourne, 870 km away by the shortest road route. To Brisbane it's at least 980 km, to Adelaide it's at least 1420 km, Perth is 4100 km away and the shortest road to Darwin is 4000 km long. Sydney to Darwin via Adelaide is 4450 km, and it's nearly 5000 km going via Townsville.

Train

Interstate trains can be faster than buses and there are often special fares which make the prices competitive. On interstate journeys you can arrange free stopovers if you finish the trip within two months (six months on a return ticket).

Caper fares offer considerable savings on the standard fare, up to 30% off. You're supposed to book two weeks in advance but this is sometimes waived, and there are often other 'promotional' fares anyway – you have to ask for them. There are limited discount seats available on any one train, so it is advisable to book well in advance. Caper fares are non-refundable and you can only make a stopover if your journey is between two capital cities.

Interstate routes and fares from Sydney are:

To/From Canberra Two trains run daily. The trip takes about 4½ hours and costs $35/48 in economy/1st class.

To/From Melbourne A nightly XPT, 10 hours, $49/$79 in economy/1st class; sleeping berths are available for $135. (These fares are artificially low and could skyrocket.)

To/From Brisbane A nightly XPT, about 12½ hours, $95/137 in economy ($67/96 Caper fare), $217 with a sleeper. In conjunction with this train there's a connecting bus from Casino to the NSW far north coast and Queensland's Gold Coast. You can also take the train between Sydney and Murwillumbah, just south of the Queensland border, from where there's a connecting bus to the Gold Coast.

To/From Adelaide & Perth There's the twice-weekly Indian-Pacific, costing $104 in economy, $199 in an 'Econoberth' sleeper ($139 Caper fare) and $317 in a standard sleeper ($222 Caper fare). The trip takes nearly 26 hours. There's also Speedlink, a daily bus/train connection which is cheaper ($99/105 in economy/1st class) and five or six hours faster.

The Indian Pacific goes on to Perth, nearly 70 hours from Sydney. Fares are $883 in 1st class, with a sleeper and including meals, $600 in economy, with a berth but not including meals, and $230 sitting all the way. This is called a Super Sitter fare, and you'd need to be a super sitter to survive it!

Bus
It pays to shop around for fares. Students, YHA members and maybe backpackers in general get discounts of at least 10% with many long-distance companies. On straight point-to-point tickets there are varying stopover deals. Some companies give one free stopover on express routes, others charge a fee, maybe $5 for each stopover. This fee might be waived if you book through certain agents, notably some of the hostels.

There is only one truly *national* bus network – Greyhound Pioneer Australia (☎ 13 2030), which consists of the former Greyhound/Pioneer and Bus Australia. All were once separate companies and the buses

are still done out in their original paint-jobs. McCafferty's (☎ (02) 361 5125) and Kirklands (☎ (02) 281 2233) are the next largest, although they don't run Australia-wide. There are quite a few other companies running less extensive routes.

Major interstate routes and fares from Sydney are:

To/From Canberra Murrays (☎ (02) 252 3599) has three daily express (under four hours) buses to Canberra for $28 or around $20 if you pay in advance. Greyhound Pioneer Australia has the most frequent Canberra service ($28) including one direct from Sydney Airport ($32).

To/From Melbourne It's a 12 to 13-hour run (more if you go via Canberra) by the most direct route, the Hume Highway. Firefly Express (☎ (02) 211 1644) currently charges just $35, other companies charge around $50. As well as the Hume route, Greyhound Pioneer Australia runs up the prettier but much longer (up to 18 hours) Princes Highway coastal route ($58). For destinations along the Princes Highway within NSW, Pioneer Motor Service (no relation to the national company) has the best fares.

See the Tours section of the Getting Around chapter for the excellent three-day trip with Straycat.

To/From Brisbane By the Pacific Highway it takes about 16 hours and can cost $55 or less; the 'standard' cheap fare is around $60. You often need to book ahead. Not all buses stop in all the main towns en route. Companies running on the Pacific Highway route to Brisbane include Greyhound Pioneer Australia, Kirklands, McCaffertys and Lindsay's (☎ 1800 027 944 toll-free).

Fares between Sydney and some destinations within NSW include: Port Macquarie $36 (seven hours), Coffs Harbour $44 (9½ hours) and Byron Bay $60 (13 hours).

Greyhound Pioneer Australia, McCafferty's and Border Coaches (book at Sydney's Eddy Ave bus terminal) also have services on the inland New England High-

---

Cargo Boats

A traveller who sailed on a small freighter serving the South Pacific found things quite comfortable:

'As a passenger on a small cargo ship, you become an honorary officer. You dine in the officers' mess with dinner-gongs, typed menus and white-coated stewards. You drink with them at duty-free prices in the saloon. The few passenger cabins are large, comfortable and air-conditioned. But as the only folk on board without jobs to do, you must expect to be gently ignored. You have the run of the ship, from the claustrophobic racket of the engine-room up to the bridge for a yarn with the officer on watch. Other than that, settle down on the fo'c'stle deck, feel the great rise and fall as the swells roll under, and open up your copy of *Ulysses* or *War & Peace*.' ■

---

way which takes an hour or two longer but can cost about the same.

To/From Adelaide Sydney to Adelaide takes 18 to 25 hours and costs from about $90. Services run via Mildura ($70) or Broken Hill ($90). Travelling Sydney/Melbourne/Adelaide with Firefly might be a little cheaper than travelling Sydney/Adelaide with other companies. Countrylink's daily Speedlink service is a train to Albury then a bus to Adelaide and costs about $90.

To/From Elsewhere The fare is about $245 for the 52 to 56-hour trip to Perth. To Alice Springs it's about 42 hours (plus some waiting in Adelaide) and $211, and all the way to Darwin it's 67 hours and about $320, via either Adelaide or Brisbane.

Bus Passes If you're planning to travel around Australia, check out Greyhound Pioneer Australia's excellent bus-pass deals – make sure you get enough time and stopovers. See the Sydney Getting There & Away section for addresses of some travel agents which specialise in backpacker travel. They will know of the current deals and can advise on the pass that's best for you.

Broadly, there are set-distance passes which give you a year to cover a pre-determined distance (minimum 2000 km for $180, rising in multiples of 1000 km) and set-route passes which give you six or 12 months to cover a set route. There are about 20 routes to choose from and they can work out cheaper than a set-distance pass, but

you're locked into a route and you can't backtrack.

The third type of pass is the set-duration pass which allows travel on a set number of days during a specified period. There are no restrictions on where you can travel, and passes range from $343 for seven days of travel in one month up to $2100 for 90 days of travel in six months (what a nightmare!).

Car & Motorbike

See the Getting Around chapter for details of road rules, driving conditions and information on buying and renting vehicles.

The main road routes into NSW are the Hume Highway from Melbourne to Sydney (a freeway in Victoria but much of it is pretty narrow in NSW); the Princes Highway from Melbourne to Sydney via the coast (longer than the Hume but prettier and carrying less traffic until you reach the Shoalhaven area, beginning near Ulladulla); the Pacific Highway between Brisbane and Sydney via the coast (passing through or near all the north-coast beach resorts, but not a fun road to drive); and the route from Adelaide to Sydney via Broken Hill and Dubbo (wide open spaces and empty roads – except for kangaroos). The Newell Highway is a good road running from Victoria to Brisbane, crossing much of rural NSW along the way.

SEA

Cruise liners regularly call at Sydney, as do yachts. The liners aren't really a feasible way of travelling from point A to point B, but yachts looking for crew might be, especially if point B is a Pacific island. Ask around at yacht clubs and check hostel noticeboards. *Sydney Afloat* is a free monthly paper which occasionally has ads for crew. You'll find a copy at most yacht clubs. If you're determined to try yacht-crewing and have some spare time and money, it might help for you to do one of the sailing courses offered in Sydney.

It might be possible to travel on a cargo ship. This will be more expensive than flying (although much cheaper than a cruise ship), but could be interesting. Try agents such as the Sydney Sea & Air Centre (☎ 283 1199).

To/From Indonesia

Goden Shipping, based in Bali, has a vessel which sails roughly twice a month in each direction between Darwin and Bali. While cargo is the main concern, the vessel, which has an Australian skipper and Indonesian crew, has accommodation for 20 passengers in two, four and eight-berth cabins. The accommodation is described as 'basic but comfortable', all meals are provided and there's a bar on board. The trip takes from six to seven days non-stop, and the cost is A\$340/300/270 per person in two, four or eight-berth cabins. This service started in 1994 and we don't yet have any feedback on it, but it sounds interesting. For full details contact the shipping company, or its agent in Darwin:

Bali – Golden Shipping, Denpasar (☎ 289508; fax 287431)
Darwin – All Points Travel, Anthony Plaza, Smith St Mall (☎ 41 0066; fax 41 1602).

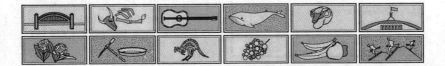

Getting Around

AIR

Ansett Express and Eastern Australia, which are subsidiaries of Ansett and Qantas, have intrastate flights, and there are several regional operators such as Hazelton, Kendell and Oxley. Most flights are between Sydney and major country centres (see the chart for fares), with few flights linking country centres. It would be difficult to put together a tour of the state by scheduled flights without a lot of backtracking to Sydney.

TRAIN

The NSW government's Countrylink rail network is the most comprehensive in Australia. The trains, in conjunction with connecting buses, take you quite quickly (if not necessarily very frequently) to most sizeable towns.

As well as the high-speed XPT trains (some with sleepers) there are the new Explorer trains, also pretty nippy. The introduction of the Explorers means that NSW has actually expanded its rail network. It's still much smaller than it once was ('the disused railway station' is a landmark common to many towns), but this is a step in the right direction. Trains run as far as Albury (and on to Melbourne), Armidale, Canberra, Broken Hill (and on to Adelaide and Perth), Dubbo, Kyogle (and on to Brisbane), Moree and Murwillumbah.

On point-to-point tickets, Countrylink's prices can be comparable to the private bus lines and there are sometimes special deals. You can make free stopovers, but they must be booked when you buy the ticket. With a one-way ticket you have to complete the journey within a week, and on a return ticket the outward half must be completed in a week and the return half within two months.

Countrylink promises that rail passes will soon be available, but don't hold your breath – I was first told that they were imminent back in 1991.

Most Countrylink services have to be booked (☎ (02) 217 8812 or 13 2232 outside Sydney, 6.30 am to 10 pm daily).

Intrastate one-way economy fares from Sydney include Albury, 643 km, $62; Armidale, 530 km, $58; Bathurst, 240 km, $25; Bourke, 841 km, $70; Broken Hill, 1125 km, $86; Byron Bay, 883 km, from $70; Coffs Harbour, 608 km, $62; Cooma, 446 km, $47; Dubbo, 431 km, $47; Griffith, 631 km, $62; Orange, 323 km, $30; Tamworth, 455 km, $51 (direct rail), $45 (bus).

CityRail, the Sydney metropolitan service, runs frequent electric trains south through Wollongong ($8.60) to Bomaderry ($14), east through the Blue Mountains to Katoomba ($8.60) and Lithgow ($18), north to Newcastle ($13.60) and south through the southern highlands to Goulburn ($17). Some of these services duplicate Countrylink services and while they are a little slower they are much cheaper, especially if you buy a day-return ticket. You can't book seats on CityRail trains.

New South Wales Air Fares

All fares in Australian Dollars
One-way economy air fares

Coolangatta
254
Coffs Harbour
Port Macquarie
Dubbo
190
155
156
Newcastle
Broken Hill
68
337
SYDNEY
138
209
162
CANBERRA
Cooma
Albury

BUS

The most comprehensive bus network is Countrylink's system of coordinated buses and trains.

The major bus lines also serve many towns on their express runs from Sydney to other capitals – see the Getting There & Away chapter for routes and fares. However, travelling short distances within NSW on an interstate bus is likely to be expensive, and because of regulations the interstate lines might not be allowed to take you on some sectors. Countrylink and a few local services fill these gaps.

Once you arrive at a major town there will usually be local services to smaller places nearby, but these services are rarely frequent.

CAR

If you want to visit a lot of places and don't have forever to do it in, a car is essential.

Road Rules

Although overseas licences are acceptable for overseas visitors, an International Driving Permit is even more acceptable.

Driving in NSW and the ACT holds few real surprises. Australians drive on the left-hand side of the road just like in the UK, Japan and most countries in south and east Asia and the Pacific. There are a few local variations on road rules. The main one is the 'give way to the right' rule. This means that even if you're driving along a main road and somebody appears on a minor road on your right, you must give way to them – unless they are facing a give-way or stop sign. At nearly all intersections they will be, but it's wise to be careful on minor roads in country areas, as some intersections aren't sign-posted and the 'give way to the right' rule applies – or, more likely, drivers just assume that on this lonely road there will be no other traffic and shoot straight though the intersection without thinking about rules.

Seat Belts All new cars are required to have seat belts back and front, and if your seat has a belt then you're required to wear it. Small children must be belted into approved safety-seats.

Speed Limits The speed limit is 100 km/h (roughly 60 miles per hour), except where otherwise indicated. On freeways, other divided roads and some rural highways this is sometimes raised to 110 km/h. Some dangerous sections of rural roads have a limit of less than 100 km/h. The usual limit in towns is 60 km/h, sometimes rising to 80 km/h on the outskirts and dropping to 40 km/h in residential areas. Speeding in towns is not uncommon (if stupid), but near schools *everyone* observes the 40 km/h limit.

Speed cameras catch people who exceed these limits, but they generally operate only in cities and on major roads, which leaves country drivers to speed unhindered on narrow back-roads where head-on collisions are a real possibility.

Alcohol The blood alcohol limit in NSW is 0.05%, which most people reach after drinking two full-strength beers in an hour (although there is a lot of variation between individuals). Bus drivers must not have any alcohol in their system when they get behind the wheel. These limits are enforced with random breath-checks and the penalties for exceeding them are heavy, which accounts for the new-found popularity of low-alcohol beer.

Parking Parking in Sydney can be a nightmare – there are just too many cars for those narrow streets. Beware of tow-away zones! A lot of cheaper accommodation in Sydney has no parking, so you're left with the choice of paying for commercial parking or constantly shifting your car to avoid fines.

Outside of Sydney, parking meters are rare. Many country towns insist on rear-to-kerb angle parking. This takes a while to master, and also means that the car in front of you will signal a left turn then move to the middle of the road, hopefully stopping to see that you are behind them before reversing into the parking space.

On the Road

Australia is not crisscrossed by multi-lane highways, and although the east of NSW is reasonably closely settled (well, compared with the Northern Territory, not compared with Sussex), don't expect to find major roads everywhere you want to go.

You'll certainly find stretches of divided road, particularly on roads out of Sydney, but elsewhere highways are usually only two lanes wide. I met a very strung-out couple who had arrived in Sydney, hired a car and driven up to Byron Bay the same night. The 900 km they drove might have been on the Pacific Highway, but, as they found, it's a narrow, winding road carrying a lot of traffic.

Between cities, signposting on the main roads is generally OK, but once you enter the maze of rural backroads you'll need a map – the NRMA's series of regional roadmaps should see you right. In towns the street-signing can be very poor.

Fuel Petrol and diesel are available from stations sporting the well-known international brand names. Prices vary from place to place and from price-war to price-war, but generally it's in the 65c to 75c per litre range (say around $2.70 to $3.20 per imperial gallon). In remote areas the price can soar, and some outback service stations are not above exploiting their monopoly position. Distances between fill-ups can be long in the far west, so make sure you have enough fuel.

Outback Driving

There are very few sealed roads in the state's far west, but there are plenty of unsealed tracks. Some are in good condition and carry a relatively large amount of traffic (you might see a car every hour or so), but others are very lonely, very remote and potentially very dangerous if you break down. You often don't need 4WD to tackle these roads, but you do need to be prepared. Backtracking hundreds of km to pick up a replacement for some minor malfunctioning component or, much worse, to arrange a tow, is unlikely to be easy or cheap.

You will of course need to carry a fair amount of water in case of disaster. Food is less important – the space might be better allocated to an extra spare tyre.

If you run into trouble in the back of beyond, *stay with your vehicle*. It's much easier to spot a car than a human being from the air. Also, the heat can quickly kill you once you leave the shelter of your car.

The number-one rule of outback driving is to seek local advice, preferably from the police. They will know of the road conditions (sections of road can still be boggy many days after the last rain) and can advise whether your vehicle is suitable for a particular track – many outback routes are perfectly OK for 2WD vehicles, but you might need high clearance to cope with ruts and washouts if the road hasn't been graded since the last rains, for example.

C&LM's tourist map of the outback is informative, but if you plan to drive on the minor unsealed roads you should supplement it with more detailed maps. There's a recorded message (☎ (02) 11571) detailing road conditions for all of NSW. If you're heading further into the outback (this really is 4WD country) you'll want to know about conditions in the north of South Australia (☎ (08) 11 633) or Queensland (☎ (07) 11 655). You should still contact a local police station before setting out.

4WD or 2WD? You see an awful lot of 4WD (four-wheel drive) vehicles, but many never leave the sealed roads and fewer still do any serious rough-terrain work. Do you need one? If you are sticking to routes which are regularly maintained, a 4WD's main advantage is its high clearance which can cope with minor flooding and deep ruts. Of course, they are also designed not to fall apart under the strains of outback travel, and they are generally big bastards, so you can carry a lot of fuel and luggage.

My 2WD sedan easily coped with the 30,000-odd km of research for this guide, a lot of it on unsealed roads. On the other hand, I had to postpone a couple of sections because of rain. Once, I didn't postpone long enough and ended up bogged a long way from anywhere. (Cutting down thornbushes – to provide traction – with a pocket knife was not much fun at all. Carry a hatchet and a shovel!)

If you do have a 4WD, don't go crazy with it. After rain, some outback roads are closed, not necessarily because 4WDs can't get through but because of the damage they will do to the road in trying. Some drivers see a Road Closed sign as a challenge and stuff things up for everyone else. 'Bush-bashing' (making your own road through the bush) is definitely a no-no.

Hazards

Local drivers on little-used rural roads often speed, and they often assume that there is no other traffic. Be careful of oncoming cars at blind corners on country roads.

Animals Animals are common hazards on country roads, and a collision is likely to kill the animal and seriously damage your vehicle. Kangaroos are most active around dawn and dusk, and they travel in groups. If you see one hopping across the road in front of you, slow right down – its friends are probably just behind it. In remote areas many people avoid travelling altogether between 5 pm and 8 am, because of the hazards posed by animals. If an animal appears in front of you, hit the brakes (gently if you're on dirt) and only swerve to avoid the animal if it is safe to do so. The number of people who have been killed in accidents caused by swerving to miss an animal is high – better to damage your car and probably kill the animal than kill yourself and others with you.

Other animals with no road sense include cows, sheep (they are incredibly *stupid)* and emus. Once again, if you see one you can expect more to be following.

In the country, even on quite major roads, it's fairly common to meet a herd of sheep or cattle being driven (droved?) along the road. Sometimes you will have been warned of this by signs placed on the roadside, but often you'll come around a corner and find the road crammed with animals. Stop and see what the situation is (the drover won't appre-ciate it if you scatter a herd that he/she and the dogs have just rounded up), then drive through *very* slowly. Beware of stragglers.

Dirt Roads You don't have to get very far off the beaten track to find yourself on dirt roads. Most are regularly graded and reason-ably smooth (although rain can alter that), and it's often possible to travel at high speed. Don't.

If you're travelling along a dirt road at 100 km/h and you come to a corner, you won't go around that corner – you'll sail off into the bush. If you put on the brakes to slow down you'll probably spin or roll. If you swerve sharply to avoid a pot-hole you'll go into an exciting four-wheel drift then find out what happens when your car meets a gum tree. Worst of all, if another car approaches and you have to move to the edge of the road, you'll lose control and collide head-on.

On dirt roads that are dry, flat, straight, traffic-free and wide enough to allow for unexpected slewing as you hit potholes and drifted sand, you could, with practise, drive at about 80 km/h. Otherwise, treat dirt like ice.

Gates & Grids Rural roads, especially access roads to national parks and out-of-the-way waterfalls etc, sometimes run through private property where you might encounter closed gates and cattle grids. Cattle grids (usually sections of railway tracks laid across a pit) stop stock from wan-dering and they're usually no hasssle to drive across, unless the road has been washed out on either side of them, in which case you'll get an almighty jolt. It always pays to slow down for grids. The essential rule about gates is: *always leave a gate as you find it.* If it's open, leave it open; if it's closed, close it after you.

One-Lane Bridges These are fairly common on minor roads. They're usually signposted, but not always.

Buying a Car

Australian cars are not cheap – another consequence of the small population. Locally manufactured cars are made in small, uneconomic numbers, and imported cars are heavily taxed. If you're buying a second-hand vehicle (which is what nearly all travellers do) reliability is all-important.

You can buy through a dealer (you'll probably pay more, but you'll get a guaranteed title and help with paperwork), or privately by checking the classified ads or hostel noticeboards. If you're buying an old car, remember that the further you get from big towns, the better it is to be in a Holden or a Ford Falcon. Life is much simpler when you can get spare parts anywhere from Bourke to Bulamakanka, and every scrap-yard in Australia is full of good ol' Holdens and Falcons. This isn't so much of a problem in NSW unless you have a very exotic car, but elsewhere in the country it might be.

Sydney is the best place to buy a car. Parramatta Rd is lined with used car lots, and there are other setups geared especially for travellers. There's a car market (☎ (02) 358 5000) at the Kings Cross Parking Station on the corner of Ward Ave and Elizabeth Bay Rd, which charges sellers $35 a week (daily rates available). This place can help with paperwork and insurance and is becoming something of a travellers' rendezvous. The Sunday Flemington Car Market (☎ 0055 21122) near Flemington Station charges sellers $50 and has a shuttle bus that picks up in Kings Cross.

Several dealers, such as Mach 1 Autos (☎ (02) 569 3374) at 495 New Canterbury Rd in Dulwich Hill, will sell you a car with an undertaking to buy it back at an agreed price. Always read the small print. We've heard of deals where the seller agreed to buy the vehicle back at 60% of sale price, minus 1% for every 1000 km travelled, minus the cost of repairing any damage, and the buyer ended up with next to nothing. A buy-back deal with a private seller (such as a hostel manager) is risky, as they might not have enough ready cash when you want to sell.

Before you buy it's worth having the car checked by a mechanic. If you, or a friend, are a member of the NRMA you can get a vehicle checked over for $98. It costs $72 to join the NRMA (☎ 13 2132), but members of interstate and some overseas motoring organisations pay only $36. Some garages do inspections for much less.

For full details of the paperwork required to buy a car, pick up a copy of the Roads & Traffic Authority (RTA) pamphlet 'Six Steps to Buying a Secondhand Motor Vehicle', available at RTA and NRMA offices. Motor Registry offices also have information and there are many of them. If you're buying privately it's essential to check that the registration is still valid, that the vehicle isn't stolen or actually owned by a finance company, and whether there are any outstanding fines – the pamphlet tells you how to do this.

Every registered vehicle has third-party insurance – a Green Slip. This covers you against injuries you might cause but not damage to other people's property, so it's a very good idea to have third-party property insurance. The major insurance companies don't sell third-party property insurance to travellers, but the Kings Cross car market (and some dealers) can arrange it, even if you didn't buy the car there.

When the time comes to sell the car, fill in a Notice of Disposal card (available from a Motor Registry), or you might be liable for fines incurred by the new owner.

Renting a Car

If you've got the cash, there are plenty of car rental companies ready and willing to put you behind the wheel. Competition is pretty fierce, so rates tend to be variable and lots of special deals pop up and disappear again. Whatever your mode of travel on the long stretches, it can be very useful to have a car for some local travel. Between a group of people, it can even be reasonably economical.

The three major companies, Budget, Hertz and Avis, have agents everywhere. Thrifty is a second-string outfit which also has a wide network. Then there is a vast number of local firms. The big operators often have higher rates than the local firms, but not always.

You'll need to calculate insurance, km rates and all the other fine print. The big companies usually allow one-way rentals, although there might be extra charges and other restrictions.

Be aware that the insurance usually has an excess – if you have a prang, the excess is the amount you have to pay before the insurance company takes over. With some of the small companies this can be very high. Most companies prefer to rent to people over 21, and some require you to be over 25, although there are a few who will rent to 18-year-olds (often with higher insurance premiums or a greater excess).

The major companies offer unlimited km rates in Sydney and some other major centres, but in country areas it's usually a flat charge plus so many cents per km. With straightforward city rentals they're all pretty much the same price. It's on special deals, odd rentals or longer periods that you find the differences. Weekend specials – usually three days for the price of two – are usually good value.

Daily rates are typically about $70 a day for a small car (Ford Laser, Toyota Corolla, Nissan Pulsar); about $90 a day for a medium car (Holden Camira, Toyota Camry, Nissan Pintara); and about $100 to $110 a day for a big car (Holden Commodore, Ford Falcon), all including insurance. Prices start to drop if you hire for more than a day or two.

Don't forget the 'rent-a-wreck' companies. They specialise in renting older cars, typically around $35 a day. If you just want to travel around the city, or not too far out, they can be worth considering.

4WDs Renting a 4WD vehicle is within the budget range if a few people get together. Something small like a Suzuki costs around $100 per day; for a Toyota Landcruiser you're looking at around $150, which should include insurance and some free km (typically 100 km). Check the insurance conditions, especially the excess, as they can be onerous.

Hertz has 4WD rentals, with one-way rentals possible between the eastern states

and the Northern Territory. Brits Australia (☎ (1800) 331 454) hires 4WD vehicles that are fitted out as campervans. These are not cheap at $155 per day for unlimited km, plus collision damage waiver ($12 per day). Their Sydney office (☎ (02) 667 0402, toll-free 1800 331 454) is at 182 O'Riordan St in Mascot.

MOTORCYCLE

Motorcycles are a very popular way of getting around. The climate is just about ideal for biking much of the year and the many small trails from the road into the bush often lead to perfect spots to spend the night in the world's largest camping ground.

A fuel range of 350 km will cover most fuel stops. You'll need a rider's licence – a car license isn't enough – and a helmet.

If you want to bring your own motorcycle into Australia you'll need a *carnet de passages*, and when you try to sell it you'll get less than the market price because of restrictive registration requirements (not so severe in Western and South Australia and in the Northern Territory). Shipping from just about anywhere is expensive.

Unfortunately, renting a bike is pretty expensive. In Sydney try a company such as All Bike Hire (☎ (02) 707 1691) at 164 Canterbury Rd in Bankstown, which charges from around $50 a day ($250 a week, less by the month) for a 125 cc bike and $95 a day ($500 a week, less by the month) for 650 cc and over.

With a bit of time up your sleeve, getting mobile on your own two wheels is quite feasible, thanks largely to the chronically depressed motorcycle market. Australian newspapers and the lively local bike press have extensive classified advertisement sections where $2500 gets you something that will easily take you around the country if you know a bit about bikes. The main drawback is that you'll have to try and sell it again afterwards.

An easier option is a buy-back arrangement with a large motorcycle dealer, although this is not common and the major disasters that can befall bikes make agreeing on a buy-back price very much a matter for negotiation. Holiday Wheels Motorcycles (☎ (02) 718 6668) at the rear of 589 Canterbury Rd in Belmore (Sydney) sometimes has buy-back deals, and they can help arrange insurance (sometimes a problem for foreign visitors). One of the partners speaks German.

It's worth carrying some spares and tools even if you don't know how to use them, because someone else often does. The basics include: a spare tyre tube (front wheel size, which will fit on the rear but usually not vice versa); puncture repair kit with levers and a pump (or tubeless tyre repair kit with two or three carbon dioxide cartridges); a spare tyre valve; the bike's standard toolkit for what it's worth (aftermarket items are better); spare throttle, clutch and brake cables; tie wire, cloth tape ('gaffer' tape) and nylon 'zip-ties'; a handful of bolts and nuts in the usual emergency sizes (M6 and M8), along with a few self-tapping screws; one or two fuses; a bar of soap for fixing tank leaks (knead to a putty with water and squeeze into the leak); and, most important of all, a workshop manual for your bike (even if you can't make sense of it, the local motorcycle mechanic can).

Stray animals on the road can mess up a car, but if you hit them on a bike you're in serious trouble, mate. It's wise to stop riding by around 5 pm. Keep an eye out for cattle grids. As with car driving, outback travel demands that you carry plenty of water (and drink it even when you don't feel thirsty, as you dehydrate rapidly on a bike), and, if you break down, park your bike where it's clearly visible and stay with it.

BICYCLE

NSW is a great place for cycling and it's possible to plan rides of any duration and through almost any terrain. There are thousands of km of good roads which carry so little traffic that the biggest hassle is waving back to the drivers.

Bicycle helmets are compulsory, as are front and rear lights for night riding.

Cycling has always been popular and not only as a sport: some shearers would ride for huge distances between jobs, rather than use less reliable horses. It's rare to find a reasonably sized town that doesn't have a shop stocking at least basic bike parts.

If you're coming specifically to cycle, it makes sense to bring your own bike. Check with your airline for costs and the degree of dismantling/packing required. Within Australia you can load your bike onto a bus or train to skip the boring bits. Note that bus companies require you to dismantle your bike, and some don't guarantee that it will travel on the same bus as you. Trains are easier, but supervise the loading and if possible tie your bike upright, otherwise you may find that the guard has stacked crates of Holden spares on your fragile alloy frame.

See the Activities section in the Sydney chapter for some places which rent bikes.

Much of eastern Australia seems to have been settled on the principle of not having more than a day's horse-ride between pubs, so it's possible to plan even ultra-long routes and still get a shower at the end of the day. Most people do carry camping equipment, but it's feasible to travel from town to town staying in pubs or on-site vans.

You can get by with roadmaps but they don't show topography, so if you care about hills, buy C&LM maps. The scale you need depends on the terrain – mountain biking through a national park demands a detailed map; following a major road across the western plains doesn't. The 1:250,000 series is good for road work, but you'll need a lot of maps if you're covering much territory.

The Bicycle Institute of NSW (☎ (02) 212 5628) in Sydney at 82 Campbell St, Surry Hills 2010 has more information and sells guides. Some bike shops listed in the Sydney chapter can also help with information on routes and suggested rides.

HITCHING

Hitching is never entirely safe in any country in the world, and we don't recommend it. Travellers who decide to hitch should understand that they are taking a small but potentially serious risk. However, many people do choose to hitch, and the advice that

Long-Distance Cycling

Until you get fit you should be careful to eat enough to keep you going – remember that exercise is an appetite suppressant. It's surprisingly easy to be so depleted of energy that you end up camping under a gum tree just 10 km short of a shower and a steak.

No matter how fit you are, water is still vital. Dehydration is no joke and can be life-threatening. I rode my first 200-km-in-a-day on a bowl of cornflakes and a round of sandwiches, but the Queensland sun forced me to drink nearly five litres. Having been involved in a drinking contest with stockmen the night before may have had something to do with it, though.

It can get very hot in summer, and you should take things slowly until you're used to the heat. Cycling in 30°C-plus temperatures isn't too bad if you wear a hat and plenty of sunscreen, and drink *lots* of water. Be aware of the blistering 'hot northerlies', the prevailing winds that make a north-bound cyclist's life uncomfortable in summer. In April, when the south-east region's clear autumn weather begins, the 'southerly trades' prevail.

Always check with locals if you're heading into remote areas, and notify the police if you're about to do something particularly adventurous. That said, you can't rely too much on local knowledge of road conditions, as most people have no idea of what a heavily loaded touring-bike needs. What they think of as a great road may be pedal-deep in sand or bull dust, and I've happily ridden along roads that were officially flooded out. ■

follows should help to make their journeys as fast and safe as possible.

Successful hitching depends on several factors, all of them just plain good sense. The most important is your numbers – two people is really the ideal; any more makes things very difficult. Ideally those two should comprise one male and one female – two guys hitching together can expect long waits, and it is probably not advisable for women to hitch alone, or even in pairs.

Factor two is position – look for a place where vehicles will be going slowly and where they can stop easily. Junctions and freeway slip roads are good places if there is stopping room. Position goes beyond just where you stand. The ideal location is on the outskirts of a town – hitching from way out in the country is as hopeless as from the centre of a city. Take a bus out to the edge of town.

Factor three is appearance. The ideal appearance for hitching is a sort of genteel poverty – threadbare but clean. Looking too good can be as much of a bummer as looking too bad! Don't carry too much gear – if it looks like it's going to take half an hour to pack your bags aboard, you'll be left on the roadside.

Factor four is knowing when to say no. Saying no to a car-load of drunks may be pretty obvious, but it can be time-saving to say no to a short ride that might take you from a good hitching point to a lousy one. Your best bet is to wait for the right, long ride to come along.

Trucks are often the best lifts, but they will only stop if they are going slowly and can get started easily again. Thus the ideal place is at the top of a hill where they have a downhill run. Truckies often say they are going to the next town and, if they don't like you, will drop you anywhere. As they often pick up hitchers for company, the quickest way to create a bad impression is to jump in and fall asleep.

If you're visiting from abroad, a nice prominent flag on your pack will help, and a sign announcing your destination can also be useful. University and hostel notice-boards are good places to look for hitching partners.

The main law against hitching is 'thou shalt not stand in the road' – so when you see the law coming, step back.

OTHER OPTIONS
The Kindness of Strangers

If you're totally stuck in an out-of-the-way place with no bus before next Tuesday and you don't want to hitch, there are a few last-resort options. Chances are there's a school bus taking students to a high school in the area's nearest large town. The bus probably isn't licensed to take you along, but your charm might get you on board. The mail-run is usually let out to private contractors who just might let you go along, maybe for a fee, maybe not. The post office will know the contractors and their routes. Finally, there's probably some sort of carrier in town who might be persuaded to give you a lift on a delivery-run.

Don't count on these options, and remember that country people might be hospitable but they can also be wary of strangers. Arranging a lift in the pub the night before is likely to be more successful than just turning up out of the blue.

Walking

Most long-distance walking is recreational (see the Activities section of the Facts for the Visitor chapter), but 'humping your bluey' (walking with a swag, or bedroll) is a time-honoured way of getting around rural roads. You don't see many swaggies (people who carry swags) these days, but they do still exist. They resemble England's tramps or America's hobos, but their social status is traditionally a little higher: if you're down on your luck it's no disgrace to 'go on the wallaby' (hit the road) and look for work.

LOCAL TRANSPORT
Taxi

Sydney has an awful lot of taxis, but you won't see many plying for trade on the streets of country towns. That doesn't mean they aren't there, though, and even quite small towns often have at least one taxi. Taxi fares vary through the state but shouldn't be very different from the Sydney fares, unless there are local considerations such as dirt roads.

Bus & Train

Sydney has a good public transport system and in Canberra, Wollongong and Newcastle it's possible to get around by public transport. Anywhere else it becomes a bit problematic. There are buses in cities such as Wagga Wagga and Dubbo, but they are fairly infrequent.

TOURS

There are some interesting tours, although few that cover much of the state. Most are connected with a particular activity (eg, bushwalking or horseriding tours) or area (eg, outback tours from Broken Hill). See the Activities section of the Facts for the Visitor chapter and the various chapters of this book for some suggestions.

It's worth checking out what's available through the Sydney YHA, as they often run good tours themselves, or know about other tours that are available. Hostel noticeboards are also good sources of information.

Major tour companies in Sydney have programmes of tours to places such as Canberra and the Snowy Mountains; see the Sydney chapter.

A good way of travelling between Sydney and Byron Bay is with Ando's Opal Outback Tours (☎ (02) 559 2901). The trip takes a week and includes travelling inland via Lightning Ridge for a taste of opal, sapphire and gold mining. Ando (John Anderson) is quite a character and his tour gets good feedback from backpackers. At around $390 it's a bargain. Ando sometimes has other tours – ring and check.

Straycat (☎ (03) 481 2993 or 1800 800 840 toll-free) runs a 22-seater bus between Sydney and Melbourne, taking a leisurely three days on a scenic route through the mountains. The trip includes visits to Canberra and national parks, with time for outdoor activities. One night is spent at a working sheep-station in the Snowy Mountains and another in Bright (Victoria), where you have a choice of accommodation including a youth hostel – and you can stop over if you want. Everything except accommodation (and an optional caves visit) is included in the fare, excellent value at $125. There are usually two departures a week in summer, and one a week at other times.

The Pioneering Spirit (☎ (018 751 466) is a double-decker bus (with sleeping quarters on the upper deck) which runs from Sydney to Brisbane via the coast, taking six days to complete the trip and costing $32 per person a day, plus $6 food kitty – there's a chef on board. It describes itself as a 'mobile hostel'. As you're taking six days to do a trip that regular buses complete in 16 hours, there's plenty of time to explore.

See the Activities section of the Facts for the Visitor chapter for Wildwise, an outfit that runs adventure activity tours for women. Breakout Tours (☎ (02) 550 0328), GPO Box 3801, Sydney 2001, has tours that cater specifically for gays and lesbians.

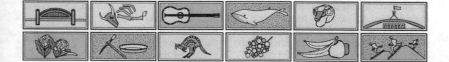

Sydney

Sydney is a glittering, lively city with a fabulously beautiful harbour at its centre.

The citizens of Australia's largest city (population 3.7 million) pursue fashion and trends with a vigour not found elsewhere in the country. Sydneysiders are not noted for their reserve! Perhaps this is because they live among some reassuringly large and constant natural features: the harbour, the Pacific Ocean and the encircling mountains.

The barriers which restricted the growth of the early colony still affect the city's outlook. Like the convicts who were convinced that China was just on the other side of the impassable Blue Mountains, Sydneysiders behave as though the outback begins at Lithgow, and as though Newcastle and Wollongong are the limits of civilisation. You're more likely to hear about the latest in New York or Paris than the news from Adelaide or Melbourne.

Despite Sydney's cosmopolitan population, there's still a strong streak of Australian larrikinism (saying to hell with formality and 'good manners') and egalitarianism.

Sydneysiders are often open and friendly. If you need help, you will either be ignored or be shown amazing solicitude. Don't expect queuing or other formal signs of politeness, though. When the train doors slide back or the ferry ramp slams onto the deck, step lively or you'll be left behind.

The mix of people is fascinating. I reckon that on every inner-city train, among all the business wear, beach-culture clothes, feral people, tourists etc, there's always at least one sprightly old man, wearing shorts, deck-shoes and a yachting slicker, on his way to an important meeting with a boat.

ORIENTATION

Sydney came into existence before the era of grand plans that was to characterise most later Australian cities, and its layout is further complicated by the harbour with its numerous arms and inlets, and by the hilly nature of the city. If you plan to explore beyond the inner suburbs, a street directory is essential.

The harbour divides Sydney into north and south, with the Harbour Bridge joining the two. The city centre and most other places of interest are south of the harbour.

City Centre

The central city area is relatively long and narrow, although only George and Pitt Sts (the main commercial and shopping streets) run the whole three km from the waterfront Rocks area south to Central Railway Station.

The historic Rocks and Circular Quay, where you'll find the Opera House and the Harbour Bridge, mark the northern boundary of the centre; Central Railway Station is on the southern edge; the inlet of Darling Harbour is the western boundary; and a string of parks borders Elizabeth and Macquarie Sts on the eastern side.

Inner Suburbs

Most of Sydney's inner suburbs have undergone at least some gentrification, and their terraces of Victorian workers' houses are now spruce – and expensive. Cafes, restaurants, interesting shops and good pubs, often with entertainment, are scattered throughout the inner suburbs.

East of the city centre are Kings Cross,

Woolloomooloo and Paddington. Further east again are some of the more exclusive suburbs south of the harbour and then beachfront suburbs like Bondi. The airport is some way south of this area, beside Botany Bay, which is Sydney's second great harbour.

South-east of the city centre are the inner suburbs of Darlinghurst and Surry Hills; to the south-west is Glebe, a bohemian suburb famous for its eateries, and west again is arty Balmain.

North of the Harbour

Across the Harbour Bridge from the city centre is North Sydney, an important business centre with its own collection of tall office buildings. North-shore suburbs such as Hunters Hill are among Sydney's most expensive places to live. The beachside suburb of Manly is on both the harbour and the ocean, near Sydney Harbour's sea entrance. North from here, a string of ocean beaches leads up to Palm Beach, which also fronts Pittwater, a large inlet. On the west side of Pittwater is Ku-Ring-Gai Chase National Park (see the Around Sydney chapter).

Greater Sydney

The suburbs stretch westward beyond Parramatta, 25 km west and once a country retreat for the colony's governor, to Penrith at the foot of the Blue Mountains. South-west of the city there's a similar sprawl of housing developments, swamping old towns such as Campbelltown and Liverpool. These red-tile-roofed, triple-fronted suburbs are where most Australians live – not in the outback or beside a harbour or beach.

INFORMATION
Tourist Offices

The New South Wales Government Travel Centre (☎ 231 4444) is at 19 Castlereagh St and is open weekdays from 9 am to 5 pm. The Sydney Information Booth (☎ 235 2424) is nearby in Martin Place (sharing a booth with Halftix) and is open the same hours. You might be served more quickly here.

The Tourist Information Service (☎ 669 5111) answers phone queries from 8 am to 6 pm daily. In the Eddy Ave bus station (outside Central Railway Station), the Travellers' Information Service (☎ 281 9366) makes bus and accommodation bookings (but not hostel bookings).

Money

At the airport's international terminal, a Westpac agency is open daily from around 5.30 am until after the last flight, around 10 pm. You don't need to enter passenger-only areas to change money, so this is a useful emergency option.

Thomas Cook has foreign exchange branches at 175 Pitt St (☎ 229 6611), in the Queen Victoria Building and in the Kingsgate shopping centre in Kings Cross. The Pitt St branch is open Monday to Saturday, the others daily. American Express branches are

Lost?

With so much travel in central Sydney done underground, and with so many arcade exits from the stations, it's easy to emerge onto street level and not have a clue which way you're facing. There are very few policemen on foot to ask directions of, but most Sydneysiders are happy to help once you have grabbed their attention (no mean feat if they are hurrying to a train).

The city's most obvious landmark is Sydney Tower, that tall needle-and-bobbin structure. Trouble is, the tower looks the same from any direction.

If you can see the Harbour Bridge you have a pretty good idea of which way you're heading (unless things have gone totally haywire and you have ended up on the north shore), and a long street with a downhill slope is probably heading towards the bridge. ■

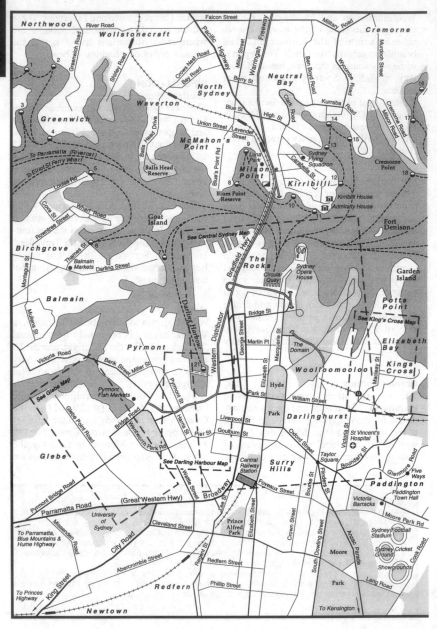

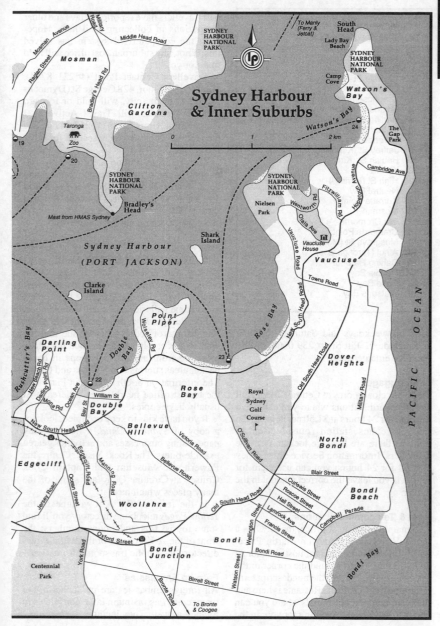

Sydney Harbour & Inner Suburbs

SYDNEY

FERRY WHARVES
(See map previous pages)

1 Northwood
2 Bay St
3 Valentia St
4 Greenwich
5 Longnose Point (Birchgrove)
6 Thames St (Balmain)
7 Darling St (Balmain)
8 McMahons Point
9 Lavender Bay
10 Jeffrey St (Kirribilli)
11 Beulah St (Kirribilli)
12 Kirribilli
13 High St (Kirribilli)
14 Neutral Bay
15 Kurraba Point
16 Mosman
17 Old Cremorne
18 Cremorne Point
19 Musgrave St (Mosman)
20 Athol (Taronga Zoo)
21 Darling Harbour
22 Double Bay
23 Rose Bay
24 Watsons Bay

open on weekdays and Saturday morning and include 92 Pitt St (☎ 239 0666, or 886 0666 for emergencies).

Left Luggage

There are cloakrooms at Central, Town Hall and Wynyard stations where you can leave luggage for 24 hours at $1.50 per item. At the Eddy Ave bus station (outside Central Station) there are luggage lockers near the Travellers' Information Service office. They cost $4 for 24 hours; you can use them for longer if you leave the correct amount in the locker.

Post & Telecommunications

The main Sydney post office, the GPO, is a grand Victorian building on Martin Place. Sadly, this old structure is almost abandoned and you have to go around the corner to the Pitt St entrance to enter the nondescript temporary post office. Poste Restante is here and there are computer terminals where you can check to see if mail is waiting for you. In the

past travellers have reported delays and other frustrations in collecting mail here. Hopefully the computerised system has solved this; if not, any suburban post office will hold mail for you.

Travellers Contact Point (☎ 221 8744), Suite 16, 8th Floor, 428 George St (Dymocks Building) in the city, will hold or forward mail for you, as will Travel Active at 3 Orwell St in Kings Cross (☎ 357 4477). See the Getting There & Away section for other travel agents.

The Telecom Phone Centre, with 100 phones (some of which accept credit – and debit – cards) is open 24 hours a day. It is at 100 King St in the city, between Pitt and George Sts.

Sydney's telephone area code is 02.

Free Publications

Index is a monthly pamphlet useful for its gallery and entertainment listings, with cafes, bookshops and other places mentioned briefly. The tourist office has copies, as do some galleries and quality bookshops.

For Backpackers, By Backpackers gives brief listings of budget places to stay and eat, what to see, etc. It appears bi-monthly and is available from hostels and shops in backpacker areas such as Kings Cross and Glebe. The information booth on Martin Place and the tourist office nearby on Castlereagh St usually have copies.

If you have kids to keep occupied, look for a copy of *Sydney's Child*, a free monthly paper listing businesses and activities geared to ankle-biters. The Rocks Visitor Centre, the Powerhouse Museum and Captain Cook Cruises at Circular Quay are some of the many places which have it.

In the front of the A-K volume of the *Yellow Pages* telephone directory you'll find some tourist tips and phone numbers; the front of the A-K volume of the *White Pages* directory has public transport information.

Foreign Embassies

All foreign embassies are in Canberra, but many countries maintain large consulates in Sydney as well. They include:

Canada
  111 Harrington St (☎ 364 3000)
France
  31 Market St (☎ 261 5779)
Germany
  13 Trelawny St, Woollahra (☎ 328 7733)
Israel
  37 York St (☎ 264 7933)
Italy
  1 Macquarie St (☎ 247 8442)
Japan
  52 Martin Place (☎ 231 3455)
Netherlands
  500 Oxford St, Bondi Junction (☎ 387 6644)
New Zealand
  1 Alfred St (☎ 247 1999)
Sweden
  44 Market St (☎ 262 1077)
UK
  1 Macquarie Place (☎ 247 7251, recorded information 0055 20273)
USA
  Corner of Park and Castlereagh Sts
  (☎ 234 9200)

Cultural Centres

Among the many cultural organisations in Sydney are the following:

Alliance Francaise
  257 Clarence St (☎ 267 1755)
British Council
  203 New South Head Rd, Edgecliff (☎ 326 2022)
Italian Institute for Culture
  424 George St (☎ 221 4087)
Japan Cultural Centre
  201 Miller St, North Sydney (☎ 954 0111)
Jewish Cultural Centre
  148 Darlinghurst Rd, Darlinghurst (☎ 360 7999)

Useful Organisations

The National Parks & Wildlife Service has an information centre at Cadman's Cottage off George St in the Rocks. The Australian Conservation Foundation has a shop at 39 George St in the Rocks, and the Total Environment Centre is not far away at 88 Cumberland St.

Books & Bookshops

A great book to read while visiting Sydney is *Sydney* by Jan Morris, one of the best travel writers around. It's available as a Penguin paperback and costs about $15. There is a

good range of guidebooks concentrating on particular aspects of the city, including:

Sydney Good Walks Guide
  Joan Lawrence, Kingsclear Books, paperback, about $15
Sydney Bushwalks
  Neil Paton, Kangaroo Press, paperback, about $13
Sydney by Public Transport
  Peter Spence, Peter Alan Books, paperback, about $6 (this book was last published in 1989 so it is out of date, but the price reflects this and it provides good general information).

The Travel Bookshop (☎ 241 3554) at 20 Bridge St is open daily and has books on Sydney and the rest of Australia and the world.

Dymocks (☎ 235 0155) and Angus & Robertson (☎ 235 1188) are two large chains with a reasonable range of stock. Dymocks branches include those at 424 George St and the Harbourside Festival Marketplace in Darling Harbour; you'll find an Angus & Robertson in the Imperial Arcade on Pitt St.

There are plenty of other shops catering to more specialised tastes. Abbey's Bookshop at 131 York St, opposite the Queen Victoria Building, is a more serious bookshop with a good range including many foreign-language titles. Other shops worth checking out include Gleebooks (☎ 660 2333) at 191 Glebe Point Rd. Gleebooks has another outlet a few blocks north-west which sells second-hand books. Paddington is known for its bookshops, such as New Edition (☎ 360 6913) at 328 Oxford St, which also has a cafc. Furthcr cast at 40 Oxford St, at the corner of West St, Ariel has a large range. The Humanities Bookshop at 240 Oxford St sells interesting secondhand titles, including first editions.

Maps

Just about every tourist brochure you pick up includes a map of the city centre. These are OK but are usually limited in their scope and, sometimes, legibility. For a very handy map of the city centre and many of the nearby suburbs including Kings Cross, look for the

The 2000 Olympics

In 1993 Sydney was chosen to host the Olympic Games in the year 2000. Life in this already exciting city will move up a gear or two as the games approach.

The partying that followed the announcement that Sydney had won the bid was quickly replaced by bickering over who should be on the committee, and by revelations that NSW probably couldn't afford to stage the Olympics. This sort of thing seems to be essential for Sydneysiders to get anything done – both the Opera House and the Darling Harbour project were built amidst predictions of economic doom and political squabbling.

The main site for the games will be the suburb of Homebush, on the Parramatta River 16 km west of the city centre. Homebush has long been a neglected area and definitely not a desirable address. Neighbouring Strathfield was where everyone wanted to be, with real estate agents using euphemisms such as North Strathfield for Homebush – that will no doubt change.

Other events will be held at Darling Harbour's Exhibition Centre, the nearby Entertainment Centre, Moore Park, Parramatta and Penrith. Yachting events will of course be held on the harbour.

Some lucky people will have about the best accommodation in the world for the games, on one of the 10 cruise liners which will be moored in the harbour. The *QE II* has already booked the prize location in Circular Quay. ∎

UBD Sydney Tourist Map. At $4.15 it's a bargain. Bookshops such as Dymocks and Angus & Robinson carry it, as does C&LM.

The NRMA has a good map (free to members) of the whole city, too unwieldy for use in a car but good for orientation. If you're planning on doing a lot of driving, a street directory is indispensable. There are a number of these, produced by companies such as UBD and Gregory's. Expect to pay between $25 and $30 for a full-sized directory, although there are smaller versions available.

For topographic maps see C&LM in the Lands Department building on Bridge St.

Newspapers & Magazines

There are two daily papers, the *Sydney Morning Herald* (the *Herald*), first published in 1831 and probably the best daily paper in Australia, and the *Telegraph-Mirror* (the *Tellie*), a tabloid. There's also the *Australian*, a national paper which takes a conservative viewpoint.

TV

Sydney has five TV channels: 2, the government-funded ABC station; 7, standard commercial fare; 9, ditto; 10, ditto; and SBS, a UHF channel devoted to multicultural pro-

grammes – which means that it has the best news, the best movies and some off-the-wall arts and music programmes.

'The Guide', the *Sydney Morning Herald*'s TV guide, comes with the Monday paper and is sometimes refreshingly blunt in its reviews: one programme was dismissed as 'slavering video vomit – a putrid poultice, sucking out the poison of the celebrity scene and presenting it as infotainment'.

Radio

Sydney's radio dial is crowded with about 20 stations, plus another dozen short-range community FM stations. The ABC has Radio National (576 AM), 2BL (702 AM) and Fine Music (92.9 FM). Triple J FM (105.7) is the ABC's 'youth' station, with a playlist of alternative/indy music. There's also the SBS multilingual station, 2EA (1386 AM).

Luggage Repairs

If your backpack or suitcase needs repairing, try Custom Luggage (☎ 261 1099) at 317 Sussex St in the city, in the block between Bathurst and Liverpool Sts.

Women's Organisations

Some of the major women's organisations

(which will be able to direct you to local bodies) are:

Royal Hospital for Women
188 Oxford St, Paddington (☎ 339 4111)
Women & Girls Emergency Centre
190 Elizabeth St (☎ 281 1277)
Women's Legal Resources Centre
(☎ 637 4597, 1800 801 501 toll-free)
Women's Liberation House
63 Palace St, Petersham (☎ 569 3819)

Cameras

Many camera shops also do repairs. Paxtons (☎ 299 2999) at 285 George St (across from the corner of Hunter St) in the city is a large camera store specialising in duty-free gear; at the other end of the scale and of the city is Jackson Lau (☎ 267 6260) who has a small shop at 605 George St near the corner of Goulburn St.

Vaccinations

Qantas has a medical and vaccination centre (☎ (02) 255 6688) in the city at the World Trade Centre on Jamison St, open weekdays.

The Traveller's Medical & Vaccination Centre (☎ 221 7133) is at Level 7, 428 George St, between King and Market Sts; and the Kings Cross Travellers' Clinic (☎ 358 3066) is at Suite 1, 13 Springfield Ave. Both are open on weekdays and Saturday morning. It's best to ring first to make an appointment.

Emergency Assistance

Dial 000 for emergency help from the police, ambulance or fire brigade from any telephone for free. Some other useful emergency numbers include:

Chemist
Emergency Prescription Service, 24 hours (☎ 438 3333)
Dentist
Dental Emergency Information Service, after hours (☎ 962 6557)
Gay & Lesbian Counselling
4 pm to midnight, daily (☎ 360 2211, 1800 805 379 toll-free)

Interpreter Service
Telephone Interpreter Service, 24 hours, over 20 languages available, particularly useful in an emergency or when seeking medical treatment (☎ 221 1111)
Rape
Rape Crisis Centre, 24 hours (☎ 819 6565)
Poisons
Poisons Information Centre, 24 hours (☎ 692 6111)
Life Crisis
Life Line (☎ 951 5555)
Salvo Care Line (Salvation Army) (☎ 331 6000)
Youth Line, noon to midnight (☎ 951 5522)

The Wayside Chapel (☎ 358 6577) at 29 Hughes St, Kings Cross, is a crisis centre and is good for all sorts of local information and problem solving.

In the city there are police stations at 192 Day St (☎ 265 6499) near Darling Harbour, and in the Rocks at the corner of George and Argyle Sts (☎ 265 6366). Sydney Hospital (☎ 228 2111) on Macquarie St and St Vincent's (☎ 339 111) on the corner of Victoria and Burton Sts in Darlinghurst are two of the many public hospitals with casualty departments.

Dangers & Annoyances

Sydney isn't an especially dangerous city, but you should remain reasonably alert. The usual big-city rules apply: never leave your luggage unattended, never show big wads of money and never get drunk in the company of strangers. Harassment of gays/lesbians and non-Anglo-Celtics is not rife, but it does happen. Use extra caution in Kings Cross, which attracts drifters from all over Australia and gutter-crawlers from all over Sydney.

Sydney is generally a safe place for women travellers, although you should avoid walking alone late at night. Gross sexual harassment is uncommon, but you should be a little wary, especially in pubs, until you come to terms with the sexist elements of Aussie male culture. Reacting strongly to infantile sexism can result in a potentially dangerous situation if you're dealing with a bunch of drunken louts. Walk away and choose a better pub – there are plenty of them.

SYDNEY WALKS

Walking routes are suggested in the following sections covering the various suburbs and areas, but don't forget that it's often feasible to walk between suburbs as well – with reasonable public transport, reasonably short distances and the absence of unsafe neighbourhoods, setting out on foot is a good way to explore Australia's largest city. There are often steep hills but they are invariably short.

See the Organised Tours section of this chapter for guided walks.

VIEWS

The highest view in Sydney is from **Sydney Tower** (☎ 229 7444), that 300-metre needle soaring up from the Centrepoint shopping centre at the corner of Market and Pitt Sts. The views extend to the Blue Mountains and far out to sea, as well as straight down to the twisting streets of inner Sydney. Riding the lift to the top costs $6 ($2.50 children). The tower is open daily from 9.30 am to 9.30 pm (11.30 pm on Saturday). To get to the tower lifts (elevators), enter Centrepoint from Market St and take the lift to the Podium level.

The **Harbour Bridge** is a good vantage point, and a footpath runs right across it. Enter from a stone staircase off Cumberland St in the Rocks, or from near Milsons Point railway station at the north-shore end of the bridge (from here it's worth walking down to Kirribilli Point for a view back to the city). In the middle of the bridge you're 50 metres above the water – that's a long way up, but it's just one metre higher than the funnel of the *QE II*, should she happen to be passing below. You can climb the 200 stairs inside the south-east pylon for panoramic views of the harbour and city. The pylon also houses the small **Harbour Bridge Museum**. Admission to the pylon is $1.50 (50c children) and it's open from 10 am to 5 pm daily.

For a view of the Opera House, harbour and bridge from sea level, walk to **Mrs Macquarie's Point**, one headland east of the Opera House. It has been a lookout since at least 1810 when Elizabeth Macquarie, wife of the governor, had a stone chair hewn in the rock, from where she would watch for ships entering the harbour or keep an eye on hubby's construction projects just across Farm Cove. The seat is still there today.

Probably the best views in town are from the ferries, and the **Manly ferries** have the best of all. The ferries which travel west of the bridge (such as the Hunters Hill ferry) are worth trying as well, both for the experience of sailing under the bridge and for the narrower waterways humming with workaday activity. There are also some fine old houses to be seen.

MUSEUMS

Some of Sydney's museums are major attractions, while others are interesting diversions.

Artillery Museum
    See the Manly section.
Australian Museum
    Sydney's main museum, with lots of activities for kids and an excellent pre-history department – see the City Centre section.
Barracks Museum
    The story of the 1817 barracks and life at the time – see the City Centre section.
Colonial House Museum
    An old house furnished in period style – see the Rocks section.
Earth Exchange
    An interactive geological and mining museum – see the Rocks section.
Elizabeth Bay House
    A fine old house dating from 1839 – see the Kings Cross section.
Hall of Champions
    Amidst all the construction for the Olympics at the State Sports Centre in Homebush, the Hall features NSW sporting heroes from 1876. It's free and open daily. To get there, take a train to Strathfield then a shuttle bus to the sports centre.
Harbour Bridge Museum
    A small museum high in a pylon – see the Views section.
Jewish Museum
    The story of Jewish life in Australia – see the Oxford St & Nearby section.
Justice & Police Museum
    A historic building housing displays about waterfront crime – see the City Centre section.

La Perouse Museum
A museum relating to the La Perouse expedition which almost resulted in a French colony – see the Botany Bay section.

Macleay Museum
At the University of Sydney, this collection (☎ 692 2274) was begun by the Macleay family, builders of Elizabeth Bay House. They seem to have been irascible people but insatiable collectors, and this museum contains everything from stuffed birds and animals to anthropology to early computers and cameras. It's free and open on weekdays from 8.30 am to 4.15 or 4.30 pm.

Manly Art Gallery & Museum
Some exhibitions relate to beach culture – see the Manly section.

Museum of Sydney
A new museum, due to open in 1994 on the corner of Bridge and Elizabeth Sts, the site of the colony's first government house. (The name is a bit of a furphy: it's a museum about early Australia.)

National Maritime Museum
A must-see – see the Darling Harbour section.

National Trust Centre
See the Rocks section.

Nicholson Museum
At the University of Sydney, the Nicholson (☎ 692 2812) displays Greek, Assyrian, Egyptian and other antiquities. It's free and open weekdays from 8.30 am to 4.15 or 4.30 pm.

Powerhouse Museum
Perhaps the best museum in town – see the Darling Harbour section.

Sportspace
Tour the Sydney Cricket Ground and the football stadium – see the Paddington section.

State Library
Extensive collections of Australiana and changing exhibitions – see the City Centre section.

Sydney Observatory
Interesting (and free) little museum – see the Rocks section.

Vaucluse House
Historic mansion – see the East of the Cross section.

Victoria Barracks Army Museum
See the Paddington section.

GALLERIES

The Art Gallery of NSW (see the City Centre section) and the Museum of Contemporary Art (see the Circular Quay section) shouldn't be missed. Nearby in the Rocks on George St is Craftspace, run by the Crafts Council of NSW. Other galleries abound, especially in the inner-eastern suburbs.

Index is a monthly pamphlet with some gallery listings. The tourist office has copies or try galleries and quality bookshops. The *Sydney Morning Herald*'s Friday 'Metro' section lists galleries and art exhibitions, but for more detailed information look for the monthly *Art Almanac* ($2) at galleries and some newsagents. It covers all of Australia. The New Edition bookshop in Paddington has a pamphlet showing the location of some galleries and bookshops in the area. You can also call the Art Gallery Info Line (☎ 0055 20437) for recorded information.

There are many, many galleries – here is a baker's dozen:

ABC Ultimo Centre Gallery
700 Harris St, Ultimo (☎ 333 2055), Monday to Saturday, changing exhibitions, often featuring photography

Artspace
The Gunnery, 43-51 Cowper Wharf Rd, Woolloomooloo (☎ 368 1899), Tuesday to Saturday, changing contemporary exhibitions

Australian Centre for Photography
257 Oxford St, Paddington (☎ 331 6253), Wednesday to Saturday

Australian Galleries
15 Roylston St, Paddington (☎ 360 5177), Monday to Saturday

Boomali Aboriginal Artists Co-op
27 Abercrombie St, Chippendale (☎ 698 2047), Tuesday to Friday and Saturday afternoon

The Cartoon Gallery
Level 2, Queen Victoria Building (☎ 267 3022), specialising in animation and comic-strip art

Coo-ee Aboriginal Art Gallery
98 Oxford St, Paddington (☎ 332 1544), daily

Ken Done Gallery
21 Nurses Walk, the Rocks (☎ 247 2740), colourful naive art by a popular designer

Pod Theatre Gallery
183 Campbell St, Surry Hills (☎ 331 7270), contemporary

Stills Gallery
16 Elizabeth St, Paddington (☎ 331 7775), contemporary photography

Tin Sheds Gallery
154 City Rd, University of Sydney (☎ 692 3115), daily (from 1 pm on weekends), contemporary

Wagner Art Gallery
39 Gurner St, Paddington (☎ 360 6069), daily (from 1 pm Sunday), big-ticket Australian art

Watters Gallery
109 Riley St, East Sydney (☎ 331 2556), Tuesday to Saturday, contemporary

BEACHES

Sydney's beaches are some of its greatest assets. They're easily accessible and usually very good – recent problems with pollution seem to have been overcome.

There are two types of beaches – harbour beaches and ocean beaches. The harbour beaches are sheltered, calm and generally smaller. The ocean beaches often have good surf.

Although they get crowded on hot summer weekends, Sydney's beaches are never really shoulder-to-shoulder. Swimming is generally safe – at the ocean beaches you're only allowed to swim within the 'flagged' areas patrolled by the famed lifesavers. Efforts are made to keep the surfers separate from the swimmers. High points of Sydney's beach life are the surf-lifesaving competitions at various beaches throughout the summer.

Shark patrols are operated through the summer months and the ocean beaches are generally netted – Sydney has only had one fatal shark attack since 1937. The shark-proof nets do not usually enclose the beaches – they run at right angles to the shore, to dissuade sharks from patrolling along the beaches.

Many of Sydney's beaches are 'topless', but some aren't – do as the locals do. There are also a couple of nude beaches.

Harbour Beaches

On the south side, out near the heads (the harbour entrance), is trendy **Camp Cove**, a small but pleasant sliver of sand popular with families, and topless. This is where Governor Phillip first landed in Sydney. Just north from Camp Cove and immediately inside the heads, tiny **Lady Bay Beach** achieved some notoriety in the process of becoming a nude beach. It's mainly a gay scene. South of Camp Cove is **Watsons Bay** with Doyle's delightful outdoor seafood restaurant. Two other popular harbour beaches are **Balmoral**, near the entrance to Middle Harbour, and **Nielsen Park** at Vaucluse (see Sydney Harbour National Park). Manly has some pretty harbour beaches and **Reef Beach**,

accessible from the Manly Scenic Walkway, is another nude beach.

South Ocean Beaches

South of the heads there's a string of ocean beaches all the way to Botany Bay. **Bondi**, with its crowds and surfies, is the best-known beach in Australia. Bondi is a favourite with New Zealanders and other young visitors to Sydney, and has a selection of cheap accommodation. See the Bondi section for transport details.

Tamarama, a little south of Bondi, is a tiny sweep of sand with strong surf. Take a bus from Bondi Junction railway station. Then there's **Bronte**, a wide beach popular with families (bus No 378 from Bondi Junction), and **Coogee**, another wide, sweeping beach where you'll also find the popular Coogee Bay Hotel with its beer-garden overlooking the beach (bus Nos 373 and 374 from Circular Quay). Other beaches towards Botany Bay, which is more for sailing than swimming due to the sharks, include **Maroubra** (bus Nos 395-398 from Circular Quay).

North Ocean Beaches

The 30-km coast up to Barrenjoey Heads is dotted with beaches beginning at **Manly**. **Freshwater**, first up from Manly, attracts a lot of teenagers, then there's **Curl Curl** (families and surfers), **Dee Why** and **Collaroy** (family beaches), the long sweep of **Narrabeen** which has some of Sydney's best surf as well as the **Narrabeen Lakes** which are home to many water birds, and further up the very safe **Newport** (families again). Up towards Barrenjoey Heads, three of the best are **Avalon**, **Whale Beach** and **Palm Beach**, the north end of which is a nude beach.

Bus Nos 136 and 139 run from Manly to Freshwater and Curl Curl. Bus No 190 from Wynyard in the city centre runs to Newport and north. From Manly take a bus to Narrabeen (eg No 155) and pick up No 190 there. A hop-on, hop-off bus tour runs a circuit of the northern beaches – see the Getting Around section.

Surf Beaches

Surfing is a popular pastime in Sydney, and with so many good beaches close at hand, it's easy to see why. Apart from **Bondi** and **Tamarama**, there's **Maroubra** and, beyond Botany Bay, **Cronulla** is another serious surf beach. North of Manly there are another dozen or so, the best being **Narrabeen**, **North Avalon** and **Palm Beach**.

PARKS & GARDENS

Sydney has many parks which, together with the harbour, make it one of the world's most spacious major cities.

A string of parks borders the eastern side of the city centre – the **Royal Botanic Gardens**, the **Domain** and **Hyde Park** (see the following City Centre section). As well as these, there are a few pocket-handkerchief parks around the city centre giving respite from the tar and cement. **Wynyard Park** is a wedge of Victoriana on York St outside Wynyard Station, the smaller **Lang Park** is a few blocks north, and north again at Circular Quay is **First Fleet Park**. In Millers Point, across the Bradfield Highway from the Rocks, **Observatory Park** is a pleasant place with old trees and good views.

From Kings Cross the nearest swathe of green is **Rushcutters Bay Park**, a pretty waterfront area. East of Surry Hills and just south of Paddington are the adjacent **Moore Park** and **Centennial Park**, large recreational areas (see the Paddington section).

North of the harbour, many points and heads along the shoreline are tipped with small parks, and narrow parks often follow creeks down to small bays – finding them without a street directory can be difficult, as the steep streets wind randomly. See the North of the Bridge section for information on **Balls Head Reserve**, a small bushland area not too far from a railway station

As well as parks, Sydney has wilder areas. Some of these, along the harbour shores, are described in the Sydney Harbour section. Another, **Garigal National Park**, is an eight-km corridor of bushland in northern Sydney, stretching from Bantry Bay on Middle Harbour up to Ku-Ring-Gai Chase National Park at St Ives. There's also **Lane Cove River National Park**, between the suburbs of Ryde and Chatswood, again north of the harbour. Both parks have extensive walking tracks, and Lane Cove River has lots of picnic areas. You may see lyrebirds in Garigal; the males make their spectacular mating displays from May to August. Cadman's Cottage in the Rocks has more information.

These parks became freeways for firestorms in the '94 fires and were extensively damaged.

Sydney is surrounded by other national parks, large areas of relatively pristine bushland. See the Around Sydney chapter for information on Ku-Ring-Gai Chase and Royal national parks, and the several parks which make up the massive bushland area of the Blue Mountains.

TARONGA ZOO

A short ferry ride from Circular Quay's Jetty 5 takes you across to Taronga Zoo (☎ 969 2777), which has one of the most attractive settings of any zoo in the world. There are over 4000 critters, including lots of Aussie ones. The zoo is beginning to show its age, but a major redevelopment is planned to

Taronga Zoo

restore Taronga to its former position as one of the world's most humane zoos.

Ferries to the zoo depart from Circular Quay half-hourly from 7.15 am on weekdays, 8.45 am on Saturday and 9 am on Sunday. The zoo is at the top of a hill and, if you can't be bothered to walk, you can take a bus or cable car (the Aerial Safari, $2.50, $1.50 children) to the top entrance. It's open daily from 9 am to 5 pm and admission is $14 ($8.50 students, $7 children). A Zoo Pass, sold at Circular Quay and elsewhere, costs $17 ($8.50 children) and includes return ferry rides, the bus to the entrance, zoo admission and the Aerial Safari.

More wildlife parks are covered in the Around Sydney chapter.

CITY CENTRE

Australia's narrowest city streets twist through the centre of its biggest city, and its newest architecture is grafted onto its oldest buildings. The city centre is a mini Manhattan of tightly-packed tall buildings, with landmarks appearing in cameo glimpses. It's a busy place. Buses shudder and roar, a monorail train hisses around a corner, pedestrians ignore the lights and plunge into the traffic, cycle couriers ricochet off kerbs, motorcycle cops blatt down the narrow canyons. It's just as frantic beneath the streets in the web of tunnels and arcades around shopping centres and underground stations, with the subterranean rumble of trains and the constant click and clomp of shoe-leather.

Yet you're never more than a few blocks from a view of the serene harbour and its wide horizon. It's like stepping from a Chinese painting – long, narrow and without perspective – into a landscape on a Cinemascope screen.

Central Sydney stretches from Central Railway Station in the south up to Circular Quay in the north; east to Hyde Park and west to Darling Harbour. The business hub is towards the north end, as are many of the older buildings, which also extend south along Macquarie St.

At the corner of Loftus and Bridge Sts,

under the shady Moreton Bay fig trees in little **Macquarie Place**, are a cannon and anchor from the First Fleet flagship HMS *Sirius*. There are several other pieces of colonial memorabilia in this square, including an 1857 drinking fountain, an obelisk indicating distances to various points in the colony and a gentlemen's convenience which is classified by the National Trust. Backing Macquarie Place is the **Lands Department building** on Bridge St.

To the east at 8 Phillip St, the **Justice & Police Museum** is housed in the old Water Police Station and is set up as a turn-of-the-century police station and court, with various displays on crime, once a major industry in the nearby Rocks. The museum is open on Sunday from 10 am to 5 pm and admission is $4 ($3 children).

If anywhere is Sydney's centre it's **Martin Place**, a pedestrian mall extending from Macquarie St to George St beside the massive GPO. This is a popular lunchtime entertainment spot, with buskers and more organised acts in the amphitheatre. At the west end is the **Cenotaph**, the war memorial. The Commonwealth Bank on Elizabeth St at Martin Place has a hugely impressive old banking chamber; Westpac on George St at the west end of Martin Place also has a fine old chamber, with an attendant to politely direct you to the next free teller. In December a Christmas tree appears in Martin Place, in the summer heat.

Barrack St, west of Martin Place and another pedestrian walk, has fruit barrows and good views back towards the GPO, with that enormous clock. Pitt St crosses Martin Place and a block south it's the busy **Pitt St Mall** with shopping arcades and department stores nearby. The pretty **Strand Arcade** runs off the mall west to George St, housing speciality shops and, upstairs, some interesting designers. Across the mall, **Skygarden** is a modern version of an arcade; take the long 'express' escalator straight to the top. **Centrepoint**, at the bottom of the **Sydney Tower**, is another large complex. Nearby on Market St are **Grace Brothers** and the more upmarket **David Jones**, two large depart-

The Bureaucrats who Won the West

The various ways in which crown land has been allotted, leased and sold have both reflected and caused major changes in the development of NSW. It was bureaucrats and barristers that settled land disputes in the Australian colonies, not sheriffs and six-guns. This is reflected in the imposing proportions of the Lands Department building (built 1876-1891) on Bridge St, a neo-Renaissance pile complete with statues of explorers, surveyors and others connected with the spread of White settlement. More than half of the 48 niches intended to contain statues remain unfilled, perhaps because politicians began squabbling over whose statues should be erected. ■

ment stores. **Gowings**, on the corner of Market and George Sts, is a big menswear shop that's like a relic of another era – the clothes are daggy but practical, inexpensive but not cheap.

The decadently ostentatious old **State Theatre** on Market St near Pitt St was built as a movie palace during Hollywood's heyday. Now it is a National Trust classified building, but it is still open for live shows – no more movies, unfortunately, except during the film festival in June. Unless you go to a show, the only way you can see the interior is to take one of the infrequent guided tours. Still, a stroll around the foyer is enough to evoke memories of the memories evoked in the era when this semiologist's dream was built.

Running up Liverpool St, into Pitt St and north to Market St, where it turns back to Darling Harbour, is the elevated **monorail** – see the Getting Around section for details.

The huge and gorgeous **Queen Victoria Building** takes up the whole block between George, Market, York and Druitt (Park) Sts. It houses about 200 shops, cafes and restaurants, but it was built in 1898 as the city's fruit and vegetable market, in the style of a Byzantine palace – they certainly don't build markets like that any more!

In the basement of the Hilton Hotel, under the Royal Arcade between George and Pitt Sts south of Market St, is the **Marble Bar**, a Victorian extravaganza built by George Adams, the fellow with the prescience to foresee Australia's gambling lust, who founded Tattersall's lotteries (Tattslotto). When the old Adams Hotel was torn down to build the Hilton, the bar was carefully

dismantled and reassembled like some archaeological wonder.

Half a block further south along George St is the 1874 **Town Hall** on the corner of Park St. Inside there's the impressive Grand Organ. Various concerts, lunchtime and evening, are held in the Town Hall (☎ 265 9554). Across the open space to the south, **St Andrew's Cathedral** was built about the same time. Today it houses an unusual two-part organ with computerised sections. Recitals are held weekly.

West of George St between Liverpool and Quay Sts is the colourful **Chinatown** around Dixon St and the **Haymarket** area, where **Paddy's Markets** have recently come home to their original site.

While the northern end of the city centre is becoming a museum of 200 years' public building, anarchically displayed, the southern end, from around Liverpool St, presents a rather odd contrast between the decaying remains of '50s and '60s Anglo-Celtic Sydney and the vibrant commercialism of Asian Sydney. There are also some large holes in the ground where big developments stalled due to lack of money in the late '80s. World Square's hole, taking an entire city block, is the biggest.

The complicated intersection of Broadway, George and Regent Sts outside **Central Railway Station** (built in 1906) is known as **Railway Square**. At the turn of the century this area was Sydney's business centre. Running beneath the railyards at Central Station is a very long pedestrian subway, emerging on the east side at Devonshire St in Surry Hills and on the west side near the Institute of Technology (not the University

SYDNEY

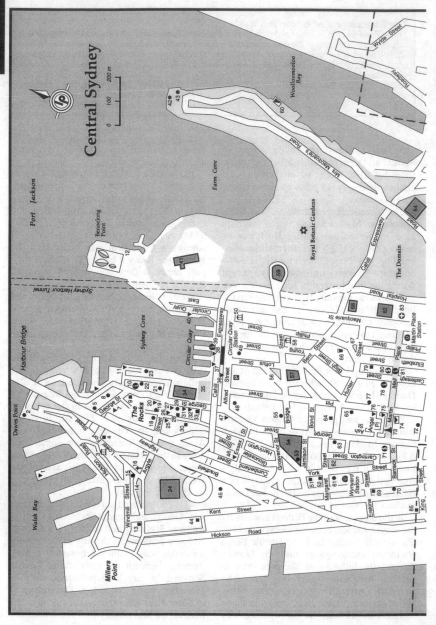

Central Sydney

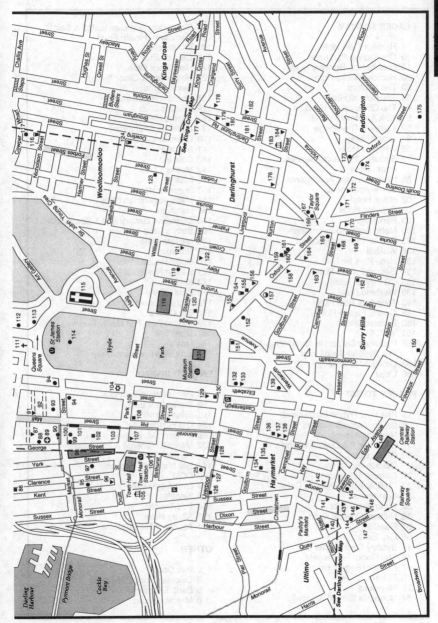

PLACES TO STAY

4 Harbour View Hotel
9 Old Sydney Parkroyal
13 Lord Nelson Brewery Hotel
28 Harbour Rocks Hotel
30 The Stafford
33 The Russell Hotel
44 The Observatory Hotel
51 York Apartment Hotel
52 Wynyard Travelodge
64 Grand Hotel
69 Wynyard Hotel
79 Sydney City Centre Serviced
  Apartments
85 Metro Serviced Apartments
86 Savoy Apartments
102 Hilton Hotel
108 Criterion Hotel
109 Park Regis
120 Metro Serviced Apartments
123 Forbes Terrace Hostel
126 Waldorf
130 Hyde Park Inn
134 George Private Hotel
135 CB Private Hotel
136 Westend Hotel
140 Travellers Rest Hotel
148 Crystal Palace Hotel
150 Excelsior Hotel
151 YWCA
155 Parkridge Corporate Apartments &
  The Park All-Suite Hotel
162 Cron Lodge Motel
180 L'otel

PLACES TO EAT

1 Pier Four (Wharf Restaurant)
6 Italian Village & Wolfies
7 Mercantile Hotel
11 Doyle's at the Quay & Bilson's
20 G'Day Cafe
25 Clocktower Centre
26 Gumnut Teagarden
27 Phillip's Foote & Rocks Cafe
31 Bakehouse
32 Ox on the Rocks
36 Nulbom Oriental Food
37 Rossini
38 City Extra
40 Sydney Cove Oyster Bar
46 The Rocks Teppanyaki
47 Kable's (Regent Hotel)
75 El Sano
76 Merivales
87 Noonan's (Strand Arcade)

91 Skygarden Complex (cafes & bars)
96 Carruthers Health Food
107 Woolworth's
110 Cafe de Pub
121 Hard Rock Cafe
122 No Names & Other Italian
  Restaurants
127 Spanish Restaurants
129 Hellenic Club
133 Cyprus Hellene
137 Diethnes Restaurant
138 Chamberlain Hotel
141 Mekong
142 Cafe Inn
143 Mother Chu's
146 Malaya
153 Burdekin Hotel
156 Metro Vegetarian Cafe
158 Hanovers
160 Downtown Darlinghurst & Spanish Deli
163 Betty's Soup Kitchen
164 Maltese Cafe
169 Riberries
170 Bagel House
171 Balkan Restaurant
172 Kim's
176 Cafe DOV
177 Michaelangelo's Cafe
178 Bar Coluzzi
179 Govinda's & The Movie Room
181 Darlo Bar
182 Una's
184 Laurie's Vegetarian Diner

ENTERTAINMENT

15 Hero of Waterloo Hotel
66 Someplace Else
116 Tilbury Hotel
124 Old Fitzroy Hotel
125 Cinema Complexes
132 Mandolin Cinema & Powercuts
  Reggae Club
147 Her Majesty's Theatre
152 DCM
154 Exchange Hotel
165 Kinselas
168 Pod Theatre
173 Albury Hotel
174 Academy Twin Cinema

OTHER

2 Pier One
3 Colonial House Museum
5 Earth Exchange
8 Metcalfe Arcade

OTHER continued

10 Rocks Visitors' Centre
12 Sydney Opera House
14 Argyle Place
16 Garrison Church
17 Argyle Cut
18 Argyle Centre
19 The Rocks Centre
21 Cadman's Cottage, NSW National
   Parks Office
22 Rockcycle Tours
23 Overseas Passenger Terminal
24 Sydney Observatory
29 Ken Done Design
34 Museum of Contemporary Art
35 First Fleet Park
39 Ferry Information
41 Government House
42 Mrs Macquarie's Point
43 Mrs Macquarie's Chair
45 National Trust Centre
48 Goldfields House (Australian Wine
   Centre)
49 Old Customs House
50 Justice & Police Museum
53 Qantas Vaccination Centre
54 Qantas (World Trade Centre)
55 Travel Bookshop
56 Macquarie Place
57 Lands Department Building
58 Museum of Sydney
59 Conservatorium of Music
60 Boy Charlton Pool
61 Countrylink Travel Centre
62 Wynyard Park
63 Paxtons Cameras
65 CES
67 Chifley Square
68 State Library
70 NRMA
71 Westpac Bank
72 Telecom Phone Centre
73 Cenotaph
74 Post Office

77 American Express
78 NSW Government Travel Centre
80 Commonwealth Bank
81 Sydney Information Booth, Halftix &
   Ticketek
82 Parliament House
83 Sydney Hospital
84 Art Gallery of NSW
88 Dymocks Bookshop
89 Traveller's Medical Centre
90 Grace Brothers
92 Imperial Arcade
93 Centrepoint & Sydney Tower
94 David Jones
95 YHA Membership & Travel Centre
97 Abbey's Bookshop
98 Queen Victoria Building
99 Gowings
100 State Theatre
101 City Centre Monorail Station
103 Town Hall Monorail Station
104 Great Synagogue
105 Aboriginal Artists' Gallery
106 St Andrew's Cathedral
111 St James Church
112 Mint
113 Hyde Park Barracks
114 Archibald Fountain
115 St Mary's Cathedral
117 The Gunnery
118 Australian Museum
119 Watters Gallery
128 World Square Monorail Station
131 Anzac Memorial
139 Women & Girls Emergency Centre
144 CES City Casuals
145 Thomas Cook Outdoor Clothing
149 Bus Station
157 Greyhound Pioneer Australia Depot
159 Remo General Store
161 Pandarra Trading Co
166 Darlinghurst Courthouse
167 Old Darlinghurst Jail
175 Victoria Barracks
183 Jewish Museum

of Technology) on Broadway at the southern end of Railway Square. It's usually crowded with commuters (and buskers), but late at night it can be a spooky place. In **Prince Alfred Park**, south-east of Central, the nighttime dangers are probably more real.

Macquarie St
Macquarie St has the greatest concentration

of early buildings. After the founding governor Phillip left in 1792, the colony was run mainly by officials and soldiers intent on making quick fortunes through the rum monopoly. It was not until Lachlan Macquarie took over as governor in 1810 that order was restored. The narrow streets of parts of central Sydney are a reminder of the chaotic pre-Macquarie period.

Macquarie commissioned Francis Greenway, a convict transported for forgery, to design a series of public buildings, some of which are still among the finest in Sydney. Excellent views of all Greenway's buildings can be obtained from the 14th-floor cafeteria of the Law Courts building on the corner of Macquarie St and Queens Square.

St James Church and the **Hyde Park Barracks** (1819), two of Greenway's masterpieces, are on Queens Square at the northern end of Hyde Park, facing each other across Macquarie St. The Barracks, originally convict quarters, are now an interesting museum of Sydney's social history, open daily from 10 am to 5 pm, admission $6 ($4 children). The museum was helped by 19th century rats which stole bits and pieces to build their nests, preserving many everyday items which would otherwise have been discarded.

Next to the Barracks on Macquarie St is the **Mint Building**, with a collection of decorative arts, stamps and coins. It is open from 10 am to 5 pm daily except Wednesday when it opens at noon. Admission is $4 ($2 children). Next door is **Sydney Hospital**, dating from the 1880s. The site was originally the central wing of the 'rum hospital' – built in 1812 by entrepreneurs whose fee was a monopoly on the lucrative rum trade. The rum hospital's other wings survive as the Mint and Parliament House, flanking the current hospital. A tour of historical aspects of the hospital is held at 11 am on the first Monday of the month. In front of the hospital is the **Little Boar**, a copy of a statue in Florence. As with the original, rubbing its snout is supposed to grant you a wish.

North of the hospital is NSW's **Parliament House**, which is, surprisingly, the oldest continually-operating parliament building in the world. There are free tours at 10 am, 11 am and 2 pm on non-sitting weekdays and a tour at 1.30 pm on sitting days which includes question time – this is usually booked out months in advance. Phone for bookings (☎ 230 2111).

Just north of Parliament House, the **State Library** (☎ 230 1414) has one of the best

collections of early records and works on Australia, including Captain Cook's and Joseph Banks' journals and Captain Bligh's log from the *Bounty* (the irascible Bligh recovered from that ordeal to become an early NSW governor and suffer a second mutiny!). Many items are displayed in the library galleries, which are open from 10 am to 5 pm Monday to Saturday, 2 to 6 pm on Sunday. There's a cafe on the premises.

Just east of Macquarie St near Bridge St, the **Sydney Conservatorium of Music** was originally built, by Greenway again, as the stables and servants' quarters of a new government house for Macquarie. Macquarie was replaced as governor before the rest of the house could be finished, partly because of the perceived extravagance of this project. Greenway's life ended in poverty because he could never recoup the money of his own that he had put into the work.

Hyde Park

Perhaps not the most spectacular urban park in the world, Hyde Park is nevertheless one of central Sydney's most pleasant places. It's large enough to offer a break from traffic and crowds, but retains a feel of being in the centre of a large city. The ibis (waterbirds) which live here look rather shabby, as though they've been sleeping rough. The park is in a slightly elevated position, and after a few hours of walking around Sydney's hilly streets, it's good to sit down on the grass and know that it's all downhill from here.

At the north end of the park is the delightful **Archibald Fountain**, which is rich with symbolism. Near Liverpool St at the south end is the severely Art Deco **Anzac Memorial** (1934) where there is a small exhibition relating to Australia's wars and a changing-of-the-guard ceremony at 12.30 pm on Thursday. Some of the pines near the memorial were grown from seeds gathered at Gallipoli.

Across College St from the park's northeast corner is **St Mary's Cathedral** (begun in 1868), one of the largest in the world, although it still lacks its spires. A free tour of the cathedral is held at noon on Sunday, departing from the College St entrance. You sometimes see high-spirited nuns on the steps of St Mary's – they are probably cross-dressers who have popped over from Oxford St. Diagonally opposite, on Elizabeth St just north of Park/William Sts is the impressive **Great Synagogue** (1873). A free tour of the synagogue takes place at noon on Tuesday and at 1 pm on Thursday.

There's an entrance to **Museum Station** in the south-west corner of Hyde Park, near the park cafe. Many people dislike Museum Station, while others find it a charming period piece. It depends, I suppose, whether those dim tunnels of glazed tiles remind you of *film noir* or of a public toilet. Museum Station and nearby St James Station date from the 1920s and were the first of Sydney's underground system.

Australian Museum

The Australian Museum, across from Hyde Park on the corner of College and William Sts, is a natural history museum with an excellent Australian wildlife collection and a gallery tracing Aboriginal history from the Dreamtime to the present. See the latter before you head off into central Australia. There's a good bookshop with publications on Aboriginal and Pacific arts & crafts. An impressive gamelan orchestra plays twice a week (☎ 339 8111, 339 8181 for recorded information for times). There are also plenty of activities to keep children gainfully amused, especially during school holidays. The museum is open from 10 am to 5 pm daily except Monday, when it opens from noon to 5 pm. Admission is $4 ($1.50 children) but free after 4 pm.

Royal Botanic Gardens

Stretching back from the harbour front, beside the Opera House, the Royal Botanic Gardens (☎ 231 8111) has a magnificent collection of South Pacific plant life. The gardens were established in 1816, and in one corner a stone wall marks the site of the convict colony's first vegetable patch. There is also an Aboriginal plant trail. The tropical display, housed in the interconnecting Arc

and Pyramid glasshouses, is worth the $5 admission ($2 children). It's open daily from 10 am to 6 pm during summer and from 10 am to 4 pm the rest of the year. The gardens are open from 6.30 am to sunset daily. There's a visitor centre where guided walks start at 10 am every Wednesday and Friday and at 1 pm on Sunday.

The Domain

The Cahill Expressway separates the Botanic Gardens from the Domain, another open space to the south. You can cross the expressway on the Art Gallery Rd bridge. On Sunday afternoons in the Domain, impassioned soapbox speakers entertain their listeners. Free events are held here during the Festival of Sydney in January, as well as the popular Carols by Candlelight in December. This is also a rallying place for public protests.

Art Gallery of NSW

In the Domain, only a short walk from the centre, the art gallery has an excellent permanent display of Australian, European, Japanese and tribal art, and from time to time has some inspired temporary exhibits. There is also a cafe. It's open from 10 am to 5 pm daily and free guided tours are held at 1 and 2 pm on Monday, 11 am, noon, 1 and 2 pm from Tuesday to Friday and 1, 2 and 3 pm on weekends. There's no entry charge, but fees may apply for some major exhibitions. Phone (☎ 225 1790) for recorded information.

Art Gallery of NSW

City Centre Walks

An introduction to the city centre might start at the Liverpool St exit from Museum Station, in Hyde Park. Walking north through the park you pass the **Anzac Memorial** and, across William St, the wonderful **Archibald Fountain**. Nearby on College St are the **Australian Museum** and **St Marys Cathedral**. (From here you could walk west to Market St which leads to Pyrmont Bridge and **Darling Harbour** – and to Pyrmont Bridge Rd on the other side of Darling Harbour, which leads to the **fish markets** and, eventually, **Glebe**.)

Keep going north for Macquarie St with its collection of early colonial buildings and, after a few blocks, **Circular Quay** and the **Opera House**. On the west side of Circular Quay, behind the **Museum of Contemporary Art**, George St runs north into the Rocks.

Walk north on George St, which curves around under the **Harbour Bridge** into Lower Fort St. Turn right (north) for the waterfront or left to climb **Observatory Hill**. From here Argyle St heads east, through the **Argyle Cut** and back to the Rocks.

Nearby on Cumberland St you can climb stairs to the bridge and walk across to **Millers Point** on the other side, from where you can take a train back to the city.

This walk covers about 6.5 km, plus whatever diversions you might make.

A walk from the city to Kings Cross is detailed in the later Kings Cross section. It's worth walking along Oxford St from Hyde Park to Paddington, and if you keep going to Bondi Junction you can take a train home. ■

DARLING HARBOUR

Darling Harbour, once called Cockle Bay, was a major shipping port from the early days of the colony right up until the 1980s, when the old wharves and railway yards were finally made redundant by Botany Bay's container terminals. Using such a large tract of vacant waterfront land, so close to the city centre, for an innovative development seems an obvious idea, but when the plans for Darling Harbour were first mooted there was much opposition, which continued through the construction delays and budget blow-outs. The final bill came to around $2 billion, but it was money well spent.

Today Darling Harbour is a huge waterfront leisure and tourist park which includes several of Sydney's top attractions. The complex covers quite a large area, and for a look around which doesn't wear out the shoe leather, take the **Peoplemover**, that incongruous mini-train which makes a 20-minute loop around the sights between 10 am and 5 pm for $2.50.

If you're bent on seeing everything on offer, consider the Darling Harbour Superticket which costs $35.50 ($19.50 children under 12) and gives you a harbour cruise, entry to the aquarium, barbecue lunch at the Craig, entry to the Chinese Gardens and a monorail ride. You can buy the Superticket (valid for three months) at the aquarium, at monorail stations, at the Chinese Gardens or through Matilda Cruises.

For recorded information on happenings at Darling Harbour, phone 0055 20261.

The main focus is **Harbourside Festival Marketplace**, across Pyrmont Bridge from Market St in the city. Harbourside is a large and graceful structure, faintly reminiscent of public buildings from the reign of Queen Victoria. There are two sections, the north and south pavilions, containing bars, restaurants, fast-food outlets and many shops which stay open until fairly late every day of the week.

Just to the south of Harbourside are the **Convention Centre** and the **Exhibition Centre** which continues the maritime theme with its roof suspended from steel masts. Like the aquarium and the maritime museum, the exhibition centre was designed by Australian architect Philip Cox, who also created the new Sydney Football Stadium, Melbourne's National Tennis Centre and the resort near Uluru (Ayers Rock).

In front of the exhibition centre, **Tumbalong Park** has an amphitheatre where there is free entertainment during most lunchtimes. Just south of the Chinese Gardens, the

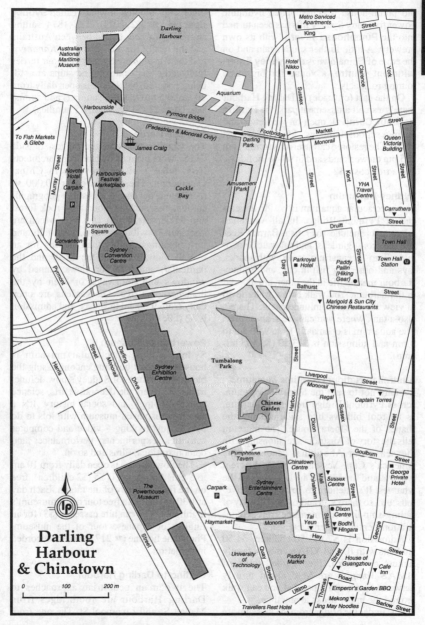

Darling Harbour & Chinatown

0   100   200 m

Darling Harbour

Australian National Maritime Museum

Aquarium

Metro Serviced Apartments

King Street

Hotel Nikko

Clarence Street

York Street

Sussex Street

Harbourside

Pyrmont Bridge

(Pedestrian & Monorail Only)

Footbridge

Market Street

Monorail

Queen Victoria Building

James Craig

Darling Park

To Fish Markets & Globe

Novotel Hotel & Carpark

Harbourside Festival Marketplace

Cockle Bay

Amusement Park

Kent Street

Carruthers Street

YHA Travel Centre

Murray Street

Convention Square

Convention

Sydney Convention Centre

Druitt Street

Day St

Parkroyal Hotel

Paddy Pallin (Hiking Gear)

Town Hall

Town Hall Station

Pyrmont

Bathurst Street

Marigold & Sun City Chinese Restaurants

Harris Street

Darling Drive

Monorail

Sydney Exhibition Centre

Tumbalong Park

Liverpool Street

Monorail

Regal

Captain Torres

Sussex Street

Chinese Garden

Dixon Street

Harbour Street

Goulburn Street

George Street

Pier Street

Pumphouse Tavern

Chinatown Centre

George Private Hotel

The Powerhouse Museum

Carpark

Sydney Entertainment Centre

Chinatown Mall

Sussex Centre

Dixon Centre

Bodhi

Hingara

Haymarket

Monorail

Tai Yuen

Hay Street

University of Technology

Quay Street

Paddy's Market

House of Guangzhou

Cafe Inn

Thomas Street

Ultimo

Emperor's Garden BBQ

Mekong

Jing May Noodles

Barlow Street

Travellers Rest Hotel

old pump-house which supplied hydraulic power for many Sydney lifts has been turned into the **Pumphouse Tavern**, with its own brewery. A little further south again and on the edge of Chinatown is the **Sydney Entertainment Centre**, a venue for big-name touring rock acts.

On the east (city side) of Darling Harbour there's a small amusement park, the **Darling Harbour Carnival**, open on weekends and during school holidays. Most rides cost $3.50. The restored carousel runs from 11 am to 5 pm on weekends and in school holidays, and a ride costs $2.

Sydney Aquarium

The spectacular aquarium is beside the east end of Pyrmont Bridge. Its all-Australian inhabitants include river fish, Barrier Reef fish and coral gardens, and saltwater crocodiles. Two 'oceanarium' tanks, with sharks, rays and other big fish in one, and Sydney Harbour marine life in the other, are moored in the harbour. You walk below water level to view the tanks from underneath. There's also a tank where you can see seals at play. The aquarium is open daily from 9.30 am to 9 pm and admission is $13.50 ($6.50 children).

Australian National Maritime Museum

It's hard not to spot the Maritime Museum, across Pyrmont Bridge from the aquarium, as its roof billows like sails, echoing the shapes of the Opera House. The museum tells the story of Australia's relationship with the sea, from Aboriginal canoes to the America's Cup. Vessels of many different types stand inside or are moored at the wharves. It's intended to be an 'interactive' museum, so there's an audiovisual display of sailing-ship life with maritime craft demonstrations, entertainments, etc.

Admission is $7 ($3.50 children, $4.50 students with ID and YHA members, family tickets available). Free guided tours of HMAS *Vampire* are held about hourly between 11 am and 3 pm, but you can walk around the upper decks at any time.

Just under the bridge from the museum are other ships moored at what's called **Sydney Seaport** (☎ 552 2011). The 1874 sailing ship *James Craig* traded between Australia and the rest of the world, and the *Kanangra* and the *Waratah* are Sydney Harbour ferries built early this century. The ships are still being restored, but the site is open daily from 10 am to 5 pm (later in summer) and admission costs $2 ($1 children, $5 families).

Chinese Gardens

The Chinese Gardens, the biggest outside China, were planned by landscape architects from NSW's sister province in China, Guangdong. The gardens cover 10,000 sq metres and have several distinct geographical features, such as mountains, rock forest and wilderness, forest and lake, which are interspersed with pavilions, waterfalls and lush plantings. Rather than looking for an overall view, seek out the small and the particular, and look for views framed by windows and doorways, or even by the branches of a tree. The gardens are open daily from 9.30 am to sunset, and admission is $2 (50c children).

Powerhouse Museum

Sydney's most spectacular museum is housed in a vast building encompassing the old power station for Sydney's now defunct trams. It covers the decorative arts, science and technology and social history. It's a superbly displayed museum with lots to do besides just looking – video and computer activities, experiments, performances and demonstrations, films and so on.

The Powerhouse is open daily from 10 am to 5 pm. Admission is $5 ($2 children), free on the first Saturday of the month. Each day at 1.30 pm there's a free tour of the museum's highlights. You can hire cassettes ($3) for an English or Japanese tour of the museum. Phone the hotline (☎ 217 0444) for recorded information.

Getting to Darling Harbour

The two main pedestrian approaches to Darling Harbour are footbridges from Market St and Liverpool St. The one from

Market St leads on to the lovely old Pyrmont Bridge, now a pedestrian-and-monorail-only route. It was world-famous in its day as it was the first electrically operated swing-span bridge in the world.

The 'Tramway' bus service shuttles between the Rocks and Darling Harbour on weekends. The $2 ($1 children) fare is good value, and all-day passes are available. Town Hall is the closest railway station, from where it's a short walk down Druitt St or Market St. You can also get there by boat: a ferry leaves Circular Quay's Jetty 4 about half-hourly from 8 am to 7.30 pm for $2.60 ($1.30 children), or you can take the private Rocket Express from Circular Quay West, across from Jetty 6, about every 20 minutes for $3 ($1.50 children).

The controversial monorail circles Darling Harbour and links it to the city centre. Some say its steel track, winding around the streets at first-floor level (that's second-floor to Americans), ruins some of Sydney's best vistas, but the initial fuss has died down – to be replaced by a controversy about a mooted tramline from George St to Pyrmont. As a transport system the monorail isn't great, but for sightseeing it is well worth $2.50. Get off at Haymarket for the Powerhouse Museum or at Harbourside for the Harbourside Festival Marketplace, the Maritime Museum and Pyrmont Bridge.

CIRCULAR QUAY

Circular Quay is a busy hub for harbour ferry commuters, and for tourists. There is no finer way of getting around Sydney than on a ferry, and just waiting for one on Circular Quay is an experience, among the crowds and the buskers. You still see Sydneysiders fishing from the quayside, oblivious to the clamour around them. A popular tale has it that the last person to be taken by a shark in the harbour was a woman who slipped off a ferry gangplank, landing in the maw of a waiting shark...

Circular Quay is the site of Sydney Cove, the landing place of the First Fleet; it was made semicircular during the 1830s. Settlement grew around the Tank Stream, a creek which provided early Sydney's water supply and ran into the harbour here. Later this was the shipping centre for Sydney, and early photographs show a forest of masts crowding the skyline.

As well as the ferries, Circular Quay is a land transport hub, with many bus routes starting here and a railway station. There are ferry and bus information booths and a Countrylink Travel Centre (☎ 241 3887). Running above Alfred St, behind the ferry wharves, the elevated Cahill Expressway is due to be demolished in time for the new millennium and the Circular Quay Railway Station will go underground.

Behind Alfred St and perhaps on the spot where Arthur Phillip pitched camp on 26 January 1788, the old **Customs House** awaits a new role. The building occupies pride of place in 'Sydney's dress circle', as Prime Minister Paul Keating put it, so any restoration should be interesting.

The east side of the Quay runs out to Bennelong Point, with the Opera House on the end. Along the west side is **First Fleet Park**, a good place to rest after pounding the pavements, the **Overseas Passenger Terminal** where liners moor, and the little bay of **Campbells Cove**, backed by the Park Hyatt Hotel.

The **Museum of Contemporary Art** (the MCA), in a stolid Art Deco building that once housed the Maritime Services Board, has a fine collection and regularly changing exhibitions of the sublime and the ridiculous. Admission is $6 ($4 concession) and it's open daily except Tuesday from 11 am to 6 pm. The bookshop sells good postcards.

SYDNEY OPERA HOUSE

At a free Sunday concert or sitting in the open-air restaurant with a carafe of wine, watching the harbour life, the Opera House is a truly memorable place. It looks fine from any angle, but the view from a ferry coming into Circular Quay is one of the best.

The Opera House sits on the end of **Bennelong Point**, named after Bennelong, an Aboriginal man who was kept for study by Governor Phillip and was later taken to England.

Before the Opera House was built, the site was used as a tram depot. A Danish architect, Jorn Utzon, beat more than 200 other competitors to win the design competition, but, at the height of the cost overruns and construction difficulties and hassles, he quit in disgust and the building was completed by a consortium of Australian architects. How were the enormous additional costs covered? Not by the taxpayer, but in true-blue Aussie fashion by a series of Opera House lotteries.

The Opera House has four auditoriums and is a venue for dance, theatre, concerts and films as well as opera. On Sunday there is free light entertainment outside on the 'prow' of the Opera House, with jazz near the Forecourt Restaurant. The **Tarpeian Markets**, with arts and crafts, are held near the front entrance on Sunday. You can often catch a free lunchtime film or organ recital in the concert hall.

As well as the theatres, the Opera House is home to a **Performing Arts Library & Archives**, open on weekdays from 9 am to 5 pm.

There are tours of the building, which are worth taking, although the inside is nowhere near as spectacular as the outside. Tours are held daily between 9 am and 4 pm for $8.50 ($5.50 students with ID and children). Not all tours can visit all theatres because of rehearsals, etc. You're more likely to see everything if you take an early tour, or phone (☎ 250 7250) to see what's available. There used to be regular backstage tours on Sunday ($13), but they are now less frequent because of the increased number of performances.

Information

For general enquiries about the Opera House, phone (☎ 250 7111).

The bi-monthly Opera House Diary gives details of forthcoming performances. A year's subscription costs $12 (A$20 overseas). Write to Diary Subscriptions, Sydney Opera House, GPO Box 4274, Sydney 2001. Make money orders payable to the Sydney Opera House Trust. You could also send in a

stamped, self-addressed envelope to receive the current diary free.

If your fax machine has a polling facility, dial the Opera House's fax number (252 1161) and press your transmission button – you should receive a list of current events.

Buying a Ticket

The box office (☎ 250 7777 for bookings) is open daily except Sunday, from 9 am to 8.30 pm. You can also book by fax (251 3943) if you quote your credit-card details, or you can book by writing to the Box Office Manager, Sydney Opera House, PO Box R239, Royal Exchange, 2000. Note that children under five aren't admitted to performances (except children's performances).

Popular performances sell out quickly, but there are often 'restricted view' tickets available at about $30 for operas. Be warned that some seats have no view at all, which might be all right for an opera but is hopeless for a ballet.

THE ROCKS

Sydney's first settlement grew up on the rocky spur of land on the west side of Sydney Cove from which the Harbour Bridge now leaps to the north shore. A pretty squalid place it was too, with overcrowding, open sewers and notoriously raucous residents. In the 1820s and '30s the *nouveaux riches* built their three-storey houses where Lower Fort St is today; their outlook was to the slums below.

In the 1870s and '80s the notorious Rocks 'pushes' were gangs of larrikins (a great Australian word) who used to haunt the area, snatching purses, beating up pedestrians, feuding and generally creating havoc. It became an area of warehouses and bond stores, then declined as more modern shipping and storage facilities were opened. An outbreak of bubonic plague at the turn of the century led to whole streets of the Rocks being razed, and the construction of the Harbour Bridge also resulted in much demolition. 'Green Bans' applied by the Builders' Labourers Federation in the '70s are responsible for today's intriguing remnants of the original Rocks.

Redevelopment has made the Rocks into a most interesting area of Sydney, and imaginative restorations have converted the old warehouses into places like the busy Argyle Centre. The Rocks is still a wonderful area to wander around, full of narrow cobbled streets and fine colonial buildings.

Orientation & Information

The main street running into the Rocks is George St, the continuation of the central city street, which curves under the Harbour Bridge and meets Lower Fort St, which leads south to Observatory Hill (also accessible via the Argyle Cut in Argyle St) and north down to the waterfront near Pier One. Running through the Rocks parallel to George St is Cumberland St. Almost all of the Rocks' attractions are jammed into the narrow paths and walkways between George and Cumberland Sts.

The Rocks Visitor Centre (☎ 247 4972; 11606 for recorded information) at 104 George St is open daily from 9 am to 5 pm. The centre sells the Rocks Ticket ($31.50, $21.50 children) which gives entry to a couple of attractions, a meal, a walking tour and a harbour cruise. You can also buy a ticket which includes admission to Taronga Zoo.

The Visitor Centre has a good range of publications and souvenirs and maps of walking tours in the Rocks for 20c and 50c. The Rocks isn't a large area but there are many small streets and hidden corners, so a map is handy. Make sure you get to some of the places on the west side of the Bradfield Highway (the elevated Harbour Bridge approach road), where there are some charming streets of old terraced houses and the Sydney Observatory.

Things to See & Do

On George St, close to the visitor centre, is **Cadman's Cottage** (1816), the oldest house in Sydney. When the cottage was built this was where the waterfront was, and the arches to the south of it once housed long boats; this

was the home of the last Government Coxswain, John Cadman. The cottage now houses the National Parks information centre (☎ 247 8861), open daily.

The **Earth Exchange** (☎ 251 2422) at 36-64 George St is a geological and mining museum with the emphasis on participation – such as experiencing an earthquake. It's open daily from 10 am to 5 pm and admission is $7 ($5 children). The always interesting **Museum of Contemporary Art** backs onto George St – see the Circular Quay section.

Susannah Place, on Gloucester St, is a terrace of tiny houses dating from 1844 and is one of the few remaining examples of the modest housing which was once standard in the Rocks.

The Rocks is full of interesting shops, with several large centres, such as **Metcalfe Arcade**, which has a number of craft shops, and **Craftspace**, a big craft gallery. The **Rocks Centre** on Argyle St has more shops, and further up Argyle St, on the corner of Playfair St, is the **Argyle Centre,** which was originally built as bond stores between 1826 and 1881. Today it houses a collection of shops, studios and the Woolshed, a theatre restaurant with Aussie sheep-station overtones.

The **Australian Conservation Foundation** (ACF) has a shop at 39 George St selling interesting souvenirs, with very good photos of Australia's more beautiful places on posters, calendars, T-shirts etc. South along George St, towards the railway overpass, are some large and upmarket duty-free shopping

Cadman's Cottage

complexes, perhaps useful for checking out prices which you might be able to better elsewhere.

On weekends the top of George St is closed off and a lively **market** is held, with jewellery, antiques, souvenirs and the usual market trash and curios. Look for the guy selling giant bubble-making devices. On a still day his huge soap-bubbles are a gorgeous sight as they quiver in the air.

There are some nice old **pubs** in the Rocks. One of Sydney's best places for a Guinness and live Irish music most nights is the Mercantile Hotel at 25 George St, near the visitor centre. Further down George St, across from the MCA, the Fortune of War claims to hold Sydney's oldest licence – a couple of other old pubs in nearby Millers Point make similar claims.

Just beyond the Argyle Centre is the **Argyle Cut**, an old tunnel through the hill to the other side of the peninsula. At the far end of the cut is the **Garrison Church** (1848), where redcoats once said their prayers. Nearby is **Argyle Place**, still a village green. The surrounding suburb is **Millers Point** (named for the flour mill which once stood on Observatory Hill), a delightful district of early colonial homes.

Close at hand are the Lord Nelson Hotel on the corner of Argyle and Kent Sts and the Hero of Waterloo Hotel on the corner of Windmill and Lower Fort Sts, which vie for the title of Sydney's oldest pub. This is not *quite* the same as claiming to have the oldest license – other pubs lay claim to the title of 'oldest continually operating pub', and the hair-splitting goes on.

Further north at 53 Lower Fort St is the **Colonial House Museum**, a private house fitted out with colonial-era furniture. It's open daily from 10 am to 5 pm and admission is just $1 (50c children).

Built in the 1850s, **Sydney Observatory** sits atop **Observatory Hill**, the highest point in this part of the world. As well as being of historical and architectural interest, the observatory has an interesting little museum with interactive displays and videos. Daytime admission is free and the observa-

tory is open from 2 to 5 pm on weekdays and from 10 am to 5 pm on weekends and during school holidays. It is also open every night except Wednesday for a tour of the building, videos and telescope viewing. Night visits must be booked (☎ 217 0485) and cost $5 ($2 children, family tickets available). This was the second observatory to be built on the hill, the first being constructed in 1821. Before that, the hill's exposed position meant that it was an ideal site for a windmill to grind wheat, and the colony's first windmill was built here in 1796. It wasn't much of a success, as the canvas sails were stolen (not surprising, considering the profession of many people living nearby) and the whole structure eventually collapsed.

Close by, the **National Trust Centre** in the old military hospital houses a museum, art gallery, bookshop and tea-rooms, open daily except Monday from 11 am to 5 pm (from noon on weekends). Admission is around $4 (students $2). Phone (☎ 258 0171), for recorded information on National Trust properties throughout the state.

Until the advent of container shipping and new port facilities in Botany Bay, the waterfront from Dawes Point down to Darling Harbour was Sydney's busiest. Darling Harbour has been reborn, but around Dawes Point the big enclosed wharves (known as finger wharves) and warehouses quietly moulder. **Pier Four** is home to the renowned Sydney Dance Company and the Sydney Theatre Company. Hour-long tours of the complex are held on weekdays for $5 – bookings are essential (☎ 250 1700). **Pier One**, right at the tip of Dawes Point and nearly under the bridge, was an attempt to turn a finger wharf into a smart shopping-centre, which seems a pretty good idea given the location and the views, but it hasn't taken off.

Just south of the Rocks on Essex St near the corner of Harrington St, up towards St Patrick's Church, you can find the site of the **public gallows**.

SYDNEY HARBOUR BRIDGE

From the end of the Rocks the 'old coat-hanger' rises up on its route to the north shore. It was the city's symbol until the Opera House came along. Some people consider it to be ugly, but there's a charm in the sheer size, symmetry and simplicity of the thing. Slide-rules, steel and muscle built the bridge and it's like an object lesson in the basic rules of geometry and engineering, on a gigantic scale.

The two halves of the mighty arch were built out from each shore, supported by cranes, while engineers crossed their fingers that their calculations had been correct and that the two halves would meet in the middle! After eight years of work, when the ends of the arches were just centimetres apart and ready to be bolted together, a gale blew up and winds of over 100 kmh set them swaying, like a pair of huge dinosaurs squabbling. It was a long night for the workers perched on top, but the bridge survived and the arch was soon completed.

The bridge was opened in 1932 – twice. Before Premier Jack Lang ('the Big Fella') could cut the ribbon, Captain de Groot charged up on horseback and cut it with his sword, declaring the bridge open on behalf of 'decent and loyal citizens'. The captain was a member of the New Guard, a mob of right-wing revolutionaries who were outraged that Lang was shepherding NSW through the Depression with socialist ideas such as feeding the starving. After de Groot was led away, Lang opened the bridge on behalf of 'the people of NSW', of whom there were an estimated 750,000 in attendance.

The bridge cost $20 million, quite a bargain in modern terms, but it took until 1988 to pay off! It took nine years to build, but just giving it a new coat of paint takes 10 years.

Driving across the bridge costs $2, southbound only; there is no toll in the other direction. There's a cycleway across the bridge (west side) and a pedestrian walkway (east side), with stairs up to them from Cumberland St in the Rocks and from near Milsons Point railway station on the north side. You can climb up inside one of the stone pylons, where there's a small **museum** – see

the earlier Views section. The pylons supported the cranes used in building the bridge, but today they are purely decorative; they don't support the bridge in any way.

THE HARBOUR TUNNEL
The bridge can no longer handle the volume of traffic crossing the harbour, so a tunnel has been built under the harbour, beginning about half a km south of the Opera House and meeting the Warringah Freeway (the road leading north from the bridge) on the north side. As with the bridge, there's a southbound-only toll of $2.

SYDNEY HARBOUR
Sydney's harbour is best viewed from the ferries. It's extravagantly colourful and always interesting. It's probably the most magnificent urban harbour in the world. Officially called Port Jackson, the harbour stretches about 20 km inland from the ocean to the mouth of the Parramatta River. The city centre is about eight km inland from the ocean.

The harbour shores are a maze of headlands and inlets. The biggest inlet, which runs north-west a couple of km from the ocean, is called Middle Harbour.

Apart from the ferries and various harbour cruises (see Getting Around), you can take trips out to some of the small islands. One of them, **Fort Denison**, or Pinchgut as it was uncomfortably named, was a punishment 'cell' for convicts who misbehaved, before it was fortified when the Empire was having a bout of Russian fears in the mid-19th century. Hegarty's Ferries (book on ☎ 241 2733; 247 6606 on weekends) has tours to Fort Denison daily except Monday at 10 am, 12.15 and 2 pm, leaving from No 6 jetty at Circular Quay. The trip takes 1½ hours and costs $8.50. There are plans to build a cafe on the island, and boats running out there should become more frequent.

Goat Island, another tiny speck in Sydney Harbour, is currently closed to visitors.

Sydney Harbour National Park
Some of the harbour shore is still quite wild and several undeveloped stretches towards

the ocean end have been declared Sydney Harbour National Park. Most of them have walking tracks, beaches and good views. On the south shore is **Nielsen Park** which covers Vaucluse Point, Shark Bay (very popular for swimming in summer, with a shark net) and the Hermitage Walk around Hermit Bay. The park headquarters (☎ 337 5355) is at Greycliffe House in Nielsen Park.

Further out there's a fine short walk around **South Head** from Camp Cove Beach, passing Lady Bay, Inner South Head, **The Gap** near Watsons Bay (a popular place for catching the sunrise and sunset), and on to Outer South Head. Bus No 325 from Circular Quay runs past Nielsen Park and the South Head area. On weekends ferries run to Watsons Bay.

On the north shore, the four-km **Ashton Park track**, round Bradleys Head below Taronga Zoo and up alongside Taylors Bay, is part of the national park. Take the Taronga Zoo ferry from Circular Quay to get to Ashton Park. From Taronga you can also walk to **Cremorne Point** by a combination of parks, stairways, streets and bits of bush. Either way you get good views of the south shore. Georges Heights, Middle Head and Obelisk Bay a little further east from Taylors Bay are also parts of the national park. See also the Manly section.

KINGS CROSS & AROUND

Kings Cross deserves its Australia-wide reputation as a hot-bed of vice – it is a genuine, full-on red light district. So much so that at times it's almost a caricature. It seems that every corruption scandal involves the exchange of money 'in a Kings Cross hotel'; that male politicians can't get themselves caught in brothels anywhere but Kings Cross; that 'underworld figures' couldn't live (and die violently) anywhere else.

The Cross has always been a bit raffish and a bit crooked, providing the goods and services denied by Australia's various prohibitions, and it boomed during the Vietnam War when Australian and American soldiers on leave flocked here. Today, the Cross retains its risky aura of 'anything goes', with

a hint of menace and more than a touch of sleaze. Sometimes the razzle-dazzle has a sideshow-alley appeal; sometimes walking up Darlinghurst Rd is about as appetising as finding a cockroach in your cornflakes.

However, there is much more to the Cross than sleaze. It's the travellers' headquarters of Sydney and has Australia's greatest concentration of backpacker hostels. With so many people beginning and ending their Australian travels here, there's a lively buzz. There are also many good (and increasingly fashionable) places to eat, and plenty of entertainment that doesn't involve watching people getting undressed. And you don't have to walk far from the neon lights to find some leafy old streets full of gracious old terraces.

There's an information booth (☎ 368 0479) in the Fitzroy Gardens, near the El Alamein Fountain, open daily (closing early on Sunday). This is largely a booking office for sightseeing tours; if it's that sort of info you're after, make sure you also check out one of the backpacker-oriented travel agents in the Cross. The Cross is a good place to swap information and buy or sell things. Travellers' noticeboards line the hostel and shop walls, and there's a car park where travellers buy and sell vehicles (see the Getting Around chapter).

Although Kings Cross is so well-known, defining its extent is not simple. Darlinghurst Rd north of the very wide three-way intersection of William St, Darlinghurst Rd and Victoria St is undoubtedly in the Cross, as is the El Alamein Fountain in the Fitzroy Gardens, where Darlinghurst Rd dog-legs into Macleay St. However, in the streets nearby the locality depends largely on the impression that people want to give. For example, all of the many backpacker hostels along Victoria St are in Kings Cross, but some more upmarket places in the same street are in Potts Point.

See the Places to Stay, Places to Eat and Entertainment sections for more on the Cross.

The old suburb of **Woolloomooloo** lies between the city and the Cross, extending from William St north to the waterfront. The 'Loo, as it's known, is yet another inner-urban area to be gentrified in the last decade or so. Near the enormous old Cowper Wharf (which might be in for some restoration soon) is Harry's Cafe de Wheels, a pie cart which opened in 1945 and is still going strong. You can try his wares for $2 and up.

If you follow Victoria St north from the Cross you enter leafy **Potts Point** and at the end of the point is **Garden Island**, a large naval base – is it just a happy coincidence that the lurid delights of the Cross are just a short stroll away?

East of Potts Point is the suburb of **Elizabeth Bay**, reached from the Cross by walking up Macleay St or Ward Ave. **Elizabeth Bay House**, at 7 Onslow Ave, is a villa in Greek revival style built in 1839 for Colonial Secretary Alexander Macleay. It fell on hard times in this century and was divided into flats (they must have been some flats!) until the Historic Houses Trust acquired it, opening the restored villa as a museum in 1977. The magnificent gardens have long been swallowed up by other buildings, but the harbour views remain. Although it isn't an especially large house, the proportions are very generous and the design, with the elliptical saloon with a stairway winding up towards the dome, is beautiful. Elizabeth Bay House is open daily except Monday from 10 am to 4.30 pm. Entry costs $5 ($3 children) or $4.50 if you have a Sydney Explorer ticket. An informative video plays in the cellar, where you can make yourself a cup of tea or coffee (50c). As well as the Sydney Explorer bus, bus No 311 from Circular Quay runs past.

East of the Cross is **Rushcutters Bay**, both a small suburb of apartment blocks and a pretty bay backed by a sizeable park.

South of William St are the interesting areas of Paddington and Darlinghurst – see the later Oxford St & Nearby and Paddington sections.

Getting There & Away
Train The simplest way to get here is on an Eastern Suburbs Line train from Martin Place, Town Hall or Central.

Bus The STA's airport express bus No 350 runs to Kings Cross, as do the private outfits KSR and Clipper/Gray Line (see Getting Around later in this chapter for more information). From Circular Quay, bus Nos 324, 325 and 327 run to Kings Cross; from Railway Square take No 311.

Walking From the city you can walk straight up William St, or there's a quieter pedestrian route. Duck through Sydney Hospital from Macquarie St, cross the Domain and descend the hill just on the right of the Art Gallery, then go down Palmer St from its junction with Sir John Young Crescent, turn left along Harmer St, and follow the paths and back-streets till you reach a flight of steps leading up to Victoria St, just south of its junction with Orwell St.

EAST OF THE CROSS
The harbourside suburbs east of Kings Cross are some of Sydney's most expensive. The main road through this area is New South Head Rd, the continuation of William St (which is called Kings Cross Rd and Bayswater Rd as it winds past the Cross).

East of Rushcutters Bay is **Darling Point**, a popular place for the early colony's merchants to build mansions, and inland from here is the suburb of **Edgecliff**. Next along is **Double Bay**, both another pretty inlet and a wealthy suburb – it's sometimes called 'Double Pay'! Bay St runs north off New South Head Rd and it's the main shopping street. It leads down to a quiet waterfront park (where the digger on the war memorial strikes an unusually aggressive pose) and the ferry wharf.

Double Bay is worth a visit if the inner-city tensions are getting to you; here, the major hassle is likely to be a badly-parked Porsche blocking the footpath. There are plenty of coffee shops and patisseries that don't necessarily charge a fortune, and you can at least window-shop for some designer clothes.

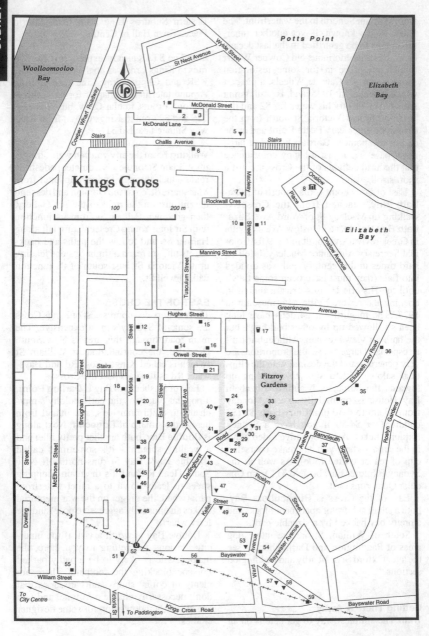

Woolloomooloo Bay

Potts Point

Elizabeth Bay

St Neot Avenue

Wylde Street

Cowper Wharf Roadway

McDonald Street

McDonald Lane

Challis Avenue

Macleay Street

Stairs

Stairs

Kings Cross

0   100   200 m

Onslow Place

Rockwall Cres

Elizabeth Bay

Manning Street

Tusculum Street

Onslow Avenue

Greenknowe Avenue

Hughes Street

Orwell Street

Victoria Street

Earl Street

Springfield Ave

Fitzroy Gardens

Elizabeth Bay Road

Roslyn Gardens

Brougham Street

Darlinghurst Road

Ward Avenue

Barncleuth Square

Roslyn Street

McElhone Street

Dowling Street

Kellett Street

Roslyn Avenue

Bayswater Avenue

Bayswater Street

William Street

Victoria St

To City Centre

To Paddington

Kings Cross Road

Ward Road

Bayswater Road

PLACES TO STAY

1	Florida Motor Inn
2	Backpackers Village
3	Rucksack Rest
4	Simpsons of Potts Point
6	Challis Lodge
9	Olims Sydney Hotel
10	Hotel Nikko Sydney
11	Sheraton Hotel
12	Kendall Private Hotel
13	Eva's Backpackers
14	Jolly Swagman Backpackers (Orwell St)
15	Downunder Hostel
16	Orwell Lodge
18	Kanga House
19	Jolly Swagman Backpackers (Victoria St)
21	Jolly Swagman Backpackers (Springfield Mall)
22	Travellers Rest
23	Bernly Private Hotel & Springfield Lodge
27	Backpackers Connection
28	Kingsview Motel
29	Fountain International Hostel
34	17 Elizabeth Bay Rd
35	Sebel Town House
36	Montpelier Private Hotel
37	Barncleuth House
38	Original Backpackers
39	Highfield House
41	Fountain Plaza Hostel
42	Maksim Lodge
46	Plane Tree Lodge
54	Metro Motor Inn
55	O'Malley's Hotel
56	Barclay Hotel
59	Backpackers Headquarters

PLACES TO EAT

5	Merivale Brasserie
7	Macleay St Bistro
20	Four Fingers
24	Yakidori
25	Astoria
26	Nick's Seafood
30	Bourbon & Beefsteak
31	Fountain Cafe
32	Fountain Bistro
40	Pad Thai
43	Geoffrey's Cafe
45	Roy's
47	Lime & Lemongrass
48	Joe's
49	Dean's
50	Cafe Iguana
53	Bayswater Brasserie
57	Cafe 59
58	Gado Gado

OTHER

8	Elizabeth Bay House
17	Joe's Garage
33	El Alamein Fountain
44	Let's Travel
51	Kings Cross Hotel
52	King Cross Station

There's a small beach near the ferry wharf and a seawater pool just east of here, by Seven Shillings Beach on **Point Piper**, which separates Double Bay from wealthy **Rose Bay**. Rose Bay has a pair of longer beaches and is also served by ferries. Running inland behind the wharf area is the Royal Sydney Golf Course.

Rose Bay curves north onto the peninsula which forms the south side of the entrance to Sydney Harbour. On the harbour side of the peninsula is **Vaucluse**, the most exclusive suburb of them all. Even in the colony's early days Vaucluse was a desirable address, but it's ironic that **Vaucluse House** (1828), one of its finest mansions, was built by William Wentworth, an outcast from high society because of his democratic leanings – he had the temerity to suggest that the Australian-born colonials were the equals of the English. Vaucluse House is open to the public from 10 am to 4.30 pm daily except Monday. Admission is $5 ($3 concession). It's an imposing turreted example of 19th-century Australiana in fine grounds. You can get here on bus No 325 from Circular Quay; get off a couple of stops past Nielsen Park. Nielsen Park is part of the scattered Sydney Harbour National Park – see the Sydney Harbour section for more information. All along this side of the harbour there are superb views back towards the city.

As the peninsula narrows down to South Head, **Watsons Bay** has a fine beach on the harbour side, and on the ocean side **The Gap** is a dramatic clifftop lookout. On the harbour north of Watsons Bay are **Camp Cove** and **Lady Bay**, small beaches with fashionable clientele. At the tip of the peninsula is **South Head**, with great views across to North Head and west to Middle Head.

Getting There & Away

The closest of these suburbs to a railway station is Double Bay, which is east of the Edgecliff Railway Station on the Eastern Suburbs Line. Take the New South Head Rd exit from the station, turn right and follow New South Head Rd to the nearby corner of Ocean Ave. Head down to the corner of Cooper St which leads you to Bay St. Alternatively you could just stay on New South Head Rd until you meet Bay St, but it's a less pleasant walk.

Infrequent ferries run from Circular Quay to Double Bay and Rose Bay and, on weekends, to Watsons Bay. See Meals With a View in the Places to Eat section in this chapter for private boats to Watsons Bay. The non-nautical could take a bus, Nos 324/5 from Circular Quay to Watsons Bay.

BONDI BEACH

Australia's most famous beach is receiving a huge facelift to ready it for a National Estate listing.

Campbell Pde is the main beachfront road and the corner of Campbell Pde and Hall St is the hub. The main road into Bondi Beach is Bondi Rd, which branches off from Oxford St east of the mall in Bondi Junction. This is the same Oxford St that begins at Hyde Park and runs through Darlinghurst and Paddington.

Bondi Beach post office is on the corner of Jacques Ave and Hall St, a block back from Campbell Pde. A little further up Hall St you enter a Jewish area, with kosher shops and the Hakoah Club.

Bondi **markets** are held on Sunday at the school at the north end of Campbell Pde.

You can hire surfboards and boogie-boards from the Bondi Surf Company, on Campbell Pde just north of the corner of Lamrock Ave, for $15 for three hours or $25 for the whole day. This includes a wetsuit if you want one. In-line skates are rented by Bondi Boards & Blades, on Curlewis St just back from Campbell Pde, for $15 for the first hour and $5 for subsequent hours, with cheaper rates for longer rentals. You get all the protective gear including a helmet. Kites are sold from a shop on the corner of Campbell Pde and Curlewis St.

Some of Australia's easiest-reached **Aboriginal carvings** are a short walk north of Bondi Beach – outlines of fish on a flat rock on the golf course.

Note that although Bondi Beach is usually referred to simply as Bondi, the suburb of Bondi is actually inland, between Bondi Junction and Bondi Beach. Immediately south of Bondi Beach is the tiny suburb of Tamarama.

Getting There & Away

Bondi Junction is the nearest railway station to Bondi Beach, and from here you can take bus No 380 to Bondi and Bondi Beach. A combined rail/bus ticket works out cheaper than buying separate tickets.

A spectacular coastal footpath runs along the clifftops from Bondi Beach to Coogee Beach, passing Tamarama, Bronte, Clovelly and Gordon's Bay.

COOGEE BEACH

About four km south of Bondi Beach, Coogee is geographically almost a carbon copy of its more famous neighbour, but without the crowds or increasingly glitzy development. Coogee is much more a suburb that happens to be on a great beach. However, backpackers are now finding Coogee increasingly attractive – usually a sign that an area is about to boom.

The main beachfront street is Arden St, and the corner of Arden St and Coogee Bay Rd is just about the centre of town.

The main attraction of Coogee is its patrolled beach. Surfworld, at 250 Coogee Bay Rd not far from the corner of Arden St, will rent you a boogie-board for $5 an hour, $15 for half a day or $25 for a whole day. A block away on Alfreda St, Pro Dive (☎ 665 6333) runs courses for about $345 (much less if there is more than one of you) and rents snorkelling gear for $10 a day – and this is a great spot for a snorkel. If you want to buy a kite, see Kite Site on the corner of Beach and Bream Sts, behind the Coogee Palace.

Getting There & Away
Bus Nos 373/4 run from Circular Quay to Coogee, Nos 371/2 run from Railway Square (near Central Station) and Nos 314/5 run from Bondi Junction.

OXFORD ST & NEARBY
Running south-east from Hyde Park in the city centre, Oxford St is a famous and lively thoroughfare which forms the border between the interesting inner suburbs of **Darlinghurst** to the north and **Surry Hills** to the south. This whole area is full of interesting shops and fashionable but often inexpensive places to eat, and it is home to some interesting people. **Taylor Square**, the junction of Oxford, Flinders and Bourke Sts, is the area's heart. Oxford St has been declared a Gay & Lesbian Precinct, but whatever your sexual preference(s) you'll find it an interesting place.

Facing Taylor Square is Darlinghurst Courthouse (1842) and behind it is the old **Darlinghurst Jail**, now a college, where author Henry Lawson was several times incarcerated for debt. Lawson called it 'Starvinghurst Jail' and dreaded 'a cell like a large-sized coffin' where he was not allowed to write. The **Jewish Museum** at the corner of Darlinghurst Rd and Burton St is open from Monday to Thursday from 10 am to 4 pm, from 10 am to 2 pm on Friday and from noon to 5 pm on Sunday. Admission is $5 ($2 children).

South-east of Taylor Square, Darlinghurst Rd and then Victoria St run north off Oxford St to Kings Cross, while Oxford St continues on through Paddington and Woollahra, eventually reaching Bondi Junction. Many buses run along Oxford St, such as No 378 from Central Station and No 380 from Circular Quay.

Gays & Lesbians
Oxford St, especially around Taylor Square, is the centre of what is probably the second-largest gay community in the world. The Gay & Lesbian Mardi Gras is the most colourful event on the Sydney social calendar. It culminates in a spectacular parade which winds down Oxford St and ends in a huge party at the showgrounds.

In 1994 the ABC, the national broadcaster, decided that it could no longer ignore an event which draws crowds of 500,000 people and is one of the major tourist attractions in the country, and showed highlights of the parade. The reaction from the rest of Australia demonstrated that there is some catching-up to do in liberal attitudes outside Sydney. Even in Sydney there's still a strong streak of homophobia among dinkum Aussies, and violence against homosexuals is not unknown.

Free papers such as *Capital Q* and the *Sydney Star Observer* have extensive listings of venues and events.

For the record, it is illegal in NSW for a man to have sex with a man under the age of 18, and for a woman to have sex with a woman under the age of 16. Note that laws in other states differ. ■

PADDINGTON

The inner suburb of Paddington, four km east of the city centre, is one of the most attractive inner-city residential areas in the world. 'Paddo' is a tightly packed mass of terrace houses, built for aspiring artisans in the later years of the Victorian era. During the lemming-like rush to the outer suburbs after WW II, the area became a slum. A renewed interest in Victorian architecture (of which Australia has some gems) combined with a sudden recollection of the pleasures of inner-city life, led to the restoration of Paddo during the '60s.

Today it's a fascinating jumble of often beautifully restored terraces, tumbling up and down the steep streets, and is one of the world's finest examples of totally unplanned urban restoration. The best time to visit Paddo is Saturday, when you can catch the **Paddo Bazaar** at the corner of Newcombe and Oxford Sts with all sorts of eccentric market stalls.

The New Edition bookshop and tea-rooms at 328 Oxford St has a pamphlet with a map showing the whereabouts of some of the area's many galleries and bookshops.

South of Paddington and bordering Surry Hills, **Moore Park** has playing fields and a golf course as well as the **Showgrounds**, historic **Sydney Cricket Ground** (SCG) and the new **Football Stadium**. Sportspace (☎ 0055 21058 for bookings) is a behind-the-scenes guided tour of these facilities, with historic displays featuring great players from all the sports played here – and some of the commentators. Tours are held daily at 10 am, 1 pm and 3 pm (except on match days when times change and tours may be shortened) and cost $15 ($9 children) for two hours, $8 ($6 children) for one hour.

East again (and south of Woollahra) you

A Paddington Stroll

Separating Oxford St's Darlinghurst/Surry Hills section from its Paddington section are the **Victoria Barracks** (the street numbers begin again here). The huge sandstone barracks are used by the army and have been since they were built by mainly convict labour between 1841 and 1848; at that time the area was mainly sand dunes and swamps! On Thursday morning you can visit Victoria Barracks from 10 am to hear a military band and see the **Army Museum**. The museum is also open on the first Sunday of the month. These days and times change fairly frequently, so, if you're planning a special trip, ring (☎ 339 3000) before you arrive. Note that the changing-of-the-guard ceremony is no longer held here, but you can see it in the city at the Anzac Memorial in Hyde Park on Thursday at 12.30 pm.

Just opposite the barracks look for Shadforth St leading north off Oxford St; this is one of the original streets with tiny terraces. Keep wandering and find Spring and Prospect streets which give an idea of the meandering nature of the original village.

Wander out of these streets again onto Oxford St and see the attractive white **Town Hall**. The former Chauvel Cinema is found in the Oatley St entrance – it's now the **AFI Cinema** (Australian Film Institute) and is a must for film buffs.

Diagonally opposite you can see a magnificent home with formal gardens and lawns leading down to Oxford St. This is the National Trust's **Juniper Hall** which was built as a family home in 1824 from the profits of gin, by a man called Robert Cooper – the father of 24 children! Currently it isn't open to the public.

From Juniper Hall, turn left into Underwood St, then follow Heeley St to reach **Five Ways**, a meeting of streets around which are some most interesting shops and places to eat, including the lovely old **Royal Hotel**.

Some favourite spots include Paddington St, further east, which is shady and leafy and has some of the finest terraced houses; William St, narrow and not as pretty but housing some of the most interesting speciality shops; and the trendy strip of Oxford St where cafes, books and boutiques vie for attention. Take time for a rest or a snack along here before a browse among the many antique shops of Queen St east from Centennial Square. ■

Paddington terraces

come to the adjacent **Centennial Park**, Sydney's biggest park, with running, cycling and horse tracks, duck ponds, barbecue sites and lots more. Black swans and many other birds nest here. You can hire bikes from several places on Clovelly Rd, Randwick, near the southern edge of the park (see Getting Around), or horses from several operators at the Showgrounds on Lang Rd. At the southern edge of Centennial Park is **Randwick Racecourse** and just south of here is the **University of NSW**, on Anzac Pde (which becomes Flinders St and runs into Taylor Square). Many buses run down Anzac Pde from the city, including No 336 from Circular Quay.

SOUTH OF THE CITY CENTRE

South-west of Central Station, the small inner suburb of **Chippendale** is a maze of Victorian terrace houses, like an unscrubbed version of Paddington. Just south of Railway Square near the corner of Lee (George) and Regent Sts, the quaint neo-Gothic **Mortuary Station** was where coffins and mourners once boarded funeral trains bound for Rookwood Cemetery.

Chippendale borders the east side of the

University of Sydney, Australia's oldest, although much newer than the architecture of buildings such as the Great Hall would have you believe.

On the south side of the uni is **Newtown**, another suburb influenced by its student population. Walk down King St between the uni and Newtown railway station for a long string of diverse places to eat, elaborate political graffiti, some good second-hand bookshops and pubs where interesting young bands play. On the north side of the uni is the more established student suburb of Glebe – see the following section.

Also south of Central Station but on the east side of the tracks, **Redfern** is one of the last inner suburbs to remain unrenovated and predominantly working class. A few sections come close to being Australia's only real slum. Redfern tends to buck the system, and relations between the police and the community (especially the large Aboriginal community) are at times very bad. The **Eveleigh Locomotive Workshops**, at the corner of Garden and Boundary Sts, has a display of Victorian steam-powered blacksmithing equipment, open from 3 pm on Fridays only ($3).

PLACES TO STAY

1 Glebe Point YHA Hostel
2 Glebe Village Backpackers
5 Haven Inn
8 Hereford YHA Lodge
9 Wattle House
12 Rooftop Motel
22 Alishan International
   Guesthouse

PLACES TO EAT

3 Perry's Pizza
4 Lilac Cafe
6 Moghul Curry House
7 Lilac & Lien
11 The Craven
13 Pudding Shop &
   Flavour of India
14 Abbey Restaurant
16 Le Chocoreve
17 Thai Intra Restaurant
19 Bogarts Pizza
20 Caffe Troppo
23 Rasputin
25 Yak & Yeti
28 Badde Manors
30 Rose Blues

OTHER

10 Valhalla Cinema
15 Excelsior Hotel
18 Post Office
21 A Natural Practice
24 Friend in Hand Hotel
26 Gleebooks (new)
27 Glebe Markets (open
   Saturdays)
29 Inner-City Cycles

GLEBE

Glebe is a relaxed suburb which has been a haven for students long enough to be now thoroughly mainstream in a bohemian sort of a way – real estate and cappuccino prices are high. The main street, Glebe Point Rd, runs north from Broadway to Glebe Point and in under two km there are scores of places to eat. Glebe is also a backpacker accommodation centre and there are also several other reasonable places to stay. Alternative health care is another feature of the area. A Natural Practice (☎ 566 4038) at 161A Glebe Point Rd has flotation tanks ($20), various massages and a wide range of other services.

To get here from the airport you can take the KST bus; from the city and Railway Square bus Nos 431, 432, 433 and 434 run along Glebe Point Rd. On foot you can head south on George St and Broadway, turning into Glebe Point Rd about a km south-west of Central Station. A more interesting walk begins at Darling Harbour's Pyrmont Bridge (at the end of Market St) which leads to Pyrmont Bridge Rd. After passing the **Pyrmont Fishmarkets** on Blackwattle Bay this road becomes Bridge Rd and eventually crosses Glebe Point Rd. This route passes through some industrial areas which are pretty quiet after hours, so you might not feel like walking this way at night.

BALMAIN

Once a tough neighbourhood, Balmain attracted artists in the '60s and has been prime real estate for some time. However, it remains an idiosyncratic area which has staunchly resisted the trendier aspects of gentrification. This might be partly due to its relative isolation, on its own little peninsula. There are no special things to do or see here, but there are some good places to eat and pleasant walks, and it's a nice place to be. Another attraction is that it's accessible by ferry (Hunters Hill).

The inner suburbs between Balmain and Glebe, **Annandale** and **Leichhardt** (dubbed 'dyke-heart' by its lesbian population), are also attracting interesting people and places to eat.

Top: Sydney (PS)
Bottom Left: Darling Harbour, Sydney (PS)
Bottom Right: Chinese Garden, Darling Harbour (JM)

Top: Haute couture, Mardi Gras Festival, Sydney (BP)
Bottom Left: City to Surf Fun Run, Sydney (MA)
Bottom Right: Life guard, Sydney (PS)

NORTH OF THE BRIDGE

The northern shores of Sydney Harbour have some pleasant suburbs and patches of national park.

Kirribilli & Milsons Point

At the end of Kirribilli Point, east of the bridge, stand **Admiralty House** and **Kirribilli House**, the Sydney pieds-à-terre of the governor general and the prime minister respectively (Admiralty House is the one nearer the bridge).

Luna Park was at its peak in the 1930s, when thousands of people flocked across the harbour on the new bridge. The park closed in the '70s, sparking a long battle for the prime site between preservationists and developers. The goodies have won, and the Luna Park site has been proclaimed a public reserve. The amusement park is being restored and will retain a quirky sense of fun. The idea is to recapture something of the past, not to build a new hi-tech park.

Martin Sharp, a Sydney artist with a fascination for the odd, has been involved in the fight to restore Luna park for many years, and the resurrected park will bear the stamp of his and other artists' creativity. The new gondolas on the ferris wheel will be worth seeing, as they are being created by Chris O'Doherty (aka Reg Mombassa, member of the band *Mental as Anything* and designer of 100% Mambo clothing).

The new Luna Park was due to open in 1993, but things are running well behind schedule. When it does open there will be no admission charge to the reserve and there will be some free entertainment along the midway, as well as pay-as-you-go rides, including a revamped Big Dipper.

Some ferries will be routed via the park. Other ways of getting there include walking across the bridge and taking a North Shore line train to Milsons Point station.

McMahons Point

The next headland west is McMahons Point, tipped by the evocatively-named **Blues Point**, where there's a small reserve. Blues Point is named after the Jamaican-born Billy Blue who ferried people across from Dawes Point in the 1830s.

Balls Head Reserve

On the north shore of the harbour two headlands west of the Harbour Bridge, Balls Head Reserve is a park with great views of the harbour and also old Aboriginal rock paintings (in a cave) and carvings. Take a North Shore line train to Waverton and follow the signs from the station.

Hunters Hill

On a spit at the junction of the Parramatta and Lane Cove rivers, Hunters Hill, with the adjacent suburb of Woolwich, is full of elegant Victorian houses. The National Trust's **Vienna Cottage** at 38 Alexandra St, Hunters Hill, is a stone cottage built in 1871 and open on the second Sunday and the last weekend of the month; admission is $4. Hunters Hill ferries from Circular Quay stop at Woolwich's Valentia Street wharf.

North Sydney

There are now enough tall buildings in North Sydney to furnish a respectable city centre. The area has bloomed because of high costs in the CBD, and job prospects for working travellers tend to be brighter on this side of the bridge.

A km or so further along the Pacific Highway from North Sydney is **Crows Nest**, with a growing number of good places

---

A Balmain Walk

At the intersection of Darling St and Rowntree Rd, turn right into Rowntree Rd and follow it down to turn right into Ballast Point Rd, cutting through at Lemm St into Wharf Rd. This is a most attractive stretch of waterfront homes. Follow Wharf Rd west and turn left into Grove St and right into Cove St and then right again into Louisa Rd which winds down to Long Nose Point and its ferry and reserve. The whole area is extremely attractive, with pretty Victorian homes in abundance. ■

to eat. The 1880s Sexton's Cottage at 250 West St, next to the old St Thomas's Church, has displays relating to early life in the area.

Further North

Mosman and **Cremorne**, on the large chunk of land separating Middle Harbour from the main harbour, have good shopping centres and some nice walks along the shore. **Balmoral**, near Mosman and facing Middle Harbour, has a long beach with a netted area.

The main road through this part of the world is Military Rd, which branches off the Warringah Freeway (the north side of the Harbour Bridge) near North Sydney. Military Rd crosses the Spit Bridge (which opens to let boats through) over Middle Harbour then runs north, changing names several times, bypassing Manly and eventually reaching Palm Beach, the northernmost beachside suburb. Bus No 190 runs a limited-stops route from Wynyard to Palm

Beach; to get to Mosman and Cremorne take bus No 182 from Wynyard. You can also get here from St Leonards.

MANLY

'Seven miles from Sydney and a thousand miles from care'. This old tourist slogan still applies: Manly is a relaxed little resort with superb beaches, only half an hour by ferry from Circular Quay (or 15 minutes by JetCat). It's a place you must visit and it's worth considering as a place to stay.

Manly was one of the first places in Australia to be named by Europeans – Captain Arthur Phillip named it for the 'manly'-looking Aborigines he saw here in 1788.

Manly straddles the narrow isthmus leading to North Head, and has both ocean and harbour beaches. The ferry wharf is on Manly Cove, on the harbour side, and from here the Corso runs across to the ocean side where you'll find the famous **Manly Beach**,

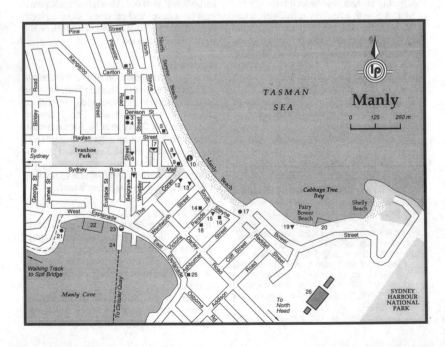

lined with Norfolk Island pine trees. Most of the Corso is a pedestrian mall.

The Manly Visitors Information Bureau (☎ 977 1088), open daily from 10 am to 4 pm, is on Manly Beach near the Corso. There are lockers where you can leave your valuables while you go for a swim. A **craft market** is held near the information centre on weekends. Pick up a copy of the *Manly Daily* newspaper to see what's going on in and around Manly. Several venues in Dee Why, just north of Manly, regularly have big Australian touring bands.

The long ocean beach north of the Corso is **North Steyne Beach**; the shorter stretch of beach running south is usually called **Manly Beach** but it's technically South Steyne Beach. The beachfront road is called North Steyne and South Steyne. At the south end of Manly Beach is the surf-lifesaving club, and from here a path leads around the rocky headland to tiny **Fairy Bower Beach**, which has a small rockpool. Further around is beautiful little **Shelly Beach**. North Steyne Beach runs on up to **Queenscliff Beach**, near the steep Queenscliff headland. There's a lifesaving club here as well. Around the headland (although not simple to get to on foot) is **Freshwater Beach**.

That large building on the hill south-east of the town centre is **St Patricks Seminary** (1889).

Across on the harbour side on **Manly Cove** is another stretch of sand, backed by the East and West Esplanade. In the centre is the rejuvenated **Manly Wharf**. You could spend most of your visit to Manly here, as there are cafes, restaurants, shops and a small amusement park.

On the headland at the west end of Manly Cove is **Oceanworld** (☎ 949 2644), a good oceanarium. It's open daily and admission is $11 ($5 children). Qualified divers can dive with the sharks! Shark dives must be booked and cost $55 (plus equipment). They are held daily at 1 pm and in the evening on Wednesday, Thursday and Friday. Friends can watch evening dives for $5; during the day they pay the normal admittance.

Next to Oceanworld, the **Manly Art Gallery & Museum** has exhibitions concentrating on beach themes and local history (much the same thing in Manly), with old photos and historic cossies (bathers, swimsuits), as well as contemporary ceramics and other artworks. It's open from 10 am to 4 pm from Tuesday to Friday and from noon to 5 pm on weekends; admission is $2 (children free).

You can continue past Oceanworld to join a 10-km walking track, the **Manly Scenic Walkway**, which follows the shoreline all the way back to the Spit Bridge over Middle Harbour. Points of interest on the way, from the Manly end, include Fairlight, Forty Baskets and Reef beaches (the latter, a nude

PLACES TO STAY

1	Manly Beach Resort Backpackers & Motel
2	Manly Astra Backpackers
5	Pacific Parkroyal Hotel
9	Steyne Hotel
14	Eversham Private Hotel
16	Radisson Kestrel Hotel
18	Manly Lodge
25	Periwinkle Guesthouse

PLACES TO EAT

6	Cafe Tunis
8	Luis
11	Malacca Straits Satay Restaurant
12	Cadillac Cafe
13	Pan Tip Thai
15	Cafe Steyne
19	Bower Restaurant

OTHER

3	Aloha Surf
4	Manly Cycle Centre
7	Post Office
10	Information Office
17	Surf Lifesaving Club
20	Rock Pool
21	Oceanworld
22	Netted Swimming Area
23	Bus Interchange
24	Manly Wharf/Ferries
26	St Patrick's Seminary

Daylight Swimming Legal!
While you're enjoying Manly Beach, thank William H Gocher that you're not breaking the law by swimming in daylight. Such immorality was illegal until Gocher, a local newspaper editor, announced in 1902 that he would take a dip in daylight and defied the authorities to arrest him. He had to swim three times before he was arrested, but the subsequent court case led to the legalisation of daylight bathing. ■

beach, involves a slight detour from the main track), great views between Dobroyd Head and Grotto Point, and ancient Aboriginal rock-carvings on a sandstone platform between the Cutler Rd Lookout and Grotto Point. Collect a leaflet detailing the walk from the information centre. Buses run from the Spit Bridge to Sydney city centre.

North Head
Spectacular North Head at the Sydney Harbour entrance is about three km south of Manly and offers good views from several lookouts. Most of the headland is in Sydney Harbour National Park – including the **quarantine station** which housed suspected disease carriers from 1832 until 1984. The station is now controlled by National Parks and you have to book a guided tour to visit (☎ 977 6229). Tours are held most afternoons and cost $6 ($4 children).

The centre of the headland is an off-limits military reserve, but you can visit the **Regimental Museum of the Royal Regiment of Australian Artillery** (☎ 976 1138), to use the full name, which is open from noon to 4 pm on weekends. Admission is $3 ($1 children).

Manly Coach Tours (☎ 938 4677) runs passenger services between Manly Wharf and North Head. On weekends quite a few buses run all the way to the North Head lookout, but on weekdays you might have to get off at Manly Hospital and walk the rest of the way. The return fare is about $3.

Activities
Swimming & Surfing During summer there's a netted swimming area on the harbour beach between the ferry wharf and Oceanworld. There's also sheltered swim-

ming across on the ocean side at Shelly Beach.

When the wind tends towards the northwest the surf is usually good at Queenscliff and North Steyne; south-westerlies make for good waves at South Steyne and Fairy Bower. Sometimes there's a huge reef break off the Queenscliff bombora – for experienced surfies only.

Aloha Surf (☎ 977 3777) on the corner at 44 Pittwater Rd rents both surf and boogie boards for $15/25 for a half/full day's hire (until 7 pm). Wetsuits go for $5/10.

Cycling & In-Line Skating With less hectic traffic and long cycle paths, Manly is one of Sydney's better places for cyclists. You can hire good bikes from the Manly Cycle Centre (☎ 977 1189) at 36 Pittwater Rd for $5 an hour, $25 a day, $40 a weekend or $60 a week.

The cycle paths are also popular for in-line skating, and there are a couple of rental outfits where you can get skating gear: Manly Beach-Hut on South Steyne rents skates for $10 an hour, $15 for two hours and $20 for a day. This place is mainly a beachwear shop, so beginners might want to try Manly Blades, an in-line specialist not far away on North Steyne, where you can have lessons. Equipment hire costs $15 for the first hour and $5 for subsequent hours or $28 for 24 hours. Lessons cost from $10, less if there is more than one person. You can usually find Manly Blades' discount vouchers at the information centre.

Diving The dive shops have regular boat dives, and you can make beach dives from Shelly Beach. Dive Centre Manly (☎ 977 2095) at 10 Belgrave St runs PADI courses for around $300, and they hire snorkelling gear (including wetsuit) for $20. There's also Moby Dive (☎ 976 3297) on Manly Wharf, and Pacific Coast Divers (☎ 977 5966) at 169 Pittwater Rd.

Other Activities As well as diving, Moby Dive (☎ 976 3297) on Manly Wharf can arrange skydiving, paragliding and abseiling – in fact they'll put all four activities together into a discount package for you.

Kiteworks (☎ 976 2771) on Manly Wharf sells kites, and you'll find the staff flying kites on Manly Beach most days. Every second Sunday a kite club meets at Tania Park on Dobroyd Head, just west of Manly.

Getting There & Around

See this chapter's Getting Around section for details on ferries to Manly.

Taxis (☎ 977 9111) can usually be found near the corner of the Corso and Belgrave St. Alternatively, you can drive your own tuk-tuk (the three-wheeler transport which is a feature of Asian cities) for $15 an hour, minimum two hours. Contact Tuk-Tuk Hire (☎ 976 3657) at Manly Wharf. These tuk-tuks have seatbelts and carry three people – not the half-dozen or so that manage to cram on board in Asia.

NORTHERN BEACHES

A string of beaches and oceanfront suburbs stretches north up the coast from Manly, ending in beautiful, affluent **Palm Beach** and the spectacular **Barrenjoey Heads** at the mouth of Broken Bay, 30 km from Manly. Fans of Aussie TV soap-operas will want to make a pilgrimage to Palm Beach, as many outdoor scenes in *Home & Away* are shot here. Barrenjoey Head and its lighthouse feature in the title sequence.

From Palm Beach you can take cruises on **Pittwater**, a fine inlet off Broken Bay, or the Hawkesbury River, or get ferries to Ku-Ring-Gai Chase or across Broken Bay to **Patonga**. The latter is part of an interesting alternative route north: from Patonga there are buses to Gosford, where you can get a bus or train heading up the coast.

Bus Nos 136 and 139 run from Manly to Freshwater and Curl Curl. Bus No 190 from Wynyard in the city centre runs all the way to Palm Beach. From Manly take a bus to Narrabeen (eg No 155) and pick up No 190 there.

BOTANY BAY

It's a common misconception amongst first-time visitors that Sydney is built around Botany Bay. Actually Sydney Harbour is Port Jackson and Botany Bay is 10 to 15 km south, although the city now encompasses Botany Bay too. Botany Bay was Captain Cook's first landing place in Australia and was named by Joseph Banks, the expedition's naturalist, for the many botanical specimens he found here.

This is the stretch of water you sometimes see as you approach or depart Sydney by plane.

The suburb of **Sylvania Waters**, now infamous because of a pommie TV series 'exposing' Aussie materialism, is on the Georges River near the southern shore of Botany Bay.

In **Botany Bay National Park** at Kurnell, on the south side of the bay, Captain Cook's landing place is marked with various monuments. The Discovery Centre relates to Cook's life and explorations, as well as to the surrounding wetlands. It's open from 10.30 am to 4.30 or 5 pm daily; the rest of the site, with bushland walking tracks and picnic areas, is open from 7.30 am to 7 or 8 pm. From Cronulla Station (10 km away) take bus No 987. Entry costs $7.50 per car.

On the northern side of the bay entrance is **La Perouse**, where the French explorer of that name arrived in 1788, just six days after the arrival of the First Fleet. He gave the poms a good scare, as they weren't expecting the French to turn up in this part of their empire quite so soon. La Perouse and his men camped at Botany Bay for a few weeks, then sailed off into the Pacific and totally disappeared. It was not until many years later that the wrecks of their ships were discovered on a reef near Vanuatu.

At La Perouse there's a monument to the

expedition (built in 1828 by a French expedition searching for signs of La Perouse), and a museum with relics from the La Perouse expedition and a collection of antique maps. The museum is open daily from 10 am to 4.30 pm and entry costs $2 ($1 children). Guided tours in English or French can be booked (☎ 311 3379). Offshore from the museum is **Bare Island** with a decaying concrete fort built in 1885 to discourage a feared Russian (yes, Russian) invasion of Australia. Bus Nos 394 and 398 run here from Circular Quay.

ACTIVITIES
Canoeing & Kayaking
Canoe Specialists (☎ 969 4590), at the south end of the Spit Bridge in Mosman, rent sea kayaks to paddle on Middle Harbour, or even out into Sydney Harbour if it isn't too rough. They'll give basic lessons to beginners. Single kayaks cost $10 for the first hour and $5 for subsequent hours. Double kayaks cost twice that. Natural Wanders (☎ 555 9788) has kayak tours of the harbour, paddling under the bridge and stopping in secluded bays where you can take short walks. No kayaking experience is necessary. A tour of about five hours costs $65. You might be able to book this at YHA hostels.

Cycling
See the Getting Around section at the end of this chapter.

Diving
There's good diving from ocean beaches, and shipwrecks to explore from boat dives. Plenty of outfits will take you diving and many run dive courses, including Pro Dive (☎ 665 6333) in Coogee, Manly Dive Centre (☎ 977 2095) and Moby Dive (☎ 976 3297) in Manly.

Qualified divers can dive with the sharks at Manly's Oceanworld ($55 plus equipment).

Golf
The most central of Sydney's 40-odd public golf courses is Moore Park (☎ 663 3960) on

Centennial Ave, which charges $14 for 18 holes on the weekend and $10 on a weekday. Other public courses reasonably close to the city include Bondi (☎ 30 1981) on Military Rd in North Bondi and Barnwell Park (☎ 713 9019) on the corner of William St and Lyons Rd in Five Dock.

Horseriding
Several outfits offer rides in Centennial Park, such as Blue Ribbon Riding School (☎ 361 3859), Centennial Park Horse Hire (☎ 361 4513), and Eastside Horse Riding Academy (☎ 360 7521), all based at the Showgrounds (so they don't operate during the Royal Easter Show). They all charge around $18 per hour. Bookings are necessary.

In-Line Skating
Many places rent in-line skates and the protective equipment that beginners will make plenty of use of. See the Manly and Bondi sections for some hire shops.

Running/jogging
The many pathways of Centennial Park attract joggers, as do the shorefront paths at Bondi and Manly. Running across the Harbour Bridge is a popular way for north-shore people to get to work in the city.

Surfing
See the earlier Beaches section for surf beaches, some of which have board-hire shops, especially Manly and Bondi.

Swimming
See the earlier Beaches section for information on harbour and ocean swimming. As well as the beaches, there are more than 100 public swimming pools, such as the saltwater Boy Charlton pool on Woolloomooloo Bay near the Domain, the North Sydney pool next to Luna Park in Milsons Point and the pool in Prince Alfred Park, near Central Station and Surry Hills.

Tennis
There are tennis courts for hire all over the city, including: Coogee (☎ 665 1387) at 35

Division St; Darling Harbour (☎ 212 1666) at the corner of Day and Bathurst Sts; Double Bay (☎ 389 9259) in Cooper Park, off Suttie St; Manly (☎ 977 1309) on Pittwater Rd; Moore Park (☎ 313 8000) and Prince Alfred Park (☎ 698 9451) between Surry Hills and Central Station.

Sailing & Windsurfing
There are several sailing schools, most running courses for crew on larger yachts. If you want to learn to sail a dinghy (and what better place could you do it?), see an outfit such as Northside Sailing School (☎ 969 3972), at the south end of the Spit Bridge in Mosman. On a sailboard you'll pay $100 for three two-hour lessons, in a dinghy it's $200 for four three-hour lessons, and in a yacht it's $250 for four three-hour lessons. They also hire sailboards and dinghies for $15 per hour.

Balmoral Marine (☎ 969 6006) at 2 The Esplanade, Balmoral, on Middle Harbour, hire sailboards ($15 per hour) and cats ($20 per hour). They can arrange tuition.

Pittwater is more than twice the size of Sydney Harbour and is very beautiful. Put this together with adjacent Broken Bay and you have some of the world's best sailing. Scotland Island Schooners (☎ 99 3954) at Church Point cruises the area in an old 65-foot schooner, Bon Ton. They can drop off and pick up at the YHA's Pittwater Hostel in Ku-Ring-Gai Chase National Park (a great way to get there) and you can organise to be picked up from the Avalon Beach Hostel. A day on the water costs around $30 (BYO barbecue or pay $6 extra) and, judging from travellers' comments, it's worth it. This outfit is also a sailing school specialising in ocean going boats. It would take you some months to earn your internationally recognised Certificate of Competency – but what a nice qualification to have!

Out of Town
The Blue Mountains offer activities such as bushwalking, abseiling, canyoning and climbing. See the Around Sydney chapter for some Katoomba-based adventure outfits.

The *Sydney Morning Herald*'s Friday

'Metro' guide lists activities in the Out & About section; noticeboards at hostels are usually crammed with suggestions and Kings Cross travel agents often have packages (day-trips or longer) for backpackers and others.

ORGANISED TOURS
There's a vast array of conventional city and area tours. Ask at the Travel Centre of NSW on Castlereagh St for details, and check out the give-away magazines from hotels and so on. Australian Pacific, Ansett Pioneer, AAT King's, Newmans, Murrays, Clipper Grayline and Great Sights Tours carry most of the tourists around town.

Clipper Grayline (☎ 241 3983, 24 hours) has various tours in Sydney ($30 for a half-day tour), the Blue Mountains (from $50) and as far afield as Canberra ($60) and the Hunter Valley ($75).

National Parks runs occasional tours of Sydney's historic forts. The tours cost $6 ($4 children) and you'll need to bring a torch (flashlight). Phone (☎ 977 6229) for details.

Blue Thunder Bike Tours (☎ 018 235 686) will show you Sydney from the back of a Harley Davidson for anything from $10 for a very short ride up to $250 for eight hours. They have set tours or you can plan your own itinerary.

Another interesting way to see Sydney is by helicopter; not the cheapest way to go, but if you're ever going to take a flight in a helicopter it might as well be here over this beautiful harbour. Companies offering flights include Heli-Scenic (☎ 317 3402), which has a variety of flights from $95 per person.

See the Getting Around section for some hop-on, hop-off bus tours.

Harbour Cruises
There is a wide range of cruises offering relatively inexpensive excursions onto the harbour. You can book most at the Quayside Booking Centre (☎ 247 5151, 24 hours) at Circular Quay's Jetty 2. Captain Cook Cruises (☎ 206 1111) has its own booking office at Jetty 6. STA ferries offer some good

value cruises, such as a 2½ hour trip for $16 ($12 children, family tickets available). Buy tickets from the ferry information office behind Jetty 4 at Circular Quay.

The Sydney Harbour Explorer, run by Captain Cook Cruises, is a hop-on, hop-off service around the harbour with stops at Circular Quay (Jetty 6), the Opera House, Watsons Bay, Taronga (for the zoo) and Darling Harbour. Boats run two-hourly from 9.30 am until evening, and the fare is $16 ($12 students, $10 children).

Hegarty's Ferries (☎ 201 1167) has tours of Fort Denison daily except Monday at 10 am, 12.15 and 2 pm, departing from Jetty 6 at Circular Quay and costing $8.50 ($6 children).

Solway Lass is a restored 40-metre schooner which offers two-hour harbour cruises under sail twice a day for $22 ($12 children) or $35 ($18 children) with a buffet lunch. There is also a three-hour dinner cruise on Friday and Saturday nights for $45. The *Solway Lass* sails from Darling Harbour's Aquarium Wharf. Bookings (☎ 264 7377) are essential.

Sail Venture Cruises (☎ 262 3595) sails big cats around the harbour several times a day, from Darling Harbour's Aquarium Wharf and picking up at Circular Quay's East Pontoon on the way (you get a longer cruise for the same price if you go from Darling Harbour). The cruise takes about two hours and costs $22 ($11 children). There's a lunch option ($38, $19 children) and a dinner cruise for $55.

Another sailing cruise is on the *Bounty*, a replica of the ship lost by Captain Bligh in the famous mutiny. This ship was made for the film starring Mel Gibson. Cruises cost $45 ($22.50 for children under 16, free for children under 6).

Walking Tours
Several people offer guided walks in Sydney, such as Maureen Fry (☎ 660 7157), who has a wide range of walks, mainly for groups of about eight people but she can take individuals or perhaps fit you in with a group. The Rocks Walking Tours (☎ 247 6678) at 39 Argyle St (near Harrington St) has regular walks for about $10 ($6 children) and individual tours are available.

Bicycle Tours
World Beyond (☎ 555 9653) has a couple of day-long rides concentrating on the harbour and beaches, for around $75 per person. Original Sydney Bike Tours (☎ 411 1618) has three-hour tours of the Rocks and across the harbour for about $40 per person.

The Art of Mud (great name) has mountain-biking weekends in the Blue Mountains for about $170. Book through an agent such as Inner City Cycles (☎ 660 6605) at 31 Glebe Point Rd, Glebe.

Rockcycle Tours can help you arrange a do-it-yourself tour – see the Getting Around section.

FESTIVALS & EVENTS
Sydney likes fireworks and the harbour makes a superb venue for a big display, with plenty of vantage-points and all those hills and tall buildings to echo the whistles and bangs.

In addition to the state-wide holidays and events (see the Facts for the Visitor chapter), Sydney has some celebrations of its own.

Spring
The Royal Botanic Gardens Spring Festival, held in mid-September, involves more than just looking at flowers, with music and other events. Some of the best spring flowers are displayed in the David Jones store, which is

decked out in a spectacular fashion in early September.

Bondi Beach welcomes spring with the Festival of the Winds on the second Sunday in September. It's a kite-flying festival with a multicultural theme, and amazing creations hover and swoop above the beach. There are competitions for the best home-made kites, including a category for good old newspaper kites.

The big Manly Jazz Festival is held over the Labour Day long weekend in early October. Styles range from trad and big-band to fusion, bop and contemporary. Among the many international performers there is always at least one band from Japan, as a Tokyo suburb has an annual jazz competition at which the first prize is a trip to the Manly festival.

The week-long Taylor Square Arts Festival is held in mid-September and involves a wide range of events, many involving local cafes and businesses.

The rugby league grand final is held at the Football Stadium in September.

Summer

Not officially sanctioned and perhaps soon to be banned, the huge impromptu Christmas party on Bondi Beach is a favourite with travellers.

Sydney Harbour is a sight to behold on Boxing Day, 26 December, when boats of all shapes and sizes crowd onto its waters to farewell the yachts competing in the gruelling Sydney to Hobart Yacht Race. It's a fantastic sight as the yachts stream out of the harbour and head south.

On New Year's Eve, Circular Quay and Darling Harbour are popular places.

Taking up most of January, the Festival of Sydney is the umbrella for a wide range of very different events and activities, from opera (outdoors in the Domain – free) to roller-blading, and there are fireworks most nights in Darling Harbour. In Chinatown, Chinese New Year is also celebrated with a bang and falls in January or February.

Which event generates more tourist dollars than any other in Australia? Sydney's spectacular Gay & Lesbian Mardi Gras! This month-long festival (held during February and sometimes splashing over into March) includes events as various as sports carnivals, the Blessing of the Mardi Gras, plenty of theatre and other entertainment and *lots* of parties. It culminates in an amazing parade (with an audience of half a million people) and the Mardi Gras Party at the Showgrounds. Because of the many visitors to Sydney for the Mardi Gras, there are usually accommodation and tour packages available. Contact the Mardi Gras office (☎ 332 4088) for a brochure.

Autumn

The Royal Easter Show is a big occasion, when the best of the state's animals and produce are brought to town and there are plenty of events to entertain the city slickers. The Showgrounds also hosts events through the year, some with an agricultural flavour, some not. Phone (☎ 0055 21111) for recorded information.

Chinese dragon

The Australian Motorcycle Grand Prix, a round of the 500cc world championships, is held at the Eastern Creek circuit, west of Sydney.

Winter

The Sydney Film Festival (☎ 660 3844) is held in June. It's cheaper to subscribe to the whole season, but it's usually possible to buy tickets to individual screenings. In even years the Sydney Biennale, an arts festival, is held.

In July, many guesthouses and restaurants in the Blue Mountains celebrate Yulefest, and there might even be snow.

On the second Sunday in August more than 40,000 runners pound the 14 km from Park St in the city to Bondi Beach in the City to Surf Run. Some contestants are deadly serious, some are in it for fun and everyone gets their name and finishing position published in the *Sydney Morning Herald*. If you want to participate, entry forms start appearing in the *Herald* months before the race, although you could enter on the day if you wanted. There's a fee of about $20.

WORK

Many backpacker hostels boast that they can find work for guests, but, while that might be true, much of the work involves collecting for charities or door-to-door sales. Some of the door-to-door outfits will want you to put up a deposit for their stock which you will be carrying around. Hostels and contacts with other travellers are likely to be your best source of work, unless you have the skills (and the clothes) to apply for office work. If you have, there are a number of temp agencies – see the *Yellow Pages*.

The CES (Commonwealth Employment Service) can help you find work. Overseas visitors must present their work-permit when using the CES. Some travellers say that their visit to the CES was helpful, others that it was a waste of time. The main city office is at 105 Pitt St, near the corner of Hunter St. In the same building is the CES's Temp Line service (☎ 227 9333), specialising in filling casual office vacancies.

For temporary (usually one day only) non-office jobs in the city, see the CES's City Casuals office (☎ 201 1166) at 10 Quay St which is open from 6.30 am to noon, Monday to Friday. Most jobs involve physical work, some heavy, and most jobs come in before 10 am. If you arrive before 7 am and still haven't got a job by 10 am you will be placed on a shortlist for the next day.

PLACES TO STAY

Sydney's inner-city hotels and motels take in well over $500,000 every night from around 3500 occupied rooms. That works out at about $150 a room. Some people must be paying a lot more than they need to, however, as there are plenty of good places to stay for less than $100 a night. Of course, you can also spend $3000 a night for a suite at the ANA Hotel.

Summer is the busy season for Sydney's accommodation, and just about every place, from hostels to five-star hotels, lifts its rates or at least cancels special deals. In winter when things are slow it's worth ringing around to see if there are any bargains. Specials are often available if you book through an agency such as the NSW Government Travel Centre (☎ 231 4444) at 19 Castlereagh St. Remember that many of the expensive hotels cater primarily to business people, so their rates might be lower on weekends.

For longer-term stays there are places in the 'flats to let' and 'share accommodation' ads in the *Sydney Morning Herald*, especially on Wednesday and Saturday. Many travellers find flat-shares through other travellers they have met in hostels. Hostel noticeboards are good sources of information.

Places to Stay – bottom end

Caravan Parks Sydney's caravan parks are a long way out of town. Listed here are some within 25 km of the centre.

Meriton North Ryde (☎ 88 72177), corner Lane Cove and Fontenoy Rds, North Ryde, sites $18 double, cabins from $50.

East's Lane Cove River Van Village (☎ 805 0500), Plassey Rd, North Ryde, sites from $15 double, on-site vans from $44, cabins from $50.

Sheralee Tourist Caravan Park (☎ 567 9211), 88 Bryant St, Rockdale, sites from $12.

Lakeside Caravan Park (☎ 913 7845), Lake Park Rd, Narrabeen, camping from $14, cabins from $55.

The Grand Pines Caravan Park (☎ 529 7329), 289 The Grand Parade, Ramsgate, no camping, on-site vans from $40 double.

Hostels After remaining static for years, rates at Sydney hostels have finally broken the $10-a-night barrier. This isn't such a bad thing, as there is now a greater choice between standards. You'll still find a dorm bed for ten bucks (and maybe less in winter), with average hostels charging $12 or so and some higher-quality places charging $15 or more.

Most hostels charge less by the week and most are acutely aware of what the competition is charging. The prices quoted here could easily fluctuate by a few dollars, depending on demand.

The largest concentration of hostels is still in Kings Cross, but hostels are appearing in some new areas such as Newtown.

Some hostels have set hours for checking in and out, although all have 24-hour access once you have handed over your cash.

If you are Australian, just finding a hostel which will accept you might be a problem. Partly to stop locals using hostels as doss-houses, and partly because of unpleasant experiences with lecherous drunks, a few Sydney hostels ban Australians altogether. Many others are suspicious of Australians who aren't travelling (some demand a passport as ID), although in the off-season these standards sometimes mysteriously vanish in the quest for a buck.

Of course, the YHA hostels (both in Glebe) will accept members of any nationality and are better-run and cleaner than many backpackers' places. The YHA's Membership & Travel Centre (☎ 261 1111) at 422 Kent St can book you into any Australian YHA hostel and many others around the world. This is also a domestic and international travel agency. The YHA also operates

a summer hostel at St Andrews college at Sydney University, charging $15 in dorms and $17 per person in twins.

As well as the backpacker-only hostels, there are plenty of places such as pubs and boarding houses which have decided to fill their spare rooms with bunk beds and rake in the money – having six people paying $12 each seems a better idea than letting a double room for $50 a night. Some of these places are perfectly OK, but most lack the hostel atmosphere (and the essential information grapevine), and they are unlikely to offer services such as airport pickups and discounted bus-tickets which you'll find at many backpacker places.

City Centre The only real hostel in the city is the *YWCA* (☎ 264 2451) on Wentworth Ave at the corner of Liverpool St. With Hyde Park across the road, plenty of buses and trains nearby, both the city centre and Oxford St a short walk away, the Y has an enviable position. The standard of accommodation is high as well, with simple but spotless and well-furnished rooms. There's an inexpensive cafeteria. Unfortunately, there's a fairly high price to pay for all this: $42/60/75 for singles/twins/triples, or $60/85/100 for rooms with attached bathrooms. There are cheaper weekly rates, but you have to stay at least a month to qualify for them. There is also dorm accommodation at $18 a night, but the maximum stay is three nights. Both men and women can stay.

The big *CB Private Hotel* (☎ 211 5115) at 417 Pitt St (between Goulburn and Campbell Sts) has some dorm rooms at $10 per person, and from time to time other old pubs in the city centre decide that they'll try to lure backpackers.

The *YMCA* (☎ 264 1011) still hasn't built its new hostel (the old one was destroyed by fire).

South of the City Centre *Kangaroo Bakpak* (☎ 319 5915) is at 635 South Dowling St in Surry Hills, just north of the corner of Cleveland St. This is a very friendly place which gets consistently good feedback. Dorm beds go for $12 ($70 per week). To get here from Central Railway Station, take bus Nos 372, 393 or 395.

A pub but also a member of the BRA hostel group, the *Excelsior Hotel* (☎ 211 4945) is also in Surry Hills at 64 Foveaux St, on the corner of Bellevue St and only a few blocks from Central Station. Unlike some other inner-city pubs this is a small place with a good atmosphere. Most of the rooms offer reasonable pub accommodation (with shared bathrooms), with a few large dorms. Dorm beds are $13 ($80 per week) and doubles are $35 ($30 if you stay more than a couple of days and $180 per week). There's a backpackers' kitchen and common room.

Across the road from Prince Alfred Park at 207 Cleveland St in Redfern, the *Alfred Park Private Hotel* (☎ 319 4031) has been a high-quality, low-cost place for a few years, and is now concentrating on backpackers. Dorm beds cost from $15, singles from $25 to $35 and twins from $40, around $50 with bathroom. It's run by the people who have the Forbes Terrace Hostel, a good place near the Cross.

At 83 Regent St near Redfern Station, the *Regent St Hotel* (☎ 698 2793) is a pub but also a reasonable hostel with variable rates that tend to be a little lower than those in the Cross.

The *Sydney Working Holiday Hostel* (☎ 698 1195) at 94 City Rd in Chippendale, near the corner of Cleveland St, is a relaxed (ie, things can get untidy) place in an old house with weekly rates of $70 in dorms or triples, $80 in twins and $95 in singles. Bus Nos 422, 423, 426 and 428 run past here from Central, but it's not far to walk.

Billabong Gardens (☎ 550 3236) at 5 Egan St in Newtown is a good new hostel, purpose-built by one of Sydney's original hostel owners. Dorm beds cost from $12, twins/doubles from $35 or $50 with an attached bathroom. There are also triples ($60) and a family room ($65) with attached bathrooms. Weekly rates are available. It's clean, quiet and there's a very small pool. They do airport pickups between 9 am and 9 pm. To get here from Railway Square take

bus No 422, 423, 426 or 428 which run up Newtown's King St; get off at Missenden Rd. By train go to Newtown station and turn right into King St; Egan St is about four blocks along, on the left.

Kings Cross & Nearby Heading north along Victoria St from Kings Cross station, the first hostel you come to is *Plane Tree Lodge* (☎ 356 4551) at No 172. This is pretty much a standard large Kings Cross hostel, with a variety of rooms. Winter rates are $12 ($75 per week) in a four-bed dorm, $11 ($70 per week) in a six-bed. There are some singles at $20 (no weekly rate), twins at $25 ($170 per week) and doubles at $30 ($190 per week).

Next down the street at No 166 is *Highfield House Private Hotel* (☎ 358 1552) – the sign hanging over the footpath just says Budget Accommodation. It caters exclusively to overseas travellers and is run by friendly Swedes. It's secure, clean enough and has a good atmosphere. The rates stay much the same all year, with singles/doubles for $25/40 ($150/240 per week). You can share a twin for $15 per person or share a triple for $12 per person. Bathrooms are shared. There are cooking facilities in the small common room and you can eat at the inexpensive cafe.

The *Original Backpackers* (☎ 356 3232) at No 162 *is* the original backpacker place in this part of the world, and it's still going strong, with more accommodation in other houses nearby. The atmosphere is good, it's reasonably clean and there are good-sized common areas. Dorms cost between $10 and $13 (from $70 per week), and singles/doubles are $20/28 ($120/160 per week). The noticeboard here is one of the larger ones. Nearby *Travellers Rest* (☎ 358 4606) is very clean, with well-equipped rooms (fridge, sink, TV, kettle). Some rooms have balconies overlooking Victoria St. This place is well run, with a resident owner. The rates, which tend to stay the same year-round, are: dorms (three-bed) $13 ($72 per week), singles $22, twins $28, twins/doubles with attached bathroom $30.

Across the road at No 141, *Kanga House* (☎ 357 7897) is a pretty basic place with winter rates of $10 ($60 per week) for dorms and $15/24 ($90/144 per week) for singles/doubles.

Back on the east side of Victoria St, at No 144 you'll find one of the three busy *Jolly Swagman* hostels, also called *Sydney Central Backpackers*. They all charge the same rates: dorms $11 ($66 per week), singles/doubles $24/26 ($144/156 per week). These rates might drop a little in winter and probably rise a little in summer. All Jolly Swagman rooms have fridges and cooking facilities. As well as the Victoria St hostel (☎ 357 4733) there are also Jolly Swagman hostels at 16 Orwell St (☎ 358 6600) and 14 Springfield Mall (☎ 358 6400).

On Orwell St at No 6, *Eva's Backpackers* (☎ 358 2185) is family-owned and operated, and it's clean and friendly. There's a rooftop barbecue area and big kitchen/dining room. The high-season rates are $14 in dorms, $16 per person in twins or doubles and $48 for a three-person room with attached bathroom. If you stay two nights they'll refund your airport bus fare. Prices drop in winter, when there are also weekly rates.

The big *Downunder Hostel* (☎ 358 1433) at 25 Hughes St has recently been renovated and is looking much more spruce than it once did. Dorms cost $11 or $12 ($70 per week) and doubles are $30 ($160 per week). Downunder is popular and lively. There are free excursions, such as outings to Palm Beach.

Completely renovated and refurbished, the big *Backpackers Headquarters* (☎ 331 6180) at 79 Bayswater Rd is squeaky-clean. Rates are a fraction higher than you can get at other places, from $13 in dorms and from $17 per person in doubles.

Fountain International Hostel (☎ 358 6799) at 22 Darlinghurst Rd, next to the Bourbon & Beefsteak restaurant, has fairly large dorms scattered through a warren of corridors. This place tends to be among the cheapest of the Cross's hostels and currently charges about $10 ($60 per week) in dorms. There are some twin rooms from $20.

One of the most popular Kings Cross hostels is *Barncleuth House* (☎ 358 1689), often known as the Pink House. It is slightly away from the main drag, in a quieter street at 6 Barncleuth Square, east of Darlinghurst Rd. It has a courtyard garden and log fires when the weather is cold. Dorm beds are $11 ($70 per week) and doubles are $12 per person (around $80 per week). Some of the dorms have double-bed bunks (!) which go for $10 per person. Winter rates are a little lower.

Pretty much a crash-pad, *Bargain Backpackers Hotel* (☎ 357 4730), upstairs at 40 Darlinghurst Rd, charges from $8 in dorm beds and $25 for a double. Australians pay more.

At 9 McDonald St, off Macleay St north of the El Alamein Fountain (and technically in Potts Point), *Rucksack Rest* (☎ 358 2348) is a long-established hostel, quiet, clean and in fairly good condition. Sam, the owner, lives in the hostel. The rooms are fairly small, but they are comfortable and the dorms don't have more than three people in them. Dorm beds go for $12 or $13, twins/doubles are about $28 and singles are $20. If you stay a week you only pay for six nights. A couple of doors away at 3 McDonald St, *Backpackers Village* (☎ 358 2808) is quite a large hostel in a block of flats. All rooms have TV and cooking facilities.

One of the higher-quality hostels which are beginning to crop up is *Forbes Terrace* (☎ 358 4327), at 153 Forbes St in Woolloomooloo, just north of William St. It's new, clean, quiet and has a good courtyard area. Each room has a TV, fridge and tea & coffee-making facilities. The Forbes Restaurant next door is owned by the same people and there are special deals such as a $2 breakfast and a three-course meal for under $10. Dorm beds go for $15, singles are $25 to $35 and twins cost from $40.

A number of other places have jumped on the backpacker bandwagon lately. *Fountain Plaza* (☎ 358 6799) on the corner of Darlinghurst Rd and Llankelly Place was once a private hotel but is now more like a hostel. Shared rooms cost $10 per person

($60 per week) and singles/doubles are just $16/25 ($100/140 per week). The accommodation is reasonable and many travellers stay here. The *Astoria* (☎ 356 3666) at 9 Darlinghurst Rd is a tizzy hotel from the '50s – Regency wallpaper, fussy light-fittings and all – which is fading fast but is still in fair condition. All rooms have attached bathrooms, TV, air-con and fridges, but don't expect everything to work. The office is staffed 24 hours a day. Per-person rates are $13 ($75 per week) in four-person rooms, $15 ($85) in twins and $25 ($150 per week) for a single room.

The *Lido* (☎ 358 4844), also known as *Backpackers Connection*, at 2 Roslyn St, just off Darlinghurst Rd, is a large motel which is concentrating on the backpacker trade. It must have once been an above-average motel and it isn't all that old. The rooms are a bit run-down (compared with motel rooms, not compared with hostels) but they are large and have been recently painted. Each room has a TV, bathroom, ceiling fan and air-con, plus a phone (incoming calls only). Dorm accommodation costs $12 ($73.50 per week) in four-bed or more crowded six-bed dorms. Motel rooms cost $45 for a single or a double. There's a very basic kitchen on the roof.

Glebe Glebe is a good place to stay, with several very different hostels, plenty of places to eat and good entertainment options.

At 44 Hereford St, *Wattle House* (☎ 692 0879) is a small hostel in a pleasant old house. It is very clean, newly renovated and decorated, and has some nice touches such as free linen and doonas (duvets). The friendly owners live in the hostel. This is *not* a hostel for party animals. The rates here are a touch higher than at other hostels, but they are worth it for the standard of accommodation and they don't deter guests – Wattle House is often full. A bunk in a three or four-bed dorm costs $14 ($85 per week) and twin rooms are $17 per person ($105 per week).

There is also high-quality shared accommodation to be found at the excellent *Alishan*

International Guesthouse (☎ 566 4048) at 100 Glebe Point Rd, with dorm beds at $18 a night ($105 per week). See the following Places to Stay – Middle for more information.

The YHA has two large, clean and friendly hostels, *Hereford YHA Lodge* (☎ 660 5577) at 51 Hereford St, and *Glebe Point YHA Hostel* (☎ 692 8418) at 262 Glebe Point Rd. Hereford Lodge has a small rooftop pool and an inexpensive cafe. There are six-bed dorms at $15 ($95 weekly), four-bed at $17 ($110 weekly) and twin rooms at $44. Glebe Point has six-bed dorms at $15, four-bed at $16 ($95 weekly) and twin rooms at $40. Bess O'Mattick (!) has painted some murals here. Both hostels offer a large range of activities, both store luggage and both deduct the airport busfare from your bill.

At the north end of Glebe Point Rd, near the YHA hostel, *Glebe Village Backpackers* (☎ 660 8133) is a large place in two big houses. There's something of the rabbit-warren about it and it's well-worn, but many people like the lively atmosphere. Dorms cost $14 or $15 and singles/doubles are $20/40.

For long-term accommodation, *Pat's Place* (☎ 660 0988) at the corner of Bridge Rd and Clare St, three blocks south-west of Glebe Point Rd, has small rooms with cooking facilities. This is a quiet place for travellers only, and Australian men might have a tough time getting in. There is a three-bed dorm for women only at $60 per week (the minimum stay). A single costs from $85 per week and twins are $140. The twin rooms are available to women and heterosexual couples only – apparently because of the rowdiness of two men sharing, rather than homophobia.

Bondi Beach The most famous of Sydney's beaches, Bondi has a range of accommodation and lots of long-term working travellers – but only one real hostel. *Lamrock Hostel* (☎ 365 0221) is at 7 Lamrock Ave, a block back from Campbell Pde on the corner of Lamrock and Jacques Aves. It's a well-worn but bright house with dorms at $15 ($80 weekly) and twins for about $40. These rates stay the same all year, unlike most other budget accommodation in Bondi. They also have long-term beds in the building next door at about $60 weekly. This place has been running for years and it's friendly and popular.

Other places in Bondi have shared rooms; see the following Hotels & Guesthouses section.

Coogee Coogee is becoming popular with backpackers and there are now several hostels. As Coogee is a bit further from the city than Bondi, off-season specials can be lower than elsewhere. It's worth ringing before arriving, as some hostels have limited office hours.

Closest to the beach is *Surfside Backpackers Coogee* (☎ 315 7888) at 186 Arden St (the entrance is around the corner in Alfreda St), above McDonald's and across the road from the bus stops. The hostel is in a newly renovated building and there are balconies, some with views down to the beach which is just across the road. There are also lots of stairs! Off-season rates are around $13 ($75 per week) in the dorms, rising to about $15 a night (no weekly rates) in summer. There are also double rooms which go for $34 all year.

A block inland at 116 Brook St, on the corner of Alfreda St, *Aaronbrook Lodge* (☎ 665 7798 or 315 8222) is in a rambling old house. Off-season dorm rates are $12 ($70 weekly) and $28 for a double/twin ($160 weekly).

A short but stiff walk up a hill, the popular *Coogee Beach Backpackers* (☎ 665 7735) is at 94 Beach St – Beach St runs beside the Coogee Palace centre at the north end of the beach. The hostel is in a Federation-era house with a more modern block next door. Dorms are $15, doubles $32, a little less in winter. There's a once-off compulsory sheet-hire charge of $1. *Indy's* (☎ 315 7644) is at 302 Arden St on the corner of Dudley St. It's on the hill south of the beach and is a smaller place in a pleasant old Victorian-era house.

About one km up Coogee Bay Rd at No 40, the *Aegean* (☎ 398 4999), also known as *Coogee Bay Rd Backpackers*, has shared accommodation in self-contained flats for around $12 (from $65 weekly), with twins from about $26. There's a range of rates and good deals in winter.

See the following Hotels & Guesthouses section for information on the Grand Pacific Private Hotel, which is right on the beach and has backpacker rates.

North of the Bridge In Kirribilli, *Kirribilli Court Private Hotel* (☎ 955 4344) at 45 Carabella St has dorm beds for just $10 and singles/doubles for $20/30. The *Harbourside Hotel* (☎ 953 7977) at 41 Cremorne Rd on Cremorne Point isn't a hotel, it's a large, loose hostel catering mainly to backpackers and young locals working in Sydney. There are good views and the atmosphere is something like a large shared house. It won't suit everyone (it can be very noisy), but it's worth checking out. Dorms cost between $10 and $12, with singles/doubles from $20/25, and there are also weekly rates. Take a ferry to Cremorne Wharf and walk up the hill a couple of hundred metres.

Manly has great ocean and harbour beaches and few city hassles, but it's just 30 minutes by ferry (15 minutes by JetCat) from Circular Quay. *Manly Beach Resort Backpackers* (☎ 977 4188) is part of a motel on the corner of Pittwater Rd and Carlton St, but backpackers have their own section in a newly-renovated house. The four dorms ($14) are spacious and clean; by now there should be twin rooms (from $30). The long-running *Manly Astra Backpackers* (☎ 977 2092) is nearby at 68-70 Pittwater Rd. Bunks in dorms or twin rooms go for $13 per person ($78 weekly).

For a break from city life, try the relaxed northern beachside suburb of Avalon, near Pittwater, where the purpose-built *Avalon Beach Hostel* (☎ 918 9709) at 59 Avalon Pde is a good place to stay. It's clean, friendly and well-run. The emphasis here is on activities rather than just a roof over your head. Avalon Beach is a couple of blocks away and the hostel has boards and bikes for hire. They can also arrange a variety of outdoor activities and outings, such as abseiling at nearby Barrenjoey Head or in the Blue Mountains, sailing, hiking and wine-tasting in the Hunter Valley. The hostel has its own boat. Dorms cost $12 a night ($80 per week) or $14 in a smaller dorm. Singles/doubles are $28/32. To get here take bus No 190 from Wynyard Park on York St in the city. Ask for Avalon Pde. The trip takes about 1¼ hours and costs $4.20.

Hotels & Guesthouses A wide variety of accommodation falls into this category. Places well worth checking out include Challis Lodge near Kings Cross, Hotel Bondi and Bondi Beach and St Leonards Mansions in St Leonards.

City Centre & Nearby Near Central Station there are several places to stay, although the Great Southern Hotel no longer has accommodation and the West End Hotel has moved upmarket a notch or two – see the later Places to Stay – middle section.

Close to the station but out of the central city is the *Central Private Hotel* (☎ 212 1068) at 356-358 Elizabeth St, at the corner of Randle St. This is a friendly place and comfortable enough. Singles/doubles with shared bathroom cost from $25/35 (from $120/180 a week); a double with bathroom is $45.

At 417 Pitt St near the corner of Goulburn St, the *CB Private Hotel* (☎ 211 5115) first opened for business in 1908 and it's still going strong. It was once the largest residential hotel in the country, with over 200 rooms, mostly singles. It is plain, clean and fairly well-maintained, although it gets a lot of wear. Daily rates are $25/40/50 for singles/doubles/triples with shared bathroom. They also have backpackers' rooms for $10 per person. The weekly rate in single rooms (only) is $99.

A block west at 700A George St, just south of the corner of Goulburn St, the *George Private Hotel* (☎ 211 1800) is also plain and clean. The rooms are much more spartan than the foyer area suggests, but they are

passable. There is a kitchen for guests to use, and laundry facilities are also available. Singles/doubles with common bathrooms are $30/45 and a double with TV and attached bathroom is $60. There are weekly rates, and the daily rates might drop a little in winter.

Further south at 789 George St, near the corner of Valentine St, the *Crystal Palace Hotel* (☎ 211 0957) is a pub which has single/double rooms for $35/55 ($125/175 per week). All rooms have fridges; all the double rooms have attached bathrooms, as do a few of the singles. The *Criterion Hotel* (☎ 264 3093) on the corner of Pitt and Park Sts is a large pub with rooms from $40/50, or $60/70 with attached bathroom.

Right in the Rocks, on the corner of Lower Fort St and Cumberland St, the small *Harbour View Hotel* (☎ 252 3769) should have been renamed the 'Bridge View' in 1932 – it's right next to one of the approach pylons. There's some noise from trains on the bridge and much more from the bands in the bar, but with clean rooms at $35/40 for singles/doubles (including a light breakfast) it's great value for the location.

Close to Darling Harbour in Pyrmont, the *Woolbrokers Arms* (☎ 552 4773) at the corner of Allen and Pyrmont Sts is a pub charging $60 a double for B&B.

Kings Cross & Nearby One of the accommodation bargains in the Cross is *Challis Lodge* (☎ 358 5422) at 21 Challis Ave. It's a pair of big old terraces which have somehow survived their transformation into a budget guesthouse without becoming dowdy or tacky as a result. The rooms are simple but clean and well-maintained, and they charge just $28/34 ($120/154 per week) for singles/doubles with shared bathrooms and $36/42 ($154/168) with attached bathrooms. There are also a few larger rooms at the front which have balconies and go for $54 ($266 per week). The people who own Challis Lodge (and also Springfield Lodge) are due to open a new place at 71 Macleay St.

There are some quite reasonable hotels in the heart of the Cross. *Springfield Lodge*

(☎ 358 3222) on Springfield Ave has simple guest-house style accommodation, clean and well-maintained. All rooms have fridges, TVs and tea & coffee-making facilities. Rooms with shared bathrooms start at $30/38 ($140/168 per week) and with an attached bathroom you'll pay from $42/44 (from $182/196 per week). You're advised to book. Nearby at 15 Springfield Ave, the *Bernly Private Hotel* (☎ 358 3122) has more modern rooms. All the rooms share toilets, but some rooms have private showers. Singles/doubles/triples cost $40/50/60 or $45/55/65 with shower. Prices haven't risen for years and the friendly manager emphasises that the rates are negotiable.

Nearby at 37 Darlinghurst Rd, *Maksim Lodge* (☎ 356 3399) has singles/doubles for $55/65, less by the week and at slow times of the year. Backpackers can share triples ($60). Each room has a bathroom, fridge and TV. *Orwell Lodge* (☎ 358 1745) at 18-20 Orwell St charges about $30/40 ($140/160 per week) for singles/doubles with shared bathroom.

The *Montpelier Private Hotel* (☎ 358 6960) at 39A Elizabeth Bay Rd, south of the corner of Greenknowe Ave, sometimes has single/double rooms from as little as $25/30 ($130/150 per week).

Bondi Beach Check out *Hotel Bondi* (☎ 30 3271) on the corner of Campbell Pde and Curlewis St. It's a grand old seaside hotel where the very reasonable accommodation rates have actually fallen since the previous edition of this guide was researched. Another plus is that the rates stay the same year-round. Unfortunately this also means that vacancies can be scarce over summer. Singles/doubles cost from $25/27.50 or $27.50/35 with attached bathroom. In the off-season there are also cheaper weekly rates.

Rates at most other bottom-end places in Bondi vary a lot depending on demand. The rates quoted here are about average and you can expect price-hikes in summer but also better deals when trade is slow.

Thelellen Beach Inn (☎ 30 5333) at the south end of the beach strip at 2 Campbell Pde (on the corner of Francis St), dates from the '30s and its 70 rooms are in fair condition, each with a fridge, TV and tea & coffee-making facilities. There's a large rooftop area with views down to the beach. Singles go for $30 and doubles from about $35 to $42. Some rooms sleep up to four people and an extra person costs $5. They let shared rooms for $15 per person. In winter deals are possible and from May to December there are cheaper weekly rates (single $140, double $150 to $170).

These people also have *Thelellen Lodge* (☎ 30 1521), a boarding-house at 11A Consett Ave, between Lamrock and Hall Sts. It's smallish and quite well kept, with a good new kitchen. The rates are theoretically the same as at the Thelellen Beach Inn (although there are no shared rooms) with lots of off-season specials. Next door at No 11, *Bondi Beach Guesthouse* (☎ 389 8309) is perhaps marginally better and has similar rates. There is some off-street parking here. On the corner of Consett and Lamrock Aves, *Merrimeads Flatettes* (☎ 30 5063) has off-season specials such as shared 'flatettes' from $12 per person or $65 per week.

Back on Campbell Pde, between Hall and Roscoe Sts, the run-down *Biltmore Private Hotel* (☎ 30 4660) charges from $25/35 a single/double (from $105/140 per week). Check the room before handing over your cash.

A little south of the main beach area (and technically in the suburb of Tamarama) *Bondi Boutique Hotel* (☎ 365 2088) at 63 Fletcher St, on the corner of Dellview St, is apparently worth checking out. Their advertised rates are from $30 per person, including a big breakfast and dinner, with dorm beds from $10.

Coogee The *Grand Pacific Private Hotel* (☎ 665 6301) is right on the south end of the beach, at the end of Carr St. Although it has seen much better days it's an attractive building and some rooms have balconies. All rooms have a TV, fridge and tea & coffee-making facilities; bathrooms are communal and there is a guests' kitchen and laundry. The rates are low and stay the same year-round. Singles cost $20 or less and doubles between $24 and $60, a single/double room with a balcony costs $17/28 and there are cheaper weekly rates. They also have shared rooms for backpackers at $12 per person. If you have the slightest interest in Taiwan, see the manager who is a Taiwan buff.

Also try the *Metro Private Hotel* (☎ 665 1162) on Arden St at the north end of the beach, near the corner of Dolphin St.

North of the Bridge *St Leonards Mansions* (☎ 439 6999) at 7 Park Rd, St Leonards, occupies three well-kept old houses and has well-equipped, clean rooms for $45 a single, plus $10 for each extra person, up to six people, or $35 plus $10 with shared bathrooms. Most rooms have phones, fridges and cooking facilities. A light breakfast is free and there are laundry facilities. Some rooms have balconies with city views. There is parking and a well-kept garden that attracts plenty of birds. It's a nice place and good value. To get here from St Leonards station, head west along the Pacific Highway (towards the hospital), and Park Rd is the second street on your left.

At 310 Miller St in North Sydney, near Falcon St and across from St Leonards Park, *Tielgreen Lodge* (☎ 955 1012) is a guesthouse charging from $70 a single or double.

Just north of the bridge, the suburb of Kirribilli has a number of guesthouses. You can take a ferry to Kirribilli Wharf or a train to Milsons Point Station and walk down. *Tremayne Private Hotel* (☎ 955 4155) at 89 Carabella St (near the corner of Fitzroy St) is a large, clean guesthouse originally built as accommodation for country girls attending school in Sydney, and it retains a spartan but quality feel. The weekly rates (only) are from $115/180 a single/double, including meals. Bathrooms are shared. There are some units with bathrooms for about $200 per week for a double. Not far away at 45 Carabella St is *Kirribilli Court Private Hotel* (☎ 955 4344) with singles/doubles for $20/30 and also dorm beds ($10). Further

south on Carabella St at No 12A, *Glenferrie Private Hotel* (☎ 955 1685) is in a very large old house. Some rooms are dowdy (to put it mildly), others have been renovated. Rates, which include breakfast and dinner, vary a lot. Singles/doubles in the old rooms range from $90/120 a week and in the new rooms from about $110/160. Daily rates from about $20/40 are possible and you can negotiate lower rates if you don't want meals.

In Neutral Bay on the corner of Kurraba Rd and Hayes St and not far from the ferry wharf, the *Neutral Bay Motor Lodge* (☎ 953 4199) is more like a guesthouse than a motel. Several travellers report that it's a reasonable place to stay and rates start at $50/55.

Manly Manly is particularly susceptible to summertime price rises.

The *Eversham Private Hotel* (☎ 977 2423) on Victoria Pde near the corner of South Steyne is a large, basic place where the rates haven't risen for years. Singles go for $123 to $133 a week (only) and doubles are $150. There is a dining room and some deals include meals. A major renovation is about to take place, but they say that prices won't rise.

Ask at *Manly Lodge* (☎ 977 8655), across Victoria Pde at No 22, about *Lansdown Court* and *Manly Cove*, where dorm beds go for around $20 ($110 per week) and singles/doubles are $40/50 ($145/180 per week). The three places are owned by the same people, and you have to check in at Manly Lodge.

Colleges Many residential colleges are now a lot keener to take casual guests than they once were. Unless it's otherwise mentioned, all these places accept non-students and both men and women. Also, unless otherwise stated, these rooms are available during vacations only, mainly the long break from mid-December to late January. It's possible that some will have rooms available during shorter breaks during the year.

The rates shown here are those which I was quoted, but it is not unusual for different staff members to quote different rates. Also, although most places quote B&B or full-board rates it is often possible to negotiate a lower bed-only rate. Ask about weekly or fortnightly rates which might be cheaper.

University of Sydney is south-west of Chippendale and not far from Glebe.

Darlington House (☎ 692 3322), terrace houses sleeping four to eight, $350 to $400 a week.
International House (☎ 950 9800), rooms for $30. During term, three serviced rooms are available for students or visitors connected with the university, from $55 B&B.
St Johns College (☎ 394 5200), doesn't always stay open for all of the long vacation. When it does, rooms with bathroom and all meals go for $250 a week; rooms with shared bathrooms are $210.
Wesley College (☎ 565 3333), rooms available during any vacation except Easter, $40 B&B (students $32.50), $51.50 full board (students $45.50).
Women's College (☎ 516 1642), students and YHA members pay $32 B&B; $37 dinner, B&B; and $42 full board. Everyone else pays $40/46/52. There are also some twin rooms which go for $53/64/72 for students and YHA members and $60/72/80 for others.
Try also *St Pauls College* (☎ 550 7444) and *Sancta Sophia College* (☎ 519 7123).

University of NSW is in Kensington, further from the centre but closer to the beaches and not too far from Oxford St.

International House (☎ 663 0418), full board $35 students, $45 others. For a few weeks around Christmas there are also B&B rates, $25 students, $35 others.
New College (☎ 697 8962), sometimes has accommodation at other vacations as well as the long break. B&B $25.
Try also the *Kensington Colleges* (☎ 663 8111) and the better *Shalom College* (☎ 663 1366).

Places to Stay – middle

This section covers places charging between about $60 and $150 for a double room. It's a wide price-span and standards vary accordingly.

B&B Bed & Breakfast Sydneyside (☎ 449 4430), PO Box 555, Turramurra, NSW 2074, will find you accommodation in a private home in Sydney for about $40 to $65 a night for a single, $55 to $95 a double. This is a

good way of meeting locals and getting inside advice on things to see and do. For those who don't want B&B accommodation but still want to meet Sydneysiders, they can sometimes arrange lunches.

Hotels & Motels Some of the hotels in this section are basically pubs where the accommodation is a little better than average.

City & Nearby The *Wynyard Hotel* (☎ 299 1330) on the corner of Clarence and Erskine Sts is a pleasant pub that has rooms for $45/55/65 for singles/doubles/twins, with cheaper weekly rates. Each room has a TV, fridge and tea & coffee-making facilities, but bathrooms are shared. Weekly guests can use the hotel's cooking facilities. The rooms are plain but clean and comfortable, and the manager says that they will soon be renovated. For the location this is excellent value, especially for singles. Another inner-city pub with accommodation is the *Grand Hotel* (☎ 232 3755) on Hunter St just west of Pitt St, where prices are a little higher at $50/70.

The *Westend Hotel* (☎ 211 4822) at 412 Pitt St has 13 floors of motel-style rooms, all equipped with bathrooms, TV, fridge, air-con, phone, etc. Singles/doubles go for $60/70 – reasonable value, especially if you get a room at one end of the building, which means big windows and views. There are weekly rates but you have to stay a month and pay in advance – and it's strictly non-refundable. There's a bar and an inexpensive restaurant on the premises.

The *Wynyard Travelodge* (☎ 299 3000) has a good downtown location on the corner of Margaret and York Sts, across from Wynyard Park, a tiny patch of green in the city centre. Rooms cost around $130, but the rate changes often.

The *Park Regis* (☎ 267 6511) on the corner of Park and Castlereagh Sts is a fairly sparse motel-style place with rooms for around $110, with seasonal specials. *Hyde Park Inn* (☎ 264 6001) at 271 Elizabeth St charges from $130/140.

Right in the Rocks is the *Lord Nelson Brewery Hotel* (☎ 251 4044), on the corner of Kent and Argyle Sts, where doubles cost between $60 and $100. The *Russell Hotel* (☎ 241 3543), a small private hotel at 143A George St charges from around $100 for rooms with shared bathrooms and from $140 with attached bathroom.

Close to Chinatown and Darling Harbour, the *Travellers Rest Hotel* (☎ 281 5555; 1800 023 071 toll-free bookings) at 37 Ultimo Rd in Haymarket is newly renovated and is a bargain for a reasonable hotel this close to the city centre. Singles/doubles cost from $58/68 or $68/78 with attached bathroom. There are also 'mini apartments' for $85 (plus $10 for each extra person) and a family apartment for $120. They have a four-bed room which they will let at $27 per person.

Also near Darling Harbour, by the Entertainment Centre at 64 Harbour St, *Metro Inn Sydney* (☎ 281 0400) charges from $130.

In Surry Hills at 289 Crown St, a little way south of Oxford St, *Cron Lodge* (☎ 331 2433) is a motel charging from around $70.

Kings Cross & Nearby On the corner of William and Brougham Sts, a block west of the Darlinghurst Rd/Victoria St junction, *O'Malley's Hotel* (☎ 357 2211) is a pub dating from 1907 which has been renovated into a mid-range hotel, and with rooms at $50/60 a single/double it's good value. The rooms are well-furnished and have air-con. Some twin rooms share a bathroom but all the doubles have attached bathrooms.

On Bayswater Rd just east of Darlinghurst Rd, the *Barclay Hotel* (☎ 358 6133) has a wide range of rooms, some starting at under $50. At 30 Darlinghurst Rd, the Flag *Kingsview Motel* (☎ 358 5599) has recently been renovated and charges about $85. The *Metro Motor Inn* (☎ 356 3511) at 40 Bayswater Rd charges about the same.

L'Otel (☎ 360 6868), at 145 Darlinghurst Rd just south of William St, is a stylish boutique hotel with individually designed rooms (some in retro '50s style, others more traditional) charging from $80 a double (no twins).

At 122 Victoria St, right in the heart of it all but offering a quiet retreat from the street-

life, the *Kendall Private Hotel* (☎ 357 3200) is a comfortable boutique hotel in a pair of restored terrace houses. There's a large jacuzzi, security parking and a pleasant little courtyard. Single/double rooms go for $100/115 including continental breakfast, but ring to ask about specials. The honeymoon suite ($145) has a four-poster and a balcony from which you can watch the world go by.

The *Sheraton Hotel* (☎ 358 1955) at 40 Macleay St has rooms from $90 and good-value stand-by rates of under $60. Phone for details.

More expensive places in the Cross include the *Florida Motor Inn* (☎ 358 6811) at 1 McDonald St, charging from $110, and the *Century Radisson* (☎ 368 4000) at 203 Victoria St, which charges from $130.

Woolloomooloo Waters (☎ 358 3100), at 48 Dowling St in Woolloomooloo, charges from around $100/150.

East of the Cross, *Bersens Cosmopolitan Hotel* (☎ 327 3207) is at 2B Mona Rd, near the intersection with New South Head Rd (the continuation of William St/Kings Cross Rd). Edgewater railway station is nearby. Each room has a mini-kitchen with a fridge and microwave and some of the rooms have good views. There's also a roof garden. Singles/doubles start at $75/85. Further east in Double Bay, a pleasant upmarket enclave, the *Savoy Double Bay Hotel* (☎ 326 1411) at 41-45 Knox St is a small place which charges from about $70 a double, rising a little when things are busy. It's worth paying an extra $15 for a superior room, which is good value compared to other places charging around the same price.

In Rushcutters Bay at 85 New South Head Rd, the *Bayside* (☎ 327 8511) is a member of the Flag chain and has rooms from $150. Add $10 for harbour views.

Glebe *Alishan International Guesthouse* (☎ 566 4048), at 100 Glebe Point Rd, is something like an upmarket hostel, with well-travelled and multilingual staff, very good common areas including kitchen and laundry facilities, and a small garden with a barbecue. Singles/doubles with ensuite bathroom go for $65/75, dropping to around $50/65 when things are slow. An extra person costs $15 and a family room is available ($90).

As well as hostel accommodation, the YHA's *Hereford Lodge* (☎ 660 5577) at 51 Hereford St has some motel-style rooms and you don't have to be a member to stay in one. The rooms are large, clean and comfortable, although they lack phones. A single costs $60 plus $5 for each extra person, up to four. YHA members are given a discount of around 10%.

The *Rooftop Motel* (☎ 660 7777) at 146-148 Glebe Point Rd is a fairly simple motel charging $70 per room, with variations in busy or slack times. Further north at 196 Glebe Point Rd, the *Haven Inn* (☎ 660 6655) is quite a good motel with large rooms (for an inner-city motel) going for $140, sometimes dropping to around $90 at quiet times. There's a heated swimming pool, secure parking and a restaurant. Their courtesy bus will take you into the city and other nearby destinations.

Bondi Beach Hotel *Bondi* (☎ 30 3271), an impressive old pile on the corner of Campbell Pde and Curlewis St, has newly renovated suites from $60 to $80 and other rooms with beach views from $50. These prices stay the same year-round, so it's great value in summer, when you'll probably have to book ahead. There are also much cheaper rooms.

The *Bondi Beach Motel* (☎ 365 5233) at 68 Gould St, a block back from Campbell Pde off Curlewis St, is a reasonable motel which boasts that 'Gary Puckett & the Union Gap chose to stay at the Bondi Beach Motel on their 1993 Young Girl Oz Tour'. Hmm. Singles/doubles go for $60/70, more in the summer.

At 152 Campbell Pde, on the corner of Roscoe St, *Bondi Beachside Inn* (☎ 30 5311) has older-style motel rooms which are being upgraded. The rooms are a little small but each has a kitchen and a balcony and it's fair value at $69 for an older single or double, up

to $88 for a renovated room with a beach view. On the opposite corner is *Breakers Motel* (☎ 365 3300) at 164-176 Campbell Pde, more modern and with a small pool. Doubles cost from $90 ($560 per week) to $110 ($700 per week), rising by about 10% in summer. An extra person costs $10.

Ravesi's (☎ 365 4422, 365 4483 AH) is an interesting three-star place in a recycled building on the corner of Campbell Pde and Hall St. There are only 16 rooms and suites, some with their own terraces. Rates start at $88 but you'll have to pay at least $110 for a beach view. Split-level suites with terraces cost from $165. There are often special deals in winter and spring.

Coogee The *Coogee Sands Motor Inn* (☎ 665 8588) is across from the beach on Dolphin St, which runs off Arden St at the north end of the beach, and charges from $100 to $120 or so. There are a few other motels, including the *Corban International* (☎ 665 2244) at 183 Coogee Bay Rd, from around $80/90 and *Alice Motel* (☎ 30 5231) at 30 Fletcher St from about $50/60.

Manly Because of its beach-resort atmosphere, many places at Manly have seasonal deals; always ring around to find out what's on offer.

The *Steyne Hotel* (☎ 977 4977) on the corner of the Corso and North Steyne has rooms, most with shared bathrooms, from $40/60. *Manly Beach Resort* (☎ 977 4188) at 6 Carlton St, at the corner of Pittwater Rd, is a reasonable motel with rooms for $70/75, plus a $10 surcharge in December and January. There are a few other motels in this price range, such as *Manly Paradise* (☎ 977 5799) at 54 North Steyne and *Manly Surfside* (☎ 977 2299) at 102 North Steyne.

Periwinkle Guesthouse (☎ 977 4668), a restored Victorian house facing the harbour beach at 19 East Esplanade, has guesthouse accommodation for $70/80. Kitchen and laundry facilities are available.

Manly Lodge (☎ 977 8655) at 22 Victoria Pde is a guesthouse, but not in the usual musty sense of the word – there's a holiday atmosphere here. Thomas Power continues to improve his pleasant establishment – the latest additions are a licensed restaurant (main courses around $15) and a honeymoon suite with a spa. Each of the 32 rooms has a ceiling fan and an attached bathroom (the honeymoon suite has air-con). There is quite a variety of rooms – most are small but all are well-furnished. They cost from around $70 a double, with prices rising over summer when there are no weekly rates. In winter or slack times there are sometimes good deals.

Places to Stay – top end
This section covers places charging more than $150 a night. With a dozen five-star hotels and many more four-star places, there are plenty to choose from. Travel agents in other states or countries can book many of these places and will probably have access to special deals and packages.

Airport The *Sydney Airport Hilton* (☎ 597 0122; 1800 222 255 toll-free bookings) is at 20 Levy St, Arncliffe and charges from $150/230 a single/double.

City & Nearby In the Rocks, *The Stafford* (☎ 251 6711) at 75 Harrington St is a pleasant new place with self-contained studio and single-bedroom apartments (some in a row of restored terrace houses) from $170 a night. Diagonally opposite at 34-52 Harrington St, the *Harbour Rocks Hotel* (☎ 251 8944; 1800 251 210 toll-free bookings) is in a renovated old building, although it was never a hotel. Rooms start at $165, or $105 with shared bathrooms.

Also right in the Rocks, on George St at the corner of Mill Lane, the *Old Sydney Parkroyal* (☎ 252 0524) charges about $260, with various specials offering hefty discounts, such as weekend nights for $150.

On the corner of Kent and High Sts, on the Walsh Bay side of the Bradfield Highway, the *Observatory Hotel* (☎ 256 2222) is large for a boutique hotel, small for a five-star hotel, charging from $340 to $1200 a night. Not far away at 176 Cumberland St is the big *ANA Hotel Sydney* (☎ 250 6000), with more

than 600 rooms (from $200) and suites (from $350).

On Carrington St across from Wynyard Park, the *Menzies Holiday Inn* (☎ 299 1000; 1800 221 066 toll-free bookings) has rooms from $230 to $265 and suites from $350 to $540.

The *Sydney Hilton* (☎ 266 0610; 1800 222 255 toll-free bookings), on Pitt St between Market and Park Sts, charges from $220/260 up to $850. There are specials in winter and at other times. The *Regent* (☎ 238 0000) at 199 George St, near Circular Quay and the Rocks and with great views from the upper floors, charges from around $300.

At Darling Harbour, the 700-room *Hotel Nikko* (☎ 299 1231) backs onto Sussex St and charges from $250. On the other side of Darling Harbour, behind Harbourside Festival marketplace, is the 530-room *Novotel Sydney* (☎ 934 0000, 1800 024 499 toll-free) charging from $180.

East of the City At 8 Challis Ave (a short walk to the heart of Kings Cross), *Simpsons of Potts Point* (☎ 356 2199) offers large, well-furnished rooms with attached bathrooms in a superb old house. Singles/doubles start from $155/165. Definitely worth a look.

Olims Sydney Hotel (☎ 358 2777; 1800 266 466 toll-free bookings) at 26 Macleay St in Potts Point, near the corner of Challis Ave, charges around $160 with specials available.

The *Sebel Town House* (☎ 358 3244; 1800 222 266 toll-free bookings) at 23 Elizabeth Bay Rd in Elizabeth Bay has a reputation for celebrity guests, especially from the music industry. It has some quality touches such as its own gym and a rooftop heated pool – and you can open the windows in your room. Rates begin around $200, with seasonal specials and good deals on weekends.

Hotel Nikko Sydney (☎ 368 3000) at 81 Macleay St charges from around $240.

In Double Bay, the very plush *Ritz-Carlton* (☎ 362 4455; 1800 252 888 toll-free bookings) at 33 Cross St charges from $180, right up to $1800 in the Ritz-Carlton suite. If you think they don't build 'em like they used to, this is the place for you – an opulent interior with lots of marble and olde worlde touches has been fitted into a big new building. George Bush stayed here on his presidential visit to Australia.

The top-dollar place to stay on Bondi Beach is the big *Ramada Grand Hotel* (☎ 365 5666; 1800 222 431 toll-free bookings) on the corner of Campbell Pde and Beach Rd. The entrance is on Beach Rd. Suites cost from $170 up to around $500. There's a *Holiday Inn* (☎ 315 7600) on Arden St at the corner of Carr St, charging from $150 to about $600.

North of the Bridge *The Rest* hotel (☎ 955 1111; 1800 807 356 toll-free bookings) is across from Milsons Point station at the corner of Cliff and Alfred Sts, right at the northern end of the bridge and one stop from both Wynyard and North Sydney. It's a stylish four-star hotel oriented to business customers, and rooms cost from $160 a single/double. There are good discounts on Friday and Saturday nights.

Manly *Manly Pacific Parkroyal* (☎ 977 7666) at 55 North Steyne charges from $220, and the *Radisson Kestrel* (☎ 977 8866) at 8 South Steyne charges from around $150. *Manly Waterfront Apartment Hotel* (☎ 976 1000) at 1 Raglan St (on the corner of North Steyne) has serviced apartments from $170.

Serviced Apartments
Serviced apartments – which can be anything from a hotel room with a fridge and microwave oven thrown in, to a full-size apartment – can be good value, especially for families.

City & Nearby Well worth checking out is *City Centre Serviced Apartments* (☎ 233 6677 or 223 3529) at 7 Elizabeth St, between Martin Place and Hunter St. Each apartment is fully equipped, down to the washing machine and drier. The apartments are bedsits, but they are a reasonable size. Rates start at $60 a double, plus $10 for each extra person.

The *Metro* chain has a couple of serviced

apartments in the city, on the corner of Sussex and King Sts (☎ 290 9200) at $120 a double, and 2 Francis St (☎ 360 5988) just east of Hyde Park at $100 a double. They sometimes have good weekend specials. *Savoy Apartments* (☎ 267 9211) at 37 King St charges from around $130 and the *Waldorf* (☎ 261 5355) at 57 Liverpool St is a little more expensive.

Top-end serviced apartments include *Quay West* (☎ 240 6000) at 98 Gloucester St which charges from $260 a double, $330 for three people. *Carrington Sydney City Centre Apartments* (☎ 299 6556) at 57 York St near the corner of Barrack St charges from $180. Others in the same range include the *York Apartment Hotel* (☎ 210 5000) at 5 York St, the *Park All-Suite Hotel* (☎ 331 7728) at 16 Oxford St and *Parkridge Corporate Apartments* (☎ 361 8600) at 6 Oxford St.

Kings Cross & Nearby In Elizabeth Bay, just down the road from the Cross, *17 Elizabeth Bay Rd* (☎ 358 8999; 1800 251 917 toll-free bookings) has well-equipped serviced apartments from $110 ($560 per week) for a single-bedroom apartment and from $140 ($735 per week) for a two-bedroom apartment sleeping four. *Oakford Executive Apartments* (☎ 358 4544, toll-free 1800 818 224) at 10 Wylde St (the northern continuation of Macleay St) charges from $140 and way up, and *Medina Executive Apartments* (☎ 356 7400) at 68 Roslyn Gardens charges from $100/120.

The Lodge (☎ 327 8511) at 38-44 New South Head Rd in Rushcutters Bay has studio (ie, small) apartments for about $60 a double ($320 per week). Check in at the Bayside Motel diagonally opposite.

PLACES TO EAT
Sydney seems to be between cuisines at the moment, having surfeited on Thai food. Restaurants which have won awards lately tend to serve modern Australian food – something like an amalgamation of Mediterranean, South-East Asian and Californian styles, with a look and taste that's distinctively Australian. With the best fresh produce in the

world to work with, Australian chefs have a head start.

You can easily save for a big night out at one of the top restaurants and still eat well, as there are scores of places serving good food at reasonable prices. The obvious solution is to cook for yourself, but even those on the tightest budgets can eat well at Chinese and Vietnamese places. Pub counter meals, becoming less common in central Sydney, are also good for solid, inexpensive food.

Guides for the Serious Foodie

There are several books to help you choose between the vast array of eating places. *Cheap Eats in Sydney* (Universal Consumer Guides, large-format paperback, about $8) lists hundreds of places where you can eat two courses for less than $22. Canberra and the Blue Mountains are also covered. The only drawback with the book is that it shares Sydney's fascination for the new, and old favourites are dumped to make way for new and happening places.

The other annual guide is the *Good Food Guide* (paperback, about $16). The restaurants listed aren't exactly cheap, but it's well worth considering a splurge at one of them. It is published by the *Sydney Morning Herald*, which has restaurant reviews in its 'Good Living' section on Tuesdays.

SBS, the multicultural broadcaster, has a *Guide to Ethnic Eating* in Sydney, by Maeve O'Meara and Joanna Savill, which includes

tips on shopping as well as places to eat (Text Publishing Company, paperback, about $15).

Bargains

One of Sydney's cheapest places to eat is *Mekong*, an Asian place at 711 George St where you can choose two dishes and rice and still have change from $5. There are other Mekongs, at 570 Oxford St in Bondi Junction and on Anzac Pde a few blocks south of the University of NSW.

The city's various food halls offer similar prices for predominantly Asian food. Try the food hall in the basement of the *China Centre* on Chinatown's Dixon St.

At the south end of the city centre, upstairs at 373 Pitt St (just north of Liverpool St), *Mamma's Kitchen* has pasta from $3.50 to $5.50, with weekday lunch and dinner and Saturday dinner. The *Astoria* on Darlinghurst Rd in Kings Cross is a rare old-style cafe and serves honest tucker such as roast lamb or beef for just $5.

For a rather more expensive bargain, try *Kable's* at the Regent Hotel on George St near the Rocks. It's one of Australia's best restaurants and the prices reflect this, but there's a lunchtime deal where you can choose from the full menu and pay $37.50 for three courses or $32.50 for two courses.

Meals with a View

On Manly Wharf, where the ferries berth, and with outdoor tables overlooking Manly's pretty harbour beach, *Armstrong's* (☎ 976 3835) has a very good reputation for modern Australian food. Seafood is emphasised and main courses approach $20.

Another restaurant accessible by water is *Doyles' on the Beach* (☎ 337 2007) at Watsons Bay, where seafood is the speciality and main courses average around $25. Bookings are advisable. On weekday lunchtimes you can take Doyle's own water taxi from Commissioners Steps on the west side of Circular Quay. The taxi costs $7 return and services start at 11.30 am. An ordinary water taxi would cost about $50 between four people. Ferries run from Circular Quay to

Doyles' on the Beach, at Watsons Bay

Watsons Bay on weekends, but not very frequently and only until 6 pm or so. The non-nautical could take bus Nos 324/5 from Circular Quay. Next door to Doyles' is the Watsons Bay pub, which shares the views.

The Doyle family has been serving seafood to Sydneysiders for generations and has two other waterfront eateries, *Doyles' at the Markets*, a bistro and takeaway at the Pyrmont Fishmarkets, and *Doyles' at the Quay* on the west side of Circular Quay, in the International Passenger Terminal. You can sit outdoors, the atmosphere is relaxed (although the service has production-line overtones on busy weekends), the seafood is good and the prices are reasonable. There's a minimum food order of $14.50 per person, with main-course seafood costing from around $20. Note that they don't take Amex cards. Upstairs from Doyles' and sharing the views, *Bilson's* (☎ 251 5600) is more formal but has an equally good reputation for seafood. At lunch main courses are $20 and up; at dinner you'll pay $30 and up.

There are more good views from the other side of Circular Quay. The *Sydney Cove Oyster Bar* is a small place right on the waterfront and offers purely Australian produce, including a good wine list. Oysters cost from $16/$9 a dozen/half dozen, with other dishes from $12. It's open from mid-morning until about 8 pm in winter, until 11 pm or later in summer. Just next door is a cheaper takeaway place with some outdoor tables.

Further around at the Opera House there are three restaurants with good views. The *Forecourt* restaurant and bar is on the lower concourse – you might have to stand up to see the water. The menu (of the steak, seafood and spatchcock variety) has main courses from $14 to $17. It's open for lunch daily and for dinner daily except Sunday. There's also a bar which is open until late most days. The *Harbour* (☎ 250 7191) is right at the 'prow' of the Opera House and there's an outdoor area. All entrees are $8.50, all main courses are $15.50. The Harbour is open for lunch and dinner daily except Sunday. Next door is the *Harbour Take-Out*

Bar, open daily, with takeaways such as fish & chips from $5.50. Upstairs at the classy *Bennelong Restaurant* (☎ 250 7578), main courses cost from $20, with an after-show buffet for $12.50. It is open for dinner daily except Sunday.

The prize for the highest view in Sydney is easily won by the restaurants slowly spinning on top of the Sydney Tower. Bookings are suggested (☎ 233 3722). At Level 1 the *International Revolving Restaurant* has main courses for around $25 and also fixed price menus from about $30 on weekdays. It's open for lunch on weekdays and for dinner (two sessions) from Monday to Saturday. The *Level 2 Revolving Restaurant* is an all-you-can-eat buffet with a large selection of meats, some seafood and plenty of Asian dishes, but little for vegetarians. There is a variety of prices depending on when you go, from $25 for lunch from Tuesday to Saturday to $33 for Saturday dinner, with children less than half price. It's open for lunch and dinner (two sessions) daily, except Monday. Restaurant patrons are not charged for the ride to the top of the tower, so you're $6 ahead before you sit down.

City

There's no shortage of places for a snack or a meal in the city, on weekdays anyway. They are clustered around railway stations, in shopping arcades and at the bases of office towers.

North of Liverpool St If you want a quiet cup of tea or coffee away from the city bustle, take the lift or climb the stairs to Level 2 of the pretty Strand Arcade, which runs between the Pitt St Mall and George St. Here you'll find *Noonan's* and a wide choice of teas for just $2 for a one-person pot. There are also cakes and salads. Noonan's also does a good breakfast, such as bacon & eggs for $7.50, including tea or coffee, and muesli or porridge for $4.50.

Not far away is the stylish collection of eateries and bars at the top levels of the *Skygarden*, a new complex in a recycled building on Pitt St Mall. Take the long 'express' elevator to get directly to the top.

For a lunchtime vegetarian snack, drop into *Carruthers*, a takeaway place on Druitt St near Clarence St, where there are tasty sandwiches, salads, vegie burgers and the like at low prices. More substantial vegetarian meals with a South American flavour are sold at *El Sano*, downstairs on the north-west corner of Pitt St and Martin Place. A little way north at 125 Pitt St in the old Angel Hotel is *Merivales*, a stylish (and busy) coffee shop and bar, with snacks for about $6 and main courses from under $10. It's open on weekdays from 7.30 am until late. There's another city *Merivales* on Pitt St, just north of the mall at No 194. Here you can buy snacks such as pizzettes for $5.40 and a good selection of cakes. Good coffee is $1.80.

The *Centrepoint Tavern*, downstairs on the Pitt St Mall near the corner of Market St is a plush cafeteria with main courses between $8 and $12. It's a popular place for weary locals to feed up between bouts of shopping.

On the corner of George and Park Sts, the 2nd floor (that's 3rd floor to Americans) cafeteria in *Woolworths* has meals from $6; a roast will set you back about $7. Better value is the small food hall in the basement where there's a variety of shops with dishes, mainly Asian, from $4.50 or less.

On Pitt St at the corner of Bathurst, the Edinburgh Castle Hotel has the upstairs *Cafe de Pub*, not as trendy as it sounds and serving interesting and relatively inexpensive food.

Liverpool St to Central Station There is a small collection of Spanish places along Liverpool St between George and Sussex Sts. *Captain Torres* has a $15 lunch deal, tapas in the bar from $3.50 and main courses between $9 and $18. A few doors closer to George St, *Cafe Espana* charges under $10 for most dishes. The *Grand Taverna* at the Sir John Young Hotel on the corner of George St is another popular place where most main courses are around $12.

At 152 Elizabeth St, just south of Liverpool St, the *Cyprus Hellene Club* is open Monday to Saturday. Most main courses are $7.50, with steaks for $8.50. A little dearer is the *Hellenic Club*, upstairs at 251 Elizabeth St, across from Hyde Park (yes, it's over Liverpool St), where steaks are between $9.50 and $12 and Greek lamb dishes are $9.50. At 336 Pitt St, *Diethnes* is a large and friendly Greek restaurant. It's open Monday to Saturday, and many main courses are under $9.

You'll find a good collection of inexpensive eating places in the streets around Central Station. These are a diverse mix of Asian places spilling over from Chinatown, old-style cafes and a few pubs with inexpensive counter meals, such as the *Chamberlain Hotel* on the corner of Pitt and Campbell Sts which has $5 meals. Along George St there are plenty of cafes where you can buy breakfast for less than $6, such as the *Cafe Inn* at No 768, across from Ultimo Rd. Breakfast here is $5 and includes tea or coffee. Their other meals are also cheap.

Carriages in Central Station itself serves inexpensive cafeteria-style meals, a little on the stodgy side. Roast beef with vegies goes for $7.50, and there are other dishes for much less. One of Sydney's cheapest places to eat is *Mekong*, an Asian place at 711 George St where you can choose two dishes and rice and still have change from $5. A little further south on George St at No 735 is *Mother Chu's*, more expensive but a rare Chinese restaurant which serves vegan food. They don't use MSG, onion, garlic or chives! It's open for lunch and dinner daily and has main courses for around $8 to $10, plus many cheaper snacks.

Nearby on the corner of Valentine St, the *Malaya* was once a very cheap Chinese/Indonesian/Malaysian eatery patronised by students. It has moved upmarket in recent years but still has plenty of main courses between $8.50 and $14, with cheaper vegetarian dishes. It's open daily for lunch and dinner, and takeaways are available.

Chinatown
Officially, Chinatown consists only of the pedestrian mall on Dixon St, but there are

also good Chinese restaurants in the streets nearby, notably in the small Haymarket area at the south end of the Chinatown mall. There is a dense concentration of Chinese restaurants, cafes and takeaways, plus shops catering to the Chinese community. You can spend a small fortune at some outstanding Chinese restaurants with internationally-famous chefs, or eat well for next to nothing in a food hall. Weekend yum cha brunch is popular in Sydney and you may have to queue to get into some of the many places offering it.

Although Chinese food is the dominant cuisine, there are also some Thai, Vietnamese and Japanese places.

For a quick sample, the best place to start is the food hall downstairs in the *Chinatown Centre*, the pagoda-style building on the corner of Dixon and Goulburn Sts. There is a wide range of eateries, including Korean and Thai, and there are many dishes for $4.50 with few above $6. The food hall is open daily from 10 am to 10 pm. There are also food halls in the *Sussex Centre*, on Dixon St (running through to Sussex St) diagonally across from the Chinatown Centre and in the *Dixon Centre*, on the corner of Dixon and Little Hay Sts.

Hingara at 82 Dixon St has some more interesting dishes than the normal Chinese menu allows – fried fish with corn sauce, for instance – but the favourites are there too. Nearby is *Bodhi*, a vegetarian restaurant with low prices. Others worth checking out are the large *Tai Yuen*, at 110 Hay St, which has been around a long time and has a good reputation, and the *New Tai Yuen* at 31 Dixon St – both have main courses for around $11 to $15.

House of Guangzhou on the corner of Thomas St and Ultimo Rd is a long-established place with a reputation for seafood. Main courses cost around $10 to $19 (seafood can be more). Downstairs, there's an inexpensive *Japanese takeaway*, with a few tables. Across the road, still on Thomas St, the *Emperor's Garden BBQ* is a cafe-style Chinese eatery, popular with the Chinese community, as is *Jing May Noodles* further along Thomas St, upstairs in the Princes

Centre, with little over $15. Both of these places are open daily.

The two big *Marigold* restaurants, at 299-305 Sussex St and upstairs at 683-689 George St serve Cantonese food with great style (and high prices to match), and there's a lunchtime yum cha at George St. Very popular for Sunday yum cha is the *Regal* at 347-353 Sussex St, another more expensive place.

Darling Harbour

There are many, many food outlets in the Harbourside Marketplace. Most concentrate squarely on the tourist trade, but with a terrace table on a fine day, who cares? Stroll around and take your pick. *Jo Jo's* and *Jordan's* are two of the more expensive places. *Bobby McGees* is a big drinking/dining/dancing complex, with performing waiters and the like. The *Craig Brewery* in the North Pavilion, near a monorail station, has main courses for well under $10. Upstairs is the *Virgin Video Cafe*. Down near the Entertainment Centre, The *Pumphouse Brewery Tavern* has above-average pub meals starting under $10. In the Parkroyal Hotel on the corner of Day and Bathurst Sts, *Arizona* is one of a small chain of 'western' bar/restaurants, popular for drinking and snacking. There's another on Pitt St, just south of the mall.

If you want to get away from Darling Harbour and eat with the locals, the *Glasgow Arms Hotel* at 527 Harris St (not far from the Powerhouse Museum), has a good bistro with reasonable prices.

Circular Quay

Right behind the ferry wharves, amidst the crowds and buskers, *City Extra* is reasonable for coffee, snacks and meals, as is nearby *Rossini*, although you pay for the position. The several cafes right on the wharves aren't great value, although they're OK for a cup of coffee – be warned that the floor sways a little! If you're after fuel rather than views or great food, head for *Nulbom Oriental Food*, behind the quay on the Alfred St median strip at the corner of Pitt St; it's a kiosk selling reasonable Asian food starting at under $5.

The *Museum of Contemporary Art* has a suitably stylish cafe, dwarfed by its setting in the cavernous foyer of the old Port Authority building; there are also some tables outside with views of Circular Quay. The food is good and interesting, with entrees and specials for around $10, main courses around $13, desserts $6.50 and coffee $2.50. The service is a little overdone and isn't lightning fast.

In the Overseas Passenger Terminal at Circular Quay West, *Doyle's* and *Bilson's* are two good seafood places, and across the other side of Sydney Cove near the Opera House is the *Sydney Cove Oyster Bar*. In the *Opera House* itself are three restaurants, a couple of bars and a seafood takeaway. See the earlier Meals with a View section for all these places.

At the Campbell's Stores Complex, between the Overseas Passenger Terminal and the Park Hyatt Hotel, there is a collection of restaurants such as *Italian Village* and *Wolfies*, with large outdoor areas overlooking the quay and main courses in the $18 to $25 area.

The Rocks

At the top of George St, just before it goes under the bridge, the *Mercantile Hotel* is a restored pub with counter meals. Keep going up George St, turn left after you've gone under the bridge, and you'll come to the unrestored *Harbour View Hotel* where meals are basic but good value.

At 101 George St, *Phillip's Foote* has cafe meals from $6 to $10 at lunch, more at dinner, and an outdoor barbecue area where you cook your own steak or fish for $15; the price includes a glass of wine, but salads are extra. Next door at No 99, *Rock's Cafe* is a bit cheaper and has snacks and light meals from 8 am to 7 pm during the week and till late on Friday and Saturday nights. *G'Day Cafe* at No 83, just north of Argyle St, is similar but cheaper still – surprisingly so, with breakfast from $3.50, focaccia from $2 and other light meals. It's open from 5.30 am

to midnight. Further south on George St, the *Bakehouse* has good coffee and cakes as well as takeaways.

Next to the Fortune of War pub on George St, *Ox on the Rocks* is a restaurant with main courses from $16 to $20, more for steaks. *Rockpool* at 109 George St has superb seafood for around $30 for main courses.

In Metcalfe Arcade, near the Hickson St entrance, *Pancakes at the Rocks* is a member of the Pancake Parlour chain, has the usual huge menu and stays open long hours.

Gumnut Teagarden on Harrington St near Argyle St is in an old house and also has a courtyard where you can have coffee, cake and light meals for under $10. There's a small food hall in the *Clocktower Centre*, a modern building across Harrington St on the corner of Argyle St.

Walk under the bridge and down to Pier One to the *Harbour Watch* seafood restaurant, which has main courses around $25. There are several other eating places here, including *Harbourside Brasserie*. Not far away on Pier Four, the *Wharf Restaurant* (☎ 250 1761) is a smart restaurant serving modern Australian food, where you'll spend around $30 per person.

There are a couple of upmarket places on Cumberland St at the corner of Essex St. *The Rocks Teppanyaki* is a Japanese restaurant with set-menu lunches for $20, $25 and $40, and a la carte dishes from $12 to $20. Next door is *Lilyvale* with a solid French/modern Australian menu with main courses around $30.

Kings Cross & Nearby

Victoria St is gaining some fashionable cafes. *Joe's* has breakfast from $7, focaccia from $5 and other snacks and light meals. This is definitely a place to be seen, and on weekends the patrons being seen include fashionable stockbrokers and designer Harley riders. Further down and more of a restaurant than a cafe, *Four Fingers* has a $22.50 two-course deal, choosing from an interesting menu of modern Australian food. In the same area is *Roy's*, a slick vegetarian place with huge servings and prices under

$10. For something completely different, the *Turquoise Cafe* in front of Highfield House is a small place with plain food at low prices. Cooked breakfasts start at $5, salads at $3 and pasta around $5.50.

Along William St around the corner from Darlinghurst Rd/Victoria St is a string of cafes with inexpensive food. You can usually find one offering a full breakfast for under $5. *Golden Days* on the corner of Brougham St will sell you a kangaroo burger for $2.50. Across Brougham St, *O'Malley's Hotel* has lunches for less than $7, with pasta at $5. On the south side of wide William St, on the corner of Darlinghurst Rd (and thus in Darlinghurst), *Michelangelo's* is a 24-hour cafe.

On Llankelly Place near the corner of Darlinghurst Rd, *Pad Thai* is a tiny takeaway with a few tables, selling meals from $5 or $6. A bit further down on the other side is the equally inexpensive *Yakidori*. Not far away on Darlinghurst Rd, the *Astoria* has old-fashioned tucker such as roast lamb or beef for just $5. Just a few doors away, where Darlinghurst Rd bends around to become Macleay St, *Nick's Seafood* has a fish dinner (grilled fish, salad and chips) for $4.50.

On Darlinghurst Rd near the El Alamein Fountain there are several popular eateries. The attraction here is the pavement tables where you can watch Kings Cross go by in all its glory. *Bourbon & Beefsteak* is open 24 hours and has breakfast (all day) for about $9, steaks for about $16 and many other dishes in the same price-bracket. Next door, the *Fountain Cafe* is similar but a little cheaper. Right in the plaza, the *Fountain Bistro* is a little less expensive again. Another place with outdoor tables is *Geoffrey's Cafe* on Roslyn St near the corner of Darlinghurst Rd. The large menu has nothing over $10 and many dishes under $8, with steaks from $7. Breakfast is $4.90.

Gado Gado is a long-established Indonesian restaurant at 57 Bayswater Rd, where most main courses are under $10, more for some seafood. It's open every night for dinner and for lunch on Friday. Try *Cafe 59* next door for a coffee and a good but inexpensive focaccia. At No 32, the *Bayswater Brasserie* is a very good restaurant where you don't have to spend a fortune if you choose carefully, especially at lunch.

On Kellet St there are several places catering to late-night eating and drinking for those with deeper pockets, such as *Deans* and *Cafe Iguana*. Nearby at 42 Kellet St, *Lime & Lemongrass* serves good Thai food in a brasserie setting, with main courses around $15.

There's a string of more upmarket cafes along Macleay St north of the Cross – technically in Potts Point. Perhaps the smartest is the *Merivale Brasserie* on Macleay St at the corner of Challis Ave. Entrees are all $8.50 and main courses are all $12.50. If you go around the corner to Challis Ave, you'll find the *Espresso Bar*, part of the same establishment and equally fashionable but with fewer business suits at the tables. A little way south is the popular *Macleay St Bistro*, with main courses between $12 and $18.

Forbes Restaurant at 155 Forbes St, just north of William St, is a new brasserie-style Italian place with some good deals. It's open for dinner every night and from 7 am on weekdays.

Darlinghurst & East Sydney

A popular place for a drink is the *Darlo Bar*, taking up its own tiny block at the corner of Darlinghurst and Liverpool Sts – this must be the narrowest pub in Sydney. It is pretty much a neighbourhood pub, but it's a very interesting neighbourhood. Good food and cocktails are available (along with beer, of course) and the service is friendly.

Not far away on the corner of Victoria and Burton Sts, *Laurie's Vegetarian Diner* is open for lunch and dinner daily. Great smoothies are $3.50, soups are $4 and there's a varied, interesting and tasty menu of vegetarian delights from about $5.50 (more at dinner).

You'll find more vegetarian food at *Govinda's*, the Hare Krishnas' smart restaurant at 112 Darlinghurst St, just south of William St and Kings Cross. Currently they offer a $12.50 all-you-can-eat smorgasbord nightly between 6 and 10.30 pm. This also gives you admission to the cinema upstairs, so it's a great deal. See the later Entertainment section for more details.

The northern end of Victoria St, as it nears William St and Kings Cross, has plenty of cafes and restaurants, most of them new, trendy and probably transient. Not so *Bar Coluzzi*, a Sydney institution for coffee. Nearby is *La Bussola*, which has some of the best pizzas in the city. Another stayer is *Una's*, just south of Surry St. This Austrian-style cafe is an institution for its solid, inexpensive food, from breakfast ($5.60 and up) through to about 11 pm. All main courses cost $7.50 or less, with some specials under $6. Una's is BYO and charges a token 20c per person corkage.

Above the Arch Coffee Lounge at 81 Stanley St, *No Names* is a simple, inexpensive and popular Italian restaurant. This stretch of Stanley St is crammed with Italian eating places, from the inexpensive *Bill & Toni's* to *Beppis*, one of Sydney's best Italian restaurants.

At the corner of Forbes and Burton Sts, *DOV* is a popular BYO cafe (too popular for a quiet meal) in an old sandstone building, with interesting and delicious Israeli/Mediterranean-inspired food. There are only a couple of main courses each day (about $11), but there's a long list of very tasty cold dishes ($6.50) or you can sample a mixed plate ($8.50). DOV is also open for breakfast.

Very popular for its atmosphere and rock-star memorabilia (Elvis's suit, Jimi's hat, Johnny Rotten's jacket, etc) the *Hard Rock Cafe* at 121-129 Crown St has surprisingly inexpensive food, with many main courses from around $10. It's open daily from noon to at least midnight.

Oxford St Right at the western end of Oxford St, the *Burdekin Hotel* at No 2 has an eclectic and pricey menu – that striking bar might prove irresistible for at least a drink. Just off Oxford St at 26 Burton St, *Metro* is a pleasant little vegetarian restaurant open for dinner nightly except on Saturday (yes, closed Saturday). Main courses cost from $6

and desserts are $3. You'll probably have to wait for a table.

Hanovers, on the south side of Oxford St just west of Crown St, has great cakes and coffee plus meals such as deluxe burgers from $10. Across Crown St and on the north side of Oxford St, *Downtown Darlinghurst* is a cheaper but still stylish cafe with pastas for about $7.50 and other main courses around $8.50. The *Spanish Deli* further along provides big breakfasts for $3.50 and stays open until late for supper.

Bagel House, just off Taylor Square on Flinders St, is a cafe upstairs from a bakery where they make 'real' boiled bagels. You can sample one from just $1 for a buttered bagel, up to around $7 for the most expensive filled bagel. It's open from 8 am to 5 pm daily. Other food is also available, including breakfast for $6.50. The atmosphere is relaxed, the coffee is good and the staff are friendly. Across from here, upstairs at 2A Flinders St, the *Taylor Square Restaurant* serves modern Australian food with some old favourites such as roast chook and bread-and-butter pud. There are fixed-price menus from about $25.

On Campbell St near Denham St and just back from Taylor Square, the *Sanctuary Cafe* is in a small enclave of avant-garde galleries and studios and is a relaxed place for a coffee or a snack. In the same area, on Crown St, *Betty's Soup Kitchen* has soup for $4 and a few other dishes, slightly more expensive. Not far away is a small *Maltese cafe*, selling good and inexpensive *pastizzi* and pastas – you'll get macaroni for less than $3.

You might have cuddled a koala, but have you eaten a kangaroo? For a taste of Australian fauna try *Riberries* (☎ 361 4929) at 411 Bourke St, a block south of Taylor Square. As well as animals, Australian plants are on the menu, but despite the ingredients the style of cuisine is French. It's an intriguing combination. There are set menus offering four choices for each course (including vegetarian dishes), costing $32 for two courses and $38 for three. Bookings are essential for lunch (Thursday and Friday) and are suggested for dinner (daily except Sunday).

BYO alcohol, but leave your cigarettes at home.

Two prime people-watching places are the *Open Kitchen* on the corner of Crown and Oxford Sts and *Cafe 191* right on Taylor Square.

Along Oxford St just east of Taylor Square is a clutch of inexpensive restaurants serving cuisines ranging from Cambodian to Californian. My favourite is the long-established *Balkan* at 209 Oxford St. It specialises in those two basic Balkan dishes – *raznjici* and *cevapcici*. Ask for a *pola pola* and you'll get half of each. It's very filling and definitely for real meat-eaters only. Most dishes cost around $13. *Kim's* at 235 Oxford St is a small Vietnamese restaurant which has been popular for years, for both the quality of its food and its low prices (from $7 for main courses).

Paddington

Oxford St continues through Paddington. Across from the west end of the Victoria Barracks, *Feasts & Fancies* is open every night and on Saturday for lunch, with a varied menu based loosely on Spanish cuisine and main courses around $14. The *Fringe Bar & Cafe* at the corner of Hopewell St is a fashionable place in a renovated pub. The cycles of fashion mean that not a lot of renovation was required to meet the brief.

The no-smoking *New Edition Tearoom* at 328 Oxford St, attached to the good New Edition Bookshop, is a great place to read your new purchases – if you can get a seat. *Sloane Rangers* at 312 Oxford St is a busy vegetarian cafe open during the day and everything under $10. The courtyard is a bonus.

On William St just north of Oxford St, *Sweet William* has chocolates and sweets.

Five Ways, the junction of Glenmore, Goodhope, Heeley and Broughton Sts, is perhaps the centre of Paddington. Here there are several places to eat and drink, including the iron-laced verandah of the wonderful old *Royal Hotel. Creperie Stivel* is a pleasant cafe with a courtyard where you can eat crepes, pannequets, gallutes and blintzes for

between $5 and $11. It's open for dinner from 6 pm and for lunch from Wednesday to Sunday. Nearby, the *Delannay Brasserie* is a French restaurant with antipodean dishes such as kangaroo fillets on the menu. Main courses are about $15.

Surry Hills

Surry Hills is developing into a restaurant area. Around the corner of Cleveland St and Elizabeth St there is a large cluster of Lebanese places, all charging much the same for good food. The original restaurants are still there, *Abdul's* on one corner of Elizabeth and Cleveland Sts and *Nada's* across the road. Abdul's is the more basic, but it's relaxed and friendly. Many dishes cost under $5, more are under $6 and most are under $8. The $15 set menu is good value. Nada's and most other places charge about the same, with *Fatima's* and *Emad's*, on Cleveland St west of the corner of Elizabeth St, perhaps a little cheaper.

Turkish *pide* (sort of a Turkish pizza) is also popular along Cleveland St. You can try it at *Ericyes*, near the corner of Young St (where almost everything on the menu is $7, except for the dips which are about $4), and several other places, including *Golden Pide* on the corner of Bourke St. There is a growing number of inexpensive Indian places along here as well, including the *Southern-Indian Chef's Cafe* with many dishes around $5.

L'Aubbergade (☎ 319 5929) at 353 Cleveland St has been serving good French food for nearly 30 years, and with a $20 three-course set menu it's good value. It's open on weekdays for lunch and dinner, with dinner on Saturday as well.

There seems to be still only one South American restaurant, the Uruguayan *Casa-pueblo* on Bourke St just south of Cleveland St. It's open for dinner from Tuesday to Saturday and main courses cost between $9.50 and $13.

Surry Hill's other main area for good eats is along Crown St, north of Cleveland St. The *Da Ly* has Vietnamese and Malaysian dishes, most under $8, with some Thai dishes. It's a long-time favourite for many people. Across the road, the *Thai Orchid* is a more upmarket restaurant, although you can spend under $20 on a meal. Just north of here is the simpler *Thai Cotton*. *Meera's Dosa House*, across the road at 567 Crown St, has a small menu of dosas from $6 to $10 and main courses from $11 to $13. It's run by Indian cookbook author Meera Blakely and is usually open only for dinner.

For something completely different, such as a trendy salad or pasta or a quick coffee, *Planet*, further north on Crown St, should fit the bill. Main courses are about $8. There's more modern eating up on the corner of Crown and Devonshire Sts, with the *Rustic Cafe* on one side (modern food, lots of suits at lunchtime but reasonable prices) and *The Elephant's Foot* (bar and cafe), on the other.

La Passion de Fruit on the corner of Bourke and Devonshire Sts is an inexpensive and popular cafe, with snacks for around $5 and main course dinners under $10 (it's closed Monday). *Johnnie's Fish Cafe*, on Bourke St near the corner of Foveaux St, has fish & chips with salad for $8. This is basically a fish & chip shop with a few tables, but by a quirk of fashion it became a place to be seen, so designer clothes mingle with locals.

Glebe

Glebe Point Rd was Sydney's original 'eat street' and it still has one of the best and most varied collections of places to eat. Listed here is a sample of the 50 or so cafes and restaurants; you should really start at the bottom of Glebe Point Rd and work your way north to see what appeals.

If you're staying in Glebe and don't want to eat out all the time, visit *Russells*, a huge health-food store on the corner of Cowper St, for supplies. There are no large supermarkets in the area, but there are several small ones and also a few groceries.

At the south end, not far from the intersection with Broadway, *Rose Blues* has focaccia for $7.50, pasta from $10 and other main courses for around $14. Another long-running cafe, popular with locals and visitors

alike, is *Badde Manors* on the corner of Francis St. It's casual (sometimes hectically so) and there's almost a hint of incense in the air. Focaccia is $5.50, pasta and other meals cost about $7.50, with salads from $4. There are some great cakes and desserts. Weekend breakfasts are popular here.

Across Francis St, *Yak & Yeti* is a Nepalese place with vegetable dishes for around $6.50 and others from $11 to $14. For Russian food, *Rasputin* is open for dinner and has main courses from $9.20 to $13.50, with specials from $9. Further along is *Caffe Troppo*, brightly-decorated and with a huge (and fairly pricey) menu – bruschettae are $8, burgers go for $11 to $15. For tapas at about $4.50, try *Different Drummer* near the corner of St John Rd.

Thai Intra is a fairly large, licensed Thai restaurant in a well-decorated old house at 209 Glebe Point Rd. The MSG-free food is good and the prices are lower than the decor would suggest, with most main courses under $11, except for seafood. Other Thai Intras are at Bondi and Taylor Square.

Despite Glebe's 'students and bohemians' tag, many eateries are edging into higher price-brackets, so it's good to see that the *Craven* remains an inexpensive place for a relaxed coffee, snack or meal. The food is pretty good, too. It's open daily until 10.30 pm, except on Sunday and Monday when it closes at 6.30 pm. As well as cafe fare, lunch is served from noon to 2.30 pm and dinner from 6 to 10 pm. Good salads cost about $6.50 and other dishes are under $8. You can have bacon & eggs for breakfast from $5.

Several Vietnamese/Chinese places offer excellent value. *Lien* near the corner of Wigram Rd has vegetable dishes for $6, beef and chicken for $7 and seafood for $9.50. The nearby *Lilac* has main courses between $7.50 and $12.50, and there's another *Lilac* in the next block, a much cheaper cafe-style place.

Probably the least expensive pizzas are available from *Perry's Pizza & Ribs*, along from the Lilac cafe, but locals recommend paying a little more at *Bogarts Pizza*, between Bridge Rd and St Johns Rd.

Top: Sydney Harbour Bridge at sunset (PS)
Bottom Left: Sydney Town Hall (MF)
Bottom Right: Sydney Opera House (PS)

Top: Settlers' Arms Inn, St Albans, near Sydney (JM)
Bottom Left: Masonic Lodge, Maitland, Hunter Valley (JM)
Bottom Right: Roxy Cinema, Parramatta, near Sydney (JM)

There are many places along Glebe Point Rd where counting calories would spoil all the fun. Most of the cafes have a great selection of cakes and desserts, and *Le Chocoreve* near the corner of Bridge Rd has a window display that borders on the indecent. The nearby *Pudding Shop* is another source of the sweet and sticky.

Balmain

Balmain has some good eating places and, because much of their trade is local, the service is usually friendly and the standards consistent. There's a lot of choice, mostly along Darling St; the following is just a sample.

The French *L'Ironique* at 246 Darling St is open for dinner nightly except Sunday and has a $22 set menu except on Friday and Saturday. *La Lupa* at No 332 is an Italian place with pastas for around $10 and other main courses around $14. *Ji Yu No Omise* at 342 Darling St has Japanese food with main courses around $15. The restaurant at the *Cat & Fiddle Hotel* at No 456 has a large menu with lots of seafood and prices around $14 for main courses. Down towards the Darling St ferry wharf at No 81, *Pelicans Fine Foods* is open for snacks and soups during the day, plus breakfast.

Newtown

Newtown's long King St has a huge range of eateries, many budget-priced. None are cheaper than the *Hare Krishna* place near the railway station. There's an African cafe, *Le Kilimanjaro* at No 280, and plenty of other ethnic cuisines: Chinese, Middle Eastern, Vietnamese, Indian, Italian...

A popular place to meet and eat is the *Green Iguana Cafe* at the east end of King St near the intersection with Darlington Rd. Breakfast costs $6, main-course pasta is $7.50 and there are various snacks available. The noticeboard outside gives a good cross-section of Newtown activities. On the other side of King St a bit further west is *Hard Nox Cafe*, a reasonably priced vegetarian and seafood place.

There's also *Goodfellas* at 111 King St,

between Missenden Rd and tiny Elizabeth St, which was judged Sydney's best new restaurant in 1993. The food is modern Australian, main courses cost from $15 and it's open for dinner daily.

Crows Nest

Crows Nest, the next suburb north-west from North Sydney, has many popular eating places. Most are clustered around the three-way intersection of the Pacific Highway, Falcon St and Willoughby Rd. If you're shopping for food there's a *Woolworths* supermarket near the intersection on Falcon St and just around the corner on Willoughby Rd there's a much more expensive but very tempting *gourmet supermarket*.

Some places to try include *Bombay Heritage* at 82 Willoughby Rd, with main courses under $13; the crowded *Ten-Sun* at 103 Willoughby Rd, with fast-service Japanese noodles and set meals for $10; *Blue Elephant* at 471 Pacific Highway, with Sri Lankan food under $10; *Eric's Fish Cafe* at 316 Pacific Highway, with main courses under $15; and *Prasit's Northside Thai* in the Union Hotel at 271 Pacific Highway, with main courses around $15. A few blocks further along the Pacific Highway in St Leonards there are a few more places, including the good *Pinocchio's* Chinese restaurant at No 22, with a big menu and main courses around $12.

If you're seriously into pizza, you'll want to visit *The Red Centre* (☎ 906 4408) at 70 Alexander St, where the dish is elevated to an art form. They even have pizza desserts. Main course pizzas cost $12.50 and up.

Bondi Beach

Campbell Pde is one long string of eating places. Right at the south end of Campbell Pde, down from Thelellen Beach Inn, *Taks* is a tiny Thai place selling inexpensive food to eat there or take away. Most dishes cost $7.50 or less. Further north, *Shelley's Cafe* is just south of the corner of Sir Thomas Mitchell Rd and is a bright modern place with $6 breakfast specials. Also modern but in the stark vein is *Dog's Diner*, further north near the corner of Lamrock Ave. You'll pay more for your breakfast here, but it's a good place to show off your shades.

Ya Habibi has Middle Eastern food with felafels and kebabs around $4 and main courses ranging between $6 and $16.

There's more good-value Middle Eastern food at the *Avivim* cafe on Hall St near the corner of Consett Ave. It's BYO, but your wine must be kosher! Luckily there's a deli selling kosher wine a block or so up Hall St. Further up Hall St, O'Brien St branches off and near the corner is the *Russian Lodge* (☎ 365 1997), which has a menu of Russian dishes. Entrees cost between $5 and $8 and main courses from $12 to $16. It's open for dinner from Thursday to Sunday, with live music from Friday to Sunday.

Back down Hall St near the corner of Jacques Ave, *Gusto* is a popular little deli with streetfront seating where you can eat healthy snacks at fairly low prices.

Back on Campbell Pde, *Il Puntino* is a simple Italian restaurant where most main courses are under $12 and there are sometimes good specials, such as main-course pasta for $5.50. Further north, just before the corner of Beach Rd, *Le Chocoreve* has sinfully delicious cakes and confectionery, plus sugar-free soups and snacks. Next door is the dreadfully named *Hog's Breath Cafe*, part of a small chain selling reasonably priced food and drink.

Bondi

At 87 Bondi Rd, near the corner of Bennet St and about one km west of the beach, *Rasoi* is a popular Indian restaurant. Dosas cost from $4, vegetarian dishes from $7.20 and other main courses from $10.50. On the same block a little further east is *Shree Punjab* with $6 lunch specials. Further down the hill at 175 Bondi Rd, *Kawanna* is a fairly basic Indonesian place where most dishes are under $7.50.

Bondi Junction

If you're feeling hungry while swapping between train and bus at Bondi Junction,

head west on Oxford St (which is a mall near the railway station) to No 288, near the corner of Denison St. Here you'll find *Sennin*, a long-running vegetarian restaurant with interesting snacks and meals and prices starting under $6. If Sennin's low prices are too much for you, head east on Oxford St to No 570, where *Mekong* has ridiculously cheap meals, such as two dishes plus rice for less than $5.

Also on Oxford St, just past the eastern end of the mall, *Billy the Pig's* (more sedately known as the Bondi Junction Hotel) has specials such as pasta and a drink for $5.

Coogee

There are plenty of places to eat along Arden St and Coogee Bay Rd. The *Congo Cafe* on Arden St north of Coogee Bay Rd is popular, colourful and inexpensive. Nearby, *La Casa* is more basic but even cheaper, with $5 pasta meals. At the north end of the beach on Dolphin St, there's a food hall in the big Coogee Palace complex, as well as other restaurants and cafes nearby, such as *Venice Beach* which has breakfast specials. The *Fishermans Net* (☎ 665 5549) on the first floor of the Coogee Sands Motor Inn on Dolphin St sometimes has an offer of two courses for $20.

Renato's at 237 Coogee Bay Rd is a busy Italian restaurant, good value with main courses under $14. Nearby at No 240, *Erciyes 2* is an offshoot of the popular Erciyes Turkish pide-and-kebab house in Surry Hills. The food is tasty and inexpensive, with nothing over $8.

Manly

The Corso is jammed with places to eat and there are others along North and South Steyne. You don't have to go any further than the Wharf to find eateries, including *Armstrong's* – see the earlier Meals with a View section.

For an inexpensive Thai meal to eat in or take away, try the tiny *Pan Tip Thai* on South Steyne, near the corner of Wentworth St. It's open daily from 9 am to 10 pm. From 6 to 9 pm there's a minimum charge of $15, which would be difficult to achieve as most dishes are under $6. Simple but good food with large servings.

There are several other Thai places, including *Wi Marn* on North Steyne which has seafood dishes from $14 and vegetarian dishes between $4 and $9. They don't use MSG. *Malacca Straits Satay Restaurant* on the corner of Sydney Rd and Whistler St has a good reputation and features reasonably priced Malay and Thai dishes. Main courses go from around $8 to $12.

Cafe Steyne on South Steyne has everything from daiquiris to melts (toasted sangers), and its outdoor tables are popular. About average on the large menu is pasta for $8.

On North Steyne, *Luis* is a licensed Italian place with excellent pizzas from a wood-fired oven and other Italian dishes such as osso bucco ($13). Next door are a couple of seafood specialists, *Alexanders* and *Fishmongers*, both with main courses in the $15 region.

At 27 Belgrave St, *Cafe Tunis* has good coffee and interesting food, and is open most days and nights. Pasta costs from $8.50 and main courses are between $8 and $14.

Following the foreshore path east from the main ocean beach, you come to the *Bower Restaurant* (still called Faulty Bowers on some brochures). It's a small place pleasantly situated on pretty Fairy Bower Bay, with linen on the outdoor tables and snacks, coffee and main courses of modern Australian food for around $10 for an entree and from $15 for main courses. It's BYO and is open for lunch daily, and for breakfast as well on weekends. Further around at Shelly Beach are two upmarket places, *Le Kiosk* (with a chef who has cooked on Onassis yachts) and *La Rampa* which has Italian food.

There are a couple of seafood buffets, at the *Manly Pacific Parkroyal* on North Steyne, where a buffet lunch from Wednesday to Sunday costs $29.50; and at the *Radisson Kestrel* on South Steyne, where the Monday to Saturday buffet lunch is $17.50.

Other Suburbs

There are good places to eat all over Sydney. On the north shore you'll find *Watermark*, *Bathers Pavilion* and *Beaches* at Balmoral, and there's a long string of eateries on Military Rd in Cremorne and Mosman. Leichardt is gaining a reputation for interesting eateries, and you'll find a string of good Italian places, some inexpensive, along Norton St.

ENTERTAINMENT

The *Sydney Morning Herald*'s 'Metro' section is published on Friday and lists most events in town for the week. For more specialised music listings, pick up one of the free weekly papers such as *Drum Media* and *3D World*. The Metro lists galleries and art exhibitions, but for more detailed information look for the monthly *Art Almanac* ($2) at galleries and some newsagents.

Halftix sells half-price (or thereabouts) last-minute seats to various performances and events from a booth on Martin Place near Elizabeth St. You have to buy a ticket to a show that night and they don't post lists of which shows are available until noon, so it's a little hit-and-miss – but that's why the tickets are cheap. The booth is also a Ticketek (☎ 266 4800) agency, so if you miss out on cheap seats you can always buy full-price ones. Halftix is open from noon to 5.30 pm on weekdays and from noon to 5 pm on Saturday. The Ticketek side of the business is open from 9 am to 5 pm on weekdays and from noon to 4 pm on Saturday.

Try to see something at the Opera House – they have films, ballet, theatre, classical music, opera and even rock concerts.

A lot of evening entertainment takes place in Leagues Clubs, where the profits from the assembled ranks of poker machines – 'pokies' – enable the clubs to put on big-name acts at low prices. They may be 'members only' for locals, but as an interstate or (even better) international visitor you're generally welcome. Simply ring ahead and ask, then wave your interstate driving licence or passport at the door. Acts vary from Max Bygraves to good Australian rock, but whatever the show you'll see a good cross-section of Sydneysiders. The most lavish is the St George Leagues Club on the Princes Highway, Kogarah. More centrally there's the City of Sydney RSL Club on George St or the South Sydney Leagues Club at 263 Chalmers St, Redfern.

Music & Dancing

Sydney doesn't have the same pub music scene as Melbourne, but there are plenty of clubs and you can count on something most nights of the week. Five-star hotels often have big-name cabaret artists and sometimes more adventurous acts at prices that aren't outrageous if you watch what you drink.

A few of the many, many venues are:

The Basement, 29 Reiby Place, Circular Quay – good jazz, sometimes big international names

Bat & Ball, corner of Cleveland and South Dowling Rds, Surry Hills – pub with young bands

Cat & Fiddle Hotel, corner of Darling and Elliott Sts, Balmain – pub rock usually Friday to Sunday nights

Cauldron, 207 Darlinghurst Rd, Darlinghurst – popular dance club

Cock'n'Bull Tavern, corner Bronte & Ebley Sts, Bondi Junction – bands (often free) or disco most nights

DCM, 33 Oxford St, Darlinghurst – Don't Cry Mamma is a big gay disco

Golden Sheaf Hotel, 429 New South Head Rd, Double Bay – pub with free bands several nights. Good food, popular with travellers

Goodbar, 11 Oxford St, Paddington – popular dance club

Harbourside Brasserie, Pier One – a variety of fairly big acts, often jazz or comedy

Joe's Garage, Macleay St, Kings Cross – party atmosphere nightly, popular with backpackers for its happy hours, inexpensive food (at lunchtime) and entertainment such as horizontal bungee-jumping

Kings Cross Hotel, junction of Victoria St, Darlinghurst Rd and William St – open 24 hours, and with plenty of pokies. Several travellers have reported that this is, surprisingly, a reasonable place for a night out

Kinselas, 383 Bourke St, Darlinghurst – a renovated funeral parlour, now a large venue with various levels and interesting acts. Sometimes free (ground floor) up to $20 (top floor), depending on who's playing. Always worth checking out

Lansdowne Hotel, corner of Broadway and City Rd, Chippendale – lively young bands nightly except on Tuesday

On Sight, 171 Victoria St, Kings Cross – dance club, various theme nights, from $5

Powercuts, 150 Elizabeth St (south of Liverpool St), city – reggae and Afro club on Friday and Saturday from 10 pm

Rose, Shamrock & Thistle Hotel ('the three weeds'), 139 Evans St, Rozelle – the gentler end of the rock spectrum (sometimes big names), plus jazz, folk etc

Royal Hotel, Bondi Rd at Bondi Beach – bands, free

Sandringham Hotel, King St, Newtown – young bands

Selina's (in the Coogee Bay Hotel), Coogee Bay Rd, Coogee – rock, often top Australian bands for which you can pay $20 or more. Main nights Friday and Saturday, but sometimes cheaper bands other nights

Strawberry Hills Hotel, 451 Elizabeth St (corner Devonshire St), Surry Hills – something interesting most nights, often jazz

Studebakers, 33 Bayswater Rd, Kings Cross – club with '50s and '60s theme

Tom Tom Cafe, 22 Bayswater Rd, Kings Cross – bands and/or DJs Tuesday to Sunday until 7 am, busy and lively. Big-name bands sometimes play here semi-incognito. From $6 to $8; backpackers might get in for half-price midweek

Performance

The major commercial theatres are Her Majesty's (☎ 212 3411) at 107 Quay St near Railway Square and the Theatre Royal (☎ 202 2200) in the MLC Centre on King St. The opulent State Theatre (☎ 264 2431) at 49 Market St is usually the venue for big-budget productions.

The top mainstream company is the Sydney Theatre Company, which has its own theatre at Pier Four on Hickson Rd, across from the Rocks. The similarly prestigious Sydney Dance Company is also here. At NIDA (National Institute of Dramatic Art), 215 Anzac Parade, Kensington, student shows are staged regularly. The Seymour Centre at the corner of Cleveland St and City Rd, Chippendale (near Sydney University), has varied and interesting productions. The Footbridge Theatre at Sydney Uni is also worth keeping an eye on.

The Pod Theatre on Campbell St in Surry Hills, back from Taylor Square, is mainly a gallery but also has interesting events from time to time. There are many experimental and off-beat places, including the Bay St

Theatre at 75 Bay St in Glebe, the Belvoir Street Theatre at 25 Belvoir St in Surry Hills, and the Rep Theatre at 1 Brown Lane in Newtown.

The small Ensemble Theatre (☎ 929 0644) at 78 McDougall St in Milsons Point presents mainstream theatre in a great setting on the waterfront at Careening Cove, a few blocks from Milsons Point station. There's also a restaurant here (☎ 956 8250) with pre-show, three-course, set-price meals at $30.

The Comedy Store (☎ 564 3900) on the corner of Crystal St and Parramatta Rd in Leichardt is open from Tuesday to Saturday. Tuesday, when new comics try out, is the cheapest night.

Pubs & Bars

Many pubs have a totally different atmosphere during the week than they do on weekends when the hordes are out on the town.

One of the nicest places for a quiet Guinness on a weeknight is the Molly Bloom's Bar at the Mercantile Hotel on George St in the Rocks – appropriately but coincidentally, the outside is tiled in green. There is often good Irish music here.

Kitty O'Shea's in Paddington at 384 Oxford St is popular with Irish visitors and residents alike and also has good music.

In the Opera House, the Mozart Bar near the box office is open before and after performances – it's intended for patrons, so you might stand out without evening wear.

The Craig at Darling Harbour has $1 schooners on Thursday until 10.30 pm. It's very popular with backpackers. There is often entertainment here, usually of the 'show' variety (fake Elvises, fake Madonnas etc).

Over in Glebe, the Friend in Hand at 58 Cowper St has earned a reputation as a party pub amongst backpackers. There are events such as crab-racing, music on weekends and generous and frequent discounts on drinks and food. Glebe's other popular pub, the Harold Park Hotel at 115 Wigram Rd, also has a packed entertainment programme but

one more in keeping with the suburb's arty image. Instead of the standard pub 'Pool Comp with Ca$h Prizes', the Harold Park has a chess competition (currently Thursday night) – with ca$h prizes! The Writers at the Park programme presents some well-known writers reading their work (currently on Tuesday nights); on other nights there are comedy acts and on weekends there are bands.

On the other side of town, the Cricketers Arms at 106 Fitzroy St in Surry Hills is also popular with backpackers. Kings Cross also has plenty of watering holes. Backpackers congregate in the Soho Bar at the Piccadilly Hotel at 171 Victoria St. More expensive places include Deans and Cafe Iguana on Kellet St.

The Old Fitzroy at the corner of Cathedral and Dowling Sts in Woolloomooloo has poetry some nights and also has a cafe. The Tilbury Hotel (☎ 357 1914, bookings are usually essential) in Woolloomooloo at the corner of Forbes and Nicholson Sts often has high-class cabaret. The Woolloomooloo Bay Hotel at 2 Bourke St is popular at lunchtime on weekends.

The Albury Hotel at 6 Oxford St in Paddington is a gay pub which often has good entertainment. The Lizard Lounge at the Exchange Hotel at 34 Oxford St in Darlinghurst is popular with lesbians. Other good places on Oxford St include the Burdekin at No 2. Not far away is Q, a cavernous bar and pool hall, above Central Station Records at 46 Oxford St. In Woollahra, the Lord Dudley Hotel on Jersey St is as close as Sydney gets to an English pub atmosphere.

Someplace Else, in the city on Bligh St, beneath the Sheraton Wentworth, is a more upmarket bar with eating places and live entertainment. Over on the north shore, The Oaks on Military Rd in Neutral Bay packs out at lunchtimes.

Cinema

Mainstream shows cost a ridiculous $11 or so; some major city cinemas are cheaper on Tuesdays, except during school holidays. There is a cluster of cinema complexes on

George St between Bathurst and Liverpool Sts. The Ritz (☎ 399 9840) at 43 St Pauls St in Randwick (not far from Coogee) shows mainstream movies and charges just $7, every day.

For more unusual fare, try independent cinemas such as the Dendy at 624 George St and under the MLC Centre on Martin Place, the Mandolin at 150 Elizabeth St, the Academy Twin on the corner of Oxford and South Dowling Sts in Paddington, the Valhalla Cinema at 166 Glebe Point Rd in Glebe, and the Encore Cinema at 64 Devonshire St in Surry Hills. The Australian Film Institute screens interesting new work and classics at the AFI Cinema in the Paddington Town Hall on the corner of Oxford St and Oatley Rd.

In Darlinghurst, the Movie Room is above Govinda's, the Hare Krishna restaurant at 112 Darlinghurst Rd. It shows a wide range of good movies: mainstream blockbusters, some of the more accessible arthouse fare and some old favourites. There's a slight catch to seeing movies here – or an incredibly good deal, depending on whether you like Hare Krishna food. Admission costs $12.50, but with that you get an all-you-can-eat smorgasbord at Govinda's. There are two screenings every night, the first at about 7 pm. Govinda's is open from 6 pm. Phone (☎ 380 5162) to see what's showing or to get a monthly programme.

A sight in itself is the State Movie Theatre on Market St between Pitt and George Sts – they don't make them like this any more! It's now used for live shows, except during the Sydney Film Festival in June.

Cinema complexes on the north shore include the Greater Union (☎ 969 1988) at 9 Spit Rd in Mosman and the Manly Twin (☎ 977 0644) at 43 East Esplanade. The Walker (☎ 959 4222) at 121 Walker St in North Sydney shows non-mainstream films. The Hayden (☎ 908 4344) on Military Rd in Cremorne is an Art Deco masterpiece.

Gambling

By far the most common form of gambling is on the pokies (poker machines). They're everywhere.

Sydney's horse-racing venues are Randwick (closest to the city, near Centennial Park), Canterbury (south-west of the city centre), Rose Hill (near Parramatta) and Warwick Farm (near Liverpool). The major events are run during the spring and autumn carnivals.

A bit further down the social scale are trotting (harness-racing) meetings at Harold Park and greyhound racing at Wentworth Park, both in Glebe.

Free Entertainment

On summer weekends there is free music in parks. There's music at lunchtime in Martin Place and at Darling Harbour, and the State Conservatorium of Music on Macquarie St has free lunchtime concerts on Wednesday and Friday during term.

Spectator Sports

Sydneysiders don't place the same emphasis on spectator sports as do Melburnians – there's just too much else to do in this city. Even so, you'll find vocal crowds and world-class athletes in action on just about every weekend of the year.

Football Sydney is the world capital of rugby league (as opposed to the more gentlemanly – and more widely-played – rugby union). The main competition is the Winfield Cup, which now includes interstate sides and will become international with the inclusion of an Auckland side. Winfield Cup games are played at various grounds, with the sell-out finals played at the football stadium in Moore Park in September.

The other big rugby league series is the State of Origin matches against Queensland, which generate a lot of passion ('Origin of the Species' was the slogan of one series, which was just a wee bit nasty, given the Neanderthal image of some league stars). These games are sometimes played in Brisbane, sometimes in Sydney.

Rugby union has a less fanatical competition but the Australian rugby union team, the Wallabies, are world-beaters and you can sometimes see them in action against international teams.

Aussie Rules football, partly based on Gaelic football but tougher and faster than just about any other game, wasn't traditionally played in NSW until the Victorian league decided to go national. A struggling Melbourne club was transplanted to Sydney and renamed the Sydney Swans. The poor old Swans haven't exactly set the world on fire but it might be interesting to see a match, played at the Sydney Cricket Ground. You won't have any trouble getting a seat.

Cricket In summer the Sydney Cricket Ground in Moore Park is the venue for sparsely-attended Sheffield Shield matches, well-attended test matches and sell-out World Series Cup (day/night) matches.

Tennis Major matches are held at White City (in Rushcutters Bay) or indoors at the Entertainment Centre (near Darling Harbour).

Yachting On weekends there are an awful lot of yachts weaving around the ferries and ships on Sydney Harbour. Many of them are racing and the most spectacular are the speedy 18-footers. These honed-down skiffs carry a huge sail area for their size, and their crews have to be extremely agile, using platforms and trapezes to control them.

The 18-footer races carry big prize-money and the boats are covered with sponsors' logos, like racing cars. On race days a special spectator ferry follows the action and you can even make a bet on board. The ferry leaves from Commodores Steps on the western side of Circular Quay at 2.15 pm and costs $9 ($5 children). The 18-footer racing season runs from mid-September to late March. The oldest and largest 18-footer club is the Sydney Flying Squadron (☎ 955 8350) near Milson Park and on Careening Cove on the north side of Kirribilli Point. There's a restaurant here which is open to visitors.

The great yachting event on Sydney Harbour is the Boxing Day (26 December) start of the classic Sydney to Hobart race. The harbour is crammed with competitors, media boats and a huge spectator fleet, all getting in each other's way as the yachts tack up the harbour in the race to the heads and the open ocean.

Basketball Australia now has a basketball league with all the razzmatazz of American pro basketball (and quite a few American players), thanks largely to TV coverage of the games. The Sydney sides are the Kings (men) and the Flames (women).

Netball, a version of basketball, is Australia's number-one sport in terms of participation rates. Netball is played almost exclusively by women and attracts zero media attention. Hmm.

THINGS TO BUY

Shopping complexes in the city include the Royal, Strand and Imperial arcades, Centrepoint and the impressive Queen Victoria Building. David Jones and Grace Brothers are city-centre department stores. The Rocks and the Harbourside Festival Marketplace at Darling Harbour teem with shops which are open daily (the shop at the Powerhouse Museum in Darling Harbour has some intriguing gadgets and souvenirs). Oxford St tends to galleries and bookshops in Paddington, and to the bizarre in Surry Hills. Then there are all the large suburban shopping complexes.

The old Foys building on Elizabeth St at the corner of Liverpool St, once a grand department store, is to be renovated as a shopping complex similar to the Queen Victoria Building, although this plan has been on the drawing-board for some time. The store's impressive facade gave rise to a Sydney expression which describes a brash person as having 'more front than Foys'.

On the corner of Oxford and Crown Sts, the Remo General Store is a modest but expanding attempt at getting some interesting things to buy under the one roof. The store is open from 10 am but the cafe opens at 8.45 am.

In Redfern, clustered around the corner of Regent and Redfern Sts, are many factory outlets, seconds shops and the like. They sell mainly clothing, but other bargains are also available. If you're serious about bargain-hunting, buy yourself a copy of *The Bargain Shoppers Guide*, about $8.

The biggest shopping centre in North Sydney is Greenwood Plaza, above North Sydney railway station.

Military Rd on the north shore is one long string of shops.

Aboriginal Art

There are several Aboriginal Art Centres, including 117 George St in the Rocks and a large showroom at 7 Walker Lane, opposite 7A Liverpool St, in Paddington. They have a lot of bark paintings and, as usual, these are attractive but costly. The Aboriginal Artists Gallery in Civic House, 477 Kent St (behind the Town Hall), has a large range of traditional and contemporary Aboriginal and Islander work. Quality is high, prices competitive.

New Guinea Primitive Arts, on the 6th floor at 428 George St, and also on Level 2 of the Queen Victoria Building, has a big range of artefacts from PNG and some Aboriginal work.

Bennelong Boomerangs, at 29-31 Playfair St in the Rocks, is owned by a guy who's been the Australian boomerang-throwing champion a few times, so he can tell you it isn't as easy as it looks. Another champion is at 14 Blues Point Rd in McMahons Point.

Australiana

Arts & crafts, T-shirts, souvenirs, designer clothing, bush gear and the like are sold practically everywhere. Much of this stuff is high quality, with prices to match, though you can pick up the odd bargain. Check out the huge range sold in the Rocks and Darling Harbour to see what's available, then compare prices in other areas.

For bush gear, try Morrisons at 105 George St in the Rocks, Goodwood Saddlery at 237-9 Broadway, or Thomas Cook at 790 George St.

The Wilderness Shop at 92 Liverpool St has high quality posters and books on wilderness issues, as well as great T-shirts and other good souvenirs. It's open all week. At the Gardens Shop in the Royal Botanic Gardens Visitors' Centre there are souvenirs, posters and books with an Australian plant theme.

In the Strand Arcade, just off the Pitt St Mall, several leading fashion designers and craftspeople have shops.

The Australian Wine Centre in Goldfields House behind Circular Quay at 1 Alfred St is open daily and stocks wines from every Australian winegrowing region. There are sometimes tastings, especially on Friday or Saturday.

On Oxford St across from Victoria Barracks, the Coo-ee Australian Emporium sells souvenirs of better quality than what you'll find at many other places.

Aussie Clothing A must-buy item is an Akubra hat. These are sold everywhere tourists gather, but if you want good advice and the right size try the Strand Hatters (☎ 231 6884) at 8 Strand Arcade on the Pitt St Mall. This excellent shop also sells many other types of hat (none very cheap) and the staff are friendly and knowledgeable.

Thomas Cook (no, not the travellers' cheque people) is a long-established manufacturer of Aussie outdoor gear. There is a Thomas Cook shop at 790 George St, on the corner of Rawson Place.

If you're planning to visit Tamworth's Country Music Festival you might want to stock up with full-on C&W wear, available at the Pandarra Trading Company, at 96 Oxford St in Darlinghurst.

Opals Many Sydney jewellers and duty-free shops sell opals. See as many stones as you can before making a purchase. If you're planning to visit Lightning Ridge or White Cliffs, two of the state's opal-mining towns, have a look at prices and standards in Sydney before you go, to get an idea of value. You'll find plenty of opals in the Rocks.

Outdoor Gear

Outdoor suppliers are all over the city, but there's a good selection of shops on Kent St near Bathurst St, not far from the YHA Travel Centre. If you're staying in Bondi, there's an outdoor shop on Oxford St in Bondi Junction, east of the mall and near the Mekong restaurant.

It's also worth checking out 'disposals' stores (they handle ex-army gear among many other things) for rugged clothing and less hi-tech gear which is a hell of a lot cheaper than the specialist stuff. One of Sydney's many disposals stores is Kings Disposals on the corner of George St and Quay St near Railway Square.

Galleries & Antiques

Paddington and Woollahra have some 30 art galleries, most featuring Australian art and artists. Sydney Antique Centre is an agglomeration of 60 shops at 531 South Dowling St, Surry Hills, open daily. Woollahra Antiques Centre at 160 Oxford St, across from Centennial Park, has 50 shops.

Crafts Metcalfe Arcade at 80-84 George St houses the Society of Arts & Crafts and has a gallery and sales, and there's Australian Craftworks at 127 George St in the old police station.

Duty-Free

Duty-free shops abound in the Rocks and the city centre. Remember that a duty-free item might not have had much duty on it in the first place and could be available cheaper in an ordinary store.

Music

Big stores selling recorded music include HMV and Virgin, both on Pitt St Mall, Virgin at Darling Harbour and Brashs at 244 Pitt St. There are many specialist shops – see the *Yellow Pages* under Records, CDs & Tapes.

If you have a penchant for guitars and stringed instruments, wander into the Guitar Centre (☎ 380 5104) at 30 Oxford St, just east of South Dowling St. Rick Falkiner has some very fine instruments in stock and can often hunt up oddities and specialities.

Markets

Sydney has lots of weekend flea-markets. The most interesting is Paddo Village Bazaar, held in the grounds of the church on the corner of Oxford and Newcombe Sts on Saturday. It's quite a scene. Balmain's Saturday market is also good; it's in the church on Darling St, opposite Gladstone Park. Glebe's weekend markets are held in the school at the corner of Glebe Point Rd and Derby Place. On weekends the top end of George St in the Rocks is closed for a market and there's a Sunday craft market outside the Opera House.

Paddy's Markets, an institution which was banished to the suburbs for a few years, has returned to Haymarket, at the corner of Hay and Thomas St, and is open on weekends. The Paddy's on Parramatta Rd in Flemington still operates (along with the Flemington fruit and vegetable market) on Friday and Sunday.

GETTING THERE & AWAY
Air

Sydney's Kingsford Smith Airport is the busiest in Australia. It's fairly central, which makes getting to or from it easy, but it also means that jet flights have to stop at 11 pm due to noise regulations. Although a third runway is under construction, delayed flights will continue to be a feature of travel to/from Sydney.

Sydney Harbour Seaplanes (☎ 918 7472, 1800 803 558 toll-free) flies between Rose Bay and Newcastle Harbour five days a week for $95. They also have joy flights.

See the Getting There & Away chapter and the various towns throughout this book for more information on flying to and from Sydney.

Train

All interstate and principal regional services operate to and from Central Station. Call the Central Reservation Centre (☎ 217 8812, 13 2232 outside Sydney) or contact a Countrylink Travel Centre. There's one at Circular Quay (☎ 241 3887), near Wynyard Station at 11-31 York St (☎ 224 2742), and another in

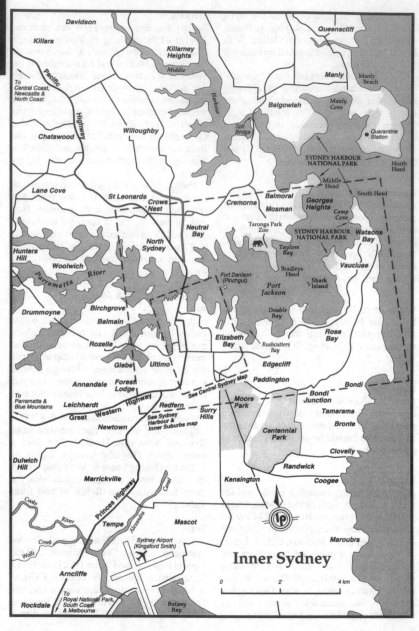

Inner Sydney

0   2   4 km

the Queen Victoria Building Arcade near Town Hall Station (☎ 267 1521). Countrylink Travel Centres are fully-fledged travel agencies and keep pretty much to business hours, but you can buy a train ticket at the Sydney Booking Office at Central Station every day from 6 am to 9.35 pm.

You can also make phone bookings (☎ 217 8812) between 6.30 am and 10 pm and collect your tickets from a Countrylink Travel Centre or a railway station.

For information on timetables and fares there's a recorded-message service (☎ 0055 20202) but this costs 50c per minute. If this seems exorbitant, call a Travel Centre for just 30c.

See the Getting Around chapter for routes and sample fares.

Bus

The Sydney Coach Terminal (☎ 281 9366) is on Eddy Ave near Pitt St, outside Central Station. A few companies maintain their own depots, notably Greyhound Pioneer Australia which is at the corner of Oxford and Riley Sts. McCafferty's has a depot near Kings Cross at 179 Darlinghurst Rd, but they also pick up on Eddy Ave. Many lines stop in suburbs on the way into or out of the city, and some have feeder services from the suburbs.

See the Getting There & Away chapter for some routes and fares.

Eddy Ave's long colonnade is one of the few places in central Sydney where you can be pretty sure that you'll be hassled for small change, and at night it is a bit creepy – but there are always other travellers around.

Car & Motorbike

Main Routes The main road routes out of Sydney are: the freeway running north to Newcastle, becoming the Pacific Highway (cross the Harbour Bridge and follow the Pacific Highway to the start of the freeway in Hornsby); the Western Motorway running west to Penrith and the Blue Mountains, becoming the Great Western Highway to Bathurst and beyond (follow Parramatta Rd west to Strathfield); the Hume Highway

running south-west to Goulburn and on to Melbourne (follow Parramatta Rd west to Ashfield); and the Princes Highway running south to Wollongong and the south coast (follow South Dowling St south from Surry Hills).

Car Rental – New Cars The major companies, Avis (☎ 902 9292), Budget (☎ 13 2727) and Hertz (☎ 13 1918), have offices at the airport and around the city.

Thrifty is a smaller national company offering good deals, with agents in all capital cities and many larger towns. They are especially good on limited-km rates – 50 to 100 km free – from about $40 per day including insurance. You lose your insurance cover if you take these cars onto unsealed roads. There are Thrifty offices at the airport (☎ 669 6677) and in the city at 75 William St (☎ 380 5399)

The *Yellow Pages* is crammed with other outfits, many offering deals which appear much better than those offered by the major companies, but at least one of the second-string companies has misleading ads, so read the small print carefully.

Car Rental – Old Cars There are plenty of places renting older cars which range from reasonable transport to frustrating old bombs, although there are no great bargains. Check for things like bald tyres and bad brakes *before* you sign anything – some of these outfits have all the compassion of used-car salespeople (which some of them are). Also check the fine print regarding insurance excess – the amount you pay before the insurance takes over. It can be pretty bloody high. The following list is a fairly random sample; hostel noticeboards are good places to find others.

Bayswater Car Rental (☎ 360 3622) at 120 Darlinghurst Rd, just south of William St, rents new and recent-model cars for pretty good prices, but be very sure that you know all the charges before signing anything.

Pricerite Auto Rentals is at 86B Mount St in Coogee (☎ 665 7745) and 38-40 Anzac Pde in Kensington (☎ 662 7757) and charges from $35 a day including insurance for the metropolitan area, but not including free km. Rates reduce with hires of three days or more. They will rent to anyone over 21 but you need good ID.

Kings Cross Rent-a-Car (☎ 361 0637) at 169 William St in the Cross charges from $35 a day (less for six or more days) with free km in the Sydney metropolitan area. However, they also charge $12 a day for insurance. You need to have held your licence for more than a year, and they prefer you to be over 25.

Rent-a-Ruffy (☎ 977 5777) at 48 Pittwater Rd in Manly, which charges from $40 for 24 hours including 100 free km or from $50 a day if you want to go more than 150 km from Sydney.

Travel Agents

Let's Travel Australia (☎ 358 2295) at 165 Victoria St in Kings Cross is a backpacker-oriented travel agency, which means that they have dealt with just about every possible permutation and combination of the travel jigsaw. They can help with tricky details such as car insurance. Eden Travel (☎ 368 1271) at 2 Springfield Ave in Kings Cross also sees a lot of backpackers, as does nearby Travel Active (☎ 357 4477) at 3 Orwell St and Travel Oz (☎ 368 1282) at 4 Llankelly Place.

The head office of STA Travel (not STA as in State Transit Authority) is at 732 Harris St in Ultimo, near the corner of Broadway (☎ 212 1255), and there are offices around the city.

The Airport Express

GETTING AROUND

The State Transit Authority (STA) controls almost all public transport. For information on STA buses, ferries and trains, phone 13 1500 between 6 am and 10 pm daily. You'll also find bus and ferry information in the front of the A-K volume of the *White Pages* phone book. Children (under 16) pay half price on STA services.

To/From the Airport

The international and domestic terminals at Sydney Airport are across the runway from each other, and about a five-km bus trip apart ($2.50 with STA).

The Airport Express is a special STA service to/from the airport via Central Station, with No 300 going on to Circular Quay and No 350 going on to Kings Cross. Airport Express buses have their own stops and are painted green and yellow. The one-way fare is $5 and a return ticket, valid for two months, is $8. The trip from the airport to Central Railway Station takes about 15 minutes, while to Circular Quay or Kings Cross takes 30 minutes.

Airport Express buses depart from Circular Quay and Kings Cross every 20 minutes, but both stop on Eddy Ave at Central Station (across the road from the colonnade), so a bus leaves there every 10 minutes. The first service is at about 5.15 am and the last at about 9.30 pm.

Kingsford Smith Transport (KST) (☎ 667 0663, 24 hours) runs a door-to-door service between the airport and places to stay (including hostels) in the city, Kings Cross and Darling Harbour. The fare is $5. Heading out to the airport, you have to book at least three hours before you want to be collected. Clipper/Gray Line (☎ 319 6600, 5.30 am to 10 pm) offers a similar service for $6 ($4 children) or $10 return ($6 children).

A taxi from the airport to Circular Quay should cost between $15 and $20, depending on traffic.

STA Fare Deals

The Sydney Pass offers great value if you would have bought its components separately. If you just want transport, you're better off buying a Travel Pass (see below). Sydney Pass gives bus and ferry transport, travel on Tramway and Sydney Explorer buses, harbour cruises and a return trip on the Airport Express. A three-day Sydney Pass costs $50 ($40 children), five days costs $65 ($55 children) and seven days is $75 ($65 children). Family tickets are available. The trip back to the airport is valid for a month, but it must be your last trip, as you surrender the ticket.

Designed for commuters but very useful for visitors, Travel Pass offers cheap weekly or quarterly travel. There are various colour-coded grades offering combinations of distances and services. The Green Travel Pass is valid for extensive train and bus travel and all ferries except the RiverCat and the Manly JetCat. At $24 for a week, it's a bargain. If you buy a Travel Pass after 3 pm, your week doesn't begin until the next day. They're sold at railway stations and STA offices.

A Travel 10 ticket gives a sizeable discount on 10 trips.

Several transport-plus-entry tickets are available on STA services, and these work out cheaper than paying separately. Zoo Pass pays for your ferry to/from Taronga Park Zoo, the short bus ride from the wharf to the zoo entrance, zoo entry and the 'aerial safari' ride and costs $17 ($8.50 children, family tickets available). The Wildlife Explorer costs $49 ($37.50 children; family tickets available) and combines an hour-long visit to the Australian Wildlife Park in the morning with a Sydney Explorer Pass which you can use in the afternoon. It's a fast-paced way to see a lot of things, but is perhaps more attractive for those with limited time.

Train
Quite a lot of Sydney is covered by the suburban rail service, which has frequent trains and is generally much quicker than the bus network. Getting around the city centre by train is feasible (if disorienting).

The rail system has a central City Circle and a number of lines radiating out to the suburbs. The stations on the City Circle, in clockwise order, are Central, Town Hall (on George St near Park St), Wynyard (York St at Wynyard Park), Circular Quay, St James (north end of Hyde Park) and Museum (south end of Hyde Park). A single trip anywhere on the City Circle or to a nearby suburb such as Kings Cross is $1.20. Most suburban trains stop at Central Railway Station and usually one or more of the other City Circle stations as well. If you have to change trains, buy a ticket to your ultimate destination – it's cheaper.

Trains generally run from around 4 am to about midnight, give or take an hour. After the trains stop, Nightrider buses provide a skeleton service.

Automatic ticket machines are being installed at stations, and for these you'll need coins (any except five-cent coins) or $5 notes.

After 9 am on weekdays and at any time on weekends you can buy an off-peak return ticket for not much more than a standard one-way fare. City Hopper costs $2.20 and gives you a day of unlimited rides in the central area after 9 am on weekdays and at any time on weekends. You can go as far north as North Sydney, as far south as Central and as far east as Kings Cross. If you buy City Hopper at a suburban station, the higher price includes the return fare.

Bus
The bus information kiosk on Alfred St (running behind Circular Quay) at the corner of Loftus St is open daily. There are other information offices on Carrington St by Wynyard Park and in the Queen Victoria Building on York St.

Buses run almost everywhere, but they are slow compared to trains. Some places – including Bondi Beach, Coogee and the north shore east of the Harbour Bridge – are not serviced by trains, so you do need buses to get there. On the Eastern Suburbs line you can get a combination bus-rail ticket from some stations such as Kings Cross (but not Central), so you can change to a bus for a destination such as Bondi Beach. This works out cheaper than buying the tickets separately.

Circular Quay, Wynyard Park on York St and Railway Square are the main bus stops in the city centre.

Special Bus Services The red Sydney Explorer is an STA bus running a continuous loop around many inner-city attractions, approximately every 20 minutes between 9.30 am and 9 pm every day. There's an on-board commentary, you can get off and on as often as you like and your ticket entitles you to discounted entry to many of the attractions. As well as seeing a lot of sights, this is a good way to orient yourself to the city. The 22 Explorer stops are marked by green and red signs. You can buy the ticket on the bus, from STA offices and elsewhere. Tickets cost $20 ($15 children, family tickets available) – it would be much cheaper to get around these places by ordinary buses (in fact it's possible to walk around the circuit), but the Explorer's easy as you don't have to work out routes. You can use the Explorer ticket on ordinary buses between Central Railway Station and Circular Quay or the Rocks until midnight. The ticket also entitles you to big discounts on some tours – conditions apply.

The route is from Circular Quay to the Opera House, down Macquarie St to Hyde Park, up to Mrs Macquarie's Chair, back down to the Art Gallery of NSW, across to Kings Cross and Elizabeth Bay, through Woolloomooloo, down to Central Railway Station, to several stops around Darling Harbour, back up George St and around the Rocks to Circular Quay. The Kings Cross stop is at the railway station near Darlinghurst Rd.

The Bondi & Bay Explorer operates on similar lines to the Sydney Explorer, running a much larger circle from Circular Quay to Kings Cross, Double Bay, Vaucluse, Watsons Bay, the Gap and Bondi Beach, and returning up Oxford St. Just riding around the circle takes two hours, so if you want to get off at many of the 20 places of interest along the way you'll need to start early. The bus runs half-hourly (hourly after 1.30 pm

on weekdays) between 9 am and 6 pm daily. The ticket entitles you to use ordinary buses south of the harbour until midnight. Ticket prices are the same as for the Sydney Explorer, or you can buy a two-day pass for $35 ($25 children, family tickets available) which gives you the use of both the Sydney Explorer and the Bondi & Bay Explorer.

Operating on similar lines to the Explorer services is a new privately-run operation, Boomerang Bus Tours (☎ (02) 913 8402), which runs a continuous loop between Manly and Palm Beach, stopping at 15 places of interest along the way, including North Head, Church Point, Avalon and several places in the Palm Beach area. The whole route takes about three hours, plus whatever stops you make, and the trip includes a commentary. The bus leaves from near Manly wharf on Thursday, Friday and Saturday, with the first bus departing at 9.15 am and the last at 5.15 pm during daylight savings time and at 2.15 during the rest of the year. Three buses run the three-hour route and there are nine circuits in summer, six during the rest of the year. The fare is $20 ($15 children) and there are discounts for YHA and VIP members.

The Tramway, a bus disguised as a tram, shuttles between Circular Quay and Darling Harbour every 15 minutes between 9.30 am and 6 pm daily. A one-way ticket costs $2 (children $1, family tickets available) or you can buy an all-day pass for $3 (children $2, family tickets available). The all-day ticket is a good way of getting around central Sydney at a rock-bottom price, as the Tramway stops at several places of interest. Tramway stops are marked with yellow and black signs like railway signals.

Nightrider buses provide a skeleton service after the regular buses and trains stop running.

Ferry
Sydney's ferries are one of the nicest ways of getting around in Australia. As well as the ferries there are speedy JetCats to Manly and RiverCats running up the Parramatta River to the John St Wharf near Parramatta – more

often only as far as Meadowbank ($2.60). During the '94 fires, a JetCat ventured out through the heads into the open sea, travelling up the coast to rescue people from Pittwater.

All the ferries (and Cats) depart from Circular Quay. The STA, which runs most of the ferries, has a ferry information office on the concourse behind Jetty 4, open daily. Many ferries have connecting bus services.

Getting to Manly you have the choice of a roomy ferry which takes about 30 minutes and costs $3.40 ($1.70 children) or a JetCat which does the trip in half the time and costs $4.60 (no concessions). The ferry trip is much more pleasant, as you can walk around and there's usually a snack-bar. The JetCats have only a small outdoor area, and if you're inside the windows can be a long way away. After 7.40 pm the JetCat is the only craft running to Manly, but you can take it for the normal ferry fare. If you're staying in Manly consider buying a Ferry 10 pass (10 trips for $22.80) or, better, a Green Travel Pass ($24 for a week of train, bus and ferry travel).

Hegarty's Ferries (☎ 247 6606) departs from Jetty 6 at Circular Quay and runs to wharves directly across the harbour: Lavender Bay, McMahon's Point and two stops in Kirribilli. These services cater to peak-hour commuters and stop early in the evening.

STA ferry routes (all subject to change) are as follows:

Cremorne & Mosman
Departs Jetty 4, stops at Cremorne, Musgrave St, Old Cremorne and Mosman. First ferry departs Circular Quay at 5.35 am, last ferry departs Mosman at 11.35 (all stops, 12.20 limited stops). On Saturday first ferry 6 am, last ferry 11.55 (all stops, 12.25 limited stops); on Sunday first ferry 9 am, last ferry 7.20 pm (limited stops all afternoon). On Sunday this ferry runs via Taronga Zoo.

Darling Harbour
Departs Jetty 5, stops McMahons Point, Thames St, Darling St, Darling Harbour (Aquarium). First ferry departs Circular Quay 8.05 am, last ferry departs Darling Harbour 7.35 pm all week.

Hunters Hill
Departs Jetty 5, stops McMahons Point, Darling St, Thames St, Longnose Point, Elliot St, Greenwich St, Cockatoo Is, Valentia St, Wolseley St (not weekends). No services stop at all wharves. First ferry departs Circular Quay 5.55 am, last ferry departs Wolseley St 6.25 pm, departs Valentia St 11.55 pm. On Saturday first ferry departs 6.25 am, last ferry departs Valentia St 11.55 pm; on Sunday first ferry 9.50 pm, last ferry departs Valentia St 6.10 pm.

John St (Rydalmere) RiverCat
Departs Jetty 5, stops McMahons Point and John St. First ferry departs Circular Quay 7.15 am, last ferry departs John St 4.45 pm. No weekend service.

Manly Ferry
Departs Jetty 3, runs direct to Manly. First ferry departs Circular Quay at 6 am; after about 7.30 pm you can travel on the JetCat at a ferry fare. On Saturday first ferry 7.15 am, on Sunday first ferry 8 am.

Manly JetCat
Departs Jetty 2, runs direct to Manly. First JetCat departs Circular Quay at 6 am, last JetCat departs Manly at 11.50 pm. On Saturday first JetCat 6.10 am, last JetCat 11.50 pm, on Sunday first JetCat 7.15 am, last JetCat 11.25 pm. If you miss the last JetCat, go to Wynyard station, from where buses run to Manly through the night – infrequently.

Meadowbank
Some services RiverCat, some ferry: Departs Jetty 5, stops McMahons Point, Wolseley St, Gladesville, Meadowbank. Not all services stop at all wharves. On weekends also stops Darling Harbour. First ferry departs Circular Quay 7.40 am, last ferry departs Meadowbank 5.55 pm. On weekends first ferry 8.45 am, last ferry 6.15 pm.

Neutral Bay
Departs Jetty 4, stops Kirribilli, High St, Hayes St and Kurraba Rd. First ferry departs Circular Quay 5.50 am, last ferry departs Kurraba Rd 12.05 am. On Saturday first ferry 6.12 am, last ferry 11.50 pm; on Sunday first ferry 9.10 am, last ferry 6.35 pm.

Rose Bay
Departs Jetty 4, stops Darling Point, Double Bay, Rose Bay. On weekdays, morning services run direct to Rose Bay, afternoon services run direct to Circular Quay. First ferry departs Circular Quay 7.10 am, last service departs Rose Bay 6.30 pm. On weekends use the Taronga Park ferry.

Taronga Park
Departs Jetty 4, stops Taronga Zoo wharf and Cremorne wharf. First ferry departs Circular Quay 7.15 am, last ferry departs Taronga Zoo wharf 7 pm. On Saturday first ferry 8.45 am, last ferry 7 pm; on Sunday first ferry 8.30 am, last ferry 6.35 pm. On weekends this ferry also runs to Rose Bay and Watsons Bay; on Sunday you can also get to the zoo on the Cremorne & Mosman ferry.

Monorail

The monorail circles Darling Harbour and links it to the city centre. The full circuit takes 12 minutes and there's a train every three or four minutes. A single circuit costs $2.50 ($1.20 children). For $6 you can ride as often as you like between 9 am and 7 pm. City monorail stations are World Square (on Liverpool St between Pitt and George Sts), Park Plaza (at the corner of Pitt and Park Sts) and City Centre (at the corner of Pitt and Market Sts). Stations in Darling Harbour are Harbourside (near Harbourside Festival Marketplace), Convention (near the Convention Centre) and Haymarket (near the Powerhouse Museum and the Entertainment Centre).

Tram

In the '30s Sydney had more than 250 km of tramway, but by 1960 the last tram had lowered its pantograph and that fine metaphor for a hasty departure, 'pulled out like a Bondi tram', became meaningless. There is talk of re-establishing a tram route in George St, perhaps linking the southern end of the city with Pyrmont. Bringing back trams seems a good idea, but the proposed route would probably be another monorail in terms of usefulness to commuters. Also, it's hard to see how Sydney's narrow streets could cope with both modern traffic and trams – Melbourne's wide boulevards have difficulty accommodating both.

The Rocks/Darling Harbour Tramway is not a tram, it's a bus – see the Special Bus Services section.

Taxi

Taxis are easily flagged down in the city centre and the inner suburbs. You'll also find many (usually) in taxi ranks at Central, Wynyard and Circular Quay railway stations, and at the large rank just off George St in Goulburn St.

The four big taxi companies offer a reliable telephone service: Taxis Combined (☎ 332 8888), RSL Taxis (☎ 581 1111), Legion (☎ 289 9000) and Premier Radio Cabs (☎ 897 4000). Taxis Combined made a quantum leap in service standards recently, and the other companies probably won't be far behind.

Taxi fares are: $1 booking fee, $1.80 flagfall, 95c per km; the waiting fee is 45c a minute and there's a maximum luggage charge of 50c (often waived). These fares apply to any time of day or night. Tipping is not mandatory, but 'rounding-up' the bill is common – if the fare is $9.20 you might say 'Call it $10, mate'. Occasionally, the driver will say the same to you if the fare is $10.20.

Water Taxi Water taxis are pricey but are a fun way of getting around the harbour. Companies include Taxis Afloat (☎ 955 3222) and Harbour Taxis (☎ 555 1155). Up to four people can travel from Circular Quay to Watsons Bay for about $50; to one of the harbour islands it's about $35.

Car

You will definitely need a street directory if you plan to drive around the city – and with such good public transport, why bother? Parking is hell in most of the inner area and tow-away zones lurk in wait.

Some of the many commercial parking stations in the inner area include the Goulburn St Parking Station on the corner of Goulburn and Elizabeth Sts, KC Park Safe at 521 Kent St, Grimes Parking on Gateway Plaza at Circular Quay and Kings Cross Car Park on the corner of Ward Ave and Elizabeth Bay Rd.

For car rental companies, see the Getting There & Away section earlier in this chapter.

Bicycle

The Bicycle Institute of NSW (☎ 212 5628), at the corner of Campbell and Foster Sts in Surry Hills, publishes a handy book, *Cycling Around Sydney* (paperback, $10.50), which details routes and cycle paths in and around the Sydney area. They also publish a series of booklets on cycling throughout the state. Before you visit, it would be a good idea to phone to see if they have moved. Their postal address, GPO Box 272, Sydney 2001, will stay the same even if the office moves. Another guide to cycling in Sydney is *Seeing Sydney by Bicycle* by Julia Thorne (Kangaroo Press, paperback, about $13).

The RTA (Roads & Traffic Authority) publishes a map showing recommended bike routes around greater Sydney, mainly for cycle commuters. It costs $3.50 and is available from the Bicycle Institute and bike shops such as Rockcycle Tours (see below).

You can take your bike on suburban trains, but you'll have to buy it an adult fare.

Places *not* to ride are Darling Harbour and Martin Place, where cycling is banned. Apparently plain-clothes police on bikes patrol the city centre, busting the cycle couriers for their indiscretions.

Bicycle Hire Most of the bicycle hire places require hefty deposits, but they'll accept credit cards.

Rockcycle Tours (☎ 247 7777) on Circular Quay West, across from the Overseas Passenger Terminal and behind the Rocks visitor centre, is a friendly new outfit renting good mountain bikes for $9 an hour, $25 for half a day and $39 a day, with big discounts for students and backpackers. They know interesting and bike-friendly routes around the Rocks and the inner city, and you get a map when you hire a bike. They can also help with information on rides further afield.

In Kings Cross on Orwell St near Eva's Hostel, Roo Bikes rents well-worn mountain bikes at $12 for a half-day, $15 for the day after 10.30 am and $20 for the whole day. Inner City Cycles (☎ 660 6605) at 31 Glebe Point Rd in Glebe rents quality mountain bikes for $30 a day, $45 for the weekend (from Friday afternoon to Monday morning) and $100 a week. They're friendly and knowledgeable and can help with touring queries.

The Australian Cycle Company (☎ 399 3475) at 28 Clovelly Rd in Randwick (near the three-way intersection of Darley Rd, Clovelly Rd and Wentworth St) rents bikes, and there are several other places nearby, handy for rides in Centennial Park.

At 82 Oxford St in Paddington, across from Victoria Barracks, Woolys Wheels (☎ 331 2671) might by now be renting quality mountain bikes. Over in Manly, you can hire good bikes from the Manly Cycle Centre (☎ 977 1189) at 36 Pittwater Rd for $5 an hour, $25 a day, $40 a weekend or $60 a week.

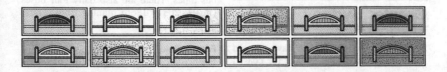

Around Sydney

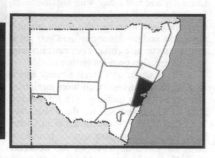

Sydney sprawls over a coastal plain, surrounded by rugged country on three sides and the Pacific Ocean on the fourth.

The city is at the centre of the largest concentration of population in Australia, with at least 100 people per square km all the way from Wollongong to beyond Newcastle. More than two-thirds of the state's population is crammed into this area; about a quarter of all Australians live within 150 km of Sydney.

Most people live on the coast or around the lakes of the central coast – the slopes and forests of the Great Divide have halted westward expansion, except along a ridge-top corridor through the Blue Mountains.

This might sound like a recipe for overcrowding, but as well as the development there are some pretty little towns, stunningly beautiful waterways, uncrowded beaches and vast tracts of forest. The proximity of Sydney means that public transport is often quite good and you can see a lot of the area on day-trips even if you don't have your own vehicle.

Greater Sydney

Sydney's sprawling suburbs have covered much of the accessible land of the coastal plain, with corridor development running out along the Great Western Highway to Penrith and south along the Hume Highway past Liverpool. In the hilly areas to the north-west, settlement is sparser but is increasing rapidly.

WILDLIFE PARKS
As well as Sydney's popular Taronga Zoo, there are several other places where you can see native animals – often at cuddling range. As well as the larger places listed below, you can meet native animals at **Australian Pioneer Village** near Wilberforce (see the following Macquarie Towns section). The **Australian Reptile Park** (☎ (043) 28 4311), near Gosford, has many native animals and birds as well as reptiles and is open daily.

Koala Park
If koalas are all you're interested in, Koala Park (☎ 484 3141) on Castle Hill Rd in West Pennant Hills in north-west Sydney is open daily from 9 am to 5 pm and admission is $8 ($4 children). The koalas are fed at 10.20 am, 2 and 3 pm. Take a train to Pennant Hills Station, and from there take any bus from No 661 to No 665.

Waratah Park
The popular Waratah Park on Namba Rd, Terrey Hills, on the edge of Ku-Ring-Gai Chase National Park, is another place where you can meet koalas. The TV series *Skippy* was filmed here. It's open daily, and admission is $10.80 ($5.80 children). You can get here on Forest Coachlines bus No 284, which meets trains at Chatswood, but there are only three a day and fewer on weekends. A recorded message (☎ (02) 450 1236) gives bus times. There are also daily tour buses (☎ (02) 20319 1266) running from central Sydney.

Featherdale Wildlife Park
Featherdale Wildlife Park (☎ (02) 671 4984

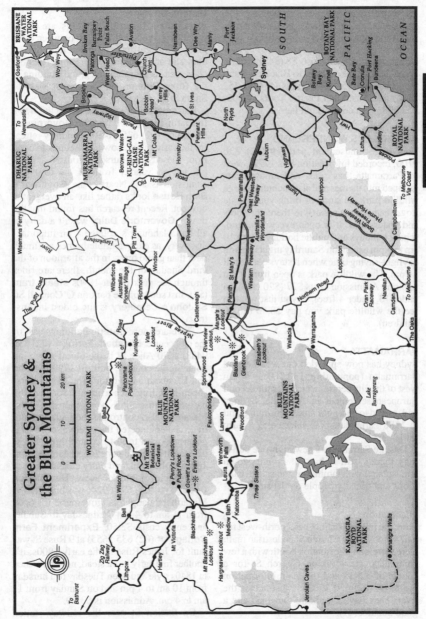

Greater Sydney &
the Blue Mountains

for recorded information) on Kildare Rd, Doonside, about halfway between Parramatta and Penrith, is a 'koala cuddlery' with plenty of other native fauna as well. Featherdale is open daily and costs $8 ($4 children). From the city, take a train to Blacktown and then bus No 725. AAT Kings (☎ (02) 252 2788) and Australian Pacific Tours (☎ (02) 252 2988) run coaches out here.

AUSTRALIA'S WONDERLAND

This large amusement park (☎ (02) 830 9100; recorded information 832 1777), west of Parramatta, has rides and amusements grouped into themes and also includes a large **wildlife park**. In summer bring your cossie (togs, bathers, swimsuit), as there are pools and waterslides. It is open every weekend, school holidays and public holidays from 10 am to 5 pm except on Saturday nights during daylight-saving time when it stays open until 11 pm. The wildlife park is open from 9 am to 5 pm. Admission costs $27 ($20 children under 13, under 4 free). If you just want to see the wildlife park you pay $8.50 ($6.50 children).

PARRAMATTA

Sydney has now sprawled out well beyond Parramatta (population 130,000), 24 km west of the city centre, which was the second European settlement in Australia. Sydney had proved to be a poor area for farming, and in 1788 Parramatta was selected as a farm settlement.

Despite Parramatta's new high-rise buildings there's still a hint of country-town atmosphere, with lamingtons on sale in cake shops and friendly people on the street.

Information

From the railway station, head north-west for half a block to the Church St pedestrian mall. Here there's an information booth with a few pamphlets; go north on Church St for a couple of blocks and the main information centre (☎ (02) 630 3703) is just across the river. They have a walking-tour map and a good booklet ($1).

Historic Buildings

Parramatta's historic buildings are fairly widely scattered, and walking between them gives an insight into the much more recent domestic architecture of this lower-middle class area. A more recent grand building is the **Roxy Cinema** on George St west of Smith St.

Parramatta Park was the site of the area's first farm. Here you'll find **Old Government House** (☎ (02) 635 8149), a country retreat for the early rulers, now a museum and open from Tuesday to Thursday from 10 am to 4 pm and on Sunday from 11 am to 4 pm; admission is $4. Nearby, the **Governor's Bath House** looks rather like an overgrown dovecot. Recent research has found that the nearby **Governor's Dairy** wasn't a dairy at all but a labourer's cottage – an important discovery, as early humble homes are much rarer than grand ones. In the afternoon of the third Sunday of the month, there are rides through the park on an 1890s **steam tram** ($2). Just south of the park on O'Connell St, **St John's Cemetery** is the oldest in Australia.

There are more historic buildings east of the city centre. **Elizabeth Farm** (☎ (02) 635 9488) at 70 Alice St is the oldest surviving home in the country, built in 1793 by John and Elizabeth Macarthur. The Macarthurs' sheep-breeding experiments formed the basis for Australia's wool industry. John Macarthur also controlled the lucrative rum trade and engineered the removal of several governors who tried to control him! Elizabeth Farm is open daily except Monday from 10 am to 4.30 pm, and entry costs $5.

A couple of blocks away, **Hambledon Cottage** (☎ (02) 635 6924) was built for the Macarthurs' daughters' governess. It's open from 11 am to 4 pm Wednesday to Sunday and entry costs $2.50. **Experiment Farm Cottage** (☎ (02) 635 5655) at 9 Ruse St was built for James Ruse in the early 1800s; it's another fine early homestead, now furnished in 1840s style and open Tuesday to Thursday from 10 am to 4 pm and on Sunday from 11 am to 4 pm. Admission is $3.50.

On Station St near the railway station

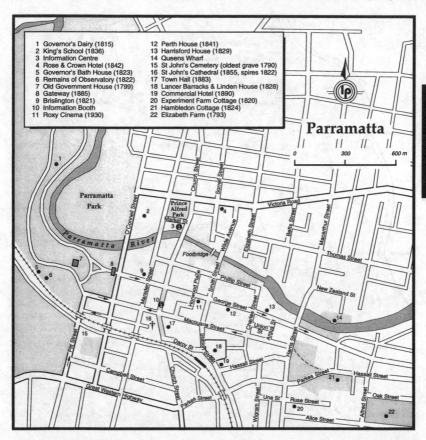

1 Governor's Dairy (1815)
2 King's School (1836)
3 Information Centre
4 Rose & Crown Hotel (1842)
5 Governor's Bath House (1823)
6 Remains of Observatory (1822)
7 Old Government House (1799)
8 Gateway (1885)
9 Brislington (1821)
10 Information Booth
11 Roxy Cinema (1930)
12 Perth House (1841)
13 Harrisford House (1829)
14 Queens Wharf
15 St John's Cemetery (oldest grave 1790)
16 St John's Cathedral (1855, spires 1822)
17 Town Hall (1883)
18 Lancer Barracks & Linden House (1828)
19 Commercial Hotel (1890)
20 Experiment Farm Cottage (1820)
21 Hambledon Cottage (1824)
22 Elizabeth Farm (1793)

Parramatta

0   300   600 m

(itself a notable building) are the barracks of the **Royal NSW Lancers** (☎ (02) 635 7822) with a museum open on Sunday.

Getting There & Away
Suburban electric trains run to Parramatta from Central Station and other stations.

By car, follow Parramatta Rd west from the city centre. You have a choice between taking the Great Western Highway or the Western Freeway (a toll road).

ROYAL NATIONAL PARK
Once, this was just *the* national park, Australia's first, and the second in the world after Yellowstone in the USA. Sticklers for accuracy point out that while Yellowstone was founded first, it wasn't actually *called* a national park until after the National Park had been founded. (The 'royal' tag was added after Queen Elizabeth visited the park in 1954.)

Thirty-six km south of the city, Royal National Park stretches about 20 km south from Port Hacking and has a large network of walking tracks through varied country, including a two-day, 26-km trail along the coast, with spectacular clifftop stretches.

The park was devastated in the bushfires of '94 and it will be many years before it

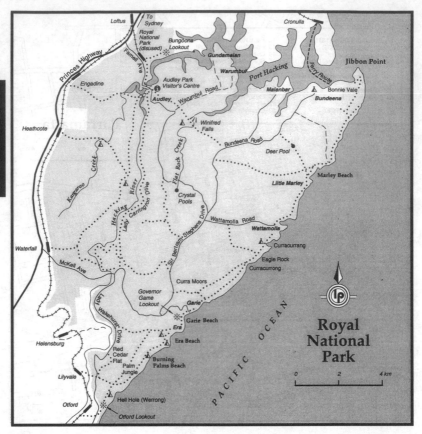

recovers fully. However, much of the superb rainforest in the southern end of the park survives, most of the facilities are intact and the walking tracks should have re-opened by now. The beaches were not affected.

The visitor centre (☎ (02) 542 0648) is at **Audley**, about two km from the park's northern entrance, off the Princes Highway. You can hire rowing boats on the river here. Park entry costs $7.50 per car, but is free for pedestrians and cyclists. You can drive through the park from end to end and down to the coast in a few places.

The sandstone plateau at the northern end of the park is a sea of low scrub. You have to

descend into the river valleys for tall forest, and there's more at the southern end where the park meets the Illawarra escarpment. In late winter and early spring the park is carpeted with wildflowers.

There are good surfing and swimming beaches (although surfing at Marley is dangerous), and there are swimming spots along the Hacking River which runs right through the park, and Lady Carrington Drive (a walking and cycling trail) follows the river south from Audley. At **Wattamolla Beach** there's a picnic area and a lagoon for more serene swimming and at **Garie Beach** there's a kiosk (not always open) and a surf lifesaving club. Road access to the beaches is closed at sunset.

Bundeena, across Port Hacking from Sydney's southern suburb of Cronulla, is a sizeable town surrounded by Royal National Park. Bundeena has its own beaches, or you can walk 30 minutes to **Jibbon**, nearer the ocean coast, which has another good beach and Aboriginal rock art. Bundeena is also the starting-point for longer coastal walks. Coastline Dive (☎ (02) 523 2296) offers boat dives.

Places to Stay

There's a *campsite* with showers at Bonnie Vale near Bundeena, the only campsite accessible by car. *Bush camping* is allowed in several other areas, with a permit from the visitor centre – Burning Palms Beach towards the south is one of the best places. The small, basic (no electricity or phone) and secluded *Garie Beach Youth Hostel* is near one of the best surfing beaches. Beds cost $5. You need to book, collect a key and get detailed directions: see the YHA Travel Centre at 422 Kent St in Sydney (☎ (02) 261 1111).

Getting There & Away

Train The Sydney to Wollongong railway line forms the western boundary of the park. The closest station is Loftus, four km from the park entrance and another two km from the visitor centre. Bringing a bike on the train is a good idea. Other stations (Engadine, Heathcote, Waterfall and Otford) are near walking trails.

Ferry An interesting way to reach the park is to take a train to Cronulla, then a Cronulla Ferries boat to Bundeena (☎ (02) 523 2990 for timetables). Cronulla Ferries also cruises up the Hacking River on Sunday, Monday and Wednesday for $8 and usually gets as far as Audley (it depends on the tide), but there's no longer a wharf at Audley so you can't disembark there.

Car & Motorbike By road you reach the park from the Princes Highway – from Sydney

turn off south of Loftus – or from the south via Otford, a beautiful drive through thick bush.

KU-RING-GAI CHASE NATIONAL PARK

Ku-Ring-Gai Chase (☎ (02) 457 9322 weekdays, 457 9310 weekends) lies between Sydney and the Hawkesbury River, 24 km north of the city centre. Its east side borders Pittwater. With over 100 km of shoreline, lots of forest and wildlife and many walking tracks, this is a very good national park to find on a city's doorstep.

Large areas of Ku-Ring-Gai Chase, especially around West Head, were burned in the fires of '94. However, neither the camping area at the Basin nor the YHA hostel was directly affected.

High points in the park offer superb views across deep inlets like Cowan Water and the wide Pittwater, and from West Head at the park's north-east tip there's another fantastic view across Pittwater to Barrenjoey Point at the end of Palm Beach. You may see **lyrebirds** at West Head during their May to July mating period.

There are Aboriginal **rock carvings** in the park, and one group is thought to depict a star chart, tens of thousands of years old.

The **Kalkari Visitor Centre**, open daily, is on Ku-Ring-Gai Chase Rd about four km

Lyrebird

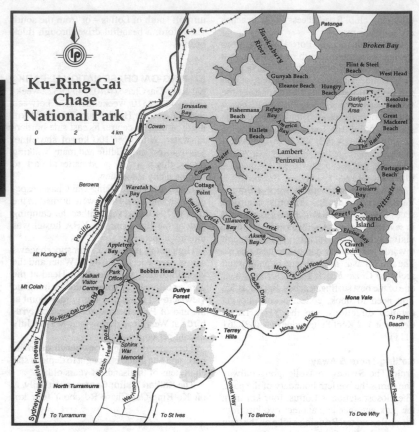

Ku-Ring-Gai Chase National Park

into the park from Mt Colah, near Bobbin Head. There's an adjoining nature trail. This road descends from the visitor centre to Bobbin Head on Cowan Water, where you can hire rowing boats, then goes round to the Turramurra entrance.

At Akuna Bay on Coal and Candle Creek, off Cowan Water, there's a **marina** (☎ (02) 450 2709) with a variety of craft for hire.

Places to Stay

Camping ($10 for two people, $15 in school holidays) is allowed only at the Basin, on the west side of Pittwater and a walk of about two km from the West Head road, or a ferry

ride from Palm Beach. Book campsites in advance (☎ (02) 451 8124). The idyllic *Pittwater YHA Hostel* (☎ (02) 99 2196) is a couple of km south of the Basin and is noted for friendly wildlife. Beds cost $13 or $16 per person in a twin room. If you stay only for Saturday night it costs a little more. You must book in advance.

Getting There & Away

There are four road entrances to the park – from Mt Colah (on the Pacific Highway) and Turramurra in the south-west, and Terrey Hills and Church Point in the south-east. Hornsby Buses (☎ (02) 457 8888) run fairly frequently from Turramurra railway station to the nearby park entrance ($1.80), with a few services continuing on to Bobbin Head ($2.50). Roads reach Akuna Bay and West Head from the Terrey Hills or Church Point entrances, which are served by Forest Coachlines (☎ (02) 450 2277) and STA buses respectively. It's quite a walk in from these entrances.

Boat From Palm Beach, ferries (☎ (02) 918 2747) run to the Basin hourly from 9 am to 4 pm (5 pm on weekends), $6 return. A ferry departs Palm Beach for Bobbin Head (running via Patonga on the north side of the Hawkesbury River) every day at 11 am, returning at 3.30 pm. The one-way fare is $10 ($5 children) plus a dollar or two for bikes or big backpacks. A private water taxi (☎ 018 238 190) runs from the Newport Hotel.

For the YHA, take a ferry from Church Point to Halls Wharf from where it's a short walk. (YHA members get ferry discounts.) Several bus routes run from central Sydney to Church Point, some involving a change of buses at Mona Vale. You can get a direct bus from Manly. Scotland Island Schooners (☎ (02) 99 3954) at Church Point will drop you off at the Basin or the hostel by arrangement.

HAWKESBURY RIVER

The Hawkesbury River enters the sea 30 km north of Sydney at Broken Bay. Dotted with coves, beaches, picnic spots and some fine riverside restaurants, it's one of Australia's most attractive rivers. The Hawkesbury's final 20-odd km before it enters the ocean expands into bays and inlets like Berowra Creek, Cowan Water and Pittwater on the south side, and Brisbane Water on the north. The river flows between a succession of **national parks** – Marramarra and Ku-Ring-Gai to the south; Dharug, Brisbane Water and Bouddi to the north. About 100 km upstream are the towns of Windsor and Richmond – see the following Macquarie Towns section.

An excellent way to get a feel for the river is to go along with the **Riverboat Postman**

which runs up the river every weekday from Brooklyn at 9.30 am and returns at 1.15 pm. There's also an afternoon run on Wednesday and Friday, departing at 1.30 pm and returning at 4.15 pm. It costs $20 ($10 children), and the 8.16 am train from Sydney's Central Station will get you to Brooklyn (the station is called Hawkesbury River and a ticket from Sydney costs $3.80, $4.80 off-peak return) in time to join the morning run. By car, take the Newcastle freeway or follow the old Pacific Highway, which passes through Sydney's northern suburbs then along a winding route through the hills. The Riverboat Postman people also run other Hawkesbury services, including Brooklyn to Windsor **cruises** and a cruise between Brooklyn and Patonga on the north shore daily except Friday ($10 return; $4 children). Bookings (☎ (02) 985 7566) are necessary.

There's also a daily ferry between Palm Beach, Patonga and Bobbin Head in Ku-Ring-Gai Chase National Park. From Patonga, Peninsula Bus Lines (☎ (043) 41 4133) has infrequent buses to Gosford where you can catch a bus or train going north.

Another interesting way to see the river is to hire a **houseboat** from one of several outfits. As a very rough guide, *Hawkesbury Holidays-A-Float* (☎ (02) 985 7368) in Brooklyn offers three midweek days on their cheapest two- to four-berth boat for around $275 between May and late September, $330 from late September to mid-December, $510 from mid-December to early January and $430 until the end of February. There are different types and sizes of boats and different deals for longer rents and weekends. Other companies include *Able Hawkesbury River Houseboats* (☎ (045) 66 4308) at Wisemans Ferry and *Ripples* (☎ (02) 985 7333) in Brooklyn.

The small town of **Berowra Waters** is on a narrow, forested waterway. It's a very pretty location, with boat hire and walking tracks through the bush, but the main reason Sydneysiders come here on weekends is to eat at the *Berowra Waters Inn* (☎ (02) 456 1027), one of Australia's best-known restaurants. It's open for lunch and dinner on

Friday and Saturday and for lunch only on Sunday. The food is excellent modern Australian and the set menu, including a glass of French champagne, costs $85 per person. Bookings are essential. If the Inn is beyond your means, there are several cafes in town.

Wisemans Ferry & Around

The tiny settlement of **Wisemans Ferry** (see the Central Coast & Lake Macquarie map) is a popular spot up the river. The town is on a sharp bend in the Hawkesbury River, opposite the entrance of the Macdonald River. The historic *Wisemans Ferry Inn* (☎ (045) 66 4301) has rooms for $50 a double. There are several caravan parks in the area; the cheapest sites ($8 a double) are at *Rosevale Farm Resort* (☎ (045) 66 4207) a couple of km north of the village centre. There's a National Parks shop (☎ (045) 66 4382) which has information on the area.

Across the river, **Dharug National Park** (14,850 hectares) is noted for its Aboriginal rock carvings which date back nearly 10,000 years. Forming the western boundary of the park is the **Old Great North Road**, built by convicts in the 1820s to link Sydney and Newcastle. Most of the road, which hasn't been used since the 1930s, is badly dilapidated, but a two-km section (running north into the national park from the sealed road across the river from Wisemans Ferry) has been restored, although there is no vehicle access. There are *campsites* at Mill Creek and Ten Mile Hollow.

On the south side of the Hawkesbury is **Murramarra National Park** (11,760 hectares), with vehicle access from the Old Northern Rd south of Wisemans Ferry. You can bush-camp here. Contact the National Parks office in Gosford (☎ (043) 24 4911) for more information.

Unsealed roads on both sides of the river run north from Wisemans Ferry to the hamlet of **St Albans**. It's a pretty drive, with bush on one side and the serene flats of the Macdonald River on the other side, with the occasional old sandstone house. In St Albans, the friendly *Settlers Arms Inn* (☎ (045) 68 2111) dates from 1836, and the

public bar is worth a beer. They have a few pleasant rooms from $80 a double, and there's a basic *campsite* opposite the pub. There's also B&B accommodation in the *old courthouse* (☎ (045) 68 2170).

Getting There & Away A road leads to Wisemans Ferry from Pitt Town, near Windsor. You can also get there from Sydney on the Old Northern Rd, which branches off Windsor Rd north of Parramatta.

If you've arrived at Wisemans Ferry by either of these routes, you have a choice of two ferries. The ferry on the west side of town (it's the one at the bottom of the steep hill) takes you to St Albans Rd which runs up to St Albans; the ferry on the north-east side (a little way out of town, near the park) takes you to Settlers Rd which also runs up to St Albans and in the other direction takes you to Central Mangrove and, eventually, the central coast or the Sydney to Newcastle Freeway.

From St Albans an unsealed road runs north-east to Bucketty, from where you can get to Wollombi and Cessnock in the Hunter Valley.

MACQUARIE TOWNS AREA

The riverflats of the upper Hawkesbury, under the lee of the Blue Mountains, offered the young colony fertile land for growing much-needed food. After early settlements were flooded out several times, Governor Macquarie established the five 'Macquarie towns' on higher ground in 1810 – Windsor, Richmond, Wilberforce, Pitt Town and Castlereagh. The area is still intensively cultivated.

The upper Hawkesbury is popular for water-skiing, but if you're tempted to get into the water, check that there isn't an algae problem. Outbreaks of toxic blue-green algae have occurred in recent years, and just because you can't see any doesn't mean that the water isn't affected. During the first outbreak, several government agencies knew that the algae levels were dangerously high but none of them told anyone because it wasn't their job! Backsides were kicked and now there's a reporting system to match the monitoring system. There have been no problems in the lower reaches of the river.

Information

The main information centre for the upper Hawkesbury area (☎ (045) 88 5895) is on the road between Richmond and Windsor, across from the Richmond RAAF base. It's open daily from 9 am to 5 pm. Windsor has its own information centre (☎ (045) 77 2310) in the 1843 Daniel O'Connell Inn on Thompson Square, off Bridge St.

In Richmond there's a National Parks office (☎ (045) 88 5247) at 370 Windsor St.

Windsor

In Windsor, the **Hawkesbury Museum of Local History** is in the same old building as the information centre. It's open daily and admission is $2.50 (50c children). You can book cruises on the Hawkesbury here.

Windsor's other old buildings include the convict-built **St Matthew's Church**, completed in 1822 and designed, like the old **courthouse**, by convict architect Francis Greenway. George St has other historic buildings, and the **Macquarie Arms Hotel** is reckoned to be the oldest pub in Australia (there are a few 'oldest pubs'). It was built in 1815 under orders from the governor. Happily, its history hasn't gone to its head and it's still very much a small-town pub.

On the edge of town is the **Tebbut Observatory**, featured on the $100 note. You can look through the telescopes on Friday and Saturday night tours ($10), but you must book a fortnight in advance (☎ (018 611 232).

Wilberforce & Around

Wilberforce, six km north of Windsor, is a tiny town on the edge of the riverflat farmland. Here, **Australian Pioneer Village** (☎ (045) 75 1457) is a collection of old buildings gathered from around the district to form a small historic park. It includes **Rose Cottage** (1811), probably the oldest surviving timber building in the country (and occupied by members of the same family

until 1961). There are also native animals and regular entertainment. The village is open daily, except Monday and Friday, from 10 am to 5 pm and admission is $7 ($2.50 children, $15 families). Next to the village is a **butterfly farm**. You can get here by public transport, by train to Windsor and then by bus – phone to check times, as the bus isn't frequent. At nearby **Ebenezer**, the Presbyterian church, built in 1809, is said to be the oldest in Australia still regularly used. The old **Tizzana Winery** near Ebenezer is open on Saturday afternoons.

Pitt Town & Around

Pitt Town, a few km north-east of Windsor, is another Macquarie Town with more old buildings including the restored Bird in Hand Hotel (1825). The small **Cattai State Recreation Area**, with canoe hire and horseriding, is north of Pitt Town on the road to Wisemans Ferry.

Richmond

Richmond, eight km west of Windsor, dates from 1810 and has some more early buildings, including the **courthouse** and **police station** on Windsor St and, around the corner in Market St, **St Andrew's Church** (1845). **St Peter's Church** dates from 1841 and a number of notable pioneers are buried in its cemetery. There's a village-green-like park in the middle of town.

Up the Putty Road

The Putty Road is a scenic route from Windsor to the upper Hunter Valley via Wisemans Ferry (see the Getting There & Away section following). The road runs through dense bush, amid a sea of forest-covered ranges (somewhat blackened by the '94 fires). On the Putty Road about 20 km north of Windsor, there's a long descent to the lovely **Colo River**. The nearby hamlet has a shop and a caravan park (☎ (045) 75 5253) where you can arrange various adventure activities, or contact a company such as Colo River Expeditions (☎ (045) 65 9280). Further along, off the main road, Saddlebums (☎ (065) 79 7039) in the hamlet of

Putty has day rides in the mountains for about $65 and overnight rides for $120.

Getting There & Away

Train Suburban trains run from Sydney to Windsor and Richmond. Neither town is too large to see on foot, but getting to the other Macquarie towns involves connecting with an infrequent local bus service.

Car & Motorbike From Sydney the easiest routes to Windsor are on Windsor Rd (Route 40), which is the north-western continuation of Parramatta's Church St (you'll have to wind around the Church St mall); and via Penrith, heading north from either the Western Freeway or the Great Western Highway on Route 69 (Parker St and the Northern Rd).

The Putty Road runs north from Windsor to Singleton, 160 km north in the upper Hunter Valley. From Windsor take Bridge St across the river then turn right onto the Wilberforce road (Route 69).

From Richmond, Bells Line of Road runs west up into the Blue Mountains. This is a more interesting (but considerably longer) route to Katoomba than the crowded Great Western Highway.

PENRITH

Now Sydney's westernmost suburb, Penrith is bounded on the west by the serene Nepean River (which becomes the Hawkesbury a few km downstream). Across the river the forested foothills of the Blue Mountains rise above the Nepean's riverflats and the plains of western Sydney come to an abrupt end. Europeans arrived here soon after the colony's founding, in search of land to grow food, and a road between Penrith and Parramatta was built in 1818.

The information centre (☎ (047) 32 7671) is in the car park of the Penrith Panthers complex.

Things to See & Do

The **Museum of Fire** contains displays of historic fire-fighting equipment and some interesting educational items about fire and its dangers. There's a very graphic display on the disastrous effects of fire. The museum is open daily from 10 am to 3 pm (until 5 pm on Sunday) and admission is $3 ($2 children). It's off Castlereagh Rd (the main road to Richmond), just east of the railway line.

Looking for a touch of Sylvania Waters? Try the huge **Penrith Panthers** complex, a leagues club with just about everything you could wish for: glitzy surroundings, plenty of pokies, flash restaurants, a free cinema, lavish amusements such as cable water-skiing, and an expensive *motel* (☎ (047) 21 7700, 1800 024 911 toll-free). Perhaps a visit here on the way to the Blue Mountains will give you a better appreciation of the bush.

The *Nepean Belle* (☎ (047) 33 1274) cruises the river several times a week.

Getting There & Away

Train Frequent electric trains stop at Penrith on the run between Sydney and the Blue Mountains.

Car & Motorbike The Western Freeway (a toll-road) from Sydney runs past Penrith, and the Great Western Highway runs through it. The Northern Road (Route 69) runs south from Penrith to the towns of Camden and Picton (see the Macarthur Country section) and north to Windsor (see the Macquarie Towns section).

AROUND PENRITH

Another extravagant curiosity is **Notre Dame** (☎ (047) 73 8599), near the hamlet of Mulgoa, 15 km south of Penrith on Mulgoa Rd (Route 73). It's a '20th century castle' with lots of antiques, a private zoo and dancing horses (at noon daily). Admission is $13.50 ($7.50 children under 12).

In **Emu Plains**, on the highway in the foothills of the Blue Mountains, the **Arms of Australia Inn** is an old pub which is now a small museum. It's open Sunday afternoon.

MACARTHUR COUNTRY

The Hume Freeway heads south-west from Sydney, flanked by the rugged Blue Mountains National Park to the west and the coastal escarpment on the east, following a rising corridor. This cleared and rolling sheep country (see the Southern Highlands & Macarthur Country map) has some of the state's oldest towns, although many have been swallowed up by Sydney's steamrolling suburbs. For a closer look at the countryside than the freeway allows, take the **Northern Road** between Penrith and Narellan (just north of Camden).

The main information centre for this area (☎ (02) 821 2311) is in the outer suburb of Liverpool, at the corner of the Hume Highway and Congressional Drive. **Liverpool** is now a fairly unattractive outer suburb of Sydney, and **Campbelltown**, 20 km further south, is going the same way. Both towns do have some interesting old buildings, and tour brochures are available at the Liverpool information centre.

History

This area was originally called Cow Pastures because a herd of escapee cattle from Sydney Cove thrived here, but it was John and Elizabeth Macarthur's sheep, arriving in 1805, which made the area famous. The couple's experiments with sheep-breeding led to the development of merino sheep suited to Australian conditions, and these became the foundation of the Australian wool industry.

Activities

Balloon Aloft (☎ (046) 55 9892; 1800 028 568 toll-free) has early-morning hot-air flights from Camden for about $200, less for standby passengers.

Camden Area

Camden is a large country town (population 8000) on the verge of becoming a dormitory suburb of Sydney. The town retains its integrity, but the surrounding countryside is fast filling up with weekend attractions for Sydneysiders. John Oxley Cottage on the northern outskirts houses the information centre (☎ (046) 58 1370), open from 10 am to 3 pm on weekends and holidays. At other times the library on John St has information. Pick up a walking tour leaflet. Behind the library at 40 John St is the **museum**, open on weekend afternoons ($1, 10c children).

The Macarthurs' home, **Camden Park House** (1835), is only open to the public on the last weekend in September.

At **Narellan**, near Camden, **Gledswood** is an old (1810) homestead now housing a winery and a restaurant. There is also sheep-shearing, boomerang-throwing and other activities. **Struggletown** on Sharman Close is a collection of galleries and studios in some historic cottages. Not far from Narellan, **Australiana Park** (also called El Caballo Blanco) has a grab-bag of things to see and do, including sheep-shearing, water-sliding, horse-riding and koala-cuddling. The star attractions are the Andalusian Dancing Stallions; phone (☎ (02) 606 6266) for performance times. Admission is around $15 ($8 children).

Midway between Camden and Campbelltown, the **Mount Annan Botanic Garden** is an offshoot of Sydney's botanic gardens and displays native flora on its 400 hectares. It's open daily from 10 am and admission is $5 per car, $2 for pedestrians. You can get here on bus No 896, which runs approximately hourly from Campbelltown railway station to Camden.

Picton Area

South of Camden and more rural, pretty **Picton** is an old village originally called Stonequarry. Today coal is mined in the area (and there are subsidence problems under those rolling hills and sheep paddocks). A number of buildings from the early days still stand, including the railway station and the **George IV Inn** which dates from 1839 and now brews its own beer. Upper Menangle St has been listed by the National Trust. On weekends there's a tourist information booth on the main street.

The **Elizabeth Macarthur Institute** (☎ (046) 29 3333) is a research station northeast of Picton which takes in the site of the Macarthurs' first farm in the area and is being developed as an educational attraction. Most historians now agree that Elizabeth supervised most of the sheep-breeding projects while the irascible John was embroiled in political disputes with a succession of governors.

Just south of Picton in **Thirlmere**, the **Rail Transport Museum** is well worth visiting if you have the least interest in old trains. Their collection of engines and rolling stock is huge, with many more awaiting restoration. The museum is open from 10 am to 3 pm on weekdays and from 9 am to 5 pm on weekends. Admission is $5 ($2 children). There are occasional steam-train excursions; phone (02) 744 9999 for upcoming dates.

The small **Thirlmere Lakes National Park** (630 hectares) is just south-west of Thirlmere and protects five small lakes and the surrounding bush, where there are walking trails.

The **Merigal Dingo Education Centre** (☎ (046) 84 1156), near Bargo about 20 km south of Picton, is open on the first Sunday of the month between 10.30 am and 3 pm. The centre is run by the Australian Native Dog Training Society which aims to get a better deal for dingoes. Their first goal is to have dingoes legally recognised as dogs, not vermin.

The Blue Mountains

The Blue Mountains, part of the Great Dividing Range, have some truly fantastic scenery, excellent bushwalks and all the gorges, gum trees and cliffs you could ask for. The hills rise up just 65 km inland from Sydney, and even a century ago this was a popular getaway for affluent Sydneysiders who came to escape the summer heat. Despite the intensive tourist development, most of the area is so precipitous that it's still only open to bushwalkers.

The blue haze which gave the mountains their name is a result of the fine mist of volatile oil given off by eucalyptus trees – which is also why eucalypt forests can explode into firestorms.

During the '94 fires, large areas on the east and south-east sides of the Grose Valley were burned, but the Blue Gum Forest escaped almost intact. A low-intensity fire in the undergrowth raced through without causing too much damage to the larger trees.

There are two distinct attractions to the Blue Mountains – the national parks with their superb scenery and opportunities for walking and other activities, and the guesthouses with their hill-station atmosphere. Of course, it's possible to combine both. There's nothing like coming back to a log fire in an Edwardian house after a day of walking through the bush.

History
The first Europeans into the area found evidence of extensive Aboriginal occupation but few Aborigines. It seems quite likely that catastrophic diseases had travelled up from Sydney long before the explorers.

The colonists at Port Jackson attempted to cross the mountains within a year or so of their arrival, driven not just by the usual lust for exploration but also by an urgent need to find land suitable for growing food for the new colony. However, the sheer cliffs, blind valleys and tough terrain defeated their attempts for nearly 25 years. A member of one unsuccessful expedition described the journey as like 'travelling over the tops of houses in town'. Meanwhile, many convicts came to believe that China, and freedom, was just on the other side of the mountains.

The first crossing was made in 1813, by Blaxland, Wentworth and Lawson. They followed the ridge-tops and their route is pretty much the route of today's Great Western Highway. The first road across the mountains was built in just six months, and the great expansion into the western plains began.

After the railway across the mountains was completed in the 1860s, wealthy Sydneysiders began to build mansions here, as summer retreats from the heat and stench of Sydney town. By the turn of the century, grand hotels and guesthouses had opened to cater for the increasing demand. This early tourist boom tapered off by the 1940s, but today there is a resurgence of interest, with some of the old guesthouses making a come-back and new resorts being built.

One of Australia's first conservation battles was won in the Blue Mountains in 1931, when members of the Sydney Bush-walking Club came across loggers about to cut down Blue Gum Forest. They reached an agreement with the loggers to buy out their rights to the timber, and spent the next two years raising the money – just £150 for Blue Gum Forest!

Geography
The Blue Mountains do rise up to 1100 metres, but they are really a sandstone plateau riddled with spectacular gorges. Unlike one eminent visitor, you shouldn't throw stones into those gorges!

It is not easy to conceive a more magnificent spectacle than is presented to a person walking on the summit-plains, when without any notice he arrives at the brink of one of these cliffs, which are so perpendicular, that he can strike with a stone (as I have tried) the trees growing at the depth of between one thousand and one thousand five hundred feet below him; on both hands he sees headland beyond headland of the receding line of cliff, and on the opposite side of the valley, often at a distance of several miles, he beholds another line rising up at the same height...
Charles Darwin, 1836

Climate
Be prepared for the climatic difference between the Blue Mountains and the coast – you can swelter in Sydney but shiver in Katoomba. However, even in winter the days are often clear, and down in the valleys it can be warm.

Although the Blue Mountains are pro-moted as a cool-climate attraction, they're worth visiting at any time of year. With none of the summer haze, winter can be the best time for bushwalks, but beware of sudden changes of weather and come prepared for freezing conditions. Autumn's mists and drizzle can make bushwalking a less attrac-tive proposition, but Katoomba in a thick Scotch mist is an atmospheric place.

It usually snows some time between June and August.

Orientation
The Great Western Highway from Sydney follows a ridge from east to west through the Blue Mountains. Along this less-than-beau-tiful road, the Blue Mountains towns often merge into each other – Glenbrook, Spring-wood, Woodford, Lawson, Wentworth Falls, Leura, Katoomba (the main accommodation centre), Medlow Bath, Blackheath, Mt Vic-toria and Hartley. Just west of Mt Victoria township, the road falls down Victoria Pass, with sharp bends and a gradient of one in eight. On the western fringe of the mountains is Lithgow, occupying a similar position to that of Penrith on the eastern side.

To the south and north of the highway's ridge the country drops away into precipi-tous valleys, including the Grose Valley to the north, and the Jamison Valley south of Katoomba. There's a succession of turn-offs to waterfalls, lookout points or scenic alter-native routes along the highway.

The old Bells Line of Road, much more scenic (and less congested) than the Great Western Highway, is a more northerly approach from Sydney; from Richmond it runs north of the Grose Valley to bring you out on the main highway at Mt Victoria, or you can follow it all the way to Lithgow.

National Parks Large areas to the north and south of the Great Western Highway make up the Blue Mountains National Park. Wollemi National Park, north of Bells Line of Road, is the state's largest forested wilder-ness area (nearly 500,000 hectares), and it stretches almost up to Denman in the Hunter Valley, offering good rugged bushwalking. It has lots of wildlife and similar landscape to the Blue Mountains. Large tracts of Wollemi burned in the '94 fires, but much was untouched, especially the beautiful Colo Valley. At the north-east end of Wollemi is the new Yengo National Park, a wilderness area with no facilities and limited road access.

Kanangra Boyd National Park, west of the southern section of the Blue Mountains National Park, has bushwalking possibilities and grand scenery, and also includes the

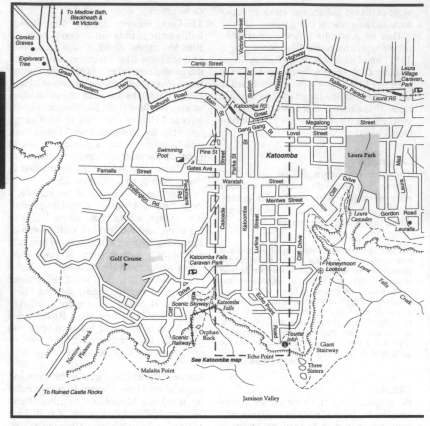

spectacular Kanangra Walls Plateau which is entirely surrounded by sheer cliffs and can be reached by unsealed roads from Oberon or Jenolan Caves.

Information

There is an information centre on the highway at Glenbrook (☎ (047) 39 6266) and another one at Echo Point in Katoomba (☎ (047) 82 0756). The excellent National Parks visitor centre – the Blue Mountains Heritage Centre (☎ (047) 87 8877) – is on Govetts Leap Rd at Blackheath, about three km north of the highway. On weekends a second National Parks visitor information

centre is open in Glenbrook (☎ (047) 39 2950) on Bruce Rd.

Katoomba has its own tourist radio station (87.7 FM), which plays a tape about tourist attractions. You'll hear exhortations to visit 'our woolly friends', but there is some interesting history and other information among the puff.

Books & Maps The National Parks heritage centre in Blackheath is the best place to ask about walks, and they also sell maps and some books. Maps suitable for walking are also sold at information centres. Rockcraft in Katoomba also has maps and books. Mega-

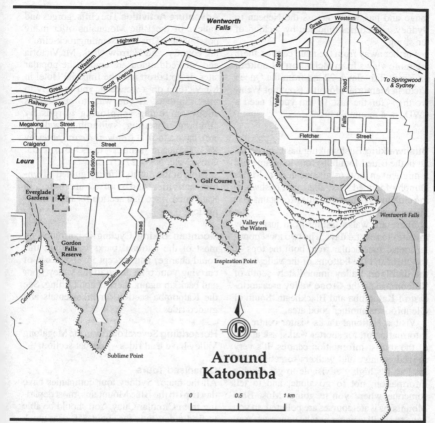

Around Katoomba

0   0.5   1 km

long Books, at 82 Railway Pde in Leura, stocks books about the Blue Mountains. It's open daily.

How to See the Blue Mountains by Jim Smith (Megalong Books) is useful and has details of day walks. Neil Paton's *Treks in NSW* (Kangaroo Press) includes walks in the Blue Mountains, and Lonely Planet's *Bushwalking in Australia*, by John and Monica Chapman, details the walk in Blue Gum Forest.

Things to See & Do

Lookouts Blue Mountains views have been clichés for so long that it's a little surprising to find that they *are* breath-taking. Don't miss **Echo Point** at Katoomba, where you'll see the famous Three Sisters. **Cliff Drive**, running along the edge of the Jamison Valley between Leura and Katoomba, also has some great views. Make sure you get to **Govett's Leap** (near Blackheath, close to the National Parks heritage centre) and **Evans Lookout** (north of the highway, turn off before Blackheath) for spectacular views. Less well known but at least as spectacular are the viewpoints off Bells Line of Road, such as **Walls Lookout**. **Hawkesbury Heights**, on the road between Springwood and Bell's Line of Road, is on the eastern face of the range and has views across the Nepean to Sydney, sometimes muddied by a cloud of tan smog.

Further away from the main centres, there are more views from **McMahon's Lookout** on Kings Tableland, 22 km from the Queen Victoria Memorial Hospital (south of Wentworth) – for the last 10 km you'll need a 4WD (or a mountain bike).

Bushwalking Bushwalking has been popular in the Blue Mountains for a long time and it might even have originated here, as Myles Dunphy founded Australia's first bushwalking club in 1914 and the Blue Mountains was his favourite area.

There are walks lasting from just a few minutes to several days. The two most popular areas, spectacular from both the tops of the cliffs and the bottoms of the valleys, are the **Jamison Valley** immediately south of Katoomba and the **Grose Valley** area northeast of Katoomba and Blackheath. South of Glenbrook is another good area.

Visit a National Parks visitor centre for information or, for shorter walks, ask at one of the tourist information centres. It's very rugged country and walkers sometimes get lost, so it's highly advisable to get reliable information, not to go alone, and to tell someone where you're going. Most Blue Mountains watercourses are polluted, so you have to sterilise water or take your own. And be prepared for rapid weather changes.

Walkabout Backpackers in Katoomba takes guests to trailheads. Private parking for bushwalkers' cars is offered near the trailhead for the Grand Canyon walk on Evans Lookout Rd. It costs $2 a day.

Outside the national park, there's a fairly easy three-day walk from Katoomba to Jenolan Caves along the **Six Foot Track**. C&LM (Department of Conservation & Land Management) has a brochure detailing the walk. More challenging is the 140 km **Ensign Barralier Walking Track** from Katoomba to Mittagong in the southern highlands. See the Southern Highlands section for more information.

Adventure Activities The cliffs, gorges and valleys of the Blue Mountains offer many possibilities. This is outstanding rock-climbing country, and Narrow Neck, Mt Victoria and Mt Peddington are among the popular sites. If you drop into the Imperial Hotel in Mt Victoria on a weekend, you're likely to meet climbers. If you want to get serious about canyoning (exploring gorges by climbing, abseiling, swimming, walking etc), have a look at *Canyons Near Sydney* by Rick Jamieson (send $7 to PO Box 2753, Grose Vale, NSW 2753).

Most of the outfits offering guided adventure activities and courses are based in Katoomba – see that section for more information.

Mountain Biking Cycling is permitted on most of the national parks trails (but this could change) and, except for the hassle of carrying your bike down to the valley floor and back up again, there is good riding. See the Katoomba section for bike rentals and guided rides.

Horseriding Several outfits in the Megalong Valley have trail rides – see that section.

Organised Tours

All the major Sydney tour companies have day trips to the Blue Mountains, most departing from Circular Quay. You should be able to find a day tour for about $50 or a quick half-day visit for about $30.

On weekdays you can buy a rail/bus sightseeing ticket at Sydney's Central Station for about $40. On weekends the hop-on, hop-off Explorer bus meets trains – see the Katoomba section.

The Wonderbus, popular with backpackers, runs day tours of the Blue Mountains ($30) and overnight trips which include the Jenolan Caves ($74), dorm accommodation at the Katoomba YHA hostel (you don't have to be a YHA member; private rooms might be available for a small extra fee) and a visit to the Australian Wildlife Park where you can cuddle a koala. The tariff covers everything except entry to the Jenolan Caves (which ranges from $10 to $12) and meals other than breakfast on the overnighter. Book in person at the Sydney YHA Travel Centre or either of their Glebe hostels. The Martin Place information booth also takes bookings. Day trips leave from Tuesday to Saturday and the overnighter departs on Sunday. It's possible to arrange a stopover in the Blue Mountains.

Another inexpensive tour operator which gets good feedback is Oz-Trek (☎ (02) 360 3444), at 318 Crown St in Sydney's Darlinghurst. A little bit pricier (but offering backpacker rates), Wild Escapes (☎ (02) 482 2881) has 4WD tours which get off the beaten track.

One way to see the area from the road is on the back of a Harley Davidson with Cliff-Edge Cruisers (☎ (047) 82 4649). For something a little bit slower, the Hillcrest Coachman (☎ (047) 84 3265) in Leura has superb old coaches.

From the air the mountains are even more spectacular, and a short flight costs about $30 (minimum two people) with Mountain Aviation (☎ (047) 82 2892) at Katoomba airfield, a few km from Medlow Bath.

Photographers might want to go along on a Go-Anna Photographic Trek (☎ (047) 84 2246), costing about $150 for a full day of walks plus a scenic flight, on which you receive lessons on photography. There's a less elaborate half-day trek for $50.

See the Jenolan Caves section for tours specifically to the caves.

Yulefest

It usually snows in the Blue Mountains some time between June and August, and the region has a Yulefest in July, when many of the restaurants and guesthouses have good deals on 'Christmas' dinners.

Places to Stay

There's a great deal of accommodation in the Blue Mountains, from campsites and hostels to super-expensive guesthouses and resorts. Katoomba is the main accommodation centre. Most places charge more at weekends, and guesthouses tend to be booked out

on long weekends. In the national park you might need a permit to camp, and in some parts camping is banned, so check first.

This book gives details of the area's backpacker accommodation, and a sample of the other places, but there isn't room to list all the options. Information centres (including the NSW Travel Centre in Sydney) stock copies of the *Blue Mountains Holiday Book*, a free brochure which details the more expensive places. You're advised to check prices before heading off to the Blue Mountains because of the numerous packages available and price-hikes at various times of the year. Information centres (and some travel agents) book accommodation in the Blue Mountains and will know of current specials and packages.

Getting There & Away

Katoomba is now almost an outer suburb of Sydney, 109 km from the centre, and trains run frequently on the two-hour trip. The standard one-way fare to Katoomba is $8.60; an off-peak return fare is $10.60. Countrylink buses meet trains at Mt Victoria on Tuesday, Friday and Sunday for the run to Oberon.

Getting Around

The Katoomba-Leura Bus Co (☎ (047) 82 3333) runs between Leura, Katoomba, Medlow Bath, Blackheath and Mt Victoria, with some services running down Hat Hill Rd and Govetts Leap Rd which lead respectively to Perrys Lookdown and Govetts Leap. They'll take you to within about one km of Govetts Leap, but for Perrys Lookdown you will have to walk about six km from the last stop. Services are sparse, with few on Saturday and none on Sunday. In Katoomba the bus leaves from the top of Katoomba St.

The Katoomba-Woodford Bus Company (☎ (047) 82 4213) runs between Leura and Katoomba and east as far as Woodford. They run from the Skyway and Katoomba railway station daily except for Sunday and public holidays.

Ask Fantastic Aussie Tours (Golden West

Travel), outside Katoomba railway station, for details of other local bus services.

GLENBROOK TO KATOOMBA

From Marge's Lookout and Elizabeth's Lookout, just north of Glenbrook, there are good views back to Sydney. The section of the Blue Mountains National Park south of Glenbrook contains **Red Hand Cave**, an old Aboriginal shelter with hand stencils on the walls. It's south-west of the National Parks information centre, an easy walk of about seven km (return).

The famous (and infamous for his cheerfully erotic art) artist and author Norman Lindsay lived in **Springwood** (☎ (047) 51 1067) from 1912 until he died in 1969. His home at 128 Chapman Parade is now a gallery and museum, with exhibits of his paintings, cartoons, illustrations and, in the garden, sculptures. It's open from 11 am to 5 pm Friday to Sunday and public holidays, and admission costs $5 ($2.50 children). The streets in the new housing developments nearby are named after characters from Lindsay's children's masterpiece *The Magic Pudding* – just the sort of kitsch that Lindsay hated.

Just south of the town of **Wentworth Falls** there are views of the Jamison Valley and of the 300-metre Wentworth Falls themselves, from Falls Reserve which is the starting point for a network of walking tracks. In Wentworth Falls, Yester Grange is a restored 19th-century premier's home, open Wednesday to Sunday from 10 am to 4 or 5 pm. Admission costs $4 ($2.50 children).

Sublime Point, south of Leura, is another great lookout. In **Leura**, Leuralla is an Art Deco mansion with a fine collection of 19th-century Australian art, as well as a toy and model-railway museum. The house is a memorial to H V 'Doc' Evatt, a former Labor Party leader who was the first president of the United Nations; it's open from Wednesday to Sunday and admission is $5 ($2 children). In Leura Strand Arcade, the Candy Store has a huge range of items more properly called lollies. **Gordon Falls Reserve** is a popular picnic spot, and from here you can

follow the road back past Leuralla, then take the Cliff Drive or the even more scenic Prince Henry Cliff Walk to Katoomba (it's about four km to Echo Point).

Places to Stay

The *Leura Village Caravan Park* (☎ (047) 84 1552) has tent sites (from $14), on-site vans (from $32) and cabins (from $40). It's at the corner of the Great Western Highway and Leura Mall. There's plenty of expensive hotel, motel and guesthouse accommodation. *Leura House* (☎ (047) 84 2035) at 7 Britain St is a grand Victorian home (c 1880) with a range of accommodation. Mid-week, singles/doubles are around $85/135 with breakfast, but there is a cheaper room ($55/92) and specials in summer. On weekends there are packages.

There are National Parks *camping areas* which can be reached by car at Euroka Clearing near Glenbrook, Murphys Glen near Woodford and Ingar near Wentworth Falls. For Euroka Clearing you need a permit from the National Parks office at Richmond (☎ (045) 88 5247). The dirt track to Murphys Glen is bad in wet weather and is sometimes impassable.

The *YHA hostel* at Springwood was destroyed in the '94 bushfires, but there are plans to replace it. The new hostel might not be in the same place, but it will be similarly simple and designed for people who want to experience the bush.

One of the top places to stay in the Blue Mountains is the big (210 rooms) *Fairmont Resort* (☎ (047) 82 5222) on Sublime Point Rd. It's right on the edge of the escarpment and charges from $190.

KATOOMBA

With its adjacent centres of Wentworth Falls and Leura, Katoomba (population 17,500) is the tourist centre of the Blue Mountains. It has always catered to visitors, being an Australian equivalent of an Indian 'hill station', where plains-dwellers escape the summer heat. Despite the numbers of tourists, Katoomba retains the atmosphere of a town from another time and place, with its Art

Deco and Art Nouveau guesthouses and cafes, its thick mists and occasional snow.

Information

The tourist information centre (☎ (047) 82 0756) is at Echo Point, about two km from the railway station, down Katoomba St.

PLACES TO STAY

1   Walkabout Backpackers
2   Katoomba Hotel
4   Hotel Gearin
12 Carrington Hotel
18 Cecil Guesthouse
19 Katoomba Mountain Lodge
20 Bibury Cottage
28 Katoomba YHA Hostel
30 Clarendon Motel
32 3 Sisters Motel
33 Three Explorers Motel
34 Lilianfels Blue Mountains
35 Echo Point Motor Inn

PLACES TO EAT

3   Chilli Pepper
8   Avalon Cafe Gallery
13 Savoy
14 Satay Sultan
15 Paragon & Blues Cafes
22 Priya's Place
23 Romi's Kitchen
26 Tom's Place & Grillers in the Mist
27 Stirling's
29 Chork Dee
31 RSL Club

OTHER

5   Golden West Travel
6   Renaissance Centre
7   Main St Markets
9   Carrington Bar
10 High & Wild
11 Last Resort
16 Post Office
17 Summit Gear
21 Shopping Centre
24 Rockcraft
25 Mountain Designs
36 Echo Point Lookout
37 Information Centre

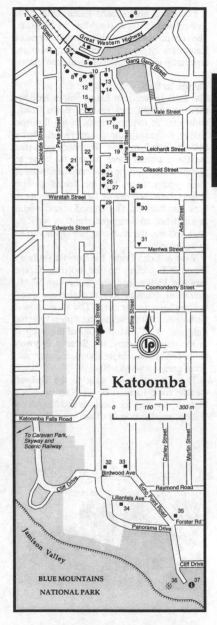

There's a noticeboard laden with New Age-related items at the Main St Markets. The second-hand bookshop at the top end of Katoomba St is worth browsing through, especially if the owner is playing the piano.

Things to See
The Cliff Drive from Leura passes **Honeymoon Lookout** then reaches **Echo Point**, with some of the best views of the Jamison Valley including the magnificent **Three Sisters** rock formation. The story goes that the three sisters were turned to stone to protect them from the unwanted advances of three young men, but the sorcerer who helped them died before he could turn them back into humans. The Three Sisters floodlit at night are an awesome sight. A walking track follows the road and goes even closer to the edge.

West of Echo Point, the **Scenic Railway** drops 200 metres to the bottom of the Jamison Valley (one-way $2, return $3.60, extra for backpacks) and there's good bushwalking in the area. The railway was built in the 1880s to transport miners to a coal mine and its 52° incline is one of the steepest in the world. Nearby, the **Scenic Skyway** cable-car crosses high above a gorge and gives great views ($3.60).

The 12 km return walk to the **Ruined Castle** rock formation on Narrow Neck Plateau, dividing the Jamison and Megalong Valleys another couple of km west, is one of

The Three Sisters

the best – watch out for leeches after rain. The **Golden Stairs** lead down from this plateau to more bushwalking tracks.

The **Explorers Tree**, just west of Katoomba near the Great Western Highway, was marked by Blaxland, Wentworth and Lawson, the first Europeans to find a way over the mountains in 1813.

Activities
At least three places offer abseiling and other adventure-type activities. The competition means that the deals are usually similar – expect to pay about $60 for a day's abseiling. High 'n' Wild (☎ (047) 82 6224), across from the station at the top of Katoomba St, is run by an enthusiastic pair of ex-travellers. They concentrate mainly on abseiling but can help with other enquiries, and they have a rough but handy photocopied guide to some of the walks in the Blue Mountains.

Further down Katoomba St, at No 182, Rockcraft (☎ (047) 82 2014) also offers abseiling. Their speciality is climbing and they run the Australian School of Mountaineering. A two-day basic rock-climbing course costs about $160. There has been good feedback on this. Their bush survival courses (from $170 for two days) also sound interesting. Not far away, upstairs in the Mountain Designs shop, the Blue Mountains Adventure Company (☎ (047) 82 1271) also has abseiling and a variety of tours, with the possibility of 4WD trips starting soon. They also have some interesting mountain bike rides from about $50 a day.

Extreme Mountain Bike Tours (☎ (047) 87 7281, ask for Philip) is a small outfit offering experienced mountain bikers some great riding. Philip works at Mountain Designs and can help bikers with tracknotes.

Places to Stay – bottom
Katoomba Falls Caravan Park (☎ (047) 82 1835) on Katoomba Falls Rd has tent sites from $7 and on-site vans from $35.

Katoomba's *YHA Hostel* (☎ (047) 82 1416) is in a nice old guesthouse on the corner of Lurline and Waratah Sts, near the centre of town. Dorm beds cost from $11 and twins/doubles are around $17 per person. Many of the rooms have attached bathrooms. Nearby, *Katoomba Mountain Lodge* (☎ (047) 82 3933) at 31 Lurline St is a guest-house and hostel charging from $22 per person for singles/doubles with shared bath-rooms, and from $11 for dorm beds. There are also more expensive rooms in the guest-house section.

Walkabout Backpackers (☎ (047) 82 4226) at 190 Bathurst Rd (the westward continuation of Main St) is close to the railway station and has large dorms for $12 (three nights for $30) and good twins for $30. This place isn't as immediately attractive as the other two backpacker places, but it is popular and receives consistently good reviews from travellers. They'll drive you to any of the trail-heads in the area.

Hotel Gearin (☎ (047) 82 4395), always known as Gearin's Hotel, is good for a local pub and has rooms for $25/45. Some of the rooms are much better than average pub rooms. The *Katoomba Hotel* (☎ (047) 82 1106) also has rooms, for $20/40 midweek and $25/50 on Friday and Saturday nights. Both pubs sometimes have share rooms which they let to backpackers for about $20 per person.

Places to Stay – middle & top end

There are many motels and even more guest-houses in and around Katoomba. Rates tend to rise at weekends, and on long weekends accommodation can be scarce.

The *Clarendon Motel* (☎ (047) 82 1322), at the corner of Lurline and Waratah Sts, has guesthouse-style singles/doubles from $40/60 midweek, and other more expensive rooms. There's a theatre restaurant/cabaret here, with shows on Friday and Saturday nights – some of the acts are big names.

Rates at most of the more expensive places vary widely, depending on the time of the week and the time of the year. The *3 Sisters Motel* (☎ (047) 82 2911), at the bottom end of Katoomba St, is an average cheaper motel, charging from around $50 to $85 a single or double.

In the style of the grand guesthouses but with a lower tariff than many, the *Cecil Guesthouse* (☎ (047) 82 1411) at 108 Katoomba St (there's a larger frontage on Lurline St) charges from around $50 per person with breakfast.

At the top of the hotel scale is the *Hydro Majestic Hotel* (☎ (047) 88 1002), a few km west of Katoomba at Medlow Bath, a massive relic of an earlier era. Doubles with breakfast cost from around $130, more on weekends. The equally grand *Carrington Hotel* (☎ (047) 82 1111) in the centre of Katoomba is due to reopen after a major refit. *Lilianfels Blue Mountains* (☎ (047) 80 1200, 1800 024 452 toll-free) near Echo Point is one of the top places in the Blue Mountains and charges from about $240 a double.

Places to Eat

Katoomba St has plenty of good places to eat. The *Savoy* is a bright new place with a large and interesting menu of the focaccia, pasta and Asian-inspired variety. Main courses come with steamed vegetables. It's pleasant and the prices are reasonable. Salads cost from $4.50 and entree-size pastas from $6; the servings are large. For some reason you can't get focaccia after 5 pm, but everything else is available until 9 pm, later on weekends.

Across the street is the *Blues Cafe*, a coffee shop/cafe with interesting snacks for about $5 and main courses for about $12. It has Art Deco decor, but nearby is Katoomba's undis-puted Art Deco palace, the *Paragon Cafe*. While the menu here doesn't go much beyond what you'll find in country-town cafes all over NSW, the surroundings are wonderful and it's worth a visit if only for a cup of coffee. Check out the particularly gaudy cocktail lounge at the back. Of course, once you're inside you might not be able to resist one of their cakes. Meals are around $10 and up. Both the Blues Cafe and the Paragon are open only during the day, except perhaps on weekends and at peak times.

Back on the other side of the street is *Satay Sultan*, a combination of a coffee shop and a

Malaysian restaurant. Small serves cost $6 and main courses with rice, salad and side-dishes are $13.50. Vegetarian meals are about $9. Further down Katoomba St is Romi's Kitchen, a small coffee-shop open during the day which also sells curries for about $6.

Towards the corner of Waratah St at 200 Katoomba St, *Tom's Place* has meals for well under $10. It's open from 11 am to 11 pm during the week and till 1 am on weekends. Nearby *Grillers in the Mist* (groan) sells fresh and frozen seafood and puts together some interesting takeaways, such as grilled sardine rolls for $3.50. Next door is *Stirlings Restaurant* (☎ (047) 82 1298), open for BYO dinner from Tuesday to Saturday and with a menu featuring such standards as rack of lamb, trout and beef. Main courses are around $17. Across Waratah St, the Thai *Chork Dee* has vegetarian dishes for around $7 and other main courses for under $10. At 43 Waratah St, the *Curry Shop* is open for dinner nightly and for weekend lunches.

On Main St next to the railway station, *Chilli Pepper* serves Asian food, with plenty of vegetarian dishes, for around $8 to $11 for a main course. It's open for dinner from Wednesday to Monday, daily at peak times. Upstairs and along some corridors from 82 Main St, near the station, the *Avalon Cafe Gallery* is a relaxed and pleasantly eccentric place, open for lunch and dinner Wednesday to Saturday and for dinner on Sunday. Main courses are around $9 for pasta and $14 for other dishes.

Both *Gearin's Hotel* and the *Katoomba Hotel* have counter meals; Gearin's has the better atmosphere.

At 13 Cliff Drive, near the highway towards Blackheath, the *Arjuna Cafe* has Indian and Asian food, vegetarian meals and home-made cakes. It's a pleasant place with mountain views, open for dinner from Wednesday to Monday. In Leura, the *Little Cafe* in Leura Mall has Indian vegetarian meals for $7 on Sunday evening.

Some way from the town centre on the corner of Cliff Drive and Merriwa St, the *Rooster* is a French restaurant with three-course a la carte dinners for $30 and light lunches served on the verandah overlooking Jamison Valley.

For late-night eating and drinking, try the *Last Resort* restaurant and bar at 8 Gang Gang St, open from 6 pm to 3 am daily. Most meals are $10 or less.

Entertainment

The Carrington Hotel, apparently saved from developers, might be reopening soon. Meanwhile, the hotel's revamped bar, with an impressive tiled facade, is open. There are some dress regulations, but that doesn't stop them from holding events such as horizontal bungee-jumping. The bar at the Last Resort on Gang Gang St stays open until 3 am nightly. There's jazz here on Sunday afternoons and sometimes music at other times. For local bands, try Gearin's Hotel or the Katoomba Hotel on weekends, and there's a blues jam at Gearin's on Monday nights.

See the Mt Victoria section for information on a night out at the Mt Vic Flicks.

Getting Around

If you're driving, be aware of the parking restrictions, as they're strictly enforced by the 'Brown Bomber'.

Bicycle You can hire mountain bikes at the YHA hostel for $20 a day ($15 for guests) and $12 for a half-day ($10 for guests). If all their bikes are out, try the Cecil Guesthouse, further up Lurline St; the rates are similar. Better bikes are available from the Blue Mountains Adventure Company (☎ (047) 82 1271) on Katoomba St for $30 a day (24 hours), less for longer.

Bus A bus service (☎ (047) 82 4213) runs from opposite the Carrington Hotel to the Scenic Railway, approximately hourly until about 4.30 pm on weekdays and a few times on Saturday ($1.60). On weekends and holidays the Blue Mountains Explorer Bus around Katoomba and Leura is a hop-on, hop-off service for which you buy an all-day ticket ($15, $7.50 children). Contact Fantastic Aussie Tours, also called Golden West

Travel (☎ (047) 82 1866), outside Katoomba railway station; the same people run Blue Mountains and Jenolan Caves tours.

Car Rental Cullens (☎ (047) 82 5535) at 60 Wilson St rents cars from $60 a day including insurance and 250 free kms. Other local companies such as Cales (☎ (047) 82 2917) have similar rates.

BLACKHEATH

A relatively large town (population 4000) presenting an ugly face to the highway, Blackheath has the closest railway station to the National Parks' **Blue Mountains Heritage Centre**, about three km north-east along Govetts Leap Rd. The turn-off for the beautiful **Megalong Valley** is in Blackheath too.

There are superb lookouts near Blackheath, among them **Govett's Leap** with the adjacent **Bridal Veil Falls** (the highest in the Blue Mountains), **Evan's Lookout** (turn off the highway south of Blackheath) and **Pulpit Rock** and **Perry's Lookdown** to the north, some km along Hat Hill Rd.

A long cliff-edge track leads from Evan's Lookout to Pulpit Rock and there are walks down into the Grose Valley itself and on the valley bottom – all involve at least a 300-metre descent and ascent. Get details on walks from the National Parks Heritage Centre. Perry's Lookdown is at the beginning of the shortest route to the beautiful **Blue Gum Forest** in the valley bottom – about four hours return, but you'll want to spend longer.

To the west and south-west of Blackheath lie the Kanimbla and Megalong valleys, with yet more spectacular views from places like **Hargreaves Lookout**.

Places to Stay & Eat

The nearest National Parks campsite is Acacia Flat in the Grose Valley, near Blue Gum Forest and a steep walk down from Govetts Leap or Perrys Lookdown, but you can camp in the car park at Perrys Lookdown.

Blackheath Caravan Park (☎ (047) 87 8101) has tent sites from $7 a single and vans from $35 a double. It's on Prince Edward St, off Govetts Leap Rd, about 600 metres from the highway. *Lakeview Holiday Park* (☎ (047) 87 8534) on Prince Edward St has cabins from $40 to $60 a double. *Gardners Inn* (☎ (047) 87 8347) on the highway in Blackheath, just north of the Govetts Leap Rd corner, is the oldest hotel in the Blue Mountains (1831) and charges about $35 per person, including breakfast.

On the road to Evan's Lookout, *Federation Garden Lodge* (☎ (047) 87 7767) has two-bedroom apartments from $80 a double. The grounds are large and the facilities are good. Further along is *Jemby-Rinjah Lodge* (☎ (047) 87 7622), in bushland and with good self-contained cabins from $80.

There are several cafes along the highway, including the *Banksia* which serves breakfast ($8.50 for 'the works') light meals and good coffee. The *Blackheath Cake Shop* gets rave reviews from one muffin fan. On weekends, the *Bush Rock Cafe* on the road to Evan's Lookout has inexpensive meals and vegetarian dishes. At the other end of the price scale, *Cleopatra's* on Cleopatra St is an excellent restaurant, winner of many awards. There's also accommodation, in the region of $200 per person including meals.

THE MEGALONG VALLEY

Unless you walk or take Katoomba's Scenic Railway down to the valley floor, the Megalong Valley offers about the only chance to see what the gorges of the Blue Mountains look like from the bottom rather than from above. The valley feels like rural Australia, a big change from the quasi-suburbs strung out along the ridge-tops.

The valley is largely cleared farmland, but it's still a beautiful place. The road down from Blackheath passes through some lovely **rainforest**, and there is at least one place where you can stop and walk. Just as the road levels out for the run down the valley, look for an orchard on the right in front of a huge old timber homestead.

Megalong Valley Farm (☎ (047) 87 9165) has shearing, milking and other activities as well as Clydesdale horses and native animals. You can book a ride on a Clydesdale. It's open daily from 10 am to 5 pm. There is also accommodation here, with camping from $3 per person and a bunkhouse with dorm beds for $12.

There are several **horseriding** outfits, such as Werriberri Trail Rides (☎ (047) 87 9171) near Megalong Farm and Packsaddlers (☎ (047) 87 9150) at the end of the valley in Green Gully. There was no road to Green Gully until the '50s and no electricity until the '60s, and Packsaddlers is run by one of the district's longest-established families. Both these outfits offer riding by the hour and longer treks, and accommodation.

MT VICTORIA

Mt Victoria is a small place (population 800) with some nice old buildings and a less suburban feel to it than some of the other highway towns. It was popular as a holiday spot early, and Henry Lawson worked here as a house-painter, decorating the new houses that his father had built. Today the town is classified by the National Trust.

Everything is an easy walk from the railway station, where there's a **museum**, open on weekend afternoons. Interesting buildings include the Victoria & Albert guesthouse, the 1849 Tollkeeper's Cottage and the 1870s church.

Mt Vic Flicks (☎ (047) 87 1577 for programme details and bookings) is a movie theatre of the old school, with 'usherettes' and door prizes. They show mainstream films and the more popular arthouse releases. On Thursday and Friday nights it costs just $5, and on Saturday night $10 gets you a double feature plus supper at interval! It used to be possible to take a train from Katoomba to the Mt Vic Flicks and another home again – a pleasant outing. However, the last train currently leaves at about 10.30 pm, which might be too early – the Saturday night double ends long after the last train. The owners (Mr and Mrs Flicks, as they're known) can *sometimes* drive people back to Katoomba by prior arrangement – but please don't abuse their generosity.

Off the highway at **Mt York** there's a memorial to the explorers who first found a way across the Blue Mountains. There's a short stretch of the original road across the mountains here.

Places to Stay & Eat

The *Imperial Hotel* (☎ (047) 87 1233), a very fine old hotel indeed, has what are probably the best backpackers' rooms in the Blue Mountains, at $20 for a dorm bed. They also have singles/doubles from about $30/50 to $70/100, with various packages. The hotel faces both the highway and quieter Station St. The Imperial is the weekend wateringhole of rock climbers, so this is a good place to make contacts.

Down Station St from the Imperial is the *Victoria & Albert* (☎ (047) 87 1588), a guesthouse in the grand old style. B&B costs from $45/90, $15 more with attached bathroom. There's a cafe and in the evening a good restaurant offering two-course dinners for $24.50 and three courses for $30. Another old-style guesthouse is the *Manor* (☎ (047) 87 1369) on Montgomery St with rooms from $75 per person, including dinner and breakfast. The Duke of York, later King George VI, had afternoon tea here in 1927.

HARTLEY HISTORIC SITE

In the 1830s, after the Victoria Pass route made it easier to travel inland from the coast, increasing numbers of travellers crossed the Blue Mountains. However, the discomforts of the old road via Mt York were soon replaced by the discomforts of being bailed up by bushrangers. The government established Hartley as a police post, and the village became a popular place to break the journey, partly because it was safe and partly because of the pubs. Some fine sandstone buildings were constructed, notably the Greek Revival courthouse (1837). Many of these buildings remain today, although the village is now deserted. National Parks (☎ (063) 55 2117) runs tours of Hartley at 10 am, 11 am, noon, 2.15 and 3.30 pm, at $2 per person per building visited.

BELLS LINE OF ROAD

Constructed in 1841 as an alternative route across the mountains, Bells Line of Road runs from near Richmond across to Lithgow, although you can cut across to join the highway near Mt Victoria. It's much quieter than the highway and instead of the strip of close settlement along the highway there are small farms and apple orchards, especially around Shipley.

Not far from the old village of **Kurrajong Heights**, on Bells Line of Road about 15 km from Richmond, Grass Carting (☎ (045) 67 7184) has hi-tech billy-carts and a steep, grassy slope to ride them down. The carts have four-wheel steering and brakes and there's even a lift to get you back to the top of the slope. The first hour costs $8 and it's $5 for subsequent hours. There's also grass skiing. The centre is open on weekends and holidays.

Mt Tomah Botanic Gardens

Midway between Bilpin and Bell, the Mt Tomah Botanic Gardens is a cool-climate annexe of Sydney's botanic gardens. As well as native plants there are exotic species including a magnificent display of rhododendrons. There's a restaurant and a shop with a range of books on Australian flora. The gardens are open daily and admission is $5 per car and $2 for pedestrians and cyclists.

Mt Wilson

Mt Wilson is eight km north of Bells Line of Road; the turn-off is seven km east of Bell. Like Katoomba, Mt Wilson was settled by people with a penchant for things English, but unlike Katoomba with its guesthouses and Art Deco cafes, Mt Wilson is a spacious village of hedges, lines of European trees and houses with big gardens. Near the Post House there's an information board with details of gardens open to the public and some walks in the area, ranging from one to four hours.

A km or so from the village centre is a lovely section of rainforest thick with tree-ferns, the **Cathedral of Ferns**.

Places to Stay & Eat The *Post House* (☎ (047) 56 2000) serves teas and can arrange B&B accommodation, or you could try *Blueberry Lodge* (☎ (047) 56 2022), a pretty house sleeping up to six and costing from $130 a double.

The Zig Zag Railway

The Zig Zag Railway by which, until 1910, trains descended from the Blue Mountains, was built in 1868 and was quite an engineering wonder in its day. A section has been restored, and steam trains run on weekends and in school holidays. The railway is on Bells Line of Road about 10 km east of Lithgow. The fare is $10 ($5 children) and you can phone for timetable information (☎ (02) 858 1480).

JENOLAN CAVES

South-west of Katoomba and on the west edge of Kanangra Boyd National Park, these are the best-known limestone caves in Australia. One cave has been open to the public since 1867, although parts of the system are still unexplored. Three caves are open for independent viewing, and you can visit a further nine caves by guided tours which go about 10 times a day from 10 am to 4 pm, with an evening tour at 8 pm. Tours last 1½ to two hours and prices vary from $10 to $12. At holiday time it's advisable to arrive early, as the best caves can be 'sold out' by 10 am.

Walks

There's a network of walking trails through the bush surrounding the Jenolan caves.

The Six Foot Track from Katoomba to the Jenolan Caves is a fairly easy three-day walk. C&LM has a detailed brochure. Great Australian Walks (☎ (02) 555 7580) has guided walks on the track for about $300. They carry everything for you.

Organised Tours

See Organised Tours at the start of the Blue Mountains section for information on the popular Wonderbus tour. Fantastic Aussie Tours (☎ (047) 82 1866; (02) 281 7100 in

Stalactites, Jenolan Caves

Sydney) has day tours to the caves from Katoomba for about $46 (plus cave entry). Walkers can be dropped off at and collected from the Six Foot Track at Jenolan for $30, but you have to book. They also have a day-trip from Sydney for $62, and the overnight Jenolan Caves Breakaway Pass which costs about $100 (plus $37 single supplement) and includes transport to the caves from Sydney via Katoomba, sightseeing in the Blue Mountains, accommodation at Jenolan Caves House, dinner and breakfast.

Places to Stay
Jenolan Caves House (☎ (063) 59 3304) is a big old-style guesthouse, built in 1889, which has been considerably revamped. Dinner, bed & breakfast packages cost from $90/150. There's a four-course buffet lunch for $19.50. You can also *camp* near Jenolan Caves House.

Binda Bush Cabins (☎ (063) 59 3311), on the road from Hartley about eight km north of the caves, can accommodate six people in bunks for $75 per night. In the town of Oberon, about 30 km north-west of the caves, there are other cheaper options including a *caravan park*.

LITHGOW
Nestled in the western foothills of the Blue Mountains, the Lithgow Valley was first settled by Europeans in the 1820s, but the town didn't begin to grow until the coal was mined in the 1870s to supply the trains which crossed the mountains on the Zig Zag Railway. Today Lithgow is an industrial town (population 12,000) with a rural feel.

There are two information offices, one on Main St (☎ (063) 51 2307), the road into town from the Great Western Highway, and another in the council chambers on the corner of Mort and Eskbank Sts.

Eskbank House on Bennet St (off Inch St which is north of the railway line) is a gracious home built by the founder of Lithgow's coal industry in 1842 and now housing a museum. Admission is $2 and it's open from Thursday to Monday between 10 am and 4 pm. There are fine views from **Hassan Walls Lookout**, five km south of town.

The first steelworks in Australia were established in Lithgow last century, but all that remains is a few crumbling buildings in **Blast Furnace Park** (great name) off Inch St. There are plans to develop walks and explanatory notices.

Places to Stay
Lithgow Caravan Park (☎ (069) 51 4350) on Cooerwull Rd has tent sites for about $8 for two people, on-site vans from $25 and self-contained cabins from $40.

There are several pubs with accommodation from around $15/25, such as the *Courthouse* (☎ (063) 51 3234) on Main St, and several motels such as *Parkside Lodge* (☎ (063) 52 1232) on the highway, charging around $50/60, and the cheaper *Lithgow Valley Inn* (☎ (063) 51 2334), off the highway on Cooerwull Rd.

Getting There & Away
Train Lithgow is on the main western rail-

way line to Bathurst, Orange and Dubbo. Electric trains also run from Sydney ($18).

Bus Countrylink buses (☎ (063) 52 3099) connect with some trains and run to Orange, Bathurst, Dubbo, Coonabarabran, Mudgee, Gulgong, Forbes and Parkes, but not daily.

Car & Motorbike Lithgow is on the Great Western Highway running between Sydney and Bathurst. You can head south on smaller roads to Oberon (from where still smaller roads lead south to Goulburn) and north to Mudgee and Gulgong (turn off the highway about seven km on the Bathurst side of town).

AROUND LITHGOW
The road from Lithgow north towards Mudgee runs parallel to the western escarpments of the Blue Mountains and there are some good views, especially from **Pearsons Lookout**, 40 km north of Lithgow. See the Bathurst to Mudgee section of the Central West chapter for information on places further along this road.

At Lidsdale, on the Mudgee road about 10 km north of Lithgow, a road which degenerates into a rough track runs 30-odd km to **Newnes**, a ghost town where the pub still functions. There's a five-km walk to a disused railway tunnel full of glow-worms and access to the wild Wollemi National Park. An 11-km walking track leads north to the ghost town of **Glen Davis**, where there's a museum open on weekends.

The Southern Highlands

The southern highlands was one of the first inland areas to be settled, and most of it was quickly cleared of unruly native foliage to make way for English-style villages. This development was early enough in Australia's history for the settlers to regard themselves as English landed gentry rather than Australian farmers, and their unease at being so far from home is reflected in their landscape of

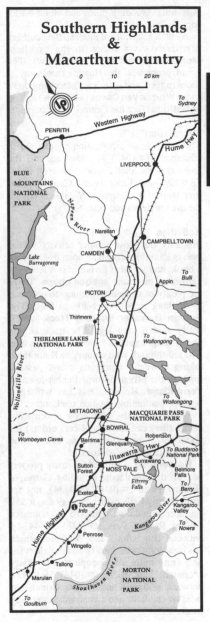

Southern Highlands & Macarthur Country

bare hills, brooding pines and stone buildings.

As well as historical interest, the southern highlands gives access to the excellent **Morton National Park** (see below). The country north of the Hume expressway is more rugged, and there's an interesting drive to the **Wombeyan Caves** (see below) and on to **Bathurst** (see the Central West chapter).

Information
The area's main information centres are in Mittagong (☎ (048) 71 2888) and off the freeway at the Shell Service Centre (☎ (048) 78 9369) near Sutton Forest. Craigie's *Visitors Map of the Southern Highlands* covers the area in detail and costs $3.95.

Activities
Probably the most popular activity in the area is lounging around an open fire reading a book, and the next favourite is a leisurely perusal of the many **antique shops**. There are plenty of more active things to do, such as walking in Morton National Park. The **Ensign Barralier Walking Track** would really stretch your legs. The track begins near Mittagong at Lake Alexandra and winds 140 km through wild country to Katoomba, taking a week to nine days and passing through the privately-owned ghost-town of **Yerranderie**. Robert Sloss has written a booklet containing detailed tracknotes; it's available from the Mittagong information centre (they can mail credit-card orders) for about $9. Information centres in the Blue Mountains might also stock it.

Horseriding is offered on many properties on the highlands, including Carringal Holiday Farm (☎ (048) 86 4234), not far from Fitzroy Falls, which charges about $50 for accommodation and $16 an hour for riding; Roslyn Park (☎ (048) 84 4434), between Bundanoon and Wingello, which has hour-long rides for $18 and day rides for $85 (minimum two people); and Misty Mountain Trail Rides (☎ (048) 41 0243), between Wingello and Tallong, which has rides by the hour and can arrange three-day treks.

Festivals & Events
The Mittagong Country Fair is held in late March and the Bowral Tulip Festival is held in late September. Over the Queen's Birthday long weekend in June, the village of Burrawang holds a folk music festival.

Guesthouses
In the 1920s a bout of nostalgia for 'home' afflicted the area and lavish country-house-style guesthouses catered to the wealthier Sydneysiders. Few remain, but those that do are enjoying a resurgence in popularity. This can be a bleak place in winter, with grey skies and winds off the snow, so log fires and hearty meals have their attraction and certainly offer a contrast to Sydney, not far away on the Hume expressway. As in the Blue Mountains, many guesthouses here celebrate Christmas in winter.

The larger places are almost in the resort class, and the words 'exclusive' and 'luxury' figure highly in their advertising. The NSW Travel Centre and some travel agents in Sydney have glossy brochures about the more expensive places and will know about packages and special deals.

Getting There & Away
Train Some trains on the Sydney to Canberra run stop at Mittagong, Bowral, Moss Vale, and Bundanoon; the XPT to/from Melbourne stops at one or more of these stations; timetables change.

Bus Long-distance buses running on the Hume Highway between Sydney and Melbourne call in at Mittagong, but most of them don't go on to Bowral and Moss Vale. The Mittagong information centre sells tickets for most bus-lines; you can buy Countrylink tickets at the railway station, a few blocks away. Note that buses don't necessarily come off the expressway into Mittagong unless they know that someone is waiting, so you have to book.

Firefly stops at the information centre, Pioneer Greyhound Australia stops at the Caltex service station and Countrylink stops at the railway station.

Berrima Coaches (☎ (048) 71 3211) runs fairly frequent weekday services between Mittagong, Moss Vale and Bowral, with a few continuing on to Berrima, Sutton Forest, Exeter and Bundanoon. On Saturday morning there are buses between Mittagong, Moss Vale and Bowral. Buses also link Wollongong and Moss Vale, some running via Bundanoon.

Car & Motorbike The Hume Expressway runs past Mittagong and Bowral. The Illawarra Highway links the area with the coast and runs through Moss Vale.

MITTAGONG & BOWRAL
These two large towns have almost blended into each other and **Moss Vale**, just south of Bowral, is heading the same way. The total population of this area is approaching 20,000.

If you're driving between Bowral and Mittagong, take the scenic route over **Mt Gibraltar**, which gives good views down the valley.

In Mittagong, the three-dimensional **Castle Maze** on the corner of Bowral and Bessemer Sts is open daily from 10 am to 5 pm. It will cost you $4 ($3 children) to get lost. **Butterfly House** on Bessemer St has a large collection of live butterflies and is open daily. Admission is $5 ($3.75 children).

Bowral's claim to fame is that Sir Donald Bradman began his cricketing career here. A large **Bradman Museum** (☎ (048) 62 1247) is being developed, and the first stage has been completed. It's a museum in a purpose-built pavilion by a cricket ground and contains plenty of memorabilia. You can see videos of the Don's career and other pieces of cricketing history. The museum is on St Jude St, a few blocks east of the main street. It's open from 10 am to 4 pm daily, and admission is $3 ($1 children).

Places to Stay
The *Mittagong Caravan Park* (☎ (048) 71 1574) on the old highway has tent sites for about $10, on-site vans for about $25 and cabins from $30. The *Moss Vale Village Park* (☎ (048) 68 1099) off Argyle St (the Illawarra Highway) south of the town centre is a little more expensive.

The *Mittagong Hotel* (☎ (048) 71 1923) on the old highway has accommodation from about $35/50 a single/double, although they sometimes advertise backpacker specials.

Motels range from the *Melrose* (☎ (048) 71 1511) and the *Mittagong* (☎ (048) 71 1277) on the highway in Mittagong, charging from about $40/50, to the swag of expensive places in Bowral such as the *Oxley View* (☎ (048) 61 4211) on Moss Vale Rd, which also has cheaper rooms starting at around $50.

Braemar Lodge (☎ (048) 71 2483) off the old highway just north of Mittagong is a big old mansion in large grounds with rooms from about $40/50 midweek. There's an Indian restaurant here.

In Robertson, on the Illawarra Highway between Bowral and the coast, *Ranleigh House* (☎ (048) 85 1111) was built in 1924 as a big, exclusive guesthouse. It went through some changes, becoming a friary, a country club and a hotel, but is now back in business as a guesthouse, with 60 renovated rooms. Deer and peacocks roam through the

Our Don Bradman
If you need to read this section you must come from one of the barbaric nations which don't play cricket. If you do come from a cricketing country there's probably no need to read this section. Anyway...

Sir Donald Bradman is probably the greatest batsman cricket has ever seen, retiring in 1948 after a test career of 20 years, with a test batting average of 99.9! The average would have been over 100 had he not been dismissed for a duck (0) in his last innings, and it's a mark of the man's character that he didn't play another match to boost the average. ■

extensive grounds, and apparently a friendly ghost roams the hallways. B&B rates start at about $50 per person, more on weekends.

Top-end places to stay include *Links House* (☎ (048) 61 1977), *Berida Manor* (☎ (048) 61 1177) and *Milton Park* (☎ (048) 61 1522), all in or near Bowral.

WOMBEYAN CAVES

These interesting caves are reached by an even more interesting mountain road. The caves reserve is a pretty little valley, with mown lawns shaded by poplars and pines. The surrounding bushland is a nature reserve with some walking trails and plenty of wildlife. You can walk to a swimming-hole at Limestone Canyon.

Organised Tours

Guided tours of the caves cost $8 ($4 children), and there's one cave which you can inspect by yourself for $6. For $500, a party of up to 10 people can spend a whole day underground, undertaking more strenuous exploration. You have to book six weeks ahead (☎ (048) 43 5976).

Places to Stay

There are campsites ($7), on-site vans ($40), cabins with ensuites ($55) and a three-bedroom cottage ($65) at the caves reserve (☎ (048) 53 5976 for bookings). There's a kiosk, and also a well-equipped communal kitchen for campers.

On the Mittagong road, just before the steep ascent into the Wombeyan Nature Reserve, *Wollondilly Station Campsite* (☎ (048) 88 9239) has some lovely camping areas on the banks of a broad, shallow river, for $4 per person ($2 children). They also rent out tents. Off the road, a bit further back towards Mittagong, is *River Island Retreat* (☎ (048) 88 9236) with camping and other accommodation. There's a small store here.

Getting There & Away

Coming from Canberra or Melbourne, the Goulburn/Taralga route is quickest and involves only four km of narrow, winding road; coming from Sydney, take the road running west from Mittagong. This route is direct but it involves about 45 km of narrow, steep and winding mountain road – very scenic but slow. This is a popular drive, and on weekends there must be a lot of other cars to meet at the blind corners.

Fuel is available at the caves reserve.

BERRIMA

The first Europeans travelled through the Berrima area early in the 19th century, on an expedition to prove to Sydney's convicts that China (and thus freedom) did *not* lie on the other side of the Great Dividing Range. The site for Berrima was chosen by explorer Thomas Mitchell, and the town was founded in 1830. It blossomed as a stopping-place on the way to the wide lands west of the mountains. However, the road proved too steep for easy travel, bushrangers infested the route and eventually the railway bypassed the town. Berrima's population dropped to just eight people by 1900, meaning that the town suffered little from further development.

Berrima's main street is a stretch of coffee shops, antique shops and craft places catering to Sydneysiders on Sunday drives – but don't be deterred, as the town is well worth a look for its buildings. The best is the neo-classical **courthouse**, built in 1838. The court now houses an excellent little museum, and for $2 ($1 children) you can see an audiovisual show on Berrima's history and visit the courtroom set up as it was during the trial of a notorious murderer – complete with lifelike dummies and a soundtrack. The courthouse is open daily and also has tourist information (☎ (048) 77 1505).

There's another museum at the other end of the main street, opposite the Alpaca Centre. It's open on weekends; admission is 50c (20c children). The nearby **Surveyor General Inn** claims to be Australia's oldest continually operating hotel (ho-hum). The first owner of the pub built himself a large house on Wilkinson St, **Harper's Mansion**, which is open for inspection from Saturday to Monday.

Berrima Bicycle Hire is at Armfield Cottage on the old highway.

Places to Stay

The *White Horse Inn* (☎ (048) 77 1204) on Market Place was built in 1832 but has much more recent motel units from about $60, as does the *Berrima Bakehouse Motel* (☎ (048) 77 1381). The *Surveyor General Hotel* (☎ (048) 77 1226) on the main street charges $50/80, including breakfast. Ask the information centre about the several B&B places, most of which are pricey.

BUNDANOON

Bundanoon (population 1500) is a village midway between Sydney and Canberra, handy for the southern highlands and the north side of Morton National Park. Tourists discovered the town early and in the 1920s Bundanoon was the guesthouse capital of the southern highlands, with over 50 guesthouses. There are far fewer today, but you can still experience some of that stuccoed charm.

There are plenty of craft studios in the area but not many other services. Bundanoon has a couple of cafes and a pizzeria and ANZ and Westpac bank agencies, neither of which is open every day.

Ye Olde Bicycle Shoppe (☎ (048) 83 6043), next to the post office and not far from the railway station, has tourist information and rents bikes from $15 per day; cycling is a popular way to get around the area's villages. The shoppe is closed on Wednesday.

Bundanoon's main attraction is its proximity to the northern escarpments of **Morton National Park**, and there are a number of lookouts and walking trails within easy reach of the town. **Glow-worm Glen**, best visited at night, is in Morton National Park and is a half-hour walk from the end of William St in Bundanoon.

Exeter, a hamlet seven km north of Bundanoon, will satisfy Anglophiles in search of walled parks, gloomy lanes of pine trees and stone houses.

Places to Stay

The *YHA Hostel* (☎ (048) 83 6010) is on Railway Ave (the main street), about one km east of the station. It's an old boarding-house in a large, leafy yard. The manager might not be around if you arrive during the day, but the common areas are left unlocked. Dorm beds are $12, twins/doubles are $16 per person.

The *Bundanoon Country Hotel* (☎ (048) 83 6005) is a well-equipped place charging from $50/90. It's across the tracks from the railway station. Most other places to stay are much cheaper midweek than on weekends, when you might have to take a package including meals. *Killarney Guesthouse* (☎ (048) 83 6224) on Ellsmore Rd dates from 1897 and is in six hectares of garden. It's a big setup, with a theatre restaurant and various accommodation options, from about $50 per person midweek with weekend packages from about $180 per person. *Mildenhall* (☎ (048) 83 6643) at 10 Anzac Pde has weekend packages including Friday and Saturday night accommodation and most meals for $220/380 with shared bathroom or $250/410 with ensuite. Bring your own alcohol.

Getting There & Away

Train Bundanoon is on the Sydney to Canberra line.

Bus Countrylink runs to Wollongong daily, via Moss Vale. Taking a train to Wollongong then a bus up Macquarie Pass would be a long but interesting way to get here from Sydney.

MORTON NATIONAL PARK

Covering more than 160,000 hectares, this wilderness area has magnificent sandstone cliffs and waterfalls which drop down to the deep forests in the valleys below.

The main information centre (☎ (048) 87 7270) for the park is at Fitzroy Falls. Ask here about camping in the valleys below the escarpments – you'll probably have to walk in. The closest road access to the park is around Bundanoon and Fitzroy Falls, and on the road from near Kangaroo Valley to Tallowa Dam on the Shoalhaven River. There's also the road running to Sassafras (surrounded by the park) from either Nowra or Braidwood.

The spectacular **Fitzroy Falls** drop a total of 120 metres, and the less well-known **Twin Falls** are a km or so from here. The corner of the park near Bundanoon has a character of its own, with many lookouts. In the south of the park is the **Pigeon House**, a curiously-shaped mountain. See the South Coast chapter for information on climbing it.

Twin Falls Bush Cottages (☎ (02) 977 1159 for bookings) are self-contained and sleep six people in two bedrooms, or up to four in a single-bedroom cabin. They are on their own patch of bushland. Nightly rates are $80 a double up to $150 for six people, plus a linen hire charge unless you bring your own. Weekend rates are higher. There's a minimum stay of two nights.

On the north-east edge of Morton is the smaller **Budderoo National Park**, with more waterfalls, lookouts and walking trails. On the west side of the park is the **Minnamurra Rainforest Area** (see the Kiama section of the South Coast chapter). Access is from Robertson to the north or from Jamberoo near Kiama.

KANGAROO VALLEY

From Fitzroy Falls to Kangaroo Valley the road descends the steep escarpment. Kangaroo Valley is a lovely place, largely cleared but with steep, forested mountains and escarpments encroaching onto the valley floor.

You enter the valley through the castellated **Hamden Bridge** (1898), a few km north of the township of Kangaroo Valley. Near the bridge is **Pioneer Farm**, an old homestead with historic displays and some native animals in a refuge. Markets are held here on the last Sunday of the month. You can also visit **Sharply Vale Fruit World**, a big fruit orchard. There's also a *caravan park* (☎ (044) 65 1223).

In Kangaroo Valley township, *Glenmack Caravan Park* (☎ (044) 65 1372) is a very pleasant place to pitch a tent ($10) and has cabins from $35. It also has tourist informa-

tion. There are several craft studios, including Collections (☎ (044) 65 1621) which is open at weekends and displays the work of Don Sheil, a metal artisan.

The Shoalhaven and Kangaroo rivers are popular for canoeing, and Kangaroo Valley Canoe Adventures (☎ 1800 805 742 toll-free) has day trips and longer journeys, usually on weekends. There's a minimum group size of six, but ring Geoff Whatmore and he might be able to fit you in with a group. Day trips cost $40 per person and overnight trips are $200.

The road from Kangaroo Valley to Berry is beautiful. Take the turn-off to the left just out of Kangaroo Valley township on the road to Nowra. This narrow little road takes you up through thick forest to a neatly farmed plateau, then plunges down again through the forest, about 20 km in all. Take it easy – the road is narrow and winding and there are school buses.

Up here is the *Skyfarm* (☎ (044) 65 1651), a small, luxurious farmstay catering to one group of up to six people at a time. You'll pay $240 a night for the whole place midweek, and $330 a night on weekends. Between a few people, this is good value for a touch of luxury.

Illawarra & Wollongong

Illawarra is the coastal strip and the spectacular escarpment behind it, running from Royal National Park down past the cities of Wollongong and Port Kembla.

The region was explored by Europeans in the early 19th century, but apart from timber cutting and dairy farming there wasn't much development until the escarpment's coalfields attracted miners. By the turn of the century Wollongong was a major coal port. Steelworks were developed in the 1920s, and today the region is one of the country's major industrial centres.

Despite the industry, there is spectacular natural scenery and some great beaches.

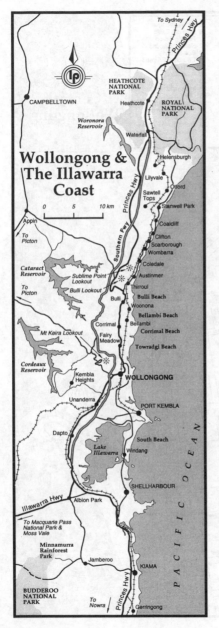

AROUND SYDNEY

WOLLONGONG

Wollongong (population 214,000), 80 km south of Sydney, is the state's third largest city and now sprawls south to the biggest steelworks in Australia at Port Kembla. Despite the industry, Wollongong's city centre is pleasant enough and there are some excellent beaches, especially north of the centre where the Illawarra escarpment draws closer to the beach.

Wollongong has a bit of a reputation as a tough town, but if you've successfully negotiated the streets of Kings Cross you won't have any trouble here. It's a hard-working industrial city without the edgy weirdness of inner Sydney – a day trip to Wollongong can be a good break. You don't even have to drive: the train trip from Sydney takes less than 1½ hours and a day-return ticket costs $10.60. It's an interesting ride through tunnels and the bushland of the Illawarra escarpment, and there are great beaches awaiting you at the end. Beachside suburbs such as Bulli offer plenty of sand and waves and most have railway stations.

Orientation & Information

The GPO is at 296-98 Crown St near the railway station, but you might find the Wollongong East post office near the tourist information centre more convenient.

Bushcraft on Stewart St has hiking and camping gear.

The tourist information centre (☎ (042) 28 0300) on the corner of Crown and Kembla Sts is open daily. West of here, Crown St is a pedestrian mall for two blocks, emerging on Keira St, part of the Princes Highway. Through traffic bypasses the city on the Southern Freeway.

Things to See & Do

Wollongong has an interesting harbour, with the fishing fleet based in the southern part called **Belmore Basin**, which was cut from solid rock in 1868. There's a fish market, a couple of seafood restaurants and an **old lighthouse** (1872) on the point. The old lighthouse is open weekends from noon to 4 pm (1 pm to 5 pm during daylight-saving

PLACES TO STAY

3 Novotel Hotel
15 Keiraleagh House
31 Piccadilly Motor Inn
32 Tattersalls Hotel

PLACES TO EAT

1 The Lagoon & Kiosk
4 North Beach Gourmet
5 Jodie's
6 Beach House Restaurant
7 Ocean View Chinese
 Restaurant
16 Market Street Bistro

17 Cafe on the Mall
 & Terrace Cafe
18 Pot of Gold & Frenchies
19 Il Faro
21 Tannous
22 Thai Carnation
24 Lorenzo's
29 Plant Room
35 Angelo's Trattoria
36 Som Chay

OTHER

2 Wollongong North
 Railway Station
8 Swimming Pool

9 Old Lighthouse
10 Belmore Basin
11 Fishing Co-op
12 New Lighthouse
13 Bus Station
14 Church of England
 Cathedral
20 Harp Hotel
25 Museum
26 Information Office
27 City Gallery
27 Oxford Tavern
28 City Bus Terminal
30 Post Office
33 Wollongong Railway
 Station & Countrylink
34 Bushcraft

Central Wollongong

0   250   500 m

To Corrimal, Bulli
& Sydney

Fairy   Creek

Stuart
Park

PACIFIC

OCEAN

Bode   Ave

Blacket   St

Bourke   Street

Edward   Street

Gipps   Street

Gipps

Throsby   Drive

Campbell

Smith   Street

Market   Street

Victoria   Street

Crown   Lane

Rawson St

Crown

Burelli   Street

Stewart   Street

McCabe
Park

Ellen   Street

Bank   Street

To Kiama
& Nowra

To Port Kembla
(8 km)

Harbour

Endeavour
Drive

North   Beach

Wollongong   Beach

time); don't confuse it with the larger, newer lighthouse on the headland.

North Beach, north of the harbour, generally has better surf than the south beach (Wollongong Beach). The harbour itself has beaches which are good for children. Other beaches run north up the coast.

The interesting **City Gallery** on the corner of Kembla and Burelli Sts is open from Tuesday to Friday and weekend afternoons. This is the largest regional gallery in the country and its collection focuses on 20th century Australian painting and sculpture and Aboriginal paintings.

The **museum** of the Illawarra Historical Society, on Market St, is open Wednesday from 10 am to 1 pm and weekend afternoons ($2). The museum includes a reconstruction of the 1902 Mt Kembla village mining disaster.

Port Kembla's industrial area has been renamed **Australia's Industry World** (it sounds like a theme park), and the bicycle path from downtown Wollongong leads through it.

The **Wollongong Botanic Garden** on Northfields Ave, Keiraville, has both tropical and temperate plants and a lily lake.

If you're interested in seeing a **rugby league** match, check whether the Illawarra Steelers, members of the Sydney competition, are playing a home game in front of adoring fans.

On the second Sunday of the month (every Sunday in January and all long weekends) you can ride an old tram or steam train at the **Illawarra Light Railway Museum** on Tongarra Rd in Albion Park. Admission is free and rides cost up to $1.50.

A big **surf-lifesaving carnival** is held on Australia Day.

North of the City Wollongong sprawls north nearly to the edge of Royal National Park, but the beachside suburbs are almost individual towns by the time you get this far. **Bulli** and **Thirroul** (where D H Lawrence lived during his time in Australia; the cottage where he wrote *Kangaroo* still stands) are both popular. In Bulli the Heritage Centre

Museum at the railway station is open on Sunday from 10 am to 4 pm. At **Coalcliff** (appropriately named – coal was mined near this cliffside for most of the 19th century) the road heads up the escarpment. Shortly after, near **Stanwell Park**, it enters thick forest for the drive through Royal National Park.

Up the coast there are several excellent beaches. Those with good surf include **Sandon Point**, **Austinmer**, **Headlands** (only for experienced surfers) and **Sharkies**.

On the road to the village of **Otford** and Royal National Park, the **Lawrence Hargrave Lookout** at Bald Hill above Stanwell Park is a superb clifftop viewing-point. Hargrave, a pioneer aviator, made his first attempts at flying in the area early this century. Hang-gliders fly there today, and Aerial Technics (☎ (042) 94 2545) has courses. **Symbio Koala Gardens** (☎ (042) 94 1244) on Lawrence Hargrave Drive in Stanwell Tops (above Stanwell Park) has kangaroos and other animals. Near Otford, Otford Valley Farm Riding School (☎ (042) 94 2442) has **horseriding** for $15 an hour, and there are several other outfits in the area.

South of Wollongong Just south of Wollongong, **Lake Illawarra** is very popular for watersports. The world windsurfing titles were held here in the summer of '93/94. South of Lake Illawarra, **Shellharbour** is a popular holiday resort. It's one of the oldest towns along the coast and was a thriving port back in 1830, but it declined after the construction of the railway lines. The name Shellharbour comes from the number of shell middens (remnants of Aboriginal feasts) the early Europeans found here. There are good beaches on the Windang Peninsula north of the town. The Windang Boatshed hires boats and canoes.

Views The most popular viewpoint in the area is the spectacular **Bulli Scenic Lookout** high on the escarpment off the highway, with enormous views down to the coastal strip and out to sea. Nearby **Sublime Point** and **Bald Hill Lookout** in Stanwell Tops are similarly breathtaking. **Mt Keira Summit Park**

on Queen Elizabeth Drive on Mt Keira offers an even higher viewpoint. For something completely different, try the **Hill 60 Lookout** on Military Rd in Port Kembla, which has views of the vast industrial landscape.

Illawarra Escarpment State Recreation Area
Taking in land donated by the BHP company, this area is good for bushwalking. There is no vehicle access. The park is comprised of a number of separate pieces from Bulli Pass down to Bong Bong, so it isn't all that large, but the country is spectacular. Contact National Parks (☎ (042) 29 4756) for information on bush camping.

Places to Stay
The information centre books accommodation and will know of any specials.

Caravan Parks & Camping You have to go a little way out before you can camp. The council runs *camping areas* on the beach at Corrimal (☎ (042) 85 5688), near the beach on Farrell Rd in Bulli (☎ (042) 85 5677) and on Fern St in Windang (☎ (042) 97 3166), with beach and lake frontage. From central Wollongong, Corrimal is about six km north, Bulli is 11 km north, and Windang is 15 km south, between Lake Illawarra and the sea. All charge about $12 for campsites (two people) and from $40 for vans or cabins, with prices rising sharply during school and Christmas holidays. Buses run from the railway station to within walking distance of all these. There are quite a few privately owned *caravan parks* in the area – the tourist office has information.

Hostels There's no formal hostel, but *Keiraleagh House* (☎ (042) 28 6765) at 60 Kembla St north of Market St is a large place catering mainly to long-term students, although they will let you have a bed for $15 a night if there's room. Weekly rates are $75 to $95. *Piccadilly Motor Inn* (☎ (042) 26 4555) next to the railway station has a few units available to backpackers at $20 per person sharing.

Pubs Several hotels have fairly cheap accommodation, such as *Tattersalls Hotel* (☎ (042) 29 1952) at 333 Crown St, just down from the station, charging $25/40/50 for singles/doubles/triples, and the *Harp* (☎ (042) 29 1333) in the centre of town on Corrimal St near Crown St which charges a little more (and has bands).

Pubs up the coast near the beaches have accommodation, such as *Ryan's Hotel* (☎ (042) 67 1086) on George St in Thirroul ($20/30), and the *Corrimal Hotel* (☎ (042) 84 4086) on the highway in Corrimal ($17/27).

Middle & Top End About the only inexpensive motel in the area is the *Cabbage Tree Motel* (☎ (042) 84 4000) at 1 Anama St (behind the Cabbage Tree Hotel) in Fairy Meadow, off the Princes Highway 3.5 km north of the city centre. Singles/doubles cost from $30/35 to $40/45. Just about any bus heading north from the railway station will get you to Fairy Meadow.

Metro Motor Inn (☎ (042) 28 8088) at the corner of Crown and Keira Sts charges from around $50, and the *Piccadilly Motor Inn* (☎ (042) 26 4555) near the railway station at 341 Crown St has similar rates. The *City Pacific Hotel* (☎ (042) 29 7444) at 112 Burelli St has a wide range of rooms, starting at around $50, up to around $130.

Park St Serviced Apartments (☎ (042) 27 7999) at 1 Park St in North Wollongong charges from about $70; *Belmore Deluxe Apartments* (☎ (042) 24 6500) at 39 Smith St has serviced apartments from about $110. The top place to stay is *Novotel Northbeach* (☎ (042) 26 3555) with rooms starting around $130, or less with special deals.

Places to Eat
For good coffee, snacks and meals it's hard to go past *Tannous*, a Lebanese cafe on Crown St at the corner of Corrimal St. Various shishkebabs, felafel and other takeaways are $3, or $5 if you eat in. Eat-in meals come with large serves of houmous, tabouli and bread. There's also a good selection of cakes and sweets.

There are plenty of other places in the area. The *Cafe on the Mall* and the *Terrace* at the corner of Church and Crown Sts are open long hours for snacks and meals. *Lorenzo's* on the Crown St mall near Kembla St is a highly-rated restaurant with an interesting Italian-inspired menu; main courses are around $15. Nearby in Kembla St there's the *Pot of Gold*, a Mexican place with main courses around $10. Across the street is *Il Faro*, a pizza place.

The *Market St Bistro* on Market St west of Corrimal St is open daily except Sunday for dinner and from Tuesday to Friday for lunch. Steaks are around $15; there are some dress restrictions.

Angelo's Trattoria at the International Centre, 28 Stewart St, between Kembla and Corrimal Sts, serves moderately priced Italian food plus steaks and seafood. It's popular with the local Italian community and is open for lunch and dinner daily. There's no sign on the street – walk along the verandah to the back of the building.

Down at Belmore Basin, the *Harbourfront Seafood Restaurant* is open daily for lunch and dinner, and until 7.30 pm the menu is available at special prices, with most main courses under $15. More seafood is available at the *Lagoon* (☎ (042) 26 1766) in Stuart Park behind North Beach. It has a great location and is open daily for lunch and dinner, and for breakfast on Sunday. The adjacent *Kiosk* is less expensive.

The relaxed *Plant Room* on Crown St opposite the corner of Gladstone Ave, just up the hill from the railway station, opens during the day for coffee and snacks and at night for meals, with main courses around $12. It has a relaxed atmosphere and a cosmopolitan menu. This is a good place for a late-night coffee.

On Bourke St at North Beach, *Jodie's* and *North Beach Gourmet* are cafes serving breakfast and light meals.

Entertainment
Several of the pubs in the centre of town have bands, usually on weekends. Your best chance of hearing an interesting young band

is at the Harp on Corrimal St and the Oxford Tavern nearby on Crown St. There are many clubs and other pubs with live entertainment scattered throughout the area. Bear in mind that this is a steel town where hair gets let down on weekends.

Getting There & Away
Train Many fast electric trains run to/from Sydney (about 80 minutes, $8.60, off-peak day-return $10.60), and a fair number continue south along the coast to Kiama, Gerringong and Bomaderry (Nowra). On weekends a tourist train runs to Moss Vale ($5), inland near the Hume Highway and Morton National Park.

Bus The bus station (☎ (042) 26 1022) is on the corner of Keira and Campbell Sts. There are several daily services to Sydney ($15, sometimes much less) and one to Canberra ($28) which runs through Moss Vale and the southern highlands. Greyhound Pioneer Australia's Sydney to Melbourne ($58) coastal route runs through Wollongong. Direct buses to Brisbane with Pioneer cost $75. Pioneer Motor Service (a Nowra company, not the national giant) runs through Wollongong along the south coast as far as Eden ($47) and also connects with buses to Canberra.

Car & Motorbike The Princes Highway (a freeway near Wollongong) runs north to Sydney, or you can follow the coast road up through Otford and Royal National Park, rejoining the highway near Sutherland. The highway also runs south to Kiama and the south coast, and eventually ends in Melbourne.

The Illawarra Highway runs up the escarpment to the southern highlands.

Getting Around
You can reach a lot of Wollongong from the railway line, and trains are fairly frequent. There are also some buses; the main stop is in Crown St where it meets Marine Drive.

Although it's definitely urban cycling, bringing a bike on the train from Sydney and riding around the area is a good idea. A cycle path runs from the city centre north to Bulli and south to Port Kembla. You can hire bikes in Stuart Park behind North Beach.

The Central Coast & Lake Macquarie

The central coast is a strange combination of the beautiful and the awful – superb surf beaches, lakes and national parks combined with huge swathes of rampant suburban housing. The central coast's population is over 200,000, with more urban areas around Lake Macquarie immediately to the north, blending into the sprawling city of Newcastle. While you're stuck in one of the central coast's suburban-style traffic jams, you might want to ponder on the possibility of this mess taking over the entire east coast of Australia. It's a depressingly likely scenario.

The central coast's tourism symbol is the pelican, and the huge birds are everywhere, paddling around in search of a meal or gliding overhead and looking about as manageable as jumbo jets. Some have learned the trick of perching on street lights, like weighty gargoyles.

Australian pelican

Orientation
As well as the long string of surf beaches, the central coast includes some lovely inland waterways. **Broken Bay** in the south is the wide and beautiful mouth of the Hawkesbury River, with many wide bays and inlets, including Brisbane Water which runs up to Gosford. Next north is Tuggerah Lake, which meets the sea at the Entrance. North of Tuggerah Lake is the smaller Lake Budgewoi near Toukley, and just north of here is Lake Munmorah. These three lakes are actually contiguous. A few km north of Lake Munmorah is Lake Macquarie, which runs all the way up to outer Newcastle.

West of the lakes in the low **Watagan Mountains** are 13 state forests running up to the Hunter Valley. There are walking trails and camping is permitted, except in picnic areas. The old village of **Cooranbong** is the main access point for the Watagans. This area bore the brunt of the fires of '94 and is extensively burned. West again you come to the vast national parks of the **Blue Mountains** – see that section.

Gosford is the main town in the area, blending into the surrounding urban areas. Larger beachside centres are Terrigal and the Entrance. On the eastern side of Lake Macquarie, Swansea is the start of a long strip of suburbs up to central Newcastle.

Information
The Gosford information centre (☎ (043) 25 2835) is at 200 Mann St near the railway station, and is open from 9 am to 5 pm on weekdays and until 2.30 pm on weekends. Gosford City also has information centres at Terrigal (☎ (043) 84 6577) and Umina (☎ (043) 43 2200). There's a large information centre on Marine Pde at the Entrance (☎ (043) 32 9282) and others in Toukley, at the corner of Victoria St and Main Rd (☎ (043) 92 4666), and at Railway Square in Wyong (☎ (043) 51 2277).

Lake Macquarie's information centre (☎ 1800 802 044 toll-free) is in Swansea, on the highway north of the bridge. It's open daily. The lake's only sea entrance is at Swansea.

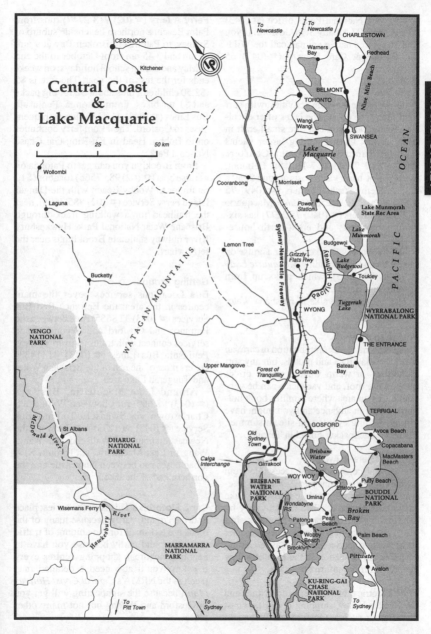

There's a National Parks office (☎ (043) 24 4911) at 207 Albany St in Gosford. If you find an injured native animal, call the Wildlife Rescue & Care Society (☎ (043) 65 1121).

Activities

Watersports are the main activities, with surf right along the coast. The lakes offer excellent boating and you can hire small craft in many towns. Outfits renting larger yachts include Summertime Yacht Charters (☎ (049) 47 7036) at 7 Hill St, Belmont, whose eight-berth yacht costs around $250 a day. Alchemy Yacht Charters (☎ (049) 75 3297) is a little cheaper. Lake Macquarie Holiday Cruisers (☎ (049) 75 2177) has six-berth motorboats and eight-berth houseboats.

Several boats will take you for a cruise on Lake Macquarie, including *Macquarie Lady* (☎ (049) 73 2513), which picks up from Toronto and Belmont.

There are good walks in Brisbane Water National Park.

Places to Stay

There is plenty of accommodation in caravan parks, holiday flats and motels, but any sort of holiday or warm weather sends prices through the roof, and vacancies can be very scarce. It's an area where families book holidays a year in advance and you might have trouble finding even a tent-site in summer. There's a backpacker hostel in Terrigal.

Getting There & Away

The central coast is easily accessible from Sydney, via the Sydney to Newcastle freeway and a variety of public transport. Lake Macquarie can be reached from Sydney by car (exiting the freeway at Wyong is simplest) but by public transport access is easier from Newcastle. See the Newcastle Getting There & Away section in the Hunter Valley chapter for more information.

Train Electric trains run between Sydney and the Hunter Valley, stopping at central coast destinations such as Gosford and Wyong.

Ferry A ferry (☎ (02) 918 2747) runs from Palm Beach, a northern beachside suburb of Sydney, to Patonga in Broken Bay at 9 am, 11 am and 3.45 pm from October to the end of May and during school holidays; on weekends for the rest of the year. The fare is $5 ($2.50 children), plus about $2 for big packs and $1 for bikes. From Patonga, Peninsula Bus Lines (☎ (043) 41 4133) has infrequent buses to Gosford. The 11 am ferry continues on to Bobbin Head in Ku-Ring-Gai Chase National Park.

From Brooklyn you can get to Patonga on a cruise boat (☎ (02) 985 7566) for about $10 return, or to Wobby Beach with the Dangar Island Ferry Service (☎ (02) 985 7605), near the trailhead for a walking track through Brisbane Water National Park. Hawkesbury River railway station in Brooklyn is near the ferry wharf.

Getting Around

Bus Local bus services cover the main centres in the area: the Entrance Red Bus Services (☎ (043) 32 8655) runs between the Entrance and Gosford and Wyong. Some services connect with trains to/from Sydney. Peninsula Bus Lines (☎ (043) 41 1433) covers most of the rest of the Brisbane Water and Tuggerah Lake area.

Around Lake Macquarie, Busways (☎ (043) 92 660) runs between Wyong and Charlestown via Swansea. Toronto Bus Service (☎ (043) 59 1233) runs between the Newcastle suburb of Wallsend and Wangi Wangi on Lake Macquarie, via Toronto. STA urban buses run between Newcastle and the northern end of the lake.

Car & Motorbike This isn't the easiest place to drive around, partly because many of the roads are too small for the amount of traffic they carry, and partly because you have to negotiate suburban shopping centres every few km. You'll also need a detailed map (such as the NRMA's *Central Coast Holiday Map*), because the signposting will get you to Gosford and Wyong but not many other places.

GOSFORD & AROUND

Gosford is the largest town in the area, some way inland with a frontage onto Brisbane Water. There are good transport connections to Sydney, and Gosford might be a good base for visits to **Brisbane Water National Park**, but otherwise it's just another large town. It blends into **Woy Woy**, which blends into **Umina**.

Europeans first settled this area in the 1820s, attracted by the timber, and boat-building followed. After the railway from Sydney was built in the 1880s, tourism began and large guesthouses were built.

Just south of Brisbane Water National Park is **Patonga**, a small fishing village on Broken Bay. There's a *caravan park* here. Off the road to Patonga is **Warrah Lookout**, with great views over Broken Bay.

Not far away but screened from the housing estates of Umina and Woy Woy by a steep road over Mt Ettalong, **Pearl Beach** is a lovely hamlet surrounded by the national park. Pearl Beach is a National Trust town with restrictions on development, so it is likely to retain its charm – a fact which is appreciated by the media personalities who have weekenders here. The only way to stay here is to rent a holiday house or apartment, and there aren't many. A two-bedroom house on the beach will cost around $1000 a week at peak times. Contact Pearl Beach Real Estate (☎ (043) 41 7555) for more information. Right on the beach, *Pearl Beach House* is open for lunch on weekends and for dinner from Thursday to Saturday. Seafood is the specialty and main courses are around $18.

Things to See & Do

Off the freeway nine km south-west of Gosford, **Old Sydney Town** (☎ (043) 40 1104) is a major reconstruction of early Sydney with non-stop street theatre retelling events from the colony's early history. It's open from 10 am to 4 pm Wednesday to Sunday and daily during school holidays. Admission is $14.50 ($8 children). The Narara Dancers perform a daily corroboree in the woolshed for $15 ($5 children). Pen-

insula Bus Lines runs here from Gosford and several tours run here from Sydney.

Just north of Gosford on the road to Ourimbah (Mann St) is the **Australian Reptile Park** (☎ (043) 28 4311), which has many native animals and birds as well as reptiles and is open daily. Admission costs $9.50 ($4 children). Off Brisbane Water Drive in West Gosford is **Henry Kendall Cottage**, a small museum in the home of an early poet. It's open on Wednesday and weekends, and daily in school holidays. Admission is $2 ($1 children). Other attractions in the Gosford area include the **Forest of Tranquillity** (turn west off the freeway at Ourimbah), a private forest reserve. Admission is $6 ($3 children).

As well as the area's national parks there are several smaller reserves around Gosford with walking trails, such as **Rumbalara Reserve**. The information centre has pamphlets.

The historic MV *Lady Kendall* (☎ (043) 23 2974) cruises Brisbane Water from Gosford Wharf at 10.15 am and 1 pm from Saturday to Wednesday, daily during school holidays.

Brisbane Water National Park

On the north side of the Hawkesbury River, across from Ku-Ring-Gai Chase National Park, Brisbane Water National Park extends from the Pacific Highway in the west to Brisbane Water in the east – despite its name the park has only a short frontage onto that body of water.

In rugged sandstone country, the park is known for its wildflowers in early spring, and there are many walking trails. South of the township of Kariong is the turn-off for the **Bulgandry Aboriginal Site**, where there are interesting rock carvings.

The main road access is at Girrakool; travel west from Gosford or exit the Sydney to Newcastle freeway at the Calga interchange. Wondabyne Railway Station, on the line between Sydney and Newcastle, is right in the park and near several walking trails (including part of the Great North Walk). You have to tell the guard that you want to get off at Wondabyne, and you have to travel in the rear carriage. Ferries from Palm Beach run to Patonga and ferries from Brooklyn run to Wobby Beach, on a peninsula south of the park and near some walking trails.

Large areas of the park were burnt during the fires of '94. For more information contact the National Parks office (☎ (043) 24 4911) in Gosford.

TERRIGAL & AROUND

Terrigal, about 12 km east of Gosford and on the ocean, is probably the most upmarket of the central coast's beachside towns, and a big *Holiday Inn* (☎ (043) 84 9111; 1800 024 966 toll-free) dominates the foreshore. The steep streets are leafy and the houses are on large blocks, but it's still suburbia. There's also a new hostel, *Terrigal Beach Backpackers* (☎ (043) 85 3330), with dorm beds for $14 and a double or triple room for $35. It's a block from the beach at 10 Campbell Crescent.

South of Terrigal the houses are a little further apart, and **Copacabana** is tiny by comparison. North of Terrigal, Bateau Bay is adjacent to the southern section of the small Wyrrabalong National Park. It's popular for surfing and the beach is patrolled. There are a number of caravan parks.

Bouddi National Park

Bouddi National Park extends south from MacMasters Beach to the north head of Broken Bay. It also extends out to sea in a marine reserve; fishing is prohibited in much of the park. Vehicle access is limited, but there are walking trails leading to the various beaches. The park is in two sections on either side of Putty Beach which does have vehicular access. The Maitland Bay Centre has information on the park but it's open only on weekends. There are *campsites* in the park but you have to book through the National Parks office in Gosford (☎ (043) 24 4911).

THE ENTRANCE & NORTH

The Entrance (the town is on the Tuggerah Lakes' sea inlet) is the only place you need to visit if you want to see the best and worst of the central coast. It's a large urban area of relentlessly cheerful cream-brick and introduced palm trees, plastic chairs on footpaths, happy urchins and beer-bellied parents – all on a supremely beautiful lake and a superb surf beach.

Daily at 3.30 pm the **pelicans** are fed on the beachfront near the information centre.

The **Entrance Boathouse** (☎ (043) 32 2652), under the bridge, rents canoes, rowing boats and motor boats.

Given the decidedly hedonistic surroundings, it seems a bit odd to find an excellent second-hand bookshop in the Entrance, but **Richard's Old Books** is just that. As well as shelves of thrillers and romances, there are plenty of older standards at reasonable prices. It's one of those infuriatingly interesting shops where the books are shelved two-deep, so you're never quite sure that you've seen everything. Richard's is in the main street, just up the hill from the main group of shops.

At the Entrance **Sunday markets**, held by the beach near the main shopping centre, keep an eye out for the excellent wooden toys and models made by J & L Greve.

The Entrance is home to the central coast **Irish Athletic Club**, which holds a Celtic Festival in late November, with games, music, dance and poetry, plus a ball on the opening night.

The peninsula north of the Entrance is the small **Wyrrabalong National Park**, with walking trails and diverse flora habitats. There's another chunk of the park south of the Entrance around Bateau Bay.

North of the national park, between Tuggerah Lake and Budgewoi Lake, is the town of **Toukley**, and north on the isthmus separating Budgewoi Lake and Lake Munmorah is **Budgewoi**. Running up the coast for 12 km is the **Lake Munmorah State Recreation Area**. It books out at peak times and you must book campsites in advance at the office (☎ (043) 58 1649), off the road just south of Elizabeth Bay. There are two *camping areas*, Freemans Beach and Frazer Beach. The day-use fees are $6.50 per car ($3 for motorbikes and pedestrians), and camping costs $10 a night for two people plus $2 per extra person. You have to pay the day-use fee for the first night you stay, so it's an expensive overnight stop if you're alone.

Near Warnervale, on the west side of the lakes, the **Smoky Mountain & Grizzly Flats Steam Railway** has steam-train rides on Sunday and at other times during school holidays. Admission is by donation.

Dawsons Scenic Cruises (☎ (043) 32 9282) cruises on Tuggerah Lake and up the Wyong Creek.

Places to Stay
Just across the bridge at the end of the spit separating the sea from the lake, *Dunleith Caravan Park* (☎ (043) 32 2172) is close to the surf and has good facilities. Tent sites cost from about $18 (there are no unpowered sites), on-site vans from $45 and self-contained cabins from about $55. Like everywhere else on this coast it's shoulder-to-shoulder in the peak seasons. Other caravan parks include *Blue Bay* (☎ (043) 32 1991) and *Pinehurst* (☎ (043) 32 2002).

The *Entrance Hotel* (☎ (043) 32 2001) is near the water at the bottom of the main street, near the post office. Singles/doubles cost from $30/66 including breakfast. Some rooms have attached bathrooms for the same price. You're unlikely to find a vacancy here in summer.

Places to Eat
There are plenty of reasonable places for a meal. *Preecha Thai* is an inexpensive takeaway on the main street in the Entrance. Just downhill from here is *Taste 'n' Tell*, with an interesting menu including salads, seafood and curries. Main courses are around $7 at lunch and twice that at dinner. It's open from Wednesday to Sunday. Down near the post office, *Boua Thai* has main courses at

around $10 and the nearby *Pelican Pizza Trattoria* is reasonable. Around the corner on Coral St there's the upmarket *Kohinoor Tandoori Restaurant. Casanova Oysters,* under the bridge at the Entrance Boathouse, sells oyster, prawn and crab meals to eat in or take away daily except Monday.

LAKE MACQUARIE
Lake Macquarie is Australia's largest coastal lake and covers four times the area of Sydney Harbour. It lies immediately to the north of the Tuggerah Lakes, separated by a narrow strip of land, and extends up to outer Newcastle. The suburban development here is a little older than that on the central coast and there's a little more room to move.

The main centres on Lake Macquarie are **Charlestown** and **Belmont**, outer suburbs of Newcastle, and **Swansea**, a long-time holiday resort for the working town of Newcastle and now also merging into the city's sprawl. The two or three caravan parks here tend to have cheaper tent-sites than those further south. **Nine Mile Beach** runs north from Swansea to **Redhead**, where there's a caravan park. The western shores of Lake Macquarie are relatively undeveloped, but they certainly aren't virgin bush. **Toronto**, another Newcastle satellite suburb, is on the west shore at the northern end.

On **Wangi Point** on the west shore, near Swansea on the opposite shore, there are walking trails through the bush and a caravan park. Also on the point is **Dobell House**, where artist William Dobell lived and worked. It's open on Sunday from 2 to 4 pm.

Vales Point power station and the adjacent colliery are at the south end of the lake. It's possible to arrange a visit (☎ (043) 52 6111). The area's two other power stations aren't open to visitors.

The Hunter Valley

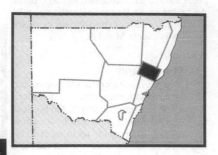

The Hunter is best known for its wines, with about 50 vineyards in the lower Hunter (mainly around Cessnock and Pokolbin) and half a dozen more in the upper Hunter (around Denman). Coal is another important commodity and accounts for Newcastle's name. The first export of coal was in 1814, in exchange for a cargo of rum. Electricity is another product flowing out of the Hunter Valley; 75% of the state's power is generated here.

For a relatively small area, the Hunter includes some very different landscapes. West of Newcastle there's a large urban agglomeration (linked by poorly maintained roads clogged with irritable traffic); further west, beyond Cessnock, you come to the lower Hunter wineries, a very pretty area of gentle hills which continues west into the upper Hunter. The Hunter River itself flows past some of the oldest towns in the country. Although there are rolling farmlands in the Hunter, there are also some stretches of rugged ranges, harbouring lush stands of cool-climate rainforest in the Barrington Tops National Park.

Down on the coast there are excellent surf beaches and the tranquil waterways of Myall Lakes National Park, an estuarine lakes system, and nearby Port Stephens, a large bay which is home to dolphins – see the North Coast chapter for these.

History

The Hunter was settled early in the history of NSW, as it offered a large expanse of relatively flat land, with coastal access. Before the Great Divide was crossed, such land was at a premium.

In 1804 intractable convicts were sent to Coal River (later Newcastle) because of the area's remoteness, but the settlement was moved up the coast to Port Macquarie in 1824 after the growing influx of graziers, timber cutters and coal miners diluted the isolation.

Finding a route from the Hunter to the plains beyond the mountains proved almost as difficult as crossing the Blue Mountains. For thousands of years Aborigines had used the rocky gorges of what is now the Goulburn River National Park as a route between the inland and the Hunter Valley (and thus the sea), but the Europeans, encumbered with their wagons, flocks and herds, had to settle for the long, steep climb up the Liverpool Ranges near present-day Murrurundi. The current road closely follows one of the first routes out of the Hunter.

Vines were first planted in the valley in the 1820s, and by the 1860s there were 2000 hectares under cultivation. This enthusiasm for wine in what was in other matters a somewhat puritan colony reflects the problems that harder drinks were causing. A Hunter champagne made its way to Paris in 1855 and was favourably compared to the French product. However, most of the Hunter wineries gradually declined, and it wasn't until the 1960s that winemaking again became an important industry.

At the Golden Grape Estate on Oakey Creek Rd near Pokolbin there's a museum devoted to the history of winemaking in the area.

Geography

The Hunter Valley cuts a triangular swathe

through the Great Divide, broadest on the coast and tapering as it approaches Denman. On the southern side of the valley rise the sandstone ranges of the Wollemi and Goulburn River national parks; the northern side is bordered by the high, rugged ranges leading up to Barrington Tops National Park.

Getting There & Away

Air See the Newcastle and Cessnock sections of this chapter for routes and fares.

Train Trains run up the valley en route to Armidale and Moree, and north-coast line trains stop at Maitland, Dungog and Gloucester. These trains don't run into central Newcastle, but electric trains from Sydney do – see the Newcastle section.

Bus The major interstate lines pass through Newcastle on their Pacific Highway run up the north coast, but you're better off taking a train from Sydney to Newcastle. Batterhams Express (☎ 1800 043 339 toll-free; in Sydney book at Eddy Ave) has at least one bus a day running from Sydney's Eddy Ave to Tamworth via the Hunter towns of Cessnock ($18 from Sydney), Singleton ($23.50), Muswellbrook ($27) and Scone ($33), but not Newcastle. Border Coaches (☎ (02) 281 9366, 1800 028 937 toll-free) and McCafferty's run up the New England Highway on their service between Sydney and Brisbane.

Car & Motorbike There are several routes into the Hunter Valley from Sydney. The quickest way is to take the Sydney to Newcastle freeway, which doesn't actually reach Newcastle but stops short near Minmi, west of the city. The alternative is to come by the slow roads of the central coast, entering Newcastle through its southern suburbs.

Much longer than these but more interesting is the road between Windsor and Singleton, known as the Putty Road. See the Macquarie Towns section in the Around Sydney chapter. There's also an interesting route (including some unsealed roads) from Wisemans Ferry, passing through Wollombi.

The Pacific Highway, the main coastal route north, emerges from Newcastle and branches off from the New England Highway at the big Hexham Bridge over the Hunter River, not far north-west of Newcastle's outer suburbs. Heading north, the Pacific Highway runs through Raymond Terrace and Bulahdelah, but bypasses the region's coastal attractions.

See the North of Newcastle section in this chapter for information on the Bucketts Way, an interesting diversion from the Pacific Highway.

The New England Highway runs up the valley and climbs up to the New England tableland near Murrurundi; the other western exit from the valley is through Denman and Sandy Hollow to Merriwa.

NEWCASTLE

Newcastle (population 265,000) doesn't have much of a reputation among Sydneysiders – they still think of it as a dirty industrial city with little to offer. But Sydneysiders are wrong. If you must think of Newcastle as an industrial city, picture the English city of Newcastle (which is about the same size), then imagine it with a warm climate and superb surf beaches a stone's throw from the city centre. Also, the old cliche about working towns being very friendly places still applies here.

A recent survey judged Newcastle as the best Australian city to live in, and with its good services, excellent climate, great beaches and easy access to national parks it isn't hard to see why.

For a look at how the city once saw itself, visit the murals in the lobby of the Great Northern Hotel on the corner of Scott and Watt Sts. One romanticises heavy industry, the other early beach culture.

Strangely, the name of this working town is pronounced new-*cah*-sel, not new-*cass*-el.

History

Originally named Coal River, the city was founded in 1804 as a place for the most intractable of Sydney's convicts and was known as the 'hell of New South Wales'. The

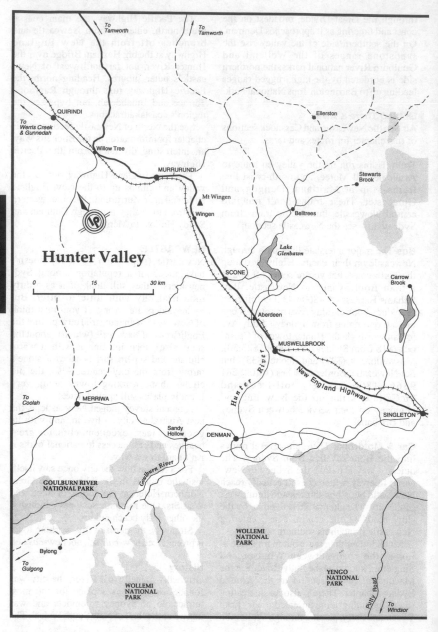

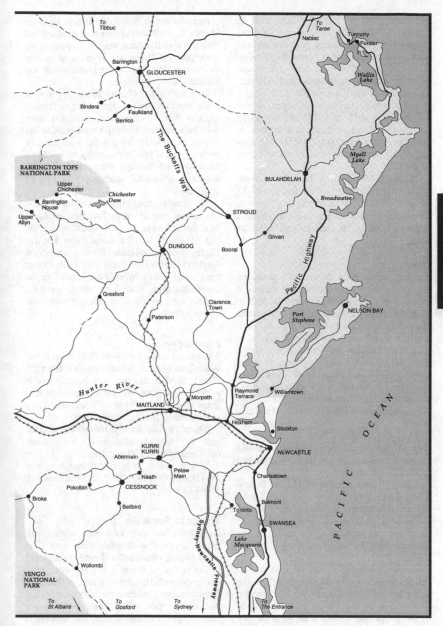

breakwater out to Nobby's Head with its lighthouse was built by convicts, and the Bogey Hole, a swimming pool cut into the rock on the ocean's edge below the pleasant King Edward Park, was built for Major Morriset, an early commander and strict disciplinarian. It's still a great place for a dip.

Large-scale coal-mining began in the 1850s and in 1915 the BHP company set up steelworks. Once, just about everyone in Newcastle was employed by BHP, but now the workforce is down to 4000 and will drop to 2000.

In late 1989, Newcastle suffered Australia's most destructive earthquake, with 12 people killed and a lot of property damage. There are still a few signs of the earthquake – props holding up facades and buildings being restored.

Orientation

The city centre is on the end of a peninsula separating the Hunter River from the sea. It tapers down to the long sandspit leading to Nobbys Head, just east of the city centre. Hunter St is the three-km-long main street, and it's a pedestrian mall between Newcomen and Perkins Sts. Hunter St's shops continue west for a long way, well out of the city centre, and Hunter St eventually becomes the northbound Pacific Highway; southbound, the Pacific Highway is Stewart Ave, which meets Hunter St west of the city centre.

The railway station, the long-distance bus stop, the post office, banks and some fine old business buildings are at the north-east end of the city centre.

King St runs parallel to Hunter St and along the bottom of steep Cook Hill. Up on the hill you get great views of the city and the coastal lands beyond, and here there are some fine old terraces of houses. Church St and tree-lined Tyrrell St run along the top of the hill.

Across the railway lines (there's a footbridge beginning in Hunter Mall) is the waterfront and the Queens Wharf complex. The swimming beaches are on the other side of the peninsula, a short walk from the city

centre. To get to Newcastle Beach head up Hunter St, walk across the pleasant plaza and then through the 'time tunnel' – a pedestrian underpass which contains some good murals of Newcastle's beach-life history, not *too* vandalised.

Just across the Hunter River (by now a wide estuary called Port Hunter) from Queens Wharf is Stockton, a modest town with beaches and striking views back to the city of Newcastle. It's not far from the city by ferry, but if you're travelling by road you have to wind through the docks and some dramatic industrial landscapes, a trip of about 20 km.

Newcastle's sprawling suburbs and satellite towns run down to Swansea on Lake Macquarie and north to Hexham, where the big Hexham Bridge carries the Pacific Highway over the Hunter River and the New England Highway branches off for its run up the Hunter Valley. West of Newcastle are the coalfields and more large urban centres; further west are the lower Hunter vineyards and wineries.

Information

The tourist office (☎ (049) 29 9299) is in the waterfront Queens Wharf complex; from the Hunter St Mall take the elevated walkway. It is open from 9 am to 5 pm on weekdays and from 10 am to 3.30 pm on weekends. They sell excellent heritage walk maps.

There's a cloakroom at the railway station, near the Watt St entrance. It's for day-use only and costs $1.50 per item.

If you need to get vaccinations, see TravelSafe (☎ (049) 29 1321) on Level 2, 160-173 King St.

Things to See & Do

Newcastle is well endowed with clean beaches, many with world-class surf. The main beach, **Newcastle Beach**, is adjacent to the centre of town; it has an ocean pool and good surf. Just north of here is **Nobby's Beach**, more sheltered from the southerlies and often open when other beaches are closed. South of the centre, **Bar Beach** is

HUNTER VALLEY

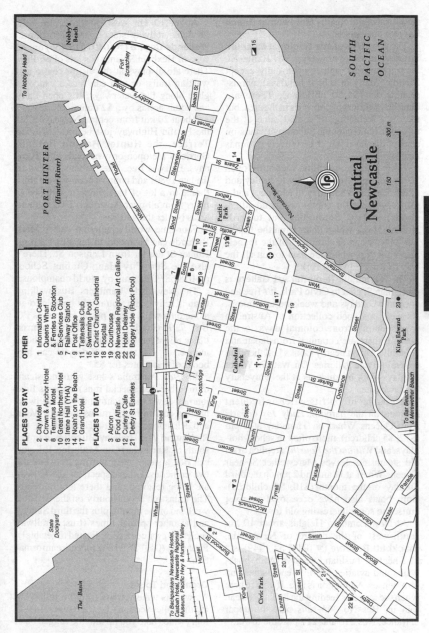

PORT HUNTER
(Hunter River)

To Nobby's Head

Nobby's Beach

Fort Scratchley

Nobby's Road

Beach St

Parnell Pl

Stevenson Place

Telford Street

Bond Street

Pacific Park

Pacific Street

Zaara St

14

15

SOUTH PACIFIC OCEAN

Central Newcastle

0   150   300 m

Newcastle Beach

Ocean St

Esplanade

Shortland

Wharf Road

Scott Street

7

Hunter Street

Bolton Street

10
11 12
13

Ocean St

8
9

17

19

18

King Edward Park

23

State Dockyard

The Basin

Mall

Footbridge

6

King Street

Church Street

Perkins Steps

Steps

Brown Street

Cathedral Park

16

Barker St

Ordnance Street

Wolfe Street

Newcomen Street

To Bar Beach & Merewether Beach

Wharf Road

Bolton St

Burwood St

McCormack Street

Tyrell Street

3

Parade

Anzac Parade

Kitchener Parade

Swan Street

Brooks Street

Darby Street

Laman Street

Queen St

Civic Park

4
5

2

20

21

22

23

To Backpackers Newcastle Hostel,
Casbah Hotel, Newcastle Regional
Museum, Pacific Hwy & Hunter Valley

PLACES TO STAY
2   City Motel
4   Crown & Anchor Hotel
8   Terminus Motel
10 Great Northern Hotel
13 Irene Hall (YHA)
14 Noah's on the Beach
17 Grand Hotel

PLACES TO EAT
3   Alcron
6   Food Affair
12 Curley's Cafe
21 Derby St Eateries

OTHER
1   Information Centre,
    Queens Wharf
    & Ferries to Stockton
5   Ex-Services Club
7   Railway Station
9   Post Office
11 Tattersalls Club
15 Swimming Pool
16 Christ Church Cathedral
18 Hospital
19 Courthouse
20 Newcastle Regional Art Gallery
22 Hotel Delaney
23 Bogey Hole (Rock Pool)

floodlit at night. Nearby **Merewether Beach** has two huge pools.

The good **Newcastle Regional Museum** is housed in an old brewery at 787 Hunter St, Newcastle West, and is open daily except Monday (daily in school holidays); admission is $3 ($1.50 children). There are currently no tours of collieries in the area, but there's a recreation of a coal mine at the museum. It includes the Supernova hands-on science displays. Wickham railway station is nearby.

There is a free **maritime museum** (open 10 am to 5 pm from Tuesday to Friday and afternoons from Saturday to Monday) and a military museum (open weekend afternoons) in **Fort Scratchley** out towards Nobbys Head, which dates from the 1880s. For $1 you can explore part of the tunnels under the fort which are said to run all the way to King Edwards Park.

The **Newcastle Regional Art Gallery** is on Laman St next to Civic Park. It's free and is open weekdays and weekend afternoons. As well as a good collection of Australian works dating from colonial days to the present, there are ceramics from Japan and Australia. Up on nearby Cooks Hill there are several private galleries. On Watt St, **Watts** displays work by students at the University of Newcastle.

A couple of outfits offer infrequent **cruises** on the harbour. *Lady Joy* departs from Queens Wharf on Thursday at 2 pm ($12, $5 children), more often in school holidays, and *William the Fourth*, a replica of an old steamship, leaves Merewether St near Queens Wharf at 11 am and 2 pm on the third Sunday of the month ($10, $5 children). Both boats also have occasional up-river cruises to some interesting old towns.

At New Lambton Heights about 10 km south-west of the centre of Newcastle, **Blackbutt Reserve** (☎ (049) 52 1449) is a 182-hectare bushland reserve with bushwalks and aviaries, wildlife enclosures and fern houses. Admission is free. If you're here when the ranger is feeding the koalas you can join in. Bus No 363 runs past the upper entrance, Nos 216 and 217 past the lower.

About 10 km west of the centre near Sandgate railway station, the **Shortlands Wetlands Centre** (☎ (049) 51 6466) on the edge of Hexham Swamp has lots of birdlife. There are displays at the visitor centre and walking trails, or you can hire a canoe to glide along the waterways. It's open daily and admission is by a $2 donation.

About 20 km from central Newcastle, off the Pacific Highway just before Raymond Terrace, the **Hunter Region Botanic Gardens** are open on weekends and Tuesdays. Entry is free. The gardens opened in the late 1980s and contain mainly local flora (home to a lot of local fauna), with specimens from all over Australia. Two wetland areas border the gardens.

Four-time world champion surfer Mark Richards can be found in his surf shop on Hunter St not far from Denison St. There's also the Sun City Hang-Gliding School (☎ 018 687 020), run by world champions.

The Newcastle Ramblers Bushwalking Club is active, and you might be able to go along on a walk. Their postal address is PO Box 719, Charlestown 2290; the tourist office might have the current contact phone number. At the tourist office you can buy books of tracknotes for $5.

In 1987 Australia's last working steam train (other than special runs) made its final journey down the Richmond Vale Railway, hauling coal from the mines at Pelaw Main and Richmond Main to Hexham. At the **Richmond Vale Railway Museum**, four km south of Kurri Kurri on Mulbring Rd, you can ride a steam train puffing between the two collieries. Other aspects of the railway are being restored, and there is a museum. The trains run about hourly on the first full weekend of the month, plus the third Sunday and at other special times (trust a railway society to produce a complicated timetable!). Phone (☎ (049) 36 1124) for more information.

Organised Tours

As well as winery tours (see the following Up the Valley section) there are several 4WD tours which take you up into the rugged bush on the northern side of the valley. Outfits such as Bush Ranging Tours (☎ (049) 92 1614) will take you to Barrington Tops and other destinations for about $70 (minimum two people).

Festivals & Events
The Newcastle Show is held in February, and Beaumont St hosts a Jazz & Arts Festival in March. Steam engines take over several locations during the Hunter Valley Steamfest in May. The Newcastle & Hunter Valley Folk Club holds its annual music festival in Wollombi in mid-September.

Places to Stay – bottom
Caravan Parks *Stockton Beach Caravan Park* (☎ (049) 28 1393) is on the beach in Pitt St. Sites are $14 a double, on-site vans cost from about $35. Stockton is handy for Newcastle by ferry but it's 20 km by road. There are several caravan parks south of Newcastle, around Belmont and on the ocean at Redhead Beach.

Hostels There are now two hostels in Newcastle, with the YHA operating part of *Irene Hall* (☎ (049) 29 3324) at 27 Pacific St as a hostel. Irene Hall is a large building which was once the nurses' home for the nearby hospital but is now student accommodation. The main advantage of this place is that it's right in the centre of the city and a short walk from the beaches. The disadvantage is that it has a definite institutional feel to it. Still, you do get to meet students during term time. Dorm beds are $12 (YHA members only), singles are about $20 and twins are $15 per person. Checking in after 9.30 pm on weekdays or 8.30 pm on weekends could be a problem.

Further from the centre (but with free pick-ups when you arrive and free bikes to get around on) is *Backpackers Newcastle* (☎ (049) 69 3436), at 42 Denison St. This is a very clean, very friendly place and is recommended. Dorm beds are $12 and doubles are $28. There are free surfboards and one of the owners is a keen surfer who can help you learn. They also have trips to beaches up the

coast and there might be excursions to the lower Hunter wineries. Denison St runs off Hunter St, but if you're driving it's best to come up Parry St (the continuation of King St), to avoid the necessity of making an illegal manoeuvre to get into the top half of Denison St.

Hotels Once a very grand hotel but now terminally past its prime, the *Great Northern Hotel* (☎ (049) 29 4961) on the corner of Scott and Watt Sts is worth a look even if you don't stay there. Check out the murals in the foyer and also the first-floor bar (which stays open until 3 am). The rooms are no worse than standard pub accommodation (and a lot better than many), but the atmosphere of hard times overtaking an aristocrat is a bit dismal. Singles/doubles are $26/41 with shared bathroom, and $33/48 with attached bathroom. There are also triples with bathroom for $63. Weekly rates are much cheaper.

The *Crown & Anchor* (☎ (049) 29 1027) on the corner of Hunter and Perkins Sts has singles/doubles for $25/35; groups can pay $12.50 each in a five-bed family room. The *Lucky Country Hotel* (☎ (049) 29 1997) on Crown St near the corner of Hunter has rooms for $25/35.

Places to Stay – middle & top end
More expensive than most pubs but also much more comfortable is the *Grand Hotel* (☎ (049) 29 3489) on the corner of Bolton and Church Sts in the city centre, across from the courthouse. This fine old pub has been well renovated and the large, pleasant rooms go for $40/42, or $50/52 with attached bathroom. This would be a much nicer place to stay than a cheap motel. The *Terminus Motel* (☎ (049) 26 3244) at 107 Scott St, also known as the *Harbourside Motel*, is central and has rooms for $45/50. The *City Motel* (☎ (049) 29 5855) on the corner of Darby and Burwood Sts, is reasonably central but costs $60/65. In Belmont, about 15 km south, there's a string of cheaper motels along the Pacific Highway.

Noahs on the Beach (☎ (049) 29 5181) on

HUNTER VALLEY

Shortland Esplanade faces the ocean, and standard rates start at $90/95, but there are often specials. The *Radisson* (☎ (049) 26 3777) on the corner of King and Steel Sts starts at about $100 a double, with lower standby and weekend rates.

Places to Eat

From Monday to Wednesday during term, you can put together a main course and dessert for around $5 at the *Hunter TAFE College* on King St.

There are several good places for snacks and meals at the top end of Hunter St. *Vera's Cafe* on the corner of Pacific and Hunter Sts has footpath tables and a wide range, including breakfast for around $6. *Curley's* (the illuminated sign says Vienna Cafe), just around the corner on Pacific St, is a nice place with focaccia for $4.50, pasta from about $6 and other main courses for $8. Also on Pacific St, the *Irene Hall Cafeteria* has inexpensive meals for the students (and hostellers) living above, but anyone can eat there. Breakfast is served from 7 to 9.30 am, lunch from 11 am to 2 pm and dinner from 5 to 7 pm.

At Queens Wharf, *Sinbad's* has seafood in the $15 to $18 range, and also breakfast for around $7. Upstairs, the *Foreshore Restaurant* has all-you-can-eat smorgasbords for $12.90.

Up the escalator on Hunter mall is *Food Affair*, a small food hall. The Chinese place here offers three dishes plus rice for $5.40.

Darby St has a good stretch of varied eating places, most between Queen and Bull Sts. They include: *Taco Bill's* (Mexican), *The Bistro* (interesting menu with entrees around $9 and main courses from $16 to $20), *Natural Tucker* (health-food shop with small cafe), *The Taj* (Indian grocery with fine takeaway section), *Splash* ('the finest fish & chips in the known universe' for $4.20), and *Cravings* at Hotel Delaney (nice new restaurant area, main courses around $10 to $15). Across Bull St is *Lan's Vietnamese* with main courses from around $8.50, and across Darby St from Hotel Delaney is *Al-Oi*, a Thai restaurant (not the metallurgists' delight it

sounds) with similar prices. Next door is *Emilo's Trattoria*. Further down is the *Rattlesnake Club*, a restaurant and bar with vaguely Tex-Mex dishes. Main courses are around $15 to $25; lunch specials are $10.

Voquet, on Darby St near Taco Bill's, is a new place well worth checking out, with stylishly idiosyncratic decor, French food and reasonable prices. Antoine, the enthusiastic owner, wants to create Parisian cafe atmosphere, with a large dollop of chic. Not far away, up on the Church St hill, is *Alcron*, perhaps the oldest restaurant in Australia. The views are good, there's a hint of elegance and main courses are around $20.

Beaumont St, in Hamilton just south of the Pacific Highway as you enter the town, is another street where you'll find lots of places to eat. Italian restaurants such as *Little Swallows*, *Milano's* and *Trieste* still form the mainstay, but there is now a sprinkling of other cuisines.

Seaspray at Noah's On The Beach hotel on Shortland Esplanade specialises in seafood and has good views of the waves.

Entertainment

There's something happening on most nights; get the Wednesday *Newcastle Herald* for an entertainment lift-out or pick up a copy of the weekly *Wire* pocket guide.

The Cambridge Hotel at the corner of Hunter and Dennison Sts has bands, as does Tattersalls Club (Tatts) on Watt St, popular with students. The Kent Hotel on Beaumont St has jazz. Hotel Delaney is a relaxed little pub on the corner of Darby and Council Sts, with music most nights. The popular Brewery, at the Queens Wharf complex, brews its own.

In Merewether the Beach Hotel has bands mainly on weekends. The Bar on the Hill out at the university usually has bands on Thursday nights.

Poetry readings are held at the Newcastle Hotel on the corner of Scott and Market Sts, from 7.30 pm on the second Monday of the month. The Grand Hotel on the corner of Church and Bolton Sts also sometimes has poetry.

Irish music is played at the General Roberts Hotel in New Lambton from 4 pm on the second Sunday of the month.

The Hunter Valley has an active folk music scene and there's likely to be a bush dance on somewhere in the area. The monthly *Green Newsletter* is the best source of information, if you can find a copy.

If you're in the mood for a tasteless night out, try the 24-hour Bellevue Hotel on the corner of Hunter and Hannell Sts. From Thursday to Saturday there are strippers until midnight, then karaoke until dawn...

Getting There & Away

Air Aeropelican flies several times a day between Sydney ($68) and Belmont, just south of Newcastle. For both convenience and the experience, it might be worth paying a little extra and flying with Sydney Harbour Seaplanes (☎ (049) 29 2677; 1800 803 558 toll-free), flying from Newcastle Harbour to Sydney's Rose Bay on weekdays for $95.

Oxley flies between Newcastle and Brisbane ($233), Lismore ($206), Port Macquarie ($126) and Taree ($106). Eastern also flies out of Newcastle. Oxley and Eastern fly from Williamtown, north of Newcastle.

Train Sydney suburban trains run from Central Station to Newcastle about 25 times a day, taking nearly three hours. The one-way fare is $13.60, off-peak return is about $18. Long-distance trains heading north from Sydney bypass central Newcastle, stopping at suburban Broadmeadow. Frequent buses run from here to the city centre. An XPT from Central Station to Broadmeadow takes about 2¼ hours ($17.90).

Bus From Sydney to Newcastle you're better off taking the train, but if you're heading up the coast from Newcastle buses offer a much better service. Nearly all long-distance buses stop on Watt St near the railway station, although there is talk of building a bus station somewhere else.

Cheapish fares from Newcastle include: Sydney $14.50, Port Macquarie $30, Byron Bay $48, Brisbane $50. Jayes Travel (☎ (049) 26 2000) at 285 Hunter St near Darby St handles most major bus-lines. Sid Fogg's runs to Canberra ($43) four times a week, daily in school holidays, and up the valley to Dubbo ($43) three times a week. Book at Tower Travel (☎ (049) 26 3199), 245 Hunter St on the corner of Crown St, or phone the depot (☎ 1800 045 952 toll-free).

Rover Motors (☎ (049) 90 1699) runs to Maitland and Cessnock ($7).

STA (State Transit Authority) buses run down to Charlestown and Swansea on Lake Macquarie. There are frequent services.

Car Rental As well as the regular places, you can hire used cars from places such as Cheep Heep (☎ (049) 61 3144) at 107 Tudor St, Hamilton, from about $20 a day.

Getting Around

STA buses cover Newcastle and the eastern side of Lake Macquarie. There are fare deals similar to those on offer in Sydney. The bus information booth at the west end of the mall (corner of Perkins St) has timetables; if it's closed, see the tourist office or phone the Travel Information Centre (☎ (049) 61 8933) between 8.30 am and 4.30 pm. For sightseeing try route Nos 348, 350 or 358 to Swansea or Nos 306, 307 or 327 to Speers Point.

Bus No 118 runs to Stockton, but the ferry from Queens Wharf is much quicker.

Trains run along the western side of Lake Macquarie with connecting buses to the south-western shores.

Ferry The ferry from Queens Wharf to Stockton costs $1.30 (65c children) and departs about half-hourly. The service runs from 5.15 am to 11 pm Monday to Thursday, and to midnight on Friday and Saturday. On Sunday and public holidays the service runs from 8.30 am to 8.30 pm. The ferry office on Queens Wharf, near the tourist office, has timetables. Buy tickets there or on board.

Tricycle Trikes are hired in the tourist office car-park (Queens Wharf) on weekends.

HUNTER VALLEY

Up the Valley

Once you leave Newcastle and the urban centres on the south-east side of the valley, the Hunter becomes a pleasant area of vineyards, old towns and rolling pastures, bordered by ranges on both sides.

Organised Tours
Most tours go to the lower Hunter wineries. Hunter Vineyard Tours (☎ (049) 91 1659) has daily departures from Newcastle and other Hunter centres and charges $45 ($28 children) or $29 without lunch.

Grapemobile (☎ (049) 91 2339) offers two-day bike rides through the wineries, with a support bus, accommodation and all meals for $160 per person. They also have day tours.

Several Sydney companies offer day tours of the Hunter wineries. Try Great Sights (☎ (02) 241 2294), or Manly In-Sight Tours (☎ (02) 905 1350) which charges $40 – good value.

Tours to Rosemount Estate and the Cruikshank Callatoota Estate in the upper Hunter are run from the Scone Information Centre (☎ (065) 45 2907, 45 1526) every Sunday at 10 am, if at least eight people book at $12.50 a head. For other tours of the upper Hunter contact the Scone or Denman information centres.

Getting Around
Bus Rover Motors (☎ (049) 90 1699) runs between Newcastle and Cessnock ($7) frequently on weekdays, less often on Saturday and not at all on Sunday. Sid Fogg's (☎ 1800 045 952 toll-free) has a daily bus from Newcastle to Denman ($21). See this chapter's Getting There & Away section for Batterhams' service from Sydney to various towns in the Hunter.

Car & Motorbike The main road through the Hunter is the New England Highway, running north-west from Newcastle through the old towns of Maitland, Singleton and Muswellbrook and climbing up to the New England tablelands near Murrurundi. This road carries a lot of traffic and passes through built-up areas, so travel is quite slow. The 300-km-long Hunter River comes from further west and meets the highway at Singleton.

Bicycle You can hire bicycles from Grapemobile (☎ (049) 98 7639), at the corner of McDonalds & Gillards Rds near Pokolbin. They charge $25 for a day and $15 for half a day.

LOWER HUNTER WINERIES
With more than 50 vineyards concentrated in a small, pretty area, the lower Hunter wineries are a very popular tourist destination, especially for weekenders from Sydney. If you can arrange it, visit midweek.

Orientation
Most of the lower Hunter wineries are north-west of Cessnock, the closest town to the winery area. Although it's a good base for winery visiting, Cessnock isn't especially attractive. Pokolbin Village, right among the wineries, is just a shop, motel and bistro; nearby Hungerford Hill Wine Village is similar but larger.

Broke is a hamlet on the northern edge of the vineyards. Further south, getting into the ranges, is picturesque little Wollombi.

A scenic but bumpy road runs between Broke and Wollombi. Wollombi is also accessible from both Cessnock and Sydney (via Wyong or Wisemans Ferry; either would be an interesting drive).

Although the Hunter wineries don't acknowledge their existence, the quieter wineries around Mudgee (see the Central West chapter) aren't far away, and if you have time you can compare the products of the two districts.

Information
The region's information centre (☎ (049) 90 4477) is in Cessnock on the corner of Wollombi and Mount View Rds. It's open from 9 am to 5 pm on weekdays and slightly

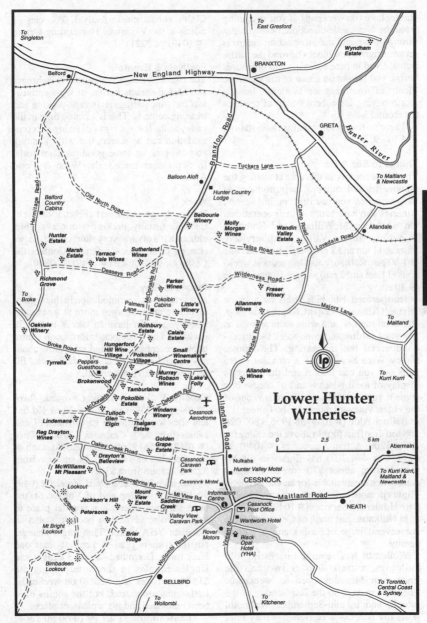

Lower Hunter Wineries

shorter hours on weekends. If you're coming from the Newcastle direction, head straight through town and the information centre is on your right a few blocks beyond the traffic lights. Drop in here for maps and brochures before you set out on a tour of the wineries. Plenty of free maps are available, but it's worth buying Broadbent's map of the area for around $4.

There's a tourist information radio station, FM 107.9.

Things to See & Do

The major activity in this area is visiting the 50 wineries and sampling their products. At most wineries you just drop in, but several wineries also have **tours** of their operations. On weekdays McWilliams and Rothbury Wineries, Hunter Valley;IRothburyhave tours at 11 am and 2 pm and Tyrrells has one at 1.30 pm. Rothbury also has tours at weekends (11 am and 2 pm) as does Hunter Estate (9.30 am).

Hungerford Hill bills itself as a 'wine village'. It has a restaurant, handicrafts shop, 'farmers' market' and wine tours as well as the usual tasting and wine sales facilities – commercial but interesting. The Hunter Valley Wine Society has a pleasant bistro here and you can look round the society's display of local wines – and of course buy some if you want! Nearby, Tyrrells is one of the oldest vineyard names in the Hunter.

Balloon Aloft (☎ (049) 38 1955, 1800 028 568 toll-free) has **flights** above the valley for about $200. Action Aerobatics (☎ (049) 30 6234, 018 474 307) has flights in old biplanes from about $70 for 20 minutes. Aerobatics are available for an extra charge. Flights in more ordinary planes are available with Hunter Air Services (☎ (049) 90 3737).

In **Nulkaba**, just north of Cessnock, there are several huge old kilns and a pottery nearby.

Wollombi has several interesting old buildings, a craft shop or two and the Endeavour Museum, open on weekends. There's a market on the last Sunday of the month, and in mid-September Wollombi hosts the Newcastle & Hunter Valley Folk

Club's annual music festival. You can go riding at the Wollombi Horseriding Centre (☎ (049) 98 3221).

Festivals & Events

The Hunter Vintage Walkabout in February and March attracts hordes of wine enthusiasts for wine tasting, and grape-picking and treading contests. This is a hectic time in the valley as the harvest is in full swing. Accommodation can be scarce, but with planning you can pick up some good package deals. In September there's the Wine & Food Affair.

Work

During the grape harvest (February/March) there is usually picking work available, although it's often at very short notice. Experienced pickers are preferred. Contact the Cessnock CES office (☎ (049) 91 0800).

Places to Stay

Almost all the accommodation in this region, including pubs, charges more at weekends, when you might have to take a two-night package. The Cessnock information centre books accommodation and will know about any special deals. Accommodation can fill up, so it pays to book ahead.

Cessnock *Valley View Caravan Park* (☎ (049) 90 2573) on Mount View Rd has tent sites for $8, on-site vans from $17 and cabins from $30. *Cessnock Caravan Park* (☎ (049) 90 5819) off Allandale Rd north of Cessnock has sites for $10, on-site vans from $25 and cabins from $30.

The friendly *Black Opal Hotel* (☎ (049) 90 1070), at the top end of Vincent St, the main shopping street, is a popular place to stay – you're advised to book. It's also an associate YHA hostel. That might change, but the owners plan to keep at least one bunk-room. Dorm beds are $13 a night and singles/doubles in the hotel rooms are $15/30 midweek and $20/40 on weekends. Bathrooms are shared, but the rooms have been renovated and it's a pleasant place.

The *Wentworth Hotel* (☎ (049) 90 1364)

at 36 Vincent St charges about $30/50 with breakfast. Other Cessnock hotels include the *Royal Oak* (☎ (049) 90 2366) on the corner of Vincent and Snape Sts and the *Cessnock Hotel* (☎ (049) 90 1002) on Wollombi Rd opposite the post office.

Midweek prices at some Cessnock motels include $42/52 at the *Cessnock Motel* (☎ (049) 90 2699) and $40/48 at the *Hunter Valley Motel* (☎ (049) 90 1722), both on Allandale Rd. Prices rise steeply at weekends.

Vineyards There is a lot of accommodation out in the vineyards. Most goes well over the $100-a-night mark on weekends, but midweek there are a few places charging around $60 a double, such as *Hunter Country Lodge* (☎ (049) 38 1744), about 12 km north of Cessnock on Branxton Rd; *Belford Country Cabins* (☎ (049) 91 2777), on Hermitage Rd north of the Hunter Estate; and *Potters Inn* (☎ (049) 98 7648), on DeBeyers Rd south of Pokolbin Village. *Pokolbin Cabins* (☎ (049) 98 7611) on Palmers Lane is a large complex with cabins sleeping from four to 14 people and costing from $30/40 midweek.

Probably the top place to stay in the area is *Peppers Hunter Valley Guesthouse* (☎ (049) 98 7739) on Ekerts Rd, which charges from $150 a double midweek.

Elsewhere As well as the Cessnock pubs, several others in the area have accommodation. *Hotel Denman* (☎ (049) 30 4212), which is not in Denman but in Abermain, about 10 km before Cessnock on the road from Hexham, charges $20 per person (including breakfast) all week. The *Neath Hotel* (☎ (049) 30 4270) is a grand old place in the small town of Neath, just before Cessnock on the road from Kurri Kurri and Hexham. During the week singles/doubles cost $35/55 with breakfast and there are weekend packages including dinner for $85 per person. In Bellbird, just south of Cessnock, the *Bellbird Hotel* (☎ (049) 90 1094) charges $60 a double, including breakfast, and $75 on weekends. The *Ellalong Hotel*

(☎ (049) 98 1217) is in the small town of Ellalong, off the road between Cessnock and Wollombi. They charge $25 per person, including breakfast, and $5 more on weekends.

In Wollombi there are several guesthouses such as *Wollombi House* (☎ (049) 98 3340) and the more expensive *Mulla Villa* (☎ (049) 98 3254). The Wollombi Horseriding Centre (☎ (049) 98 3221) has riverside cabins.

Places to Eat
The dining room at the *Black Opal Hotel* in Cessnock has a good reputation, with main courses in the $12 to $16 bracket. There are also cheaper counter meals.

Many of the wineries have cafes or restaurants. There's a *bistro* at Hungerford Hill Wine Village. *Arnold's Restaurant* at Pokolbin Village has a good reputation, and *Chez Pok* at Peppers Hunter Valley Guesthouse is an upmarket restaurant, open daily. *Cafe Max* is in the Small Winemakers Centre on McDonald's Rd near Pokolbin. If you're watching your budget, though, bring a cut lunch.

Getting There & Away
Air Yanda Airlines (☎ (065) 72 3100 or book through Ansett) flies between Sydney and Cessnock on weekdays for $89 or $70 ($134 return) if you book a week in advance. Yanda also flies to other destinations in the Hunter and up into the north-west of the state.

Bus Rover Motors (☎ (049) 90 1699) is a local company which runs between Cessnock and Newcastle for $7. There are about seven services on weekdays, but only three on Saturday and none on Sunday. The last bus from Newcastle to Cessnock departs from Watt St at 6.30 pm on weekdays and at 4.45 pm on Saturday. There are also services between Cessnock and Maitland. Rover's office is on Vincent St in Cessnock, opposite the Black Opal Hotel.

A little further down Vincent St is Batterhams Express (☎ (049) 90 5000), which has two services to Sydney on weekdays and one on weekends, for $18. Going the other way, all these services run at least as far as Scone. In Sydney, book at the Eddy Ave bus station (☎ (02) 281 9366).

Car & Motorbike Coming from Newcastle, the simplest route is to take the New England Highway and turn off to Kurri Kurri and Cessnock about four km past Hexham Bridge. You can also get here from the Sydney to Newcastle freeway.

See the Getting There & Away section at the start of this chapter for routes into the Hunter Valley.

MAITLAND

Maitland (population 46,000) has been a large town since the early days of European settlement in the Hunter Valley. It was long seen as a more desirable address than Newcastle and even had brief dreams of rivalling Sydney as the colony's most important city.

One of Maitland's most famous citizens was Les Darcy, a boxer who became a national hero but died – perhaps under mysterious circumstances – in the USA in 1917. When Phar Lap, a racehorse but also a national hero, likewise died in the USA in 1932, there was no shortage of conspiracy theories!

Orientation & Information

Maitland's main street is High St, which follows the winding route of the original trail through the town. Part of the street is now the Heritage Mall, so driving through town is not simple. The information centre (☎ (049) 33 2611) is in East Maitland, on the highway at the corner of Banks St. It's open on weekends.

Things to See

The city's 19th-century wealth is reflected in the elaborate Georgian and Victorian buildings which remain. East Maitland, which was established in 1833 after floods in the original town, has its share of old buildings, and the nearby village of **Morpeth**, once the area's main riverport, is also well endowed with architectural gems, especially along Swan St.

The **City Art Gallery**, open on Thursday, Friday and Saturday afternoon and from 10.30 am on Sunday, is in Brough House (1870) on Church St. The **museum** of local history is next door in **Grossman House** (1870) and is open on weekends. The extraordinary **Masonic Lodge** on Victoria St and the **courthouse** (1895) at the west end of High St are some of the many interesting old buildings in Maitland.

Over in East Maitland, have a look at the **old jail** and the nearby **courthouse** on John St, and the **Lands Department Offices** on Newcastle Rd.

Maitland Show, held in late October, is one of the biggest in the state.

About 15 km north-west of Maitland is **Windermere**, a homestead built by Captain Winder in 1821 and later the home of William Wentworth, crosser of the Blue Mountains and colonial politician. Captain Winder is today less well known than Wentworth, but he apparently planted the Hunter Valley's first vines. Windermere and its museum are open for inspection by appointment (☎ (049) 30 7204). A guided tour costs $10 per person.

Places to Stay & Eat

The *Hunter River Hotel* (☎ (049) 33 7244) at 10 Melbourne St in East Maitland has singles/doubles for $20/40 and a backpacker rate of $15 if there is a spare room. There is plenty of other pub and motel accommodation, much of it in East Maitland, and also a *caravan park* (☎ (049) 33 2950). *Cintra* (☎ (049) 32 8483) is a large Victorian house with accommodation at $90 a double.

On High St east of the mall, *Pepperina Books & Coffee* is a nice place to relax after a stroll around. There are several Chinese restaurants and other eateries, but fewer interesting places to eat than you would expect in a large town near the wineries. The *Old George & Dragon Restaurant* (☎ (049) 33 7272) at 48 Melbourne St in East Maitland is in a restored pub dating from the 1830s and offers Anglo-French food. Main courses are in the region of $24 and you can arrange a dinner, bed and breakfast package for $160 a double during the week (more on weekends).

SINGLETON
Europeans first came to this area in 1820 and farms were soon established on Patricks Plains. By 1835 the village which was later to be called Singleton was established. The current population is 12,000.

On weekends, an information centre (☎ (065) 72 3973) is open from 10 am to 3 pm in Townhead Park, off the highway.

In the old courthouse by shady Burdekin Park there's a **museum** with displays on local history. It's open on weekends and admission is $1 (20c children). For other early buildings, take a stroll down George St.

The **Royal** (at the time of writing) **Australian Army Infantry Corps Museum** is at Singleton Army Camp. According to the army, it's a 'top-class infantry weapons collection'. As well as the guns there are memorabilia from most of the wars that the Australian infantry has been involved in. The camp is four km south of Singleton and you can get there from the New England Highway before Singleton or from the Windsor road just out of Singleton. The museum is open from Wednesday to Sunday (but closed in October or November each year) and admission is $2 ($1 children).

Singleton also boasts the world's largest sundial.

Places to Stay
Country Acres Caravan Park (☎ (065) 72 2328) on Maison Dieu Rd has sites, on-site vans and cabins.

The *Caledonian Hotel* (☎ (065) 72 1356) on the highway near the town centre has accommodation. Things might be quieter at one of the pubs along John St, such as the *Imperial* (☎ (065) 72 1290). Motels range from the *Benjamin Singleton* (☎ (065) 72 2922) on the highway, which charges about $45/55, to the *Mid-City Motor Inn* (☎ (065) 72 2011) at 180 John St, which charges around $90.

Pelerin (☎ (065) 72 2780) at 30 Edinburgh Ave was one of the area's first homes,

although the current impressive house dates from the 1880s. The one guest-room is available for about $40 per person.

UPPER HUNTER WINERIES
With far fewer wineries, the upper Hunter is less visited than the lower, but the country is pretty and the wineries worth seeing. The upper Hunter **Wine Weekend** is the first weekend in August.

Most of the upper Hunter wineries are close to the small town of Denman, but don't miss **Serenella Estate**, near the hamlet of Sandy Hollow and in a beautiful valley. **Verona Winery** is just north of Muswellbrook.

Denman
Denman, the nearest town to the upper Hunter wineries, is a sleepy little place (population 1500) close to the forested sandstone ranges bordering the southern side of the Hunter Valley.

The information centre (☎ (065) 47 2731) is on the main street, by Benjamin's Lock, Stock & Barrel Inn, a restaurant in an old railway carriage. There's a **museum** in the old courthouse on Palace St.

Places to Stay As well as the plentiful accommodation in nearby Muswellbrook and Singleton, there are some local places. *Denman Van Village* (☎ (065) 47 2590) has sites for $11, on-site vans from $20 and cabins from $30. There's another *caravan park* (☎ (065) 47 4575) in Sandy Hollow. The *Denman Hotel* (☎ (065) 47 2207) has pub rooms for $15 per person, and the even more basic *Royal Hotel* (☎ (065) 47 2226) nearby charges just $10. The *Denman Motor Inn* (☎ (065) 47 2462) charges from $42/48.

Ask the information centre about B&B accommodation in the area.

Getting There & Away Sid Fogg's (☎ 1800 045 952 toll-free) has a daily bus from Newcastle to Denman ($21) and from Denman to Dubbo ($28).

MUSWELLBROOK

Like other towns in the Hunter Valley, Muswellbrook (population 10,000) was founded early in Australia's history and has some interesting old buildings, surrounded by spreading residential areas.

Bridge St (the New England Highway) is Muswellbrook's main shopping street. The closest thing to an information centre in Muswellbrook is the lobby of the Bridgecourt Motor Inn (☎ (065) 43 2170) towards the north end of Bridge St.

The National Parks office (☎ (065) 43 3533) is also on Bridge St, across from the RSL Club. There's also a National Parks sub-station at Bulga (☎ (065) 74 5275), on the Putty Road and at the edge of Wollemi National Park.

The **Weidman Cottage Heritage Centre** on Bridge St near the centre of town has displays on the area's history.

St Albans Church on Brook St dates from 1867. It is quite small and quite dark, which makes the stained glass blaze on sunny days.

Historic *Eatons Hotel* (☎ (065) 43 2403) on the main street at the north end of town charges $18/30 a single/double.

SCONE

Scone (which *isn't* pronounced skonn) is a pleasant old upper Hunter town (population 3500) known for its horse studs – there are more than 40 in the area. It is perhaps the world's second-largest stud district, and the *Mare & Foal* sculpture in Elizabeth Park is a local landmark. Like Muswellbrook, Scone is a handy jumping-off point for the upper Hunter wineries.

Just east of Scone the Hunter River is dammed to form **Lake Glenbawn**, a popular watersport area with camping (☎ (065) 43 7752).

About 25 km north-east of Scone, just off the interesting road across to Barrington Tops and Gloucester, **Belltrees** is an old sheep station with a beautiful and very grand homestead. The family of Patrick White, Australia's Nobel Prize-winning author, has owned the property for 150 years, and it appears as 'Kudgeri' in White's novel *The Eye of the Storm*. Belltrees isn't open to visitors, but there is a guesthouse on the property – see the Places to Stay section for more information.

Orientation & Information

Kelly St (the New England Highway) is the main shopping street of Scone. Liverpool St runs off Kelly St and becomes the road to Merriwa.

The information centre (☎ (065) 45 2907, 45 1526) is off Kelly St on the north side of the town centre, near the *Mare & Foal* statue. There's a cafe and you can buy souvenirs here, starting at just 10c for a rock! Information and souvenirs are also available at the Station Gallery & Cafe at the railway station.

Australian Stock Horses
Although it wasn't formally defined as a breed until 1971, the Australian stock horse participated in most of the major events of European-Australian history. Originally called Walers (from New South Wales) the breed served as cavalry horses in India, South Africa and during WW I. They carried the 4th Australian Light Horse in the world's last cavalry charge at the taking of Beersheba in 1916.
The headquarters of the Australian Stock Horse Society (☎ (067) 45 1122) is in Scone. ∎

Horse Studs

You can visit the horse studs (or the upper Hunter wineries) with Helen Sinclair's tours (☎ (065) 45 3337) from around $120 for four people on a tour lasting around 2½ hours. The information centre might be able to help you arrange a self-drive visit to studs for considerably less.

Burning Mountain

Coal seams beneath this mountain were burning when the first Europeans arrived in the area (they thought it was an active volcano), and calculations based on the burning rate of a metre per year suggest that the fire started as long as 6000 years ago. The mountain is a nature reserve, and a three-km walking track leads through some diverse terrain up to the smoking vents. The turn-off from the New England Highway to Burning Mountain is about 20 km north of Scone.

Festivals & Events

Horse Week, with equestrian competitions and displays, is held in mid-May.

Places to Stay

Caravan Parks There are a couple of caravan parks, the *Scone* (☎ (065) 45 2024), with sites and cabins, and the smaller *Highway* (☎ (065) 45 1078) with sites and on-site vans.

Hostel The rural *Scone YHA Hostel* (☎ (065) 45 2072) is actually 10 km east of town at Segenhoe. Dorm beds in this historic building (an old school) cost $12.

Hotels & Motels The *Belmore Hotel* (☎ (065) 45 2078), on Kelly St not far from the railway station and the information centre, is a pleasant place with a fine beer-garden. Its good rooms are in the process of being renovated into excellent rooms. Singles/doubles are currently $20/30.

The *Golden Fleece Hotel* (☎ (065) 45 1357) on the corner of Kelly and Liverpool Sts charges $15/24, and the *Thoroughbred Hotel* (☎ (065) 45 1086) at the south end of Kelly St charges $15/35. The *Royal Hotel*

(☎ (065) 45 1305) on the corner of Kelly and St Aubins Sts has pub rooms for $20/25 and motel-style rooms for around $40/50.

Airlie House Motor Inn (☎ (065) 45 1488) on the highway near the town centre takes in a large Victorian house and charges around $60/65. Less expensive motels include *Isis* (☎ (065) 45 1100), further south on the highway.

Belltrees Country House (☎ (065) 45 1668) is part of a working farm, on the old Belltrees property 25 km north-east of Scone. Dinner, bed & breakfast costs $140 per person and there's a two-night package which includes one night in a mountain retreat ($390 per person). Children are allowed during school holidays only.

Places to Eat

At the information centre, *Le Café au Lait* is open daily for light meals (maximum $6) and snacks. The *Station Cafe* at the railway station has similar fare and is also open for dinner on Friday. They prefer you to book (☎ (065) 45 2144).

The *Summerhouse Cafe* on Kelly St across from the Civic Theatre is a pleasant place for coffee, cake and light meals during the day from Monday to Friday, and dinner on Friday and Saturday with main courses around $12.

Further down Kelly St, across from the Village shopping centre, *Asser House* is open daily except Sunday for snacks and light meals (up to $10, many less), and for dinner on Friday and Saturday with main courses costing around $11 to $13. There's an outdoor area and the interesting menu is worth checking out.

HUNTER VALLEY

The *Country Cottage* (☎ (065) 45 1140) at 101 Liverpool St, across the railway line from Kelly St, is open for dinner on Friday and Saturday. They prefer you to book, and you can arrange meals at other times.

MURRURUNDI

This small town (population 1000) is right at the head of the Hunter Valley and from here the highway climbs steeply up the Liverpool Ranges. There's a small museum, several interesting craft shops and some fine old buildings.

MERRIWA

Although on the upper fringes of the Hunter Valley, Merriwa is very much a country town (population 1100), at no risk of the Hunter's creeping urbanisation. You have now entered pastoral country, which this area has been since the 1820s.

The information centre (☎ (065) 48 2505) is on a side-street next to the shire offices and is theoretically open daily. If no-one is there, try the shire offices.

This is a sandstone region and there are several early stone buildings here and in the surrounding area. The **Colonial Cottage Museum** on the main street is in one such building, a quite modest structure built in 1847. In the hamlet of **Cassilis**, about 45 km north-west, there are a few more sandstone buildings, not worth a special trip but interesting if you're passing through.

The new **Goulburn River National Park** at the upper end of the Hunter Valley follows the river as it cuts its way through sandstone gorges. This was the route used by Aborigines travelling from the plains to the sea, and the area is rich in rock art and other sites. You can camp but there are no facilities. Access is from the road running south to Wollar and Bylong. The Muswellbrook National Parks office (☎ (065) 43 3533) has information.

Lazy Wombat Walks (☎ (063) 73 4330), based in nearby Wollar, offers 'stress-free strolls' in the area's beauty spots.

Places to Stay & Eat

There's a basic *caravan park* (☎ (065) 48 2494) by the river on the western edge of town. The *Fitzroy Hotel* (☎ (065) 48 2235), a fine old sandstone pub, charges $15/30, and the *Royal Hotel* (☎ (065) 48 2285) charges $20 per person. Both are on the main street. *El Dorado Motel* (☎ (065) 48 2273) is on the main street east of the shopping centre and charges about $45/50. For a mock-Spanish-American motel it's quite a nice place.

Glenburnie (☎ (065) 47 6073) has farm holidays in self-contained cabins for about $35 with all meals or $350 per week for four people self-catering.

The *bakery* on the main street sells some of the best pies in the land.

Getting There & Away

Bus Sid Fogg's (☎ 1800 045 952 toll-free) stops in Merriwa on the service between Dubbo ($25 from Merriwa) and Newcastle ($28).

Car & Motorbike Merriwa is a modest travel crossroads, with roads leading to the upper Hunter (via Sandy Hollow and Denman), to Gulgong and Mudgee (via Cassilis), to Dubbo (via Dunedoo or Gulgong) and to Coonabarabran (via Dunedoo or Cassilis).

North of Newcastle

The inland routes running north from Newcastle and the rugged ranges on the northern side of the Hunter Valley have some attractions that are very different from the genteel vineyards.

THE BUCKETTS WAY

This old road is an alternative to the Pacific Highway as a route north, branching off the highway about 15 km north of Raymond Terrace and rejoining it just south of Taree. This road is longer and narrower than the highway but it carries much less traffic and passes through some interesting country.

The Australian Agricultural Company
By the 1820s the idea that NSW might be a good place to make money had filtered back to England. Floated in 1825, the Australian Agricultural Company raised £1,000,000 from British investors, a colossal sum, and was granted a huge tract of land from Port Stephens to the Manning River. The company also took over the Hunter coalfields and renamed the port Newcastle. A manager and workers (including convicts who were essentially slave labour) were sent out to farm sheep and cattle, and they began in the Karuah Valley around the company-built village of Stroud, named for the landscape's resemblance to the English Cotswolds.

Unfortunately, while the country is lush, well-watered and beautiful, the soil lacks essential trace elements and, along with the sheep, the company failed to thrive. Just about every other form of agriculture was tried, including growing silk worms, but the land refused to turn its fertility into cash crops.

Taking up more land in the Tamworth area (which didn't look like England at all) proved to be more successful, but the company's plans for a closely-settled private empire with an English social structure never materialised. Today the company still owns large properties in Queensland and the Northern Territory. ■

HUNTER VALLEY

Stroud

Stroud is a small village (population 600), but it's the main town in this part of the Karuah Valley. Founded by the Australian Agricultural Company in 1826, Stroud has several convict-built buildings such as **Quambi**, once a company residence and now a museum (intermittently open). Next door to Quambi is the Anglican church, and in its graveyard are some interesting old headstones, including one which pronounces, rather ominously, 'Vengeance Is Mine, Saith The Lord'.

The road running past Quambi leads to **Silo Hill**, where there are some wheat silos built in the early days of the Australian Agricultural Company. These aren't your ordinary phallic silos – they are buried in the hill and you can climb down into one of them. There isn't a lot to see down there, but the echo is weird.

Further down the main street is the old **courthouse**, which you can inspect by arrangement. Next door is **Stroud Treasure**, a local craft and second-hand shop that's several notches above the usual. It's open from Thursday to Sunday.

Festivals & Events Stroud's annual brick-throwing contest, held in mid-July, is an international affair, linked to similar contests in the English and Canadian Strouds. (Ladies throw rolling pins.)

Places to Stay There's a basic but pretty *camping area* at the showgrounds, near the river. The *Central Hotel* (☎ (049) 94 5197) is the only hotel in town, despite the name, and might be persuaded to give you a room.

In the hamlet of Booral, seven km south of Stroud, *Gundany House* (☎ (049) 94 9246) is an impressive Georgian house offering guest accommodation at about $30/50. It's a non-smoking, non-drinking, vegetarian household.

The YHA's *Girvan Hostel* is about 15 km from Stroud, on the Bulahdelah road (turn east off the Bucketts Way at Booral). See the Bulahdelah section of the North Coast chapter.

Getting There & Away Countrylink buses stop in Stroud on the weekday run between Newcastle and Taree. There's also a school-day-only run from Bulahdelah to Raymond Terrace and Newcastle via Stroud. This is pretty slow.

Gloucester

Offering the best access to the Barrington Tops National Park, Gloucester is a busy country town (population 2500) on the banks of the Gloucester River.

For tourist information see Gloucester Caravan Park by the river on Denison St or phone the tourist association (☎ (065) 58 1408). The **museum** at the southern end of

Church St is open on Thursday and Saturday, plus Tuesday during school holidays.

As well as the national park, there are extensive state forests in the area offering good walks and drives. The **Forestry Office** (☎ (065) 58 1005) on Queen St has information. The route of a planned 250 km walk from Barrington Tops down to the coast has been surveyed but not yet formalised.

Close to town, there are good views from up on **Mograni Lookout**, five km east on the Bucketts Way.

The Barrington River rises in the Barrington Tops and flows down past Barrington, just north-west of Gloucester. **Canoeing** is possible, although some stretches are practically whitewater and the upper reaches are isolated. The Barrington General Store rents canoes and can advise on the best places.

The Mountain Maid goldmine (☎ (065) 58 4303), one km from Copeton and 15 km east of Gloucester, has underground tours.

Places to Stay *Gloucester Caravan Park* (☎ (065) 58 1720) on Denison St has sites and cabins.

The *Avon Valley Inn* (☎ (065) 58 1016) on Church St has accommodation, and there's also *Gloucester Country Lodge* (☎ (065) 58 1812) near the golf course charging from $50/55.

Getting There & Away North-bound trains stop at Gloucester, but coming in the other direction you'll have to change to a bus at Taree. The buses don't run on weekends.

Countrylink buses don't stop in Gloucester on the weekday run between Newcastle and Taree.

The Bucketts Way runs south to Stroud and beyond, and winds east to the Pacific Highway just south of Taree. From near Barrington, a village just west of Gloucester, you can head north on a partly-sealed road to Walcha or branch off to Terrible Billy (great name!) from where a sealed road runs to Tamworth. If you keep heading west from Barrington, you'll be on a spectacular unsealed road which winds past Barrington

Tops National Park, eventually reaching the New England Highway near Scone.

WOKO NATIONAL PARK
Smaller than nearby Barrington Tops National Park, Woko is similarly undeveloped and rugged and also protects rainforests as well as other vegetation types. The Manning River offers swimming. Access is from Gloucester, about 30 km south-east; head for Rookhurst and take the left fork shortly after. Near the park entrance is a campsite on the Manning River. The National Parks office in Raymond Terrace (☎ (049) 83 1031) has more information.

BARRINGTON TOPS NATIONAL PARK
Barrington Tops (39,000 hectares) is a World Heritage Area of wild forest, with two 1500-metre plateaux that fall away steeply to just 400 metres. The 'tops' are a series of monolithic hills known as bucketts, a corruption of an Aboriginal word meaning 'big rock' (hence the road called the Bucketts Way). As well as the Barrington Tops, the park takes in the Gloucester Tops. With rare pockets of rainforest and beautiful Antarctic beech trees, it's a stunning area. There are walking trails, but be prepared for snow in winter and cold snaps at any time. Boil your drinking water. The National Parks office in Raymond Terrace (☎ (049) 83 1031) has more information.

Places to Stay
There are *campsites* in the Gloucester River area to the east of the national park, or you can bush-camp. *Barrington Guesthouse* (☎ (049) 95 3212), dating from the 1930s, is on the southern edge of the park, 43 km from Dungog, and charges about $75 per person with meals. Activities such as horseriding are available. In a small chunk of the park east of the main section and toward the headwaters of the Gloucester River, *Gloucester Tops Riverside Caravan Park* (☎ (065) 58 3155) has sites for $8 and on-site vans. The caravan park is about 40 km south-west of Gloucester; phone to ask about the best route, especially after rain.

Getting There & Around

There are 4WD tracks through the park (accessible from Dungog and Gloucester), but if the park is declared a wilderness area these will be closed. Even now they are often closed in winter. The only other road through the park is the steep, largely unsealed and very scenic road running between Gloucester and Scone. This doesn't traverse much of the actual national park, but the surrounding state forests are beautiful and on the eastern side the views from the escarpment are superb. The gate on this road is part of a fence keeping dingoes out of the sheep country further west. There are several campsites on and near this road.

Other roads run to the edge of the park from Dungog, Gresford and via Berrico, near Gloucester.

DUNGOG & AROUND

Dungog is a quiet country town (population 2500) in the steep hills to the north of the Hunter Valley, and is the closest town to the southern side of Barrington Tops National Park. There are also many state forests in the area. Established in the 1830s as a military post with the task of eradicating bushrangers

(it failed), Dungog is today a service centre for the area's farms.

There are a number of small and picturesque villages in the area, such as **Clarence Town**, **Gresford** and **Paterson**, although getting to them on the winding roads can be time-consuming.

Places to Stay There's a motel, the *Tall Timbers* (☎ (049) 92 1547), on Dungog's main street, and accommodation at pubs including the *Courthouse Hotel* (☎ (049) 92 1615) on Brown St. Along the Chichester Dam road, running north from Dungog, there are several farmstay options, such as *Bellbird Valley* (☎ (049) 95 9266) and *Ferndale Park Camping Reserve* (☎ (049) 95 9239). Camping is permitted in the area's state forests.

Getting There & Away

Train Trains on the main northern line stop at Dungog.

Car & Motorbike Dungog is about 20 km west of Stroud (the turn-off from the Bucketts Way is at Stroud Road, seven km north of Stroud), or you can get here from Singleton on the Gresford road.

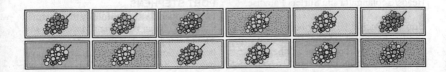

The North Coast

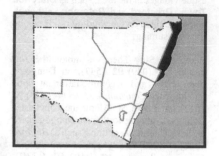

The north coast of NSW stretches from Port Stephens right up to the Queensland border at Tweed Heads. Most of the places from Coffs Harbour north, especially Byron Bay, are travellers' meccas, but it's worth taking your time on a trip north from Sydney as there are excellent beaches and rugged bushland all the way up. There are also some interesting places in the ranges behind the coast.

The central coast, between Sydney and Newcastle, is covered in the Around Sydney chapter.

Getting There & Around
Air See the Port Macquarie, Coffs Harbour, Grafton and Ballina sections for details of flights and fares.

Train & Bus The nightly XPT from Sydney to Brisbane runs up the coast. Connecting buses at Casino run to Lismore, Ballina, Byron Bay, Mullumbimby and Tweed Heads/Coolangatta. Another XPT makes a daylight run from Sydney to Murwillumbah, from where connecting buses run to Tweed Heads/Coolangatta and Surfers Paradise.

Bus The Pacific Highway between Sydney and Brisbane probably has the hottest competition of any bus route in the country. Getting to Brisbane takes about 16 hours and

costs around $60. All the resorts except Port Stephens (and with the occasional exception of Forster-Tuncurry) are serviced by long-distance buses, but not all bus services stop everywhere. Some typical fares from Sydney are Port Macquarie $36 (seven hours), Coffs Harbour $44 (9½ hours) and Byron Bay $60 (13 hours). You often need to book ahead on this route.

Companies running the Pacific Highway route to Brisbane include Greyhound Pioneer Australia, Kirklands, McCafferty's and a Port Macquarie company, Lindsay's (☎ 1800 027 944 toll-free).

Car & Motorbike The Pacific Highway runs all the way up the coast, although it does bypass some of the coastal towns, notably Nelson Bay and Forster-Tuncurry. It is not a great road to drive on, often narrow and often passing through quite densely populated areas. And there are all those bloody caravans!

If you have time, consider taking the longer New England Highway which begins in Newcastle and runs inland to Tamworth and then north, offering many opportunities to turn off to coastal towns along the way. Most of these side-trips to the coast involve a spectacular descent of the Great Divide.

Lower North Coast

The coast from Port Stephens north to Port Macquarie is easily accessible from Sydney but doesn't attract as much attention as the resorts further north.

PORT STEPHENS
Port Stephens is a beautiful bay that charmed Captain Cook and Governor Macquarie, saw a lot of shipping while the cedar forests were being cut down, was mooted as a major naval base but has since been left to its own

devices. This is a good thing, as it's a beautiful area.

Port Stephens is a good weekend getaway from Sydney, about three hours away by bus, and it is much less developed than the central coast. There are also plenty of connections to nearby Newcastle.

History
Captain Cook sighted the entrance to Port Stephens in 1770, but the colony of New South Wales was seven years old before the first survey of the area was made – the first official survey, that is. Escaped convicts had fetched up here five years earlier and were living with the local Aborigines in what must have seemed like heaven after their time in Sydney.

Orientation & Information
Port Stephens has a long way to go before it's in the same league as the crowded central coast, but it's headed in the same direction, with land sales and new housing-estates everywhere you look. The largest town on Port Stephens is Nelson Bay (population 7000), near the south head. The tourist office (☎ (049) 81 1579) is at the end of the main street, near the d'Albora Marina complex, and is open daily from 9 am to 5 pm.

Just west of Nelson Bay, and now nearly merged with it, Shoal Bay is a smaller and perhaps nicer place. Shoal Bay is on a long, sheltered beach with great views across to hilly islands, and it's a short walk to surf at Zenith Beach.

Back down the Tomaree Peninsula from Shoal Bay is Anna Bay, with access to both the bay and ocean beaches.

Samurai Beach at the north end of One Mile Beach on Anna Bay (some way east of the town of the same name) is a nude beach. One Mile Beach is one of the area's best surf beaches. On the west side of Anna Bay township, the wide Stockton Beach runs all the way back to Newcastle. Watch out for vehicles on Stockton Beach, as driving is permitted on it. The stretch of coast between Tomaree Head (Shoal Bay) and Anna Bay is the small Tomaree National Park.

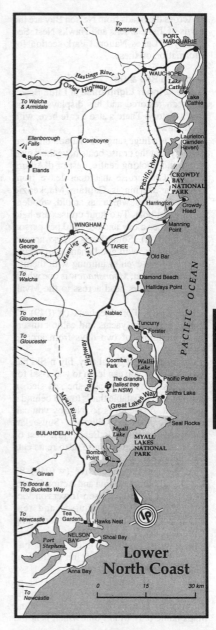

Lower North Coast

0   15   30 km

NORTH COAST

Across the heads from Nelson Bay are the towns of Tea Gardens and Hawks Nest. See the Myall Lakes National Park section for information on these.

Things to See & Do

The 1872 **Inner Lighthouse** at Little Beach has been restored and has displays on the area's history. There's also a cafe here, with good views.

There is a huge range of **cruises** on offer, so many that the cruise boats have their own wharf and booking centre, east of d'Albora Marina. One cruise that does leave from d'Albora Marina is Captain Mackenzie Classic Charters, which has an old, wooden, gaff-rigged boat. Two-hour cruises are held several times a day and cost $20 per person ($15 children). Some boats cruise around Port Stephens, with good chances of seeing dolphins (and even swimming with them if the boat has a net; *Moonshadow* is one which does), and others head across to the Myall Lakes.

Sail Cruise Port Stephens (☎ (049) 82 2399) rents large yachts and cabin cruisers for a minimum of two days from around $300.

On the beach at Shoal Bay, Fly'n'Ski has paragliding or you can learn to water-ski for $20 a lesson. There's also the sea sled, a sausage-like inflatable that's towed behind a speedboat. A ride costs $6. Nearby you can hire cats, canoes and sailboards. Sunseeker Sailboards on Bagnalls Beach, just west of the Nelson Bay town centre, also rents cats and sailboards.

At Nelson Bay, Pro Dive (☎ (049) 81 4331) at d'Albora Marina and Action Divers (☎ (049) 81 2491) in Nelson Towers on Victoria Pde run diving courses and rent equipment. Pro Dive also has snorkelling trips. *Advance II* (☎ 018 494 386) is a long-range motor/sailing yacht which has live-on-board dive courses for up to four people – pricey but fun.

On the Tilligerry Peninsula (west of Nelson Bay between Soldiers Point and the entrance to Lemon Tree Passage – some maps name only Mud Point which is at the tip of the peninsula) there is a large colony of **koalas** living in bushland.

Tomaree Toboggan Run, near the Salamander Shopping Centre, is a one-km steel track which you can shoot down on a toboggan for $4 (less for more rides).

Organised Tours

Horizon Safaris (☎ 018 681 600 or book at the tourist office in Nelson Bay) has various tours of the district, including a tour of the Hunter Valley wineries for $25.

Places to Stay

In winter there are often good package deals at the more expensive places. Contact the tourist office to see what's available.

Caravan parks The closest caravan parks to Nelson Bay are *Halifax* (☎ (049) 81 1522) at Little Beach, right on Nelson Head, about two km north of town, and the council-run *Alex McDonald* (☎ (049) 81 1427) in Shoal Bay. Both have sites and cabins and both are expensive at peak times.

Hostels An associate YHA hostel has opened at Shoal Bay, in the *Shoal Bay Motel* (☎ (049) 81 1744). The hostel section takes up the upper floor of one wing and it's quite good. The motel is on the beachfront road, just along from the caravan park. Dorm beds cost $13 and there are some motel-style rooms for $18 per person (minimum two people). Unusually for a YHA place, these rates rise during holiday periods, and it would be wise to book at any time.

In Anna Bay, *Samurai Beach Bungalows* (☎ (049) 82 1921) is a new backpacker hostel with a bush setting and dorm beds in bungalows from $10. It's at the corner of Frost Rd and Robert Connell Close. Buses from Newcastle run past.

Motels The *Shoal Bay Motel* (☎ (049) 81 1744) is worth considering for non-hostel accommodation. In the off-season they charge $45/49 a single/double, rising by increments to $125 a double in the peak season.

There are many motels in Nelson Bay, all very expensive at peak times. In the off-season, the *Central* (☎ (049) 81 3393) at the corner of Government Rd and Church St and the *Marlin* (☎ (049) 81 1036), east of town on Shoal Bay Rd, charge around $40 a single or double. *Leilani Court* (☎ (049) 81 3304) on Gowrie Ave (the road that runs up to the Nelson Head lighthouse) has serviced apartments from $50 in the off-season.

Self-catering Letting agents include L J Hooker (☎ (049) 81 3844) at 89 Magnus St and Raine & Horne (☎ (049) 81 1577) at 5 Stockton St.

Places to Eat
Good, cheap meals are available at the big *RSL Club* between Nelson Bay and Shoal Bay and at the *Bowling Club* on Stockton St.

In the d'Albora Marina complex there's a coffee shop and, upstairs, the *Hog's Breath Grill* (yuk!). Further along the waterfront, at the Fishing Co-op wharf, there's the *Fisherman's Wharf Restaurant*, with smorgasbords on weekends. You can buy fresh fish here, too. *Waves Seafood Family Restaurant* in Nelson Square on Donald St has an all-you-can-eat deal for about $15.

Getting There & Away
Bus Port Stephens Buses (☎ (049) 81 1207, (02) 281 9366 in Sydney, 1800 045 949 toll-free) runs to Newcastle ($9) frequently and to Sydney ($20) daily.

Heading north up the coast it's a little more complicated. You could backtrack to Newcastle and pick up a long-distance bus there (and that's what most people do), but if you can persuade one of the cruise boats to take you over to Tea Gardens (they'll charge around $8 for the short trip) you can pick up a Great Lakes Coaches (☎ (049) 83 1560, 1800 043 263 toll-free) service which runs up to Forster-Tuncurry, where you can usually pick up a bus travelling north. This service doesn't run frequently and you'd be advised to check the current timetable before heading across to Tea Gardens.

Car & Motorbike If you want to drive north up the coast from Nelson Bay, you will have to backtrack a long way to the Pacific Highway at Newcastle or Raymond Terrace, or join the highway north of Raymond Terrace by taking the Medowie road and then an unsealed road. On the highway near the Tea Gardens turn-off you'll pass the Ayers Rock Roadhouse, a monstrous piece of kitsch.

Getting Around
There are a couple of bike-hire places. One is in Nelson Bay across from the tourist office, where you'll pay $4 an hour or $15 a day, plus $2 for a helmet. There's another in Shoal Bay, a block back from the beachfront road, next to the caravan park. It's worth hiring a bike, as there is a good network of bike paths in the area.

BULAHDELAH & AROUND
A small town on the Myall River and the Pacific Highway, Bulahdelah is the jumping-off point for Myall Lakes and, a little way north of town, the Great Lakes Way route to Seal Rocks and Forster-Tuncurry. Some interesting old towns, such as Stroud, and the spectacular Barrington Tops National Park are inland from Bulahdelah, but they are more easily reached from towns in the Hunter Valley and have been included in that chapter.

The pub at Bulahdelah has an excellent beer-garden with lawns running down to the river, where there might be boats for hire. The pub also supplies tourist information (☎ (049) 97 4285).

Looming over the town is **Mt Alum**, the largest above-ground deposit of alum (a salt used in various industrial processes) in the world. The mining has ceased and the mountain is now the **Bulahdelah Mountain Reserve** with some walking trails to historic sites. The entrance is a couple of blocks from the highway, on the same street as the police station. In November there's a race to the top.

The mists which often wreath Mt Alum occur all over this area and the combination of warmth and moisture is ideal for lush forests. Not far from Bulahdelah, the tallest tree in the state towers over dense rainforest. **The Grandis**, a 400-year-old flooded gum *(Eucalyptus grandis)* is an awesome sight. On a humid, misty day, with the strange calls of whip birds echoing off the palm trees and tall timber, the atmosphere is almost primeval. With its immensely tall, straight trunk it's amazing that the Grandis, and some of its slightly shorter relations, survived the logging which continues in this area. To get here, take the Great Lakes Way and then the signposted turn-off 12 km from Bulahdelah. The Grandis is six km further on, down a bumpy all-weather road. You can also get here from the Pacific Highway, on a road that is part of a driving tour of the area's state forests.

The Forestry Commission office (☎ (049) 97 4206) in Bulahdelah has maps of this drive and other places of interest in the area. At the **O'Sullivans Gap** picnic area, which is off the Pacific Highway nine km north of Bulahdelah, there are walking trails through some interesting forest and you might meet goannas begging for food.

On the Violet Hill road into Myall Lakes is the **Bulahdelah Logging Railway**, a recreation of a timber train. It's open on Friday and Saturday (daily except Sunday during school holidays). Pony rides and horseriding are available nearby.

Places to Stay

Bulahdelah has a *caravan park* (☎ (049) 97 4565) and several motels, all just highway stops. Campers are better off heading to one of the nearby beaches, at Seal Rocks or Myall Lakes National Park. Ask at the Forestry Commission offices (☎ (049) 97 4206), near the entrance to Bulahdelah Mountain Park, for information on camping in the area's state forests.

There are two *houseboat* hire places in Bulahdelah, both on the river near the turn-off to Myall Lakes. See the Myall Lakes National Park section for details.

Near Girvan, a sub-hamlet about 20 km west of Bulahdelah on the winding road to Booral, is the simple *Girvan YHA Hostel*

(☎ (049) 97 6639). The hostel is an old school and it's a secluded, pleasant place in bushland with a walking trail nearby. There are hot showers but pit toilets. The hostel is about 13 km from Booral and 16 km from the highway turn-off south of Bulahdelah. It might pay to ring before you arrive so they know you're coming – no calls after 10 pm.

Getting There & Away

Bus Great Lakes Coaches (☎ (049) 83 1560, 1800 043 263 toll-free) comes through Bulahdelah on the daily run between Forster and Sydney ($28 from Bulahdelah) via Newcastle ($14). There are also rather slow schoolday-only runs to Taree, and to Raymond Terrace and Newcastle via Stroud.

Car & Motorbike The Pacific Highway runs through Bulahdelah, but if you're heading to Forster-Tuncurry take the Great Lakes Way, a scenic road that winds through state forest and passes Myall Lake, the turn-off to Seal Rocks and some other beaches, then runs between the ocean and Wallis Lake up to Forster. The Great Lakes Way leaves the highway just north of Bulahdelah. In town is the turn-off to Bombah Point in Myall Lakes National Park, 11 km away. The road to Girvan and Booral (and the Bucketts Way) leaves the Pacific Highway three km south of Bulahdelah.

MYALL LAKES NATIONAL PARK

This park (31,560 hectares) combines some beautiful lakes with ocean beaches and is one of the few remaining coastal lagoon systems in the state. The park was proclaimed partly to save the lagoons from being mined.

Orientation & Information

Bombah Point, 11 km from Bulahdelah, is the main settlement within the national park. Just outside the southern end of the park, **Tea Gardens** and **Hawks Nest** are two sizeable towns near the north head of Port Stephens. You can travel by road between Tea Gardens and Bulahdelah, through the national park and crossing the lake on the Bombah Point punt, but to get to **Seal Rocks**, an idyllic hamlet at the far north of the park, you have to return to the Great Lakes Way.

Organised Tours

Warren Anderson (☎ (049) 97 1071) runs 4WD tours of the area for about $35 for a half day and $60 for a full day.

Places to Stay

There are a number of National Parks *camping sites*, including Korsmans Landing, Violet Hill, River Mouth and Bungwahl on the inland side and Mungo Brush, Broadwater and Shelly Beach on the ocean side. Camping fees are $5 for two people, plus the $7.50 once-only park-use fee. Sites can be scarce at peak times.

At Bombah Point, *Myall Shores* (☎ (049) 97 4495) (which was once called Legges Camp) has a variety of accommodation, all of which becomes more expensive around Christmas and other peak times. Tent sites cost from $13 for two people, a bed in a shared cabin costs from $12.50 (rising to $17.50), and a cabin to yourself costs from $40. There's a substantial shop, a kiosk and a licensed restaurant.

There are caravan parks and motels in Tea Gardens and Hawks Nest.

Several outfits will rent you a houseboat to cruise the lakes, and it would be a pretty nice way to go. At Bulahdelah, *Myall Lake Houseboats* (☎ (049) 97 4221) has an ageing fleet of boats including some small two-person boats. Their two-person boats cost from $200 to $420 for three midweek nights, depending on the season. Next door, *Luxury Houseboat & Cruiser Hire* (☎ (049) 97 4380) has a newer fleet of more upmarket boats. Their two-to-six person boats cost from $570 to $720. They also have yachts for hire. In Tea Garden there are another couple of places. There's a bewildering array of rates varying with the time of week, the time of year, the size of the boat and the number of people, and there are special deals from time to time. The least expensive time is midweek from about May to September; the peak time is from Christmas to late January and on long weekends.

Getting There & Away

Access is via either Bulahdelah or Tea Gardens. At Bombah Point a vehicle-carrying punt runs half-hourly from 8 am to 6 pm, shuttling between the ocean and the western sides of the park. The fare is $2.50 for cars and 50c for pedestrians. If you're staying at Myall Shores you can arrange a lift from Bulahdelah, free at 9 am and 3.30 pm on schooldays and $5 at other times. Whenever you go, you'll have to book your lift (☎ (049) 97 4495).

Tea Garden and Hawks Nest are close to Nelson Bay by water, but distant by road. See the Port Stephens section for more information.

Seal Rocks

At the north end of Myall Lakes National Park, Seal Rocks is a small hamlet on a great beach. There's a shop, a few houses and not much else. The actual Seal Rocks are some distance offshore.

You can visit the **lighthouse** on Sugarloaf Point at night, on Thursday from April to October and on Saturday as well from November to March. The tour, which includes a snack, costs $8 ($4 children). There are cheaper daytime tours on Thursdays at 3.15 pm, at various times on Saturdays from November to March and during school holidays.

Humpback **whales** swim past Seal Rocks and can sometimes be seen from the shore. In 1992 a large pod of false killer whales beached at Seal Rocks, but most were saved after a massive effort by locals and people from all over the Hunter Valley.

Place to Stay The simple *caravan park* is a bit of a walk from town but is next to an excellent beach. Sites cost $8.50 or $51 for a week. It's the sort of place where you'd seriously consider staying a week in summer.

Getting There & Away Seal Rocks is 11 km down a partly-sealed road from the Great Lakes Way; turn off at Bungwahl, which is about 30 km from Bulahdelah and a little further from Forster-Tuncurry.

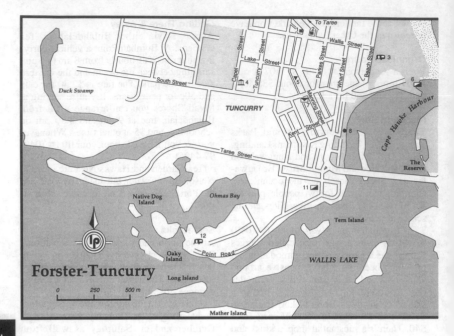

FORSTER-TUNCURRY

Forster and Tuncurry (population 16,000) are twin towns on either side of the sea entrance of Wallis Lake. In summer this is a very popular beach resort and there are plenty of great beaches and things to do, but the area is less developed than resorts both up and down the coast from here.

Orientation & Information

Forster-Tuncurry is at the north end of Wallis Lake, on a narrow spit of land that runs between the lake and the ocean. As well as the lake there are some excellent sea beaches near town and many others in the area.

At the south end of the spit, the **Pacific Palms** area is pretty and has some more good beaches. A little further south is **Smiths Lake**, where there's a koala colony which is under threat from the housing developments. On the west shore of the lake is the village of **Coomba Park**.

Forster (pronounced foster) is the larger of

the twin towns, and here you'll find the helpful information centre (065) 54 8779) on Little St (the lakefront road) near the town centre. It's open daily from 9 am to 5 pm. **Miles Island** is just across from Little St, and in the centre of the lake is big **Wallis Island**. The post office is near the roundabout that marks the town centre. The main street through Tuncurry is Manning St, which crosses the long Wallis Lake bridge and becomes Head St in Forster. The main shopping street in Forster is Wharf St.

Things to See & Do

The **museum** is on Capel St in Tuncurry, off South St, which runs off Manning St at the Tuncurry post office. The museum is open Sunday afternoon and admission is $2 ($1 children).

A walking track leads to the lookout on top of **Cape Hawke**, a few km south-east of town, and the views from up here are good.

On the way south to Pacific Palms you

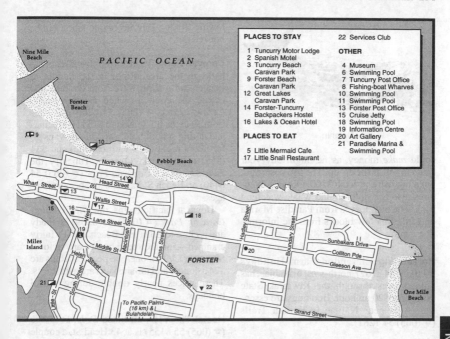

PLACES TO STAY
1 Tuncurry Motor Lodge
2 Spanish Motel
3 Tuncurry Beach
   Caravan Park
9 Forster Beach
   Caravan Park
12 Great Lakes
   Caravan Park
14 Forster-Tuncurry
   Backpackers Hostel
16 Lakes & Ocean Hotel

PLACES TO EAT
5 Little Mermaid Cafe
17 Little Snail Restaurant

22 Services Club

OTHER
4 Museum
6 Swimming Pool
7 Tuncurry Post Office
8 Fishing-boat Wharves
10 Swimming Pool
11 Swimming Pool
13 Forster Post Office
15 Cruise Jetty
18 Swimming Pool
19 Information Centre
20 Art Gallery
21 Paradise Marina &
   Swimming Pool

will pass the **Green Cathedral**, an open-air church created in 1941.

Swimming & Surfing As well as the lake, which is great for paddling about, there are some excellent sea beaches right near the town. Nine Mile Beach at Tuncurry is consistently the best for surf, but Forster Beach and Pebbly Beach can be just as good. There are large swimming pools at Forster Beach and near the harbour entrance in Tuncurry. Another pool is on the lakefront near Paradise Marina on Little St.

Cruises *Amaroo II* has a two-hour cruise on Wallis Lake three or four times a week, for $16 ($10 children). There are several dolphin-watching cruises, such as Dolphin Watch Cruises (☎ (065) 54 7478), which gives you the opportunity to get in the water with the dolphins. They say that the dolphins recognise their boat.

Boats & Canoes Most of the marinas along Little St hire boats and other forms of water transport.

Down at Smiths Lake, the Frothy Coffee Boatshed rents boats, catamarans and canoes and also dispenses their frothy coffee which, it is claimed, cures thirst, hunger, loneliness, shyness, unhappiness and boredom!

Diving Three outfits offer dives and courses: Action Divers (☎ (065) 55 4053) on the main street in Tuncurry; Forster Dive Centre (☎ (065) 54 5255) at the Tikki Boatshed on Little St; and Forster Dive School (☎ (065) 54 7478). A PADI course costs about $350. Popular dives in the area include the *SS Satara*, the largest diveable wreck in Australia (this is a deep dive), and Seal Rocks, where there are grey nurse sharks.

Fishing Ocean Adventures (☎ (065) 59 2692) is run by a professional fisherman, Chris Denton. On his game-fishing trips you

Dolphin

could *make* money, as he might buy your catch to sell at the co-op. The trip costs $50, but a big fish can fetch $100. Ocean Adventures also has dolphin and whale-watching trips. The boat leaves from Paradise Marina on Little St a few blocks from the information centre.

Horseriding Clarendon Farm Holidays (☎ (065) 54 3162), north-west of Nabiac, has guided rides through the Kiwarrak State Forest for $20 an hour. Bookings are essential. Also near Nabiac is Eureka Trails (☎ (065) 54 1281).

Organised Tours

Aboriginal Ranger Heritage Tours (☎ (065) 55 5274) explain the traditional meanings and significances of the area. Tours cost from $20 per person for the local area and $40 for a day trip and they are apparently good. Local-area tours are available during the week and day-tours on weekends. You'll need a minimum of three people.

Fair Dinkum Bush Tours (☎ (065) 55 4956) runs 4WD tours into some of the nearby state forests, as do various other outfits. There are some other tours of the area; the information centre has details.

Festivals & Events

There's a market at the Reserve, at the bridge end of Head St in Forster, on the third Sunday of the month. The annual Oyster Festival is held in early October.

Places to Stay

Over summer, especially the two weeks following Boxing Day, accommodation can be booked out.

Caravan Parks There are almost 20 caravan parks in the area. Right in the middle of Forster and a short walk from the lake and ocean, the council-owned *Forster Beach Caravan Park* (☎ (065) 54 6269) has sites from $9 in the off-season to $15 at Christmas and during school holidays. On-site vans go for $20 a night ($30 with ensuite) and $34 ($55) at the peak. Over in Tuncurry the *Tuncurry Beach Caravan Park* (☎ (065) 54 6440) on Beach St has lake and ocean frontages.

Down at Pacific Palms, the *Pacific Palms Caravan Park* (☎ (065) 54 0209) is shady and is close to Elizabeth Beach, but it's fairly cramped – and the speed bumps are vicious! Sites cost $5/9 for one/two people, cabins are $24 a double and on-site vans are a little less. These prices nearly double during school holidays.

Hostel The YHA-affiliated *Dolphin Lodge* (☎ (065) 55 8155) is at 43 Head St, a couple of blocks from the Forster post office. Coming from the town centre it's on the left just before the road makes a right-angle turn to the right. This is a new hostel in a renovated block of flats. It's very clean and airy and gets good reports. It has a surf beach pretty well at its back door, where you might be able to swim with dolphins. Dorm beds are $12 and there are doubles for $25. Boogie boards, surfboards and bikes are free.

Hotel & Motels Although there are 20 motels, you'll be lucky to find a bed around Christmas and the prices reflect this, but in the off-season there are some good deals on motel rooms, with doubles from $35 or less. Try the *Spanish Motel* (☎ (065) 54 7044) on the corner of Manning and Wallis Sts in Tuncurry.

The *Lakes & Ocean Hotel* (☎ (065) 54 6005) is on Little St near the information centre and it's a pleasant place. You won't get a room at Christmas unless you book months in advance, but in the off-season singles/doubles with shared bathroom are about $25/30 and that's fair value for the location, although not much cheaper than you'd pay in a motel.

Down in Pacific Palms, the *Pacific Palms Resort* (☎ (065) 54 0300) is a well-designed time-share resort with space for casual guests. Self-contained bungalows sleeping six people cost from $95 a night in the off-season and up to $1300-odd for a week around Christmas.

Self-Catering There are a lot of holiday apartments. The cheapest go for around $90 a week in the off-season and about $300 at Christmas. You can pay an awful lot more than this. Letting agents include Hilton Mason (☎ (065) 54 6333) at 17 Wallis St, Forster.

Across the lake in the quiet waterfront village of Coomba Park, *Bream Cottage* (☎ (065) 54 2035, (02) 651 2311 in Sydney) is well equipped and can sleep up to six people (probably more comfortable with four). It costs $190 to $550 a week, starting Saturday, depending on the time of year. If you stay longer the rates drop sharply, and if there's a vacancy they might let the cottage by the night. The turn-off from the Great Lakes Way to Coomba Park is just south of Pacific Palms, but after you arrive it's a 15-minute row to Forster-Tuncurry in the boat that comes with the cottage. What a good way to go shopping!

Places to Eat

The bistro at the *Lakes & Ocean Hotel* on Little St has pub standards for about $9 and the beer garden overlooks the lake. The plush *Services Club* on Strand St has a coffee shop, an inexpensive bistro and a restaurant.

Veta's Fresh Pastas in the Dolphin Arcade off Manning St has eat-in, takeaway and cook-yourself (at home) pastas plus salads and bread. *Il Pozzo* at 24 Wharf St is a pizzeria with some pasta, veal and seafood dishes.

Forster Indian Tandoori Restaurant on Little St across from the Amaroo II cruise jetty is open daily for dinner and most days for lunch. Tandoori main courses cost around $12 and most others are under $10; under $7 for vegetarian dishes. Down at Green Point, off the road to Pacific Palms about five km south of Forster, the *Green Point Gallery & Restaurant* (☎ (065) 54 5816) also has Indian food. It's open from Wednesday to Sunday for lunch and dinner (bookings required for dinner).

Over in Tuncurry, the *Little Mermaid* restaurant (☎ (065) 55 5144) is run by a Danish chef, a nice young guy, and presents good Australian and Scandinavian food. Main courses are around $14 and there is a $20 set menu, with cheaper set menus at times. It's open for dinner daily and for lunch most days, but you might have to let them know you're coming to lunch in the off-season. It's at 98 Manning St opposite the Bi-Lo supermarket.

With French food and a good reputation, the *Little Snail* (☎ (065) 55 6355) serves seafood and game. It's in Forster at 26 Wallis St, on the corner of West St.

Getting There & Away

Bus Great Lakes Coaches (☎ (049) 83 1560) has daily buses to Newcastle ($20) and Sydney ($34). Some services to Newcastle connect with trains to Sydney. There are also buses from Tea Gardens (on Port Stephens). Eggins Coaches (☎ (065) 54 8699, 52 2700 in Taree) runs to Taree ($11) four times on weekdays and twice on Saturday.

In summer one of the companies running between Sydney and Brisbane usually stops here, but there isn't always a service in winter.

Car & Motorbike Forster-Tuncurry is off the Pacific Highway, on the scenic but winding Great Lakes Way which leaves the highway at Bulahdelah and rejoins it about 20 km south of Taree. A more direct road from the highway to Forster-Tuncurry is planned.

Getting Around

Car Hire Coastwise, at 112 Manning St in Tuncurry (☎ (067) 54 6673) and also at the corner of Little and Wallace Sts in Forster,

(☎ (065) 54 7547) rents cars from $60 a day (100 km free) and has unlimited km rates for rents of more than three days.

THE MANNING VALLEY

The Manning Valley extends from the delta islands of the two mouths of the Manning River (near Old Bar and Harrington) westwards through farmland to Taree and Wingham, then through forests to the Bulga and Comboyne plateaux.

About 150 km of the meandering Manning River is navigable – see the Taree section for some cruises. It's possible to canoe 60 km down the Manning River from Bretti (a small town near the north side of Woko National Park, 35 km north of Gloucester) to Wingham, but seek local advice about conditions. You could start 45 km further upstream on the Barnard River at Corroboree Flat, although this stretch of river flows through private property and you technically need permission to land.

History

The valley was home to the Biripai, Ngamba and Worimi peoples when the first Europeans arrived, around 1830. The densely forested valley with its animals and subtropical fruits and the bountiful river must have made for a good life.

John Oxley was the first European to visit the valley (1818), although Captain Cook had sailed past in 1770 and named (or renamed) mountains in the area. In 1829 Governor Darling set the Manning River as the northernmost limit of the colony, but this was ignored by the cedar cutters. A land grant to William Wynter in 1831 saw permanent European settlement on the Manning. Taree, the valley's main town, was developed through subdivision of private lands, which was unusual in this government-dominated colony.

Taree

This large town (population 17,000) is the service centre for the farms of the fertile Manning Valley. It's also the nearest large town to a long strip of coast. The **Big Oyster**,

at the Viennaworld service station on the highway north of town, acknowledges the area's large oyster-farming industry.

Taree's long main street is Victoria St (the Pacific Highway); the centre of town is probably the block between Pulteney and Manning Sts, although the shops continue a long way east. The post office is in this block. A block south of Victoria St is the Manning River and the narrow **Queen Elizabeth Park** runs along the bank for the length of the city centre.

The information centre (☎ (065) 52 1900, 1800 801 522 toll-free) is on the highway north of the town centre, about three km from the post office. It's open daily from 9 am to 5 pm. Next to the information centre is the town's **art gallery**, open from noon to 4 pm from Thursday to Sunday.

Several boats cruise the river, including the MV *Surprise* (☎ (065) 52 4767) and the *Taree II* (☎ (065) 52 4767).

Places to Stay Taree is about 15 km inland, so if you're interested in beaches it's better to stay at one, but there are many options in town if you just need a bed for the night.

Caravan Parks Taree's two caravan parks, *Taree* (☎ (065) 52 1751) and *Twilight* (☎ (065) 52 2857), on the highway north and south of town respectively, have sites, on-site vans and cabins.

Hotels & Motels The *Exchange Hotel* (☎ (065) 52 1160) on the corner of Victoria and Manning Sts has singles/doubles for $12/20. A block away on the corner of Pulteney and Victoria Sts, *Fotheringhams Hotel* (☎ (065) 52 1153), known as Fogg's, is a bit better and a bit more expensive.

There are 20-odd motels in this highway town. Although their rates drop in the off-season they don't go as low as those in Forster-Tuncurry, not too far away and a nicer place to stop in. In summer you're more likely to find a vacancy in Taree, though.

Houseboats *Manning River Holidays Afloat* (☎ (065) 52 6271) has four to 12-berth houseboats for a wide range of seasonal rates. Outside summer, school holidays and long weekends, a four-berth boat costs about $450 per week.

Places to Eat On the south side of Victoria St between Pulteney and Manning Sts there are a few places worth trying. The large *Healthy Cafe* has 'alternative' overtones. Breakfast (muesli, free-range eggs) is served and throughout the day there are snacks and more substantial meals such as pasta and Thai curry for about $7. Their coffee is good. You're likely to meet some of the interesting people who live in the hills behind Taree.

A little north-east of here is the completely different *Elite Cafe*, a country-town cafe complete with booths, but a thoroughly renovated one. In between these two is the *Royal Bar & Brasserie*, renovated in spare style.

Local seafood is served at the town's oldest restaurant, *Manuel's*, in Manuel's Arcade at 103 Victoria St. *Laurent's* (☎ (065) 52 1455) is a French restaurant in the Alabaster Motel on the highway two km north of town and is open for dinner from Tuesday to Saturday.

The RSL's *Dallas Restaurant* on Pulteney St serves lunch and dinner daily and the *Viennaworld* restaurant beneath the Big Oyster is open 24 hours.

Getting There & Away Countrylink buses run to Newcastle (via the Bucketts Way) where they connect with trains to Sydney ($35). Great Lakes Coaches (☎ (049) 97 4287, 1800 043 263 toll-free) also runs to Sydney for about the same fare.

If you're driving north to Port Macquarie consider making an inland detour through Wingham to Wauchope, passing through some interesting villages and great scenery. Of course, this way you would miss out on the drive through Crowdy Bay National Park...

Wingham

Wingham (population 4900) is a quiet town serving the upper Manning Valley. It has a long association with the timber industry.

The main streets surround **Central Park**, a large, grassy square which was once the town's common and still hosts cricket matches. The huge brush-box log on the common is a memorial to Captain Cook, but it could equally be a memorial to the Manning Valley's vanished forests. On Farquar St, running along the south side, is the **museum** (☎ (065) 53 5823), open daily from 10 am to 4 pm.

Just east of the town centre, down Farquar St, is a picnic spot on a bend in the wide Manning River and **Wingham Brush**, a seven hectare vestige of rainforest. It's a very pretty place and the Brush is alive with bird calls and the twitter of flying foxes.

Wingham's **market** is held on the second Saturday of the month near the Wingham Hotel.

Places to Stay There are no camping areas close to town. The *Australian Hotel* (☎ (065) 53 4511), facing Central Park on the corner of Farquar and Bent Sts, has accommodation, as does the *Wingham Hotel* (☎ (065) 53 4007) across the park at the corner of Isabella and Wynter Sts. The Australian has a well-renovated lounge area; the Wingham is made of timber, unusual for a large hotel. There's also the *Wingham Motel* (☎ (065) 53 4295) on Bent St near the Australian Hotel, with singles/doubles for about $45/50.

Getting There & Away The railway line between Sydney and Brisbane runs through Wingham. The station is at the west end of Isabella St.

Mountains & Forests

Inland from Wingham there is some wild and rugged bushland, less well-known than the forests of the Walcha area. Woko National Park is west of Wingham but is more easily reached from Gloucester – see the Hunter Valley chapter.

There are quite a few small communities in the area with alternative lifestye tendencies, especially around Elands and Bulga. There are also plenty of art & craft galleries

– the Taree information centre has a brochure.

The **Bulga State Forest** is currently the scene of a protracted battle between conservationists and loggers who want to get their hands on some of the last stands of old-growth forest in the whole state. Draconian measures, such as declaring the state forest off-limits to anyone faintly tinged with green, have been tried, but the protests continue. However, it seems likely that the loggers will win, so have a look before the ancient trees are cut down.

Also on the Bulga Plateau, the spectacular **Ellenborough Falls** plunge 160 metres and are perhaps the highest single-drop falls in the southern hemisphere. To get here from Wingham take the Comboyne turn-off from the Oxley Highway about 10 km north of town. The falls are about 25 km west of Comboyne. In the same area you can visit **Blue Knob Lookout** and the **Wautui Falls**.

Places to Stay WWOOFers have several options in the area (see Useful Organisations in the Facts for the Visitor chapter).

Near Comboyne is the *Comboyne Hideaway* (☎ (065) 50 4230), which has quality accommodation and great views. Dinner, bed & breakfast costs $110 in the homestead; and in the self-catering dairy (sleeps six) or cottage (sleeps at least two) it's $250 for the weekend or about $110 per night. Near Elands there's *Winmurra Bush Cabin* (☎ (065) 50 4596) on a property concerned with alternative agriculture, and *Bulga Plateau Cottage* (☎ (065) 50 3045). There are various other farmstays in the area – see the Taree information centre for a complete list.

Beaches

On the coast south of the Manning's southern arm and 16 km from Taree is **Old Bar**, a village with a popular surf beach. There's a *caravan park* (☎ (065) 62 7254) with sites, on-site vans and cabins. For holiday apartments contact L J Hooker (☎ (065) 53 7650). Just south of Old Bar is **Wallabi Point** where there's a lagoon for swimming.

Near the south side of the northern arm is **Manning Point**, a hamlet serving the oyster farms along the river. Manning Point is on a large, flat river island which supports intensive dairy farming. There are several caravan parks in the area. Across on the north bank of the northern arm is **Harrington**, a small village (turn off the highway at Coopernook). There is swimming in the lagoon and surf beaches nearby. Harrington is developing into a mini-resort and there are plenty of motels and caravan parks, plus the Railway Crossing fun park.

Crowdy Head is a small fishing village four km north-east of Harrington. The views from the old lighthouse on the high head are superb, out to the limitless ocean, down to the deserted beaches and back to the apparent wilderness of the coastal plain and mountains. The only place to stay is the pleasant *Crowdy Head Motel* (☎ (065) 56 1206), which charges about $40/60 a single/double.

North of Harrington and Crowdy Head, **Crowdy Bay National Park** runs up the coast, backing a long and beautiful beach sweeping north to **Diamond Head**. A rough road leads into the national park from just before Crowdy Head village. It is very corrugated and if you want to avoid the bumps you can enter the park from the Pacific Highway just north of Moorland, which is six km north of Coopernook. You can also enter from Laurieton at the north end of the park. There are basic but very pretty campsites at Diamond Head and Indian Head but you might need to BYO water.

North of the national park and accessible from the Pacific Highway at Kew is **Camden Haven**. This area is composed of Laurieton, North Haven and Dunbogan, villages clustering around the wide sea entrance of Queens Lake, and there are good beaches. North Brother mountain towers over Camden Haven. There are walking trails in the state forests behind Laurieton, and the dive shop (☎ (065) 59 7181) on Ocean Drive in North Haven offers courses. The *Beachfront Caravan Park* (☎ (065) 59 9193) in North Haven is close to the surf beach.

North of here the coast road runs past

Top: Post office, Maitland, Hunter Valley (JM)
Bottom Left: Showground pavilion, Grafton, north coast (JM)
Bottom Right: Courthouse, Grafton, north coast (JM)

Top: Byron Bay Community Centre, Byron Bay, north coast (JM)
Middle: Food van, Seal Rocks, north coast (JM)
Bottom: Government sign Nimbinised, Nimbin, north coast (JM)

Lake Cathie (pronounced cat-eye), both a town with a caravan park and holiday apartments and a lake with shallow water suitable for kids, and then enters the sprawling outer suburbs of Port Macquarie.

PORT MACQUARIE

Port Macquarie (population 30,000), usually called just Port, is at the southern end of the state's subtropical coast. Winters are cool but short, while summers can be sticky.

Although tourist development in Port has been gaining momentum for the last 20 years or so, the city still has a relaxed small-town feel to it. With a series of surf beaches, the winding lower reaches of the Hastings River and its tributaries, and some excellent bush in the mountains behind the coast, this is a good place to spend some time.

History

Port Macquarie was only the third town to be established on the Australian mainland. John Oxley was the first European in the area, in 1818. Governor Macquarie established a penal settlement here in 1821, designed as punishment for convicts who found life in Sydney Cove too easy.

Orientation & Information

The city centre is at the mouth of the Hastings river, on the south side. Running south from the city centre is a long string of excellent beaches.

Horton St, the main shopping street, runs down to the water and there are views across to North Beach on the other side of the river-mouth. West of the city centre at the base of the Settlement Point peninsula is the big Settlement City shopping centre, the RSL's new club and entertainment centre (with an aggressively large Australian flag) and the Port Marina.

The information centre (☎ (065) 83 1077, 1800 025 935 toll-free) is at the corner of Hay and Clarence Sts. It's open daily.

Bookshops There's a big Angus & Robertson at the corner of Horton and William Sts. For a good trashy paperback to read on the beach, go to Mainly Books, a second-hand place at the north end of Hay St.

Historic Buildings

Few buildings from the early days of the penal settlement still stand. Most of the survivors are near the city centre: **St Thomas' Church** (1828), on William St near Hay St (admission $1, 30c children); the **Garrison** (1830) on the corner of Hay and Clarence, now housing a collection of cafes; the **courthouse** (1869) across the road which is being restored; and the nearby building housing the **museum** (1830).

Museums

The museum, in a historic building at 22 Clarence St, is open daily from 9.30 am to 4.30 pm, from 1 pm on Sunday. Admission is $3 (50c children). An old pilots' cottage above Town Beach is now a **Maritime Museum**, open daily from 10 am to 4 pm. Admission is $2 ($1 children).

Koalas

Koala habitats and new housing developments compete for space in this area, and guess which loses out? Koalas living near urban areas are at risk from traffic and domestic animals, and many end up at the **Koala Hospital** (☎ (065) 84 1522) off Lord

Koala

St about one km south of the town centre. The convalescent koalas are in outdoor enclosures and you can visit them daily; tours of the actual hospital are by arrangement only.

The koala hospital is in the grounds of **Roto**, a historic homestead which also houses the National Parks office. Roto is open on weekdays from 9 am to 4 pm, although the grounds are always open.

You can meet undamaged koalas and other animals at **Kingfisher Park** (☎ (065) 81 0783), off the Oxley Highway. Admission is $6 ($4 children). **Billabong Koala Park** (☎ (065) 85 1060) is further out, just past the Pacific Highway interchange. It's open daily and admission is $5 ($3 children, free for children under five).

Nature Reserves

The **Kooloonbung Creek** Nature Reserve is close to the town centre at the corner of Gordon and Horton Sts, but its 50 hectares of bush is home to many bird species. There are trails and boardwalks (suitable for wheelchairs). In the reserve is a cemetery dating from the earliest days of European settlement.

Five km south of the centre of Port Macquarie, between Miners Beach and Pacific Drive, the National Parks' **Sea Acres Rainforest Centre** (☎ (065) 82 3355) is a 70-odd hectare flora & fauna reserve protecting a surviving pocket of coastal rainforest. There's an ecology centre with displays and a 1.3-km long elevated boardwalk, suitable for wheelchairs. Entry is $8.50 ($4.50 children). As the centre points out, the world loses an area of rainforest twice the size of Sea Acres every second of every day.

Wineries

The **Cassegrain Winery** (☎ (065) 83 7777) is off the Pacific Highway just north of the Port Macquarie interchange. It's open for wine sales and tastings and there's a restaurant here as well. In the same area is the **Immeslake Vineyards** (☎ (065) 81 0381), open from 2.30 to 4.30 pm on weekdays and all day on weekends and holidays.

PLACES TO STAY

3	Lindel Travellers Hostel
6	Flag Motel
8	Royal Hotel
9	Port Macquarie Hotel
11	El Paso Motel
12	Sundowner Breakwall Caravan Park
14	River Motel
25	Historic Well Motel
31	Backpackers Headquarters
34	Beachside Backpackers (YHA)
35	Port Macquarie Cabins

PLACES TO EAT

13	Toro's Cantina
16	The Intersection
17	Macquarie Seafoods
20	Garrison & Cafes
22	The Tickled Trout
23	Yum Yums
30	Yuen Hing
32	Shades

OTHER

1	Settlement City Shopping Centre & RSL
2	Port Marina
4	Koala Hospital & Roto Homestead
5	Sea Acres Rainforest Centre
7	Post Office
10	Old Courthouse
15	Fishermen's Wharf (cruises & fishing co-op)
18	Lindsay's Buses
19	Information Office
21	Museum
24	Jetset Travel
26	Lookout
27	Observatory
28	TC's Nightclub
29	Down Under Nightclub
33	Tower
36	Bowling Club
37	Maritime Museum
38	Port Pushbikes

Across the Hastings River

A vehicle ferry crosses the river at Settlement Point, leading to two interesting roads north. A very rough dirt road (4WD may be required) runs along the coast, past the

NORTH COAST

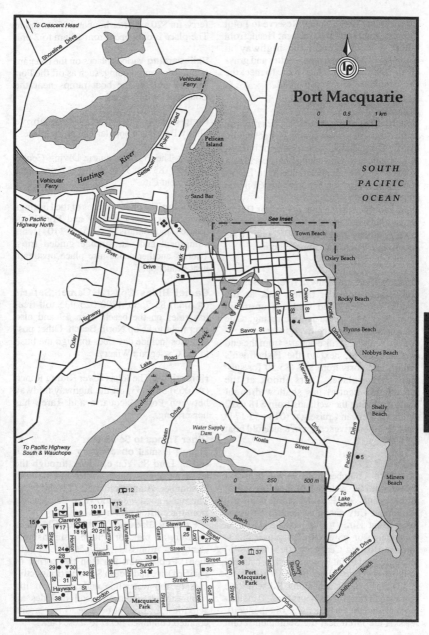

Limeburners Creek Nature Reserve to Point Plomer (good surf) and Crescent Head, from where you can rejoin the highway at Kempsey. The second road – better and gravelled – takes a more inland route to meet the Crescent Head to Kempsey road.

Activities

Beaches The string of surf beaches running south from the town centre is backed by Pacific Drive and a lot of apartment blocks. A footpath also runs along the beachfront from Town Green on Clarence St to Lighthouse Beach, the southernmost beach in the city area.

A favourite surfing spot is **Plomer Point**, across the river and about 30 km north of town on a very rough road (4WD might be necessary). There's a campsite here.

Cruises There are plenty of river cruises and you should consider taking one, as the system of creeks and wetlands upstream from Port Macquarie is fascinating. One section is known as the Everglades.

Port Venture's cruise departs from the end of Clarence St, next to the Fishermen's Wharf, and costs from $15 ($5.50 for subteens). Everglades Tours (book at the information centre) has shallow-draught boats exploring the wetlands from $18 ($12 children). Pelican Cruises (☎ (018 652 171) has a five-hour river cruise in a nice old boat for $25.

Boat Hire A number of places will help you get out onto the water, all of them on Settlement Point. At Port Marina, near the Settlement City shopping centre, Hastings River Boat Hire (☎ (065) 83 8811) has a wide range of powered craft plus canoes. Jordans Boating Centre (☎ (065) 83 1005) on Settlement Point Rd rents yachts, cats and sailboards. Gypsy Boat Hire (☎ (065) 83 2353) at 52 Settlement Point Rd will give you a small boat for six hours for $30 including fuel, and they have a range of other craft. Jet-skis are hired near the Settlement Point

ferry, for $20 a quarter-hour and $50 an hour. The place is only open from 10 am to 2 pm.

Sailboarding Various places on the river are popular for sailboarding, such as off the Port Marina and off the boat ramps near the Country Comfort motel.

Hang-Gliding Harry's Lookout above Shelly Beach is a popular launching place.

Diving The Port Macquarie Diving Centre (☎ (065) 83 8483) is at the Marina near Settlement City.

Canoeing The upper reaches of the Hastings River offer good canoeing and Port Macquarie Canoe Safaris (☎ (065) 81 1107) rents equipment and can arrange guided trips. There's another canoe-hire place upstream near Wauchope.

Camel Rides Coastal Camel Safaris (☎ (065) 83 7650, 1800 025 935 toll-free) has rides on the beach from $9 and also overnight treks up North Beach. Other possibilities include day rides through the bush to the Cassegrain Winery.

Horseriding The Johns River Riding Ranch (☎ (065) 56 5353) off the highway midway between Port Macquarie and Taree has horseriding.

Other Things to See & Do

There's a small **observatory** at the beach end of Lord St. You can look through the telescope at 7.30 pm in winter and 8.30 pm in summer. Admission is $2 ($1 children). There are good views down to the beaches from the clifftop near here.

Fantasy Glades on Parklands Close is a big fairytale park for children, surprisingly elaborate. Admission is $6.50 ($4.50 children). **Peppermint Park** on the corner of Pacific Drive and Ocean St has various activities of the waterslide and mini-golf ilk. Admission is about $10 and includes all activities. You might be able to buy a discounted combined ticket to these parks.

Organised Tours

Port Explorer (☎ (065) 82 1235) has half-day tours of the town on Friday for $10 ($7.50 children) and several day-tours of the area for $18 ($14 children).

Places to Stay – bottom

Caravan Parks The most central caravan park is the expensive *Sundowner Breakwall* (☎ (065) 83 2755) at 1 Munster St, near the river mouth and Town Beach, with sites from $15 and on-site vans from $35. There are cheaper places near Flynns Beach and inland along the river.

Hostels & Cabins There are currently three hostels, all in hot competition.

Beachside Backpackers (☎ (065) 83 5512) is a YHA associate hostel at 40 Church St, near the corner of Grant St. The telecommunications tower across the street is a landmark. This place is clean, friendly and popular. Dorm beds are $12. It's about five minutes' walk from both the town centre and the beach and they'll collect you from the bus stop. An attraction here is water-skiing trips which are great value at about $20.

Lindel Travellers Hostel (☎ (065) 83 1791) is slightly further from the centre but they meet the buses and there are free bikes to ride once you get here. They also do a daily run to the beaches. Lindel is in a well-kept old house and has a reputation for being friendly and well run. There's a small swimming pool. Dorm beds are $12 and a twin room costs $24. There's a once-only fee of $1 for linen hire.

Backpackers Headquarters is at 135 Horton St (☎ (065) 83 1913). The previous managers were planning a cafe on the ground floor, but they moved on and now there's a pawn shop instead of a cafe. This is the cheapest hostel in town at $10 for a dorm bed and only $8 for VIP and YHA members (the hostel is *not* a YHA affiliate). There are also singles for $15, doubles for $25 and twins for $30. It's a bit of a rabbit warren and is looking very tired, and the atmosphere is depressing and reportedly sleazy.

Despite Port's spreading veneer of glitz,

Port Macquarie Cabins (☎ (065) 83 1115) is still very much in business. These old fibro cabins are well-worn but clean enough, and cheap at $24 for two people and just $1 for each extra person. The weekly rate is $120. At Christmas and other peak times the charge for two people rises to $39 plus $5 per extra person and the weekly rate is $210. Each cabin has a double bed and three singles, all in the same room, and each has an attached bathroom (and a garage!) and cooking facilities. You can hire linen if necessary. The cabins are at 24 Lord St, not far from the corner of Church St. The sign is small and the entrance isn't on the street – go down the driveway next to the fish & chip shop.

Across on the north shore (take the ferry), *Limeburners Lodge* (☎ (065) 83 8000) has dorm accommodation geared to large groups but they might have space for individuals and there are a few family rooms.

Places to Stay – middle

Hotels It's a sign of how this town has grown from small beginnings, and of the sort of people who have moved here, that there are only two pubs. Superbly located at the north end of Horton St, the *Port Macquarie Hotel* and the *Royal Hotel* (☎ (065) 83 1011 for bookings at either hotel) both have very reasonable rates. The Port Macquarie has motel-style units for $45/55, rising to $75 a double (only) at Christmas and Easter. There are also pub rooms with attached bathrooms for $25/35 (rising to $50, double only) and small rooms with shared bathrooms for $20/30 (up to $30/45). At the Royal there are motel-style units overlooking the water for just $32/40 (up to $55, double only) and pub rooms with attached bathrooms for $25/30 (up to $45, double only).

The pub rooms at the Port Macquarie are a bit better than those at the Royal, but at either place check the bed and listen for noise such as jukebox music wafting up from the bar, or industrial-strength air-con ducts outside the window. The reception desk at the Port Macquarie handles accommodation at both hotels.

Motels There might not be many pubs in town but there are plenty of motels – more than 30 at last count. The cheapest are furthest from the beaches, not surprisingly. In town, the *River Motel* at 5 Clarence St near the corner of School St has off-season doubles for around $40 and several nearby holiday apartments have similar deals. Other less expensive places are along Hastings River Drive.

There are several motels along Stewart St/Pacific Drive, such as the *Historic Well Motel* (☎ (065) 83 1200) at the corner of Lord St, close to Town Beach, charging from around $50 a double in the off-season, rising to around $90 in summer.

Places to Stay – top end

The *Flag Motel* (☎ (065) 83 2166) on the corner of Clarence and Short Sts is a highrise, very centrally located. Doubles are about $70, plus $10 for each extra person. There's a $20 surcharge on long weekends and around Christmas.

Further east on Clarence St, next to the old courthouse, the *El Paso Motel* (☎ (065) 83 1944) is an old-style motel now basking in a fashionable paint-job and renovations. (It won't be long before motels like this get National Trust listings for their unique architecture.) The prices aren't cheap, around $80/90 a single/double, plus $10 for each extra person, with a $20 surcharge at Christmas and Easter.

Midway between the centre and Settlement City, the *Country Comfort Motel* (☎ (065) 83 2955) is on the waterfront and charges from around $75/85. *Sails Resort* (☎ (065) 83 3999, 1800 025 271 toll-free bookings) is on the waterfront near Settlement City. Rooms cost from $150; $170 with a view of the water.

Self-Catering There are a great many apartments and holiday flats. They are expensive at peak times, but in the off-season you might find a two-bedroom apartment for about $200 a week. Letting agents include Town & Country Real Estate (☎ (065) 84 1007) on the corner of Short and Clarence Sts.

On Clarence St, on the corner of Murray St, *Port Pacific Resort* (☎ (065) 84 9024) is a large block of timeshare apartments, some of which are available to let. In the low season you'll pay about $90 for two people in a single-bedroom apartment and $100 in a two-bedroom apartment. Each extra person costs $12, and daily servicing costs another $10. Prices rise by about 15% over Christmas, Easter and other school holidays.

Places to Eat

Port has a wide range of eating places with over 50 restaurants. Outside peak times many have good-value meal deals.

If you want to cook your own seafood, head down to the Fishermen's Co-op at the west end of Clarence St where they sell fish straight off the boats.

Snacks & Cafes Perhaps the cheapest place for breakfast is *Yum Yums*, a small place on Short St near the corner of William St. Around $4 should get you going for the day. Plenty of other places serve breakfast, such as the many coffee shops in the arcades running off Horton and William Sts. Across from the hostel on Horton St is *Shades*, a fairly standard coffee lounge that serves light meals and has outdoor tables.

On William St near the corner of Short St is *Zars Cafe*, which has a pleasant terrace although there's not much of a view. They have reasonably-priced breakfasts, snacks and light meals such as lasagne ($6.50) and stirfried prawns ($7.50) as well as cakes, coffees and smoothies. Next door there's a 24-hour deli.

At the historic Garrison building, on the corner of Hay and Clarence Sts, *Margo's Cafe* has tables outside and is a pleasant place for a coffee and a snack. It's licensed and prices are reasonable. Fish & chips are $5, nachos $6 and pastas $6.50. The big menu includes crepes, quiches and other light meals. There are several other cafes in the Garrison building. Diagonally opposite is the *Pancake Place* with a large menu of crepes for around $10.

At the corner of Short and Clarence Sts is

another place with footpath tables, *The Intersection*. The large menu includes snacks and light meals. Focaccia goes for $6. Across Short St is *Macquarie Seafoods*, a takeaway place that doesn't pre-cook the food and uses vegetable oil. Basic fish & chips costs $3.80. The fish is superb but the chips are almost as slim as the unsatisfying fries of that well-known hamburger chain.

Across the road, on Clarence St, the *Hog's Breath Cafe* has snacks such as nachos (from $7) and burgers (from $8) and main meals for around $15.

Restaurants On Murray St there are a couple of Mexican places, *Toro's Cantina*, which has main courses around $10 to $12, and nearby *Bruno's Pizza & Mexican*. Bruno's is a little more expensive, but it gets rave reviews. It was up for sale at the time of writing, so things might have changed.

There are a couple of Chinese places on Horton St south of William St, the *Wah Hing* and the *Yuen Hing*. Both have special deals and sometimes smorgasbord lunches for well under $10.

Riverview Terrace (☎ (065) 84 14446) overlooks the water at the Royal Hotel and is open for lunch and dinner from Tuesday to Sunday. Main courses are in the $16 region, with cheaper options at lunch.

The *Tickled Trout* at 2 Clarence St is open nightly and has main courses for around $12. Half-a-dozen oysters will set you back $6. They also have takeaways in the evenings, with fish & chips for $4.

Cray's, overlooking the river at Fishermen's Wharf, specialises in seafood, especially crayfish, and has main courses from $18. Their off-season specials are worth a look. Next door is *Al Dente*, an Italian restaurant with main-course pasta for about $12 and other main courses under $20.

Chula, the small Thai restaurant at the corner of Short and Clarence Sts, is open daily except Monday for lunch and from Tuesday to Saturday for dinner. Main courses are around $10. There's another Thai place upstairs in the arcade on Horton St near the corner of Clarence St.

On Horton St not far from here is the *Treasure of India* which has main courses for less than $10, or a whole tandoori chicken for $12. They have lunch specials for $7.50 in the off-season.

At the top end of Hay St is *Dang*, not a disgruntled cowboy place but a Vietnamese and Malaysian restaurant where main courses are around $11, with seafood dishes around $16. Further along and with sea views is *Pottsy's Place* with grills and seafoods for around $15. *Harpo's* on Flynns Beach is popular with locals.

At the Sails Resort near Settlement City, *Spinnakers* has harbour views and off-season specials such as three courses for $30. Not far away, *Scampi's* in the Port Marina centre is a pleasant place that's open for dinner. Seafood features heavily, but there are other dishes as well. Main courses are around $15 to $20, with daily specials. The $64 seafood platter for two sounds very interesting.

Entertainment
There are currently three nightspots: Lachlans, between the Port Macquarie and Royal hotels, TC's on William St and Down Under around the corner on Short St. When the RSL's new big complex at Settlement City gets underway there should be a lot of entertainment there as well.

Getting There & Away
Air There are at least three flights a day to Sydney, on Oxley ($156) and Eastern ($162). The standard one-way fare to Brisbane is $196. The Oxley agent is Jetset Travel (☎ (065) 84 1411) on the corner of Horton and William Sts.

Train The nearest railway station is at Wauchope.

Bus Port Macquarie Bus Service (☎ (065) 83 2161) runs to Wauchope about four times a day for $5.40. This service stops outside the Lindsay's office at the corner of Clarence and Horton Sts, as do Lindsay's long-distance services. All other long-distance bus services stop outside the old RSL building on Short St, but a new bus terminal might be developed near the information centre.

Long-distance bus lines include Port Macquarie on their Sydney to Brisbane route, but not every service stops here. Lindsay's (☎ (065) 53 1277, 1800 027 944 toll-free) runs to Newcastle ($33), Sydney ($36), Brisbane ($45), Armidale ($35) and Tamworth ($50). Prices to destinations closer to Port Macquarie are high – it costs $30 to get to Coffs Harbour, $26 to Dorrigo. Port Macquarie Bus Service also has a daily run to Sydney.

Car & Motorbike The next major town on the Pacific Highway is Kempsey, about 50 km north. The Oxley Highway runs west from Port Macquarie through Wauchope and eventually reaches the New England tableland near Walcha. It's a spectacular drive.

The Settlement Point ferry runs to the north side of the Hastings River and costs $1 per car. It runs only a few times each day, so ask the information centre for the current timetable before you head out there. To get to the ferry, keep going past the RSL club and follow the signs to Settlement Point.

Getting Around

Bike Rental Port Pushbikes on Hayward St rents ungeared bikes for $8 a half day, $15 for a day and just $25 for a week. Graham Seers Cyclery at Port Marina near Settlement City also rents bikes.

Car Rental There are no super-cheap outfits, only the major companies. Budget (☎ (065) 83 5144) is at the corner of William and Short Sts.

WAUCHOPE

Wauchope (pronounced 'war hope') is a timber town of long standing. There's no tourist office but you can phone for information (☎ (065) 85 2017),

The town's main attraction is the big **Timbertown** historic park, with the emphasis on the history of the timber industry. It's one of the better theme parks and is well

worth visiting. Admission is $12.50 for adults, $11 for YHA members and students, $6 for children and free for children below school-age.

Just before Wauchope on the road from Port Macquarie is the turn-off to **The Big Bull**, billed as 'the world's largest fibreglass bull'! It's a pretty kitsch idea but apparently it's worth a visit, especially if you have kids, who will enjoy the hay-ride and the animal nursery. Admission is $5 ($3 children).

The turn-off to Lilybank Canoe Hire (☎ (065) 85 1600) is nearby. For $10 an hour (less for longer hires) you can paddle on the beautiful river, and they can organise five-day trips down the Hastings River from Mt Seaview.

Cowarra Homestead (☎ (065) 85 3531) has horseriding.

Places to Stay

The YHA associate *Rainbow Ridge Hostel* (☎ (065) 85 6134), 11 km west of town on the Oxley Highway, was once the only hostel between Sydney and Queensland. Times have changed! It's still an old-style hostel: quiet, friendly and definitely not the place for party animals. There are bushwalks nearby, including a six-hour climb to the top of Bago Bluff, but many people come just for the good night's sleep they don't get in livelier places. Dorm beds are $10 or you can camp for $5 per person.

Coming from Wauchope, the hostel's driveway is on the right just before the Comboyne turn-off. Keep a look-out after you cross the Mahers Creek bridge. With prior arrangement you can probably get a lift from Wauchope, or ask around town for information on schoolbuses running out this way.

In Wauchope the *Hastings Hotel* (☎ (065) 85 2003) on the main street near the railway line has accommodation and there are a couple of motels, the *Wauchope* (☎ (065) 85 1487) on the main street in town and the *Broadaxe* (☎ (065) 85 1355) on the highway near Timbertown. There's also a *caravan park* here.

Off the Oxley Highway about 60 km west of Wauchope, *Mt Seaview Resort* (☎ (065)

87 7144) is a large complex on the Hastings River and not far south of Werrikimbe National Park. There's horseriding and 4WD tours. It might not be everyone's cup of tea but with inexpensive camping and bunkhouse accommodation (as well as a range of rooms and suites) it might make a good base for exploring the area.

Getting There & Away
Train Wauchope is on the main line between Sydney ($51) and Murwillumbah ($51) or Brisbane ($64).

Bus Port Macquarie Bus Service (☎ (065) 83 2161) runs to/from Port Macquarie about four times each day for $5.40. Lindsay's (☎ (065) 53 1277, 1800 027 944 toll-free) comes through on the run to Armidale.

Mid-North Coast

MACLEAY VALLEY
Rising in the New England tableland, the Macleay River flows east through the fertile Macleay Valley, entering the sea near South West Rocks, although until a flood in 1893 its entrance was near Grassy Head. The main town in the valley is Kempsey, on the Pacific Highway and about 20 km inland from the nearest ocean beach at Crescent Head. North and south of Crescent Head there are long, uncrowded beaches.

Before Europeans arrived, the valley was owned by the Dangaddi people, but in 1827 the penal settlement in Port Macquarie established a camp in the valley to cut cedar and rosewood. Land grants were made in 1835 and the town of Kempsey (named because of the country's supposed resemblance to the Kempsey Valley in Worcestershire) was established by 1840. Beef cattle and dairying were early agricultural ventures and they remain the mainstay of the area, with tourism forming the third leg of a stable and prosperous tripod.

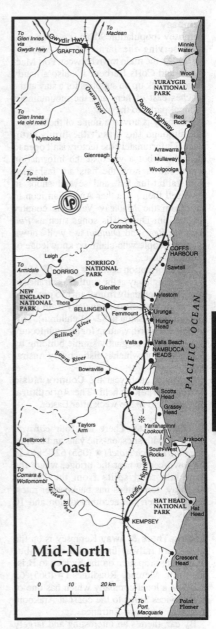

Mid-North Coast

NORTH COAST

Kempsey

Kempsey (population 9000) is a large rural town serving the farms of the Macleay Valley. As the main town between Port Macquarie and Coffs Harbour it's also a handy place to stock up on supplies for a stay at the beaches east of here and the mountainous national parks to the west.

Kempsey is now the home of the Akubra hat, although this wasn't the firm's birthplace. Unfortunately the factory isn't open to the public, but a video at the information centre shows how the hats are fashioned from rabbit-fur felt, and several shops in town sell them. Another Australian icon to hail from the Macleay Valley is country singer Slim Dusty. His songs such as *Pub With No Beer* and *Duncan* are well known even by people who claim no knowledge of country music.

The information centre (☎ (065) 63 1555) is off the highway at the southern entrance to town; it's open daily from 9 am to 5 pm. Also here is the **museum**, open daily from 10 am to 4 pm. Admission is $2 ($1 children). This complex is worth visiting for the architecture alone – it's an elegantly simple building by Glenn Murcutt which is distinctively Australian.

In March each year the **Country Music Heritage Week** is held. The **Agricultural Show** is held in the week after Easter.

Places to Stay There are four *caravan parks,* all with sites, on-site vans and cabins. The *Pearl Perch Hotel* (☎ (065) 62 4586), in the town centre near the bridge, where the Armidale road splits from the Pacific Highway, sometimes has backpacker rates. There is other pub accommodation and 10 motels.

Getting There & Away Kempsey is on the north-coast railway line, and the major bus companies stop here on the Sydney to Brisbane run. Mercury Roadlines (☎ (065) 62 4201) is a local company which has one or two services a day to the coast at Arakoon, Trial Bay and New Entrance.

By car, there's an interesting and largely unsealed route running west to Wollomombi (on the Dorrigo to Armidale road); head north-west to Bellbrook.

Crescent Head

This small village (population 1100), 20 km south-east of Kempsey (turn off the highway near the information centre), has both a quiet front beach and a surf-washed back beach. There's quite a lot of new holiday development, but the village is far enough off the highway to remain relaxed. South of the town is the **Limeburners Creek Nature Reserve** (☎ (065) 83 5866), with walking trails and camp-sites. North of town is Hat Head National Park (see below).

Places to Stay The *Crescent Head Caravan Park* (☎ (065) 66 0261) is right on the beach and has sites from $9 and cabins from $40, rising to $70 in holidays.

There are plenty of holiday apartments in town and they might be cheaper than a cabin at the caravan park. In the off-season they should be available by the night, but in summer you might have to rent by the week. The cheapest one-bedroom apartments go for $30 a night, rising to $45 in school holidays. See one of the two estate agents on the main street (☎ (065) 66 0500 or 66 0306).

Bush & Beach Retreat (☎ (065) 66 0077) is about three km north of town on Loftus Rd (turn off the main road at the Mediterranean Motel) with bushland behind and the beach not far away. It's a modern building in 'colonial' style, but much nicer than most fakes. B&B packages start at around $70 a double. *Killuke Lodge* (☎ (065) 66 0077) is three km south of Crescent Head on the Point Plomer road and has accommodation in good cottages sleeping up to six people, from $275 a week (much more in holidays). Outside holiday time you might be able to rent for as few as three days.

Hat Head National Park

This coastal park (6500 hectares) runs north from around Hat Head to Smoky Cape (just south of Arakoon), protecting scrubland, swamps and some excellent beaches backed

by significant dune systems. Bird-life is prolific on the wetlands. Rising up from the
generally flat landscape is Hungry Hill, near
Hat Head, and sloping Hat Head itself, where
there's a walking track.

Surrounded by a national park, the village
of **Hat Head** is a much smaller and quieter
place than Crescent Head. The *Hat Head
Caravan Park* (☎ (065) 65 7501) is pleasant
and not far from a good beach. Sites cost
from $9 to $11.50 in the peak season.

You can camp at Hungry Hill, five km
south of Hat Head, and at Smoky Beach, but
BYO water to the latter.

The park is accessible from the hamlet of
Kinchela, on the road between Kempsey and
South West Rocks. It's possible to get a lift
on a schoolbus from Kempsey to Hat Head.
Phone the caravan park for details.

South West Rocks

The wide Macleay River enters the sea a few
km from South West Rocks at New Entrance.
Here you can cruise up the river on the
Leisurely Lady (☎ (065) 66 6192) from $12.
South West Rocks Marine Centre (☎ (065)
66 6474) hires diving equipment, and some
of the area's dive sites, such as Fish Rock
Cave, are widely known. Kids might enjoy
feeding the fish at the Everglades Aquarium.

Places to Stay The *Horseshoe Bay Caravan
Park* (☎ (065) 66 6370) is a small place
running along the slope behind pretty little
Horseshoe Bay near the town centre. Sites
cost from $12 and on-site vans from $24.
Prices rise in summer and vacancies are rare
at Christmas and other major holidays.

The *Costa Rica Motel* (☎ (065) 66 6500)
sometimes has share accommodation for
about $15, and South West Rocks Dive
Centre (☎ (065) 66 6474) at 100 Gregory St
has bunkhouse accommodation for divers,
but they might let others stay. In the off-
season you might get a single-bedroom
apartment for $150 a week. Contact an estate
agent, such as L J Hooker (☎ (065) 66 6313).

Midway between the Pacific Highway and
Stuarts Point (a short way north of South
West Rocks but accessible only from the

highway), the *Kurrabi Rainforest Retreat*
(☎ (065) 69 0809) accommodates eight
people in a bushland setting. Daily rates are
$105/180, including meals. No smokers or
children.

Trial Bay & Arakoon State Recreation Area

Three km east of South West Rocks is **Trial
Bay Gaol**, on the headland. This imposing
edifice was a prison in the late 19th century
and housed German POWs in WW I. The
POWs were kept on a loose rein and were
allowed to fish, so their confinement can't
have been too irksome. The jail is now a
museum with wonderful views, open daily
($2.50; $1 children). Trial Bay is named after
the brig *The Trial* which was stolen from
Sydney by convicts in 1816 and wrecked
here. **Smoky Cape Lighthouse**, a few km
down the coast from the jail, can be inspected
on Thursday (and Tuesday in school holidays) from 10 to 11.45 am and 1 to 2.45 pm.

The beaches on the ocean side of the peninsula are unsafe, but those on the bay side
are safe and good. The sea has a habit of
scouring sand from some bay beaches and
dumping it on others, so if your beach
doesn't have much sand try the next one
along.

On the shores of the bay behind the old jail
is the *Arakoon SRA Camping Area* (☎ (065)
66 6168), with sites from $8 for two adults
and two children and on-site vans from $18
during the week and $30 on weekends.
You'll pay more for waterfront sites and all
prices rise considerably during school holidays and in summer. During the season you
can hire cats and boats on the beach here.

NAMBUCCA HEADS

At the mouth of the Nambucca River (the
'bucc' rhymes with buck, not book), this
small resort town (population 6000) is one
of the better stops on the north coast.

History

The Nambucca Valley was owned by the
Gumbaynggir people when the European
timber-cutters arrived in the 1840s, and there

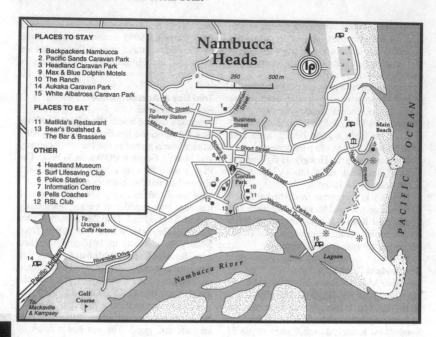

PLACES TO STAY

1 Backpackers Nambucca
2 Pacific Sands Caravan Park
3 Headland Caravan Park
9 Max & Blue Dolphin Motels
10 The Ranch
14 Aukaka Caravan Park
15 White Albatross Caravan Park

PLACES TO EAT

11 Matilda's Restaurant
13 Bear's Boatshed &
     The Bar & Brasserie

OTHER

4 Headland Museum
5 Surf Lifesaving Club
6 Police Station
7 Information Centre
8 Pells Coaches
12 RSL Club

NORTH COAST

are still strong Aboriginal communities in Nambucca Heads and up the valley in Bowraville.

Orientation & Information

Nambucca can be a little difficult to get a handle on. The town is a km or so off the highway and the road in, Riverside Drive, runs alongside the wide estuary of the Nambucca River then climbs a steep hill to Bowra St, the main shopping street. Most of the older part of the town is up on this headland.

Main Beach, the patrolled surf beach, is about one km east of the centre. Follow Ridge St (running off Bowra St) and take Liston St when it splits. If you take Parkes St at this junction you'll eventually reach North Head, where there are good views from Pilot Lookout. To get to the river-mouth (where there is more good surf for experienced surfers), turn off Bowra St at the Mobil station onto Wellington Drive, which winds

down past Gordon Park. This is a very scenic spot.

The helpful information centre (☎ (065) 68 6954) is on Ridge St, next to the post office on the corner of Ridge and Bowra Sts. The information centre is open daily from 9 am to 5 pm (shorter hours on Sunday), and they will let you leave luggage here while you go exploring. The town's **Headland Museum** is on Liston St near the Main Beach car park. As well as displays on local history, the museum has 'many other interesting exhibits difficult to place into categories'! $1 seems a small price to pay.

Among the places offering **boat hire** are Bears Boat Shed (☎ (065) 68 8138) on the waterfront at Gordon Park. The *Jungle Queen* (☎ (065) 64 7865) cruises up the Nambucca River, with two-hour trips for $12.50 ($5 children) and day trips for $25 ($14 children). It departs from the RSL car park.

At Valla, just up the highway (not Valla

Beach), the **Big Fat Worm Farm** will let you pick, pack and even race worms for $5 ($2 children), on weekends from 10 am to 4 pm.

Places to Stay

Caravan Parks There are several caravan parks. As usual, prices rise in holidays and you might have to stay by the week at peak times. *Foreshore Caravan Park* (☎ (065) 68 6014) is on Riverside Drive not far from the highway and overlooking the estuary, with a beach nearby. Sites are from $8, on-site vans from $20 and cabins from $32.

The *White Albatross* (☎ (065) 68 6468) is near the river-mouth at the end of Wellington Drive. There's a lagoon for swimming as well as the surf beach. Sites cost from $11 a double (more for waterfront sites and during school holidays), on-site vans are from $22 and cabin vans with bathrooms are from $32. There's a campers' kitchen. Around near the main surf beach are *Headland* (☎ (065) 68 6547) and *Pacific Sands* (☎ (065) 68 6120).

There are other caravan parks further out. Near the small town of **Valla Beach**, off the highway eight km north of Nambucca Heads, the *Valla Beach Resort* (☎ (065) 69 5106) is on a lagoon not far from the surf. It has its own bar and restaurant. Sites cost between $10 and $15 and cabins between $30 and $50. They prefer families at Christmas, when they're usually booked out anyway.

Hostel & Guesthouse *Backpackers Nambucca* (☎ (065) 68 6360) at 3 Newman St is a very good hostel and a great place to relax for a few days. Dorm beds are $13 for the first night, $12 for subsequent nights; doubles are $28 for the first night, $26 for subsequent nights; and singles, when available, are $20. There are sometimes specials available in less busy times. The friendly managers offer trips in the area and can arrange whitewater rafting. They lend snorkel gear and boogie boards. It's a one-km walk through bush to the beach, and you might meet wallabies in the evening.

The Ranch (☎ (065) 68 6386) at 4 Wellington Drive is a guesthouse in the building which was the first hotel in the Nambucca Valley. From the outside this looks like a place to drive past without stopping, but inside it's a different story. The amiable Irish owners decided to renovate the interior before the exterior so as not to disappoint people – commendable, but bad for business. Currently there are large, newly-renovated rooms for $35 including breakfast. Bathrooms are shared but the next phase of renovation will be to add ensuites. There are also a couple of bunkrooms for backpackers, who pay $10 a night (more in summer) and can use the kitchen facilities. Dorm beds might not be available in summer. The view from the Ranch must be equal to the best in the world.

Motels Sharing the view from the other side of Gordon Park are a couple of moderately-priced motels, *Max Motel* (☎ (065) 68 6138) and the *Blue Dolphin Motel* next door. Max Motel is an old-style place with few luxury touches, but it's clean and the view is worth a lot more than the $36/50 charged (less in the off-season). The Blue Dolphin is newer and costs a few dollars more. Both these places are entered from Fraser St, the southern continuation of Bowra Street.

Places to Eat

The *Bowling Club* on Nelson St and the *RSL* on Fraser St both have restaurants with good-value meals. The *Golden Sands Hotel* has pub meals, and *Midnight Express* behind the pub is worth trying. On Wellington Drive near Gordon Park is *Matilda's* with char-grill and seafood for around $15 a main course. It's open for dinner daily and for lunch from Wednesday to Friday. They prefer you to book (☎ (065) 68 6024). Nearby on the waterfront is the *Bar & Brasserie*, which has seafood and other dishes for around the same prices.

Getting There & Away

Train The railway station is about three km out of town: follow Bowra St then Mann St. The fare to Sydney is $58. The hostel picks up guests (for a fee); otherwise there's no transport between the station and town.

Bus All the long-distance buses stop at Nambucca, but Lindsay's is the only line which comes into town. The others stop on the highway at the Shell station (southbound) or the Aukaka Motel (northbound). With Kirklands the fare is about $42 to Sydney, and about $38 to Byron Bay. Harvey World Travel (☎ (065) 68 6455), on Bowra St opposite the police station, handles bookings.

Pells (☎ (065) 68 6106), the local bus company, runs to Coffs Harbour on Tuesday and Thursday, departing at 9.30 am from the police station on Bowra St. The return fare is $6. You can go along on Pells' schoolbus runs to Macksville and Valla Beach on school days. Jessup's (☎ (066) 53 4552) has a service between Bellingen and Coffs Harbour, running via Nambucca, Mylestom and Urunga, on school days only. Joyce's (☎ (066) 55 6330) has about four runs a day (fewer in school holidays), weekdays only, between Bellingen, Urunga and Nambucca Heads ($6.80).

AROUND NAMBUCCA HEADS

The Nambucca Valley is much narrower than the Macleay Valley to the south and the Bellinger Valley to the north. The main roads running up the valley turn off from the old town of **Macksville**, on the highway about 12 km south of Nambucca Heads. Near **Taylors Arm**, a hamlet about 25 km west of Macksville, Nambucca Trails (☎ (065) 64 2165) at Bakers Creek Station offers horseriding through the mountains, and you can also hire canoes there. Taylors Arm is the home of the **Pub With No Beer**, immortalised in a song by Slim Dusty which was one of the first Australian songs to sell well overseas – it stayed at the top of the Irish charts for more than two months! There's plenty of beer there now and often acoustic music at weekends.

South of Macksville, off the road to the seaside village of **Scotts Head** (good surf), an unsealed road leads up through the Way State Forest to **Yarrahapinni Lookout** which has great views down to the coast and back into the hinterland.

Bowraville

This small town is very different from its booming coastal neighbours. It's a close-knit community of old families, the descendants of the cedar-getters who arrived in 1842 and the Aborigines who are somewhat longer-established residents.

Along the main street you'll find several interesting craft shops and the big **Bowraville Folk Museum**. The museum is open during school holidays, on Sunday and Tuesday, on Wednesday morning or by request (☎ (065) 62 7251). Admission is $1 (50c children). Even if you aren't interested in the museum, have a look at the wonderful Max Hill Memorial Gates at the entrance. Just along from the museum is a building which claims to be a guesthouse, but it's just a facade and is now part of the museum. It was used in the film *The Umbrella Woman* which was shot here.

Festivals & Events On Saturday morning the popular Bowraville Country Market is held in a building on the main street. The market has its own tea-rooms, a great place to meet locals.

The annual Back to Bowra Festival is held over the October long weekend. Among many other events there is billy-cart racing.

Places to Stay The *Royal Hotel* (☎ (065) 64 7208) has rooms for as little as $12 per person. The *Bowra Hotel* (☎ (065) 64 7041) is one of the few old brick buildings in town. They will probably let you have a room for $20/25 a single/double.

Getting There & Away The only public transport is schoolbuses. By car you can get here from Macksville, and interesting back-roads lead north to Bellingen and Dorrigo and south to Taylors Arm, where you can join a network of largely unsealed roads which eventually lead up to the New England table-land at Wollomombi, east of Armidale.

Urunga

On the highway about 12 km north of Nambucca there's a strip of tacky highway motels which get down to $25 a double at slow times. Urunga, just east of the highway, is a nicer little place than this would indicate. It is on the estuary of the Bellinger/Kalang River, with surf beaches not far away at **Hungry Head**.

There are several caravan parks in the area and the *Ocean View Hotel* (☎ (066) 55 6221) in Urunga is a fine old pub overlooking the estuary with pub rooms for $25/35 with breakfast. The double rooms are fairly large and some have views; the smaller singles and twins are at the back. On the highway, the Honey Place, a nursery and craft shop with live bee displays, has tourist information (☎ (066) 55 6160).

See the Bellingen, Nambucca Heads and Coffs Harbour sections for transport information.

Mylestom

About five km north of Urunga and just south of the big Raleigh Bridge over the Bellinger River is the turn-off for the **Raleigh Winery** (☎ (066) 55 4388), open for tastings and sales daily from 10 am to 5 pm. North of this bridge you come to the turn-off for Mylestom, also called **North Beach**, about five km east of the highway.

This quiet hamlet is in a great location on the north bank of the Bellinger River estuary and also has good ocean beaches.

Places to Stay & Eat *North Beach Caravan Park* (☎ (066) 55 4250) is close to the beach and has sites from $7.50 ($11.50 school holidays) and on-site vans from $19.

Caipera Riverside Lodge (☎ (066) 55 4245) is a backpacker hostel on the main street across from the river. It's the third house on the left as you enter town. Beds in two-bed 'dorms' are $13. They can help organise activities such as whitewater rafting and horseriding, and there are bikes to explore the area. They can usually give you a lift from Coffs Harbour if you give a day's notice.

Beaches, also on River St, is a restaurant with snacks (minimum order $5) and main courses from around $13. Seafood features on the menu here. Beaches is open for lunch from Thursday to Sunday and for dinner from Thursday to Saturday.

See the Bellingen, Nambucca Heads and Coffs Harbour sections for transport information.

BELLINGEN

Bellingen is a small town (population 1600) in hilly country, on the banks of the Bellinger River. It is reached by turning off the Pacific Highway near Urunga, about halfway between Nambucca Heads and Coffs Harbour. It's a pleasant and interesting place, and a centre for the area's artistic and alternative people.

History

The Kumbaingeri people owned this area until European timber cutters arrived in the 1840s. The first settlement here was at Fernmount, about five km east of Bellingen, but later the administrative centre of the region was moved to Bellingen. Rivercraft were able to come up here until the 1940s when dredging was discontinued. Until tourism boomed at Coffs Harbour in the 1960s, Bellingen was the most important town in this area.

Information

There's no information office, but the Yellow Shed craft shop (☎ (066) 55 1189) on Hyde St (the main street) has pamphlets and can help with enquiries. The Environment Centre, up a lane running off Church St, is a friendly place, and someone here can probably help with enquiries about the area's forests.

Things to See & Do

The small **museum** is behind the old wooden library on Hyde St and is open from 2 to 4 pm daily and also from 10 am to noon on Wednesday and Friday. At other times you can phone (☎ (066) 55 1262) to see if there's someone available to open it for you.

Admission is 50c. Talking to the volunteers who staff the museum might be as informative as looking at the exhibits. The huge old **Commercial Emporium** on Hyde St is worth a look.

There are plenty of craft shops in town, and a short way out on the road east to the highway is the **Old Butter Factory** which houses several craft workshops and galleries. There's a cafe here.

A huge colony of **flying foxes** lives on Bellingen Island, near the caravan park, during the breeding season from December to March. There are **platypuses** living in the river nearby.

You can hire canoes ($10 for the first hour, $32 for the day) at the Oasis Cafe at the Old Butter Factory. Bushwhacker Expeditions (☎ (066) 55 8607) also has canoeing and various other tours, including guided walks through the rainforests. Most tours begin at Thora, about 15 km from Bellingen on the road to Dorrigo.

The **Syndicate Walking Trail** is a strenuous day-long walk of 15 km from Gleniffer up onto the plateau, following the route of a tramline once used by the timber cutters.

Phil & Margaret's Motorcycle Tours (☎ (066) 53 7725) offers rides on the back of a Harley, at $20 for 15 minutes.

Festivals & Events

The Community Market, held in the park on the third Saturday of the month, is a major event, with more than 250 stalls. People from all over the valley show up and there's live music. The annual Jazz Festival is held in late August.

Places to Stay

The *caravan park* (☎ (066) 55 1138) is across the river – turn onto Wharf St from Hyde St (the post office is on the corner), cross the bridge and follow the road around to the left, then turn left down Dowle St. You can walk from town.

Bellingen Backpackers (☎ (066) 55 1116) (also called *Belfry Lodge)* should have opened by now. It's on Short St (behind the Federal Hotel) in a renovated old house that

overlooks the river. Beds cost around $15 and they will pick you up from Urunga.

There is pub accommodation, including rooms at the *Federal Hotel* (☎ (066) 55 1003) for about $15/30. The *Bellingen Valley Motor Inn* (☎ (066) 55 1824) is on the west edge of town and charges from about $60/70, rising to about $100.

B&B places are springing up in town and around the nearby countryside. *Rivendell* (☎ (066) 55 0060) is close to the centre of town at 10 Hyde St and charges from $45/55. *Jelga* (☎ (066) 55 2202) is across the river at 1 Wheatley St, and the self-contained stone cottage costs from $75 a double plus $10 for each additional person up to six or seven (at a pinch). The price includes breakfast, but you have to cook it yourself. See the directions for the Flying Fox Cafe. *Koompartoo Retreat* (☎ (066) 55 2326, best before 10.30 am or after 3.30 pm) is on a property at the southern edge of Bellingen, at the corner of Rawson and Dudley Sts, and has good self-contained cabins. *Blue Gum* (☎ (066) 55 1592), about eight km south-west of town near Gleniffer, charges about $50/70. *Jasmine Retreat* (☎ (066) 55 8632) is about 30 km north-east near Upper Thora (turn off the Dorrigo road at Thora) and charges from $40/75 including all meals.

Places to Eat

On Hyde St, towards the top end, *The Carriageway* is a coffee shop that's stylishly decorated but country-town friendly. It's open daily and in the evening from Wednesday to Saturday. They serve breakfast (muesli $3.50, omelettes from $5) and light meals. There are a few places on Church St, including *Martha & Mario's*, a pasta place with murals on the wall and patchouli oil in the air, open daily for lunch (except Monday) and dinner. Main-course pasta costs around $10.

Don't miss the *Flying Fox Cafe*. It's a relaxed place but the food is innovative and excellent. Prices are reasonable, with main courses around $10 at lunch and $14 at dinner, plus cheaper vegetarian options. To get here follow the directions for the caravan park but keep going to the roundabout just up from Dowle St; turn left here onto Wheatly St and the cafe is nearby. You can walk from town.

Getting There & Away

Bus The bus stop is at the corner of Church and Hyde Sts, diagonally opposite the courthouse. Lindsay's (☎ (066) 53 1277, 1800 027 944 toll-free) comes through on the run up to Armidale, but they aren't allowed to carry you on short sectors such as Coffs Harbour to Bellingen. They can do Coffs to Dorrigo ($9.70) or Bellingen to Armidale ($17.20).

Joyce's (☎ (066) 55 6330) has about four runs a day (fewer in school holidays), on weekdays only, between Bellingen, Urunga ($3.20 from Bellingen) and Nambucca Heads ($6.80). Jessup's (☎ (066) 53 4552) runs to Coffs Harbour via Nambucca Heads, Mylestom and Urunga on school days only, departing Bellingen at 8 am. On any Tuesday they have a service from Bellingen to Coffs via Urunga and Mylestom only, departing Bellingen at 9.35 am.

It might be possible to get to Dorrigo by schoolbus, but you'd have to change at least once on the way and hope for a connection.

Train The nearest station is at Urunga.

Car & Motorbike Bellingen is about 12 km west of the Pacific Highway; turn off just south of the Raleigh Bridge. From Bellingen the road climbs steeply up to Dorrigo – a spectacular drive. From Dorrigo you can continue west to the Armidale to Grafton road. A network of unsealed roads leads south to Bowraville and some tiny mountain settlements.

DORRIGO

This mountain town (population 1200), close to the edge of the Great Divide's eastern escarpment, was one of the last places to be settled in the eastward push across the New England tableland. It had the usual cedar-getting pioneers and was on a railway to Glenreagh. It was (and still is) an important stop on the road between Armidale and the coast.

Today Dorrigo is just a quiet country town with wide streets and a few architectural reminders of its history. As the largest town on the Dorrigo Plateau it makes a good base for visiting the area's outstanding national parks. Dorrigo National Park is covered later in this chapter, the others in the New England chapter.

The information centre (☎ (066) 57 2486) is in the Dorrigo Hotel/Motel and is usually open on weekdays. The hotel is at the corner of Cudgery and Hickson Sts, the two main streets of this little town.

Things to See

The **Railway Museum** isn't open yet, but you can see a long line of matte-black steam engines queued up at the old railway station. Head down Cudgery St and take the first right after the bridge. The museum is part of a project to run steam trains on the disused Dorrigo to Glenreagh line, a project that is foundering under the weight of bureaucracy but might yet succeed.

A few km north of town on the road to Leigh are the picturesque **Dangar Falls**.

Places to Stay

Dorrigo Mountain Resort (☎ (066) 57 2564), a caravan park with some substantial cabins, is just out of town on the road to Bellingen. Sites cost from $8.50 ($10 in school holidays and on long weekends), self-contained cabins cost from $42 to $50 and there are cheaper on-site vans.

The *Dorrigo Hotel/Motel* (☎ (066) 57 2017) has motel units for about $40 and cheaper pub rooms. An interesting brochure on the history of the hotel is available at the information centre. The other pub, the *Commercial Hotel* (☎ (066) 57 2003), has motel units in a new section, for $30/40, but no pub accommodation in the wooden main building.

The *Lookout Motor Inn* (☎ (066) 57 2511), further out on the Bellingen road not far from the national park entrance, charges from around $55/70. The *Tallawalla Retreat*

(☎ (066) 57 2315) is about a km out of town on the old Coramba road and has B&B for about \$40/80.

Places to Eat The *Dorrigo Hotel/Motel* has a bistro and there might be meals available in the old dining room. On Hickson St, *Nick's* is a country-town cafe. There's a *Chinese restaurant* at the Bowling Club, open daily except Monday for lunch and dinner.

Getting There & Away

Bus Lindsay's (☎ (066) 53 1277, 1800 027 944) comes through on its run from the coast to Armidale, but they aren't allowed to take you on the sector between Bellingen and Dorrigo. A community bus runs to Coffs Harbour on Monday at 9 am from Hickory House at the top of Hickson St. This bus can be full of locals going shopping and you can't book. It departs from Coffs at about 1.30 pm. Contact John Rowe (☎ (066) 57 2233) if you need more information.

There are no other buses except for schoolbuses, and none of them runs direct; for Bellingen you'll have to get off at Thora and hope to pick up another bus there. Talk to a schoolbus driver in Bellingen to see if it's feasible.

Car & Motorbike Coffs Harbour is about 60 km away via Bellingen, or there's an interesting, partly unsealed route via Leigh and Coramba. You can get to Armidale or Grafton by heading west to the Armidale to Grafton road; to Grafton there's also a partly unsealed route that passes through Leigh and Glenreagh.

DORRIGO NATIONAL PARK

The astonishingly dense rainforest of Dorrigo National Park (7900 hectares), a World Heritage Area, is known for its orchids. The **Dorrigo Rainforest Centre** has an elevated walkway and good displays as well as a National Parks office (☎ (066) 57 2309) and a cafe. A walking track leads to the Glade rest area from where there's a 5.5 km walk through the forest. It's well worth making the drive down to the Never

Never rest area in the heart of the national park, from where you can walk to waterfalls or begin overnight walks. Walkers in this area can bush-camp, but otherwise no camping is allowed. The turn-off to the park is just south of Dorrigo.

COFFS HARBOUR

Coffs Harbour is a major resort town and the centre of rampant housing development. The town centre is busy and nothing to write home about, but there's a harbour and some interesting headlands, and a string of good beaches stretches north.

History

Originally called Korff's Harbour, the town was settled in the 1860s. The jetty, built in 1892 to load cedar and other logs, is in disrepair and its future depends on funds being raised to restore it. Bananas were first grown in the area in the 1880s but no-one made much money from them until the railway was built in 1918, giving access to markets and also bringing a huge workforce of hungry labourers.

The recent boom in tourism and retirement housing has seen intense development in the area and the ecology is beginning to grumble. Just supplying all the newcomers with water is proving to be a headache.

Orientation

Coffs is quite spread out, with several distinct areas. The Pacific Highway is called Grafton St on its run through town and passes through the main shopping and business district. The corner of Grafton and High Sts is just about the city centre. High St is a pedestrian mall here, but on the other side of the mall it's the main road to the **Jetty** area, three km east. This is where you'll find the railway station, some shops and a string of restaurants. Across the railway tracks is the actual Coffs Harbour with its historic jetty.

From here High St heads north along the coast, becoming Orlando St then Ocean Pde after it crosses a bridge over Coffs Creek, taking you to the **Park Beach** area. Towards the north end of Ocean Pde, Park Beach Rd

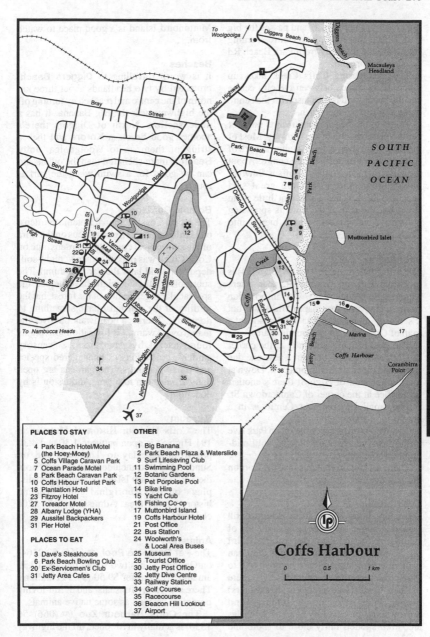

NORTH COAST

PLACES TO STAY

4 Park Beach Hotel/Motel
  (the Hoey-Moey)
5 Coffs Village Caravan Park
7 Ocean Parade Motel
8 Park Beach Caravan Park
10 Coffs Hrbour Tourist Park
18 Plantation Hotel
23 Fitzroy Hotel
27 Toreador Motel
28 Albany Lodge (YHA)
29 Aussitel Backpackers
31 Pier Hotel

PLACES TO EAT

3 Dave's Steakhouse
6 Park Beach Bowling Club
20 Ex-Servicemen's Club
31 Jetty Area Cafes

OTHER

1 Big Banana
2 Park Beach Plaza & Waterslide
9 Surf Lifesaving Club
11 Swimming Pool
12 Botanic Gardens
13 Pet Porpoise Pool
14 Bike Hire
15 Yacht Club
16 Fishing Co-op
17 Muttonbird Island
19 Coffs Harbour Hotel
21 Post Office
22 Bus Station
24 Woolworth's
  & Local Area Buses
25 Museum
26 Tourist Office
30 Jetty Post Office
32 Jetty Dive Centre
33 Railway Station
34 Golf Course
35 Racecourse
36 Beacon Hill Lookout
37 Airport

Coffs Harbour

0   0.5   1 km

runs back to the highway and passes the big Park Beach Plaza shopping centre. Turning right onto the highway from Park Beach Rd can be a major pain.

The meandering Coffs Creek takes up much of the space between the city centre and the beach, and is the reason for the centre being so far from the beach.

To get to the beaches and resorts north of Coffs you have to take the highway. Most of the resorts are just past the satellite suburb of **Korora**, five km north of the centre. About the same distance south of Coffs is **Sawtell**, on a lagoon and with more great surf beaches. Sawtell has a pleasant little main street but the rest of the town is sprawling housing developments which merge into Coffs Harbour.

Information

The information centre (☎ (066) 52 8824) is in Urana Park on Grafton St, near where Moonee St branches off. The information centre has several free maps of the town, but it's worth spending $3.95 on Broadbent's map of Coffs and the surrounding area.

The post office is currently at the corner of High and Grafton Sts, but a new one due to open in the mall might replace it. Down at the harbour end of High St there's another post office at the corner of Camperdown St.

The small Environment Centre is in a health-food shop on the mall.

The Woolworths supermarket on Park Ave in the town centre is open daily, until midnight on weekdays.

There's a laundromat in a lane off Gordon St, near the mall.

The Harbour

There are good views from **Beacon Hill Lookout** above the harbour up at the top of Edinburgh St, and from **Corambirra Point** on the south side of the harbour. You can walk out along the northern harbour wall to **Muttonbird Island**, a nature reserve where mutton birds (wedge-tailed shearwaters) breed. They lay eggs in underground burrows. In June and July humpback whales are often spotted fairly close to shore and Muttonbird Island is a good place to watch from.

Beaches

It is worth travelling to **Diggers Beach**, protected by two headlands about three km north of the centre and reached by turning off the highway near the Big Banana. It has a nude section. North of Diggers there's another good beach at **Korora** and then a string of them up to Woolgoolga. **Jetty Beach** is more sheltered than the others and can be good for a swim when the surf is rough.

Botanic Gardens

The North Coast Regional Botanic Gardens, on Hardacre St off High St, focus on the flora of the subtropical coast. The gardens' site on Coffs Creek was once the town's 'night-soil' depository and later the garbage dump. The subtropical climate might have helped the spectacular regeneration of the forest, but the fertility of the soil must have something to do with it. There's a boardwalk out over the mangrove swamp, information on plants found useful by Aborigines, a 'sensory garden', collections of endangered species and other plantings. The gardens are open daily from 9 am to 5 pm. Admission is by donation.

Museum

The Coffs Harbour Historical Museum at 191 High St is open between 1.30 and 4.30 pm from Tuesday to Thursday and on Sunday. Exhibits include the old 'optic' from the South Solitary Island lighthouse and displays on the Aboriginal and European history of the area. Admission is $1 (20c children).

Animals

The **Pet Porpoise Pool** (☎ (066) 52 2164) on Orlando St has two shows daily at 10.30 am and 2.15 pm for $9.50 ($4.50 children). There are 'funny fur seals' and a 'fun-loving porpoise', as well as some native animals.

The **Coffs Harbour Zoo** (☎ (066) 56 1330) is actually in Moonee, off the highway

12 km north of Coffs. The emphasis is on native animals and the koalas are 'presented' at 11 am and 3 pm daily. You can go horseriding and there's a restaurant. The zoo is open daily and admission is $9 ($5 children).

Fruit Farms

Coffs' best-known symbol, the **Big Banana**, stands outside a tropical fruit plantation (☎ (066) 52 4355) with theme-park exhibits which you visit by travelling on a mini railway system. There's a restaurant, a cafe or two and crafts. Entry to the complex is free but it costs $9 ($5 children) to take the tour.

For something rather different, visit **Kiwi Down Under**, a biodynamic tropical fruit farm four km west of the highway from Bobville (12 km south of Coffs). You can drop in between 1.30 and 4.30 pm on weekends and from Wednesday to Sunday in school holidays. A guided tour starts at 2.30 pm.

Activities

You can book attractions and activities at a kiosk in the mall, at the Grafton St end. However, they don't necessarily give you a choice of all the possibilities (they book only one of the whitewater rafting outfits, for example) so if you're shopping around for deals you should contact the companies directly. Backpackers will find the best deals at the hostels, especially Aussietel.

Cruises *Commissioner II* (☎ (066) 51 3271) cruises past South Solitary Island each day for $20 ($8 children). The MV *Laura E* (☎ (066) 51 1434) has deep-sea fishing trips for $65 and during the whale-spotting season (April to October) they have a two-hour cruise for $25.

Diving The Jetty Dive Centre (☎ (066) 51 1611) at 396 High St has courses ($350) and dives ($25 for a single dive, plus equipment hire). They also rent snorkelling gear ($15 a day for the full set, including weights and wetsuit, or less if you need less gear). Up in Mulloway there's also Dive Quest (☎ (066)

54 1930). Both can take you to the interesting Solitary Islands.

Flights Fly Scenic (☎ (066) 51 3244) has sightseeing flights in the area. Balloon flights are available with Bananacoast Balloons (☎ (066) 58 1236) from around $100 per person.

High Flyer Parasailing (☎ (066) 51 5200, booking essential) will whisk you up above the harbour for $40. Their office is at the jetty. Direct Parasailing (☎ (018 65 7034; 1800 67 0417 toll-free) is nearby, on the breakwater out to Muttonbird Island, but their flights are outside the harbour, above the ocean. They also charge $40, or $50 with a pick-up from Coffs or a resort.

Horseriding South of Coffs near the hamlet of Valery, Valery Trails (☎ (066) 53 4301) charges about $25 for two hours and $55 for a day. In the same area, Bonville Forest Stables (☎ (066) 53 4537) is on Butlers Rd just south of Bonville, 16 km south of Coffs. Both places can arrange longer trips.

Surfing The best local beach is Diggers Beach, north of Park Beach. Diggers isn't patrolled, but, as with several other beaches in the area, there are alarm buttons on the beach which will bring lifesavers quickly.

Boards are hired at Coopers Surfshop at 380 High St in the Jetty area, and Northside Surf in Northside Shopping Centre on Park Beach Rd has surf-skis as well.

The East Coast Surf School (☎ (066) 52 4727) is rapidly developing a reputation for teaching novices to surf. Helene Enevddson guarantees that you'll be able to stand up on a board after six lessons, or subsequent lessons are free! The fee, $14 an hour or a $72 for a six-lesson course, covers all equipment, including wet-suits at cooler times of the year. Backpackers get discounts on lessons booked through hostels. Helene also runs weekend surfing camps in school holidays for $80.

Whitewater Rafting The Nymboida River inland from Coffs offers some excellent

NORTH COAST

whitewater thrills, and there are a couple of outfits which get good reports. Whitewater Rafting Professionals (☎ (066) 51 4066) at 20 Moonee St (next to the bus station) has day trips for $95 and overnight trips for $245. Wildwater Adventures (☎ (066) 53 4469) at 4 Butlers Rd in Bonville offers much the same, plus four-day trips and more challenging trips on the Gwydir River, near Inverell in New England.

Other Activities Outer Limits Abseiling (☎ (066) 51 4066) at 22 Moonee St has day-trips with instruction for about $85. You can hire a jet ski for $20 for 15 minutes, cheaper for longer, near the mouth of Coffs Creek. The Thunderdome on Hogbin Drive, south of the racecourse, is open daily from 10 am to 10 pm and has exciting go-karts to drive (on and off-road), plus arcade entertainment.

Organised Tours

Coffs Harbour Coaches (☎ (066) 52 2686) has various day tours of attractions in and around Coffs from $20 ($12 children). They will pick you up.

4WD Adventure Safaris (☎ (066) 58 1871) has various tours of the town, the beaches and the bush, from around $35 ($20 children) for a half-day tour. Mountain Trails 4WD (☎ (066) 55 1961) has similar tours at similar prices. Check at the information centre for other outfits.

Festivals & Events

Every Sunday from 8 am to 2 pm there are markets at the Jetty Village shopping centre at the harbour end of High St, and there's another at the Park Ave car park.

The Gold Cup, Coffs' premier horserace, is run on a Thursday in early August. It's a big day out, capping off a big week of entertainment in Coffs. Entry to the racetrack is only $5.

A busking festival is held in late October.

Places to Stay

Except in the hostels, expect prices to rise in school holidays by about 50% mid-winter

and about 100% at Easter and Christmas/New Year.

Caravan Parks The huge *Park Beach Caravan Park* (☎ (066) 52 3204) on Ocean Parade, one km north of the harbour and just north of the mouth of Coffs Creek, is right next to the beach and has tent sites at $12 a double, on-site vans from $26 and cabins from $35. There are lower weekly rates, but not at peak times. *Coffs Harbour Tourist Park* (☎ (066) 52 1694) on the highway a couple of blocks on from the Ex-Services Club has sites from $10, on-site vans from $20 and cabins from $30. There are plenty of other places along the highway north and south of town.

Hostels There are two hostels. Both are in good modern buildings and can arrange discounts on just about everything in town.

Aussitel Backpackers Hostel (☎ (066) 51 1871) at 312 High St, about 1.5 km from the town centre and 500 metres from the harbour, is a lively place with dorm beds at $13 and $15 per person in doubles. It has all the usual hostel facilities plus a pool. The enthusiastic management will help arrange whitewater rafting, diving, surfing and other activities, and will pick you up on arrival and give rides to the beach during the day or to the pub at night. There's a stretch of creek across the road from the hostel and canoes are free.

Albany Lodge (☎ (066) 52 6462), the YHA hostel at 110 Albany St, a block from High St and one km from the town centre, is a friendly place. Dorm beds cost $12 and there are a few double rooms for $12.50 per person. Bikes and surfboards are free and there's a spa. The hostel is open all day and can usually pick you up – at night phone in advance to ask. They arrange trips and activities here and have excursions such as day trips to the Dorrigo area.

Hotels Many of the town's hotels have accommodation. In the off-season you're better off hunting around for a motel with deals, but pub prices tend to stay the same year-round so they can be great value in summer.

Officially on Moonee St (although it actually looks as if it's on Grafton St), the *Fitzroy Hotel* (☎ (066) 52 3007) is an old-style neighbourhood pub with singles/doubles for $15/30. Further down Grafton St, opposite the Ex-Services Club, the *Plantation Hotel* (☎ (066) 52 3855) has rooms from $20/25 for singles/doubles. It's OK, but the rooms are pretty stark, the communal bathrooms could be cleaner and there are bands...

Down near the harbour on High St, the *Pier Hotel* (☎ (066) 52 2110) has a few large, clean, old-style rooms for $18 per person. One has an attached bathroom, but the rest share clean communal facilities. The owners live on the premises, so they are a little choosy about who they will take as guests.

Motels There's a string of motels on Grafton St across from the tourist office, such as *Toreador* (☎ (066) 52 3887) and *Golden Glow* (☎ (066) 52 2644). In the off-season prices fall as low as $40 a double. There's another bunch in the Park Beach area with similar rates. You'll pay around $40 a double at *Ocean Parade Motel* (☎ (066) 52 6733), but in the high season their rates are around $60 a double (no singles). The *Park Beach Hotel-Motel* (☎ (066) 52 3833) – the Hoey-Moey – has old-style motel units for $25/30/35 a single/double/triple, or less when trade is slack.

If you're just passing through, the motels on the highway further south, such as those in Urunga, can get down to $30 a double in the off-season.

Better quality motels include the *Big Windmill* (☎ (066) 52 2933), on the highway south of the town centre and not too pricey in the off-season; *Royal Palms* (☎ (066) 52 4422) on Park Beach Rd; and the *Country Comfort* (☎ (066) 52 3832) on the highway north of the town centre.

Self-Catering There is a huge range of holiday apartments and houses. In the off-season, the cheapest of the two-bedroom apartments go for around $45 a night (less by the week) and $90 a night in the high season, which is not too bad between a group. Of course, there are many which are vastly more expensive. Many places are available only by the week in the high season. The tourist information centre has a free booking service (☎ 1800 025 650 toll-free), and there are plenty of real estate agents.

Resorts The resorts are responsible for Coffs' upmarket image – without them it would be just another thriving coastal town. Most of the resorts are off the highway past Korora, about five km north of Coffs. Most have lower weekly rates.

Novotel's *Opal Cove* (☎ (066) 51 0510) is a large place which includes a residential development and a golf course – it looks pretty bare of foliage. There's a nightclub and a huge pool. Rooms cost around $150.

Nautilus on the Beach (☎ (066) 53 6999; 1800 029 966 toll-free bookings) is part of the Flag motel chain and is a large collection of small buildings. It feels a bit cramped, but for the price it's reasonable value. Rooms sleeping three cost from $85, rooms with kitchens sleeping four cost from $110 and suites cost from $135. Add $10 per person for more than two people and add $30 during school holidays.

Next door, the more stylish *Pelican Beach Resort* (☎ (066) 53 7000; 1800 028 882 toll-free bookings) is run by the Travelodge motel chain. Double rooms start at $99, rising to $120 around Christmas, and suites cost from $185, rising to $250. There are plenty of packages and deals offering large discounts, NRMA members get 20% off if rooms are available.

The five-star *Aanuka Beach Resort* (☎ (066) 52 7555) is closer to town than the others – turn off the highway just after the Big Banana. It's the most pleasant of the resorts, with only 48 suites, lush gardens and a beach without rips. The cheapest suites go for $180 in the low season, rising to $250 during holidays.

Down in Sawtell, off the highway six km south of Coffs, the *Boambee Bay Resort*

(☎ (066) 53 2700; 1800 028 907 toll-free bookings) is partly a time-share resort and is on the lagoon rather than the beach. It's nice enough, but nothing out of the ordinary. Accommodation in a long terrace of two-bedroom apartments starts at $115 a double, rising to $200 at peak times.

B&B *Illoura* (☎ (066) 53 1690 after 4 pm), about one km off the highway seven km south of Coffs (get full directions when you book), has great views, wildlife and one guest suite which goes for $60/90. No children under 16.

Places to Eat
Some of the best cheap eats can be found in the clubs, such as the *Ex-Services Club* on the corner of Grafton and Vernon Sts and the *Catholic Club* on High St, about one km inland from Grafton St.

City Centre There are a number of snack places on the mall, including a *bakery* with $1 mini-pizzas across from the mini-McDonald's. At the intersection in the middle of the mall *Brent's on the Mall* has coffee, snacks and light meals, and tables to eat at. The nearby *Island Cafe* is similar, although the coffee isn't great.

The pubs in this area all have counter meals, with the cheapest being lunches at the renovated *Legendz* bistro at the Plantation Hotel on Grafton St, where lunch specials can include a meal and a drink for $5.

Pancakes All Round on High St near the corner of Gordon St, has pancakes and crepes from $6 to $10, plus pasta from $8 to $10. It's licensed and is open for lunch and dinner daily. Across the road a little further east is the *Tequila Mexican Restaurant* with main courses from $9 to $14.

On Park Ave across from Woolworths, the Chinese *Phoen Wong* has Thursday lunch smorgasbords for $6.50 and early dinner smorgasbords for $12 from Friday to Sunday. The ordinary menu includes quite a few vegetarian dishes for under $6. Another of the several Chinese restaurants is the *Unicorn* upstairs in the 176 Arcade, off the mall. It has been recommended by travellers for its good food and its occasional great deals such as big $3 main courses.

Jetty For choice you can't beat the cluster of restaurants at the Jetty end of High St, although none is especially cheap. You can eat seafood, Italian, Indian, Chinese, French and, nearby, Thai. There are also pub bistro meals and $5 breakfasts at the *Pier Hotel*.

The *Fishermans Katch* (☎ (066) 52 4372) is one of Coffs' better seafood restaurants (you're advised to book), but it isn't too expensive, with seafood dishes from $12. It's open for dinner from Monday to Saturday (all week during holidays) and for lunch from Wednesday to Friday.

There are three Italian places. *Pasta Mamas* is family-oriented and has a large menu with main-course pasta around $12.50, but also excellent year-round specials such as half-price pizzas between 6 and 7 pm. *Avanti*, with a Swiss-trained chef, is a little more expensive but much more adventurous. At *Gigolo's* entrees are under $5.50 and main courses are under $10 – in the off-season, at least. The food is simple but good.

The other places also have plenty of off-season specials, such as three courses for $20 at the French *Peter's Peppermill* (licensed). Main courses are in the $17 to $22 range.

In the Jetty Village shopping centre across the road, *River Kwai* has Thai food with main courses between $9 and $13. Not far away on Orlando St is *Barhn Thai*.

Takeaways are sold at the *Fishermen's Co-op* on the harbour.

Park Beach Compared to Jetty and the centre there's a dearth of eating places in this area, but you won't starve. *Le Joint*, on Ocean Pde opposite the bowling club, is basically a milkbar but it has a fine verandah where you can eat breakfast and other meals. The nearby *Hoey-Moey* has a bistro with specials such as $5 meals. Next door, the *Park Beach Bowling Club* also has meals.

In a house across the road from the

bowling club is the French *Affaire de Coeur*, with main courses from about $15.

At 99 Park Beach Rd, over York St, *Dave's Steakhouse* has steaks from $14 and seafood from $15.

Entertainment

Nightclubs come and go. Most are open until early morning every night; currently popular are High St 66 and The Sovel (formerly Oscars), both on the mall. Crystal's Night Club in the Ex-Services Club has bands and/or a disco.

The Hoey-Moey has bands at weekends, sometimes quite big touring bands. The Plantation Hotel on Grafton St has free local and touring bands from Wednesday to Saturday. Up the street, the Coffs Harbour Hotel is the place for karaoke if that's your vice.

Down at the Jetty, near the strip of eating places, Beach Street has party nights, usually with a beach theme. Velcro 'bar flying', a mechanical surfboard and other devices help the fun along – as do various deals on cheap drinks.

The cinema complex on Vernon St across from the Ex-Services Club has $5.50 films from Sunday to Tuesday.

Getting There & Away

There are plenty of travel agents around town. Near the long-distance bus stop on Moonee St, Lindsay's (☎ (066) 51 3022) handles bus bookings (not just Lindsay's), and a few doors away Coffs Harbour Coaches & Travel (☎ (066) 52 2686) will fix you up with bus, air and Countrylink tickets.

Air Coffs Harbour has a busy airport with direct flights to Sydney ($190) and Brisbane ($165). The odd charter flight from New Zealand lands here, and there are moves to have the runway extended so that scheduled international flights can land.

Train The railway station (☎ (066) 52 2312) is near the harbour at the end of High St. The fare to Sydney is $62.

Bus – long-distance All the long-distance lines on the Sydney to Brisbane route stop at Coffs, and Lindsay's has services up to Dorrigo and Armidale. The main stop is in Moonee St just west of Grafton St. Some fares from Coffs include: Byron Bay $32, Brisbane $41, Nambucca Heads $10, Port Macquarie $30, Sydney $44, Dorrigo $9.70 and Armidale $18.30. As usual, it pays to ask about special deals, and check noticeboards at the hostels.

Bus – local area Most local-area buses pick up at the multi-storey car-park next to Woolworths on Park Ave and at the Park Beach Plaza shopping centre.

Ryan's (☎ (066) 52 3201) runs to Woolgoolga ($5) via beachside towns off the highway. There are four services on weekdays, two on Saturday and none on Sunday.

Bradley's (☎ (066) 54 1516) has a weekday service between Coffs and Grafton, running via Woolgoolga and, north of Woolgoolga, some of the beachside towns off the highway such as Red Rock and Arrawarra. From Coffs there are departures at 3.15 pm plus 9.15 am on Monday, Wednesday and Friday. The fare to Woolgoolga is $5 (just $6 return) and to Grafton it's $8.50 ($13 return).

Jessup's (☎ (066) 53 4552) has a service that runs on schooldays only between Coffs and Bellingen, via Mylestom, Urunga and Nambucca Heads. This departs from Park Ave at 3.15 pm. On any Tuesday there's a service from Coffs to Bellingen via Mylestom and Urunga only, departing from Coffs at 1.45 pm; and on any Thursday there's a service to Urunga only, departing from Coffs at 2 pm.

Car & Motorbike Heading north there's an alternative to the Pacific Highway which runs inland, following the railway line through some pretty country and the small town of Glenreagh, and up to Grafton.

Boat Coffs is a good place to pick up a ride along the coast on a yacht or cruiser. Ask around or put a notice in the yacht club at the harbour – the hostels sometimes know of boat owners who are looking for crew.

Getting Around
A bus service connects the centre, the Jetty and Park Beach, but services are infrequent, with none on Sunday. The information centre has timetables.

Taxi companies include Coffs Radio Cabs (☎ (066) 51 3944). There's a taxi rank on the corner of High and Gordon Sts.

Bob Wallis Bicycle Centre (☎ (066) 52 5102) on the corner of Collingwood and Orlando Sts rents bikes.

Car Rental As well as the major companies Hertz (☎ (066) 51 1899), Avis (☎ (066) 51 3600) and Thrifty (☎ (066) 52 8622), local outfits offer cheaper rates, although you should compare the deals carefully. Coffs Harbour Rent-a-Car (☎ (066) 52 5022) on the corner of Marcia St and the Pacific Highway charges fairly high daily rates, around $60 for a small manual car, but includes 300 free km. JR's Car & Truck Rental (☎ (066) 52 8480) at 30 Orlando St rents older vehicles.

COFFS HARBOUR TO GRAFTON
Glenreagh
On the inland route which follows the railway line between Coffs Harbour and Grafton, Glenreagh is a small village (population 300) on the Orara River. Glenreagh had a gold rush in the 1880s and it was a railway junction town until the Dorrigo line closed in the 1970s. There's a **museum** in the old School of Arts, open from 9 to 11 am on Tuesday.

Take the left turn from the Coffs Harbour to Glenreagh road just past Coramba, then turn right on Bushmans Range Rd and you'll come to **George's Goldmine** (☎ (066) 54 5355), which is actually the old Bayfield Mine. Tours of the mine are held through the day and the surrounding bush is a nice spot for a picnic. It's open from Wednesday to Sunday and daily in school holidays.

Woolgoolga
This beachside town (population 4000) is home to a large Sikh community. On the highway north of the turn-off to the town centre is the Raj Mahal, a tourist-trap complex with shops and a restaurant. It used to dwarf the *gurdwara* (temple) on the hill at the other end of town, but a big new temple is under construction there. The rest of the town is pretty standard but much more laid-back than Coffs and its satellites.

Places to Stay & Eat The *Woolgoolga Beach Caravan Park* (☎ (066) 54 1373) is on the beach and has sites from $8 to $10, on-site vans from $22 to $32 and cabins from $33 to $50.

There are a few motels along the highway, such as the *Woolgoolga Motor Inn* (☎ (066) 54 1534), with rates a little cheaper than those in Coffs.

For Indian food there's the *Koh-I-Nor* restaurant at the Raj Mahal and the *Ramblak Restaurant* across from the new temple. For Aussie tucker try the Ex-Services Club, but take your hat off!

There has been trouble at the Ex-Services Club because Sikhs wouldn't remove their 'headgear'. Perhaps the local old soldiers don't know that Sikhs, and their turbans, have a rather longer tradition of defeating the English monarch's enemies than do Australians.

Getting There & Away The long-distance bus-lines pass through Woolgoolga. There are local services to Coffs Harbour, Grafton and nearby beaches.

Arrawarra
This quiet seaside village one km off the highway has yet another great beach, some bushland that is noisy with birds, the inlet of a small creek and a very pleasant caravan park close to the water, *Arrawarra Holiday Park* (☎ (066) 49 2753). Sites cost from $10, rising by increments to $15.50 at Christmas; on-site vans start at $24 ($40 at Christmas); and cabins are $30 ($50 at Christmas). They have canoes for rent. A short way south is **Mullaway**, and **Corindi** is a few km north; you have to return to the highway to get to either.

Red Rock

Six km off the highway, Red Rock is a sleepy village, a little larger than Arrawarra. It is both very relaxed and very neat, with well-mown lawns and tidy fibro or weatherboard holiday houses. The residents reckon it's a top spot. The small Redbank River enters the sea here and there's a beautiful inlet just across from the good *caravan park* (☎ (066) 49 2730) where sites cost from $8 and cottages are between $28 and $40. Across the inlet is Yuraygir National Park (see below), and you can hire canoes ($6 an hour or $25 a day) to explore.

Yuraygir National Park

Yuraygir (20,000 hectares) is the southern-most of a chain of small national parks and nature reserves which runs almost all the way north to Ballina. The beaches are outstanding and there are some stretches of forest offering bushwalks. The park is in three sections, from Red Rock to the Wooli River (turn off the highway north of the Red Rock turn-off), from the township of Wooli to the Sandon River (turn off the highway 12 km south of Grafton), and from near Brooms Head to Angourie (accessible from those towns). There is no vehicle access between the sections; on foot you'd have to cross the sizeable Wooli and Sandon rivers.

Walkers can bush-camp and there are basic camping areas at Station Creek in the southern section, at the Boorkroom and Illaroo rest areas in the central section, and on the north bank of the Sandon River and at Red Cliff at the Brooms Head end of the northern section. These are accessible by car; there are also walk-in campsites in the northern section: Plumbago Headland, Shelly Head and Shelly Beach.

Nearby Towns There are a number of small holiday settlements surrounded by the park. **Wooli** and **Minnie Water** are reached from a road running off the highway 12 km south of Grafton, or, if you're coming from the north, from Ulmarra.

Wooli is a straggling holiday hamlet, not especially attractive, but there are the usual great beaches and the very clean Wooli River which you can apparently canoe up for 20 km. Wooli's big event is the Goanna Pulling Championship held on the Queen's Birthday long weekend in June. This is not something the RSPCA should take an interest in – it's a tug-of-war between contestants with a leather strap around their heads. There is a *caravan park* (☎ (066) 49 7519), cabins (☎ (066) 49 7750), and the pub (☎ (066) 49 7532) has accommodation.

Minnie Water, 12 km or so north on the other side of **Lake Hiawatha**, is smaller but nicer. The *caravan park* (☎ (066) 49 7693) has sites from $7.50 ($11 at peak times) and cabins from $30 a double ($40). Some of the park's long-term residents have ancient tractors for hauling their boats over the hill to the beach. Buses run to Grafton two or three times a week and there are schoolbuses.

Brooms Head, on the coast 25 km east of Maclean, remains a quiet hamlet, popular with locals. It has good beaches (lagoon and ocean), a few holiday units, a *caravan park* and proximity to Yuraygir National Park, both north and south of the town.

The Solitary Islands

This group of five islands, strung out along the coast offshore from Yuraygir National Park, has been declared a marine park because it is at the meeting place of the warmer tropical currents and the more temperate southern currents, with some interesting varieties of fish and coral because of the unusual conditions. Cruises and dive boats from Coffs Harbour come here.

Far North Coast

As well as great beaches and a subtropical climate, rivers are a feature of this area (which is also known as the Northern Rivers district), with the mighty Clarence, Richmond and Tweed rivers sprawling through rich deltas. They are wide, deep and blue – most un-Australian.

Winters are short and warm in this part of

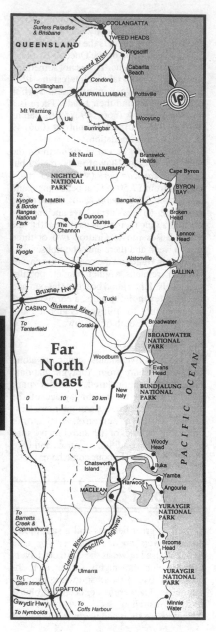

Far
North
Coast

NORTH COAST

the world, although August sometimes brings strong winds. By late winter the days are often blue and in the mid-20s and the nights are pleasantly cool (the locals think the nights are cold and shiver in woollies). By September everyone agrees that it's beach weather.

GRAFTON

Grafton is a large country town (population 17,000) basking on the subtropical banks of the wide Clarence River. Although there isn't a lot to do or see here, this isn't a tourist town or a retirement ghetto, and that makes a nice change from some of the sprawling coastal developments.

Inland from Grafton are the Washpool and Gibraltar Ranges national parks – see the New England chapter for details.

Orientation & Information

The Pacific Highway bypasses Grafton and you enter the town on a double-decker (road and rail) bridge. The Clarence River Tourist Centre (☎ (066) 42 4677) is on the highway south of the town, near the turn-off to the bridge. Before you cross the bridge a road leads off to South Grafton, a sleepy old riverside suburb.

The town is on a big bend in the Clarence River, across from Susan Island. Prince St is the main shopping street and runs north-east from the river. The corner of Prince and Fitzroy Sts, dominated by the sandstone National Bank, is the centre of town.

The National Parks office (☎ (066) 42 0613) is at 50 Victoria St, not far from the post office which is near the corner of Prince and Victoria Sts.

Things to See & Do

Pick up a free copy of the Blue Guide Handy Map from the information centre, as it has a **walking tour** around Grafton's old buildings. Victoria St is worth a look, with the old post office, courthouse and police station, shaded by big trees. On the corner of Victoria and Duke Sts is the **Anglican Cathedral**, in spare 1930s style and with older buildings in the grounds. The **Saraton Theatre** on Prince

St is a restored movie theatre where you can still see the flicks most nights.

Fitzroy St runs off Prince St and has some interesting houses, including the one that houses the **Grafton Regional Gallery** at No 158 (Wednesday to Sunday, 10 am to 4 pm, admission by donation), and, a bit further on, **Schaeffer House** which houses the local **museum** (open on Sunday and from Tuesday to Thursday, 1 pm to 4 pm, admission $2, $1 children). For local art & craft, visit the **Artisans Gallery** on Skinner St in South Grafton.

Across the river, **Susan Island** is partly covered in rainforest which shelters the largest colony of fruit bats in the southern hemisphere. The bats' departure is a spectacular sight on summer evenings. Access to the island, which has a walking trail through the rainforest and picnic areas at the southern end, is by boat. You can hire a canoe to paddle across from Acme Fibreglass (☎ (066) 42 4780) at 20 Bessie St in South Grafton.

The tourist centre can arrange visits to **farms** in the area, including a racehorse stud, a cane farm, a dairy farm, a timber factory and a brewery.

Newfoundland Trails (☎ (066) 49 4518) at Halfway Creek, off the highway about 30 km south of Grafton, has **horseriding**, for the day or longer. On weekends you can try **gliding** with the local club at Eastonville. Ask the tourist centre for the current contact number.

Banzai's Seelands Ski School (☎ (066) 44 9441) in South Grafton will teach you barefoot **water-skiing**, and they have packages including accommodation and meals for around $600 per week. Grafton is not far from Nymboida, a centre for **whitewater rafting** and **canoeing**.

About the most pleasant activity in Grafton is looking at the river, and the terrace at the Crown Hotel at the west end of Prince St is a very pleasant place from which to do just that.

See the following Clarence River section for information about houseboats and river cruises.

Festivals & Events

On the last Saturday of the month a market is held in the grounds of Alumny Creek school, on Lawrence Rd (Queen St) just north of the city.

Grafton's long avenues of lovely trees bloom during the Jacaranda Festival, held over a week in late October and early November, with a parade on the first Saturday in November. It has been running since 1935. The agricultural show is held in late April or early May.

Places to Stay

Rathgar, an old house on the southern side of town, used to offer hostel-style accommodation but it seems to have closed.

Caravan Parks *Glenwood Tourist Park* (☎ (066) 42 3466) is on Pacific Highway's southbound arm about one km south of the information centre; *Sunset Caravan Park* (☎ (066) 42 3824) is on Gwydir Highway about three km west of the information centre. Both have sites for around $10 and on-site vans from $30, and Glenwood has self-contained cabins from about $40.

Hotels & Motels Many of the pubs have accommodation, including the *Crown Hotel/Motel* (☎ (066) 42 4000). This very pleasant place overlooks the river and has pub rooms for $20/28 a single/double or $28/30 with bathroom. The motel units cost $40 a single plus $10 for each extra person up to four. See if you can get a room overlooking the river. If it's one of the small pub rooms you'll have French doors opening onto a long, wide verandah. The pub beds could be newer but it's a clean and friendly place.

Another nice old pub in the same area is *Roches Family Hotel* (☎ (066) 44 2866) at 85 Victoria St. They have rooms from under $20. Many other pubs in Grafton and South Grafton also have accommodation.

Motels near the town centre include the pleasant *Abbey* (☎ (066) 42 6122) on Fitzroy St behind the cathedral, with rooms from around $45/55, and the cheaper *Plaza*

(☎ (066) 42 1666), nearby at the corner of Fitzroy and Villiers Sts.

Places to Eat

The town centre has the usual cafes, takeaways, clubs and pub meals. In the Mid-City Arcade off Prince St between Fitzroy and Pound Sts, *Poss's Place* is open during the day for healthy snacks, drinks and light meals.

At the *Crown Hotel/Motel*, by the river at the top of Prince St, there's a bistro with pub-style meals for around $10 and in the evening the more expensive *Susan's Restaurant*.

The bistro at the Grafton Hotel on Fitzroy St, *Le Touche*, claims French food. Lunchtime main courses are from $8 to $12 and there are specials. Evening meals are pricier. Across the street, *Big Bay Pizza & Pasta* is mainly a takeaway but there are a couple of tables. You can get a pasta for under $5.

On Prince St near the corner of Pound St, *Stornelli's* is a licensed Italian restaurant with main courses between $15 and $25 and specials for about $10, and there's also a cheaper bistro with good-value pasta nights on Thursday.

Further up Prince St, past the railway viaduct, are two Chinese restaurants, *Fountain Court* and the *New Orient*.

Getting There & Away

Air Eastern flies to Sydney for $205 (about $140 with advance purchase).

Train The railway station is just south of the bridge. The station across the river in town is for freight, and freight-trains rumble across the viaducts above the streets of the town centre.

Bus – long-distance Long-distance buses stop at the Mobil station on the highway in South Grafton, not far from the information centre. The main long-distance companies come through on their run up the coast. Fares include Sydney $52, Brisbane $38 and Byron Bay $25. The fare to Coffs Harbour is

about $20 on an express bus, but you'll get a slower local service for $8.50.

Countrylink runs up the Gwydir Highway to Glen Innes (about $17) four times a week and will drop you near Washpool and Gibraltar Ranges national parks.

Bus – local area Most local-area buses leave from King St, a block back from the Market Square shopping centre, not far from the corner of Pound St. Bradley's (☎ (066) 54 1516) has a service between Grafton and Coffs Harbour ($8.50, $13 return), running via some beachside towns off the highway such as Red Rock and Arrawarra. Buses leave from King St at 7.15 am, plus 11 am on Monday, Wednesday and Friday.

The Grafton-Yamba Bus Service (☎ (066) 42 2779) runs to Maclean ($5) and Yamba ($7) several times a day from Monday to Friday, once on Saturday and twice on Sunday.

As well as long-distance services, Kirklands has a run to Lismore ($18.90), stopping at towns such as Maclean ($8.40), Chatsworth ($9.50) and Woodburn ($15.60) along the way.

Car & Motorbike The Pacific Highway runs north to Maclean and south to Coffs Harbour. Near Grafton there are several scenic routes which parallel the highway and involve ferry crossings, such as Grafton to Maclean via the north bank and the Lawrence ferry. There's also a ferry crossing between the highway and the north bank road at Ullmarra.

There's an interesting route from Grafton to Armidale via Nymboida and Ebor, passing near turn-offs to Dorrigo (and on to Coffs Harbour) and the New England and Cathedral Rock national parks. You can also get to Coffs Harbour via Glenreagh.

Heading east to Glen Innes, the Gwydir Highway passes through the superb Washpool and Gibraltar Ranges national parks (see the New England chapter for details). It's a steep 20 km climb to the tablelands and after Jackadgery, just a store and a caravan park about 50 km from Grafton, there's no fuel until Glen Innes, 130 km further west.

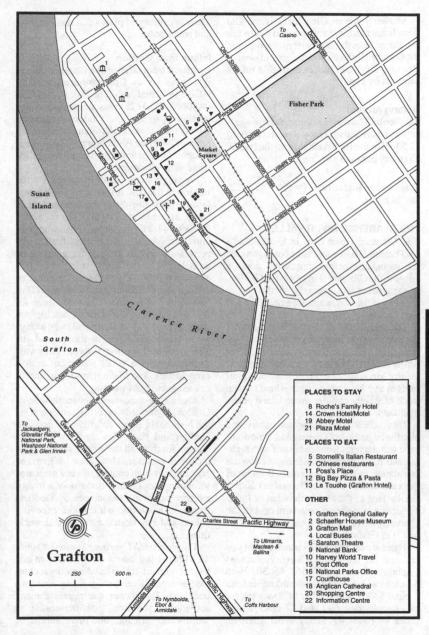

Grafton

To Casino

Fisher Park

Susan Island

Clarence River

South Grafton

To Jackadgery, Gibraltar Range National Park, Washpool National Park & Glen Innes

Market Square

Mary Street
Queen Street
Kent Street
King Street
Prince Street
Oliver Street
Dobie Street
Duke Street
Villiers Street
Bacon Street
Pound Street
Clarence Street
Victoria Street
Fitzroy Street

Cowan Street
Skinner Street
Through Street
Wharf Street
Siding Street
Ryan Street
Bright Street
Bligh Ct
Through Street

Charles Street   Pacific Highway

Gwydir Highway

Armidale Street

To Nymboida, Ebor & Armidale

To Coffs Harbour

To Ullmarra, Maclean & Ballina

0   250   500 m

NORTH COAST

PLACES TO STAY
8 Roche's Family Hotel
14 Crown Hotel/Motel
19 Abbey Motel
21 Plaza Motel

PLACES TO EAT
5 Stornelli's Italian Restaurant
7 Chinese restaurants
11 Poss's Place
12 Big Bay Pizza & Pasta
13 Le Touoho (Grafton Hotel)

OTHER
1 Grafton Regional Gallery
2 Schaeffer House Museum
3 Grafton Mall
4 Local Buses
6 Saraton Theatre
9 National Bank
10 Harvey World Travel
15 Post Office
16 National Parks Office
17 Courthouse
18 Anglican Cathedral
20 Shopping Centre
22 Information Centre

Another route to Glen Innes is the Old Glen Innes road, mostly unsealed but in fair condition. Take the Dalmorton turn-off from the Gwydir Highway about eight km west of Grafton. This road passes through a tunnel hand-cut by convicts.

Getting Around

Car Rental The major companies have agencies and there's also Handy Rentals (☎ (066) 42 3364) at the BP Roadhouse on the Pacific Highway in South Grafton.

Taxi Grafton Radio Taxis (☎ (066) 42 3622) run 24 hours.

THE CLARENCE RIVER VALLEY

The Clarence River rises in Queensland's McPherson Ranges and runs south through the mountains before thundering down a gorge in the Gibraltar Range west of Grafton. It then meanders serenely to the sea at Yamba, on the way watering a beautiful and fertile valley.

The delta between Grafton and the coast is a patchwork of farmland, in which the now immense and branching Clarence River forms about 100 islands, some very large. If you're driving, the profusion of small bridges and waterways makes it hard to keep track of whether you're on an island or the mainland.

This is the start of sugar-cane country, and also the beginning of Queensland-style domestic architecture: wooden houses with high-pitched roofs perched on stilts to allow air circulation in the hot summers. Burning of the cane-fields (May to December) adds a smoky tang to the air, reminiscent of India. To arrange a visit to a cane farm contact the Clarence River Tourist Centre (☎ (066) 42 4677) in Grafton.

There are several outfits which can set you cruising on the lower Clarence, such as Captain-a-Cruiser (☎ (066) 45 3040) in Maclean which rents a six-berth cruiser from around $300 a weekend or $600 a week for two people, plus fuel, and Clarence River-boats (☎ (066) 47 6232) at Brushgrove.

There are plenty of places that rent dinghies and small boats.

Inland from Grafton

Upstream from Grafton the Clarence is navigable as far as **Copmanhurst**, a small village in a rural area. The *Rest Point Hotel* (☎ (066) 47 3125) has accommodation. Further upstream the Clarence descends rapidly from the Gibraltar Range through the rugged **Clarence River Gorge**. The gorge is a popular but potentially dangerous site for whitewater canoeing.

Private property flanks the gorge. On the south side the land is owned by the Winters family who allow day-visitors and have cabin accommodation at *Winters' Shack* (☎ (066) 47 2173). Access is via Copmanhurst, but you'll have to ring first to get permission and to arrange for gates to be unlocked. On the north side, *Wave Hill Station* (☎ (066) 47 2145) has homestead or cottage accommodation and regular 4WD or horseriding trips to the Clarence Gorge for $50 per person ($35 without lunch); you don't have to stay at Wave Hill to go along.

On the Mann River, a tributary of the Clarence, and on the Gwydir Highway, **Jackadgery** is a small settlement with a caravan park. The Mann River is popular for canoeing and gold-panning.

Also in the mountains but south-west of Grafton, **Nymboida** is a tiny settlement on the Nymboida River and the road between Grafton and Ebor. See the New England chapter for this and the several other rugged national parks in the area. When the Nymboida is high enough this is a great area for whitewater rafting. Because of a hydro-electric pumping station, nearby Gooland Creek is a superb whitewater canoeing course and has hosted national and world titles.

The *Nymboida Coaching Station* (☎ (066) 49 4126) is just about the whole town and has a restaurant. It also has dormitory accommodation for $8 per person (bring your own bedding). The owner can organise many activities in the area, from horseriding to whitewater rafting, but there might be

Top: Spring flowers, Mootwingee National Park, far west (JM)
Middle: Sheep on road, near West Wyalong, central west (JM)
Bottom: Outback road, far west (JM)

Top: Byron Bay and Mt Warning from Cape Byron, north coast (JM)
Middle: Tallow Beach from Cape Byron, north coast (JM)
Bottom: The Entrance, Central Coast, near Sydney (JM)

minimum group sizes, so ring ahead to check.

Ulmarra

On the Pacific Highway about 15 km north of Grafton, Ulmarra (population 500) is a National Trust classified village founded in the 1850s by early cane planters. Today the town has an abundance of craft and antiques shops. The *Commercial Hotel* (☎ (066) 44 5305) has limited accommodation. A vehicle ferry (not suitable for caravans) crosses the Clarence here.

Maclean

This pretty old town (population 3000) has strong Scottish roots and at Easter it holds a Highland Gathering. Maclean is at the junction of the Clarence's main and south arms, where the river begins its lazy sprawl over the delta, and is home to a prawn-fishing fleet. It's a quiet place with excellent river views and great sunsets.

The **Bicentennial Museum** on Wharf St tells the story of the Northern Rivers area and is open from 2 to 5 pm on Wednesday and Saturday. For views over the Clarence and the canefields, Maclean Lookout on Wharf St is about two km from the town centre.

The Maclean Riding School (☎ (066) 45 2017) on Cameron St offers horseriding.

On the second Saturday of the month a market is held in the town's main car-park. There's also an agricultural show in late April and a Cane Harvest Festival in September.

Chatsworth Island

About 40 km north of Maclean the Pacific Highway crosses Chatsworth Island, bypassing the village of the same name. The village is a pretty spot, but the main attraction is the *Chatsworth Island Restaurant* (☎ (066) 46 4455). This is one of the state's better places to eat, with an eclectic French-based menu and the bonus of a view across the mighty Clarence. Prices are reasonable, with main courses around $15.50, and on Sunday from 11 am they have brunch with a variety of snacks as well as meals.

Yamba

On the coast 13 km east of the highway, Yamba (population 4000) is on the south head of the Clarence River's wide estuary, with beaches on three sides. The town has 'come on', as the locals say, and there are now plenty of motels, holiday apartments and housing developments for retirees. It would be a pretty good place to retire to, with reputedly the warmest winters in the state.

On Wednesday and Friday there are ferry cruises up the river, departing at 11 am and returning at 3 pm. The fare is $12 ($6 children).

Places to Stay There are a few caravan parks, including *Easts Calypso* (☎ (066) 46 2468) right in town and overlooking the small harbour, on Harbour St at the bottom of Yamba St, the main shopping street. Sites cost from $10, on-site vans from about $30 and cabins from $35.

On – well, *above* – the beach, the *Pacific Hotel* (☎ (066) 46 2466) at 1 Pilot St has backpacker accommodation in twin rooms from $12.50 per person and doubles for $50. Don't expect to be picked up from Maclean, despite what some brochures say.

Yamba's half-dozen or so motels have relatively low rates outside peak times. The good *Aston Villa* (☎ (066) 46 2785) on Mulgi St (the inland continuation of Coldstream St, which crosses Yamba St) charges from around $40/50.

Getting There & Away The Grafton-Yamba Bus Service (☎ (066) 42 2779) runs to Maclean ($2.60) and Grafton ($7) several times a day from Monday to Friday, once on Saturday and twice on Sunday.

A ferry runs to Iluka, on the north bank of the Clarence, four times a day for $3 ($1.50 children).

Angourie

Five km south of Yamba, Angourie is one of the coast's top spots for experienced surfers, but beware of rip-tides. Also here is the Blue Pool, a quarry next to the beach filled with fresh water from a spring.

NORTH COAST

Nat Young, legendary Aussie surfie and ex-world champion, owns a restaurant here, *Nat's at the Point*. Surfing memorabilia are displayed.

Iluka

North across the river from Yamba, Iluka is still a small place (population 2000). The town adjoins the southern end of Bundjalung National Park and a section known as the **Iluka Rainforest** has gained World Heritage listing. A short walking trail from the town centre to Iluka Bluff takes you through the rainforest.

To get here from Yamba it's either a short ferry ride or, if you have a car, a long drive back to the highway, a total trip of about 40 km.

BUNDJALUNG NATIONAL PARK

Stretching from Iluka north to Evans Head and covering 17,700 hectares, Bundjalung has long beaches, a river and a patch of rainforest at Woody Head, at the south end of the park near Iluka.

Nearby is the large Woody Head *camping area*, leased from National Parks and run privately. It has a few more facilities than most National Parks camping areas – including a kiosk and cabins – but there is no electricity, so you are spared the worst of the holiday hordes. Still, at peak times you will need to book (☎ (066) 46 6134). Sites cost $10 a double, plus $2 for each extra person and cabins go for $40/50/60 for two/four/eight people. The wallabies and kooka-burras might expect to be fed. There are also simple campsites at Black Rocks, Boorooa, Jerusalem Creek and Yabbra, with pit toilets but no water.

The Woody Head Camping Weekend of Acoustic Music, Folksong & Dance held in late August might become an annual event and is worth checking out.

There are three access points for the park: from near Iluka, near Evans Head, and, for the middle of the park, Gap Rd which runs off the Pacific Highway about five km south of Woodburn.

There were fires in the park in 1994, but the rainforest escaped and regeneration elsewhere should be swift.

NEW ITALY MUSEUM

This incongruous exhibition is on the highway about 10 km south of Woodburn. It's an unfortunately scanty museum dealing with the exciting events of the Marquis de Ray's plan to colonise the New Guinea island of New Ireland, and how the tattered survivors of that fiasco ended up here. There's also an Italian Pavilion with a lot of information on the various provinces of Italy The museum has a coffee shop and there's a licensed Italian restaurant nearby. Behind all this is the good **Gurrigai Aboriginal Arts & Crafts** shop, selling some local work along with pieces from the outback.

EVANS HEAD

A fishing town (population 2500) at the mouth of the Evans River, Evans Head has a pretty location and some accommodation, including an inexpensive pub. The views up the coast from **Razorback Lookout** are stunning – you can see Cape Byron on a clear day.

Evans Head is 10 km east of the highway; turn off at Woodburn.

BROADWATER NATIONAL PARK

Extending from north of Evans Head to Broadwater, this small (3750 hectares) coastal park has a long beach, a couple of lookouts and, unlike the others in the string of parks of which it is the northernmost, a road running through it. You can drive between Evans Head and Broadwater, a pleasant diversion from the highway. Camping isn't allowed in the park.

BALLINA

A large (population 15,000), fishing port and family holiday town on the Richmond River's north head, Ballina has no special attractions other than its climate and setting, but it's a nice place.

Orientation & Information

From the south the Pacific Highway runs

into town (passing the Big Prawn), becoming River St, the long main street. The highway turns off onto Kerr St, but River St continues beside the river, crossing North Creek then running up the coast (to Lennox Head and Byron Bay) and changing its name a couple of times in the process.

The information centre (☎ (066) 86 3484) is off River St, towards the east end, just past the fanciful old courthouse. It's open daily. The centre is also Las Balsas Museum, centred around the raft which sailed from Ecuador to Australia in 1973. A video about the voyage plays constantly.

Beaches

Lighthouse Beach is closest to town and is patrolled. Next north is the popular Shelly Beach. To get to Lighthouse Beach take River St, cross the river and take the first right after the Shaws Bay Hotel turn-off; this road will also take you to Shelly Beach, or you could just continue up the hill. The small beach curving around the Shaws Bay lagoon is a quiet place to swim.

Boats

The MV *Richmond Princess* (☎ 018 664 784 or book at the information centre) has two-hour cruises on Wednesday, Thursday and Sunday for $9. There's also a daily lunch cruise for $13.50, but this involves more lunching (ashore) than cruising. In the summer there are other options. Cruises leave from near the information centre.

The MV *Bennelong* (☎ (018 664 552 or book at the information centre) also has a variety of cruises, including a day cruise up the river to Lismore for $45 ($20 children). You can buy lunch on board. These cruises leave from near the RSL Club.

At the Ballina Quays Marina, off the highway south of the Big Prawn, you can rent dinghies (from $55 a day) and pontoon boats (from $80 a day) for day-use. Jet-skis are also available.

Places to Stay

Nearly half of all visitors to Ballina stay with friends or relations. It's that sort of town.

Caravan Parks Of the nine caravan parks, closest to the town centre is *Boomerang Park* (☎ (066) 86 3014) on River St a block east of the information centre, which has sites from $10 and cabins from $30; as does *Shaws Bay Caravan Park* (☎ (066) 86 2326) on Shaws Bay across the bridge from the town centre. *Flat Rock Camping Park* (☎ (066) 86 4848) about five km north of town on the road to Lennox Head is a tent-only park and charges about $10.

Hostel The *Ballina Travellers Lodge* (☎ (066) 86 6737) is a good, modern YHA associate in town at 36-38 Tamar St. They will collect you from the bus stop. Dorm beds cost $12 and twins are $13.50 per person. Bikes and boogie-boards are hired for $1 an hour, and there's a pool.

Motels The Ballina Travellers Lodge is worth considering if you have deeper pockets, as it's also a good motel and one of the few in town which doesn't have highway noise. In the low season singles/doubles go as low as $41/43, rising to around $70 a double (only).

There are plenty of other motels along the highway and River St. Low-season rates get down to $35 a double at some places.

Near both Shaws Bay Lagoon and Lighthouse Beach, the new *Ballina Beach Resort* (☎ (066) 86 8888; 1800 025 398 toll-free bookings) is well located, free of traffic noise and has good facilities. Accommodation includes singles/doubles from $65/75 in the low season, rising to $100 a double (only) at peak times. There are family rooms from $95 ($120 in the high season) and more expensive suites.

Houseboats At the *Ballina Quays Marina* (☎ (066) 86 4289), off the highway south of the Big Prawn, you can rent houseboats. Prices start at $90 for a small boat for one weeknight in the low season ($140 in the high season) for up to four people. The longer you hire the cheaper it gets, and with over 100 km of navigable river, there's plenty of space.

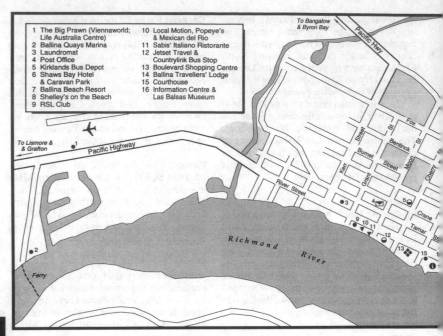

1 The Big Prawn (Viennaworld; Life Australia Centre)
2 Ballina Quays Marina
3 Laundromat
4 Post Office
5 Kirklands Bus Depot
6 Shaws Bay Hotel & Caravan Park
7 Ballina Beach Resort
8 Shelley's on the Beach
9 RSL Club
10 Local Motion, Popeye's & Mexican del Rio
11 Sabis' Italiano Ristorante
12 Jetset Travel & Countrylink Bus Stop
13 Boulevard Shopping Centre
14 Ballina Travellers' Lodge
15 Courthouse
16 Information Centre & Las Balsas Museum

Places to Eat

Shelley's on the Beach is an excellent place for breakfast (from 7.30 am), lunch and snacks. Dinner is served on Saturday and that might be extended to other days. It's a kiosk-style cafe high above Shelly Beach with superb views of the sea and, often, dolphins.

After this, most of the other places to eat are a little ordinary.

In the Boulevard shopping centre on River St near the corner of Martin St, *Palm Garden Thai* has main courses for around $9 and nearby is *Natural Addiction*, with a fairly ordinary menu despite its name. Main courses are around $12 with specials around $8, plus snacks, nachos etc.

On Moon St near the river, *Sabis' Italiano Ristorante* has main courses in the $15 area. Around the corner on River St, *Local Motion* is an above-average pasta joint, with main-course servings around $10. Nearby is *Popeye's*, a hamburger place where you can

get a sit-down curry for $5.50, and they do breakfast as well. Also in this area is *Mexican del Rio* with main courses for about $11 but lots of cheaper snacks. Across the road is *Beanz*, with healthy lunches to eat there or take away.

The *RSL Club* on Grant St near River St has meals most days, not especially cheap but seafood features – how does Balmain bug and prawn lasagne sound? The *Bowling Club* on Cherry St also does a lot of seafood at its restaurant, although their fabulous seafood nights are no more.

The restaurant at *Viennaworld*, the big service station next to the Big Prawn on the west edge of town, is reasonable for a highway stop and there are main course specials for under $10. It's open 24 hours.

Getting There & Away

Air Oxley flies from Brisbane, Air NSW from Sydney.

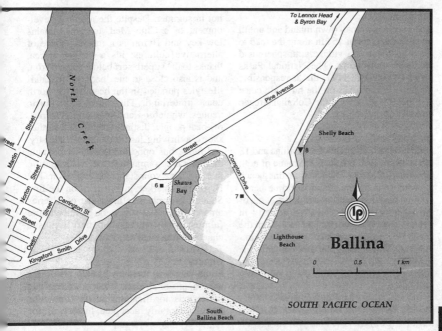

Bus The long-distance lines service Ballina, most of them stopping on the highway at the west side of town, at the Big Prawn. Kirklands has a depot in town on Cherry St and their buses come in here. Countrylink buses stop on River St outside the Jetset travel agency.

Kirklands (☎ (066) 86 5254) also has services in the local area, running to Evans Head ($8.60) and Lismore ($7.60), with connections to many other towns. Blanch's (☎ (066) 86 2144) runs from the Countrylink stop on River St to Lennox Head ($2.80), Byron Bay ($4.60) and other nearby towns. There are a fair number of buses on weekdays, fewer on Saturday and two on Sunday. The shop next to Jetset has timetables in the window.

Backsway Buses (☎ (07) 236 4163), a Brisbane company, runs to Brisbane ($25) via a few coastal towns and Murwillumbah ($12 from Ballina).

Car & Motorbike If you're heading to Byron Bay take the coast road through Lennox Head, which is not only prettier than the highway, but shorter. However, macadamia-nut fans might want to take the highway, as Macadamialand, north of Ballina, has free tastings as well as native birds and animals.

Getting Around
As well as the larger companies, try Sunray Car Rentals (☎ (066) 86 7315) at 268 River St, a local company which charges from around $40 a day plus insurance.

AROUND BALLINA
Inland from Ballina, the closely settled country of the north-coast hinterland begins, with winding, hilly roads running past tropical fruit farms, tiny villages and the occasional towering rainforest tree that somehow escaped the clearing of the forest which once covered the area.

Alstonville

Alstonville is a small town inland and uphill from Ballina, about 15 km along the road to Lismore. There's a village atmosphere and there are craft shops. The National Parks office (☎ (066) 28 1177) that is responsible for most of the parks on the far north coast and the hinterland is in the Colonial Arcade on Main St.

Lennox Head

Lennox Head, 11 km north of Ballina and 18 km south of Byron Bay, is the name of both the small, pleasant town with a fine beach and the dramatic headland (a prime hang-gliding site) that overlooks it. It has some of the best surf on the coast, particularly in winter. **Lake Ainsworth**, just back from the beach, is a freshwater lake, good for swimming and windsurfing. Its dark colour is due to tea-tree oil, supposedly good for the skin and hair, seeping in from the surrounding vegetation.

Places to Stay *Lake Ainsworth Caravan Park* (☎ (066) 87 7249) has tent sites (from $10) and cabins ($25; $45 in the high season).

People come back to *Lennox Beach House Hostel* (☎ (066) 87 7636), especially those who have been travelling for a while and want to put their feet up. It's purpose-built, very clean and very friendly. Both Lake Ainsworth and the beach are seconds away and you can use a cat and a windsurfer ($5 for as long as you stay). Boards, bikes and other sporting equipment are free. Dorm beds are $14 and there's a double for $30.

There are also a couple of motels.

Getting There & Away Long-distance buses come through Lennox Head, and Blanch's stops here on the run between Ballina and Byron Bay.

BYRON BAY

Byron Bay (population 5000) is one of the most attractive stops on the whole east coast: a relaxed little seaside town with superb beaches and a great climate – warm in winter,

hot in summer. Despite the looming development of a Club Med, tourism remains low-key and Byron is a meeting place of alternative cultures: it's a surfing mecca, thanks to the superb surf below Cape Byron, and is also close to the 'back to the land' lifestyles pursued in the beautiful far north coast hinterland. There are good music venues, wholefood and vegetarian eateries, off-beat people, distinctive craft and clothes shops, a thriving fashion and surf industry, and numerous opportunities to learn yogic dance, take a massage or naturopathic therapy, have your stars read and so on. The Byron Bay market, in Butler St on the first Sunday of each month, is one of a series around the area at which the counterculture (almost establishment up here!) gets a chance to meet and sell its wares.

History

Some people around town claim that there are remains of an ancient Egyptian ship and mysterious fortifications in the area. The more commonly accepted history of the region is prosaic by comparison, and follows the usual north-coast pattern of cedar-cutters arriving in the mid-19th century to be followed by agriculturalists and, later, tourists.

The cedar-cutters 'shot' their logs down the steep hills to the coast, hence names in the area such as Coopers Shoot.

Orientation

Byron Bay is nine km north-east of the Pacific Highway turn-off at Bangalow, or six km east of the turn-off further north. Jonson St, which becomes Bangalow Rd, is the main shopping street. The corner of Jonson and Lawson Sts is pretty well the town centre. South of the centre, along Tallow Beach, is the satellite development of Suffolk Park.

Information

The information centre (☎ (066) 85 8050) is on Jonson St near the railway station. Currently the hours are 9 am to 4 pm daily but they may be extended. You might be able to leave packs at the muralled community centre across the road, for $1.

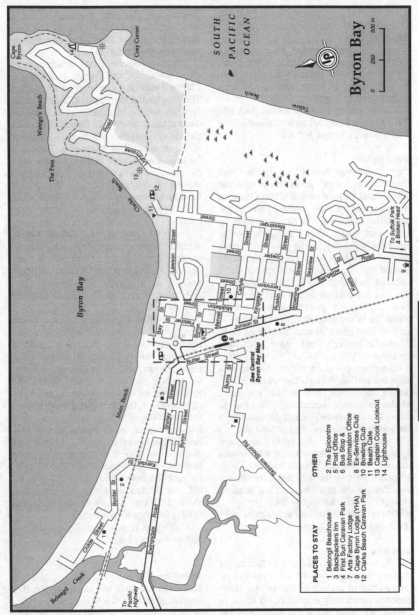

NORTH COAST

Byron Bay

SOUTH PACIFIC OCEAN

Cape Byron

Cosy Corner

Wategos Beach

The Pass

Clarks Beach

Byron Bay

Main Beach

Belongil Creek

To Pacific Highway

Tallow Beach

Lighthouse Road

Lawson Street

Massinger Street

Cowper Street

Seaview St

Bangalow Road

Keats St

Browning Street

Ruskin Street

Kingsley Street

Tennyson Street

Carlyle Street

Middleton Street

Fletcher St

Byron St

Marvell St

Bay St

Butler Street

Burns St

Jonson St

Shirley Street

Byron Street

Kendall St

Border St

Childe Street

Ewingsdale Road

Shanns Spur Rd

To Suffolk Park
& Broken Head

See Central
Byron Bay Map

0   250   500 m

PLACES TO STAY

1   Belongil Beachouse
3   Backpackers Inn
4   First Sun Caravan Park
7   Arts Factory Lodge
9   Cape Byron Lodge (YHA)
12 Clarks Beach Caravan Park

OTHER

2   The Epicentre
5   Post Office
6   Bus Stop &
    Information Office
8   Ex-Services Club
10 Bowling Club
11 Beach Cafe
13 Captain Cook Lookout
14 Lighthouse

The Byron Environment Centre (☎ (066) 85 7066) is in the Cavannah Arcade on Jonson St.

Read the quirky weekly *Echo* to get an idea of the way of life around here; the *Byron Shire News* mostly presents the view from the other side of the fence, but Rusty Miller's surfing column is worth reading.

A local community radio station, BAY FM (91.3 FM), is being set up and should have been granted a license by now.

Cape Byron

Cape Byron was named by Captain Cook after the poet Byron's grandfather, who had sailed round the world in the 1760s. One spur of the cape is the most easterly point of the Australian mainland. You can drive right up to the picturesque 1901 lighthouse, one of the most powerful in the southern hemisphere. There's a 3.5-km walking track right around the cape from the Captain Cook Lookout on Lighthouse Rd. It's circular, so you can leave bikes at the start (but lock them!). There's a good chance of seeing wallabies in the final rainforest stretch. A herd of feral goats, descendants of an early lighthouse-keeper's flock, have lived here for about 80 years.

From the top you can often see schools of dolphins surfing through the waves below. During the season (best in June and July) whales swim past, sometimes quite close to shore. The area around the lighthouse (where the best lookouts are) closes at 5.30 pm.

If you were to sail due north from Cape Byron, the next landmass you'd meet would probably be eastern Siberia; heading south the ocean rolls all the way down to Antarctica. Chile is the next stop east but heading west it's a considerably shorter voyage – you'd probably end up on the beach in front of the Belongil Beachouse.

Beaches

The Byron area has a glorious collection of beaches, ranging from 10 km stretches of empty sand to secluded little coves. **Main Beach**, immediately in front of the town, is a good swimming beach and sometimes has

decent surf. The sand stretches 50 km or more, all the way up to the Gold Coast, interrupted only by river or creek entrances and a few small headlands.

The eastern end of Main Beach, curving away towards Cape Byron, is known as **Clarks Beach** and can be good for surfing. The headland at the end of Clarks is called the Pass and the best surf is off here and at the next beach, **Watego's Beach**, apparently the only north-facing beach on the east coast of Australia. **Little Watego's Beach** is further round, almost at the tip of the cape. Dolphins are quite common, particularly in the surf off Watego's and Little Watego's. A local surfer recently survived a shark attack when a pod of dolphins drove the shark away.

South of Cape Byron, **Tallow Beach** stretches seven km down to a rockier stretch of shore around Broken Head, where a succession of small beaches dot the coast before opening on to **Seven Mile Beach** which goes all the way to Lennox Head, a further 10 km south.

The **Suffolk Park** area, behind Tallow Beach, is about five km south of central Byron Bay. One km further down the Byron to Lennox road is the turn-off to the Broken Head caravan park. About 200 metres before the caravan park, the unsealed Seven Mile Beach Rd turns off south and runs behind the rainforest of the **Broken Head Nature Reserve**. Seven Mile Beach Rd ends after five km (at the north end of Seven Mile Beach), but several tracks lead down from it through the forest to the Broken Head beaches – **Kings Beach** (for which there's a car park 750 metres down Seven Mile Beach Rd) and **Whites Beach** (a foot track after about 3.25 km) are just two good ones. Whites Beach is a nude beach.

A bike path runs all the way from Byron Bay to Broken Head.

Activities

There's a lot to do in and around Byron Bay. Hostels often have the best deals, but for a range of options it pays to check around a few hostels, and also see the information centre.

Surfing Most hostels have free boards for guests. Byron Surf Hire on Lawson St near Fletcher St hires surfboards and wetsuits for $25 a day and boogie-boards for $15 a day. The weekly rates are much cheaper. Let's Go Surfing (☎ (066) 87 1358 or 85 8768) will teach you to surf from about $20 a lesson.

Diving Diving is popular at Julian Rocks, three km offshore, a meeting point of cold southerly currents and warm northerly ones, with a profusion of marine species from both. There is cut-throat competition between the growing number of dive operators. Ask around to see who has the best deals on dives and courses.

Byron Bay Sport & Dive (also called Byron Bay Dive Centre) (☎ (066) 85 7149) at 9 Lawson St is the longest established. Sundive (☎ (066) 85 7755) has moved to the new Cape Byron Hostel complex on Middleton St. Bayside Scuba (☎ (066) 85 8333), a newcomer, has taken over Sundive's old shop at 15 Fletcher St, near the corner of Lawson. Two more newcomers are North Coast Dive (☎ (066) 85 7651), operating out of a house at 41 Cowper St, and Byron Dive Downunder, who plan to set up at 84 Jonson St near the information centre.

Prices vary widely according to the time of year and you should definitely shop around. It's a reasonably safe bet that the Byron Bay Dive Centre will be marginally cheaper than the others for a snorkelling trip, at about $20. They offer accommodation deals with courses, as does Sundive and perhaps some others.

Other Watersports Rapid Action (☎ (075) 30 8088) have whitewater rafting trips on the Nymboida River for about $95. The season is usually between November and June. As they point out, spending a day hurtling through the rapids with nine other people is a great way to get to know other travellers staying in Byron Bay.

Byron Bay Boat Charters (☎ (066) 85

7711), at the Bait & Tackle shop on Jonson St near the Plaza shopping centre, has fishing trips from $75 per person for a half-day, including bait and tackle. There's a minimum of four people but you might be able to tag along with a group. There might be other charter outfits around; ask at the information centre.

Flying Cape Byron is a great place for hang-gliding, and Flight Zone (☎ (066) 85 3178) has tandem flights and tuition. You're in experienced hands: Neil Mersham has been gliding since the mid-70s, is a former state champion and member of the Australian team, and he has lived in the area for 20 years so he knows the winds and weather. Tandem flights from Byron Bay are $75 and from Lennox Head (where he can land on the cliff and doesn't have to carry the gear all the way back up from the beach) they cost $65. Ring Neil at 10 am and he can tell you when and if there will be flights that day.

Trike flights, in ultra-light aircraft, are run by Skylimit (☎ (066) 84 3616) and cost about $70 for half an hour. They also offer tandem hang-gliding.

Byron Air Charter (☎ (066) 84 2753) has joy-flights as well as charters, and a very short flight can work out at around $10 per person. They operate from Tyagarah airport, midway between Byron Bay and Brunswick Heads. Down in Ballina, Australian Light Wing (☎ (066) 86 8658) flies two-seaters and a 20-minute flight costs $35.

Kite-flying is popular here and most days around 4 pm you'll see plenty on Main Beach or Tallow Beach, depending on the wind direction. If you want to join in, see Bernadette Graus at Byron Kites (☎ (066) 85 5299) in the Cape Byron Hostel complex. She'll rent you a good kite for $20, which includes free tuition and five hours' flying. Her shop specialises in hand-eye coordination gear, so if you want a skipping-rope or juggling equipment, this is the place to come.

Floating There are at least two flotation-tank places, Samadhi (☎ (066) 85 6905) on Jonson St opposite the Plaza shopping centre and Relax Haven (☎ (066) 85 8304) at the Belongil Beachouse. These places also do massage – at Relax Haven you can get an hour in the tank and an hour-long massage for $35.

Several other places offer massage, acupuncture and other methods of becoming pretty relaxed. If you need your *chakra* rebalanced see the Quintessence Healing Sanctuary (☎ (066) 85 5533) at 8/11 Fletcher St, next to the Misaki restaurant. They offer a wide range of services, everything from clairvoyance to sports medicine!

Falling Tandem parachute jumps (☎ (066) 80 1448) are available from the Tyagarah airstrip, off the highway about 10 km north of Byron Bay. Abseiling has been available in the past but the operator didn't seem to be around at the time of writing. The information centre might know if he has resurfaced.

Horseriding A place on Midgen Flat Rd, south-west of Broken Head, offers horseriding. They charge about $25 for 1½ hours. Phone (☎ (066) 85 3691) for bookings and directions. The Tyagarah Riding Ranch & Pet Motel (☎ (066) 84 7499) also has rides. It's near Tyagarah airport.

Cycling See the Getting There & Away section for bicycle rental.

Organised Tours

Byron Bay to Bush Tours (☎ (066) 85 5767) has a popular day-tour which gives a taste of life on the north-coast hinterland. It leaves the information centre at 9.30 am on Monday, Wednesday and Friday and costs $25. On Tuesday there's a trip to climb Mt Warning for $15, which is good value. There are plenty of other tours around, such as Damien Wilkinson's Big Scrub Tours (☎ (066) 84 5323 or see Jetset Travel on Marvell St) which has day and overnight trips to the rainforest. (Marvell St has two 'l's because it's named after the poet, not the Captain, despite the spelling on some signs.)

Byron Bay Harley Tours will show you the area from the back of a Harley Davidson

for $20 for 15 minutes, up to $250 for a day. Contact Ride On Motorcycles (☎ (066) 85 6304) on Jonson St for bookings.

Tours of the town and the immediate area are run by Aussie Paradise (☎ (066) 85 7220) and prices start at $9 for an hour-long town tour. One of the longer tours has as its highlight a drive past Paul Hogan's house...

Places to Stay

Prices are much higher at holiday times, particularly in summer.

Caravan Parks & Cabins During holidays the best sites will probably be taken, and around Christmas/January and Easter you might be lucky to find *any* site. It's unlikely that you would be able to rent a cabin for less than a week at the peak times.

If you need camping equipment, try Byron Bay Disposals in the Plaza shopping centre on Jonson St.

The council has four caravan parks, all by beaches. *First Sun Caravan Park* (☎ (066) 85 6544) is on Main Beach and is very close to the town centre, but it lacks shade. Sites start at $8 for one person, plus $4 for each extra person, rising by increments to $14 plus $6 at the peak time. There's a range of cabins, the cheapest going for $31 in the low season and $50 ($350 for a week) at the peak. *Clarks Beach Caravan Park* (☎ (066) 85 6496) is off Lighthouse Rd about one km east of the town centre and has plenty of trees. Sites are marginally more expensive here, but the cabins start cheaper, from $27 rising to $42 ($295 a week).

Down at Suffolk Park on Tallow Beach, *Suffolk Park Caravan Park* (☎ (066) 85 3353) is a friendly place with shady sites and cabins for marginally less than those at First Sun. They say that if you're camping and don't have a car they can probably squeeze you in for the night when everywhere else is full. Suffolk Park is about five km south of the town centre. Blanch's has infrequent bus services running past, and on summer weekends the local pub runs shuttle services into town.

South of here at Broken Head there's a

small council-run caravan park (☎ (066) 85 3245), superbly situated. It's on a popular surf beach and the area is surrounded by Broken Head Nature Reserve. Sites cost from $8/9 for one/two people, rising by increments to $14/15 at peak times. There are also on-site vans from $30 to $50. You'll need to bring all your supplies.

Belongil by the Sea (☎ (066) 85 8111) is an all-cabin place next door to the Belongil Beachouse hostel. The cabins are self-contained, with cooking facilities, and come with one bedroom (from $60 a double up to $120 at Christmas and Easter) or two bedrooms (from $75 for four people up to $140). There are also motel-style units (from $40 a double up to $75) with communal cooking facilities. The beach is nearby and there's a pool.

Crosby's Caravan Court (☎ (066) 85 6751) by Tallow Beach in Suffolk Park has sites from $10 for two people, rising to $15, on-site vans from $23 and cabins from $27, more during holidays, and at Christmas you'll have to stay a week and book months in advance.

Tallow Beach Resort (☎ (066) 85 3303; 1800 656 817 toll-free bookings) is a spacious place on Tallow Beach with good self-contained cabins. The cabins have two bedrooms, one with a double bed and the other with four bunks, and cost from $65 a night for two people plus $10 for each extra person (maximum $100). During school holidays you have to book for at least a week and prices range from $450 to $900, but that covers six people. There are also one-bedroom units. To get here you have to go to Suffolk Park and head back up the coast a short way, but there's a short-cut to town for cyclists and pedestrians.

The Wheel Resort (☎ (066) 85 6139) on Broken Head Rd south of the Suffolk Park shops has self-contained cabins in large, leafy grounds. The resort is designed to accommodate wheelchairs (hence the name) but you don't need a wheelchair to stay here and the facilities are good. Cabins with a double and a single bed cost from $60 a night ($100 at peak times) and a family cabin with a double and four single beds costs from $85 to $125. It might be possible to camp here but ring first.

Hostels There are now six hostels in Byron Bay and all have good points, so if you're planning a lengthy stay check them all to see which suits you best. Competition between hostels is fierce. Getting off a bus here has been reminiscent of arriving in an Asian city on the backpacker trail because of the hostel touts, but they will be banned from the proposed new bus area.

There's been an explosion of cheap accommodation here and the place has gone to the dogs.
Local businessperson

While the hostels are very keen to pick you up from the bus stop, we've had complaints that some are less willing to take you back when you want to leave. Confirm this before you check in and also ask about day-use fees which might be charged if your bus leaves in the evening.

The popular *Backpackers Holiday Village Hostel* (☎ 85 7660), at 116 Jonson St, close to the bus stop, is a clean, friendly, well-equipped place with a small pool and spa. Dorms cost from $12 or $29 for a double, and there's one double with bathroom and TV for $35. Well-maintained bicycles, surfboards and boogie boards are free, and there are plenty of them.

The hostel closest to the beach is *Backpackers Inn* (☎ (066) 85 8231) at 29 Shirley St, the main road out to the Pacific Highway, about 500 metres from the town centre. This place looks a bit anonymous from the road, but inside it's a spacious modern hostel with a pool and all the usual features of a good purpose-built hostel, including free bikes and boogie boards. To get to the beach you just walk across the lawn, cross the railway line (carefully!) and climb a sand-dune. The rates are $12 in spacious eight-bed dorms, $14 in four-share ($15 for any dorm bed around Christmas/January) and there are doubles for $30 ($60 for four people in the high season).

NORTH COAST

Byron Bay has two YHA-affiliated hostels. *Cape Byron Lodge* (☎ (066) 85 6445) is clean, comfortable and well-equipped. It's some way from the town centre at 78 Bangalow Rd (the south end of Jonson St), but only about 10 minutes' walk to Tallow Beach. There's a small pool and bikes are free. This is usually the cheapest hostel in town, with dorm beds at $11 or $12 in a four-bed dorm, and doubles for $15 per person.

The new YHA affiliate, *Cape Byron Hostel* (☎ (066) 85 8788), is close to the town centre and Main Beach, at the corner of Byron and Middleton Sts. It's a big new complex with its own mini shopping centre. There's a heated pool which is used for diver-training by Sundive, whose office is in the complex. Current prices (which might rise in summer) are $13 in a 10-person dorm, $14 in a four-person dorm, $35 in a double/twin ($28 for one person when available) and $40 for a double with bathroom.

Belongil Beachouse (☎ (066) 85 7868) is an excellent place to stay, spacious, well-run, relaxed and friendly. It's across a quiet road from the beach; bikes, surf and boogie boards are free. The cafe here is a big plus, with tasty and healthy food served between 8 am and 10 pm. There's a nightly half-price special for guests and at about $4.50 it's great value. You can store gear here for $5 a week. Dorm beds start at $12, rising to $14 during school holidays and $15 around Christmas. Singles/doubles with shared bathroom are $25/30, rising to $34 during school holidays and $38 around Christmas. There are a few doubles/triples with bathrooms starting at $40/50. During school holidays you'll pay $45 a double and around Christmas you'll have to pay the four-person rate of $70. (These rates sound more complicated than the rates at the other places, but that's mainly because Belongil is more up-front about prices than the other places.)

To get here by road follow Shirley St west about one km from the centre, then turn right onto Kendall St, cross the railway line and keep going for about 700 metres (Kendall St changes its name to Border St then Childe

St). It's a shorter walk along the beach but you'll have to ask directions because you can't see the hostel from the beach.

The *Arts Factory Lodge* (☎ (066) 85 7709) is some way from the beach but it has a nice setting and some room to move. The Arts Factory gets quite a few backpackers who have tried other places in town and want something a little looser. Just what the atmosphere is like depends on who is staying here, but you're more likely to find *some* atmosphere out here than at many places in town.

How much does it cost? That's a little hard to say. At the time of writing the owner had taken offence at a price-fixing scheme mooted by some of the other hostels and had slashed his rates to just $8 for a dorm bed and $12 per person in doubles. These prices will certainly creep back to around the same as the other hostels'. Camping on the small island in the hostel grounds costs $6 per person.

They meet most buses and will pick up anyone with a booking. Alternatively, you can have your taxi fare (about $4) deducted from your accommodation bill if you get a receipt. Day-use of the facilities (if you're catching a bus in the evening) is $2.50.

Hotel & Motels The *Great Northern Hotel* (☎ (066) 85 6454) on Jonson St has single or double rooms for $45 year-round.

Motels such as the *Wollongbar* (☎ (066) 85 8200) at 19 Shirley St, the *Bay Beach* (☎ (066) 85 7708) and *Byron Sunseeker* (☎ (066) 85 7369) at 100 Bangalow Rd have singles/doubles from around $50/60 in the off-season. Prices skyrocket around Christmas/January and Easter and to a lesser extent during other school holidays. *Bay Mist* (☎ (066) 85 6121) is a pretty standard motel but it has a good position, on Bay St. In the off-season you'll get a double room for $70 but around Christmas, January and Easter you'll pay $150.

Guesthouses & B&B There's a modest boom in guesthouses and/or B&Bs in the area, most catering to deeper pockets. *Rosewood House* (☎ (066) 85 7658) is a

PLACES TO STAY

3   Bay Mist Motel
25   Great Northern Hotel
27   Cape Byron Hostel (YHA)
42   Backpackers Holiday Village
      Hostel
43   Rosewood Guesthouse

PLACES TO EAT

2   Tucano
4   Jetty Cafe
5   Beach Hotel
6   South Indian Curry House
7   Angel Cafe
8   Munchies
9   Suppertime Blues
12   Chu's
13   Misaki
16   Kafe Kakadu
17   Athena Greek Taverna
      & Oh! Delhi
19   Earth & Sea
20   Catalina
21   Fondue Restaurant
22   Lifestream
24   Ringo's
33   Koo Kafe
34   Triados
38   Afters
41   Mexican Mick's

OTHER

1   Surf Lifesaving Club
10   Old Guesthouse
11   Byron Bay Sport & Dive
14   Bayside Scuba
15   Santo's Health Food
18   Feros Arcade
23   Byron Bay Travel Centre
26   Post Office
28   Railway Station, Railway Friendly Bar
      & Annie's Fresco Gusto
29   Information Centre
      & Bus Stop
30   Community Centre
31   Laundromat
32   Woolworths & Plaza Shopping
      Centre
35   Crystal Temple
36   Let's Go Bikes
37   Maddog Surf Shop
39   Ride On Motorcycles
40   Samahdi Flotation Centre

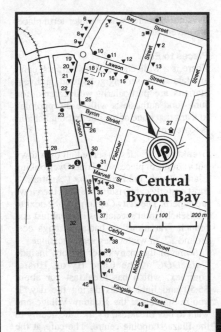

Central Byron Bay

well-restored timber house at 16 Kingsley St, near the corner of Jonson. There are three rooms, costing $120 a double for B&B, or $90 in the room without ensuite. *Coopers Shoot Guesthouse* (☎ (066) 85 3313) is in a restored headmaster's house on Coopers Shoot Rd, off the road between Byron Bay and the Pacific Highway. B&B is $95/115 or $115/165 for dinner as well. There are also weekend and week-long packages. The highly-regarded *Taylor's* (☎ (066) 84 7436) is not far away, off McGettigans Lane. B&B prices start at $135/175, or more during holidays. No children.

Self-Catering Holiday houses and apartments start at around $300 a week in the off-season, $500 during school holidays and $800 over Christmas. Several real estate agents handle holiday letting, such as Elders (☎ (066) 85 6222) on Jonson St near the station.

Some cafes, especially Suppertime Blues,

have noticeboards where longer-term places are advertised.

Places to Eat

There is a wide choice of restaurants, cafes and takeaways serving good food, and vegetarians are particularly well catered for. Junk-food enthusiasts will be disappointed to learn that none of the international chains is represented.

Breakfast Breakfast is served all over town but a couple of places stand out. Overlooking Clarks Beach, the *Beach Cafe* ('Australia's most easterly cafe') isn't cheap but the views are superb. The *Jetty Cafe* on Bay St next to the Beach Hotel specialises in breakfast and brunch. Variations on bacon & eggs cost around $7; in winter they serve porridge.

Some of the many other options include *Cafe DOC* at the Cape Byron Hostel complex, which has breakfast for about $5.50 and light meals during the day. If you're staying at the Holiday Village and want to buy breakfast, try the cafe nearby in the Plaza shopping centre. The cafe at the Belongil Beachouse is open from 8 am to 10 pm and is a great place for breakfast, lunch or dinner.

Jonson St The *Beach Hotel* has a wide range of snacks such as burgers from $4.50 and more substantial meals such as satays ($9.50) and steaks (from $11). Heading down Jonson St from the Beach Hotel, the *South Indian Curry House* is a long-time favourite and has main courses from $8 to $13, most around $10. It's open nightly for dinner. Next door, the *Angel Cafe* has breakfast from around $6.50 and specials such as lasagna for $5. *Munchies* is a very small place with hard-core healthy snacks and meals, open during the day. Further along, the larger *Suppertime Blues* has the music and decor of an old-style Byron cafe and similarly healthy food. Vegie-burgers are $4.50, smoothies from $2.50. Both places stay open until early evening, later in summer.

Still on Jonson St but east of the round-about, the old wooden guesthouse on the corner of Lawson St is due to be transformed into a bar and restaurant complex. Nearby, *Ringo's* is one of Byron's older cafes and has a large menu of snacks, drinks and meals (around $10). It's open from breakfast ($6 for bacon & eggs) until about 8.30 pm. If a 'meal deal' is on offer, grab it – around $7.50 for two courses of excellent food. Across the road, *Earth & Sea* is a popular pizza and pasta restaurant, with main-course pasta about $10 and pizzas from $9.50.

Catalina is a stylish tapas bar where you'll pay between $3 and $7 per serving, with backpacker specials on Thursday. After 10 pm Catalina becomes a nightclub – see the Entertainment section. *Lifestream* is a large health-food cafe with a huge range of goodies. You can put together a decent meal for $3 to $5. Nearby is the *Fondue Restaurant* where fondues and steamboats cost between $16 and $20. Further along, not far from the new bus stop, the popular *Byronian Cafe* is open for breakfast with omelettes for $6.50, BLT for $5.50 and other snacks and meals from around $9.

At the Railway Friendly Bar, *Annie's Fresco Gusto* is open for lunch and dinner. The food is quite innovative and not expensive.

On Jonson St at the corner of Marvell St, *Triados* is a popular place for lunch and dinner, with indoor and outdoor areas. Main courses are around $12. Nearby on Marvell St, *Koo Kafe* is a stylish coffee-and-cake place, with snacks and pasta for around $6. They might be opening in the evenings with more substantial meals. *Afters* has a good range of cakes, focaccia etc and is near the bookshop on Carlyle St near Jonson St.

Kips at the Plaza shopping centre has Malay/Singaporean and Thai food with main courses from $8 to $14. The bistro at the *Ex-Services Club* often has specials such as main courses for under $10.

Further along Jonson St is the licensed *Mexican Micks*, open for dinner from Tuesday to Saturday. It's an old favourite and is still reasonably priced, with main courses under $14 and lots of snacks on the big menu.

They sometimes have special deals for back-packers.

Elsewhere The Chinese restaurant at the *bowling club* in Marvell St has various specials and none of their main courses is over $8. *Chu's* on Lawson St has no MSG in their Chinese food, with main courses under $10. Across the road, upstairs in the Bay Centre arcade, *Oh! Delhi* is a popular Indian restaurant. Nearby, the *Athena Greek Taverna* on Lawson St has main courses for around $12.

Feros Arcade dog-legs between Lawson and Jonson Sts and has several options. The *Indian Curry Restaurant* is a small place that's open from Wednesday to Monday for dinner, with vegetarian main courses from $8 and others up to $13. *Annabella's Spaghetti Bar* is open weekdays for lunch and dinner (and maybe summer weekends), with main courses from $7 to $10. Next door, the *Raving Prawn* has an interesting modern menu with main courses from $14 to $20.

La Belle Epoque at Wategos Beach has Thursday specials at $25 a head. *Tucano Restaurant*, upstairs on Fletcher St near Bay St, is open for lunch and dinner daily and the menu ranges from main-course pasta from $11 to Thai lobster for $30; most main courses are around $17, with lunchtime specials. *Misaki Byron* (☎ (066) 85 7966) is a good Japanese cafe at 11 Fletcher St. It's open for lunch and dinner most days; main courses start at $10. They prefer you to book.

The *Fig Tree* (☎ (066) 84 7273) is a few km from town on Sunrise Lane, which is off McGettigans Lane, which is off the road between Byron and the Pacific Highway. It's open from Thursday to Saturday and on Wednesday in peak times and main courses are $20. You have to book, and remember to BYO.

Finally, you can buy late-night takeaways from the *Night Owl*, a van on Byron St behind the Great Northern Hotel.

Entertainment
No-one should miss the Railway Friendly Bar ('the Rails') at the station. It's open daily and has music most nights, with larger bands

from Friday to Sunday. Because the music area is outdoors they have to finish by 9.30 pm, but there are other venues nearby to kick on at.

The Beach Hotel on Bay St has music most nights.

Catalina on Jonson St has music and dancing from about 10 pm. There's a cover charge of about $4. Thursday is dance-party night and backpackers get half-price entry (pick up a card from your hostel), a free sangria and an inexpensive meal. Kips restaurant at the Plaza shopping centre is also a bar/nightclub. There's also a piano bar that stays open until late, with good bands and dancing some nights.

The Ex-Services Club ('the Servo'), has music on Friday and Saturday (from big touring bands to Kenny Ball) and free films on Sunday and Thursday night.

It's always worth seeing what's on at the Epicentre, on Kendall St just over the railway line. Whatever it is (and their programmes encompass a wide range of the weird) it's sure to be at least interesting. The Byron Bay Regional Gallery is here, as are several studios. The Hare Krishnas sometimes hold their feasts here and there are often performances.

The Piggery, near the Arts Factory Lodge, might be reopening as a venue for mainly local bands.

The *Echo* has entertainment listings.

Getting There & Away
Travel Agents Two of Byron's travel agents are Byron Bay Travel Centre (☎ (066) 85 6733) in Palm Court, opposite the Great Northern Hotel on Jonson St, and Jetset Travel (☎ (066) 85 6554) on Marvell St near the corner of Jonson St. The various other travel agents in town also handle most things – as with everything else in Byron Bay there's a fair degree of competition between them.

Train Byron Bay is on the Sydney to Murwillumbah line, with a daily train in each direction, plus several rail-bus services. From Sydney ($75) the quickest service is the 7.05 am XPT, reaching Byron at 7.30 pm. This train continues to Murwillumbah ($5.70) and connects with a bus to Brisbane ($24.60 from Byron).

Bus Numerous buses run through. There are also more-or-less direct buses to Melbourne ($117) and Adelaide ($147). Other approximate fares are Brisbane $22, Sydney $60, Coffs Harbour $31, Surfers Paradise $18. Kirklands' Lismore to Brisbane route passes through Byron Bay and stops in other useful places such as Murwillumbah, Ballina and Tweed Heads. Backsway Buses (☎ (07) 236 4163), a Brisbane company, runs to Brisbane ($25) via a few coastal towns.

Car & Motorcycle Rental As well as the major companies – Avis (☎ (066) 85 6373) and Hertz (☎ (066) 85 6522; 85 6262) – Earth Car Rentals (☎ (066) 85 3172 or book through a hostel) has older cars from $35 a day, including 200 free km, more recent vehicles from $45 and eight-seater vans from $45.

Jetset Travel (☎ (066) 85 6554) rents current-model cars, little Daihatsus, for $35 a day, plus 15c per kilometre. You can't go more than 300 km from Byron Bay, but that's enough to get you around the area and visit the hinterland.

Ride On Motorcyles (☎ (066) 85 6304) on Jonson St opposite the Plaza shopping centre hires bikes from $45 a day. You need a motorbike license, Australian or foreign.

Getting Around
Bus Blanch's (☎ (066) 85 6430) serves the local area with destinations such as Mullumbimby ($4) and Ballina ($4.60).

Bicycle Cycling is the perfect way to get around Byron Bay, and a bike path runs down to Suffolk Park and on to Broken Head. Blanch's (☎ (066) 85 6430) serves the local area with destinations such as Mullumbimby ($4) and Ballina ($4.60). Most hostels lend bikes of varying quality to guests. Byron Bay Cycles in the Plaza shopping centre on Jonson St has some good

single-speed bikes for $10 a day, including helmet, and geared bikes for $15 a day. Let's Go Bikes, nearby on Jonson St, also has single-speed bikes at $10 a day. Both places require a deposit of around $40.

Taxi If you need a cab, call Byron Bay Taxis (☎ (066) 85 6290).

BRUNSWICK HEADS
Brunswick Heads (population 1700) is a small fishing town that's popular for family holidays. It's quite a pleasant place, with the Brunswick River and a good beach, but nearby Byron Bay overshadows its modest attractions.

Places to Stay & Eat
The council-owned *Terrace Reserve Caravan Park* (☎ (066) 85 1233) is close to the beach and the town centre. At Christmas and Easter all accommodation, except perhaps tent-sites, is booked out well in advance. Sites cost between $10 and $15 for two people, and cabins with attached bathrooms cost from $35 to $70 at Easter and Christmas/January.

Three of the town's motels are on the highway and charge from about $40 in the off-season (twice that around Christmas). Much better positioned is the *Heidelberg Holiday Inn* (☎ (066) 85 1808), on the riverfront and not far from the beach. Single/double rooms go for about $45/50, rising to around $100 at peak times.

Places to eat include the *Happy Dolphin* on the main street, with breakfasts ($5.50), focaccia ($5), quiche and the like, and, around the corner, the *Hutt* Indian restaurant.

Just west of the highway near Billinudgel, *Pockets* (☎ (066) 80 3300) has high-quality two-bedroom cottages from about $110 a double

Getting There & Away
Long-distance buses on the Sydney ($60) to Brisbane ($21 with Kirklands) run stop here.

THE TWEED COAST
The Pacific Highway north of Brunswick

Heads curves inland to Murwillumbah (see the North Coast Hinterland section) then back to the coast at Tweed Heads. There's also a route along the Tweed Coast which is a little shorter but probably slower.

It won't be many years before the stretch of coast between Brunswick Heads and Tweed Heads is overrun by housing estates, in the all-too-familiar process whereby a superb area is ruined by tasteless developers and short-sighted local governments. Meanwhile, there are still large gaps between the cream-brick ghettos and a series of fine beaches.

The coastal road is sealed north of **Wooyung**; the Wooyung turn-off from the highway is about seven km north of Brunswick Heads. There is a basic camping area at Wooyung, and from here a dirt track, very rough and sandy, runs south along the coast to Golden Beach, near the big Ocean Shores residential development. Don't try this track after rain. **Wooyung Camel Farm** (☎ (066) 77 1632) has short rides for $4 ($3 children) and 90-minutes sunset rides to the beach for $20. They might be offering overnight rides by now. These people catch wild camels in Central Australia and you can go along on one of their expeditions (at a price). It sounds pretty full-on, with helicopter chases and trail-bike bull-dogging.

North of Wooyung, near Mooball Beach, **Pioneer Plantation** (☎ (066) 77 1215) is a banana plantation with a restaurant, bar and tours.

Next stop north is **Pottsville**, another residential development. After Pottsville you come to **Cabarita Beach** (also known as **Bogangar**) which has good surf and tends to have it even when other areas are quiet.

At Cabarita Beach there's a good purpose-built hostel. *Emu Park* (☎ (066) 76 1190) is one of the cleanest hostels around and its rooms are large. Dorm beds are still $12 and there's a great 'stay two nights, get the third night free' deal, except in the peak summer season. There are also doubles for $25 and an ensuite double with TV for $35. Bikes and boards are free, the beach is a minute away and there's some bushwalking nearby.

Camels at Wooyung

They'll drop you off at Mt Warning and pick you up five hours later for about $45, which is not bad between several people. By now they might have stitched together a deal with a Tweed Heads dive company for backpacker discounts on courses. They will collect you from Coolangatta or Murwillumbah if you phone.

Close to Cabarita is **Cudgen Lake**, a freshwater lake where you can hire cats and windsurfers ($15 an hour) and canoes (from $5 an hour). The hire shop is part of *Cabarita Gardens Lake Resort* (☎ (066) 76 2000), a motel and apartment complex with singles/doubles from $80/90 and from $95/105 in the peak season. **Kingscliff** is next north and is almost an outer suburb of Tweed Heads. It's a little older and a little less raw than the beachside developments further south. There are a couple of council-run caravan parks, *Kingscliff Beach* (☎ (066) 74 1311) and *Kingscliff North* (☎ (066) 74 1071), both of them right on the foreshore but fairly cramped for room.

Heading north from Kingscliff you have to return to the highway, where you'll come to a turn-off for **Fingal Head**, quite close to Tweed Heads as the crow flies but a fair hike by road.

TWEED HEADS

Sharing a street with the more developed Queensland resort of Coolangatta, Tweed Heads (population 5500) marks the southern end of the Gold Coast strip. The north side of Boundary St, which runs along a short peninsula to Point Danger above the mouth of the Tweed River, is in Queensland. This end of the Gold Coast is quieter than the resorts closer to Surfers Paradise.

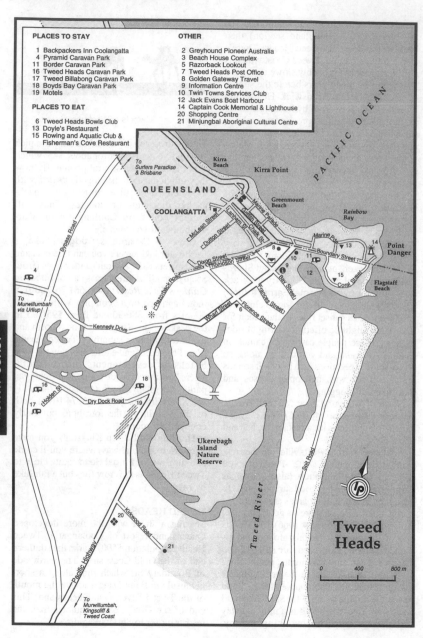

PLACES TO STAY
1 Backpackers Inn Coolangatta
4 Pyramid Caravan Park
11 Border Caravan Park
16 Tweed Heads Caravan Park
17 Tweed Billabong Caravan Park
18 Boyds Bay Caravan Park
19 Motels

PLACES TO EAT
6 Tweed Heads Bowls Club
13 Doyle's Restaurant
15 Rowing and Aquatic Club &
Fisherman's Cove Restaurant

OTHER
2 Greyhound Pioneer Australia
3 Beach House Complex
5 Razorback Lookout
7 Tweed Heads Post Office
8 Golden Gateway Travel
9 Information Centre
10 Twin Towns Services Club
12 Jack Evans Boat Harbour
14 Captain Cook Memorial & Lighthouse
20 Shopping Centre
21 Minjungbai Aboriginal Cultural Centre

PACIFIC OCEAN

Kirra Beach
Kirra Point

QUEENSLAND

COOLANGATTA

Greenmount Beach

Rainbow Bay

To Surfers Paradise & Brisbane

McLean Street
Lanham Street
Griffith Street
Chalk St
Dutton Street
Dixon Street
Thompson Street

Marine Parade

Marine Pde
Boundary Street

Point Danger

Flagstaff Beach

Coral Street

Bypass Road

Razorback Road

Bay Street

Frances Street
Florence Street

Wharf Street

Kennedy Drive

To Murwillumbah via Urliup

Holden St
Dry Dock Road

Ukerebagh Island Nature Reserve

Tweed River

Still Road

Kirkwood Road

Pacific Highway

To Murwillumbah, Kingscliff & Tweed Coast

Tweed Heads

0   400   800 m

NORTH COAST

Orientation

Tweed Heads now sprawls south of the Tweed River, but the older town centre is quite a compact area north of the Tweed. Coming from the south, after the new bypass road branches off, the Pacific Highway crosses the river on narrow Boyds Bay Bridge and becomes Wharf St, the long main street. Wharf St ends near the Twin Towns Services Club (a large cylindrical building), with Griffith St running across the border into Coolangatta and Boundary St running east up a steep hill to the end of Point Danger.

Griffith St runs north for a few blocks then meets McLean St which leads east to Marine Pde, Coolangatta's beachfront promenade.

Information

The information centre (☎ (075) 36 4244) is at the north end of Wharf St (the Pacific Highway), opposite the post office. It's open on weekdays and until 1 pm on Saturday but not at all on Sunday. There's also an information kiosk in the Beach House complex at the corner of Marine Pde and McLean St in Coolangatta, but it docsn't always open on Sunday either. The Greyhound Pioneer Australia office around the corner on McLean St *is* open on Sunday and might be able to help.

The main information centre for the Tweed region is in Murwillumbah.

Things to See & Do

At Point Danger the towering **Captain Cook Memorial** straddles the state border. The 18-metre-high monument was completed in 1970 (the bicentenary of Cook's visit) and is topped by a laser-beam lighthouse visible 35 km out to sea. The replica of the *Endeavour*'s capstan is made from ballast which was dumped by Cook after the *Endeavour* ran aground on the Great Barrier Reef and was recovered along with the ship's cannons in 1968. Point Danger was named by Cook after he nearly ran aground there too. Three km from downtown Tweed Heads there are views over the Tweed Valley and the Gold Coast from the **Razorback Lookout**.

There are several good **beaches**, most in Queensland. Coolangatta's Kirra Point is

famous for its surf, and Rainbow Bay, on the north side of Point Danger, is another patrolled beach.

On Kirkwood Rd in South Tweed Heads, the **Minjungbal Aboriginal Cultural Centre** (☎ (075) 24 2109) has exhibits on the history and culture of the Minjungbal people who once owned this area. You can also buy authentic souvenirs. The nearby *bora* ground is a traditional ceremonial site. A boardwalk runs through the mangroves of adjacent Ukerebagh Island Nature Reserve and you might be lucky enough to see a koala. The centre is open daily and admission is $4.

The **Tweed Maritime Museum** on Kennedy Drive in Tweed Heads West has old photos and other bits and pieces and is open on Tuesday and Friday afternoon; admission is $1 (50c children).

Dolphins Water Sports Hire at Jack Evans Boat Harbour rents windsurfers, canoes and other gear.

Tweed River Cruises (☎ (075) 36 8800) has a two-hour cruise ($18, $9 children), a four-hour lunch cruise ($45, $22.50 children) and a trip to Avocado Adventureland ($50, $25 children).

Places to Stay

Accommodation in Tweed Heads spills over into Coolangatta and up the Gold Coast, where the choice is more varied.

Caravan Parks There are many, many caravan parks in the area. In town on Coral St is the council's *Border Caravan Park* (☎ (075) 36 3134). It's well located but a bit cramped. There are others south of the main centre – see the map.

Hostels There's no backpacker accommodation in Tweed Heads, but in adjacent Coolangatta there's the good *Backpackers Inn Coolangatta* (☎ (075) 36 2422), at 45 McLean St. It's not far from the Greyhound Pioneer Australia terminal and within walking distance of the stop used by the other lines. This is a large, well-run place with a bar and a restaurant with specials for around $6 (breakfast from $2.50). Boogie boards and bikes are free. Dorm beds (not bunks) cost $14, singles/doubles are $19/29. There's a compulsory sheet-hire charge of $1. They also do B&B packages. A bit further up the coast in Coolangatta's suburb of Bilinga there's a YHA hostel (☎ (075) 36 7644).

Down the coast at Cabarita Beach is the good *Emu Park Hostel*. They will collect you from Coolangatta or Tweed Heads. See the earlier Tweed Coast section.

Motels Down the long strip of Wharf St south of the centre there are several motels which are feeling the pinch now that the bypass road has been completed. In the off-season you can often get a double room for $30 or less.

Houseboats *Tweed River Houseboats* (☎ (075) 72 3525) hires boats with two double and two single beds from about $500 for four midweek nights, more at peak times.

Places to Eat

The slick new *Tweed Heads Bowls Club* on Wharf St has specials such as weekday roast lunches for $3; the other clubs are also sources of cheap eats. The smaller *Rowing & Aquatic Club* on Coral St has meals for around $8.

At Rainbow Bay, on the north side of Point Danger, *Doyle's* has excellent seafood takeaways and a restaurant where main courses start at about $20. This place was until recently owned by the famous Sydney seafood family but has been taken over by one of their ex-apprentices. Also known for its seafood is *Fishermans Cove Restaurant* with entrees around $7 and main courses varying widely around $16. It's on Coral St next door to the Rowing & Aquatic Club.

Entertainment

The large Twin Towns Services Club on the corner of Wharf St and Boundary St and Seagulls Rugby Club on Gollan Drive in West Tweed Heads have regular touring acts. Seagulls is open 24 hours. The big new Bowls Club south on Wharf St from the

Services Club and the Golf Club south of town also have entertainment.

Pub entertainment is often pretty tasteless ('Miss Nude' etc). O'Rourke's on McLean St in Coolangatta is a nightclub where you won't have too many hassles.

Getting There & Away

All the long-distance buses stop in Coolangatta. Greyhound Pioneer Australia (☎ (075) 36 9966) stops at Beach House on McLean St near the corner of the beachfront Marine Pde, and the others stop at Golden Gateway Travel (☎ (075) 36 1700) a few blocks back towards Tweed Heads. Greyhound Pioneer Australia has a $15 day-return ticket to Brisbane, or $10 one-way.

Surfside (☎ (075) 36 7666) has daily services to Murwillumbah ($3.80) and to Kingscliff (some go on to Cabarita Beach, but not on Sunday) and they have deals on day-return tickets up the Gold Coast. There's a stop outside the information centre.

Getting Around

There are several car-hire places which will get you moving for $25 a day or less, such as Tweed Auto Rentals (☎ (075) 36 8000) at the information centre. There's a 24-hour taxi service (☎ (066) 34 1144).

Far North Coast Hinterland

The area stretching 60 km or so inland from the Pacific Highway in far north NSW is full of interest for its natural beauty and its population of 'alternative lifestylers', 'back to the landers', 'freaks', 'hippies', whatever label you care to apply. These settlers, the first of whom were attracted to the area by the Aquarius Festival at Nimbin in 1973, have become an accepted part of the community – although there are still occasional run-ins with the drug squad.

The country between Lismore and the coast was once known as the Big Scrub, an

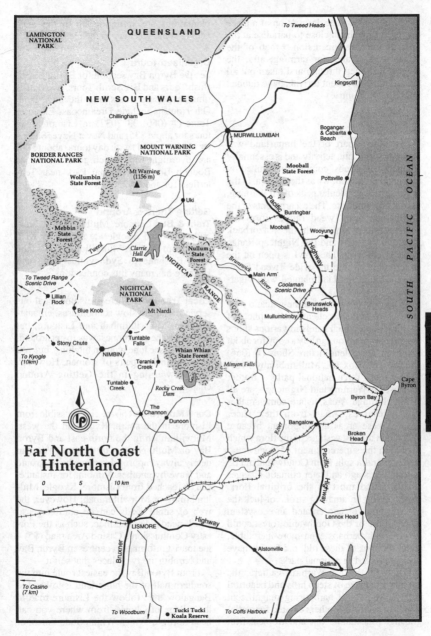

Far North Coast Hinterland

0   5   10 km

incredibly inadequate description of a place that must have been close to paradise at the time of European incursion. Much of the 'scrub' was cleared for farming, after the loggers had been through and taken out all the cedar. More recent arrivals have dubbed it Rainbow Country.

Geography

The northern part of the hinterland was formed by volcanic activity and is essentially a huge bowl, almost completely rimmed by mountain ranges known as the caldera. In the centre is the spectacular peak of Mt Warning, the old volcanic core. The escarpments of the McPherson and Tweed ranges form the north-western rim, with the Razorback Range to the west and the Nightcap Range to the south-west. The bowl is open on the eastern side, where the wide Tweed River flows through flat land planted with sugarcane.

To see just how massive the volcano was, have a look at the excellent satellite photo of the hinterland which hangs in various shops around the area. You can buy a copy for about $20 from The Silent Picture Show (☎ (066) 84 7251), PO Box 361, Mullumbimby, 2482.

The area's three national parks – Border Ranges, Mt Warning and Nightcap – are all World Heritage Areas, as are some smaller nature reserves. Apart from their sheer beauty, these areas are important because they retain the last vestiges of the flora which existed in the supercontinent of Gondwanaland. Australia split from Gondwanaland 65 million years ago and later climatic changes slowly killed most of the original flora. However, by an amazing stroke of luck the Mt Warning volcano created an ecosystem where some of the Gondwanic forest could survive and, perhaps even more incredible, small sections of these old, old forests have been preserved in national parks.

South of the Mt Warning caldera, the country is a maze of steep hills and beautiful valleys, some still harbouring magnificent stands of rainforest, others cleared for cattle-grazing. Macadamia nut and tropical fruit plantations are springing up in the area, adding some greenery to the cleared land.

Organised Tours

See the Byron Bay section for Byron Bay to Bush Tours and Big Scrub Tours, two outfits running popular tours into the hinterland. Other outfits include Dreamcoast Explorer Tours (☎ (066) 33 7037) in Lismore (day tours for about $35) and Never Never Safaris (☎ (066) 72 1031) with day tours (about $90) and overnight trips which go out as far as Boonoo Boonoo National Park near Tenterfield for about $250.

Getting There & Around

Train & Bus Lismore, Mullumbimby, Murwillumbah and Kyogle are served by XPT trains from Sydney; Murwillumbah is on the main Brisbane to Sydney bus route and Lismore has many bus connections.

Local Transport There are some local bus services, mainly slow schoolbuses, emanating from Murwillumbah and Lismore, but hitching is the commonest way to get around. You rarely see lone women hitching, but you do see plenty of pairs of women. However, see the warning in the Getting Around chapter.

Car & Motorbike The area is accessible from Lismore in the south, Kyogle in the west, Murwillumbah in the north-east and Byron Bay or Mullumbimby in the east. You can nearly always approach a place by one route and leave by another. Nimbin, for instance, can be reached from Lismore, Kyogle, Mullumbimby or Murwillumbah. However, the web of small roads can be confusing, so you'll need a detailed map, such as the Forestry Commission's Casino Area map ($5) – the tourist information centres in Byron Bay and Nimbin are two places that sell it.

From Byron Bay the easiest route into the southern half of the hinterland is to head to Bangalow then follow the Lismore road to the village of Clunes, from where you can head north to Whian Whian State Forest or north-west on the Dunoon road for The Channon and, eventually, Nimbin.

From Mullumbimby a scenic but rough track leads north to Uki and small roads lead south-west to Whian Whian, The Channon and Lismore.

From Murwillumbah and Kyogle good roads lead to Nimbin, and the Nimbin to Lismore road is also good.

Markets & Music

At the various weekend markets you can meet the colourful alternative community. The biggest market is at The Channon, between Lismore and Nimbin. Market days and locations are as follows:

Brunswick Heads
    1st Saturday, behind Ampol petrol station
Byron Bay
    1st Sunday, Butler St Reserve
Lismore
    1st & 3rd Sunday, Lismore Shopping Square
Murwillumbah
    1st Sunday, Sunnyside Shopping Centre
The Channon
    2nd Sunday, Coronation Park
Mullumbimby
    3rd Saturday, Museum
Uki
    3rd Sunday, old buttery
Bangalow
    4th Sunday, Showground
Nimbin
    4th Sunday, Showground

There are many accomplished musicians in the area and sometimes they play at the markets or in the village pub after the market (notably at Uki). Other places where you can catch good music include the Chincogan Tavern at Mullumbimby and the Kohinur Hall at Main Arm which has a regular weekly musicians' club. Between them, the *Brunswick Byron Echo* and *Lismore Echo* newspapers give notice of most musical and cultural events in the area.

LISMORE

Thirty-five km inland from Ballina on the Bruxner Highway to New England, and 48 km inland from Byron Bay, Lismore (popu-

lation 28,500) is the 'capital' of the state's far north – the centre of a productive rural district, with a student population from the Northern Rivers campus of the University of New England and influenced by the alternative community which is based in the country to the north.

Orientation & Information

Lismore is on the east bank of the Wilson River, a major tributary of the Richmond River. The Bruxner Highway becomes Ballina St as it runs through town. The main shopping street is Molesworth St.

The Information & Heritage Centre (☎ (066) 22 0122) is near the Wilson River at the corner of Molesworth and Ballina Sts. There's a good rainforest display here, costing $1 (50c children), but make sure you see the real thing as well. You can buy topographic maps here, which are essential for bushwalking and useful even if you're driving around the narrow roads in this area.

The Big Scrub Environment Centre (☎ (066) 21 3278) on Keen St also sells topographic maps, and the volunteers who staff it might know of interesting events in the area. The district's National Parks office (☎ (066) 28 1177) is in the town of Alstonville, east of Lismore on the road to Ballina.

The Outdoor & Disposals shop (☎ (066) 21 3371) on Keen St rents camping gear: a dome tent, a stove and a couple of sleeping bags would cost about $80 for a week.

Things to See & Do

The interesting **Richmond River Historical Society Museum** is at 165 Molesworth St (up from the information centre) and is open from 10 am to 4 pm on weekdays ($2), and the **Regional Art Gallery** at No 131 is open the same hours from Tuesday to Saturday (admission is free). Local artists are well represented. Across from the gallery is the interesting old post office with its iron-lace dome.

The agricultural show is held in late October.

Parks Preserving 10 hectares of the original

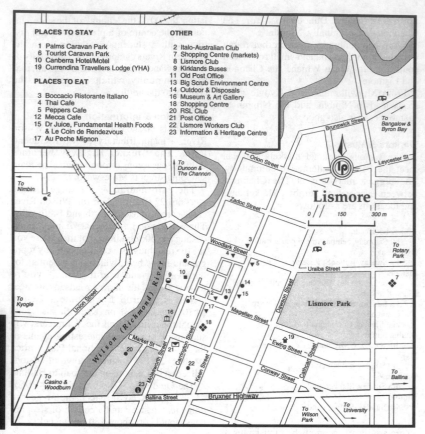

PLACES TO STAY
1 Palms Caravan Park
6 Tourist Caravan Park
10 Canberra Hotel/Motel
19 Currendina Travellers Lodge (YHA)

PLACES TO EAT
3 Boccacio Ristorante Italiano
4 Thai Cafe
5 Peppers Cafe
12 Mecca Cafe
15 Dr Juice, Fundamental Health Foods
& Le Coin de Rendezvous
17 Au Peche Mignon

OTHER
2 Italo-Australian Club
7 Shopping Centre (markets)
8 Lismore Club
9 Kirklands Buses
11 Old Post Office
13 Big Scrub Environment Centre
14 Outdoor & Disposals
16 Museum & Art Gallery
18 Shopping Centre
20 RSL Club
21 Post Office
22 Lismore Workers Club
23 Information & Heritage Centre

Big Scrub (ie rainforest), beautiful **Rotary Park** is about 2.5 km from the city centre on the continuation of Uralba St. Don't miss it. On the southern edge of town, off Wyrallah St, **Wilson Park** has a walking track.

Tucki Tucki Nature Reserve Unusually, this koala protection project was begun by local residents in the late '50s, although it is now administered by National Parks. Tucki Tucki Nature Reserve offers visitors an opportunity to see koalas in the wild. The reserve is 16 km south of Lismore on the Woodburn road (leave Lismore on Wyrallah

St). Nearby is an Aboriginal bora ring, where initiation ceremonies were held.

Activities MV *Bennelong* (☎ (066) 21 7729), a nice old boat, has several cruises on offer, ranging from a two-hour trip ($10, $8 children) to a day cruise down to Ballina on the coast ($45, $20 children).

There is good canoeing on Coopers and Wilsons creeks, and if you move quietly you might see a platypus.

The information centre has a pamphlet produced by the Far North Coast Canoe Club which details some routes. Also ask here about a contact number for the Northern Rivers Bushwalking Club.

Places to Stay

Caravan Parks *Palms Caravan Park* (☎ (066) 21 7067) by the river on Brunswick St and the small *Tourist Caravan Park* (☎ (066) 21 6581) on Dawson St are the closest to the town centre.

Hostel The *Currendina Travellers Lodge* (☎ (066) 21 6118), a few blocks north-east of the information centre at 14 Ewing St, has dorms from $12 plus single/double rooms from $15/$24 to $20/32. There's a TV lounge and a guests' kitchen, and breakfast is available. Smoking and drinking aren't permitted. This is a pleasant old wooden house, and the friendly managers can organise day tours to places of interest in the area (about $12 per person if there are a few people) and can help organise camping near Whian Whian State Forest.

Hotels & Motels The *Gollan Hotel* (☎ (066) 21 2295) on Keen St at the corner of Woodlark St has singles or doubles for $20 or $35 with bathroom. Other pubs with accommodation include the *Civic* (☎ (066) 21 2537) on Molesworth St, the *Metropole* (☎ (066) 21 4910) and the *New Tattersalls* (☎ (066) 21 2284), both also on Keen St.

The more central of the 10 motels include the *Centre Point* (☎ (066) 21 8877) at 202 Molesworth St (from $55/65), *Karinga* (☎ (066) 21 2787) at No 258 (from $50/60, and *AZA* (☎ (066) 21 9499) at 114 Keen St (from $50/60).

Guesthouses *Melville House* (☎ (066) 21 5778) on Ballina St has B&B from about $40/60 or $30/45 with a shared bathroom. Further east, off Ballina St in the Goonellabah area, *Tulloona House* (☎ (066) 24 2897) is a National Trust-classified Victorian mansion with a huge garden. Big rooms cost from $45 a double. The bathroom is shared but the rooms are furnished with antiques.

Places to Eat

Dr Juice on Keen St is open during the day for excellent juices and smoothies, and they have vegetarian and vegan snacks for around $2. On Thursday, Friday and Saturday nights cheap Indian meals are available and there are plans to open as a music cafe on the other nights. Next door is *Fundamental Health Foods*, an almost supermarket-sized health-food shop.

The large *Mecca Cafe* on Magellan St is decidedly non-vegetarian, with burgers (a Big Mec is $4.10) and other fast food.

For outdoor coffee and cake, go to *Au Peche Mignon* on Carrington St near Magellan St. There's more formal French food at *Le Coin du Rendezvous* at 142 Keen St.

Boccacio Ristorante Italiano at 55 Keen St sometimes has all-you-can-eat pasta deals for $7.50. Not far away on Keen St, *Peppers* has cheap meals, such as pasta for under $3. On Woodlark St near the corner of Keen there's a small *Thai cafe*, mainly selling inexpensive takeaways but with a few tables for eat-in meals. On Keen St next to the Big Scrub Environment Centre, the *Mandarin Palace* is a Chinese restaurant with lunch specials for around $6.

Lismore RSL Club at 1 Market St often has good value specials.

Entertainment

There are plenty of pubs and clubs with entertainment, such as Powerhouse at the Canberra Hotel on Molesworth St and the Satellite Room at the Commercial Tavern on Keen St. The Station Hotel in Union St, South Lismore, sometimes has acoustic and/or country music. The Lismore Club in Club Lane, off Molesworth St, has folk, blues and jazz on the first, second and third Thursdays of the month.

Getting There & Away

Air There are daily flights to Brisbane (Oxley) and Sydney (Hazelton).

Train The XPT train from Sydney ($70) stops here.

Bus Kirklands (☎ (066) 22 1499) is based here and runs buses around the immediate area as well as further afield. Destinations include Byron Bay ($7.90), Murwillumbah ($12.70) and Brisbane ($25.90). There's a handy service to Tenterfield in New England ($21.60).

Several local companies run to Nimbin ($8) on weekdays and one of them, Fulton's (☎ (066) 21 6231), continues on to Murwillumbah.

Getting Around

Kirklands has urban-area buses and there are taxis (☎ (066) 21 2618).

THE CHANNON

The Channon, a tiny village off the Nimbin to Lismore road, hosts the biggest of the region's markets on the second Sunday of each month. There is sometimes a dance in the town hall the night before the market (the *Lismore Echo* will have details), and often music there after the market.

The Channon Teahouse & Craftshop is a pleasant place for a snack or a light meal and there's interesting craftwork to browse through. It's open daily from 10 am to 5 pm, with dinner on Friday and Saturday nights. The village's information centre (☎ (066) 88 6276) is here as well.

About 15 km north up Terania Creek Rd is the rainforest of Nightcap National Park – see the following section.

Places to Stay

The Channon Village Campsite (☎ (066) 88 6321) is basic but pretty and costs $4 per person. Out of town on the road to Terania Creek, *Mimosa Park* (☎ (066) 88 6230) has cabins for $35 a double.

NIGHTCAP NATIONAL PARK

This park of nearly 5000 hectares is a World Heritage Area of outstanding beauty. There are three main sections.

The **Terania Creek** area, accessible from The Channon, protects a stunningly beautiful rainforest valley (some of the brush-box trees are well over 1500 years old) and very diverse bird and animal species. From the picnic area, a 700-metre walk leads to **Protesters' Falls**, named after the environmentalists whose 1979 campaign to stop logging was a major factor in the creation of the national park. If the protesters hadn't won the battle, this area, then a state forest, would have been *clear-felled*! Other state forests in NSW with similarly ancient trees are still logged today.

Mt Nardi (800 metres), a steep rise 12 km from Nimbin, has thick forest and good views. Several walking trails lead from the summit, including a one-km walk to Mt Matheson and the beautiful **Pholis Walk**, off the track to Mt Matheson. The views from **Pholis Gap** are particularly spectacular. From Mt Matheson an eight-km track connects with the **Nightcap Track**, a packhorse trail which was once the main route between Lismore and Murwillumbah.

The western end of the park, around **Mt Burrel** (933 metres), is accessible only to experienced walkers.

Places to Stay

The only camping area within the park is at Terania Creek (access is via The Cannon). It's free but you're supposed to stay only one night. No fires are allowed. By the north-east corner of Nightcap there is shared accommodation in *Nightcap Pass Bushwalkers' Cabins* (☎ (066) 79 9133) for about $20 per person. The cabins aren't far from the Nightcap Track if you're walking, or there is road access on Doon Doon road, which branches off from the Uki to Nimbin road 11 km west of Uki.

NIMBIN

Although Australia's 'back to the land' movement is past its heyday, Nimbin (population 1300), 30 km north of Lismore, is still a very active alternative centre. This was where the movement to northern NSW started with the 1973 Aquarius Festival, and there are many communes ('multiple-occupancy property' is the OK term) in the area. You're still quite likely to be asked if you

The North Coast – Far North Coast Hinterland 315

want to buy some 'green' as you walk along the street.

In 1993 Nimbin celebrated the 20th anniversary of the Aquarius Festival and many murals were added to the streetscape. The same year the more conservative elements in town and the Lismore council launched a campaign to 'reclaim the streets', in reaction to the growing transient population whose drug of choice is somewhat heavier than grass. (The campaign's major achievement so far has been cutting down a large tree.)

However, don't be misled by what you see on the streets of Nimbin. The majority of people who live in communities outside the town are hard-working idealists and if you spend a little time here you'll meet some of the friendliest (and some of the weirdest) people anywhere.

Orientation & Information

Despite the size of its reputation, Nimbin is just a tiny village – admittedly somewhat larger than life. Cullen St is the main street through town. At the north end, near the Freemasons Hotel, a street curves away to the left, crosses a bridge and becomes Blue Knob Rd; Cullen St curves away to the right and runs past the caravan park then climbs to the summit of Mt Nardi, 12 km away.

There's an information centre (☎ (066) 89 1222) next to the Ampol station on Cullen St at the south end of the shopping centre. The Environment Centre and the Community Centre, both on Cullen St, are also good sources of information.

Pick up a copy of the booklet *Nimbin & Environs* for $3. It has guides to local sights and services and gives the local history.

Nimbin People

There are a lot of different people in Nimbin, and visitors often force them into the roles of ambassadors for their various cultural perspectives. David Hallett, in his poem *Labels of Babels*, lists, among 70 others:

hippies & yuppies & greenies & junkies
smokers & tokers & dope thieves & jokers & mopers
ball-kickers & ball-hitters & ball-tearers with pit-bull terriers
drummers & dancers & dip-sticks & dobbos
yobbos & touros & musos & preggos & embryos
journos & photos & lezzos & homos
sapiens & hetero sapiens
& not-so-sapiens ■

Nimbin News, the community newspaper, is also essential reading.

Nimbin holds a good market on the fourth Sunday of the month and you may catch a good local band playing afterwards.

The Nimbin Show is held in late September. There's a good dog section.

Things to See & Do

The weird and wonderful **Nimbin Museum** is on Cullen St near the Rainbow Cafe. Admission is $2, well worth it just for the conversations you'll have before you get through the door. Many of the exhibits are for sale.

The **Rainbow Power Company**, once a shopfront on Cullen St, now has a big new building behind the caravan park. It specialises in alternative energy and has helped people all over the country, from all walks of life. The **Permaculture Village**, under construction near the showground on Curtis St, reflects the pioneering role of people in the area, especially Bill Mollison, in this internationally recognised system of sustainable agriculture.

Around Nimbin The country around Nimbin is superb. See the earlier Nightcap National Park section for information on Mt Nardi.

The Tuntable Falls commune, one of the biggest with its own shop and school – and some fine houses – is about nine km east of Nimbin and you can reach it by the public Tuntable Falls Rd. You can walk to the 123-metre **Tuntable Falls** themselves, 13 km from Nimbin. To get to **Nimbin Rocks**, with an Aboriginal sacred site, head south through the town and turn right at Stony Chute (Kyogle) Rd. After two km there's a turn-off to the left and three km along there's a signposted walking trail on the left. **Hanging Rock Creek** has falls and a good swimming hole; take the road through Stony Chute for 14 km, turn right at the Barker's Vale sign, then left onto Williams Rd; the falls are nearby on the right.

The **Nimbin Rocks Gallery** (closed Wednesday) has a large collection of local artworks. It's off the Lismore road beyond the Stony Chute turn-off.

Places to Stay

The Freemasons Hotel no longer has accommodation.

Camping, Hostel & Cabins The council's basic *caravan park* (☎ (066) 89 1402) is near the bowling club – go down the road running past the pub. Sites cost $9 and on-site vans around $28. The caravan park is due to be upgraded.

Granny's Farm (☎ (066) 89 1333), an associate YHA hostel, is a pleasant and relaxed place surrounded by farmland, with platypuses in the nearby creek. There are dorms (with beds, not bunks) for $12.50 and doubles for $15 per person. The friendly managers will sometimes give you rides to local places of interest. To reach the hostel go north along Cullen St, take the left fork near the pub and turn left just before the bridge over the creek. It's a few minutes' walk from the town centre.

Calurla Tea Garden (☎ (066) 89 7297), three km along Lillian Rock Rd (the turn-off is eight km from Nimbin on Blue Knob Rd), has a couple of better-than-average cabins for $45 a double and tent sites for around $10. This place is becoming popular, especially with people who live in the urban areas of south-eastern Queensland.

Motels Just out of town heading north, Crofton Rd branches off Blue Knob Rd, and four km along it is the quiet *Nimbin Motel* (☎ (066) 89 1420), also known as the Abode of Peace, with singles/doubles for $20/$35. As a motel it's pretty basic, but as a bed for the night in a quiet valley with bushland at the back door it's good value.

There's a new motel, *Klassic Lodge* (☎ (066) 89 9350), a few km from Nimbin on the road to Lismore. It charges $30/50.

B&B Several B&B places have opened in the past year or so, and there will probably be more by the time you get here, so ask around. In town next to the church at the south end of Cullen St, the *Old Rectory* (☎ (066) 89 1097) is in the process of being renovated and things are a little rough and ready, but it is friendly and in a great location, with views across the village. One of the owners has lived in the area on-and-off since before the Aquarius Festival, so she has good information on people and places. B&B costs $30/40/50 for a single/double/twin.

Further from the town centre and higher on a hill, with views of the valley and Nimbin Rocks, is another B&B place. The Quinns (☎ (066) 89 1113) are a retired couple who have moved to the area and have made a beautiful garden around their comfortable home. There's a spring-fed dam for swimming. B&B costs $20 per person, with full board $35. To get here head south on Cullen St to the edge of town and turn left onto High St. High St becomes Falls Rd and the Quinns' place is about one km along, on the right. It's No 103.

Nimbin Tourist Accommodation (☎ (066) 89 1493) is six km north of Nimbin and charges $40/60 for B&B.

Places to Eat
There has been a boom in eating places in Nimbin.

At the north end of Cullen St the *Nimbin Pizza & Trattoria* has pasta from $7.50 and gets good reports. It's open from Tuesday to Sunday for dinner.

The *Rainbow Cafe* has long been the most popular hangout in town. Walking in here can feel like the hippie equivalent of walking into a wild west saloon, but almost everyone is very friendly. Wholesome meals cost around $6 and delicious cakes are around $2. They do breakfasts, as does the nearby *Nimbin Rocks Cafe*, the closest thing you'll find to a standard country-town cafe, although vegie burgers are on the menu.

Across the street, *Choices* has healthy (and not so healthy) takeaways and light meals. There are outside tables.

A popular new place is *Jem's*, near the Ampol station. It's open from 10 am to 10 pm for pastries and coffee, with an interesting lunch and dinner menu with snacks from

$3.50 and most main courses under $10. It's open from Wednesday to Saturday for lunch and dinner, and on Tuesday for lunch only. Nearby is the *Espresso Bar*.

The *Freemasons Hotel* has counter meals for under $7 and the *bowling club*, the watering-hole of the town's more conservative citizens, also has meals.

When there's a film or a play at the Bush Theatre, at the north end of Cullen St, the *Mulgum Cafe* is open, serving inexpensive, healthy food.

Out of town (see Places to Stay for directions), *Calurla Tea Garden* (☎ (066) 89 7297) is open between 10 am and 6 pm daily. They do teas and lunches (up to $9.50) and a three-course dinner (bookings preferred) works out at around $25. The food is farmhouse style, the views of Mt Warning and the Border Ranges are excellent and the owners are very friendly. Ask them about arts & crafts in the area.

Entertainment
The Freemasons Hotel often has bands. The Bush Theatre, at the old butter factory near the bridge at the north end of town, has performances, and films on Friday and Saturday.

If there's a dance at the town hall don't miss it – you'll meet the friendly people from the areas outside Nimbin, and how long is it since you heard a 20-minute guitar solo? Around late Autumn you might get a chance to trip the light fantastic at the Marijuana Harvest Ball.

Getting There & Away
Train The nearest railway station to Nimbin is at Lismore.

Bus There are several buses each way between Nimbin and Lismore ($8), daily except Sunday. A Fulton's schoolbus runs to/from Murwillumbah on weekdays (leaving Murwillumbah at 7 am, returning in the afternoon). It's a slow two hours and costs $12. Students/unemployed/travellers *might* get concessions on local buses.

Car & Motorbike The main road routes to Nimbin are from Lismore to the south and off the Murwillumbah to Kyogle road 23 km west of Uki.

Hitching Hitching is pretty easy in this part of the world (but see the warning in the Getting Around chapter). Heading south, most hitchhikers stand near the church; heading north, the bridge on Blue Knob Rd is popular.

Horse Horseriding outfits, often with unfulfilled plans to offer treks down to the coast, come and go. Ask at the information centre.

MULLUMBIMBY

This pleasant little town (population 2700), known simply as Mullum, is in subtropical countryside five km off the Pacific Highway between Bangalow and Brunswick Heads. The distinctive cone of Mt Chincogan is just outside the town. Perhaps best known for its marijuana ('Mullumbimby Madness'), it's a centre for the long-established farming community and for the alternative folk from nearby areas. There's nothing like the cultural frontier mentality of Nimbin here. Perhaps the most obvious sign that the area's community is of a different mix from the usual rural Australian variety is that there's a good bookshop and several other places selling second-hand books. If you need a used copy of *The Hobbit*, this is the place to come.

Orientation & Information

Burringbar St is the main shopping street and runs off Dalley St, the main road through town.

There's an information centre (☎ (066) 84 1286) at the north end of Dalley St, near the library. It's open on weekdays. There are plenty of noticeboards around town; the best is probably at Santos Health Foods on Stuart St.

Things to See & Do

There's a short **walk** through rainforest by the Brunswick River.

This area is rich in artists and craftspeople and some of their work is displayed in the **Arts Gallery** (☎ (066) 84 1573). Entrances are near the corner of Burringbar and Stuart Sts, and it's open Tuesday to Friday from 10 am to 5 pm and from 10.30 am to 3 pm on Saturday. During school holidays it's open daily.

The **museum**, open from 1 to 4 pm (2 to 5 pm during daylight-saving time) from Wednesday to Friday, is off the south end of Stuart St, in the old post office. Although none are very grand, Mullum has some nice old buildings, and their setting in this quiet town makes them seem even finer. **Cedar House** at 140 Dalley St has been recommended for National Trust listing. Pick up a brochure on the old buildings from the information office. If the office is closed, see if The Lyrebird Motel has some.

Off the Goonengerry road about seven km south-west of Mullum, **Crystal Castle** is a large complex devoted to crystals. It also has a cafe.

The local **cycling club** has regular rides for beginners and the more experienced. Ask at the muralled bike shop on Dalley St.

Festivals & Events

A market is held at the museum on the third Saturday of the month.

The local festival is the Chincogan Fiesta, held in early September. There are bands, free camping and events such as the Chincogan Charge, a race up nearby Mt Chincogan. The agricultural show is held in mid-November.

Places to Stay

In town there's only motel accommodation: at the *Mullumbimby Motel* (☎ (066) 84 2387) at 121 Dalley St (the south end), rooms cost from $35 a single or double, rising to around $55; and at the *Lyrebird* (☎ (066) 84 1725) at the other end of Dalley St, which is fractionally dearer.

North of Mullumbimby, 12 km out on Main Arm Rd, *Maca's Camping Ground* (☎ (066) 84 5211) is an idyllic place. It's on a macadamia nut plantation, under the lee of hills lush with rainforest. It's a relaxed spot with a lot of room to move. While it is nothing like a commercial caravan park the facilities are quite good, with a communal kitchen, hot showers and a laundry. You'll need to bring all your food supplies. It costs $4 per person ($2 children) and you can hire tents from $5 a day. To get here, take Main Arm Rd out of Mullumbimby, go through the hamlet of Main Arm then the sub-hamlet of Upper Main Arm and Maca's is on the right soon after. The blue 'Camping' signs at the intersections are directing you to this place.

Places to Eat
The *Popular Cafe* on Burringbar St is Mullum's version of the country town caff, and it *is* a popular place to hang out. More stylish are *La Lu's* on Dalley St and *Kelly's Kitchen* on Burringbar St, both open during the day for coffee and light meals. Also on Burringbar St, *Bently's* is a coffee shop by day and a restaurant by night, with main courses around $13. *Buon Appetito* on Stuart St has inexpensive pastas (from $3.50) and pizzas to eat there or take away.

Mullum House at 103 Stuart St is a good Chinese restaurant with main courses under $10. It's open nightly. *The Lane* is a licensed Thai restaurant down the lane next to the National Bank on Burringbar St. Most main courses are under $12 (10% less for takeaways). There is often entertainment here.

The new *Chincogan Tavern* and the old *Commercial Hotel* have inexpensive counter meals, and the Tavern has live music a couple of nights a week. The *Ex-Services Club* on Dalley St and the *Bowling Club* on Jubilee Ave (the southern continuation of Dalley St) also have meals.

Getting There & Away
Train Mullum is on the Sydney ($70) to Murwillumbah railway.

Bus Most Kirklands buses go through Mullum on their Lismore ($8.40) to Brisbane ($20.30) run. The newsagent at the corner of Burringbar and Stuart Sts is the Kirklands agent. There's no direct service to/from Byron Bay; you have to travel via Brunswick Heads.

Car & Motorbike The most direct route to Mullum from the Pacific Highway turns off just south of Brunswick Heads, but it's worth taking the longer but prettier Tunnel Road route which leaves the highway north of Brunswick Heads, near the Ocean Shores turn-off. There's also the Coolaman Scenic Drive, which leaves the highway between Bangalow and the Byron Bay turn-off. For a superbly scenic drive to Uki and Mt Warning, head out to Upper Main Arm, pass Maca's Camping Ground (see Places to Stay for directions) and follow the unsealed road through the Nullum State Forest. Keep to the main road and watch for signposts at the few ambiguous intersections. It's a narrow road, and steep where it crosses the range, but in dry weather it's OK if you take it easy and watch out for logging trucks. Don't try it after rain or you stand a good chance of sliding off the mountain, literally.

WHIAN WHIAN STATE FOREST
Whian Whian is west of Mullumbimby and adjoins the south-eastern side of Nightcap National Park. On the south-eastern side of the state forest, **Minyon Falls** plunge 100 metres into a rainforest gorge and the surrounding area is a flora reserve with several walking tracks.

Access to the reserve is on the Minyon Drive which cuts across the south-eastern corner of the state forest. Peates Mountain Road runs off Minyon Drive and heads north to **Peates Mountain Lookout**, with views to the coast, and on to *Rummery Park*, a Forestry Commission campsite with pit toilets and cold showers. Koalas live in the nearby forest. The eastern end of the Nightcap Track walking trail emerges on the road beyond Rummery Park.

The south-western corner of Whian Whian is the **Big Scrub Flora Reserve**, the largest surviving chunk of the vegetation which once covered the Richmond Valley.

UKI

Uki (pronounced uke-eye) is a pretty village of 200 souls, dominated by the peak of Mt Warning. It's most famous for its big market, held at the old buttery on the third Sunday of the month. The Uki Trading Post (☎ (066) 79 5351) is a helpful information centre.

Places to Stay & Eat

The *Uki Village Guesthouse* (☎ (066) 79 5345) is next to the Uki Trading Post in an old wooden home. During the week B&B costs $55 for one or two people and at weekends it's $55/75 a single/double. For $160 a double you have B&B plus a five-course seafood dinner. They will pick you up from Murwillumbah. Children aren't allowed.

The licensed *Uki Trading Post* serves light meals and Devonshire teas by day and dinner at night, seven days a week. Main courses cost between $7 and $11 and vegetarians are catered for.

Around Uki There are quite a number of other places to stay in the area, geared to holiday-makers. *Mt Warning Forest Hideaway* (☎ (066) 79 7139) is 12 km south-west of Uki on Byrill Creek Rd (motel units with cooking facilities from $40/45 to $60/70); *Tyalgum Tops* (☎ (066) 79 3370) is near the village of Tyalgum on the north side of the national park and is a farmstay with various activities and weekend packages. Near Chillingham, *Crystal Creek Rainforest Retreat* (☎ (066) 79 1591) has good self-contained cabins and the property is adjacent to the forest. Cabins cost from $105 a double; children aren't allowed. *Bushrangers* (☎ (066) 79 7121), on the Doon Doon road, has a small motel (from $75/95 B&B), a cabin away from the main area (about $95 a double) and campsites ($8), plus horseriding, a bar and restaurant. Nearby *Midginbil Hill* (☎ (066) 79 7158) has horseriding and canoeing on the Clarrie Hall dam, with accommodation and camping.

Getting There & Away

Bus The Fulton's bus running between Murwillumbah and Nimbin stops at Uki.

Car & Motorbike Uki is on the main road between Murwillumbah and Kyogle. The turn-off to Mt Warning is four km north of Uki; the turn-off to Blue Knob and Nimbin is 23 km west of Uki.

See the Mullumbimby section for information on a drive through the Nullum State Forest.

MT WARNING NATIONAL PARK

The dramatic peak of this 1156-metre mountain is a landmark dominating the NSW far-north region. Mt Warning is solidified volcanic lava – the remains of the central vent of a massive volcano 20 million years old. Lava covered 5000 square km, flowing as far as 100 km out to sea, but erosion has since carved out the deep Tweed and Oxley Valleys around Mt Warning. On the far sides of those valleys, the outer flanks of the volcano remain as the Nightcap Range in the south and parts of the border ranges to the north. Mt Warning was named by Captain Cook as a landmark for avoiding Point Danger off Tweed Heads.

The road into the national park runs off the road between Murwillumbah and Uki, four km before Uki. The car park at the start of the climb to the summit is about six km along this road.

The walk from the car park to the summit is less than five km long, but the last section – you climb right to the top of that peak – is steep, so allow at least two hours. Allow five hours for the round trip. Take water.

If you're on the summit at dawn you'll be the first person on the Australian mainland to see the sun's rays that day! Climbing in the dark to catch the dawn is feasible as the trail is well-marked, but take a torch (flashlight), partly so you don't get lost and partly so you don't tread on a snake.

Even if you don't want to climb Mt Warning it's worth visiting for the superb rainforest in this World Heritage Area. Near the car park there's a short walking track in the forest.

On the east side of the national park (turn off the Murwillumbah road at the village of Chillingham), the **Limpinwood Nature**

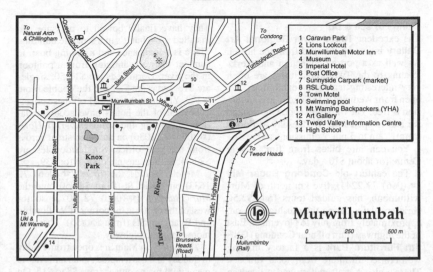

Key:
1 Caravan Park
2 Lions Lookout
3 Murwillumbah Motor Inn
4 Museum
5 Imperial Hotel
6 Post Office
7 Sunnyside Carpark (market)
8 RSL Club
9 Town Motel
10 Swimming pool
11 Mt Warning Backpackers (YHA)
12 Art Gallery
13 Tweed Valley Information Centre
14 High School

Murwillumbah

Reserve is yet another of the region's World Heritage Areas.

Places to Stay
You can't camp in the Mt Warning National Park, but *Wollumbin Wildlife Refuge & Caravan Park* (☎ (066) 79 5120), on the Mt Warning approach road, has tent sites ($10 for two people), on-site vans (from $24) and cabins ($35). The vans and cabins cost less if you stay more than one night. There are kitchen facilities and a well-stocked kiosk – and lots of wildlife in the 120-hectare refuge.

See the Uki section for more accommodation in this area.

Getting There & Away
Bus Fulton's (☎ (066) 79 5267) runs a bus on weekdays from Murwillumbah to Uki ($4.50), Nimbin ($12) and Lismore ($14), leaving Murwillumbah early in the morning and returning in the afternoon. It passes the foot of the six-km Mt Warning approach road, with some services going in as far as Wollumbin Wildlife Refuge. This is a schoolbus route so it's slow but the driver enlivens the trip with a running commentary on the out-of-the-way places you call into.

Buses in this area sometimes give discounts to YHA members and perhaps members of other backpacker organisations.

The hostels at Murwillumbah and Cabarita Beach can organise trips to the mountain, and the Uki Guesthouse should by now be running guided climbs for $15.

MURWILLUMBAH
Murwillumbah (population 8000) is in an area of banana and sugar-cane plantations in the broad Tweed Valley. It's also the main town in this part of the north-coast hinterland, and there are several communes and 'back to the land' centres in the area, plus Hare Krishna World. You're also within reach of Mt Warning and the spectacular NSW-Queensland border ranges. You can cross into Queensland by the Numinbah Rd through the ranges between the Springbrook and Lamington areas.

Information
The tourist information centre (☎ (066) 72 1340), the main one for the whole Tweed region, is on the Pacific Highway near the railway station. There is a good rainforest display.

NORTH COAST

Things to see & Do

The excellent **Tweed River Regional Art Gallery** is just up the road from the hostel. As well as a portrait collection and works relating to the Tweed area, there are often very interesting temporary exhibitions. It's open from Wednesday to Sunday and admission is free. The **museum** is on Queensland Rd and is open from Wednesday to Friday from 11 am to 3 pm. Admission is $1.

You can hire **bikes** from Jim's Cycle Centre for about $10 a day.

The century-old **Condong Sugar Mill** (☎ (066) 72 2244), five km north of Murwillumbah, has guided tours ($4, $2.50 children) daily during the crushing season, approximately from July to November. East of the highway (turn off near Condong) **Griffith Furniture Park** is a factory making well-crafted furniture from local timbers. There's also a craft gallery and a licensed restaurant here.

Stotts Island, in the Tweed River north of Murwillumbah, preserves some of the last rainforest in the Tweed Valley. Hourly cruises past the island depart from the Environment Centre on the highway between 10 am and 3 pm from Tuesday to Saturday and cost $6 ($4 children).

Avocado Adventureland, off the highway just north of Stotts Island, might make a good break for the kids, with some rides and native animals as well as many varieties of tropical fruit and a restaurant. It's open daily.

Places to Stay & Eat

Mt Warning Backpackers of Murwillumbah (☎ (066) 72 3763) at 1 Tumbulgum Rd is a YHA-affiliated hostel in a great location on the riverbank, with views of Mt Warning from the sunny verandah. You'll see the hostel on the right as you cross the bridge into town. This place has been in business for quite a while and has earned a good reputation as a relaxed and friendly place to stay. The managers try to have at least one group activity every day, such as a visit to a market, the Hare Krishna's Sunday feast, a communal meal (usually Filipino food) and the like.

They have finally bowed to pressure and installed a TV, but it's in a separate building. There is a free canoe and a rowing boat; in summer there's swimming from a pontoon in the river. Dorm beds are $13.50, singles are $18, twins are $26 and the double room is $29. YHA members get $1 off these prices.

Several of the hotels have accommodation, including the solid *Imperial Hotel* (☎ (066) 72 1036) on the main street across from the post office. Singles/doubles are $20/34, with an ensuite double for $39.

Motels include the *Town* (☎ (066) 72 1633) on Wharf St (from $40/50) and the *Murwillumbah* (☎ (066) 72 2022) southwest of the centre at the corner of Wollumbin and Byangum Sts (from $50/55). There are more along the highway.

The Eatery on Main St is open from Friday to Sunday and has a mixed Asian and Aussie menu with main courses from $8 to $15. On the first and third Sunday there's an all-you-can-eat 'mini' *rijstaffel* for $12.50.

Getting There & Away

This is the end of the northern rail line from Sydney ($75). There's a daily train which connects with a bus to the Gold Coast and Brisbane.

Murwillumbah is served by nearly all the buses on the Sydney (about $60) to Brisbane ($17) coastal run. Except for Kirklands, which goes into town, the long-distance buses stop at the railway station by the highway.

Fulton's Bus Service (☎ (066) 21 6231) runs to Uki ($4.50), Nimbin ($12) and Lismore ($14). Surfside runs to Tweed Heads ($3.80).

BORDER RANGES NATIONAL PARK

The Border Ranges National Park, a World Heritage Area of 31,500 hectares, covers the NSW side of McPherson Range, which runs along the NSW-Queensland border, and some of its outlying spurs. The park's damper areas protect large tracts of superb rainforest and it has been estimated that a quarter of all bird species in Australia can be found in the park.

NORTH COAST

There are three main sections. The eastern section, which includes the escarpments of the massive Mt Warning caldera, is the most easily accessible, via the Tweed Range Scenic Drive (see below). The smaller central section is accessible from the Lions Road (see the following Kyogle section). The large and rugged western section is almost inaccessible except to well-equipped bushwalkers, but there are good views of its peaks from the Kyogle to Woodenbong road.

The **Tweed Range Scenic Drive** – gravel but useable in all weather – loops through the park from Lillian Rock (midway between Uki and Kyogle) to Wiangaree (north of Kyogle on the Woodenbong road). The signposting on access roads to the drive isn't good (when in doubt take roads signposted to the national park), but it's well worth the effort of finding it. The road is unsuitable for caravans and large vehicles.

The road runs through mountain forest most of the way, with some steep hills and really breathtaking lookouts over the Tweed Valley to Mt Warning and the coast. The adrenalin-charging walk out to the crag called **The Pinnacle** – about an hour's walk from the road and back – is not for vertigo sufferers! At **Antarctic Beech** there is, not surprisingly, a forest of Antarctic beeches. Some of these trees are more than 2000 years old! From here a walking track (about five km) leads down to **Brindle Creek**, where there is stunningly beautiful rainforest and a picnic area. The road also runs down to Brindle Creek, so if there are a few of you, draw straws to see who gets to make the walk and who drives the car down. Cheat if you have to!

From the **Sheepstation Creek** campsite a walking track connects with the Caldera Rim Walk (three or four days) in Lamington National Park, over the border in Queensland.

Mebbin State Forest is by the eastern section of the Border Ranges National Park – this is the bush you will see if you dare to look down when you're on the Pinnacle. There's free camping at **Byrill Creek**, on the eastern side.

Places to Stay

There are a couple of National Parks camp-sites, basic but free, on the Tweed Range Scenic Drive. *Sheepstation Creek* is about 15 km north of the turn-off at Wiangaree (north of Kyogle) and *Forest Tops* is six km further on, high on the range. There are toilets but no showers. Tank water might be available but it's best to BYO.

KYOGLE

Much more a standard country town than other places in this area, Kyogle (population 3000) is a centre for the timber and beef industries. It's a jumping-off point for trips into the Border Ranges National Park and is on an inland route to Brisbane.

If you're interested in the alternative, check out the noticeboard near the small mall running off the main street diagonally opposite the Westpac bank. Amid the more prosaic ads about dances, car sales and courses, I saw a notice simply saying, 'Practise random acts of kindness and senseless beauty'.

To the west of Kyogle, the long **Richmond Range** has huge tracts of state forest. The Gorge Station near Bonalbo (see Places to Stay) has horse-trekking.

The agricultural show is held in early October.

Places to Stay

Kyogle Gardens Caravan Park (☎ (066) 32 1204) has sites and on-site vans. The *Exchange Hotel* (☎ (066) 32 1026) has accommodation, and there's also the good *Kyogle Motel* (☎ (066) 32 1070) which has singles/doubles from $40/48 to $48/55. The *Gorge Station* (☎ (066) 86 3447), near the small town of Bonalbo, has farmstays and horse trekking.

Getting There & Away

Train The XPT between Sydney and Brisbane stops here, but only if you give advance warning.

Bus Kirklands buses (☎ (066) 22 1499) run

between Kyogle and Casino ($5.90), connecting with buses to Lismore ($9.50).

Car & Motorbike Roads lead south to Casino, west into the Richmond Range and east to the Nimbin turn-off or on to Uki and Murwillumbah. Heading north you can turn off at Wiangaree, about 15 km north, for the Tweed Scenic Drive through the Border Ranges National Park. After Wiangaree the road curves west for the run to Woodenbong and eventually (after crossing the border near the intriguingly named hamlet of Legume) to Warwick. Just east of Woodenbong you can head north to the Mt Lindesay Highway to Beaudesert and Brisbane.

There's a shorter and more interesting route to the Mt Lindesay Highway, **Lions Road**, which was built by the efforts of local Lions clubs. Lions Road leaves the Kyogle to Woodenbong road five km north-west of Wiangaree, and follows the railway line

north to the border at Richmond Gap, then runs up to the highway. At Grady's Creek, seven km south of the border, there's a swimming hole and a free campsite. Further on you pass the Spiral Loop, where trains gain altitude before entering a tunnel through the McPherson Range. Just over the border there's another free camping area at Andrew Drynan Park. Note that the Grady's Creek section of the Lions Road can be cut off by floods.

See the New England map in the New England chapter for an overview of these routes.

Casino

Only 30-odd km west of Lismore but very different from towns in the hinterland, Casino is in beef country and is a typical old inland country town. The town is on the Richmond River and has a newly developed wetlands reserve as well as a folk museum.

New England

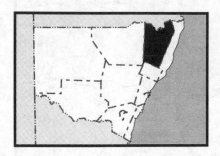

New England is the area on top of the Great Dividing Range, stretching north from around Newcastle to the Queensland border. It's a vast tableland of sheep and cattle country with many good bushwalking areas, photogenic scenery and, unlike much of Australia, four distinct seasons. If you're travelling along the eastern seaboard it's worth taking a longer route through an inland area like New England now and then, to get a glimpse of non-coastal Australia – which has a different way of life, is at least as scenic as the coast, and suffers from a great deal less tourist hype.

History
Graziers in search of new land first came to New England in the 1830s. At the time it was illegal for colonists to venture beyond the Hunter Valley, and these graziers became known as squatters because they 'squatted' on land that didn't belong to them. Although they were technically outlaws, many were eventually granted long leases on huge tracts of land and became influential citizens of the colony.

New England was once called New Caledonia, and that name should have stuck because of the large numbers of Scottish people involved in the area's settlement. Place names reflect this association – Armidale, Glen Innes, Inverell – and there's even a ring of Celtic-style 'standing stones' in Glen Innes.

Geography
New England is a large, high tableland. North of Armidale the plateau rises steeply and snowfalls are common in winter. The eastern edge of the tableland ends at the steep and often densely-forested escarpment falling to the coastal plains below. Along this edge is a string of fine national parks, some of them World Heritage Areas. Gorges and waterfalls are common features, and most parks offer at least basic camping. The western side of the tableland dwindles down to the plains.

Activities
Bushwalking Most of New England's national parks offer walking, some through very wild country.

Canoeing & Rafting The Nymboida River is popular for both canoeing and whitewater rafting. Every summer, water is released from Copeton Dam (near Inverell), turning part of the Gwydir River into a challenging whitewater course.

Two companies that offer rafting in New England are Whitewater Rafting Professionals (☎ (066) 51 4066) and Wildwater Adventures (☎ (066) 53 4469), both based in Coffs Harbour. You can probably arrange to be picked up from other places.

Horseriding Based in the Tenterfield area, Top of the Range Horsetreks (☎ (067) 37 3661) has rides ranging from half a day to six days.

Steve Langley (☎ (067) 32 1599) is based near Glen Innes and arranges 'pub crawls on horseback', lasting from three days to a week. These leisurely rides take you from village to village, staying at pubs, and cost around $900 for a week. The rides are suitable for any standard of rider (or drinker).

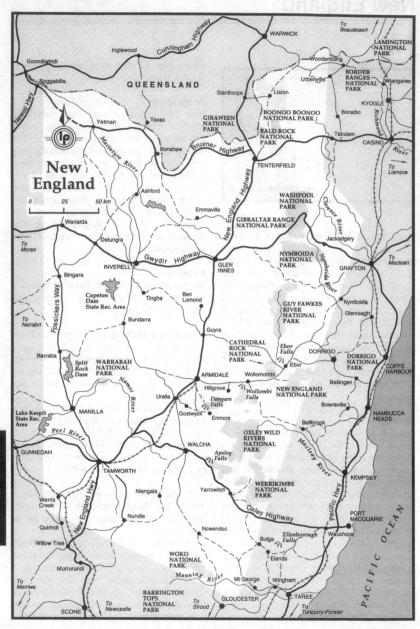

Also near Glen Innes, Paradise Creek station (☎ (067) 34 7206) offers five-day cattle-drive rides for about $500.

For experienced riders only, Double B Horseback Adventures (☎ (067) 78 2156) has rides through the rugged Blue Mountain Gorge near Enmore, south-east of Armidale. The three-day trek costs $120 per person per day, and longer rides can be arranged. A maximum of four riders can go along, and there's no minimum number. Max and Robert Brennan have mustered cattle in the area for most of their lives – Max first descended Blue Mountain Gorge at the age of 18 months, on the front of his mother's saddle.

Near Uralla, Harlow Park Riding School (☎ (067) 78 4631) has short rides and can arrange overnight or longer treks.

There are numerous other outfits in the area.

Fishing Trout fishing is popular and there are many stocked streams – the closed season is from the Queen's Birthday long weekend in June to the Labour Day long weekend in October. Other species are also fished. The various information centres have maps and further information.

Getting There & Away

Air Hazelton, Oxley and Eastern are among the airlines flying from Sydney to New England's larger towns.

Train Trains run from Sydney to Armidale ($58), from where Countrylink buses run up to Tenterfield.

Bus Several bus lines, such as Border Coaches (☎ (067) 72 5677, 1800 028 937 toll-free), Greyhound Pioneer Australia and McCafferty's run through New England from Melbourne or Sydney to Brisbane. Lindsay's runs between Tamworth and Coffs Harbour ($33.30) via Armidale. Kirklands has a Lismore to Tenterfield service ($21.60). Batterhams Express (☎ 1800 043 339 toll-free) runs between Sydney and Tamworth via the Hunter Valley.

Car & Motorbike The main route running through New England is the New England Highway, which runs up the Hunter Valley from Newcastle then heads north at Muswellbrook for its run across the tablelands to Warwick in Queensland.

An alternative route is the quieter Fossickers Way which skirts the western slopes of the tablelands as it runs between Nundle and Inverell.

Several major roads cross the tablelands and offer easy access to the coast to the east and the plains to the west. Climbing up to the tablelands from the coast is usually a spectacular trip through the forests of the Great Divide. The Oxley Highway begins at Port Macquarie, crosses the New England Highway near Tamworth and eventually runs down onto the plains and meets the Newell Highway at Coonabarabran.

The Gwydir Highway starts at Grafton, crosses the tablelands via Glen Innes and Inverell and meets the Newell at Moree on the North-Western plains. The Bruxner Highway begins near Lismore, runs through Tenterfield and meets the Newell Highway near Boggabilla.

In addition to these major east-west roads there are many smaller, often unsealed roads offering even more spectacular forest drives as they wind through the ranges. Head west on a minor road from anywhere along the coast and you'll almost guaranteed an enjoyable drive.

TAMWORTH

On the dry western slopes of the Great Divide, Tamworth (population 35,000) has little in common with the other major towns in New England. This is cattle country which ticks over to the plaintive twang of country music. The area's 'heritage' doesn't revolve around Scottish ancestors and misty moors, but around steel guitars and riding boots.

History

Much of the Tamworth area was taken up by the Australian Agricultural Company in the 1830s, after it 'traded in' its huge but unproductive land grant on the coast near Port

NEW ENGLAND

Stephens. The area wasn't opened up to small farming until early this century, when Tamworth became an important service centre for the beef, sheep and wheat farms which provide the area's wealth.

In the 1960s a Tamworth radio station organised regular concerts of country music, and in 1973 the first Australasian Country Music Awards were held. These are now the centrepiece of the big Country Music Festival held around the Australia Day long weekend (see Festivals & Events, below).

Orientation
Tamworth lies on the northern flank of the wide Peel Valley, between the river and a range of forested hills. Behind the city centre, the older residential area runs up into the hills, with fine views back across the valley. The newer areas of West and South Tamworth are south of the centre, on the flatter land across the river.

The New England Highway is called Goonoo Goonoo Rd (pronounced 'gunnag'noo') as it passes through the long sprawl of South Tamworth and crosses the Peel River to the city centre, where it becomes Brisbane St. Then, after a right-angled corner, it becomes Marius St, then Armidale Rd as it heads south-east on its way to Armidale (don't worry, it turns north some way out of Tamworth).

The main shopping area is bounded by Peel, Bourke, Marius and White Sts.

If you're standing at the corner of Kable and Brisbane Sts, waiting for those interminable lights to finally change, wander into the foyer of the swimming-pool building, where the Fisheries Department has some aquariums displaying local fish.

Information
The information centre (☎ (067) 68 4462) is in CWA Park, near the corner of Kable Ave and Brisbane St – coming from the south, turn left just after you cross the bridge.

Pick up a map of the Heritage Walk which begins at the information centre, or the longer Kamilaroi Walking Track which begins at the Oxley Scenic Lookout, high on a hill at the north end of White St. There are also maps of day tours around this interesting area.

The Lands Office next to the Post Office on Fitzroy St is in an interesting building and sells topographic maps.

For a very detailed guide to the area around Tamworth, buy a copy of Fred Hillier's *Fred's Tamworth Backtracks* at the information centre ($15).

Country Music Paraphernalia
The **Country Collection**, on the New England Highway in South Tamworth, 4.5 km south of the centre, is not hard to spot – out the front is the 12-metre-high Golden Guitar. Inside is a wax museum displaying effigies of 20 Aussie stars and, incongruously, a rock, gem and mineral display. It's open daily and admission is $4 ($2 children).

Also here is the **Longyard Hotel**, a popular venue during the festival and presenting C&W music through the year. They also hold diverse events such as cutting-horse competitions, cattle sales and highland games.

The **Winners' Walkway** in Treloar's Arcade off Brisbane St commemorates the winners of the Golden Guitar award. Near the information centre, the **Hands of Fame** are the hand-prints of country music luminaries. Not to be outdone, Tattersall's Hotel on Peel St has **Noses of Fame**! Other country music memorabilia around town include the collection of photos at the Good Companions Hotel, the guitar-shaped swimming pool at the Alandale Flag Inn Motel, and the Hawking Brothers memorial at the Country Capital Motel on Goonoo Goonoo Rd.

Tamworth's recording studios are sometimes open to visitors – ask at the information centre.

Oxley Marsupial Park
There are friendly kangaroos and other native animals at this reserve on Endeavour Drive, the northern continuation of Brisbane St. Nearby (but accessible from the top of White St) is the **Oxley Scenic Lookout**.

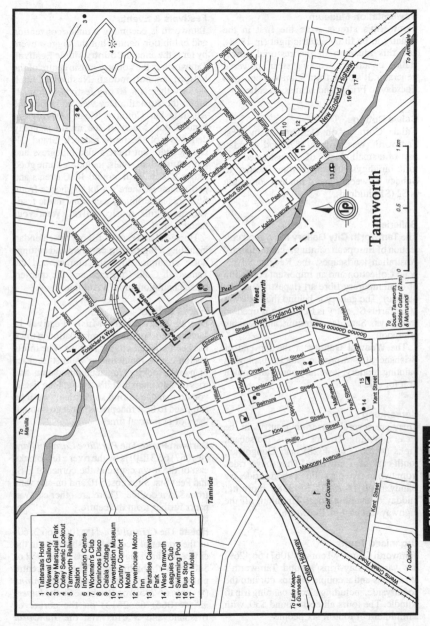

Tamworth

PLACES TO STAY
1 Tattersals Hotel
2 Weswal Gallery
3 Oxley Marsupial Park
4 Oxley Scenic Lookout
5 Tamworth Railway
  Station
6 Information Centre
7 Workmen's Club
8 Dominoes Disco
9 Calala Cottage
10 Powerstation Museum
11 Country Comfort
  Motel
12 Powerhouse Motor
  Inn
13 Paradise Caravan
  Park
14 West Tamworth
  Leagues Club
15 Swimming Pool
16 Bus Stop
17 Acom Motel

To Armidale

New England Highway

Oxley Highway

To Manilla

To Quirindi

To Lake Keepit
& Gunnedah

Wans Creek Road

To South Tamworth,
Golden Guitar (2 km)
& Murrurundi

Goonoo Goonoo Road

New England Hwy

West
Tamworth

Peel River

Taminda

Golf Course

Kent Street

Mahoney Avenue

Phillip

King

Belmore

Denison

Crown

Street

George Street

Matheute

Park Street

William Street

Bridge Street

Gipps Street

Ebsworth Street

Fossicker's Way

Peel Street

Marius Street

Kable Avenue

Macintyre Street

Darling Street

Upper Street

Brisbane Street

Jewry Street

Carthage Street

Rawson Avenue

Sheet Street

Hill Street

Napier Avenue

Dowell Avenue

Peel Street

Murray Street

Brisbane Street

Baker Street

Fitzroy Street

Bourke Street

East Street

1 km

0.5

0

Powerstation Museum

Tamworth's streets were the first in the country to be lit by electric light (in 1888), and this museum in the restored power station contains a working steam-powered generator. It's open from 9 am to 1 pm from Tuesday to Friday and admission is free.

Calala Cottage

Calala Cottage, on Denison St in West Tamworth, was built in 1875 and is today part of a small cluster of reconstructed historic buildings. It's open from Tuesday to Sunday between 2 and 4 pm and admission is $2 ($1 children).

Galleries

The **Tamworth City Gallery** has a good collection of European paintings, contemporary Australian landscapes, the Reagan Silverware Collection and an important collection of contemporary fibre art (tapestries, applique etc). The gallery is behind the library at 203 Marius St, entry is free and it is open on weekdays, Saturday morning and Sunday afternoon.

The **Weswal Gallery** at the top end of Brisbane St is a private gallery displaying painting, pottery, jewellery and crafts, much of it for sale.

Horseriding

There are several horseriding outfits in the area, including Tim & Julie's Horseback Treks (☎ (067) 69 4328) near Dungowan, south-east of Tamworth. They have rides from two to five days. For a shorter ride, try Bandyandah (☎ (067) 67 9386 morning, midday or evening), near Tintinhull off the highway just east of Tamworth.

Organised Tours

Tamworth Country Tours (☎ (067) 66 4269) has various day-trips around Tamworth's attractions and a couple of trips out into the countryside, including a gold-panning trip to Nundle. The tours all cost around $30, with a minimum of four or six people.

Festivals & Events

Tamworth is becoming a major convention and exhibition centre, but the biggest event by far is the annual **Country Music Festival**. Tamworth is the country music centre of the nation: an antipodean Nashville. Each January there's a 10-day festival, culminating in the Australia Day weekend when the Australasian Country Music Awards are handed out. Much of the music is pretty derivative of the more redneck Grand Ol' Oprey style, but there's also bluegrass and more Australian styles, including some good ratbag bands. With around 1000 events and performances, there's a lot to choose from. Still, this is definitely a *country* music festival, not a folk music festival. Wear your fanciest shirt.

Horse-related events fill out the calendar, including a big **racing carnival** and cutting-horse championships in summer, and the Tamworth Gold Cup race and the quarter-horse championships in Autumn.

Places to Stay

During the Country Music Festival in January, most of the accommodation in town has been booked out for months. The information centre maintains a 'waitlist' register of people looking for accommodation and tries to help them, but it's a long, long list. If you do manage to find something, you'll be surprised to hear that prices don't go through the roof at festival time.

Caravan Parks The *Paradise Caravan Park* (☎ (067) 66 3120) is by the river a few blocks east of the town centre at the corner of East and Peel Sts. Sites cost $10 and on-site vans from $25 a double. There are other caravan parks further from the centre.

Hotels The *Central Hotel* (☎ (067) 66 2160) on the corner of Peel and Brisbane Sts in the city centre has singles/doubles for $20/32 or $30/38 with bathroom. Other city-centre pubs include the *Good Companions* (☎ (066) 66 2850) on Brisbane St, the *Imperial* (☎ (066) 66 2613) on the corner of Brisbane and Marius Sts, the *Tamworth*

(☎ (066) 66 2923) on Marius St and the *Tudor* (☎ (067) 66 2930) on Peel St.

Motels Many of Tamworth's motels are enormous, and very few of them are cheap. At slow times of the year you might find a few motels offering rooms for $40 or $45, but don't count on it.

Along the New England Highway in South Tamworth there is a long strip of motels, and there's a smaller motel area along the New England Highway as it leaves town heading for Armidale. Here you'll find two of the largest and most expensive places, the *Country Comfort Inn* (☎ (067) 66 2903) at the corner of Murray St and the nearby *Powerhouse Motor Inn* (☎ (067) 66 7000), which describes itself as 'a boutique motel'. Further along is the reasonable *Almond Inn Motel* (☎ (067) 66 1088) which charges from $45/50, and several other places.

B&B & Farmstay There's a simple B&B at 10 Chelmsford St (☎ (067) 69 4279, 66 7276 AH), charging $40 a double. The breakfast is continental.

There are plenty of farmstays in the area; see the information centre for a complete list. *Echo Hills Station* (☎ (067) 69 4217; 1800 810 243 toll-free), 40-odd km east of Tamworth, is a working farm where there's lots to do. Backpacker deals start at $35 per person, including meals. Homestead accommodation costs $50/70 with breakfast, and a self-contained cottage sleeping three or four starts at $80 a day. Farm activities (optional) cost $25 and an overnight horseriding trip costs $80.

Places to Eat
Tamworth might be Australia's country music capital, but it isn't a cowboy town and some places to eat have dress restrictions.

There are plenty of cafes and takeaways on and near Peel St. The *Coffee Pot* on Fitzroy St is one of the larger cafes and has breakfast (bacon & eggs $6.50), steaks for around $10 and light meals such as hamburgers and salad for $5. Diagonally across the road, the *Night Owl Cafe* is a takeaway place

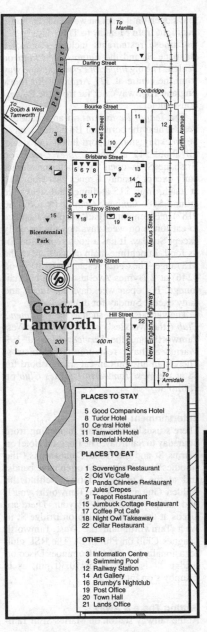

Central Tamworth

0   200   400 m

PLACES TO STAY

5 Good Companions Hotel
8 Tudor Hotel
10 Central Hotel
11 Tamworth Hotel
13 Imperial Hotel

PLACES TO EAT

1 Sovereigns Restaurant
2 Old Vic Cafe
6 Panda Chinese Restaurant
7 Jules Crepes
9 Teapot Restaurant
15 Jumbuck Cottage Restaurant
17 Coffee Pot Cafe
18 Night Owl Takeaway
22 Cellar Restaurant

OTHER

3 Information Centre
4 Swimming Pool
12 Railway Station
14 Art Gallery
16 Brumby's Nightclub
19 Post Office
20 Town Hall
21 Lands Office

NEW ENGLAND

that's open until 4 am on weekends and until midnight from Monday to Thursday.

Chinese restaurants include *Panda* on Brisbane St and the *Empress of China* on Peel St. The big *Imperial Peking* is some way from the centre at 327 Armidale Rd (New England Highway), not far from the Powerhouse motel.

The *Teapot Restaurant*, in an arcade off Peel St near the corner of Brisbane St, has a $6 weekday smorgasbord lunch and steaks for about $12 at dinner. *Jules Crepes* on Brisbane St is open for lunch and dinner daily except Sunday. Crepes cost from $10 at lunch, from $15 at dinner and steaks are around $18. *Jumbuck Cottage* (☎ (067) 66 1187) in Bicentennial Park is a pleasant place to eat lunch on weekdays and dinner daily except Sunday. It has a good reputation for its food. Lunchtime main courses are in the $13 range. The *Cellar* restaurant (☎ (067) 66 4246) at 2 Byrnes Ave also has a cocktail lounge. It's open weekdays for lunch and daily except Sunday for dinner.

The various clubs, such as the *Workmen's Club* ('the Workies') on Bridge St in West Tamworth and the *Services Club* at 199 Marius St have restaurants and bistros. There's an all-you-can-eat smorgasbord for $8 at the *West Tamworth Leagues Club* on Phillip St.

Entertainment

There's usually something happening from Thursday to Saturday. The Imperial Hotel on Marius St and the Good Companions ('the Goodies') on Brisbane St often have bands, and at the Longyard Hotel (behind the Golden Guitar in South Tamworth) you'll find music with a C&W flavour. There are discos at the Workies Club on Bridge St in West Tamworth and the West Tamworth Leagues Club on Phillip St. The RSL club occasionally has bands. Dominoes Disco on Bridge St is open from 10.30 pm, as is Brumby's on Fitzroy St.

Getting There & Away

At the railway station on Marius St in Tam-worth there is a Countrylink Travel Centre (☎ (067) 66 2357) .

Air Tamair (☎ (067) 61 5000) has five services a day between Tamworth and Sydney. Ansett, Eastern and Oxley also fly here.

Train Explorer trains run between Sydney and Moree via Tamworth. To catch the Armidale train you have to backtrack to Werris Creek.

Bus Batterhams Express runs down the Hunter Valley to Sydney at least once a day for $39, and other lines come through on the run from Brisbane to Sydney.

Getting Around

Bus Tamworth Bus Service has several services (weekdays and Saturday morning only) running from Kable St in the city centre down Goonoo Goonoo Rd to the Golden Guitar and beyond. The information centre has timetables.

Taxi You can often find a taxi on Fitzroy St near the corner of Peel St. If not, phone Tamworth Radio Cabs (☎ (067) 66 1111).

Car Rental The major companies have agencies: Avis (☎ (067) 65 2000), Budget (☎ (067) 66 7255), Hertz (☎ (067) 65 5344) and Thrifty (☎ (067) 66 9650); and there's a local company, Keft's U Drive (☎ (067) 66 2323).

WALCHA

On the Oxley Highway about 50 km east of the New England Highway, Walcha is a small town (population 1800) in pretty, rolling country. By the time you get to Walcha you have climbed onto the tablelands and there's a special feeling to the forested hills.

The information centre (☎ (067) 77 1075) is on Fitzroy St at the corner of South St, and there's a community craft shop on the premises. Walcha Taxis (☎ (067) 77 2255) offers **tours** of the town and area for $25 an hour.

A trip to Apsley Falls and back takes about three hours.

Explorer John Oxley passed through the area in 1818, and in the 1830s it was the first part of the tablelands to be invaded by graziers bringing their herds and flocks up from the Hunter Valley. The town dates from 1845, and the 1854 **Catholic church** on South St is one of the oldest remaining buildings. **Langford**, on the south side of the town, is a very impressive old homestead.

Walcha is the nearest town of any size to Oxley Wild Rivers National Park and the southern chunk of Werrikimbe National Park. The spectacular **Apsley Falls** are 18 km east of town, off the Oxley Highway.

Sheep and cattle are the important industries, but this is also timber country, and shops display signs saying that they support Forest Industries. A **Timber Expo** is held every second September. The three-day **Walcha Rodeo** is held in January.

Streams in the area are stocked with **trout**, and the season opens in October.

Places to Stay

There's a *caravan park* (☎ (067) 77 250), and pub accommodation at the *Apsley Hotel* (☎ (067) 77 2502). The *New England Hotel/Motel* (☎ (067) 77 2532) and the *Walcha Motel* (☎ (067) 77 2599) both charge from around $40/50. *Fenwicke House* (☎ (067) 77 2713) is a gallery and tearooms in an old house at 23E Fitzroy St, with accommodation for about $25 per person.

The old and atmospheric *Royal Walcha Road Hotel* (☎ (067) 77 5829) is about 20 km west on the road to Tamworth and has rooms at $25 per person with breakfast.

There are a few farmstays in the area. Contact the information centre for details.

Getting There & Away

Bus Lindsay's (☎ (065) 53 1277, toll-free 1800 027 944) comes through on the run between Armidale ($12.90 from Tamworth) and Coffs Harbour ($33.30) via Port Macquarie.

Car & Motorbike To get to Tamworth you

can travel about 50 km west on the Oxley Highway then 40 km south along the New England Highway, or there's an interesting, largely unsealed route via Nundle, about 45 km south of Walcha. See the Nundle section later in this chapter. Another pretty road, this one sealed, runs north to Uralla.

Heading east, the Oxley Highway plunges down the escarpment to Wauchope and Port Macquarie on the coast. You can also travel on small roads down to Gloucester, near the Hunter Valley.

OXLEY WILD RIVERS NATIONAL PARK

This park of scattered sections (90,270 hectares in total) east of Armidale and Walcha contains some of the best waterfalls and gorges. The **Wollomombi Falls**, 40 km east of Armidale, are the highest in Australia; **Apsley Falls** are east of Walcha at the southern end of the park. Down at the bottom of the gorges is a wilderness area, accessible from Raspberry Rd which runs off the Wollomombi to Kempsey road. The Armidale National Parks office (☎ (067) 73 7211) has information.

WERRIKIMBE NATIONAL PARK

This rugged and spectacular park (35,180 hectares) has remote-area gorge walking as well as more gentle walks around the visitor areas. Access is via the Kangaroo Flat road, about 50 km east of Walcha off the road to Wauchope. The Armidale National Parks office (☎ (067) 73 7211) has information.

URALLA

A small town (population 2300) on the highway, Uralla is a good place to break the journey. The information centre (☎ (067) 78 4496) is on the highway and is open daily. A **market** is held here on the second Sunday of the month.

Captain Thunderbolt (the dashing name taken by young Fred Ward when he turned bushranger) roamed through much of New England in the 1860s, and you'll see many sites claiming to be Thunderbolt's caves, rocks, lookouts, hideouts, etc. Thunderbolt was popular with ordinary people and seems to have performed many acts of kindness as well as robbery. He was killed by police near Uralla in 1870 and there's a statue of him on the highway in the town centre; his simple grave, still sometimes honoured with flowers, is in the cemetery. Whether or not Thunderbolt's body lies in the grave is another matter. There's a persistent rumour that he was spotted in Canada many years after the funeral.

The big **McCrossin's Mill Museum** has some Captain Thunderbolt artefacts (admission $2, 50c children). There's also a **foundry** which has been operating since 1872 and has a small museum (admission $2.50, $1 children) and **Hassett's Military Museum**. Burnet's Bookshop is a large antiquarian and second-hand bookshop on the main street, open daily.

There is a **fossicking area** with a picnic spot, about five km north-west of Uralla on the Kingstown road. Also in the area is Mt Yarrowyck, with some Aboriginal **cave paintings**. The information centre has detailed directions.

Places to Stay & Eat

There are a couple of caravan parks, the *Coachwood & Cedar Hotel/Motel* (☎ (067) 78 4110), *Thunderbolts Inn* (☎ (067) 78 4048) and one or two motels.

There were two interesting places to eat, but both were closing down at the time of writing. Hopefully something else will have opened by the time you get here. Try the pies baked by *Moon's Cakes* on the main street.

GOSTWYCK

If you're beginning to wonder how New England came by its name, visit Gostwyck, a little piece of England 11 km east of Uralla. This hamlet is comprised of the buildings and cottages of the Gostwyck sheep station. It's unusual for an Australian village to conform to the English pattern of the squire's house surrounded by the cottages of the labourers. There are long avenues of tall trees and a pretty chapel.

If you're heading to Armidale you don't have to return to the highway, as a partly-unsealed road from Gostwyck will take you there. This road passes turn-offs for the **Mihi Falls** near Enmore and **Dangar's Falls** south of Dangarsleigh.

At the Dangar's Falls turn-off you'll see a refreshingly eccentric **war memorial**, which was erected by a local landowner in honour of the people of the British Empire who 'went west' during WW I. You enter through a gate labelled Nirvana. A corporal with the same surname as the landowner is listed first on the honour roll, out of alphabetical order.

ARMIDALE

The main centre of the region and home of the University of New England (UNE), Armidale (population 22,000) is a popular halting point. The 1000-metre altitude means it's pleasantly cool in summer and frosty (but often sunny) in winter. The town centre is attractive, with a pedestrian mall and some well-kept old buildings.

With student numbers approaching 20,000 (although most students are external or study at campuses in other towns), the university has a huge influence on life in Armidale. As well, Armidale has a number of private boarding schools.

History

Graziers took up land in the Armidale area during the great White migrations up from the coast in the 1830s, and in 1839 the town appeared, named after the castle on the Isle of Skye – yet another of New England's Scots had a hand in its establishment.

Orientation

The New England Highway winds through the city, becoming Kentucky St, Dangar St, Barney St (briefly) and Marsh St. Barney St heads east to the national parks and on to Dorrigo or Grafton. The inner area of the city is a neat grid and the centre of town is the mall on Beardy St. There is some vehicle access to the East Mall between Marsh and Faulkner Sts; the block between Dangar and Faulkner Sts is for pedestrians only.

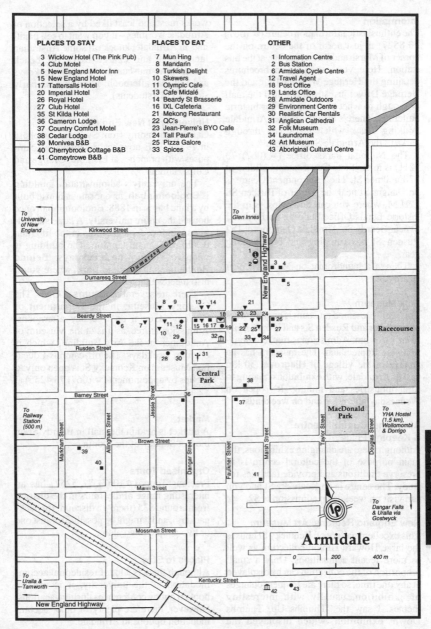

PLACES TO STAY

3 Wicklow Hotel (The Pink Pub)
4 Club Motel
5 New England Motor Inn
15 New England Hotel
17 Tattersalls Hotel
20 Imperial Hotel
26 Royal Hotel
27 Club Hotel
35 St Kilda Hotel
36 Cameron Lodge
37 Country Comfort Motel
38 Cedar Lodge
39 Monivea B&B
40 Cherrybrook Cottage B&B
41 Comeytrowe B&B

PLACES TO EAT

7 Mun Hing
8 Mandarin
9 Turkish Delight
10 Skewers
11 Olympic Cafe
13 Cafe Midalé
14 Beardy St Brasserie
16 IXL Cafeteria
21 Mekong Restaurant
22 QC's
23 Jean-Pierre's BYO Cafe
24 Tall Paul's
25 Pizza Galore
33 Spices

OTHER

1 Information Centre
2 Bus Station
6 Armidale Cycle Centre
12 Travel Agent
18 Post Office
19 Lands Office
28 Armidale Outdoors
29 Environment Centre
30 Realistic Car Rentals
31 Anglican Cathedral
32 Folk Museum
34 Laundromat
42 Art Museum
43 Aboriginal Cultural Centre

Armidale

0   200   400 m

To Glen Innes

To University of New England

Kirkwood Street

Dumaresq Creek

Dumaresq Street

New England Highway

Beardy Street

Racecourse

Rusden Street

Central Park

Barney Street

Jessie Street

Allingham Street

Markham Street

MacDonald Park

To Railway Station (500 m)

Brown Street

Dangar Street

Faulkner Street

Marsh Street

Taylor Street

Douglas Street

To YHA Hostel (1.5 km), Wollomombi & Dorrigo

Mann Street

Mossman Street

To Dangar Falls & Uralla via Gostwyck

To Uralla & Tamworth

Kentucky Street

New England Highway

42   43

Information

The enthusiastic information centre (☎ (067) 73 8527) is just north of the centre on the corner of Marsh and Dumaresq Sts, at the bus station. Here you can pick up brochures detailing the Heritage Walking Tour and the Heritage Drive; just strolling down the mall is enough to whet your appetite for historic buildings. There's also the longer Armidale Walking Track which takes you through parks to the Armidale State Forest.

The National Parks office (☎ (067) 73 7211) is in the State Government building at 87 Faulkner St. The Environment Centre is on Dangar St near the corner of Rusden St. C&LM, where you can buy maps, is in the historic Lands Office building on Faulkner St near Beardy St. Armidale Outdoors at 152 Rusden St has camping and bushwalking gear.

There's a laundromat on Marsh St near Beardy St.

Folk Museum

This well-presented museum is on the corner of Faulkner and Rusden Sts and is open daily from 1 to 4 pm. Admission is free, but donations are appreciated. The museum has an annexe in the village of **Hillgrove**, 30 km east of Armidale, with exhibitions relating to rural industries and mining. It's open on Wednesday afternoon and on weekends.

Aboriginal Cultural Centre & Keeping Place

Although there are changing exhibitions, the main purpose of the cultural centre is to preserve traditions and provide facilities for study. The centre is on Kentucky St and you can visit on weekdays; admission is $2.

New England Regional Art Museum

This excellent gallery on Kentucky St houses the large Howard Hinton collection as well as more recent acquisitions. Only a small proportion of the collection can be displayed at any one time, so there are frequent changes of exhibition, usually with interesting themes. I saw the 'Thumbs Up, Thumbs Down' exhibition, which displayed the works most and least liked by a selection of Armidale worthies – if you want to sell paintings in Armidale, knock off some Australian landscapes and charge extra for beach scenes! The museum is open on weekdays and Saturday afternoon; admission is a fairly steep $5 ($3 students).

University of New England

Gaining autonomy from Sydney University in 1938, UNE now has a network of campuses with branches at Lismore, Orange and Coffs Harbour.

The university's administration building is **Booloominbah**, an enormous house built by a land baron in 1888. Booloominbah once housed the entire university. A large stained-glass window depicts events in the life (and death) of General Gordon. The building is open to visitors on weekdays. Behind Booloominbah is a **deer park**, where you'll also meet wallabies.

There are several **museums** at UNE. The Zoology Museum in the Department of Zoology is open on weekday afternoons. Admission is free, as it is at the Museum of Antiquities in the Arts Building, which is open on weekdays. The off-campus Education Museum on Kentucky St is open only to groups by appointment (☎ (067) 73 4255) at $2 a head.

Market

A market is held in the mall in Beardy St on the last Sunday of the month.

Organised Tours

Precious Tours (☎ (067) 72 5257) has an interesting range of day tours in the district, from around $35 (there's a discount for backpackers), and it might be possible for just one or two people to go along.

Places to Stay

Although there is a lot of residential accommodation at the university, it is usually booked out by conferences during vacations. However, there are plenty of other accommodation options in Armidale.

Caravan Parks *Pembroke Caravan Park* (☎ (067) 72 6470) on Grafton Rd has sites from $11, on-site vans from $20/25 a single/double and cabins between $28/32 and $42/45. Grafton Rd is the continuation of Barney St (to the east) and the caravan park is about 2.5 km from the bus station.

The *Highlander Van Village* (☎ (067) 72 4768) on the New England Highway north of town has similar accommodation at similar prices.

Hostel Pembroke Caravan Park (see above) is also an associate *YHA hostel*, with a lot of bunk beds in one huge dorm, costing $12.50. There isn't a lot of privacy, but the facilities are quite good. Families might be offered an ensuite cabin at YHA rates.

Hotels The *Wicklow Hotel* (☎ (067) 72 2421), more often known as the Pink Pub, is on the corner of Marsh and Dumaresq Sts, across from the bus station. Beds in shared rooms are $12, singles cost from $15 and doubles are $24. The rooms are unheated and small, but they are clean and newly carpeted. Further south along Marsh St are the *Royal Hotel* (☎ (067) 72 2259) charging $20/33, and the *St Kilda Hotel* (☎ (067) 72 4459), charging $22/30 including breakfast. The problem with these three hotels is that semi-trailers grind past all night.

Tattersalls Hotel (☎ (067) 72 2247) is on the mall, so it has almost no traffic noise. Singles/doubles start at $22/34, $26/36 with shower but no toilet, and about $35/40 with ensuite facilities.

Motels There are more than 20 motels, and most of them are expensive. Cheaper places include the *Armidale* (☎ (067) 72 8122) north of town on the New England Highway (from $45/50) and the *Rose Villa* (☎ (067) 72 3872) further north (from $40/45). More central motels include the *Club* (☎ (067) 72 8777) on Dumaresq St near the bus station (from $50/60), *Cameron Lodge* (☎ (067) 72 5600) on the corner of Barney and Dangar Sts (from $60/70), the *New England* (☎ (067) 71 1011) at 100 Dumaresq St (from

$50/60) and the *Country Comfort* (☎ (067) 72 8511) at 86 Barney St (from $65/75).

B&B *Comeytrowe* (☎ (067) 72 5869), a large old house on the corner of Marsh and Mann Sts, charges $45/60. *Cherrybrook Cottage* (☎ (067) 72 4222) at 178 Allingham St and *Monivea* (☎ (067) 72 8001) at 172 Brown St are more modest places charging a few dollars less.

There are several other B&Bs a short way out of town, including *Glyngaye* (☎ (067) 75 1689), $30/50; *Poppy's Cottage* (☎ (067) 75 1277), $40/60; and *Hedgerow Farm* (☎ (067) 75 1689), $75/85.

Places to Eat
The central streets of Armidale have a wide variety of eating places.

QC's in Hanna's Arcade off the East Mall is a pleasant place with bacon & eggs from $7 and light meals through the day and some evenings. *Cafe Midalé*, further along Beardy St, has breakfast from $6 and a wide range of light meals in the focaccia/pasta vein, from $6. Still on the mall, closer to Faulkner St, the busy *IXL Cafeteria* has pasta from $4.

A reasonable place for an inexpensive meal is *Tall Paul's* on the corner of Marsh and Beardy Sts, with roasts ($7.50), steaks ($10) and a variety of less expensive eats such as burgers (from $2.70) and pasta (from $4). A short way up Marsh St is *Pizza Galore*, a pizza and pasta takeaway with sit-down meals as well. Pastas cost from around $7.50. The pizzas are good and cost from about $8.50.

On East Mall is *Jean-Pierre's BYO Cafe*, an odd combination of a country-town cafe and a French restaurant. It's open during the day and in the evening with a large menu of snacks and meals. Some dishes are French – all are cooked by a Frenchman. Beef bourguignon is $10.

On Rusden St near the corner of Marsh St, *Spices* is a licensed Indian restaurant with main courses around $10 to $13.

There are several Chinese restaurants, including *Mandarin* on Beardy St near the corner of Jessie St and the nearby *Mun Hing*

NEW ENGLAND

right on the corner. Mandarin has $5 lunch specials. *Mekong* on East Mall has weekday smorgasbord lunches for $6.50 and a smorgasbord dinner on Thursday for $8.50.

The new *Beardy St Brasserie*, upstairs near Cafe Midalé, is open from 6 pm until late for dinner and supper. It's sometimes open for weekday lunches as well. Focaccia costs from $7, pasta from $9 and main courses (including kangaroo steaks) are around $15. This is a lively place with good food and music (live on Friday and Saturday).

Squires Cottage Restaurant at the Country Comfort Motel on the corner of Faulkner and Barney Sts sometimes has an all-you-can-eat seafood buffet for $35 per person.

Entertainment
UNE is the entertainment hub, with films, theatre and music. Phone the 24-hour what's-on guide (☎ (067) 73 3100).

The Club Hotel on Marsh St has bands on weekends and the New England Hotel ('the Newie') on the mall has a dress-up disco. The Pink Pub sometimes has jazz on Sunday. Check the *Armidale Express* newspaper for other venues.

Getting There & Away
Train Armidale is a terminus for Explorer trains from Sydney ($58).

Bus Countrylink, McCafferty's, Greyhound Pioneer Australia and Border Coaches service Armidale, and there's a Lindsay's run down to Coffs Harbour and Port Macquarie, via Dorrigo. Fares from Armidale include: Sydney $49, Brisbane $44, Tamworth $12.60, Glen Innes $9.90, Byron Bay $45, Dorrigo $11.90, Coffs Harbour $18.30.

Car & Motorbike The New England Highway runs north and south from Armidale, and a good road runs east to the coast, passing through Wollomombi, Ebor and Dorrigo.

Getting Around
Taxi Phone Armidale Radio Taxis (☎ (067) 71 1455).

Bicycle Hire The UNE Sports Union (☎ (067) 73 2783) hires 18-speed mountain bikes for $17 a day, $25 for two days or $35 for a week. They also organise cycling tours in the nearby national parks. Armidale Cycle Centre (☎ (067) 72 3718) at 248 Beardy St (near Allingham St) also hires bikes.

The Failes Cycleway runs past the information centre out to UNE, a ride of five km, mainly through parkland.

Car Hire Realistic Car Rentals (☎ (067) 72 8078) at Armidale Exhaust Centre on the corner of Rusden and Dangar Sts has cars from $45 a day, including insurance and 100 free km. You must be over 23, and you can't go more than 100 km from Armidale (which rules out trips to the coast).

AROUND ARMIDALE
Saumarez Homestead
On the New England Highway between Armidale and Uralla, Saumarez is a beautiful house which still contains the effects of the rich pastoralists who built it. The station outbuildings are being restored. There are tours at 2 pm on weekdays and more on weekends. Admission is $4. One day in May a fair is held at the homestead, with hayrides and other entertainment. Saumarez is closed from June to September.

Views & Waterfalls
The Armidale area is noted for its magnificent gorges, many of which contain quite impressive waterfalls when it rains enough. Many of these falls are in national parks and there are often gorge walks at the bottom. The **Wollomombi Falls** are 39 km east of Armidale and close to the Armidale to Dorrigo road; they are the highest in Australia. Further along the same road, near the hamlet of Ebor, are the **Ebor Falls**. Closer to Armidale, off the road heading south to Gostwyck, are **Dangar's Falls**. **Apsley Falls** near Walcha rarely dry up.

NEW ENGLAND NATIONAL PARK
Right on the escarpment, New England National Park is a spectacular park of 30,000

hectares with a wide range of ecosystems. There is 20 km of walking tracks and, at the bottom of the escarpment, a wilderness area. Access is from near Ebor, and there are cabins and campsites near the entrance. Book these through the Dorrigo National Parks office (☎ (066) 57 2309).

Near the park and accessible from Ebor, *Little Styx River Cabins* (☎ (067) 75 9166 AH) date from the 1930s when they housed workers at a timber mill. They sleep up to 10 people and are comfortable but basic and there is no electricity. The cabins are close to the start of some walking trails in the national park and cost about $40 a double and $5 for each additional person. You can arrange fishing and horseriding trips.

CATHEDRAL ROCK NATIONAL PARK

Cathedral Rock National park is also near Ebor, off the Ebor to Guyra road. It's a small park (6500 hectares) with photogenic granite formations.

GUY FAWKES RIVER NATIONAL PARK

Protecting the rugged gorges of the Guy Fawkes River, this park of 35,630 hectares offers canoeing as well as walking, with camping on the pleasant riverflats. Access (not always easy) is from Hernani, 15 km north-east of Ebor. From here it's 30 km to the Chaelundi Rest Area, with campsites and water. The Dorrigo National Parks office (☎ (066) 57 2309) has information.

GUYRA

This small town (population 2000) is at the top of Devil's Pinch Pass, about 25 km north of Armidale, and at 1320 metres it gets pretty cold in winter. Guyra is at the beginning of the highlands of the New England tablelands, and nearby Chandlers Peak (1564 metres) is the highest point in the region. The C&W tear-jerker song *Little Boy Lost* tells of the desperate search in 1960 for a child who went missing 'in the wild New England Ranges' near Guyra. The town was deserted during the four days it took to find him.

The **Mother of Ducks** is a lagoon which was restored as a bicentennial project after

having been drained for farming. Birds are returning and swans again nest here. The lagoon is just west of the town centre and a path through the golf course leads to a viewing platform.

There's a **museum** on the main street, open on Sunday afternoon. Admission is $2 (50c students).

The **Lamb & Potato Festival** is held over the Australia Day long weekend in late January.

Places to Stay

There is a caravan park, the *Crystal Trout* (☎ (067) 79 1241) on the highway south of the town and pub accommodation at the *Royal Hotel* (☎ (067) 79 1005) and *Hotel Guyra* (☎ (067) 79 1018). The *Guyra Motel* (☎ (067) 79 1904) has singles/doubles for $40/50 and the *New Shiralee Motel* (☎ (067) 79 1380) charges from $35/40.

In Ben Lomond, a hamlet north-west of Guyra, *Silent Grove* (☎ (075) 33 2117) is a B&B place with woolshed accommodation, or you can camp.

Farmstays *Wattleridge* (☎ (067) 79 7593), north-east of Guyra, runs sheep, cattle and angora goats, has a large wildlife refuge, a fossicking area, horseriding and accommodation in self-contained cabins from about $35 per person. Other places include *Milani Trout Cottage* (☎ (067) 75 5735), *Shearers*

Lodge (☎ (067) 79 4235) and *Mosgeil* (☎ (067) 33 2048), a sheep and cattle property with farm holidays.

GLEN INNES

This highland town (population 6200) regards itself as the Celtic capital of New England. It does have strong Scottish roots – but having bi-lingual streetsigns (English and Gaelic) is stretching things a bit far.

The new information centre (☎ (067) 32 2397) is on Church St (the New England Highway) near the town centre. There's a National Parks office (☎ (067) 32 5133) at 87 Faulkner St.

Things to See & Do

This area was once known as the Land of the Beardies because of two hirsute stockmen on an early station who augmented their wages by selling advice to new settlers. The **Land of the Beardies History House** (☎ (067) 32 1035) in the old hospital (1875) at the corner of West Ave and Ferguson St (Gwydir Highway) is a big folk museum open from 10 am to noon and 2 to 5 pm on weekdays and weekend afternoons. Local archives are also kept here.

Grey St is well worth strolling down for its almost complete Victorian and Edwardian streetscape – above shopfront level, anyway. Have a look into Mac's Mall, once the huge MacKenzies Stores, with its impressive staircase and mezzanine levels. The Club Hotel (1906), the National Bank (1890), the town hall (1888 – see the proscenium arch in the ballroom), the courthouse (1874) and the post office (1896) stand out. The information centre has a handy guide to these buildings and a map of the longer Lands Office **town walk** which concentrates on the string of city-centre parks.

Overlooking the town from Centennial Parklands off the east end of Meade St (Gwydir Highway), the **Glen Innes Standing Stones** is perhaps the first array of standing stones to be erected for 3000-odd years. Based on the Ring of Brodgar in the Orkneys, the 33 huge 'stones' (they weigh up to 30 tonnes) were erected in recognition of the town's Celtic roots, and the traditional plan with its astronomical/mystical orientation is superimposed with other stones representing the Southern Cross.

Golden Wattle Galleries in the old butter factory at 176 Ferguson St has various arts & crafts (including blacksmithing) and a bookshop. The information centre has a brochure detailing other craftspeople in the district.

The information centre has a map of fossicking areas in the district, including **Dwyers Fossicking Reserve** where you fossick and camp for a small fee. The information centre also sells fossicking licenses ($2.50).

Festivals & Events

Glen Innes has plenty of festivals. A Celtic Festival is held on the first weekend in May. Minerama, a gem and mineral festival, is held on the first weekend in September. On the second weekend in October, the town celebrates itself in the Land of the Beardies Festival.

The Australian Bush Music Festival is held over the October long weekend and attracts about 100 artists; some are big names and an increasing number of them are Aboriginal. As the organisers point out, for an awfully long time Australian bush music was played on didgeridoos. It's a fun weekend of singing, dancing and workshops. The Koori Katerers prepare traditional bush tucker, and of course there are plenty of barbecues. Some years a special train runs to Glen Innes from Sydney and you can travel with many of the performers in antique carriages. For more information contact the organisers (☎ (065) 32 1359).

Places to Stay

The town's five caravan parks are along Church St (the New England Highway) and have sites for about $8 and on-site vans for $25 or less; most have cabins with attached bathrooms for about $35. Apparently the *Cragieburn* (☎ (067) 32 1283) on the New England Highway south of the town centre

Glen Innes

0   150   300 m

To Tenterfield

To Inverell

To Standing Stones (2.5 km) & Grafton

To Armidale

1 Swimming Pool
2 Land of the Beardies Museum
3 Royal Hotel
4 Courthouse
5 New England Motor Lodge
6 Imperial Hotel
7 Post Office
8 Great Central Hotel
9 Amber & Central Motels
10 Popular Cafe
11 Travel Agent
12 Town Hall
13 Information Centre
14 National Bank
15 New Tatts Hotel/Motel
16 Mac's Mall
17 Dragon Court Restaurant
18 Club Hotel
19 Hereford Restaurant

has a van which they let by the bunk to backpackers, and you can hire bikes here.

The impressive *Club Hotel* (☎ (067) 32 3043) on the corner of Grey and Wentworth Sts charges $25/38 or from $40 in the one room with an attached bathroom. The other pubs along Grey St – the *Great Central* (☎ (067) 32 3107), the *Imperial* (☎ (067) 32 3103) and the *Royal* (☎ (067) 32 3179) – charge a bit less.

There are several motels near the town centre, all fairly pricey but some pretty poor value. The *New England Motor Lodge* (☎ (067) 32 2922) on Church St near the

corner of Meade St is good but expensive, charging $50/57 and up.

There is another clutch of motels on the New England Highway a few km south of town, most in the $40/45 bracket.

In the village of Glencoe, on the highway 22 km south of Glen Innes, the *Red Lion Tavern* (☎ (067) 33 3271) has both atmosphere and accommodation at $30/35 for a room with attached bathroom. North of Glen Innes, about 30 km out on the Emmaville road, *Severn Valley Farm* (☎ (067) 34 7224) is a bio-dynamic farm and pottery with B&B from $25 per person and full board for $50.

NEW ENGLAND

Places to Eat

There are several cafes along Grey St. The *Popular Cafe*, next to Harvey World Travel, is average; if you want tablecloths try the *Tea & Coffee Shop* next to the town hall or the *Coffee Lounge* further south.

All the pubs have counter meals. The bistro at the *Great Central Hotel* on the corner of Meade and Grey Sts is better than average.

The very good *Dragon Court* Chinese restaurant on Grey St near the corner of Wentworth St is licensed and is open daily except Monday. There's a less grand and cheaper Chinese place further up Grey St, opposite the Westpac bank.

The restaurant at the *New England Motor Lodge* on Church St has a changing menu of interesting dishes such as emu and crocodile. The *Hereford Restaurant* at the Rest Point Motel on Church St is popular with locals for its steaks.

Getting There & Away

Air Oxley Airlines flies to Sydney at least twice daily for $189 (less with advance purchase).

Bus Long-distance buses stop near the information centre on the run between Sydney (from $48 with Border Coaches) and Brisbane (from $42 with Border Coaches). Greyhound Pioneer Australia also runs to Canberra ($73) and Melbourne ($111). Other fares include: Inverell $10, Armidale $11.10 with Countrylink but more with other companies; Warwick $36, Grafton $17.90, Lismore $36, Byron Bay $36, Moree $24.20, Tamworth $24.20.

Car & Motorbike If you're heading east on the Gwydir Highway to Grafton, note that Glen Innes has the last fuel for 130 km. The Gwydir Highway down to Grafton is a very scenic road, but to get off the beaten track take the Old Grafton Road: it turns off the Gwydir Highway about 40 km east of Glen Innes. The road, mostly unsealed but in fair condition, passes through a convict-built

tunnel, and there are good camping and fishing spots along the river.

GIBRALTAR RANGE & WASHPOOL NATIONAL PARKS

Gibraltar Range and Washpool National Parks, dramatic, forested and wild, lie south and north of the Gwydir Highway between Glen Innes and Grafton. Together they form a World Heritage Area, although it's only a decade or so since Washpool was saved from logging by a protest campaign. Except for the rest areas near the entrance, most of Washpool is a wilderness area (no vehicle access) of lush rainforest and river gorges offering challenging bushwalking; Gibraltar Range is drier country and features granite outcrops.

Countrylink buses running the Gwydir Highway from Glen Innes to Grafton stop at the Gibraltar Range visitor centre, the start of a 10 km track to the Mulligans Hut rest area, and at the entrance to Washpool, from where it's about three km to the Bellbird and Coombadjha rest areas, where you can camp and take a 10-km walking trail. National Parks offices in Grafton (☎ (066) 42 0593) and Glen Innes (☎ (067) 32 5133) have more information.

NYMBOIDA NATIONAL PARK

The Nymboida River and its tributary, the Mann River, flow through this wilderness and offer excellent canoeing and whitewater rafting. Although much of the park is rugged wilderness, the riverbanks are good places to camp. There are no facilities. To get there, head east from Glen Innes on the Gwydir Highway for 45 km, turning off onto the Narlala road and travelling another 35 km. You can reach the eastern end of the park from Jackadgery, further east on the highway. The National Parks office in Grafton (☎ (066) 42 0593) has more information.

TENTERFIELD

Tenterfield is a solid country town (population 3300), with frosty winters and clear, hot summers. To the east of Tenterfield there are

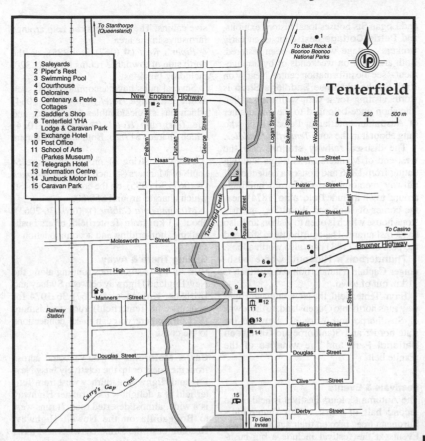

Tenterfield

1 Saleyards
2 Piper's Rest
3 Swimming Pool
4 Courthouse
5 Deloraine
6 Centenary & Petrie Cottages
7 Saddler's Shop
8 Tenterfield YHA Lodge & Caravan Park
9 Exchange Hotel
10 Post Office
11 School of Arts (Parkes Museum)
12 Telegraph Hotel
13 Information Centre
14 Jumbuck Motor Inn
15 Caravan Park

To Stanthorpe (Queensland)
To Bald Rock & Boonoo Boonoo National Parks
New England Highway
To Casino
Bruxner Highway
To Glen Innes
Railway Station
Curry's Gap Creek
Tenterfield Creek

forested ranges, but to the west the slopes of the tablelands descend to the plains and beef country. Heading north, Tenterfield is the last sizeable town before the Queensland border. At the junction of the New England and Bruxner highways, Tenterfield is also something of a travel crossroads, and is easily accessible from Lismore, so if you're staying on the far north coast the town is worth a visit to see something of the Australia that locals call 'real'.

Tenterfield claims the mantle of the town where Australia's path to Federation began, because of a speech made here by Sir Henry Parkes in 1889. (That claim is disputed by the Riverina town of Corowa.)

Information
The information centre (☎ (067) 36 1082) is on Rouse St, the main street, at the corner of Miles St.

Things to See
The School of Arts, on the corner of Rouse and Manners Sts, where Parkes made his famous speech, is now a **museum**, containing items related to the politician's career.

Centenary Cottage on the corner of High

and Logan Sts houses local history exhibits, and **Petrie Cottage** next door is an early workers' cottage which has been restored. Both are open on weekends or by arrangement – see the information centre. Nearby on High St, the old stone **Saddler's Shop** is worth visiting for a yarn with the saddler. The shop once belonged to the grandfather of Australian entertainer Peter Allen, who sang about it in the song *Tenterfield Saddler*.

The disused **railway station**, near the west end of Manners St, is a fine building dating from 1886 and houses a collection of railway memorabilia. Other old buildings around town include **Deloraine** (1874), near the corner of High and Wood Sts, an early stone house which is open to visitors and also has a restaurant. The courthouse (1885) and the post office (1881) are also worth a look.

Thunderbolt's Hideout, where bushranger Captain Thunderbolt did just that, is 11 km out of town.

From Tenterfield, the New England Highway runs north into Queensland, to the towns of Stanthorpe and Warwick. Between the state border and Stanthorpe are **Girraween National Park** and the **wineries** of the granite belt.

Festivals & Events

The Autumn Colours Festival is held in the second half of April, when Tenterfield's European trees take on their autumnal hues. Events at the festival include a big bushdance at the showgrounds.

Places to Stay

Tenterfield YHA Lodge (☎ (067) 36 1477) is a YHA-affiliated hostel/guesthouse at the west end of Manners St, near the old railway station. It's an ex-pub and most rooms have a couple of single beds and a double bed. Shared rooms go for $13 per person; a double or twin is $30. There's also a family room for $40. The hostel's kitchen and lounge are in an adjoining building, so there's no noise in the bedrooms. This place is also a small caravan park, with sites for $10, on-site vans from $22 and more expensive cabins. The managers can help arrange farmstays in the area.

Piper's Rest (☎ (067) 36 1885), on the north side of town, has rooms for about $20, including breakfast.

Several pubs have accommodation, such as the *Exchange Hotel* (☎ (067) 36 1054) which has singles/doubles for $15/25, and the *Telegraph Hotel* (☎ (067) 36 1014) which charges $17/26. Both are on Manners St.

There's a string of motels on Rouse St south of Manners St, including the *Jumbuck* (☎ (067) 36 2055), on the corner of Miles St, which charges around $50/60.

Mirrambeena Cabins (☎ (067) 36 2063), about 13 km from Tenterfield, offers bushwalking, horseriding and accommodation.

Getting There & Away

Bus As well as bus lines running along the New England Highway between Sydney and Brisbane, Kirklands (☎ (067) 36 1074 for bookings in Tenterfield) runs to Lismore ($21.60), where you can make connections to the coast.

Car & Motorbike If you've come across from the coast or up the relatively busy New England Highway, a journey west from Tenterfield is a delight – the Bruxner Highway is a wide, almost deserted road. It runs west to Boggabilla on the Newell Highway. Heading east, the Bruxner twists and turns over the ranges to Casino, then on to Lismore.

Heading south down the New England Highway, the next major town is Glen Innes; heading north, the highway continues to Warwick in Queensland. There's an alternative route to Warwick on the unsealed road that runs past Bald Rock National Park. This is a pretty drive, but be careful; although the road is wide and smooth it has a thick coating of fine dust which gives no traction at all if you have to brake or swerve.

BALD ROCK NATIONAL PARK

Bald Rock National Park (5450 hectares) is about 30 km north of Tenterfield, on an unsealed road which continues into Queensland. Not on the escarpment but in granite country, Bald Rock is a huge monolith which has been compared to Uluru. There are several walks to the summit: an easy two-hour walk, a long seven-hour walk and a steep straight-up climb. From the top you are rewarded with great views. There are basic camping areas near the base.

Access is from Tenterfield, off the road to Woodenbong, the unsealed route to Warwick.

BOONOO BOONOO NATIONAL PARK
Not far from Bald Rock, Boonoo Boonoo (2700 hectares) is an area of pretty forest where the main feature is a 210-metre waterfall which waters a pocket of rainforest at the bottom. There are no campsites, but you can bush-camp.

On the dusty road into Boonoo Boonoo, my car decided that it wanted to travel sideways, and I almost became intimately acquainted with a large tree. Be careful!

The Fossickers Way

The Fossickers Way runs from Nundle up to Warialda, then across to Inverell. It's more or less a middle north-south route between the Newell and New England highways. This interesting (and almost traffic-free) road begins high in the hills at Nundle, then skirts the western edges of the ranges and passes through rolling cattle-country, lower and drier than the tablelands to the east. Between Manilla and Warialda, the road runs between foothills of the Great Divide to the east and the rugged Nandewar Range to the west. On a hot day it's slightly reminiscent of eastern Swaziland, if you're familiar with that neck of the woods.

The Fossickers Way is so named because of the many sites where you might turn up anything from fossilised wood to diamonds. Several towns along the route have places which sell or hire the essential fossicking equipment: shovel, sieve and gold pan. You

also need a license, available from courthouses and many tourist offices for about $2.

Tamworth is on the Fossickers Way, between Nundle and Manilla, but it is also on the New England Highway and has been covered earlier in this chapter.

NUNDLE
Nundle (population 350), 63 km south-east of Tamworth, is in a valley of the Peel River, below a steep climb up onto the tablelands. In the 1850s there was a major gold rush in the area, and you can still fossick. As well as gold, sapphires and semi-precious stones can be found.

The shire council (☎ (067) 69 3205) is open for tourist information during the week, and you can pick up pamphlets any time.

The **Court House Museum** on Jenkins St is open on Sunday afternoon. Admission costs $1 (50c children).

In the hamlet of **Hanging Rock**, about 10 km east and some way up, there are views down to Nundle and winter snowfalls. You can camp here by the Sheba Dams, which were built during the gold rushes.

Places to Stay
There is a caravan park and pub or motel accommodation.

Getting There & Away
There is a sealed road from Nundle to Tamworth. A largely unsealed and hilly road runs to Walcha, passing through some lovely forest with many blooming wattles in late winter. Sadly, you'll also pass through vast pine plantations and areas where yet more irreplaceable forest is being bulldozed.

Other minor roads in the area head southeast to Nowendoc then on to Taree and Gloucester, offering spectacular drives that skirt the Barrington Tops National Park. You can also head south to Scone.

MANILLA
North of Tamworth, at the junction of the Namoi and Manilla rivers and about 40 km from Lake Keepit State Recreation Area, this small town (population 2300) is popular for

fishing. The town's name is a corruption of the name of the local Aborigines, the Manellae people.

In the early days of European expansion, Manilla developed as a stopping-place on the main route to the grazing lands of the Namoi Valley and the north-west.

The information centre (☎ (067) 85 1304) is at 210 Manilla St, the main street. The **Royce Cottage Museum**, also on Manilla St, comprises several old buildings and is open from 2 to 4 pm on Monday, Wednesday and Friday. Admission is $1 (50c children).

Dutton's Meadery (☎ (067) 85 1148), off the highway on the north side of town, is well worth a visit. Mead was probably the first alcoholic drink ever made and is mentioned in literature from many early cultures. It is still made without any chemical additives, with 12 months' fermenting taking it to 12% alcohol. It is claimed that the honey will ward off a hangover. At this quirky shop/ museum/pub you can sample meads and melomels (meads fermented with fruit juices) and perhaps buy a bottle. It's good value at $6 for the dry and semi-dry version and $8 for the full-flavoured sweet blend. They also sell honey and some souvenirs. The meadery is open daily and you're sure of a good chat with Mr Dutton.

Warrabah National Park, 35 km north-east of Manilla, is centred on a gorge in the Namoi River and has bushwalking and climbing as well as canoeing. There are basic campsites. There's a challenging three-day canoe trip from the village of Retreat, east of the park, to Lowry Creek within the park – a 250 metre drop over 15 km, with plenty of rapids and portages. It's for experienced canoeists only.

Lake Keepit State Recreation Area, south-west of Manilla and also accessible from the Gunnedah to Tamworth road, is a large artificial lake catering to watersports. There's also a soaring (gliding) club (☎ (067) 69 7640). The large *Easts Van Park* (☎ (067) 69 7620) has accommodation. With a BMX track, jet-skiing and powerboating on the lake, this isn't exactly a sleepy place during school holidays.

Places to Stay
A few km before Manilla on the road from Tamworth, you'll see a sign with the youth hostel symbol directing you to a rest area. There is no youth hostel.

Manilla St's four pubs all have accommodation, and there's the *Manilla Motel* (☎ (067) 85 1306) on the corner of Namoi and Court Sts.

BARRABA
This quiet little town (population 1400) on the Manilla River is in prime sheep country, but it's feeling the effects of the rural recession, with quite a few empty shops.

There's an information centre (☎ (067) 82 1255) in a shop near the war memorial on Queen St, the main street. Ask here about having the **museum** opened for you. There are a couple of caravan parks, a motel and several pubs with accommodation; the best is probably the *Commercial* (☎ (067) 82 1023) which charges about $20.

BINGARA
On the Gwydir River, Bingara is an even smaller town than Barraba, with a population of 1200. Finch St, the main street, is planted with orange trees as a war memorial. The oranges are left untouched until a special ceremony in mid-June when they are picked by school children.

The council (☎ (067) 24 1505) on Maitland St has tourist information, as does the Fossickers Way Motel. Pick up a brochure about the fossicking sites in this geologically diverse area. Also ask about visiting the **museum** in the old Satter's Hotel in Maitland St. The Imperial Hotel has information on **canoeing** on the Gwydir (peaceful most of the year, highly exciting in late spring) and might be able to help with canoe hire. The big **Copeton Dam State Recreation Area** is about 45 km east of town.

Places to Stay & Eat
The *caravan park* (☎ (067) 24 1209) is close to the river. It's a good place and is run by the council. The *Imperial Hotel* (☎ (067) 24 1629) is an old (1879) pub catering to 'back-

packers and travellers of all ages'. The managers can help you organise outings and activities in the district. Rooms cost $20/30. There's also the *Fossickers Way Motel* (☎ (067) 24 1371) on Finch St.

There are a few cafes and takeaways on the main street. The *Roxy Coffee Lounge* has the usual menu of grills and snacks, but it has been built in the foyer of the disused cinema and, as well as being an interesting space, it's a dim, cool retreat on a hot day. The motel has a *restaurant* and there's an *RSL Club*.

INVERELL

A large (population 10,000) and pleasant country town with some impressive public buildings, Inverell is at the centre of a sapphire mining area. Other stones, such as diamonds, are also found.

Until they are cut, sapphires aren't especially impressive. There's a story, probably apocryphal, that a few years ago the council was resurfacing a stretch of road and one truckload of gravel had a blue look to it. 'Couldn't be, there's too many of the bastards,' was the road crew's verdict, but who knows?

Orientation & Information

Inverell's main shopping street is Otho St, with another shopping strip on Byron St.

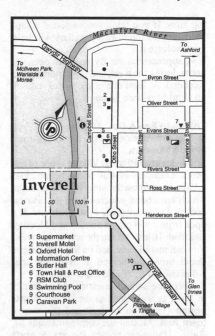

Inverell

1 Supermarket
2 Inverell Motel
3 Oxford Hotel
4 Information Centre
5 Butler Hall
6 Town Hall & Post Office
7 RSM Club
8 Swimming Pool
9 Courthouse
10 Caravan Park

The information centre (☎ (067) 22 1693) is in a converted water-tower on Campbell St, a block back from Otho St. It's open from 9 am to 4 pm on weekdays and until noon on Saturday. Pick up a map of the area's fossick-

---

The Myall Creek Massacre

In 1838, not far from present-day Bingara, stockmen from the Myall Creek station rounded up 28 men, women and children, hacked them to death with knives and swords, then made a half-hearted attempt at burning the bodies.

What is unusual about the Myall Creek massacre is not that it happened but that we know about it – the stockmen were White, their victims Aborigines. By a series of accidents, a report of the massacre reached Governor Gipps and he ordered that the stockmen be prosecuted. Amidst shocked protests from across the colony, seven of the murderers were hung. It was the first and one of the last times that Whites were hung for the murder of Aborigines.

Historians assume that such massacres were routine in the 'clearing' of new grazing lands (the Myall Creek stockmen had apparently been involved in at least one other massacre), but because the new frontiers kept pushing way past the reach of the law – and because the new settlers saw Aborigines as vermin to be casually eradicated – little concrete evidence is available.

Massacres such as Myall Creek weren't just the work of semi-barbaric station workers, who were usually following at least implicit orders. Myall Creek was owned by Henry Dangar, an educated Englishman who had helped set up the huge Australian Agricultural Company holdings in the Hunter Valley and through New England and the north-west. His voice was amongst the loudest protesting against the trial, and he raised money to pay for his stockmen's defence. ■

ing sites. If you think you've found a sapphire, any of the town's jewellers will help you evaluate it.

A supermarket on Byron St is open 24 hours during the week and long hours on the weekend. At least one of the petrol stations on Otho St is open 24 hours.

Things to See & Do

In the information centre there's a small **Mining Museum**.

The **Inverell Pioneer Village** is one of the better examples of this phenomenon. The village is composed mainly of old buildings which have been gathered from the district, and it's a pleasant place to stroll around. It's open from 2 to 4 pm on Sunday and Monday and from 10 am to 5 pm the rest of the week. You can fossick here, and on Sunday damper (bush bread) is served at afternoon tea. Admission is $3 ($1.50 children).

There are some interesting old buildings in town as well, such as the superb **courthouse** (1886) on Otho St and the nearby **town hall**. Around the corner in Evans St, Butler Hall now houses the **art & craft gallery**, open on weekdays and Saturday morning. Views over the town and the area can be had from **McIlveen Park**, west of town off Warialda St.

About five km south of Inverell, off the Tingha road, the **Goonoowigall Bushland Reserve** surrounds the site of Ferndale, a small settlement which became derelict early this century. There are several short walking tracks and quite a lot of wildlife in the bush.

Festivals & Events

Inverell's Sapphire City Floral Festival is held over two weeks in the middle of October. There's a wide range of events and a parade.

Places to Stay

Fossickers Rest Caravan Park (☎ (067) 22 2261) has sites, on-site vans and cabins.

In the centre of town on Otho St, the *Oxford Hotel* (☎ (067) 22 1101) has B&B from $20. Next door, *Motel Inverell* (☎ (067)

22 2077) charges from $40/50. There are several other motels.

West of Inverell, near the village of Delungra, *Myall Downs* (☎ (067) 23 6421) has farmstays for about $80 per person with full board, less for fewer meals, and a self-catering cottage for $30 per person. They will pick you up from Inverell.

Places to Eat

The *RSM Club* on Evans St has very cheap meals in the family restaurant, and more expensive meals in the Anzac Restaurant.

Getting There & Away

Air Harvey World Travel (☎ (067) 22 3011) at 17 Byron St (opposite the Coles supermarket) is the Eastern Australian airline agent; Inverell Travel (☎ (067) 22 2001) on Otho St is the Oxley airline agent.

Bus Long-distance buses stop at the information centre on Campbell St. Border Coaches pass through Inverell on their Brisbane to Sydney run. Fares include: Brisbane $50, Tenterfield $24, Glen Innes $10, Armidale $20, Muswellbrook $40 and Sydney $50. Countrylink has a service from Tamworth and Armidale. Harvey World Travel and Inverell Travel both handle bus bookings.

Car & Motorbike The Gwydir Highway runs west to Moree and east to Glen Innes. Smaller roads run south to Tingha and Bundarra, from where you can head west to Barraba (a nice drive) or east to Uralla on the New England Highway. North from Inverell, small roads run up to Ashford and on to the Bruxner Highway.

AROUND INVERELL

The **Dejon Sapphire Centre**, on the Gwydir Highway 20 km east of Inverell, is a working sapphire mine where you can see the sorting and cutting of the stones.

As well as sapphires, silver has been mined in the area and you can tour the old Conrad and King Conrad **silver mines** at 9 am, noon and 3 pm daily except Friday, for

$5. The mines are near the hamlet of Howell, south of Inverell near the south-east corner of the big Copeton Dam. Head south on the Bundarra road for 21 km, take the Lake Copeton turn-off and travel nine km to Wattle Grove (☎ (067) 23 3326), the reception area. There's a fossicking area nearby.

The Gilgai **winery**, about 10 km south of Inverell on the Bundarra road, was established in the late '60s, but wine was produced in this area as early as the 1850s. The winery is open for tastings and sales from 10 am to 6 pm Monday to Saturday (closed Wednesday afternoon) and from noon on Sunday.

At the village of **Tingha**, 25 km south-east of Inverell, beyond Gilgai, there was a tin-mining boom in 1870, which attracted many Chinese diggers. Large-scale mining soon took over from the small operators, and it continues today. The active Nucoorilma Aboriginal Corporation on Amethyst St sells local art & craft, and there are plans to open a roadside cafe selling bush tucker.

Green Valley Farm (☎ (067) 23 3370), 10 km south-east of Tingha, has children's rides, a museum (featuring grotesqueries such as an eight-legged kitten and 'Siamese' pigs) and a small zoo. Cabin accommodation is available.

Copeton Dam State Recreation Area, south-west of Inverell, is a large dam very popular for boating. There's a caravan park (☎ (067) 23 6269).

The **Draught Horse Centre** (☎ (067) 22 1461), a few km from Inverell town centre, raises four breeds of these magnificent beasts. They currently accept only group bookings for visits, but that might change. Ask at the information centre.

North towards the Queensland border, the **Limestone Caves** are about 30 km from the village of Ashford. Main Cave is over half a km long and leads on to Great Cave, which is almost as large. About five km north of here on the Macintyre River are the **Macintyre Falls**, with some rugged gorges, swimming holes and campsites.

WARIALDA

The local Weraerai people named the area Warialda ('place of wild honey'), and a profusion of springtime flowers blooms in the nearby bush. The town was founded in the 1840s (there are some old buildings) and has grown to become a regional centre with a population of 1400.

The council office on Hope St has tourist information (☎ (067) 29 1016). The **Koorilgur Nature Walk** through the bush on the edge of town is a good way to see wildflowers. Eight km east of Warialda, **Cranky Rock** is a small nature reserve on Reedy Creek where a 'cranky' (mad) miner last century is supposed to have jumped to his death from one of the big balancing rocks.

Accommodation is available at the *caravan park* (☎ (067) 29 1295), the *Royal Hotel* (☎ (067) 29 1444) and the *Sunflower Motel* (☎ (067) 29 1344). For information on farmstays in the area, contact Joy Tremain (☎ (067) 29 5716) or Audrey Hill (☎ (067) 29 1112).

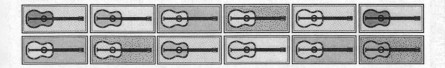

The Central West

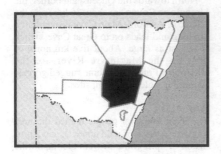

The central west takes in some of the richest farmland in Australia. Although the area has an aura of being utterly typical, it is unique in NSW (and perhaps Australia) with its relatively close settlement and liberal sprinkling of fair-sized towns. The central west is solid, respectable and, above all, rural. With some notable exceptions, such as the Western Plains Zoo in Dubbo, there isn't a lot in the way of tourist-oriented attractions – but this in itself is an attraction.

History
Much of the central west area was owned by the Wiradjuri people before the Europeans arrived.

Soon after Blaxland, Wentworth and Lawson found a path through the Blue Mountains in 1813, the young colony was able to expand to the inland plains. A road across the mountains was built in just two years and Governor Lachlan Macquarie ordered the founding of Bathurst. It was Australia's first inland town (if you don't count Sydney's satellite villages) and the first to be built on a river that flowed towards the inland.

Settlement was at first restricted because the government was concerned about convicts escaping into the vast inland, and because the size and purpose of the colony was still a matter for debate – did Britain

really *want* a huge colony on this continent? The government would have to administer and police new settlements, and this could be an expensive business if they spread too far. Anyway, the new road over the Blue Mountains was too rough to provide ready access to the Sydney markets. Sections were so steep that wagons had to be hauled up and down, and it wasn't until the Victoria Pass route was built in the 1830s that coaches were able to cross. Despite this, cattle and sheep were moved across into the new country, and before long Europeans were widely but thinly spread. Very little is known of their adventures. They were mainly illiterate shepherds and drovers who kept well away from people who might write their stories in official reports, but there must have been some interesting stories told in the pubs of Bathurst town.

Although most of the land had been taken up by squatters, the White population remained small until a string of gold rushes began at Ophir in 1851. For the next 50 years the hint of gold sent tides of diggers pouring from one hastily-built town to another, with the lucky and the disillusioned staying behind to farm or develop the township.

Geography
The area is bounded on the east by the Great Divide and to the west by the vast outback plains. North of Dubbo the Liverpool Range separates the central west from the more sparsely populated north-west of the state, and in the south the Murrumbidgee marks the beginning of the Riverina. Geographically the central west is a diverse area, including some of the Great Divide's high tablelands (around Bathurst and Orange), the western slopes (all the way from Mudgee south to Cootamundra), and the flatter land west of here, tailing off into the dry western plains.

The Lachlan River, rising in the Great Divide near Crookwell and flowing west

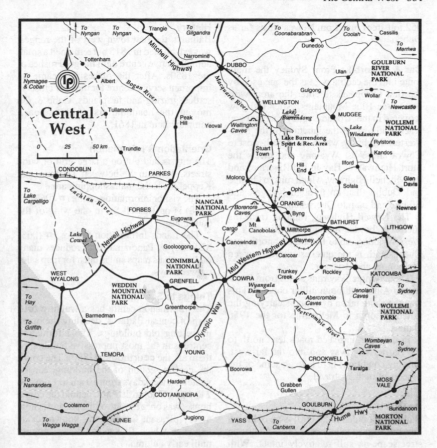

through Cowra, Forbes and Condoblin, is the heart of the area and passes through some very different but always beautiful country. Like most of the state's inland rivers, it eventually enters the Murray River (via the Murrumbidgee) and reaches the sea in South Australia.

Getting There & Around

Air The central west region is well served by air. From Dubbo ($155 from Sydney with Eastern or Hazelton) there are flights to other places in the central west and the far west of the state.

Train Trains run from Sydney to Lithgow ($18), Bathurst ($25), Orange ($35) and Dubbo ($51). From those centres, connecting buses run to most other towns, including Cowra ($37 from Sydney), Forbes ($45), Grenfell ($42) and Mudgee ($33).

Bus Major bus-lines have services running through the central west region on routes between Sydney and Broken Hill or Adelaide, and from Brisbane to Melbourne or Adelaide. Local area companies include Rendell's Coaches (☎ (068) 84 4199; 1800 023 328 toll-free). Sid Fogg's (☎ 1800 045

952 toll-free) runs from Newcastle as far as Dubbo.

Car & Motorbike From Sydney the main route into the central west is the one used by the first Europeans to enter the area: west across the Blue Mountains. After Lithgow (covered in the Around Sydney chapter) you reach Bathurst, at the junction of the Mid-Western Highway, which runs south-west to Cowra and West Wyalong and meets the Sturt Highway at Hay in the Riverina; and the Mitchell Highway, which runs to Orange and Dubbo then up through Nyngan and Bourke and on into Queensland.

The Newell Highway, running from the Victorian border through the Riverina to West Wyalong, up to Dubbo and north into Queensland, is the quickest route between Melbourne and Brisbane.

The Olympic Way runs south from Bathurst to Albury, through hillier country. This was the route taken by runners carrying the Olympic torch to Melbourne for the 1956 Games.

In the west, unsealed roads lead north to the Barrier Highway and into the far west. Driving conditions here take on some of the aspects of outback travel.

BATHURST

Bathurst (population 26,000) is an old town laid out to a grand scale, and its Victorian streetscape is still relatively intact. With European trees in the streets and a cool climate, its atmosphere is very different from other Australian country towns. Some of the city centre's streets are still lit by lines of old lamps running down the middle of the road. (This is sometimes the only street lighting and it isn't very effective. Also watch out for the metal cylinders set in the centre of wide intersections, designed to keep you on the correct side of the road. These are known as silent policemen or, colloquially, dumb cops.)

As well as its architectural and historical interest, Bathurst hosts the annual Bathurst 1000 production car race in early October.

History

Bathurst, the first town west of the ranges, was established in 1815 but remained a small administrative centre until the gold rushes of the 1850s. After the rushes it became an important service centre for the now closely-settled grazing and farmlands. Cobb & Co moved the headquarters of their coach company here in 1861.

Orientation & Information

The city is laid out on a large grid of wide streets. William St between Durham and Keppel Sts is the main shopping area.

The visitor information centre (☎ (063) 33 6288) is on Russell St, in one wing of the courthouse.

The Lands Information Centre (☎ (063) 32 8200) on Panorama Ave produces many of Australia's maps and is open for map sales on weekdays.

Things to See

The information centre has a **walking tour** map of central Bathurst, detailing the many interesting old buildings. The information centre is in the most impressive building of them all, the **courthouse** (1880). The court, the central section of the building, can be visited on weekdays from 10 am to 1 pm and 2 to 4 pm. **Machattie Park**, behind the courthouse, was once the site of the jail and is now a very pleasant formal park, known for its begonias which flower from late summer until early autumn.

Most of the town's buildings date from the boom following the gold rushes but **Government Cottage**, a small brick building behind 1 George St, was built soon after Bathurst was founded. The apricot tree is 170 years old. Another early house is **Miss Traill's House** at 321 Russell St, built around 1845. Members of the same family lived here from the time it was built until it was donated to the National Trust in the 1970s. The house is open on Sunday from 11 am to 4.30 pm.

The newly renovated **Royal Hotel** on William St near Russell St is a fine example of a boom-era pub – no longer operating as one, unfortunately. The **railway station**,

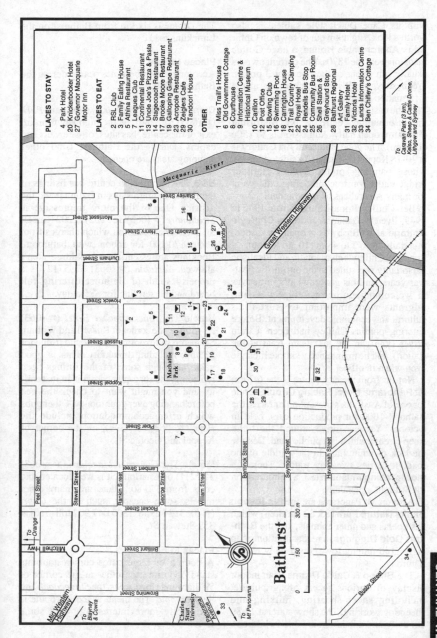

PLACES TO STAY

4 Park Hotel
20 Knickerbocker Hotel
27 Governor Macquarie
Motor Inn

PLACES TO EAT

2 RSL Club
3 Family Eating House
5 Athina Restaurant
7 Leagues Club
11 Continental Restaurant
13 Uncle Joe's Pizza & Pasta
14 Stagecoach Restaurant
17 Brooke Moore Restaurant
19 Galloping Grape Restaurant
23 Acropole Restaurant
29 Zeiglers Cafe
30 Tandoori House

OTHER

1 Miss Traill's House
6 Old Government Cottage
8 Courthouse
9 Information Centre &
Historical Museum
10 Carillon
12 Post Office
15 Bowling Club
16 Swimming Pool
18 Carrington House
21 Trail Country Camping
22 Royal Hotel
24 Rendells Bus Stop
25 Community Bus Room
26 Shell Station &
Greyhound Stop
28 Bathurst Regional
Art Gallery
31 Family Hotel
32 Victoria Hotel
33 Lands Information Centre
34 Ben Chifley's Cottage

Bathurst

with its Cape Dutch-style gables, is also worth a look. Eight km out of town on Ophir Rd is **Abercrombie House**, a huge Gothic mansion from the 1870s. The current owners usually run a tour of the house at 3 pm on Wednesday, but it's worth checking at the information centre as times change.

In the east wing of the courthouse, next to the information centre, is the **Historical Museum**, open daily. Admission is $1 (50c children). The good **Regional Art Gallery** is at 70-78 Keppel St. Grace Cossington Smith, whose paintings of the Sydney Harbour bridge under construction defined the event for many Australians, is represented.

Ben Chifley, Prime Minister from 1945 to 1949, lived in Bathurst, and **Ben Chifley's Cottage** at 10 Busby St is open for inspection daily from 2 to 4 pm (10 am to noon on Sunday). Chifley's charismatic and idealistic personality was suited to the optimistic postwar years, and his government's initiatives in welcoming European refugees as immigrants were important to Australia's cultural and economic development. Before entering politics Chifley had been a train driver (you can see his steam train at the station), and he maintained a simple lifestyle even when in office.

Not far from the city centre is the 6.2 km **Mt Panorama Motor Racing Circuit**, venue for one of Australia's most popular races, the Bathurst 1000 for production cars, held in October. You can drive around the tight, steep circuit, which is a public road. Despite the lack of white lines in the middle of the road, it carries two-way traffic. There's a **motor racing museum** ($3, $1 children) on Pit Straight, open daily.

Also on Mt Panorama are the **Sir Joseph Banks Nature Park** ($5, $2 children) which has koalas and other animals, and the **Bathurst Gold Diggings**, a reconstruction of an early gold-mining town, open daily except Saturday.

The **Sheep & Cattle Drome** is an indoor display of various facets of agriculture, including sheep-shearing, milking and sheepdog working. The show starts at 11.30 am daily and admission is $8 ($4 children).

The Drome is six km from Bathurst on the Limekilns road.

Places to Stay

Accommodation becomes scarce during the Bathurst 1000.

Caravan parks *Bathurst Caravan Park* (☎ (063) 31 8286), on the highway four km east of the centre, has sites, on-site vans and cabins. During the Bathurst 1000 other camping areas are opened.

B&B The information centre has listings of the B&Bs and farmstays in Bathurst and the district. One of the more impressive is *Strathmore* (☎ (063) 32 3252) at 202 Russell St, a Victorian mansion which charges from about $70/100 for rooms with bathroom. Bookings are essential and children aren't allowed. *Yarrabin* (☎ (063) 37 5712) is a property south of Bathurst offering full board and horseriding for $85 a day.

Hotels The *Knickerbocker Hotel* (☎ (063) 32 4500) at the corner of Russell and William Sts has en suite rooms with TV and fridge for $35/50, including breakfast. This is good value, although some of the fittings need replacing, the shag-pile carpet is in its senility and you might want to check the bed before handing over your money. Other pubs which offer accommodation include the *Park* (☎ (063) 31 3399), on the corner of Keppel and George Sts.

Motels The *Governor Macquarie* (☎ (063) 31 2211) on Charlotte St is well located and costs from $70/80. There are many other motels, some cheaper, such as the *Capri* (☎ (063) 31 2966, 1800 047 907 toll-free) at 357 Stewart St.

Places to Eat

A couple of large cafes-cum-restaurants stand opposite each other at the corner of William and Howick Sts, the *Stagecoach* and the *Acropole*. The menu at the Acropole is marginally more interesting, with some Greek dishes.

For pizza from a wood-fired oven to eat in or take away, or large servings of inexpensive pasta ($7.50 for main-course size), try *Uncle Joe's Pizza*, opposite the post office on Howick St.

Zeigler's Cafe on Keppel St is a small place, with an interesting and contemporary menu of not-too-expensive dishes. There's jazz on Thursdays and acoustic music on Saturday.

On George St near the corner of Russell St there's a group of eating places, including two or three Chinese restaurants. *Athina*, open daily for lunch and dinner, has a fairly standard menu with a few Greek-inspired dishes. The decor includes tat such as a chandelier, but prices aren't too bad, around $10 for main courses at lunch and $15 at dinner. Across the road, upstairs in the building at the corner of George and Church Sts, the *Continental Restaurant* claims to be the best in Bathurst.

Not far away from this cluster, on Howick St north of George St, the *Family Eating House* offers an all-you-can-eat smorgasbord for $7.50 at lunch and $12.50 at dinner. Asian-style dishes feature heavily but there's a good selection.

The *Galloping Grape* in an old building on William St just west of the corner of Russell St, has a standard menu of red meat, white meat and seafood, but the opulent surroundings of this restaurant make for a good night out. Main courses are under $20.

Not far away, the *Brooke Moore Restaurant* on the corner of William and Keppel Sts is another in an old building with period decor.

Tandoori House at 94 Bentinck St has Indian food.

Entertainment

This is a student town and there are a few music venues. The Family Hotel on the corner of Bentinck and Russell Sts has bands, as do the Commercial and Park hotels on George St.

Each Sunday, markets are held at the showgrounds, off the highway just east of the centre of Bathurst. The pavilions here are impressive.

Getting There & Away

Draw a wire fence and a few ragged gums, and add some scattered sheep running away from the train. Then you'll have the bush all along the NSW western line from Bathurst on.

Henry Lawson, *In a Dry Season*, 1893

Train Bathurst is on the main western line, with daily trains to Sydney and Dubbo, with connections for Broken Hill and beyond. Countrylink buses connect with some suburban services from Sydney at Lithgow and run to Bathurst.

Bus Rendell's Coaches (☎ (068) 84 4199) runs to Sydney and Dubbo from the stop on Howick St near the corner of William St. Selwoods (☎ (063) 62 7963) stops here on the run between Sydney and Orange. Greyhound Pioneer Australia stops at the Shell service station on Durham St.

If you're heading for Mudgee you'll have to backtrack to Lithgow and pick up a Countrylink bus there.

Various small towns in the area have community buses which make the journey into Bathurst, most only once a week or so. In the car park under the Grace Brothers store on Howick St there's a Community Bus Room where you might be able to get information about these services.

Car & Motorbike The Great Western Highway from Lithgow, the Blue Mountains and Sydney enters Bathurst from the east. The Mitchell Highway heads north-west to Orange, and then north to Dubbo and Bourke. The Olympic Way runs south-west from Bathurst to Cowra, eventually reaching Albury. The section to Cowra is mainly downhill, descending into the Lachlan Valley. The Mid-Western Highway (the same road as the Olympic Way until Cowra) runs south-west to West Wyalong and on to Hay.

Getting Around

Taxis (☎ (063) 31 1511) run 24 hours a day.

AROUND BATHURST

The high, cold tablelands around Bathurst were some of the first inland areas of Australia to be settled by Europeans, and there are some interesting old villages. The Around Orange section later in this chapter covers some villages to the north-west of Bathurst.

Carcoar

Established in 1833, Carcoar is a pretty village on the Belubula River. The whole village has been classified by the National Trust. Enterprise Stores (☎ (063) 67 3085) on Belubula St has tourist information, and the **museum** is in the stables of the old Stoke Hotel. There's a caravan park and accommodation at the *Royal Hotel* (☎ (063) 67 3009) and *Dalebrook* (☎ (063) 67 3149), a guesthouse.

Blayney

Although it's now growing fast, Blayney (population 2700) still has some historic buildings. Holly Folly Crafts (☎ (063) 68 2646) on Adelaide St has maps of the town and the district.

There's a caravan park, a motel and a couple of pubs with accommodation. Out of town, *Caithness* (☎ (063) 66 5082) is a cashmere goat stud and sheep property near Browns Creek with B&B accommodation for $45/70

Rockley

Rockley is a little old village about 40 km south of Bathurst with some nice stone buildings and several craft and antique shops. There's a **museum** in the old mill and across the street is a picnic area by the mill dam.

Oberon

Oberon is a high (1113 metres), cold town surrounded by farmland and extensive pine plantations. Oberon and Katoomba are the only towns in the state other than the ski resorts to regularly receive heavy snowfalls. It's a thriving rural town with a fair population (2500 people) and makes a reasonable base for visiting attractions such as the

Jenolan and Abercrombie caves and the south-western side of the Blue Mountains.

Tourist information is available from the craft shop (☎ (063) 36 1895) in the Malachi Gilmore Hall (a rigorously Art Deco building) on the main street. There's a caravan park and several motels.

On Tuesday, Friday and Sunday Countrylink buses run to/from Mt Victoria in the Blue Mountains, where they connect with trains to Sydney.

Abercrombie Caves

This group of about 50 caves is less well-known than the Jenolan Caves but is worth visiting. The Grand Arch is one of the world's largest natural tunnels and even the side tunnels are huge – in the Hall of Terpsichore you can still see the dance floor installed by miners last century. Tours of the caves are held several times daily and cost $8 ($4 children).

There are swimming places near the caves and fossicking is possible at Grove Creek. There are campsites ($7) and on-site vans (from $40). Abercrombie Caves are 15 km south of Trunkey Creek (another of the area's old villages) and 70 km south-west of Bathurst.

South to Goulburn

The high, cold plateau extends south to Goulburn. Small villages dot the area, most founded in the early 19th century, and sheep in the surrounding paddocks produce small quantities of very fine wool, perhaps the best in the world. Those old newsreels from the '30s, showing an Australian rural Arcadia with great flocks of sheep being mustered in rolling, semi-timbered country, could have been shot around here.

A network of small roads offers interesting drives. From Goulburn you can cut through this area to Bathurst or Lithgow – not a bad 'backdoor' route to the Jenolan Caves and the Blue Mountains, although some causeways flood after heavy rain. The route via Taralga involves a very steep ascent from the valley where the Bummaroo Bridge crosses the Abercrombie River. The valley is a beautiful place but the road isn't suitable for caravans. You'd reckon it wasn't suitable for semi-trailers either, but you do meet juggernauts pounding along these unsealed roads, so take care.

The largest town in the area, **Crookwell**, is a pleasant place, 45 km north of Goulburn in a highland valley. The information centre (☎ (048) 32 1988) is at the north end of Goulburn St, the main street. Ask for tips on the best trout streams in the area. The old Stephenson's flour mill is being restored and will house the local museum. Crookwell's agricultural show is held in February. Over the Anzac Day long weekend in April, several of the town's gardens are open to the public during the Autumn Festival.

The nearby village of **Taralga** is an access point for the Wonboyn Caves – see the Around Sydney chapter. The Taralga Berry Farm wins awards at Sydney's Royal Easter Show for its jams and preserves.

Places to Stay Crookwell has a small and basic *camping ground* near the town centre on the Laggan/Taralga road. The *Crookwell Hotel Motel* (☎ (048) 32 1016) has motel units ($30/40). There's also pub accommodation here and at a couple of other pubs in town. The *Uplands Pastures Motel*, a few hundred metres off the main street on the Taralga road, is good value with singles/ doubles from $40/60.

In Taralga the *Argyle Inn* (☎ (048) 40 2004) has accommodation.

In **Laggan**, a village north-east of Crookwell, the *Willow Vale Mill* (☎ (048) 37 3319) is a well-known restaurant in a historic mill, and also has accommodation in two renovated cottages. Bookings are essential. The *Laggan Hotel* (☎ (048) 37 3208) has accommodation and is also a place with a good reputation.

The Levels (☎ (048) 43 3010) is a sheep station in the Abercrombie River area. There is B&B accommodation from about $35 per person, about $100 per person for full board and participation in the station's activities. They can pick you up from Goulburn, but check the current prices for this. Other

farmstay accommodation in the area includes the *Gundowringa Shearers' Quarters* (☎ (048) 48 1244) and *Killarney Cottage* (☎ (048) 36 7225). The Crookwell information centre has details of these and other places.

BATHURST TO MUDGEE

The road running up to Mudgee curves east to run past towns on the western edge of the huge Wollemi National Park, one of the parks which protect the Blue Mountains. The Mudgee National Parks office (☎ (063) 72 3122) has information on this section of Wollemi.

Sofala

The village of Sofala (pronounced so-*fa*-la) on the fast-flowing Turon River is an old gold town, unusual because of the large number of timber buildings which have been preserved. The general store has information (including the useful booklet *A Pleasant Walk Around Sofala*, $1.50) and it's an amazing place, thoroughly cluttered with new and ancient stock.

Places to Stay & Eat As well as various tea-rooms there's the licensed *Cafe Sofala* and the pub has meals. Across the river on Maitland Point, the *Gold Commissioner's Holiday Farm* (☎ (063) 37 7025) has cabins and on-site vans for $10 per person, less if there are more people and/or you stay more than one night. The *Old Schoolhouse* and the *Old Parsonage* also have accommodation.

Getting There & Away Sofala is on the road between Mudgee and Bathurst, but schoolbuses and a weekly community bus offer the only public transport to Bathurst.

Hill End

In 1871 Hill End was one of the state's largest inland towns, with thousands of miners working a rich reef of gold. Deep mining required money, so, unlike other gold rushes, the Hill End rush attracted investment and speculators as well as diggers. Just two years later the gold ran out and the town declined rapidly.

Today, Hill End is almost a ghost town and most of its buildings no longer exist. Luckily, the town was visited by the photographer Beaufroy Merlin (see the Gulgong section), and in many of the empty spaces along the streets are photos showing the vanished buildings. Hill End isn't quite deserted and the small community lives in an enviably pretty setting.

On the hill at the edge of town is the old hospital, now a museum and information centre (☎ (063) 37 8206). The museum is open daily from 9.30 am to 4.30 pm, with an hour off for lunch between 12.30 and 1.30 pm. Ask here about tours of the Bald Hill mine. In the hospital's old morgue there's the *Morgue Cafe*, which sells 'mourning and arvo tea' for $4.50 and offers light meals.

If you fancy a fossick you can buy gold pans at the general store.

Places to Stay There are three camping areas close to the town centre. You can book at the information centre. The *Royal Hotel* (☎ (065) 37 8261), a very nice pub (and the only survivor of the 28 which were once here), has singles/doubles for $30/45, more with meals. There's also a *Holiday Ranch* (☎ (063) 37 8224) and a *Holiday Cottage* (☎ (063) 37 8207).

Getting There & Away Hill End is accessible only by unsealed roads, to Mudgee (72 km) and Bathurst (77 km). The Bathurst road is a bridle path and is often suitable only for 4WD vehicles. The other roads are OK but they are slippery after rain. The 2WD route from Bathurst is via Sofala. You'll still see sections of post-and-rail fencing which provides a very inadequate protection against the drops. The road is narrow and winding and carries some speedy local traffic, so take care. Also watch out for horses and wandering cattle.

A weekly community bus runs to Bathurst, usually on Friday morning, returning to Hill End in the afternoon. Schoolbuses run

between Hill End and Mudgee – see the Mudgee section.

Lake Windamere
This new water-storage dam on the Cudgegong River is about 25 km south-east of Mudgee and is accessible from the Ilford-Mudgee road (not to be confused with the Ilford-Kandos-Mudgee road). Boating and fishing are popular (but beware of algae), and there is a camping area. Tabrabucca Lodge (☎ (063) 58 8414) south of the lake has horseriding.

Rylstone & Kandos
Rylstone is a pretty village (population 750) with some fine sandstone buildings, including the one housing *The Bridge* restaurant. Kandos is a larger town (population 1800); it has a cement industry. Access to Wollemi National Park from these towns is on rough roads and you should seek local knowledge before using them. There's a basic *camping area* at **Dunns Swamp** (Kendells Weir), which is accessible from Rylstone, but you might have to walk in.

MUDGEE
The Mudgee area was explored by Europeans in the 1820s and a small town grew up in the 1840s, expanding rapidly with the gold rushes of the 1850s. Today Mudgee is an interesting old town (population 7500) and a thriving centre for the nearby wineries. There are some pleasant streets and interesting nooks and crannies to explore. With about 18 wineries open for sales and tastings and good transport connections from Sydney, Mudgee is ideal for a rural weekend.

Orientation & Information
Mudgee is about 120 km north of Bathurst and Lithgow, on the banks of the Cudgegong River. Most of the wineries are north of the river. The main shopping street is Church St.

The information centre (☎ (063) 72 5875) is on Market St, near the old police station.

Wineries
Most of the area's wineries are small and

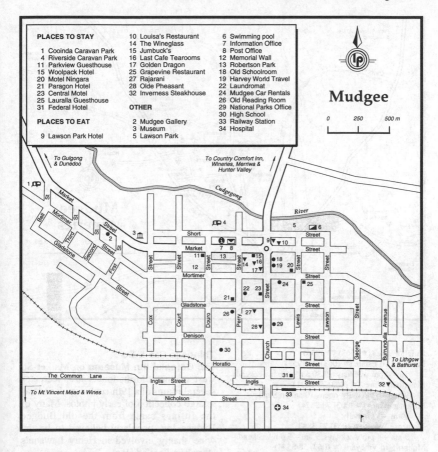

Mudgee

0   250   500 m

PLACES TO STAY

1 Cooinda Caravan Park
4 Riverside Caravan Park
11 Parkview Guesthouse
15 Woolpack Hotel
20 Motel Ningara
21 Paragon Hotel
23 Central Motel
25 Lauralla Guesthouse
31 Federal Hotel

PLACES TO EAT

9 Lawson Park Hotel

10 Louisa's Restaurant
14 The Wineglass
15 Jumbuck's
16 Last Cafe Tearooms
17 Golden Dragon
25 Grapevine Restaurant
27 Rajarani
28 Olde Pheasant
32 Inverness Steakhouse

OTHER

2 Mudgee Gallery
3 Museum
5 Lawson Park

6 Swimming pool
7 Information Office
8 Post Office
12 Memorial Wall
13 Robertson Park
18 Old Schoolroom
19 Harvey World Travel
22 Laundromat
24 Mudgee Car Rentals
26 Old Reading Room
29 National Parks Office
30 High School
33 Railway Station
34 Hospital

To Gulgong & Dunedoo

To Country Comfort Inn, Wineries, Merriwa & Hunter Valley

Cudgegong

River

To Lithgow & Bathurst

The Common Lane

To Mt Vincent Mead & Wines

locally-owned. The harvest season is later than in the Hunter because of Mudgee's higher altitude.

Craigmore, four km from Mudgee, has produced a vintage every year since 1858, making it the second-oldest continually operating winery in Australia. You can see the original cellar and some antique wine-making equipment. The restaurant here is one of the area's best – see Places to Eat.

Mt Vincent Mead & Wines produces mead, an interesting and natural fermented honey drink. There is also a new product, mead ale, which only has about 5% alcohol.

Other wineries in the Mudgee area include the following:

Augustine Vineyard (☎ (063) 72 3880)
    10 am – 4 pm daily
Botobolar Vineyard (☎ (063) 73 3840)
    10 am – 4 pm daily
Burnbrae Wines (☎ (063) 73 3504)
    9.30 am – 5 pm daily
Craigmoor Winery (☎ (063) 72 2208)
    10 am – 4.30 pm daily, closes 4 pm on Sunday
Erudgere Vineyards (☎ (063) 72 1118)
    10 am – 4.30 pm most days
Huntington Estate (☎ (063) 73 3825)
    9 am – 5 pm weekdays, 10 am – 5 pm Saturday,
    11 am – 3 pm Sunday

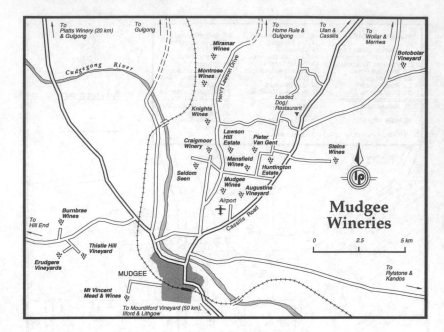

Mudgee Wineries

Knights Vines (☎ (063) 73 3954)
Lawson Hill Estate (☎ (063) 73 3953)
   10 – 4 pm weekdays, 9.30 am – 5 pm weekends
Mansfield Wines (☎ (063) 73 3871)
   9 am – 6 pm daily, opens 10 am on Sunday
Miramar Wines (☎ (063) 73 3874)
   9 am – 5 pm daily
Montrose Wines (☎ (063) 73 3883)
   9 am – 4 pm weekdays, 9 am – 5 pm weekends
Mountilford Vineyard (☎ (063) 58 8544)
   10 am – 4 pm daily (near the hamlet of Ilford,
   south of Mudgee on the Bathurst road)
Mt Vincent Mead & Wines (☎ (063) 72 3184)
   10 am – 5 pm weekdays, opens 9 am on weekends
Mudgee Wines (☎ (063) 72 2258)
   10 am – 5 pm daily
Pieter Van Gent (☎ (063) 73 3807)
   9 am – 5 pm Monday to Saturday
   11 am to 4 pm Sunday
Platts Winery (☎ (063) 74 1700)
   9 am – 5 pm daily
Seldom Seen (☎ (063) 72 4482)
   9.30 am – 5 pm daily
Steins Wines (☎ (063) 73 3991)
   10 am – 4 pm daily
Thistle Hill Vineyard (☎ (063) 73 3546)
   9 am – 5 pm daily

Things to See & Do

The **Colonial Inn Museum** on Market St, west of the information centre, recreates several rooms of a 19th-century pub and has a large collection of early photos. Many of the fittings came from the old Budgee Budgee Inn, popularly believed to be the wine shanty involved in Henry Lawson's story *The Loaded Dog*.

At the impressive old railway station, **Mandurah** is an arts and crafts co-op which is open daily.

In **Memorial Park**, at the corner of Mortimer and Douro Sts, a collection of old headstones from disused cemeteries in the area has been arranged into a wall.

Mudgee Romance Ballooning (☎ (063) 72 4087 or (02) 439 8338) organises **balloon flights** and also offers accommodation packages on the Jindalee property. The packages include horseriding.

Henry Lawson completed his schooling in Mudgee and was also encouraged in his reading by a local priest. You can still see the schoolhouse, in the grounds of the Catholic Church on Church St. The Mechanics Institute on the corner of Gladstone and Perry Sts is where Lawson first read Dostoevsky, and the old building's shingled balcony looks fairly Dostoevskian itself on a gloomy winter's day.

Lawson Park, by the river at the top of Church St, has no especial association with the writer, but it was apparently the scene of a massacre of Aborigines.

North of Mudgee, off Henry Lawson Drive, the **Eurunderee School Complex** is near the site of Lawson's childhood home and there's a restored school here, with a slab that purports to be from Lawson's slab-built home.

Work
Despite the number of wineries in the area there isn't much casual grape-picking work available, as most is done by locals and is 'pre-booked'. The four-week picking season is around February and March.

Festivals & Events
The Mudgee Wine Festival, which continues through most of September, is the area's major event. Unfortunately, it occurs at the same time as a wine festival in the Hunter Valley. If you have to choose between the two, the quality of the wine is perhaps better in the longer-established Hunter (many people would not agree) but the Mudgee area is more pleasant. This is a real rural festival and coincides with spring after a chilly winter.

The Small Farm Field Days are held on the third weekend in July at the showgrounds.

Places to Stay
If you're coming to Mudgee on a weekend you should book ahead. During the September wine festival very little accommodation is available, although if you do manage to find a bed you'll be pleased to learn that most prices stay the same all year.

Caravan Parks *Cooinda Caravan Park* (☎ (063) 72 3337) and *Riverside Caravan Park* (☎ (063) 72 2531), which is closer to the town centre, both have sites and cabins; Cooinda has on-site vans as well. *Mudgee Tourist & Van Resort* (☎ (063) 72 1090) is a few km south-east of the centre of Mudgee on Lions Drive.

Guesthouses The *Parkview Guesthouse* (☎ (063) 74 4477) on the corner of Market and Douro Sts, across from Robertson Park, has well-renovated rooms in a large old house for $60/75 and $75/85 on weekends, including breakfast. All the bedrooms have attached bathrooms. *Lauralla* (☎ (063) 72 4480), on the corner of Lewis and Mortimer Sts, is an impressive Victorian home offering B&B for around $100 a double and getting up towards $200 if you add dinner.

North of town and near the wineries, *Hithergreen Lodge* (☎ (063) 72 1022) has motel units for $48/55. On weekdays they might have backpacker specials, but phone to check first. A taxi out here costs around $4, otherwise it's a pleasant walk of about five km. *Thistle Hill Vineyard* (☎ (063) 73 3546), about 10 km west of Mudgee (and not in the main vineyard area) has a cottage for rent.

See the information centre for other places in the district.

Hotels There are some above-average pubs. The *Paragon Hotel* (☎ (063) 72 1313) on the corner of Gladstone and Perry Sts has clean, comfortable rooms for $15 per person in the simpler upstairs rooms and $20 per person in the downstairs rooms which have TVs. Staying downstairs in a pub is a great advantage, as you don't get bar noise wafting up through the floor. All rooms have washbasins and tea and coffee-making facilities. An enormous breakfast costs $8.

The *Woolpack Hotel* (☎ (063) 72 1908) on Market St is also good and the newly decorated rooms cost $15 per person. A little away from the centre is another good pub, the *Federal Hotel* (☎ (063) 72 1908) on

Inglis St near the railway station, which charges $15/24; $18/34 on weekends.

Motels Most of the motels are good but pricey. *Motel Ningara* (☎ (063) 72 1133) at the corner of Mortimer and Lewis Sts is an average good motel, charging from $50/55. Top-of-the-range is the big *Country Comfort Inn* (☎ (063) 72 4500), on Cassilis Rd north of the river, which charges from $80 a room.

Places to Eat

As well as the usual takeaways, cafes and pubs, there are some places to eat which are a cut above the usual country-town standard.

The best place for a coffee is *The Last Cafe Tearooms*, through an archway on Market St near the corner of Church St (the footpath sign says 'Tea House'). There are two vine-shaded courtyards, the coffee is excellent and the friendly owner is knowledgeable about local attractions. There are also cakes, snacks and light meals such as quiche and salad for around $8. The cafe is open daily and in summer it might stay open into the evening.

Nearby in the Woolpack Hotel, *Jumbucks* (☎ (065) 72 3159) is a pleasant licensed restaurant serving good, standard food. Most main courses are under $10 and you can get three courses for less than $20. Local wines are served with little mark-up from bottle-shop prices.

The *Rajarani* Indian restaurant on Gladstone St at the corner of Church St has just changed hands but will probably continue to serve main courses for around $13 from Tuesday to Sunday.

There are two Chinese restaurants on Church St, the *Golden Dragon*, a narrow, dim place with reasonable main courses from about $7, and the plusher *Kai Sun*, a little pricier.

Perhaps the best place to eat in town is *Louisa's Restaurant* on Market St, with an Italian menu with main courses around $15.

The *Wineglass Bar & Grill* (☎ (063) 72 3417) on Perry St across from Robertson Park specialises in grills you cook yourself

and serves local wines. Most main courses are under $10, which is good value.

The *Red Heifer* restaurant at the Lawson Park Hotel on the corner of Church and Short Sts is a popular steakhouse and has specials such as $7 roasts some weekdays. At 18 Sydney Rd, the licensed *Inverness Steakhouse* (☎ (063) 72 1701) is in an old coaching inn. It's open from Wednesday to Saturday for dinner, with weekend lunches.

Lauralla guesthouse has the *Grapevine Restaurant* with set-price meals ($25). You should book (☎ (063) 72 4480). *The Olde Pheasant* on Church St is a coffee shop by day, with a business lunch special, and a licensed restaurant at night.

Out of Town At the historic Craigmoor Winery, the *Craigmoor Restaurant* (☎ (063) 72 2208) is one of the best places to eat in the area. It has a pleasant restaurant on a mezzanine floor of the old cellars and a varied menu with main courses around $15 and cheaper lunch specials. Unfortunately it's open only on weekends for lunch and on Friday and Saturday for dinner. You must book.

Another good restaurant at a winery, the *Augustine Vineyard restaurant* (☎ (063) 72 3880), is open for lunch daily and dinner on Friday and Saturday. You must book here as well. Neither of these restaurants is far from Mudgee, so taking a taxi won't cost too much and will allow indulgence in their wines.

Further along from Augustines, *The Loaded Dog* (☎ (063) 73 3740) is in an old wine shanty, although today you must BYO. It is claimed that this is the shanty which figures in Henry Lawson's yarn of the same name. The restaurant serves dishes ranging from damper to venison and kangaroo. It's open daily for lunch (about $15 for two courses) and dinner (about $25 for three courses, reservations necessary).

Getting There & Away

Air Hazelton flies to Sydney most days. The standard fare is $140, getting down to about $110 with advance purchase.

Bus Countrylink is the only line serving Mudgee. The bus connects with trains to Sydney at Lithgow, and the total Mudgee to Sydney fare is about $40. Going the other way, these buses continue further out to Baradine, running via Gulgong, about $2 from Mudgee.

Harvey World Travel (☎ (063) 72 6077), beneath the gigantic clock on Church St (which keeps better time than the clocks on the nearby war memorial), is the Countrylink agent. Buses depart from near the post office and from the old railway station.

If you want to visit the interesting old town of Hill End you'll have to hope that there is room on Case's schoolbus (☎ (063) 72 6622), which runs from the high school on the corner of Douro and Horatio Sts and charges $3 to the village of Hargraves, where you connect with a smaller schoolbus to Hill End for another $3 or thereabouts.

Getting Around

Taxi Mudgee Radio Taxis (☎ (063) 72 3999) can usually be found on Mortimer St near Church St.

Car Rental Mudgee Car Rentals (☎ (063) 72 6332) on Mortimer St near Church St is a small local outfit which will rent you a Falcon or a Commodore for about $70 a day including petrol for the 150 free km, and other deals are possible. It's advisable to book in advance, especially on weekends.

GULGONG

Gulgong (population 2000) was known as the 'Hub of the World' during the roaring days of gold fever. Later it called itself 'the town on the ten dollar note', but, since the introduction of the plastic $10 note, it isn't.

History

Gulgong is an old gold-mining town, created almost overnight in the rush that began in 1870. After 1880 the rush tapered off but it left behind a well-established town that is today classified by the National Trust.

Author Henry Lawson spent his childhood in the area, after his parents followed the rush to the goldfields. Not that Lawson's memories of Gulgong were rosy. It was here that he learned to dislike the squalor, meanness and brutalising hard work of poverty on the goldfields. A bitterness was instilled here which never quite faded, along with a belief in the essential worth of everyday life.

Gulgong is unusual in the number of records we have of its early days – gold towns usually came and went without much trace. As well as Henry Lawson's writings, the novel *Robbery Under Arms* (written by a Gold Commissioner under the pen name of Rolfe Boldrewood) is partly set here, British novelist Anthony Trollope dropped in and wrote about what he saw, several journalists reported the rush and there are the wonderful photos of the Holterman collection.

Orientation & Information

The main road through town is Herbert St, but the delightful old main street, narrow and winding, is Mayne St. No-one remembers whether Mayne is just a fancy spelling of

The Holterman Collection

Rediscovered in 1951, the Holterman Collection is an extremely important record of early settlement and goldfields life, captured on thousands of photographic plates taken by Henry Merlin and his assistant Charles Bayliss.

Merlin had been working as a travelling photographer for many years when he met Bernard Holterman in 1871. Holterman was a struggling digger who had just struck it extremely rich and was interested in photography. He commissioned Merlin to produce an extensive series of photographs of NSW and Victoria, which he later used as a touring exhibition in Europe. Merlin died two years into the project, but the work was continued by Bayliss. It culminated in the building of a 25-metre tower to take panoramic shots of Sydney, using huge plates – one measured 1.5 metres across! The bulk of the collection is now housed in Sydney's Mitchell Library. ■

PLACES TO STAY
5 Caravan Park
6 Goldfields
Motor Inn
7 The Stables
9 Centennial Hotel
10 Ten Dollar
Town Motel
25 Gulgong Motel

PLACES TO EAT
2 RSL Club
10 Phoebe's
Restaurant
13 Saint & Sinner
15 Tea Shoppe
17 Prince of
Wales Hotel

OTHER
1 Three Ways
Gallery
3 Pioneer Museum
4 Church Hill
8 Henry Lawson
Centre
11 Old shopfronts
12 Commercial Hotel
14 Old shopfront
16 Opera House
18 Laundry
19 Olde Books
20 Post Office
21 Town Hall
22 Information Centre
23 Wylandra Hall
24 Red Hill
26 Bus stop

Gulgong

0   125   250 m

To Ulan
To Dunedoo
To Wellington
To Home Rule
To Mudgee

Memorial Park

'main' or whether the street was named after someone. Until 1872 it was called Queen St.

The information centre (☎ (063) 74 1202) has recently moved to Herbert St near the town hall. It used to be in the Olde Books shop (☎ (063) 74 2078) at the top end of Mayne St, and the owner is a good source of local knowledge; the shop is worth a look even if you don't need information.

Things to See

The **Gulgong Pioneer Museum** on Herbert St is one of the best country-town museums in the state. The huge collection of the

important and the trivial borders on chaos, but it's all fascinating. Photographs of early Gulgong from the Holterman Collection are displayed, and there are also pin-up photos of stars who drove the diggers wild at the local opera. Admission is $3 ($2 children), and that's a bargain. The museum is open from 9.30 am to 5 pm daily.

The **Henry Lawson Centre** at the bottom end of Mayne St houses part of the collection of the Henry Lawson Society. They also have a good selection of Lawson's works for sale. The centre is open from 10 am to noon daily or by appointment. Admission is $1.

Among the old buildings on Mayne St is the **Opera House**, built during the gold rushes and still occasionally in use.

Festivals & Events
From 29 December to 2 January a Folk Music Festival is held and the Foundation Day festivities take place over Easter. Some events of the eisteddfod in May take place in the Opera House.

The second weekend in June is the time for the big Henry Lawson Festival, which celebrates the author's birthday. There is music, dramatisations of Lawson stories at the Opera House, and literary awards, some sponsored by Norwegian bodies – Henry Lawson's father was Peter Larsen, a Norwegian immigrant. Sheepdog trials, parades and many other events make this a hectic weekend for the many people who attend.

Gulgong is also involved in Mudgee's September Wine Festival.

Places to Stay
The *Heritage Centre* on Red Hill has a dorm for groups. Phone (☎ (063) 74 1202) to see whether there's space for individuals.

Caravan Park There's a *caravan park* (☎ (063) 74 1294) a little way out of town on the road to Wellington.

B&B On Mayne St next to the Lawson Society, *The Stables Guestrooms* (☎ (063) 74 1668) is a pleasant B&B in a nice old house (and in the converted stables), with singles/doubles for $50/70.

Hotels & Motels The old *Commercial Hotel* (☎ (063) 74 1206) on Mayne St has pub rooms for around $20/30. The *Centennial Hotel* (☎ (063) 74 1241) at the bottom end of Mayne St at the corner of Medley St has singles/doubles for $25/35. The rooms all have attached bathrooms and they are clean enough but it isn't a very inspiring place to stay. Across the road, the *Ten Dollar Town Motel* (☎ (063) 74 1204) has units from $50/60. The *Gulgong Motel* (☎ (063) 74 1122) on Medley St charges around $40/50

and the *Goldfields Motor Inn* (☎ (063) 74 1111) on the road to Wellington charges around $45/60.

Places to Eat
Saint & Sinner (aka *Cafe de Gulgong)* is on Mayne St down from the corner of Herbert St. The menu is standard country-town cafe fare, but there are paintings on the wall and the local folk-music club has occasional meetings here. There are a couple of other cafes on Herbert St near the museum. *Phoebe's Restaurant* on Medly St just north of Mayne St has pasta for $10 and main courses from $14.

Getting There & Away
Bus Two Countrylink buses a day run between Gulgong and Sydney, via Lithgow and the Blue Mountains. Olde Books on Mayne St takes bookings.

ORANGE
The city of Orange (population 34,000) is in a fertile agricultural area but crops grown do not include oranges – the city was named after Prince William of Orange. Cool-climate fruit and vegetables are the area's main produce, although wheat was the crop grown by the first settlers.

Although it's now larger than Bathurst, Orange didn't have the administrative importance of its neighbour and lacks the grand buildings, but it is a pleasant city of wide streets and parks. The altitude (around 950 metres) means that there are four distinct seasons, with cold winters.

History
Land grants were made in the area in the early 1830s, but it wasn't until the 1840s that Orange appeared, and it remained a small village until the 1851 gold rush at nearby Ophir. By the 1880s, Orange was a large and prosperous town shipping fruit to the Sydney markets on the new railway line. Orange was briefly considered as the site for the national capital, but Victoria didn't want the capital to be located so close to Sydney and so far from Melbourne.

Map labels (clockwise/as shown):

To Molong & Dubbo; To Burrendong Sport & Recreational Area; To Botanic Gardens; To Showgrounds; Forbes Rd; To Parkes; Dalton Street; Prince Street; Rosemary Lane; March Street; Mitchell Highway; Place; To Orphir; Golf Course; Street; Street; Street; Street; Street; Lords St; Information Centre; March Street; To Lake Canobolar & Cargo; Byng Street; Street; Robertson Park; McLachlan Street; Sampson Street; Clinton Street; Hill St; Sale Street; Anson Street; Cargo Road; Summer Street; Summer Street; Woodward Street; Cook Park; Kite Street; See Central Orange Map; Orange Railway Station; Mitchell Highway; To Millthorpe & Bathurst; Moulder Street; National Avneue; Swimming Pool; Peisley Street; Warrendine Street; Anson Street; Endsleigh Avenue; Franklin Street; Orange; Barrett Street; To Mt Canobolas; Gardiner Road; 0 250 500 m; Indian Pacific Railway Station; To Airport

Orientation & Information

Suburban Orange sprawls over quite a large area, but the city centre, with its grid-pattern streets, is fairly compact and easy to get around. Summer St is the main street and the town centre begins just west of the railway line.

The big visitor centre (☎ (063) 61 5226) is on Byng St (a block north of Summer St) near the railway line and is open daily. It has a range of handy brochures including a walking tour of the city centre and day tours around the district. It also sells fossicking licenses and rents gold pans.

Things to See

The excellent **Orange Regional Gallery** in Civic Square (behind the visitor centre) has an ambitious and varied programme of exhibitions. It is open Tuesday to Saturday from 11 am to 5 pm and from 2 to 5 pm on Sunday and holidays. Not far away on McNamara St, opposite Robertson Park, is the **museum**.

The **Botanic Gardens**, begun in 1981, aims to preserve the native woodlands of the area and to grow other plants and trees suited to this cool climate, including a forest of European, North American and Asian trees. This is an interesting project, as most botanic

PLACES TO STAY

4   Metropolitan Hotel
6   Templar's Mill Motel
10 Downtown Motel
11 Mid City Motor Lodge
12 Royal Hotel
16 Tourist Hotel
18 Hotel Canobolas
25 Occidental Hotel/Motel

PLACES TO EAT

3   La Della's
7   The Wine Bar
8   Cafe 48
9   Bad Manors
14 Loc Sing Restaurant
15 Hellenes Restaurant
17 Phoenician Lebanese
    Restaurant
19 Lords Cafe
23 Hong Kong & Alfio's
    Restaurants
24 Patmos Restaurant
26 Pet Shop Cafe

OTHER

1   Civic Centre
2   Information Centre
5   Old Town Hall
13 Robertson Park
20 Post Office
21 Orange Arcade
22 CES Office

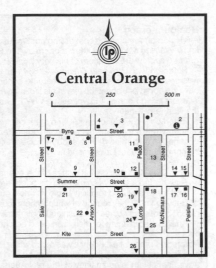

Central Orange

of the station is now **Banjo Paterson Park**, with picnic facilities. The park is about three km north-east of Orange on the Ophir road.

Work

The autumn apple-picking season lasts for about six weeks. The CES (☎ (063) 61 4144) on Anson St has a Harvest Officer who can help you find work. Some of the orchards have accommodation.

Festivals & Events

The Orange National Field Days, held during the second week in November, are the largest in the state. This is your chance to catch up on the world of tractors and chemical sprays, and also to see interesting events such as sheepdog trials.

Places to Stay

As well as the accommodation listed here, the visitor centre has details of farmstays in the area.

Caravan Parks The council's *Orange Showground Caravan Park* (☎ (063) 62 7254) has tent sites for $7.50 and a range of other accommodation, from on-site vans for

gardens in the state were established long ago and are rigidly formal, echoing the gardens back 'home' in Britain (**Cook Park** in central Orange is a good example). The first stage, including the Orchard, the Homestead Garden and the Alpine Garden, has been completed. The Botanic Gardens are on Clover Hill (with good views of the city), a couple of km north of the city centre on Kearneys Drive.

Many craftspeople live in the area and there are several outlets in town, such as **The Guildry** in Cook Park on Summer St, open daily except Monday.

Poet Banjo Paterson was born on Narrambla Station near Orange in 1864. The site

Banjo Paterson

A B Paterson remains the best-selling poet in Australia, more than 50 years after his death. If you know *Walzing Matilda* you know a poem by 'the Banjo'. *The Man From Snowy River* and *Clancy of the Overflow* are two more of his very popular ballads.

Paterson was born near Orange in 1864 and grew up here and on stations around Yass, but was sent to an exclusive Sydney boarding school at an early age. He worked as a solicitor but became bored and spent the rest of his life in adventurous activities such as reporting on the Boer War, breaking horses in Egypt during WW I, pearl diving at Broome and shooting crocodiles in the Northern Territory.

Paterson's cheerful doggerel is in stark contrast to the more sombre work of Henry Lawson, although they shared an obsession with bush themes. The poets were not friends and at one time engaged in a rhyming debate about which was the more 'authentic'. Paterson has a point when he complains about Lawson and his ilk:

With their dreadful, dismal stories of the overlander's camp
How his fire is always smoky and his boots are always damp;
And they paint it so terrific it would fill one's soul with gloom,
But you know they're fond of writing about 'corpses' and 'the tomb'.
So, before they curse the bushland they should let their fancy range,
And take something for their livers, and be cheerful for a change.

Paterson's range of experience was much wider than Lawson's, but his poetry is one-dimensional and often verges on the jingoistic. Perhaps it isn't surprising that it's Paterson who is quoted when advertisers want to add a tinge of 'the real Australia'.

And of course there's no denying that a bushman's life is tough
But a man can easy stand it if he's built of sterling stuff. ∎

$25 a double to self-contained units sleeping seven for $35/40 a single/double, plus $6 for each extra person. The showgrounds are on Margaret St, about two km north-east of the city centre. There's also the *Canobolas Caravan Park* (☎ (063) 62 7279) at 166 Bathurst Rd (the Mitchell Highway) south-east of the city centre.

Hotels & Motels *Hotel Canobolas* (☎ (063) 62 2444) on Summer St at the corner of Lords Place, is a rarity in rural Australia: a hotel built specifically to provide accommodation. Toohey's brewery built the hotel in 1939 as the flagship of its chain, and with 100 rooms it was for many years the largest hotel outside Sydney. There are lifts (elevators), a ballroom and several other grand public rooms. Time has taken some toll but the hotel is still in the business of providing accommodation and takes the job seriously. The clean rooms are not very much better than average pub rooms (although most have

attached bathrooms, steam heat, TV and a fridge) but it makes a difference staying in a hotel where your welcome isn't grudging. With singles/doubles from $25/40 or $35/55 with bathroom, it's worth a try. If you're driving, enter the car park from the bottle-shop on Summer St.

The quieter, renovated *Metropolitan Hotel* (☎ (063) 62 1353) on the corner of Byng and Anson Sts has rooms for $25/45 with breakfast. The *Parkview Hotel* (☎ (063) 62 1545) at 281 Summer St charges $15/25. The *Occidental Hotel/Motel* (☎ (063) 62 4833) charges $25/30 for pub rooms and $45/50 for motel units.

Most other motels are quite expensive. The *Mid City Motor Lodge* (☎ (063) 62 1600) at 245 Lords Place is very central and charges from $60/70.

Duntryleague Country Club (☎ (063) 62 3602) is at the golf club on Woodward St and has singles for $60 and doubles from $75, more on weekends. Duntryleague is an old

Henry Lawson

Banjo Paterson

mansion built in 1876, with the golf course constructed in its grounds in 1920.

Places to Eat

Lord's Cafe, on Lords Place just south of the corner of Summer St, is a good place for breakfast, with eggs for $3. There's an interesting collection of magazines to read.

The tiny *Pet Shop Cafe* on Lords Place near the corner of Kite St has snacks and a small but interesting menu of somewhat pricey main meals – around $11 to $14. It's open daily except Tuesday for snacks, lunch and dinner (not Sunday) from 10 am.

The *Wine Bar* on Sale St at the corner of Byng St also has an interesting menu and nothing is over $11. The kitchen stays open until midnight. There's a free Wurlitzer jukebox ('hits of the '50s and '60s') and on Wednesday night there's jazz or other live entertainment from 9 pm. The Wine Bar is open from 7 pm to 2 am from Tuesday to Saturday; it describes itself as 'the smart place to go', so dress accordingly.

Not far away at 48 Sale St is *Cafe 48*, a BYO restaurant open for lunch daily except Sunday and for dinner from Wednesday to Saturday. The menu includes the usual steak and seafood, plus curries and pasta.

La Della's at 123 Byng St is an Italian and continental restaurant open for lunch on weekdays and for dinner from Thursday to Saturday. *Patmos* is a glittery reception-centre and restaurant on Lords Place. It's licensed and the menu is mainly steak, chicken and seafood; main courses are around $12 to $16.

There are many places along Summer St. *Thavy Thai Restaurant* is upstairs next to the Orange Arcade. *Bad Manors*, although nothing like its namesake in Sydney, is a reasonable cafe with snacks and meals. *Hellenes Restaurant*, on Summer St near the railway crossing is another more upmarket place with main courses around $16. Nearby is the *Loc Sing* Chinese restaurant, with another across the road. The *Phoenician Lebanese Restaurant* is a friendly takeaway selling Lebanese food as well as hamburgers. It has a few tables.

The *Overlander* restaurant at the Mid City Motor Inn near the Courthouse on Lords Place has an Indian menu as well as the usual steaks.

The *Ex-Services Club* on Anson St has a bistro and a restaurant.

There's a member of the small *Matilda's Family Steakhouse* chain at the corner of Bathurst Rd and McLachlan St, a few blocks east of the railway line. It's squeaky-clean and has $8 all-you-can eat lunch specials with other dishes ranging from $10 to $12. Children's meals cost $5 or less.

Over in East Orange, at 176 Kite St, the *Book Cafe* offers coffee and cake, along with new and old books.

Getting There & Away
Air Hazelton (☎ (063) 61 5888) flies to Sydney ($134) at least daily. The airport is south-east of Orange, off the Mitchell Highway near Lucknow.

Train XPTs running between Sydney and Dubbo stop at the railway station (☎ (063) 61 9500) near the town centre; the Indian Pacific has its own station some way south of the centre.

Bus Rendell's Coaches (☎ (068) 84 4199; 1800 023 328 toll-free) runs to Dubbo ($30) and Sydney ($25) daily. There's also a service to Canberra ($30). Rendell's stops at the railway station. Selwood's Coaches (☎ (063) 62 7963) also runs to Sydney daily, stopping outside Hotel Canobolas. Countrylink (☎ (063) 61 9500) runs buses to Parkes, Forbes and Dubbo.

Car & Motorbike The Mitchell Highway runs south to Bathurst and north to Wellington and Dubbo. Smaller roads run west to meet the Newell Highway near Parkes and Forbes. There's an interesting alternative route to Wellington (see the following Molong section).

AROUND ORANGE
Mt Canobolas
Mt Canobolas (1395 metres) is a steep, extinct volcano 20 km south-west of Orange. The views from up here stretch a long, long way across the western plains and in winter there is often snow on the peak. You can drive to the top or there are a couple of walking tracks. The road here from Orange offers you the choice of travelling via Towac or Pinnacle; the distances are about the same.

At the bottom of the mountain is **Lake Canobolas**, where you can see deer. There's also a *camping ground* (☎ (063) 65 3224) here, open from late October to the end of April.

Borenore Caves
About 18 km north-west of Orange, these caves can be explored without a guide, but you will need a torch (flashlight). You can camp nearby. From Orange, take the Mitchell Highway (Woodward St) and turn off onto Forbes Rd.

Old Villages
South-east of Orange, **Byng** was settled by Cornish miners and retains some old buildings, notably the church. The village is only accessible by dirt roads, either from Ophir or from the Mitchell Highway near **Shadforth**, another early village. Also on the highway but closer to Orange is **Lucknow**.

Millthorpe is a neat village south of the highway and about 25 km south-east of Orange. It can be decidedly reminiscent of a northern English village on a grey winter's day, with bleak hedges and dark stone houses. When the sun is shining it's a nice place to visit. The newsagency (☎ (063) 66 3253) has tourist information. There are several craft and antique shops and B&B accommodation in the extremely impressive old Bank of NSW building on Victoria St and the adjoining manager's residence. It's called *Rosebank* (☎ (063) 66 3191) and rooms cost from $85 a single or double, more on weekends. Children aren't allowed. There is also pub accommodation at the *Railway Hotel* (☎ (063) 66 3157) and the *Commercial Hotel* (☎ (063) 66 3157).

Molong is a larger town about 35 km north-east of Orange, at the junction of the Mitchell Highway, which runs north to Wellington, and a smaller road running west to Parkes. Molong boasts more early buildings and craft shops. There's also a museum, open on Sunday afternoon. Just out of Molong on the Orange road is the turn-off for the grave of Yuranigh, a guide on several of Major Mitchell's explorations. You can still make out carvings on several nearby trees.

If you're heading to Wellington from Molong, a slightly longer and partly unsealed route runs east of the highway, through hamlets such as **Stuart Town** (originally called Ironbark and mentioned in Banjo Paterson's poem *The Man From Ironbark*) and past the entrance to Burrendong

Dam State Recreation Area (see the following Around Wellington section).

Ophir

The Ophir goldfield was the scene of the first gold rush in Australia, one that was quickly followed by other rushes in NSW and Victoria.

The Ophir field yielded nuggets rather than gold dust, so luck played as large a part as hard work. However, the easy pickings at Ophir were soon worked out, and most of the diggers had moved on to other fields a year after the rush began. After the diggers left, deep mining was begun at Ophir and continues today at Doctors Hill. There are also a few fossickers left on the field, and small finds by visitors are not uncommon. The Orange visitor centre rents gold pans and sells fossicking licences. You can also buy a license and a pan at the Gallery of Minerals in Orange (on the Mitchell Highway at the east side of town), and they will help you identify your finds.

Unlike those at Hill End, not far east but across a range and not accessible from here, Ophir's diggings did not develop into a permanent town. The rugged, bush-covered area is now a recreation reserve, with walking and fossicking the main activities. There are still signs of the diggers' activities, with mine shafts dotted all around the area (be careful – they are unmarked).

There are several walking trails and the Orange visitor centre has a map.

Places to Stay You can camp at Fitzroy Bar at the junction of Lewis Ponds and Summer Hill creeks, the site of the diggers' tent-town. There are toilets here, and drinking-water is available.

Getting There & Away To get here from Orange, head east on March St. Be careful on the access roads, as they are unsealed but carry speedy local traffic. Some sections of road within the Ophir area are very steep and are not suitable for caravans. Several of the creek crossings are impassable after heavy rain.

Wineries

An increasing number of new wineries in the Orange area are open for sales and tastings, including Cargo Road Winery (☎ (063) 65 6100) and Canobolas-Smith (☎ (063) 65 6113), both open weekends and holidays only and both on the road running south-west from Orange to Cargo; and Windowrie Estate (☎ (063) 44 3234) near Canowindra,

---

Gold!

Australia's first goldrush, the Ophir rush, began in 1851. There had been regular finds of alluvial fields before the Ophir rush, but the government had hushed up the information, fearing the wholesale movement of population and the influx of foreigners that a goldrush would produce. Labour was needed to work the sheep stations, not to hunt for gold. Also, the idea of working people getting rich quickly went against the colony's planned social structure of an aristocracy of landowners and a peasantry of agricultural labourers.

However, in 1851 the government needed help with a stagnant economy and offered a reward to the discoverer of payable gold. Edward Hargraves, who had been on the Californian goldfields, found gold in Lewis Ponds Creek, and his associate William Tom found more nearby. Tom's father suggested the name Ophir (the biblical name for King Solomon's mines) for the field.

The government had been right to fear the consequences of a rush, as the fiercely independent 'diggers' (a word used for the first time on Ophir) from all over the world brought fresh political ideas into Australia. These democratic stirrings were to culminate in Australia's first and only popular revolt, the Eureka Rebellion on the Ballarat goldfields in 1854.

The Ophir rush lasted for only a year, but gold fever had hit NSW and was not about to go away. Tens of thousands of diggers were in constant movement from field to field for the rest of the century. ∎

open daily. Windowrie also offers meals and accommodation, but you have to book.

The Orange visitor centre has a map with detailed directions to the wineries, and you should ask if any more are now open to the public.

WELLINGTON

Wellington (population 5600) was the first settlement to be established west of Bathurst and was an important stopping-place for settlers heading into the interior.

Orientation & Information

The town meanders along the east bank of the Bell River, which joins the Macquarie River just north of the town centre. Nanima Crescent, the central section of the long shopping centre, curves past the Bell River; Cameron Park runs down to the river from Nanima Crescent and across the river is Pioneer Park.

Next to the library in Cameron Park, Wellington Travel (☎ (068) 45 1733) is also the information centre.

Things to See

The **Oxley Museum** in an impressive old bank on the corner of Warne and Percy Sts is open from 1.30 to 4.30 pm daily except Saturday. Outside the police station on the corner of Nanima Crescent and Maugham St is a light-hearted statue of a policeman; the nearby courthouse, looming like a mouldering Moghul tomb, balances this frivolity.

Across the Bell River in the forested Catombal Range there's a **lookout** on Mt Arthur, about one km west of town along Maugham St.

Festivals & Events

In March the horseracing carnival culminates in the running of the Wellington Boot.

Places to Stay

There are a couple of caravan parks, the *Riverside* (☎ (068) 45 1370) by the highway on the north bank of the Macquarie, and the small *Wellington Valley* (☎ (068) 45 2778) by the highway at the south end of town.

There's also a caravan park at nearby Wellington Caves.

The *Wellington Hotel* (☎ (068) 45 2083) on Swift St near the railway station is probably the nicest of the pubs and charges $25/35 with breakfast. Swift St runs off Nanima St at the three-way intersection near the war memorial angel in the park.

Motels in Wellington include the *Garden Court* (☎ (068) 45 2288) on the highway (from $40/50), and the *Bridge* (☎ (068) 42 2555) by the river on Lee St (from $45/55).

Getting There & Away

Bus All long-distance buses leave from the post office. Greyhound Pioneer Australia runs between Sydney ($45) and Wellington daily, arriving and departing in the early hours of the morning. Rendell's has a cheaper and more convenient daily service to Sydney ($40) and a service to Canberra on Monday, Wednesday and Friday ($40).

Sid Fogg's Dubbo to Newcastle run comes through Wellington on Monday, Wednesday and Friday.

Car & Motorbike The Newell Highway runs north to Dubbo and south to Orange. Heading east to Gulgong you have a choice between a sealed road through Goolma and a partly-unsealed road to the south. To Parkes you could take the Newell to Molong and head west from there, but there's a shorter and prettier drive through the hills to the village of Yeoval and then along some unsealed stretches of road running through farmland.

AROUND WELLINGTON
Wellington Caves

Off the highway eight km south of Wellington, the caves can be seen on guided tours, held hourly from 9 am to 4 pm, with a break for lunch at 1 pm. They cost $7.50 ($4.50 children). A growing hamlet of kitsch has a few attractions such as the **clock museum**. There's a kiosk and a *caravan park* (☎ (068) 45 3188) here.

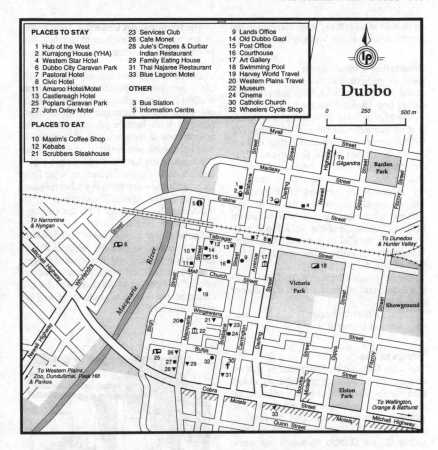

PLACES TO STAY

1 Hub of the West
2 Kurrajong House (YHA)
4 Western Star Hotel
6 Dubbo City Caravan Park
7 Pastoral Hotel
8 Civic Hotel
11 Amaroo Hotel/Motel
13 Castlereagh Hotel
25 Poplars Caravan Park
27 John Oxley Motel

PLACES TO EAT

10 Maxim's Coffee Shop
12 Kebabs
21 Scrubbers Steakhouse

23 Services Club
26 Cafe Monet
28 Jule's Crepes & Durbar
   Indian Restaurant
29 Family Eating House
31 Thai Najaree Restaurant
33 Blue Lagoon Motel

OTHER

3 Bus Station
5 Information Centre

9 Lands Office
14 Old Dubbo Gaol
15 Post Office
16 Courthouse
17 Art Gallery
18 Swimming Pool
19 Harvey World Travel
20 Western Plains Travel
22 Museum
24 Cinema
30 Catholic Church
32 Wheelers Cycle Shop

Dubbo

0   250   500 m

Burrendong State Recreation Area

About 25 km south-east of Wellington, Lake Burrendong is a large water-storage dam and is popular for watersports. Entry to the recreation area costs $3.50 per car ($1 for motorbikes). *Burrendong Park* (☎ (068) 46 7435) has camping sites ($8) and on-site vans (from $30).

The nearby **Burrendong Arboretum** is a 160 hectare, park-like place growing 2000 species of Australian plants. As well as being of botanical interest, it's a pleasant place to stroll around. It's open daily and there's no admission charge.

DUBBO

One of the larger towns in the state, Dubbo (population 29,000) is a rural centre and a transport crossroads situated at the farthest fringes of the central west region. Go north or west from Dubbo and you'll find that the population density drops dramatically and the outback begins.

History

After John Oxley passed though in 1817 it was only a few years before graziers took up land in the area. The village of Dubbo appeared by 1850 and in the 1860s first took on its role as a highway stop, catering to the people rushing to the Victorian goldfields.

Orientation & Information

Dubbo's grid-pattern city centre lies just east of the Macquarie River, with parkland bordering both banks of the river.

The Mitchell and Newell highways cross at a roundabout just west of the river. The Newell becomes Whylandra St then Erskine St as it bends east around the top end of the city centre; the Mitchell becomes Cobra St and borders the south end of the centre.

The main shopping street is Macquarie St. This is usually jammed with traffic and parking spaces are rare, so you would be better off using Brisbane St, a block east. Darling St, parallel to and east of Brisbane St, crosses the railway line and meets the Newell Highway.

The new visitor centre (☎ (068) 84 1422) is at the top end of Macquarie St, at the corner of Erskine St.

There's a laundromat on Brisbane St near the corner of Bultje St.

Things to See

The large **Old Jail** on Macquarie St is open as a museum. 'Animatronic' characters tell their stories, including that of a condemned man due for a meeting with the gallows. The gallows themselves are also on display. Admission is $3 ($1 children). Also on Macquarie St, the **Dubbo Museum** has some recreations of old shops and displays on the area's history. Admission is $3 ($1 children).

The **Regional Art Gallery** at 165 Darling St has a theme of animals in art, in a nod towards the zoo. Admission to the gallery is free.

Dubbo has the complete set of impressive old country-town buildings. The **railway station** is a fine sandstone building, and the old **pubs** along Talbragar St are suitably adorned with iron-laced verandahs. The **courthouse** at the north end of Brisbane St is an impressive neo-classical edifice. Across the street is the **Lands Department** building, which is totally different in style from the courthouse – and from any other building in town, for that matter. The visitor information centre has maps for both the Heritage Walk and the Heritage Drive.

Dundullimal is a slab house built in 1840, about two km beyond the Western Plains Zoo. It now houses craft displays and is open from 10 am to 4 pm from Tuesday to Sunday (closed in February). Admission is $4 ($2 children), but with a zoo ticket you will get a 25% discount.

A slab house

Slab Houses

Slab houses were the earliest form of permanent European housing in the newly-settled areas of NSW – the Australian equivalent of America's log cabins. The slabs were just rough-cut tree-trunks laid vertically around the frame, sometimes with mud packed into the inevitable gaps.

A slab house offered more protection than a tent but didn't require the time, tools or skills necessary for a more refined finish. Brick houses had to wait until the district was sufficiently populated to support a kiln, and stone buildings were almost exclusively the preserve of the gentry and the government.

Slab houses such as Dundullimal rarely survive, but you occasionally see more recent barns or shepherds' huts made from slabs. ∎

Koalas to the Rescue
Many of Australia's rivers are in danger of choking on the algae which feed on the nitrates and phosphates in the effluent poured into them. The phosphate problem could be solved by banning detergents which use phosphates (a simple solution, but unlikely to be implemented), but getting rid of the nitrates is more difficult.

Dubbo has been experimenting with growing plantations of trees irrigated with treated sewerage, and it seems to be successful. There's a useful spin-off from this: the koalas in the Western Plains Zoo get through a lot of manna gum leaves, and the plantations keep them in tucker. In fact, it's estimated that it takes the effluent generated by six people to grow enough trees to keep one koala happy! ∎

Western Plains Zoo

The Western Plains Zoo, Dubbo's major attraction, is off the Newell Highway about four km south-west from the town centre. The zoo is definitely worth visiting, but don't come expecting a drive-through safari park – although you can drive through, the animals are in moated enclosures. Much of the zoo's 300 hectares seems to be taken up with roads rather than space for the animals.

Of course, the animals' loss is the visitors' gain and you certainly get a good look at the inmates. The Bengal tigers and the Asiatic lions alone are worth the price of admission.

The road around the enclosures is about six km long and if it isn't too hot it's better to walk around or hire a bike ($8 for half a day) than join the crawling line of cars. Better still, hire a bike in Dubbo and ride out to the zoo (watch the heavy traffic on the highway, though).

On weekends and during school holidays, keepers give talks about the various animals. A leaflet available at the main gate has details.

The zoo is open daily from 9 am to 5 pm and admission is $14 ($7 children, family tickets available). There's a kiosk and a bistro serves lunch, with pasta dishes at about $9.

Places to Stay

Caravan Parks There are about half a dozen caravan parks in and near Dubbo. The two closest to the centre are the small *Poplars* (☎ (068) 82 4067) near the river at the west end of Bultje St and *Dubbo City* (☎ (068) 82 4820), also on the river but on the west bank and a fair distance by road from the centre, via Erskine or Cobra St.

Hostels *Kurrajong House* (☎ (068) 82 0922) is a pleasant YHA hostel at 87 Brisbane St, north of the railway line. From the bus station, head west on Erskine St. Dorm beds are $12 and there are a few twin rooms.

The managers, Noelene and Frank McCauley, are very friendly and can give good advice on travel in the area and further west. Guests get a 20% discount on zoo tickets and the YHA hires bikes for $6 a day, which is much better value than the zoo's bikes. If you don't want to ride all the way out to the zoo (it's a pretty hot pedal in summer) they can often arrange a lift with a tour company.

A couple of doors away is the *Hub of the West* (☎ (068) 82 5004). There's an old house on the street but the accommodation is behind this in a large brick building with 50 rooms resembling spartan student accommodation. It's clean and perfectly adequate, but it's not the most inspiring place to stay, especially when they have school groups there, or shearers spending their pay-cheques. Singles/doubles with shared bathrooms cost $15/30.

Hotels A number of pubs have accommodation. The *Castlereagh Hotel* (☎ (068) 82 4877) on the corner of Talbragar and Brisbane Sts is good. As usual, you don't want a room directly above the bar and you shouldn't expect everything to work perfectly, but it's clean, friendly, and many rooms have attached bathrooms (these are allocated on a first-come first-served basis). There's a pleasant dining room where a big cooked breakfast is included in the price of a room. Most importantly, the publicans are in the business of providing accommodation, not just meeting the requirements of their license. Singles cost from $25 to $30 and doubles cost $50.

Also good is the *Western Star* (☎ (068) 82 4622) on Erskine St. The meals here have been recommended and you don't have to stay here to have breakfast in the dining room.

Motels The *John Oxley Motel* (☎ (068) 82 4622) towards the south end of Macquarie St is central and cheap for Dubbo ($41/45) but the rooms are pretty small. There are more than 20 other motels, mostly along Cobra St. On long weekends and other peak times they fill up (as can all the motels along the Newell).

Places to Eat

You would expect such an important travel crossroads to have a good supply of cafes and eateries, but there are very few convenient and inexpensive places to eat. Even decent takeaways are in short supply, other than the *kebab place* on Talbragar St which has a small selection of salads. At the bus station on Erskine St there's a 24-hour cafe.

Scrubbers Steakhouse on Wingewarra St is a small place serving light meals during the day (around $8) and $20 steaks at night. There's also a member of the *Matilda's Family Steakhouse* chain at the junction of the Newell and Mitchell highways, with lunch specials from $8 and a variety of main courses for about $12. Children's meals cost $5 or less.

By far the best value is the bistro at the opulent *Services Club* on Brisbane St, where you can get a steak for about $8. Most visitors seem to end up here – three staff members were helping with the queues at the visitors' book when I arrived. As well as the bistro there's a pricey restaurant, open Wednesday to Saturday nights.

Apart from the Services Club, you're left with a handful of Chinese places along Talbragar St and counter meals at the pubs, most of which are in the $7-and-up range. There's a member of the small *Family Eating House* chain on Macquarie St, with an all-you-can-eat smorgasbord lunch for $7.50 and dinner for $12.50. Most of the dishes are Asian but there is a bit of Anglo tucker as well.

Offering an escape from mixed-grill menus is *Cafe Monet* in the Kemwah building at the corner of Macquarie and Bultje Sts. Their coffee is good and they serve both light meals (focaccia $7) and more substantial dishes (up to $15). It's open daily and from Wednesday to Saturday for dinner. A couple of doors away is *Jule's Crepes*, a little more expensive but similarly atypical of western NSW. It's licensed and is open for lunch and dinner daily. Next door is the licensed *Durbar Indian Restaurant*, open from Tuesday to Saturday for lunch and daily for dinner. On Brisbane St, next to the Catholic church with the ski-jump spire, the *Thai Najaree Restaurant* is open for lunch and dinner daily except Monday.

Several of the motels have licensed restaurants, including the French *Chez Guy* at the Forest Lodge Motel on the corner of Wheelers Lane and Myall St, north-east of the centre. You have to book (☎ (068) 84 2957). The *Blue Lagoon Motel* (☎ (068) 82 4444) at 79 Cobra St has a seafood restaurant.

Over in West Dubbo there are a couple of pasta places, including *Nino & Vince's* on Victoria St.

Entertainment

The Services Club has plenty of entertainment in the drinking-and-gambling vein. As well as the pokies there's a discreet TAB on the premises and an array of TV screens in the comfortable lounge, showing just about every event involving dogs and horses in the country. It's very tempting sit down with a beer and have a bet. Discos are held in the club on weekends.

There's a cinema on Brisbane St just south of the Services Club.

Getting There & Away

It's easiest to make bus bookings at the bus station; other travel agents include Western Plains Travel (☎ (068) 82 2833) in the Dubbo City Centre complex on Macquarie St and Harvey World Travel (☎ (068) 81 8144) nearby.

Air Eastern and Hazelton fly to Dubbo. The standard fare to Sydney is $155. Airlink flies to Bourke and some other small towns.

Train XPTs run to Sydney and the Indian Pacific stops here on its run to Perth.

Bus You can make bookings at the bus station (☎ (068) 84 2411) on Erskine St from early in the morning until 3 am the next morning. (These opening hours will give you some idea of the ungodly hours that some buses stop here.) The booking office closes on Saturday afternoon.

Most of the major bus-lines pass through on their run along the Newell, but the local company, Rendell's (☎ (068) 84 4199, 1800 023 328 toll-free), often has the cheapest fares to Sydney ($32). Sid Fogg's runs to Newcastle ($43) three times a week. To Brisbane you'll pay around $76 and the same to Broken Hill.

Countrylink has an interesting run to Lightning Ridge and services to other small towns.

Car & Motorbike Dubbo is at the junction of the Newell and Mitchell highways, so travellers who are heading for Sydney, Adelaide, Melbourne and Brisbane pass through.

Getting Around

Wheelers Cycles on the corner of Bultje and Brisbane Sts rents geared bikes for $10 a day.

AROUND DUBBO
Narromine

A sizeable but sleepy country town (population 3000) on the Mitchell Highway 30-odd km west of Dubbo, Narromine is on the very edge of the central west – there's not a lot to the west of here.

There are a couple of caravan parks, the *Narromine Hotel* (☎ (068) 89 1017) on Dandeloo St, across the railway line from the shopping centre ($18/36 with breakfast in pub rooms, $29/46 in motel units) and a couple of motels, the *Peppercorn* (☎ (068) 89 1399) and the *Stockman* (☎ (068) 89 2033).

Peak Hill

On the Newell Highway 70 km south of Dubbo, Peak Hill is a small town with several huge holes dug by gold miners. The old mines are a few blocks off the main street, on the left if you're coming from Dubbo. On the highway a few km south of Peak Hill there's a **camel farm** with rides.

PARKES

Like so many towns in the central west, Parkes (population 9000) began as a gold-rush settlement. A visit to the diggings by Sir Henry Parkes, premier of NSW, in 1871 prompted the locals to change the name of their village from Currajong and name the main street after Parkes' wife Clarinda. It is said that Parkes influenced the decision to route the railway through the town, so this sycophancy paid off.

Today, Parkes is at the junction of the railway line between Sydney and Perth and the line between Melbourne and Brisbane, and is a major freight terminal. The town is also an important rural centre and a large highway town on the Newell.

Orientation & Information

From the south, the Newell Highway takes a twisting route through the centre of Parkes, becoming Grenfell St then running up Welcome St and finally joining Clarinda St, the main shopping street, to begin its run north to Dubbo. This is a three-way intersection, with Dalton Rd, the road running west to Condobolin, also joining Clarinda St here. South of this intersection Clarinda St curves eastwards and becomes the main route to Orange.

The Parkes information centre (☎ (068) 62 4365) is in Kelly Reserve, by the highway on the Dubbo side of the town centre. It's open daily.

I stopped for a meal in Parkes on a hot Saturday night. The pubs had just closed and the main street was alive with very cheerful people. Every available flat surface held an empty beer glass and publicans were roaming around reclaiming as many as they could.

Museums
The **Henry Parkes Historical Museum** on Clarinda St displays local history from 10 am to 4 pm daily. Admission is $1.50 (60c children). **Pioneer Park**, with some relics from around the area, is open from 2 to 4 pm on Tuesday, Thursday and Saturday; admission is $1.50 (60c children).

Vintage cars are on show daily at the **Motor Museum** on the corner of Bogan and Dalton Sts (just off Clarinda St near the swimming pool); admission is $2 ($1 children).

Parkes Radio Telescope
The CSIRO's Parkes Radio Telescope, built in 1961, has helped Australian radio-astronomers become world-leaders in their science, and it was this telescope that brought you pictures of the Apollo 11 moon-landing. Parkes is now connected to the Australia Telescope array (the rest of the Australia Telescope is at Siding Springs and Culgoora). Although the actual telescope is off-limits, you can get close enough for a good look and there's a very interesting visitor centre open daily from 8.30 am to 4.30 pm, where a half-hour film is shown regularly. Admission to the visitor centre is free, the film costs $3 ($2.50 children, maximum $10 family). The visitor centre has hands-on displays and screens which show you just what the astronomers are seeing.

The telescope is four km east of the Newell Highway, about 20 km north of Parkes.

The astronomers report that one of the most consistent comments from second-time visitors is that the telescope seems to be a lot further from the highway than it used to be.

The highway hasn't changed and no-one admits to moving the telescope...

Festivals & Events
The Central West Jazz Triduum is held over the Queen's Birthday long weekend in June and there's a Country Music Jamboree on the Labour Day long weekend in early October, when there's also an antique motorbike rally. The large agricultural show takes place in late August.

Places to Stay
Caravan Parks *Spicer Park Caravan Park* (☎ (068) 62 1654) is in Spicer Park at the corner of Victoria and Albert Sts. Victoria St crosses Clarinda St four blocks north of the Dalton St intersection; head east on Victoria St and the park is four blocks away. *Currajong Caravan Park* (☎ (068) 62 3400) is by the Newell, just north of Kelly Park and the information centre. *Parkes Overnighter Caravans* (☎ (068) 62 1707) is at the corner of Dalton Rd and Bushman St, west of the centre. *Parkes Highway Caravan Park* (☎ (068) 62 1108) is on the Newell just south of town, not far from the railway station.

All have tent sites for around $10 (Spicer Park is cheapest at $8.20), all except Spicer Park have on-site vans for around $25 a double and all have cabins for about $30 a double. The cabins at Spicer Park are the best equipped.

Hotels & Motels Most of the pubs have accommodation; the cheapest are the *Royal* (☎ (068) 62 2039), the *Cambridge* (☎ (068) 62 2098) and the *Commercial* (☎ (068) 62 1526), all on Clarinda St and all charging around $15 per person. The rooms at the *Parkes Hotel* (☎ (068) 62 2498) on Welcome St (the Newell Highway) are a bit better equipped than most and cost $18/28 a single/double ($20/32 on weekends and public holidays).

Parkes is well supplied with motels. The *Clarinda Motel* (☎ (068) 62 1655) is on Clarinda St, south of the centre. With small but reasonable rooms at around $40/45 (more during holidays), it's good value.

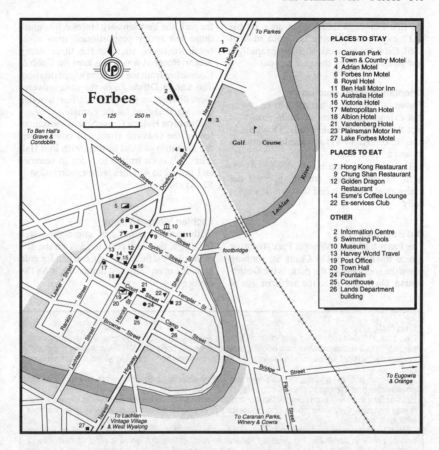

PLACES TO STAY

1 Caravan Park
3 Town & Country Motel
4 Adrian Motel
6 Forbes Inn Motel
8 Royal Hotel
11 Ben Hall Motor Inn
15 Australia Hotel
16 Victoria Hotel
17 Metropolitan Hotel
18 Albion Hotel
21 Vandenberg Hotel
23 Plainsman Motor Inn
27 Lake Forbes Motel

PLACES TO EAT

7 Hong Kong Restaurant
9 Chung Shan Restaurant
12 Golden Dragon Restaurant
14 Esme's Coffee Lounge
22 Ex-services Club

OTHER

2 Information Centre
5 Swimming Pools
10 Museum
13 Harvey World Travel
19 Post Office
20 Town Hall
24 Fountain
25 Courthouse
26 Lands Department building

There are several other places charging about the same, including the *Coachman* (☎ (068) 62 2622) on Welcome St. Of the more upmarket places, the *All Settlers Motor Inn* (☎ (068) 62 2022) on Welcome St across from Cooke Park is a fair example and costs around $52/60.

Getting There & Away

Train The Indian Pacific stops here on the run between Sydney and Perth.

Bus Trans City Tours (☎ (068) 62 3177) has a daily service to Sydney. Countrylink runs to Cootamundra and Dubbo.

Car & Motorbike As well as the Newell Highway, there are smaller roads running east to Orange and west to Condoblin and into the far west.

FORBES

A smaller town (population 8000) than nearby Parkes, Forbes has retained more of its 19th-century flavour and is worth a stop for a look around.

As with much of the state, John Oxley was

the first European through the area, on his 1817 expedition. During the gold rush of 1861 the town boomed, shrinking rapidly a few years later when the gold ran out.

Orientation & Information

Forbes is fortunate in having a town centre that extends back from the main road – in fact there are two main roads, Dowling St (the Newell Highway) and Rankin St, parallel and a block west.

The information centre (☎ (068) 52 4155) is in the old railway station, just off the highway at the north end of town. It's open daily.

Old Buildings

The **town hall** faces Victoria Park, forming a nice town square. On Court St, running down the south side of the park, is the **Courthouse**. On Spring St, on the northern side of the park, the **Vandenberg Hotel** is less grandiose but better proportioned than other hotels in town, such as the three-storey **Albion Hotel**. A watch was kept for Cobb & Co coaches from the tower on top of this pub. The **Lands Office** (now the state government offices) on Camp St is a fine wooden building, designed for the climate.

Osborne Hall on Cross St was the dancehall of the Osborne Hotel and now houses the **museum** of local history, with Ben Hall relics. It's open from 3 to 5 pm in summer and from 2 to 4 pm in winter; admission is $2 ($1 children).

Lachlan Vintage Village

With some original and some recreated buildings, the Vintage Village is on the site of the old goldfields and you can pan for gold here. It's open daily and admission is $8 ($4 children).

Ben Hall

Ben Hall (1838–1865) lived and died at a time when the ordinary people of Australia were beginning to see themselves as a people; a time when the concepts of democracy (in the social as well as political sense) and suspicion of authority were becoming ingrained in the national character.

However, political and economic power was still wielded by a British-oriented elite. Land and power were apportioned to people of quality (or at least wealth), and it was still expected that the British class system would take root in Australia. If ordinary colonials were not sufficiently servile, it was because they were crude and uneducated. The legal system was well equipped to deal with such upstarts.

Ben Hall's parents had been convicts and he grew up with a hatred of the prevailing system and of police in particular. He lived a reasonably respectable life, working as a stockman and leasing a cattle-run, until his wife left him – for a policeman! Enraged, he joined Frank Gardiner and John Gilbert and turned to bushranging.

For two years they terrorised and mocked the gentry of a large area in the Central West. Their exploits smacked of larrikinism – capturing and ridiculing police, forcing respectable folk to get drunk and sing songs, stealing racehorses, giving alcohol and cigars to the poor – and above all demonstrating that it was possible to flout the conventions of society. The gang saw themselves as latter-day Robin Hoods, and to the ordinary people of the area they were heroes. The police were unable to capture them because no-one would inform on the gang until 1865 when the government began to punish people who associated with Hall and his cronies.

Ben Hall was shot dead by police on 5 May 1865, but just how he was killed is uncertain. The official story is that he died while resisting arrest, but popular legend has it that he was shot while sleeping. His bullet-riddled body was displayed in Forbes as an awful warning to would-be renegades, but people openly mourned at his funeral and his status as a folk hero grew. Flowers are still sometimes placed on his grave in the Forbes cemetery.

A bitter folk-song, *The Streets of Forbes*, gives the popular version of his career and death.

In Farnell St in Forbes there's a replica of a house associated with another apparent rebel beloved of the common folk and still loudly mourned – Elvis Presley's Graceland. ■

Gum Swamp

Just off the Newell Highway about four km south of Forbes, this wetland area is home to many species of birds and there's a hide to watch them from.

Wineries

The **Lachlona Winery** (☎ (068) 52 2134) is west of town, off Bedgerebong Rd (the continuation of Browne St). As well as tastings (daily except Sunday) there are old underground cellars to see. **Sandhills Vineyard** (☎ (068) 52 1437) is about six km north-east of town, off Orange Rd (the continuation of Camp and Bridge Sts) and is open for tastings on Monday and from Thursday to Saturday. There's a wine museum here. There's also **Lachlan Valley Wines** (☎ (068) 52 3983), on Wandary Lane which splits from the Cowra road just after the Apex caravan park. It's open daily except Sunday.

Places to Stay

Caravan Parks The *Country Club Caravan Park* (☎ (068) 52 1957) is on the highway north of town. The *Forbes River Meadows Caravan Park* (☎ (068) 52 2694) is by the Lachlan (and the Newell) on the south-west side of town. There's also the *Apex Caravan Park* (☎ (068) 52 1929), also by the Lachlan but on the south-east side of town, near the road to Cowra.

Hotels & Motels The old *Vandenberg Hotel* (☎ (068) 52 2015), on Court St across from Victoria Park, has rooms for around $25/35. On Lachlan St, the *Albion Hotel* (☎ (068) 52 1919) is an impressive old pile.

Most of the motels are pricey. The *Lake Forbes Motel* (☎ (068) 52 2922) is about the cheapest at $40/50, although it's very close to the highway, as are many of the others. Near Victoria Park and the town centre at 22 Sheriff St, the *Plainsman Motor Inn* (☎ (068) 52 2466) is reasonable, although not cheap at $57/68. The location is quiet but some of the air-conditioning isn't.

Farmstay *Blink Bonnie Lodge* (☎ (068) 52 2344 for bookings) is on a working sheep property and offers accommodation in an impressive old homestead (1880) or a nearby lodge. It costs $105/190 or $70/100 without activities. Blink Bonnie is about 45 km south-east of Forbes; you'll get detailed directions when you book.

Places to Eat

There isn't much choice, especially for inexpensive, quick meals. On Templar St, *Esme's Coffee Lounge* has smoothies.

There are three Chinese places within a short walk of each other: the *Hong Kong*, the *Chung Shan* and the *Golden Dragon*. The *Ex-Services Club* on the corner of Sheriff and Templar Sts has a restaurant, and there are plenty of pub meals on offer.

Out at the Lachlan Vintage Village there's the *Blackridge Restaurant* which serves local wines.

Getting There & Away

Harvey World Travel (☎ (068) 52 2344) at 6 Templar St handles bus and air bookings.

Air Hazelton flies to Sydney twice a day.

Bus Being on the Newell, Forbes has a lot of long-distance bus traffic, including Greyhound Pioneer Australia and McCafferty's. Countrylink buses stop at the railway station and run to Orange, Parkes and Condoblin.

Car & Motorbike As well as the Newell Highway there are smaller roads heading east to Canowindra and Cowra, south to Grenfell and west to Condoblin and into the far west.

Getting Around

You can phone for a taxi (☎ (068) 52 2222). Car-rental companies Budget (☎ (068) 52 2245) and Hertz (☎ (068) 52 1755) have agents in town.

CONDOBLIN

Condoblin (pronounced con-*dough*-bln and often called Condo for short) is a medium-sized town (population 3500) on the Lachlan River. It's the service centre for farms in the

Lachlan Valley, but to the west and north the dry country begins.

Craft is sold in a nice ex-pub at the east end of Bathurst St, the main street.

There were once many Chinese living in the area and there's a restored section of Chinese graves in the cemetery.

The 40-hectare **Gum Bend Lake** was built as a bicentennial project in 1988 and is a venue for watersports. The lake is three km west of Condo. A couple of places in town, Taylor's Marine on Lachlan St and Parnaby's Store on Bathurst St, hire watersports equipment.

About eight km north of Condo is **Mt Tilga**, officially the geographical centre of NSW. There's a road to the bottom and you can climb to the top.

The **Overflow Station**, apparently the home of Banjo Paterson's famous Clancy, is 12 km from Bobadah (north-west of Condoblin on unsealed roads) on the Pangee road. It isn't usually open to the public but there are sometimes tours – check by phoning (☎ (068) 37 3820).

Places to Stay

The *Riverview Caravan Park* (☎ (068) 95 2036) is a shady place on the banks of the Lachlan, just south of the bridge.

There are a couple of motels, the *Condoblin* (☎ (068) 95 2233) and the *Allambie* (☎ (068) 95 2722), both on William St, and the *Condoblin Hotel* (☎ (068) 95 2040) has motel-style units. There are also a couple of other pubs with accommodation.

Getting There & Away

Harvey World Travel (☎ (068) 95 2988) on the main street handles air and bus bookings.

Air Hazelton flies daily to/from Sydney.

Bus Countrylink buses run to Cootamundra via Lake Cargelligo, West Wyalong and Temora, and to Parkes, Forbes and Orange.

Car & Motorbike Roads run east to the Newell Highway at Parkes or Forbes, and south to the Newell at West Wyalong. You can drive west to Lake Cargelligo and on to the Riverina and the far west. There are also some interesting routes north; see the following section.

NORTH OF CONDOBLIN

North of Condoblin, the farmland begins to blur into the outback. If you're heading north to the Barrier Highway there are several routes from Condoblin which don't involve backtracking to the Newell Highway. These are all at least partly unsealed, so check conditions before setting out and take a good map.

To Cobar, the Nymagee road runs through **Bobadah** (no fuel or accommodation) and **Nymagee**, a hamlet with basic services including the *Nymagee Hotel* (☎ (068) 37 3854). You can also get to Cobar on the **Kidman Way**. To get to this unsealed (but perhaps soon-to-be-sealed) route you can head west to Euabalong, about 60 km west of Condoblin, but for better roads head south-west through Lake Cargelligo and take the turn-off onto the Kidman Way midway between Lake Cargelligo and Hillston. **Mt Hope** consists of the *Royal Hotel* (☎ (068) 97 7984), a service station and a shop. It's a friendly hamlet (population 12) and used to be a large copper-mining town. If you're a motorcyclist, the annual Mt Hope Rally, held on the last weekend in May, is a good time to visit. The only other place along this road is **Gilgunnia**, where there are no facilities.

To Nyngan you can either head directly north from Condoblin (if you have a good map) or, for a better road, drive east towards Parkes and turn off to **Tullamore**, a fair-sized village with a pub (☎ (068) 92 5195), fuel and shops about 80 km north-east of Condoblin. Further on is **Tottenham**, a smaller but nicer place. There's a pub here as well (☎ (068) 92 4211). Just off this route is the small town of **Trundle**, which has what is reputedly Australia's widest street.

COWRA

Cowra (population 9000) developed because it was on the only easy crossing of the Lachlan River for some way. The town strag-

The Cowra Breakout

During WW II there was a large POW camp at Cowra, holding mainly Italian and Japanese prisoners. In the early hours of 5 August 1944 the Japanese prisoners over-ran their section of the camp and nearly 400 went over the wire in an escape attempt that never had a chance of succeeding. Of the 230 Japanese who were killed, many committed suicide.

The official report of the Cowra breakout (available at the information centre for $2) makes interesting reading. It's strange that amid the racist propaganda of WW II, the inquiry into the breakout was concerned about how much force was used on the escapees and whether the Japanese dead were treated with respect. Soldiers hunting the escapees were armed only with bayonets until one was killed.

The book *Die Like the Carp* (available at the information centre) tells the story of the breakout.■

gles up the side of a steep hill above the Lachlan River. The main landmark in town is the one set of traffic lights, on the corner of Kendal St (the Mid-Western Highway) and Brisbane St.

The information centre (☎ (063) 42 4333) is on the highway west of the shopping centre, across the bridge.

During WW II, the POW camp at Cowra was the scene of the Cowra breakout. The **Japanese War Cemetery** is a few km north of town on Binni Creek Rd (Brisbane St).

Japanese Garden

Built as a token of Cowra's connection with Japanese POWs (but with no overt mention of the war or the breakout), the garden and the attached cultural centre are well worth visiting. The large garden, serene and beautifully maintained, was a gift from the Japanese government. The cultural centre is a peaceful place with displays of modern Japanese art, some modern Japanese kitsch and some antiques. There is a collection of Ukiyo-e paintings, depicting everyday events in the lives of ordinary people in pre-industrial Japan.

The garden is open from 8 am to 5 pm daily and admission is $4.50 ($2.50 children). Drop in even if it's raining, as there are umbrellas to shelter you on a walk around.

The garden is at the top of Bellevue Hill, a steep km or so north up Brisbane St. Also on the hilltop is the **Bellevue Hill Flora & Fauna Reserve**, a complete contrast to its formal neighbour.

Steam Museum

The Cowra Steam Museum is on Campbell St and is open on weekends and holidays. It's the headquarters of the Lachlan Valley Railway Society which sometimes runs vintage trains.

Festivals & Events

The agricultural show is held in early October and Sakura Matsuri, the Cherry Blossom Festival, is held later that month.

Places to Stay

Caravan Parks The *Cowravan Park* (☎ (063) 42 1058) is by the river on Lachlan St, just south of Kendal St. There are sites and cabins.

Hotels & Motels Several hotels have accommodation, including the big *Imperial Hotel* (☎ (063) 42 1588) at the west end of Kendal St, with basic rooms for $25/30/35 a single/double/triple.

Motels include the *Cowra* (☎ (063) 42 2799) on Macquarie St (from $35/40) and the *Aalana* (☎ (063) 41 1177) at 161 Kendal St (around $50/60); the *Vineyard* (☎ (063) 42 3641) is a small place about four km southwest of town, well away from highway noise (around $55/70).

Places to Eat

The pies sold at *Royce's Bakery* on Kendal St regularly score well in the Great Aussie Meat Pie competition.

Across from the Imperial Hotel at the west end of Kendal St there's the *Ling Hing*

Chinese restaurant and a couple of pizza takeaways; up from here is the *Garden of Roses* cafe.

Ilfracombe, a historic cottage at 127 Kendal St, east of the traffic lights, now houses a good restaurant and a cafe in a new extension next door. This is an excellent place to eat and it's a little surprising to find it here among the takeaways and counter meals of a country town. The restaurant (☎ (063) 41 1511) is open for dinner from Wednesday to Saturday and has a French-based menu using local produce and serving local wines. Main courses are around $18. The cafe is open from Tuesday to Saturday for lunch and dinner, with main courses around $10 to $15. You can have a snack and one of the many variations on coffee from 10.30 am. On Saturday night you can have dinner in the cafe and get a movie ticket as well for $15.

Getting There & Away

Bus Rendell's Coaches stop at the information centre on the run between Dubbo and Canberra. Greyhound Pioneer Australia stops at the Mobil station near the information centre on its run between Melbourne and Brisbane. Countrylink stops on Macquarie St near the corner of Kendal St and runs to Bathurst and Cootamundra.

Travel agents include Lachlan Travel (☎ (063) 42 4000) on Kendal St, the Countrylink agent.

Car & Motorbike

Cowra is on the Mid-Western Highway which runs west through Grenfell to the Newell Highway near West Wyalong and north-east to Bathurst. The Olympic Way runs south-west to Young and Wagga Wagga. Smaller roads run south to the Hume Highway at Yass, south-east to Crookwell and Goulburn, also on the Hume, north to Canowindra and north-west to Forbes.

AROUND COWRA

To the west of Cowra the Lachlan River flows through fertile farmland – very pretty country. The road to Forbes (turn off the

Mid-Western Highway about five km south of Cowra) runs along the south bank of the Lachlan and is a nice drive. At Paynters Bridge, about 45 km on from the turn-off, cross the Lachlan to visit **Eugowra**, a rambling village in the shadow of bush-clad hills. Eugowra was held up by Ben Hall in 1863, and there is a re-enactment every October. Granite quarried here was used to build the new Parliament House in Canberra. You can also get here (and to Forbes) via Canowindra, on a road running down the north side of the Lachlan.

Canowindra

Canowindra (population 1750), about 30 km north of Cowra, is a sprawling village, and Gaskill St, the main street, follows the route of a bullock-cart track. In 1863 bushranger Ben Hall held the town for three days.

Canowindra has a number of old buildings and would probably be ripe for becoming a crafts/antiques ghetto were it not that the town is a service centre for the surrounding rich farmlands.

The bakery on the apex of Gaskill St's curve has limited tourist information and good pies.

The Garden of Roses Cafe is now a grocery and takeaway, but check out the old stained glass inside.

Nearby there's a shopfront displaying some of the finds from a rich fossil-bed recently discovered in the area, including a 395-million-year-old fish, *Canowindra grossi*. Many more finds are expected and eventually there may be a museum to house them. It might be possible for you to go along on a fossil-seeking expedition – the information centre at Cowra(☎ (063) 42 4333) should be able to direct you to the expedition organisers.

There's a small **museum** in the park at the end of Gaskill St, open from 2 to 4 pm on Sunday and from 11 am to noon if you phone (☎ (063) 44 1534) for someone to let you in. Admission is $2 (50c children).

The main attraction of Canowindra is **ballooning**, with several outfits offering flights, such as Balloon Aloft (☎ (063) 44 1797;

Top Left: The Golden Guitar, Tamworth, New England (JM)
Top Right: Statue, Tamworth, New England (JM)
Bottom: Club Hotel, Glen Innes, New England (JM)

Top: Roller with a roo-bar, far west (JM)
Bottom Left: Target practice, far west (JM)
Bottom Right: Bog-eye, far west (JM)

1800 028 568 toll-free) which charges from about $150.

Places to Stay The *caravan park* (☎ (063) 44 1272) is by the river, near the top end of Gaskill St. The *Canowindra Hotel* (☎ (063) 44 1407), on Gaskill St near the park, has singles/doubles for $17.50/30. The *Blue Jacket Motel* (☎ (063) 44 1002) is on the Cowra road, across the river and a couple of km from the village centre.

Grabine State Recreation Area
Taking in Wyangala Dam south-east of Cowra, this is a popular watersports area with a caravan park. There are also *houseboats* (☎ (063) 45 0877) sleeping seven or eight from around $250 for one night, less for longer.

Conimbla National Park
This is a small park (7600 hectares) in two sections, only one of which has ready access. There's some nice forest and, in the spring, wildflowers.

As yet there are no campsites within the park but the *Barryrenie Camping Ground* (☎ (063) 42 9239) is at the south-eastern end, on the main access road. This is a simple place geared to bushwalkers and the facilities are basic, but the owners are friendly and can help with information on the park. Sites cost $6 per person.

The road running through the park can be reached from Gooloogong in the north (on the road between Cowra and Forbes) or from Cowra – head east towards Grenfell for about eight km and take the signposted turn-off on the right.

Nangar National Park
This small park (4000 hectares) is 15 km east of Eugowra on the road to Cudal and Orange. Despite its size there is a range of vegetation and it offers some tough bushwalking. There are no facilities and only foot access. The National Parks office in Bathurst (☎ (063) 32 3735) has more information.

Iandra
Midway between Cowra and Young, Iandra is a 19th-century mansion built by George Henry Green in the style of an English country house. Originally the homestead of Iandra station, it was for a while a Methodist boys' home but is now a private residence. You can't actually visit the house, but you can catch a glimpse, as the road runs past the park-like grounds.

The simplest way to get to Iandra is to head for Greenthorpe (once Iandra station's own village) from the Olympic Way south of Cowra or from the Mid-Western Highway between Cowra and Grenfell. Iandra is about 10 km south of Greenthorpe. You can follow this road all the way south to Young.

Grenfell
Grenfell (population 2300) is a quiet country town, but in 1867 there were 10,000 diggers here searching for gold. Main St curves through the town centre and has some impressive buildings, notably the banks. Running parallel to it is tiny George St, the original and even more curved main street where one or two of the original buildings still stand.

Some tourist information is available from the craft shop on Main St.

The town's main claim to fame is that Henry Lawson was born here in 1867, although he and his family left for the goldfields near Gulgong when he was an infant. There's an annual **Henry Lawson Arts Festival**, held around the writer's birthday on 17 June. There is a memorial marking Lawson's birthplace, off the highway at the eastern edge of town; turn off just before the railway crossing.

For something completely different, Grenfell hosts the **National Guinea Pig Races** in June.

The *Exchange Hotel* (☎ (063) 43 1034) on Main St has rooms from $15 per person, or you could try the equally impressive *Railway Hotel* at the bottom end of Main St. The *Grenfell Motel* (☎ (063) 43 1333) is also on Main St and charges around $40/50.

Weddin Mountain National Park

Just south-west of Grenfell, Weddin is not large (8360 hectares), but it's a rugged place with some good walking trails, including a two-day walk. Holy Camp on the north-west side and Seatons Camp on the north-east side are camping areas, both with road access. You can walk between them. The Bathurst National Parks office (☎ (063) 32 3735) has more information.

WEST WYALONG

West Wyalong, a middling town (population 3500) on the Newell and Mid-Western Highways, is a rare example of stubbornness winning out over bureaucracy. A settlement grew here during a gold rush late last century, but the government decided that Wyalong, a few km east, was to be the town. A grid of streets was laid out, official buildings were erected and the government waited for the population of West Wyalong to get the message and move. They didn't. West Wyalong is still the larger town and its Main St follows the same curving path it did when it was a bullock track.

There's an information centre (☎ (069) 72 3645) in an old railway carriage in McCann Park, on the Mid-Western Highway at the east end of Main St.

Things to See

The Bland District (West Wyalong is part of this unfortunately-named shire) **museum** is at the west end of Main St and is open daily between 2.30 and 5 pm. The collection of photos of the goldfields and the town's development is interesting.

The local Aboriginal Land Council has a craft and artefact shop at 76 Main St, towards the eastern end.

In **Bardeman**, 35 km south on the Temora Rd, a huge swimming pool has been developed using an old mineshaft and a mineral spring. Whether it really has therapeutic properties is debatable, but it's a good place for a swim.

When it is full, **Lake Cowal** is the largest freshwater lake in the state. The area is an animal sanctuary and the lake supports plenty of birdlife, but getting to see it isn't simple. The lake is surrounded by farmland and even the usually accurate NRMA map has problems with the tangle of back-roads and farm tracks around the lake. I suspect that some public roads might have been closed off by farmers. Meandering around these tracks is a pleasant enough way to fill an hour or two, but don't try it after heavy rain. A road leading in the general direction of the lake leaves the Newell Highway about 15 km north of Marsden, a hamlet at the junction of the Mid-Western Highway. Good luck.

Places to Stay

There are a couple of caravan parks, the *Ace* (☎ (069) 72 3061) at the corner of the Newell and Mid-Western highways, and the *West Wyalong* (☎ (069) 72 3133) on Main St. Both have sites, cabins and on-site vans.

Tattersalls Hotel (☎ (069) 72 2030) on Main St at the corner of Monash St celebrated 100 years of ownership by the same family in 1994. It's a friendly place with pub rooms for $20/28 and cooked breakfast for $5. Across the road, the *Post Office Hotel* (☎ (069) 72 2118), which is a fair way from the post office, also has accommodation.

The *Acacia Golden Way Motel* (☎ (069) 72 2155) at the east end of Main St is good value at $45/55 for large rooms. There are about a dozen more motels, most around the same price or dearer; the *Central* (☎ (069) 72 2777) on the Mid-Western Highway at the east end of town is a little cheaper.

Places to Eat

The *New Paragon Cafe* is West Wyalong's main-street eatery, with *Rowie's* a little further along.

The pubs on Main St have counter meals. The *Tattersalls Hotel* has 'bistro meals at counter-meal prices' six days a week. There are a couple of Chinese restaurants on the main street, and the *Services & Citizens Club* on Monash St has a restaurant.

In Wyalong there's a 24-hour service station where you can buy meals.

Getting There & Away

Countrylink buses run to Cootamundra and Condoblin. The stop is on Church St, around the corner from the post office on the main street. Harvey World Travel (☎ (069) 72 2744) next to the post office takes bookings.

YOUNG

Young (population 6700) is at the edge of the western slopes of the Great Divide. East of here is rolling country; to the west the plains of the Riverina begin.

Cherries were first planted here around 1860 by Nicole Jasprizza, who arrived during one of the central west's many gold rushes. His orchard was an immediate success and expanded rapidly.

Today there are about 130 orchards producing a large proportion of Australia's crop and earning Young its Cherry Capital tag. Prunes are also an important local industry, but I guess that Prune Capital doesn't have quite the same ring.

The notorious 'White Australia policy' of Australia's early years had its origins near Young – goldfield riots at Lambing Flat in 1861 led to the government restricting Chinese immigration, a classic example of blaming the victim.

Information

The tourist information centre (☎ (063) 82 3394) is near the creek on Short St (the Olympic Way as it enters town from the south) and is open daily.

Work Cherry harvest time is in November and December. In January other stone fruits are harvested and in February the prune harvest begins. The local CES office (☎ (063) 82 3366) at 187 Boorowa St can help you find harvest work.

Things to See

On Boorowa St, the main street, across from the town hall with its memorial tower (and a soldier occupying the place where Queen Victoria or another foreign deity would usually be), is the **Millard's Building**. It was once a huge department store built by Edward Millard who started out as a 'carpenter, joiner and undertaker'. It's hard to imagine a time when it was crammed with merchandise and busy clerks.

The **Lambing Flat Folk Museum** on Campbell St displays many artefacts from the goldfields.

The information centre can tell you about **orchards** that are open for inspection.

Wineries This area produced wine grapes from the 1880s until the 1930s, when the more profitable cherry orchards took over. In the 1970s Barwang vineyard was established, and there are now about 15 small vineyards in the area, with three wineries: Woodonga Hill (☎ (063) 89 2972), northeast of Young on the Cowra road; Hercynia (☎ (063) 84 4243), south on the Prunevale road (head for Kingsvale); and Nioka Ridge (☎ (063) 82 2903), south-east on the Moppity road. All are open for sales and tastings.

Festivals & Events

The Cherry Festival is held over several weeks in late November and early December – but if you want to see the trees in blossom, come in early October, when there's a Cherry Blossom Festival.

The show is held in late September. The Young-Burragong Picnic Races are held in May, and this is one of the largest picnic race meetings in the state.

Places to Stay & Eat

The *Young Caravan Park* (☎ (063) 82 2190) on Zouch St (the Olympic Way) across the railway line north of the town centre, has tent sites for $9, on-site vans from $25 and self-contained units from $35.

A number of pubs have accommodation, the cheapest being the *Empire* (☎ (063) 82 1665) on Lovell St at $15/25 (twin $28). Most of the others charge about $20/30. The *Great Eastern Hotel Motel* (☎ (063) 82 2411) on Boorowa St charges $20/35 ($40 twin) in the hotel section and $35/45 ($50 twin) in the motel.

The other motels, including the *Cherry*

CENTRAL WEST

Blossom (☎ (063) 82 1699), the *Colonial* (☎ (063) 82 2822) and the *Tadlock* (☎ (063) 82 3300), are in the $50/60 bracket and some add a $10 holiday loading.

The information centre has details of B&Bs and farmstays in the area.

Gabriella's Place in Rialto Square on Lovell St (parallel to and a block north of Young's main street) serves Italian food from 5.30 pm.

Getting There & Away
Bus Countrylink buses run to Cootamundra and Bathurst. Greyhound Pioneer Australia stops at the railway station on its run between Melbourne and Brisbane.

Car & Motorbike The Olympic Highway runs north-east from Young to Cowra and south to Cootamundra. Smaller roads run north to Grenfell, west to Temora and south-east to Yass.

COOTAMUNDRA
Cootamundra (population 6500), by the Cooramundry Creek and with the smaller Muttama Creek flowing through town, is the service centre for the surrounding fertile farmland and is an important railway junction. The town was founded in about 1860 and was know then as Cootamundry. It wasn't until the 1950s that the current name was officially recognised.

Cootamundra wattle

The town is some way from the main through-routes and retains a coherence lacking in highway towns. Its neat grid of streets contains many fine examples of houses built in the Federation style, and there are also a few earlier Victorian gems.

Orientation & Information
Parker St is the main shopping street and its intersection with Wallendoon St, where you'll find the impressive post office, town hall and several banks, is the centre of town. There's a tourist centre (☎ (069) 42 1400) at the railway station, open daily from 8 am to 7 pm but inconveniently closing between 11 am and 5 pm on weekends.

Things to See
Cootamundra is in the foothills of the Great Divide and the town is cold in winter, sometimes receiving snowfalls. The climate means that European street trees flourish (the elms along Cooper St are 100 years old) and there are several quite formal parks, including **Albert Park** on Hovell St near the railway station and **Jubilee Park**, with an Olympic-size swimming pool built in 1935, on the other side of the city centre. Just south of town, across the Cooramundry Creek, **Pioneer Park** is a nature reserve taking in some hilly bushland with picnic places and good views. There are plans to re-introduce koalas.

The town of Cootamundra is best known for the **Cootamundra wattle** *(Acacia baileyana)*; its profuse yellow flowers are a sign that winter is nearly over. Although native to this area, Cootamundra wattle has been extensively planted throughout the cooler areas of southern Australia. The Wattle Time Festival is held in August.

Sir Donald Bradman was born here in 1908, and his family's home, a modest weatherboard house at 89 Adams St (the north-east end of Adams St), is being turned into a museum. The Bradmans moved to Bowral when he was still very young, and it's there that The Don learned his craft.

Places to Stay & Eat

The *Cootamundra Caravan Park* (☎ (069) 42 1080) is well sited in pretty Jubilee Park, beside the Muttama Creek and only a block or two from the town centre.

The *Globe* (☎ (069) 42 1446) and *Albion* (☎ (069) 42 1177) hotels at the corner of Parker and Wallendoon Sts have pub rooms. There are several motels, including the *Wattle Tree* (☎ (069) 42 2688) on Wallendoon St, not far from the railway station, which charges about $40/50.

In the hamlet of **Bethungra**, 20 km south-west on the Olympic Way to Junee, the *Shirley Hotel* (☎ (069) 43 4431) is an impressive pub with accommodation for $30 a single and $70 for a double with attached bathroom.

There aren't very many places to eat in Cootamundra. *Country Cuisine* on Parker St has coffee and light meals, such as fettuccine ($5), and next door is *The Chatterie*, a BYO restaurant. Other than that, you could try the pubs or the Country Club on Hurley St.

Getting There & Away

There's a Countrylink Travel Centre (☎ (069) 42 0446) at the railway station.

Train XPTs running between Sydney and Melbourne stop here.

Bus Countrylink buses meet the train and run to Bathurst via Cowra, Dubbo via Forbes and Parkes, Condoblin via West Wyalong and Lake Cargelligo, and to Balranald via Griffith.

Car & Motorbike The Olympic Way runs north-east to Young and south-west to Junee and Wagga Wagga. Smaller roads run north-west to Temora and south to the Hume Highway; you can also meet the Hume by heading south-east to Yass.

The North-West

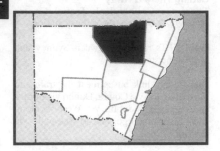

This wedge of NSW, between New England and the Mitchell Highway, is flat, dry but largely fertile country, especially in the broad valley of the Namoi River. Cattle and cotton are the main products.

Many of the towns are small, relaxed places, still conscious of the hard work that went into their establishment, and conscious that their status as outposts of settlement gives them an importance greater than their size. It is only since WW II that good roads have linked many towns, and even today they can be isolated by floods.

Except for visitors to the Warrumbungle National Park and the steady stream of traffic on the Newell Highway, the north-west doesn't see many tourists.

Geography
Unlike other regions on the west of the Great Divide, there are few significant foothills in the north-west. The Warrumbungle and Nandewar ranges straddle the fertile Namoi Valley, but the river soon meanders west onto the plains to join the Barwon River, which becomes the Darling River – which eventually joins the Murray and flows to South Australia.

Much of the area is a vast artesian basin, and there are hot artesian baths in Moree and Lightning Ridge. Bore water is often too salty for human consumption, and even

potable water can taste strongly of sulphur – if you let it stand for a while, the gases dissipate and the taste fades.

Getting There & Away
Air Airlink, Yanda Airlines (book through Ansett), Hazelton (book through Ansett), Eastern (book through Qantas) and Ansett are among the airlines serving the north-west.

Train Explorer trains from Sydney run north as far as Moree.

Bus Towns on the Newell Highway are served by Brisbane to Melbourne or Adelaide buses. Countrylink connects most other towns in the area with Sydney, usually with a train/bus combination via Dubbo, Tamworth or Moree.

Car & Motorbike The Newell Highway, running through the north-west, is a good road that provides the quickest route between Melbourne and Brisbane. The Castlereagh Highway, forking off the Newell at Gilgandra, runs more or less directly north into the rugged opal country towards the Queensland border, its surfaced section ending soon after Lightning Ridge. The Mitchell Highway heads west through Nyngan, and the Gwydir Highway runs from Collarenebri east through the region to New England.

GUNNEDAH
Gunnedah is a large country town (population 10,000) on the Oxley Highway and the edge of the Namoi Valley's plains. Back in the hills to the north-east is Lake Keepit, a big dam on the Namoi which provides water for irrigating the region's cotton crops.

There is also coal in the area, and in a few decades production might rival that of the Hunter Valley.

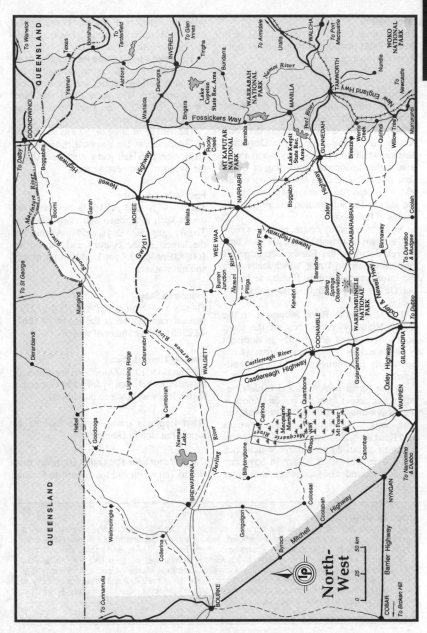

Information

The Visitors Centre (☎ (067) 1564) is in Anzac Park, just south of the railway lines from the town centre.

Things to See & Do

Near the information centre is the **Water Tower Museum**, open from 2 to 5 pm on Saturday. There are views from the roof. Nearby in Anzac Park is the **Dorothea Mackellar Memorial**. A very short-range transmitter broadcasts a recording of Dorothea Mackellar reading *My Country* on 88 FM – you have to be within 100 metres of the statue. The information centre has free copies of the poem.

At the information centre, pick up a copy of the **town tour** map. There are also brochures detailing the Lands Department's **Bindeah Walking Track**, which leads from the information centre to Porcupine Lookout. On the way you might see kangaroos and koalas.

The **Gunnedah Rural Museum** on the Oxley Highway to the west of the town boasts 'the largest gun display in northern NSW' as well as antique farm equipment. It's open daily and admission is $3 ($1.50 children).

At the corner of Abbott and Little Conadilly Sts, across from the police station, is the **grave-site of Cumbo Gunnerah**, an 18th-century Aboriginal leader known as Red Kangaroo. His burial place is marked by a bronze cast of the carved tree which once stood over the site. It is rare to have any physical reminder of individual Aborigines who lived before European contact. The events of Cumbo Gunnerah's life are related in *The Red Chief* by Ian Idriss.

The **Lake Keepit State Recreation Area** is about 35 km north-east of Gunnedah. It's a popular holiday centre, with boating and other activities. The large *Easts Van Park* (☎ (067) 69 7620) has sites from $8 and on-site vans and tents.

The village of **Breeza**, 57 km south-east of Gunnedah, is the disputed birthplace of bushranger Ben Hall, and a mural here shows the events of Ben's last years.

Festivals & Events

The show is held in April, and there are events such as a rodeo and camp drafting. The Ag-quip Field Days, held in August, are the largest in the country and can attract 100,000 people to gawk at the machinery and innovations.

Places to Stay

There's a *caravan park* (☎ (067) 42 1372), pub accommodation at the *Regal* (☎ (067) 42 2355) and a number of motels.

Getting There & Away

Air Yanda (☎ 13 1300 for bookings through Ansett) flies between Sydney and Gunnedah ($160, less with advance purchase).

Train Explorer trains on the Sydney to Moree run stop in Gunnedah.

Car & Motorbike The Oxley Highway runs east to Tamworth and south-west to Coona-

---

Ode to a New Country

While many Australians know the second verse of *My Country*, the one that begins 'I love a sunburnt country', not many know the whole poem, which is a declaration of independence from 'The love of field and coppice/Of green and shaded lanes'. These sentiments weren't very remarkable in Australia in the early 1900s, when writers and painters had already staked Australia's claim to an individual identity. However, Dorothea Mackellar came from a wealthy, landed family, the sort of people who looked to England as 'home'. That she wrote poetry not just extolling the Australian landscape but comparing it more than favourably to England is a sign that the new nation had found its feet. ■

barabran. Smaller roads run north to Boggabri and Narrabri, and south to Coolah and the upper end of the Hunter Valley.

BOGGABRI & AROUND

Boggabri, 40 km north-west of Gunnedah on the road to Narrabri, is a sleepy little town which still manages to support three old pubs. There's a small **museum**.

Gin's Leap, about six km north of Boggabri, is a sheer rockface with great views from the top. (There are probably as many gins' leaps in Australia as there are bushrangers' caves – many cliffs seem to have presented themselves as suicide places for Aboriginal women, at least in White imaginations, just as any hole in the ground is obviously the hide-out of some desperado.)

About 35 km from Boggabri and 85 km south-east of Narrabri, **Dripping Rock** is a 50-metre waterfall that is spectacular after rain and never quite dries up. To get there, take the Manilla road turn-off just north of Boggabri and turn left at the Mauls Creek sign after eight km. Three km later take the right-hand turn and travel 16 km. You'll pass through a couple of gates before you arrive at the car park, from where it's a short walk to the falls. This is a dry-weather road.

The **Wean Picnic Races** are held on the first Monday in May and attract large crowds. The racetrack is about 80 km south-east of Narrabri, 22 km east of Boggabri.

Up the Newell

GILGANDRA

This sizeable town (population 2700) on the Castlereagh River is at the junction of the Newell, Castlereagh and Oxley highways.

The visitor centre (☎ (068) 47 2045) and the small **museum** (admission $2) are in Coo-ee March Memorial Park on the Newell Highway south of the town centre. During WW I, Gilgandra was the starting point for the Coo-ee March, when 26 volunteers set off for Sydney to enlist. Along the way they attracted 237 others, and all of them were duly shipped to the trenches.

Gilgandra Observatory is a private set-up on Willie St with a 31-cm telescope, open from Thursday to Monday from 2 to 4 pm and 7 to 10 pm. There is an audiovisual of the moon landings and other space flights. Admission is $2 ($1 children).

The **Australia Collection** is a large private collection of Aboriginal artefacts. It's on the north edge of town by the Castlereagh Van Park.

For some reason, Gilgandra is well supplied with antique and second-hand shops.

Places to Stay

There are three caravan parks, including the *Rotary Caravan Park* (☎ (068) 47 2423) by the river across the bridge from town. Tent sites cost about $8 and cabins start at $28.

On the main street, the *Golden West Hotel* (☎ (068) 47 2109) has singles/doubles for $15/24; the nearby and marginally better *Royal Hotel* (☎ (068) 47 2004) charges $15/25 and $35 for triples.

As Gilgandra is a junction town, there are plenty of motels here, many charging about $40/45 or less, but prices rise on long weekends.

Getting There & Away

Bus The major lines stop here on their Newell Highway services. Countrylink buses run to Lightning Ridge and Dubbo.

Car & Motorbike The Newell Highway runs north-east to Coonabarabran (this section of it doubles as the Oxley) and south to Dubbo; the Castlereagh Highway runs north to Coonamble; and the Oxley Highway runs west to Warren and Nyngan (and north-east to Coonabarabran). A smaller road runs south-east to Dunedoo and Mudgee.

COONABARABRAN

Coonabarabran (pronounced coona-*barra*-brn) is a small country town (population 3000) which retains its shady main street (John St), despite its being both the Newell and Oxley highways.

As well as serving as a base for visits to the Warrumbungle National Park, Coonabarabran is a handy stop on the Newell, being roughly halfway between Brisbane and Melbourne (although motels tend to be cheaper further south in Gilgandra). It's about 450 km from Sydney, a fairly easy day's drive.

The town's name comes from Cooleburbarun, a squatting lease which was taken up in 1839, 20 years after John Oxley's party made the first European foray into the homelands of the Kamilario people.

The information centre (☎ (068) 42 1441) is on John St a few blocks south of the clocktower and is open from 9 am to 5 pm daily. There's also a National Parks office (☎ (068) 42 1311) on Cassilis St.

The Ryder Bros sports store on John St probably sells everything you've forgotten to bring for your camping trip to the Warrumbungles. It's a pleasantly chaotic old shop.

Things to See & Do
On the highway just north of the centre is **Crystal Kingdom**, which has local and regional crystals, gems and opals. The **Old Timers Gallery** on Dalgarno St (the road to the Warrumbungles) has local art and crafts, plus 'old wares' – goods falling somewhere between antiques and junk. Out of town on the road to the Warrumbungles you'll pass **Miniland**, with animated dinosaurs and children's playgrounds.

If you want to look at the stars, just call **Dial-an-Astronomer** (☎ (068) 42 1639) after 6 pm on a cloud-free evening, and Paul Cass will bring around his 25-cm reflecting telescope or, more likely, he will arrange to meet you at a convenient place that is suitable for viewing. It costs $5 per person ($15 per family), with a minimum charge of $35.

You can take a **scenic flight** over the Warrumbungle Range, for $40 per person (minimum two people). Contact Mike Caruana (☎ (068) 42 1560).

Tibuc is a property which uses **draught horses**, and visitors can see them in action on a daily tour at 3 pm ($15, $5 children),

have a guided ride in the morning ($30 for two hours, up to $65 for five hours). Call in at the Jolly Cauli health-food shop on the main street for details.

Places to Stay
During school holidays rooms can be scarce (and prices rise), so book ahead.

The council-owned *John Oxley Caravan Park* (☎ (068) 42 1635) is just north of the town centre. There's another caravan park, the *Wayfarer* (☎ (068) 42 1773), a few km south of town where there are also a few motels which sometimes indulge in price wars. In town there are more motels, such as the *Poplars* (☎ (068) 42 1522) which charges from around $45 a room.

The *Imperial Hotel* (☎ (068) 42 1023), across from the clocktower, is a well maintained family-run pub with singles/doubles/twins for $26/40/46, including breakfast. Rooms with attached bathroom go for $32/45/50. Other pubs in town also have accommodation.

There's an associate *YHA hostel* on the road to Warrumbungle National Park – see the following section.

Places to Eat
As well as the usual country-town cafes, pub meals and motel dining-rooms, such as the *Gunyah Restaurant* at the Country Comfort Motel (main courses about $17), there's the big *Golden Sea Dragon* Chinese restaurant with a $9 two-course deal, and a steak-house at the north end of John St. The *Jolly Cauli* (as in cauliflower – 'collie') is a health-food shop on John St with a good cafe serving salads and snacks. The smoothies ($3) are large and refreshing.

Getting There & Away
Harvey World Travel (☎ (068) 42 1566) is on Dalgarno St.

Air Yanda (book through Ansett) flies between Sydney and Coonabarabran ($166, less with advance purchase).

Bus The major bus-lines stop here on their

Newell Highway services. Countrylink buses meet some trains at Lithgow and run to Coonabarabran via Mudgee.

Car & Motorbike The Newell Highway runs north to Narrabri and south to Gilgandra and the Oxley Highway runs north-east to Gunnedah. Smaller roads run west to Warrumbungle National Park and on to the Castlereagh Highway at Gulargambone, and north to Baradine and Pilliga.

WARRUMBUNGLE NATIONAL PARK

...lofty hills arising from the midst of lesser elevations, their summits crowned with perpendicular rocks, in every variety of shape and form that the wildest imagination could paint...

John Oxley, 1818

The Warrumbungle Range makes an abrupt appearance in the midst of the region's gentle slopes. It was formed by volcanic activity 13 million years ago, and has been eroded into a strikingly rugged mountain range. The national park (20,900 hectares) is popular with sightseers, bushwalkers and rock climbers. There are many walking trails, both short and long. You need to see the rangers at the visitor centre before undertaking the longer walks or rock climbing.

The informative park **visitor centre** (☎ (068) 25 4364) is open daily. Entry fees are $7.50 for cars and $3 per person for hikers, motorcyclists etc.

There's a great range of flora and fauna, with spectacular displays of wildflowers in the spring. (Wildflowers aren't the only plants to thrive in the area – the national park suddenly grew by 620 hectares in 1993, when land confiscated from a marijuana-grower was added to it.)

Summers can be hot, but it usually cools down at night. Winter days are often sunny but there can be heavy frosts at night. The best time to visit is spring or autumn.

For more information on the park, get a copy of *Warrumbungle National Park* by Alan Fairley (National Book Distributors, paperback, about $13). Lonely Planet's *Bushwalking in Australia* (paperback, $16.95) details the Grand High Tops walk.

Siding Spring Observatory

The elevation, remoteness and clean air of the Warrumbungles make them a good place to watch the night sky. Sitting on top of the range is a cluster of observatories, like so many huge white mushrooms. They include the Anglo-Australian Telescope, with its 3.9-metre mirror. There is a visitor centre, open daily from 9.30 am to 4 pm, where you can see the 'Exploring the Universe' exhibition of hands-on displays and videos. Admission to the exhibition is $5 ($3 children, $12 families). You can ride the lift to a viewing gallery inside the Australia telescope building (free). This closes at 4 pm.

The turn-off for the steep climb up to Siding Spring Observatory is 23 km west of Coonabarabran, from the road to the national park.

Places to Stay

In the Park There are sites with electricity for $15 for two people, plus $3 for each extra person and unpowered sites for $10 for two people plus $2 for each extra person. Most of the park's camping areas are accessible by car. Hikers are charged $1 per night for bush camping. The *Woolshed* is a bunkhouse designed for groups, costing $4.50 per person with a minimum charge of $25.

Gumnuts

Nearby As well as accommodation in the park and in the towns of Coonabarabran and Coonamble, there are several options in the nearby countryside.

The *Warrumbungles Mountain Motel* (☎ (068) 42 1832), nine km west of Coonabarabran on the road to the national park, is an associate YHA hostel, charging $13 per person.

Tibuc (☎ (068) 42 1740, evenings best) is 16 km from Coonabarabran on the road to the park, and is right beside the park's boundary, under Bulleamble Mountain. It is an organic farm (it's owned by the people who run the Jolly Cauli, a good cafe in Coonabarabran) and has accommodation in four mud-brick buildings. There are differing levels of facilities, from no electricity at all, to a solar system, to full mains power. Tibuc is popular and books out during school holidays. The overnight cost is $60 for four to six people, and the longer you stay the cheaper it gets. Campsites are just $3 per person or there's a caravan for $10.

Timor View Holiday Camp (☎ (068) 42 1437) is on 12 hectares of bush and is by the park boundary, about 12 km from Coonabarabran. It can fill with groups, which is what it's geared to, but they accept individuals in cabins (from $20 a double) or camping ($5 per person).

Forest Glen (☎ (068) 42 1970) is a working farm with guest rooms, about seven km south-west of Coonabarabran. You have the choice of a double room with ensuite or a twin with private bathroom and sitting room. Dinner, bed & breakfast starts at $75 per person, or $50 for B&B only.

On the western side of the park, *Gumin-Gumin* (☎ (068) 25 4368) is an 1870s homestead with accommodation at about $20 per person. You'll need to bring your own bedding and food.

Getting There & Away

The park entrance is 33 km west of Coonabarabran and most people come via that town, but you can also get here on smaller roads from Gulargambone or Coo-namble, both on the Castlereagh Highway to the west of the park.

THE PILLIGA SCRUB

This 400,000 hectare forest, west of the Newell Highway between Coonabarabran and Narrabri, has an interesting history which you can read about in Eric Rolls' outstanding book *A Million Wild Acres*. Rolls says that the current dense forest, a beautiful place with some interesting little roads winding through it, is a new phenomenon. The early settlers cleared the land and wiped out the small marsupials which would have eaten many of the tree seedlings. After the farms failed because of unsuitable soils, the new forest exploded into life.

Baradine, north-east of Coonabarabran, is the main town in this part of the world, and roads running into the Pilliga Scrub run east from here and from Kenebri, 20 km further north. The Forestry Office in Baradine has maps of drives through the Scrub. The hamlet of **Pilliga** itself, 50 km north of Kenebri, remains much as it ever was, and in **Cuttabri**, 33 km east of Pilliga, a wine shanty still operates. **Yarrie Lake**, near the Narrabri end of the Scrub and a few km south of the Australia Telescope, has prolific birdlife. The lake might be a flooded meteorite crater.

NARRABRI

As in so many other areas of the north-west, Major Mitchell made the first European foray and was quickly followed by others taking up land as squatters. Mitchell's visit was perhaps inevitable, but it was sparked by the capture of George Clark, a runaway convict who had lived with Aborigines for six years. The unfortunate Clark was sent off to Norfolk Island, but before leaving he told of rich lands and a big river flowing to an inland sea.

Split by the Namoi River and the Narrabri Creek, this old town (population 7300) is today in danger of becoming just another highway stop on the busy Newell. However, there are good places for picnics in the riverside parks.

The visitor centre (☎ (067) 92 3583) on

the Newell Highway near the town centre has maps of drives and walks around town. The centre is open from 8.30 am to 5 pm on weekdays and from 9 am to 1 pm on weekends. There is a National Parks office (☎ (067) 92 4724) at 165 Maitland St.

The **Old Gaol Heritage Centre** on Barwan St is concerned with family history and also has displays relating to the area's history. It's open on Saturday from 9 am to 4 pm.

See if the **drive-in cinema** (maybe the last in NSW) is still operating.

Near the township of **Bellata**, off the Newell 40 km north of Narrabri, there is good fossicking, especially for agates.

Places to Stay

There are several caravan parks in town. The *Council Caravan Park* (☎ (067) 92 1294) is a block back from the highway and has a camping area by the river. The *Narrabri Motel* (☎ (067) 92 2593) on the highway south of the town centre is the cheapest of the many motels. Ask the information centre about the several farmstays in the area.

Getting There & Away

Air Eastern flies between Sydney and Narrabri at least once a day.

Train The train running between Sydney and Moree stops here.

Bus The major lines stop here on their Newell Highway services. McPhersons Coaches run to Tamworth via Boggabri several times a week. Buy tickets at the Ampol station (☎ (067) 43 4327) on the highway. Countrylink buses run to Wee Waa and other small towns.

Car & Motorbike The Newell Highway runs north to Moree and south to Coonabarabran. Smaller roads run south-east to Gunnedah, west to Wee Waa and on to Walgett, and north-east to Mt Kaputar National Park.

AUSTRALIA TELESCOPE

The Australia Telescope is an array of eight radio telescopes which form the Paul Wild Observatory. Six of them are here, five lined up on a stretch of 'railway' track and another a few km away. Another receiver is near Siding Springs in the Warrumbungles and the last is a long way south, near Parkes. When all the receivers operate together, the effective diameter of the telescope is 320 km!

This array, which began operating in 1990, helps keep Australia at the forefront of radio astronomy. One of the many wonderful facts about radio astronomy: all the radio telescopes in the world have collected less energy than is released by a raindrop falling to earth.

The visitor centre (☎ (067) 90 4070), with hands-on displays and videos, is near the railway track and one of the receivers is usually nearby. The centre is open from 8 am to 4 pm daily, and is staffed on weekdays.

The Australia Telescope is 25 km west of Narrabri. If you're entering Narrabri from the south, turn left off the Newell Highway at the roundabout just after the railway line; coming from the north follow the Newell through town and turn right just after you cross the second bridge. If you miss this turn keep going to the roundabout and turn there.

MT KAPUTAR NATIONAL PARK

A rugged park on the westernmost spur of the Nandewar Range, Mt Kaputar National Park (36,800 hectares) is popular for bushwalking and rock climbing. Visit between August and October to see the wildflowers. Mt Kaputar itself rises to 1510 metres and it has been known to snow on the summit. A road (unsuitable for caravans) runs close to the summit. From the Doug-Sky Lookout you can see 10% of the whole state of NSW.

There are two established campsites with good facilities, Dawsons Springs and Bark Hut, both accessible from the road up the mountain. There are also cabins at Dawsons Springs – you have to book through the National Parks office in Narrabri (☎ (067) 92 4724) and there's a minimum stay of two days. The park visitor centre (☎ (067) 92

1147) at Dawsons Springs isn't always staffed.

The road to Mt Kaputar runs east from Narrabri.

Sawn Rocks

Off the Bingara road about 40 km north-east of Narrabri (turn off the highway about three km north of Narrabri), Sawn Rocks is a 40-metre cliff-face of octagonal basalt rocks. A walking trail of 900 metres leads through bush from the car park.

Waa Gorge

North again, Waa Gorge is a wilderness area within the park. You should check at the National Parks office in Narrabri before visiting as roads can be closed and there are no marked walking trails. To get here take the turn-off from the Newell for Sawn Rocks, but take the left fork after about 20 km. Follow this road around the top of the park and just past the Terry Hie Hie junction you'll meet the access road. You'll pass through a number of gates on the way to the car park. From the car park it takes about 45 minutes to walk to the gorge – if you don't get lost in the rainforest-like vegetation.

WEE WAA

Wee Waa is today a quiet little town (population 2300) but it was the first town to be established in the Namoi Valley. The 'waa' in Wee Waa is pronounced 'wor' – we're lucky that the early cartographers didn't spell it 'waugh'. The grand Imperial Hotel was the first three-storey building in the north-west.

Cotton was planted near Wee Waa in the 1960s and its success sparked the widespread planting of cotton throughout the area. Cotton is planted from late September to the end of October, the bolls begin to open in late February and the picking season is April and May. The **Namoi Cotton Co-op** (☎ (067) 90 3000) in Wee Waa arranges guided tours of farms and gins (processing plants) at 10.30 am and 2.30 pm during the picking season.

Cubbaroo (☎ (067) 96 1741), 45 km west of Wee Waa, is this area's only winery and is

open from Wednesday to Saturday from 10 am to 8 pm.

Yanda (book through Ansett) flies between Sydney and Wee Waa ($175).

MOREE

Moree (population 11,000) was first settled in the 1840s and is the largest town on the north-west plains. It is the centre of a cotton and grain growing district. Although the surrounding country is often flat and bare, the lush gardens in some of Moree's residential areas show that plants can thrive here.

The information centre (☎ (067) 52 9559) is west of the highway on Alice St, south of the first bridge.

Things to See & Do

Moree's **Spa Baths** (☎ (067) 52 9554) on Anne St claim some fairly unlikely successes in the miracle cure line, but they certainly are a good way to get the cricks out of the back after a long day in a bus or car. The baths are hot (41°C) artesian water which pours out of a bore at the rate of 13 million litres a day. The spa is open from 6.30 am to 8.30 pm on weekdays and from 7 am to 7 pm on weekends. Admission is just $2.50.

The new **Moree Regional Gallery**, in an impressive old building on the corner of Frome and Heber Sts, specialises in Aboriginal art. The gallery is open from 10 am to 5 pm on weekdays, from noon to 4 pm on Saturday and from 1 to 4 pm on Sunday. **Gwydir Galleries** (☎ (067) 51 1554) at 43 Frome St sells Aboriginal artworks. The **Yurundiali Aboriginal Corporation** at 3 Endeavour Lane produces clothing using traditional and contemporary designs.

There are other interesting buildings near the regional gallery, such as the **Lands Department Office** on Frome St and the nearby **courthouse**.

The Lands Department's 9.5-km **Mehi Walking Track** begins at the tourist office and runs beside the Mehi River and past some historic buildings including the fine Lands Department office (1894).

Organised Tours

Dennis Quinn (☎ (067) 52 3841) has several **tours** of the town and district, starting at $15 ($7.50 children) for a town and pecan nut farm tour on Monday and Wednesday. There's also a day-tour to Lightning Ridge for $40 ($25 children). Book at the information centre at least a day in advance.

Droving Australia Tours (☎ (067) 52 5040), based in Moree, offer week-long rides with cattle drovers for $750, between early April and late October.

Places to Stay

Caravan Parks Caravan parks include the *Meehi* (☎ (067) 52 7188) on the river at the east end of Alice St. There are sites, on-site vans and cabins.

Hotels & Motels The *Victoria Hotel* (☎ (067) 52 5177) on Gosport St charges about $25/35 for singles/doubles and the *Royal* (☎ (067) 52 2266) on Heber St has similar rates. The *Moree* (☎ (067) 52 1644) on Alice St has singles (only) for about $20.

There are a dozen motels to choose from. Among the cheapest is the *Dover* (☎ (067) 52 4560) on Dover St near the spa.

Getting There & Away

Train Moree is the terminus of the passenger line from Sydney.

Bus The major lines stop here on their Newell Highway services. Most buses leave from Wadwell's travel agency (☎ (067) 52 4677) on Heber St across from the Regional Gallery, and you can buy most tickets here (but not Countrylink – go to the railway station). Other services run to Tamworth ($36) and you might hear about interesting mail-runs to smaller towns in the district. Countrylink has a service running east along the Gwydir Highway to New England and on to Grafton.

Car & Motorbike The Newell Highway runs north to the Queensland border at Boggabilla and south to Narrabri. The Gwydir Highway runs east to Warialda and Inverell. Heading west on the Gwydir to Collarenebri road, you pass through 140-odd km of flat scrubland, beautiful with lush growth and flowers in the spring. There's no petrol available between Moree and Collarenebri, and there are several unsealed sections. Heading north, small roads run to Boomi near the state border or, branching off at Garah, to Mungindi.

BOGGABILLA & GOONDIWINDI

Not much more than a handful of houses, Boggabilla is overshadowed by the more substantial town of Goondiwindi, 10 km north and across the Queensland border. Goondiwindi is a pleasant town and has quite a lot of accommodation options – you'll find a list with phone numbers and approximate prices on the door of the information centre in the old water tower, just off the main street. The impressive wooden *Victoria Hotel* looks like a good place to stay. The giant *New Bridge Garage* on the Goondiwindi bypass is reputed to be the busiest truck-stop in the southern hemisphere and offers fuel, meals and showers to truckies – and anyone else.

The Castlereagh Highway & Westwards

The large slice of country between the Castlereagh and Mitchell Highways is a flat artesian basin. In spring this is a beautiful area, with the vast, steamy plains bursting into life. Much of the area is black-soil country, with drier outback country beginning as you approach the Mitchell Highway.

WARREN

This small town on the Macquarie River takes its name from an old meaning of the word, a park noted for wildlife. It must have once been an attractive town, but unfortunately the old buildings along the main streets have been stripped of their verandahs and balconies.

Black-Soil

Black-soil soaks up rain and lies in wait for cars. It might not look or even feel especially wet, but it is incredibly tenacious and your tyres will collect an ever-increasing coating of mud that packs into the wheel arches like concrete. If you stop moving it's very hard to start again, as the slightest wheel-spin packs the road into a glassy-smooth surface – if you're lucky (black-soil is apparently bottomless and heavy vehicles sink to their axles). If you're driving in someone else's tracks (the only way 2WD vehicles can travel on wet black-soil) you might bottom out in the ruts.

If you become bogged the only thing to do is wait. It takes at least one day for an impassable road to dry out.

While you're waiting, ponder on the asinine but totally appropriate saying, 'You stick to black-soil in the dry and it'll stick to you in the wet'. Another more pithy aphorism applies to this situation: 'If she begins to spit, you go like shit'. ■

The visitor information centre (☎ (068) 47 3181), on the main road next to the post office, is open on weekdays from 10 am to 4 pm and on Saturday until noon.

South-east of Warren the country is suitable for farming, but to the north-west the outback begins. Although the surrounding country is dry, the river and its creeks are ribbons of greenery. Apparently you can canoe from Warren as far north as Mt Foster (about 170 km by river), although there are at least two weirs to be negotiated.

The Macquarie Marshes once extended down to near Warren, but dams and irrigation are causing the huge wetlands to recede. **Tiger Bay Wildlife Park**, off the Oxley Highway one km north-east of Warren, has been created to provide birds and other wildlife with a refuge. There's a hide from which many species can be seen.

Pleasant **Macquarie Park** runs along the river and there's a walk, starting near the bridge, which takes you to a 500-year-old river red-gum. **Warren Weir**, five km south of town, is a good spot for a picnic, and you can camp here.

Places to Stay

There are two motels, the *Macquarie Motor Lodge* (☎ (068) 47 4396) and the *Warren Motor Inn* (☎ (068) 47 4404), and pub accommodation at the *Club House Hotel* (☎ (068) 47 4923). There are also a couple of caravan parks. Ask at the information centre about camping on the district's many stock routes.

THE MACQUARIE MARSHES

This huge wetlands area was thought by Captain Oxley to be the beginning of the inland sea that he had been sent down the Macquarie River to find in 1818. Captain Sturt came the same way in 1828, but it was a drought year and the dry marshes clearly were not part of a sea. To avoid the marshes Sturt headed north and came upon the Darling River, which he realised joined the Murray (and thus flowed into the ocean), and so ended the whitefellas' inland-sea dreaming.

Birdlife on the marshes is varied and prolific, with native and migratory species breeding here. In the 1930s one casual observer reckoned that 3000 birds flew overhead in an hour. The wetlands have suffered from the damming of rivers and are receding, but while the skies are no longer dark with birds there are still plenty to be seen. The best time to visit is during the breeding season, generally in spring but varying according to the water level.

The main nature reserve on the marshes is on the west side, about 100 km north of Warren and off the sealed road running from Warren to Carinda. From here the unsealed Gibson Way runs east to Quambone and it's along here that you're most likely to see birds. A sealed road runs from Quambone back to Warren, so you can make a round trip. The Gibson Way floods in a good season, but usually doesn't close just because of rain. Other unsealed roads in this area should be treated with caution as this is black-soil country and you can easily become bogged.

COONAMBLE

The first Europeans into this area arrived in 1817, just three years after the Blue Mountains were crossed, although the town wasn't established until 1855. Not a large town, Coonamble is a pleasant place. You're well into the north-west when you get to Coonamble, and there's a relaxed feel to things. There isn't much to see but it's a pleasant place to wander around.

The Castlereagh Highway runs through town and the town centre is between the Castlereagh River and the Warrena Creek. The local roadhouse sells all the necessities of life: 'Fuel, Food, Ammo'.

The **museum** on Aberford St is in the old police station and is open on weekdays from 10 am to 1 pm and from 2 to 4 pm. **St Barnabas** is a big, wooden Anglican church on the corner of Aberford and Namoi Sts. The **Ellimatta Centre** is run by the Aboriginal community and sells arts and crafts. It's opposite the police station on Aberford St.

Places to Stay

The *Riverside Caravan Park* (☎ (068) 22 1926) on the highway south of the centre has sites only.

The impressive *Sons of the Soil Hotel* (☎ (068) 22 1009) on Castlereagh St, the main street, has single/double rooms for $20/30, including breakfast. A block back from Castlereagh St on the corner of Taloon and Namoi Sts, the quieter *Club House Hotel* (☎ (068) 21 1663) charges $15/20. The *Coonamble Motel* (☎ (068) 22 1400) is on the highway just south of the town centre and charges about $40/50. There are a couple of other motels a little further out.

Getting There & Away

Bus Countrylink buses stop here on the run between Dubbo and Lightning Ridge.

Car & Motorbike The Castlereagh Highway runs north to Lightning Ridge and south to Gilgandra. Smaller roads run south-east to

the Warrumbungle National Park and Coonabarabran. See the earlier Macquarie Marshes section for some routes west from Coonamble.

WALGETT

The small town of Walgett is near the junction of the Namoi and Barwon (a tributary of the Darling) rivers. Walgett and the Barwon feature in Banjo Paterson's poem *Been There Before*. Other than this, there isn't a lot of interest in this run-down little town. Steel shutters on shop windows (but not, surprisingly, on the bank windows) show that alcohol-induced trouble is a problem. Despite this, it's a friendly place and far enough from anywhere for people to be interested in telling you about local sights. There's an information centre (☎ (068) 28 1399) in the council chambers on Fox St.

History

Charles Sturt's 1829 expedition up the Castlereagh River brought the first Europeans to this area. Squatters followed quickly and Walgett takes its name from Walchate, a cattle station established here in the 1830s. Covering 13,000 hectares, it could support only 300 head of cattle! At this time the area was a centre for Aboriginal corroborees, but the coming of the squatters soon put an end to that. Even running 0.2 of a cow per hectare was a good enough excuse to drive the Aborigines from their lands.

By the 1880s, paddle-steamers were travelling up the Darling to Walgett, bringing in supplies and taking wool downstream.

Mechanical shears were invented on Euroka Station near Walgett in the 1870s. Australia's first artesian bore was sunk in the area around the same time.

Places to Stay & Eat

The *Two Rivers Caravan Park* (☎ (068) 28 1381) is on Pitt St near the Namoi River. There are three motels, including the reasonable *Walgett Motel* (☎ (068) 28 1355) on Fox St with singles/doubles for $40/50. Both of the hotels on Fox St also have motel-style accommodation.

The *RSL Club* on Fox St has a dining room, various pubs and motels have meals, and there's a Chinese restaurant and the odd cafe and takeaway.

Getting There & Away
Air Hazelton flies to Sydney most days. Azevedo's Gift Inn (☎ (068) 28 1433) on Fox St is the local agent.

Bus Countrylink buses stop here on the run between Dubbo and Lightning Ridge. Book at the Duncan & Duncan garage (☎ (068) 28 1781) on Fox St.

Car & Motorbike The Gwydir Highway runs east to Collarenebri and Moree. No petrol is available for the 143 km of scrub country between Collarenebri and Moree.

West from Walgett on a partly-sealed road is Brewarrina, from where a road leads to Bourke.

AROUND WALGETT
If you think Walgett is a small place, check out some of the other towns in the shire! This is not a densely populated area.

As well as the opal fields around Lightning Ridge, there are the smaller **Grawin**, **Glengarry** and **Sheepyard** opal fields, west of Cumborah, a hamlet 47 km north-west of Walgett on the road to Goodooga. You can have a drink with the opal miners at the Glengarry Hilton, or at the Club In The Scrub at Grawin.

West of these fields is **Narran Lake**, virtually inaccessible but home to a rich variety of birdlife in good seasons. If you want to visit, phone the landowner, Mr Ron Coleman (☎ (068) 74 4957) for permission and directions. The best route is off the Brewarrina to Goodooga road.

Collarenebri, the second-largest town in the area, is 75 km east of Walgett on the Moree road and is also on the Barwon River. Its name is an Aboriginal word meaning 'place of many flowers', and in spring that is very appropriate. The weir near town is supposed to be one of the best fishing-holes in the state. There are gravel pits suitable for

fossicking 10 km out of town on the Lightning Ridge road. Entertainment is provided by an outdoor cinema operating from November to April. The Great Raft Race is held on the river in the first week in March. *Tattersalls Hotel-Motel* (☎ (067) 56 2205) has accommodation, and *camping* is permitted at several sites along the river.

Tiny **Burren Junction**, 93 km east of Walgett on the road to Wee Waa, has artesian baths and hosts a gyrocopter and ultralight air show at Easter.

BREWARRINA
Brewarrina (known locally as Bree) is a pleasant little town (population 1500) with some pride in its history, both Aboriginal and European. The town is bright with coral-tree blossom from July to September.

The shire council offices (☎ (068) 39 2106) on Bathurst St (the main street) have a couple of pamphlets and can help with local information.

One of the most important Aboriginal sites in the country, the **Brewarrina Fisheries** *(Ngunnhu)* are a series of rock traps on the Darling River where the Ngemba people caught fish to feed the huge inter-tribal gatherings which they hosted, perhaps for thousands of years. Adjacent to the fisheries is the **Aboriginal Cultural Museum**, an excellent place which is open daily.

For White history, visit the **Settlers Museum** behind the well-maintained courthouse on Bathurst St. It's open on Friday afternoon between 2 and 3 pm, or you can arrange to have it opened. Admission is $2.

The annual **Festival of the Fisheries** is held over four days in early October. As well as the usual small-town events such as a parade, a decorated bicycle competition and gumboot throwing, there are sports such as a raft race, plus boomerang throwing, woomera throwing, didgeridoo playing and Aboriginal dancing – all with fairly large prizes.

Places to Stay & Eat
The council *caravan park* (☎ (068) 39 2330) is by the swimming pool on Church St.

There's another camping place on the river 6.5 km upstream from Bree. *Hotel Brewarrina* (☎ (068) 39 2019) and the *Royal Hotel* (☎ (068) 39 2283) both have accommodation, and at the *Swan Crest Motel* (☎ (068) 39 2397), on the corner of Sandon and Doyle Sts, rooms are about $40/48.

The *De-Luxe Cafe* on Bathurst St is a great old country-town cafe, with lots of the original shop-fittings, including a sign boasting 'Iced Fountain Drinks. We Excel in Sundaes, Cleanliness & Civility'.

Getting There & Away
Air Hazelton connects Brewarrina with Dubbo and Sydney.

Bus Countrylink buses run between Dubbo and Brewarrina.

Car & Motorbike You can reach Brewarrina from Bourke, from the Mitchell Highway at Coolebah or Byrock (both routes run via Gongolgon) and from Walgett. The Walgett road includes some long unsealed sections of black-soil – great when it's dry, impassable in the wet. The track north to Goodooga also has a long unsealed section. Tracks through the Macquarie Marshes area also lead here, but you'll need a good map and local advice.

LIGHTNING RIDGE
Like Coober Pedy in South Australia, Lightning Ridge is a scruffy little town, entirely dependent on opal mining and the tourism which has followed. 'The Ridge' doesn't present the same scenes of other-worldly desolation that mark Coober Pedy, but it's hot, unwelcoming country nevertheless. Although the entire town is geared towards relieving you of some cash, Lightning Ridge is no slick tourist trap. It has a decidedly eccentric feel to it and there are some interesting characters to meet.

Opal mining is still the domain of the 'battler', the little bloke (or sheila) whose hard work and tenacity pays off – sometimes. For those who don't make it, an existence of scraping a living among rusting car bodies and extremely basic huts is not considered socially demeaning. Towns like Lightning Ridge (and there aren't many) are the last refuge of 'the bushie', usually down on his/her luck but infinitely resourceful and just as wary of authority. These true-blue types sell their finds to visiting opal buyers who set up shop in motel rooms, and the meeting of these two very different worlds is an odd contrast. Some buyers come all the way from Hong Kong to buy black opals, the speciality of the area.

Most claims are 50 metres square and no-one can hold more than two claims. Each June the claims have to be renewed, and plenty of people come to town hoping to pick up one that has lapsed.

Orientation & Information
Bill O'Brien's Way, the road in from the highway, becomes Morilla St, which is the main street. The corner of Morilla and Opal Sts is pretty much the town centre. You can get tourist information from practically anyone in town, but the Lightning Ridge News office on Morilla St next to the post office acts as the visitor information centre (☎ (068) 29 1182).

Things to See & Do
On the north and west sides, the town is surrounded by intensively-mined opal fields. Be careful walking around the diggings, as they are riddled with deep, unmarked holes. Young children are especially at risk. Dropping anything down a hole won't make you popular if someone is working at the bottom.

Opal jewellery

Opals
There are various grades and types of opals. Top of the heap are black opals, which are solid opals (called stones) consisting of a black 'potch' overlaid by 'colour'. Grey and white opals are the same, but the potch is grey or white. Solid crystals are clear or opaque opals without any potch.

Prices can be astronomical, up to $2000 a carat or $3000 for a black opal, but you can pay as little as $50 for a stone of lower quality. The price will depend on flaws and the brilliance of the colour. The variation in shades of colour is enormous and if you're lucky the one you like won't be one of the most expensive.

Much less expensive are non-solid opals. Doublets are precious opals stuck (by a jeweller, not by nature) to a potch of non-precious opal. Domed doublets are worth more than flat doublets because the section of precious opal is thicker. Triplets are flat doublets with a dome of glass or quartz crystal stuck on top, protecting and magnifying the opal. ■

The **Bush Museum** (or Moozeum) is worth a visit. It's an eccentric collection of memorabilia, some genuinely historic, the rest interesting junk. There's also a large underground area in an old mine, with more displays, including cartoons from the extremely sexist but strangely innocent magazines which provided entertainment for lonely miners (and which still grace small-town barber shops). Admission is $4 ($1 children). The museum is down a dirt track off Black Prince Drive, which runs off Pandora St near the swimming pool. Look for the boat in the tree.

The **Walk-In Mine**, north of town off Gem St, is open daily and you can see a video on opal mining. Admission $4. Nearby **Spectrum Mine** also has a video (hourly from 10 am to 4 pm) but theirs is free. Off the track into the Walk-In Mine is **Bevan's Black Opal & Cactus Nursery**, with many species of cactus including some very old plants. In the same area but a km further out of town is the **Drive-In Mine**.

The **Bottle House** on Opal St is built from bottles and contains mining memorabilia as well as souvenirs and opals. **Black Queen Opal House**, off Pandora St just before the artesian baths, is a souvenir outlet in an unusual house (closed November to March).

If you need to relax, the 42°C **hot artesian baths** at the northern edge of town on Pandora St are free and open 24 hours.

About three km out of town at the southeast end of Opal St, **Kangaroo Hill** has crafts and minerals; this is a good place to see baby animals. Kangaroo Hill is open daily except Sunday and admission is $1 (50c children). Also three km out, but off Bill O'Brien's Way, **The Big Opal** has a daily mine tour at 10 am.

As well as miners and jewellers, Lightning Ridge is home to many artists and craftspeople. John Murray's engaging paintings and limited-edition prints of outback life are displayed at his **gallery** on Opal St near the corner of Morilla St, as well as some B&W photos. There are more paintings at the **Motor Village** complex further south on Morilla St – the punning sculpture *Emus on the Plane* is out the front. Graeme Anderson on Morilla St is one of several potters who work in opal clay. South of town off Bill O'Brien's Way is the **Bird of Paradise Art Gallery**.

Organised Tours
Black Opal Tours (☎ (068) 29 0666) and Victor's Opal Mining Tours (☎ (068) 29 0287) have tours of the town and area.

Festivals & Events
The Great Goat Race is held at Easter, along with horse races.

The Opal Festival is held during the school holidays in late September/early October, culminating in horse races, a parade and entertainment over the October long weekend.

Places to Stay
The cheapest place to stay is the basic *Lorne*

Holiday Station (☎ (068) 29 0366), which is about six km south-east of town (off Bill O'Brien's Way) but close to the opal fields. It has a caravan park (unpowered sites $3 per person) and a bunkhouse with shared facilities ($12 per person). There are other caravan parks in town.

In town on Morilla St, the *Tram-o-Tel* (☎ (068) 29 0448) has self-contained accommodation in old trams and in caravans for $20/30 ($120/140 per week). The trams seem to have been carefully chosen – one is a St Kilda Beach tram, a long way from Melbourne, and an old Bondi tram contains an opal shop.

There are two motels, the *Black Opal* (☎ (068) 29 0518) on the corner of Morilla and Opal St and the *Wallangulla* (☎ (068) 29 0542) on the corner of Morilla and Agate Sts. Both charge around $50/60 and neither is very luxurious. The big *Motor Village* (☎ (068) 29 0304) on Morilla St has cabins for about $40 and units from $60/70.

Places to Eat

The best but most expensive place to eat is *Nobby's Restaurant* in the Motor Village complex. The *Bus Stop Cafe* on Opal St is reasonable and there's also *Maude's* at the corner of Morilla and Opal Sts. The *Miner's Mate* on Opal St is a Chinese restaurant. The *Digger's Rest Hotel* across from Maude's has counter meals, and the *bowling club* on Morilla St has a bistro and a dining room.

Buying Opals

The main business in town is selling opals and there are outlets everywhere, ranging from The Local Guy who has a sidewalk stand on Morilla St selling bottles of opal chips for a couple of dollars, to showrooms where you can see $5000 opals on display. If you want to buy something, take your time and look at as many places as you can.

Getting There & Away

Air Hazelton flies to Dubbo. Buy tickets at the Lightning Ridge News office (☎ (068) 29 1182), on Morilla St next to the post office.

Bus Buses run north and south along the Castlereagh Highway, including the Countrylink run to Dubbo. Grahams Coaches runs on weekdays from Lightning Ridge to Toowoomba ($68) in Queensland, via St George ($23) and Dalby ($56). You can connect with various McCafferty's services.

The Log Cabin Opal Shoppe (☎ (068) 29 0277) on Morilla St opposite the post office is the bus booking agent.

Car & Motorbike The Castlereagh Highway runs south to Walgett and on to Dubbo. North of Lightning Ridge the road deteriorates, with unsealed roads leading eventually to the Queensland town of St George.

The Far West

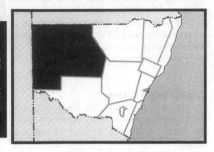

The far west of NSW is the state's 'empty quarter', but this vast expanse of dry country is one of the most interesting areas in the state and is much more diverse than it at first appears.

South of the Darling River, much of the land is taken up by precarious cattle and sheep stations, saltbush scrub and vast horizons. Elsewhere there is a surprising amount of bush, with low, tenacious trees surviving in the harsh climate. Towards the north-west corner, the long ridges of sand dunes that make up so much of central Australia begin, but even these support vegetation and it can be a beautiful place.

The outback is very sparsely populated but the people you meet are often much larger than life – they have room to grow, sometimes in pretty quirky ways.

Geography & Climate
Nearly all of the far west is the Murray-Darling Basin, red and black-soil plains riddled with usually dry waterways and clay-pans. In the north-west corner the sandy plains of outback Australia begin.

From November to February this area, especially in the north, is almost impossibly hot if you don't have air-con. By 9 am the thermometer is nudging 100°F in the shade, and by 10 am the Celsius landmark, 40°C, is passed. That leaves another 10 hours of day-

light for the current record, 51.7°C, to be broken. Winter nights can be chilly, with frosts, but the days are usually warm and sunny.

Getting There & Away
Air Broken Hill is the main centre for air traffic in the region, but small charter planes serve much of the area. There are also a few scheduled feeder services.

Bus Major bus-lines run along the Barrier Highway, and Countrylink runs up the Mitchell Highway.

Train The Indian Pacific runs between Sydney and Broken Hill, en route to Adelaide and Perth.

Car & Motorbike Two long, sealed roads skirt the edge of this area: the Barrier Highway, running from Cobar west to Broken Hill and on to South Australia; and the Mitchell Highway, beginning in Dubbo and running through Nyngan to Bourke then straight up into Queensland, through Cunnamulla to Charleville.

You'll see a lot more of the outback if you venture off the sealed roads. As long as conditions are dry (the usual state of affairs out here) you won't get into too much trouble on the main roads if you have good maps, drive carefully and are prepared for minor breakdowns. See the Getting Around chapter for more information on outback driving.

BOURKE
Nearly 800 km north-west of Sydney, Bourke (population 3400) is on the edge of the outback – 'back of Bourke' is synonymous with the outback, the back of beyond. A glance at the map will show just how outback the area beyond Bourke is – there's no town of any size for far around and the country is flat and featureless as far as the eye can see. Its very remoteness attracts a

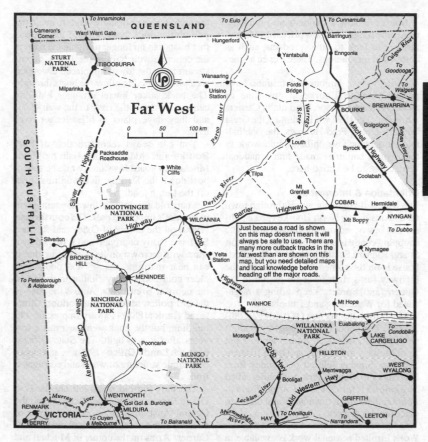

Far West

0   50   100 km

Just because a road is shown on this map doesn't mean it will always be safe to use. There are many more outback tracks in the far west than are shown on this map, but you need detailed maps and local knowledge before heading off the major roads.

steady stream of visitors. Bourke is a surprisingly pretty town and the surrounding country can be beautiful – the sheer space is exhilarating.

History

The Ngemba people lived in a large area, centred on the Brewarrina Fisheries and including Bourke and Louth. Other peoples in the area were the Barranbinja, Kula, Valaria, Kamilaroi and Wiradjuri. Early European explorers observed that local Aborigines lived in permanent structures.

The first Europeans to see this area were

the members of Captain Sturt's party of 1828. Sturt didn't think much of the country, and Major Mitchell's party of 1835 didn't manage to explore much of the area. Still, by 1860 there were enough graziers in the area for a paddle-wheeler to risk the difficult journey up to Bourke. By the 1880s many of the Darling River's 200 paddle-steamers were calling at Bourke to take wool down to the river ports at Echuca (for Melbourne) and Morgan (for Adelaide). It was possible for wool to be in London just six weeks after leaving Bourke – somewhat quicker than a sea-mail parcel today!

Bourke is still a major wool-producing area, but droughts and low prices have forced farmers to look to other products, such as cotton and rockmelons. There's even a vineyard.

Quite a few famous Australians have passed through Bourke at one time or another. Henry Lawson lived at the Carriers Arms Hotel in 1892 while painting the Great Western Hotel. Fred Hollows, the ophthalmic surgeon whose philanthropic work in third-world countries made him a national hero, chose to be buried here.

Orientation & Information

The Mitchell Highway winds through town then heads out to North Bourke (just a pub) six km away, across the old bridge. The shopping centre is on Oxley St between Sturt St and Richard St (the highway). The courthouse is on the corner. At North Bourke the highway turns right to begin its run to the Queensland border; keep going straight ahead for Wanaaring and Tibooburra.

The information centre (☎ (068) 72 2280) is at the bus depot (the old railway station) on Anson St. It is open from 9 am to 5 pm from Monday to Saturday and from 10 am to 5 pm on Sunday (closed on Sunday from November to March). Pick up a leaflet called *Swagman's Outback Mud Map Tours – Bourke*, detailing a town walk and drives to places in the district.

Work Limited seasonal work is available in the Bourke area: picking onions (around October), picking rockmelons (November or December) and cotton chipping (weeding, November or December). Contact the CES (☎ (068) 72 2511) near the Post Office on Oxley St for details. You'll notice that all these activities take place around summer and it can be *hot*!

Things to See & Do

Although the river can no longer accommodate the big paddle-wheelers there are plenty of reminders of the time when they were the town's lifeline. The **North Bourke Bridge** (1883) once lifted to let the steamboats

through. It also obligingly bends to avoid the pub on the north bank. One of the reasons that boats can no longer navigate the river is the concrete weir built in the 1940s, downstream from the town. It replaced a wooden weir which tilted to allow the boats through. The backpacker hostel arranges half-day canoe trips down the river to the weir ($20) and they have plans to offer longer river trips.

You can see a reconstruction of **Fort Bourke**, the crude stockade built by Major Mitchell to guard his stores while he took a boat down the Darling, in a wildlife refuge off the Louth road.

Many old buildings in town are reminders of Bourke's important past. The **courthouse** (1900) on the corner of Oxley and Richard Sts has a shady courtyard and is topped by a spire with a crown on it – signifying that it can hear maritime cases! Next door is an older courthouse, very similar in design to the court at Brewarrina. Across the road is the **old police station**. The **London Chartered Bank** (1888) is a very impressive old building, but the bank went bust just a few years after it was built. The State Offices, once the **Lands Office** (1900), is an elegant but simple structure of wood and corrugated iron.

The only big old **pubs** left are the Post Office Hotel on downtown Oxley St and the Central Australian Hotel on the corner of Richard and Ansen Sts. A small old pub, the Carriers Arms on the corner of Mitchell and Wilson Sts, was a watering hole of Henry Lawson. The North Bourke Hotel is a good place to meet locals. The Old Royal Hotel on Mitchell St is comparatively sedate.

Watch out for information about **bush dances**, such as the ones held at Urisino Station – a long way to go but that's why everyone has a good time.

Cotton is picked in March and April. From about May to August you can see the cotton gin in action by phoning Clyde Agriculture (☎ (068) 72 2528), or ask at the tourist office about tours of the plantations and gins.

The Back o' Bourke hostel can usually arrange aquatic activities for guests.

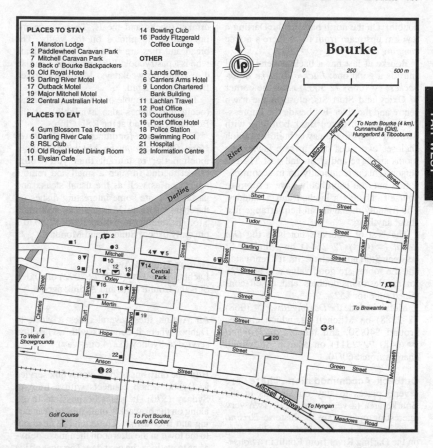

Bourke

0   250   500 m

PLACES TO STAY

1 Manston Lodge
2 Paddlewheel Caravan Park
7 Mitchell Caravan Park
9 Back o' Bourke Backpackers
10 Old Royal Hotel
15 Darling River Motel
17 Outback Motel
19 Major Mitchell Motel
22 Central Australian Hotel

PLACES TO EAT

4 Gum Blossom Tea Rooms
5 Darling River Cafe
8 RSL Club
10 Old Royal Hotel Dining Room
11 Elysian Cafe

14 Bowling Club
16 Paddy Fitzgerald
     Coffee Lounge

OTHER

3 Lands Office
6 Carriers Arms Hotel
9 London Chartered
     Bank Building
11 Lachlan Travel
12 Post Office
13 Courthouse
16 Post Office Hotel
18 Police Station
20 Swimming Pool
21 Hospital
23 Information Centre

To North Bourke (4 km),
Cunnamulla (Qld),
Hungerford & Tibooburra

To Brewarrina

To Weir &
Showgrounds

To Fort Bourke,
Louth & Cobar

To Nyngan

Central
Park

Golf Course

Organised Tours

Mateship Country Tours offers town and surrounding area tours at 10 am on weekdays if there are enough punters. Longer tours can also be arranged. Contact the information office for more details.

Festivals & Events

The Agricultural Show is held in April, with important ram and bull sales as well as a side-show alley. At Easter there is a fishing competition with other events such as wool-bale rolling, egg and spoon races and other village-green activities.

The Mateship Festival is a recent innovation and the dates haven't yet been settled on, but late September seems to be about the time. The new festival's name derives from Henry Lawson's literary theme of male bonding in the bush, a powerful strain in Aussie culture. Events are similar to those at the Easter festivities.

Places to Stay

The *Paddlewheel Caravan Park* (☎ (068) 72 2277) has tent sites ($8), vans (from $18 a double), cabins (from $30 a double) and old-style self-contained units (from $30 a double). On the north bank of the Darling a few km upstream from town there's a free *camping area*.

Bourke at last has a backpackers' hostel and it's a good one. *Back o' Bourke Backpackers* (☎ (068) 72 3009) is on the corner of Oxley and Sturt Sts, close to the town centre and the river. It's beside the impressive London Chartered Bank building, with two-bed dorms in the newer building which encloses two sides of a private lawn. The rooms are large and clean and cost $12 per person. This is technically dorm accommodation but you'll probably have a room to yourself. There's a kitchen and a laundry. The friendly manager can help arrange just about anything.

The best of Bourke's hotels is the *Old Royal* (☎ (068) 72 2544) on Mitchell St between Sturt and Richard Sts. It's renovated and the rooms are good value at $24/30/36 for singles/twins/doubles and a self-contained suite for $52.

Motels include the *Darling River* (☎ (068) 72 2288) on Mitchell St, which charges around $40/50, and the *Major Mitchell* (☎ (068) 72 2311) on Mertin St, which charges from $60/70.

Outback Accommodation There are several places to stay on stations in the Bourke area (a very large area). Two very interesting options are the historic *Urisino Station*, which has camel treks, and cruising on the Darling River from Louth in a *houseboat*.

See the following Around Bourke, Down the Darling and Bourke to Tibooburra sections for details on these and some other places, or contact the information centre, which makes bookings.

Places to Eat

There are several cafes, such as the pleasant *Gum Blossom Tea Rooms* on Mitchell St in the old Towers Drug Co building (1890), and the *Elysian Cafe*, Bourke's country-town cafe on Oxley St. Across the road in the Post Office Hotel is the *Paddy Fitzgerald Coffee Lounge*. 'Fitz's' is a pleasant cafe that serves

drinks, snacks and meals. There are some interesting old photos on the walls. The bread and pies are baked by the publican, who is a pastrycook. It's open from 10 am to 4 or 5 pm on weekdays. Meals are served from noon to 2 pm.

There are a couple of Chinese restaurants (occidental dishes also available), at the Bowling Club and at the RSL Club.

The best place for dinner is the *Old Royal Hotel Dining Room* on Mitchell St. It's a much better restaurant than you would expect to find in such a small and remote town, and as well as the usual steaks and pastas there are some interesting dishes on the changing menu. Main courses are around $15. The dining room is open from 7.30 to 9 pm daily except Sunday and Monday.

Getting There & Away

Lachlan Travel (☎ (068) 72 2092) on Oxley St is the Countrylink and Airlink agent.

Air Airlink flies several times a week to Dubbo, where it connects with a Hazelton service to Sydney ($274 one-way).

Bus The only bus is the Countrylink service to Dubbo which connects with a train to Sydney ($70). It *might* be possible to go along on the bi-weekly mail-runs to Wanaaring and Brewarrina. These tend to head out to the town in the afternoon then make deliveries to stations the next day. The post office (☎ (068) 72 2017) can put you in touch with the contractors.

Car & Motorbike The Mitchell Highway runs south to Nyngan and north to Cunnamulla in Queensland.

There's no sealed road west of Bourke in New South Wales. If you cared to drive the 713 km from Bourke to Broken Hill via Wanaaring and Tibooburra (rather than the usual route via the Mitchell and Barrier highways), it would be mostly on lonely unsealed roads. An unsealed road runs east to Brewarrina.

AROUND BOURKE

Somewhere that is 'around Bourke' can be as far away as the old Urisino Post Office, more than 200 km west on a dirt road. The Mud Map Tours brochure details some trips. If you don't already have a roadmap, pick up an NRMA map from the office on Oxley St near the Post Office Hotel.

If the roads are dry you shouldn't need a 4WD to visit places on the Bourke to Tibooburra road or the Bourke to Tilpa road, and perhaps not on the other roads mentioned here. *Wherever* you're going, check current conditions with locals, preferably the police, and carry plenty of water. If you're heading off a main route let someone know what you are doing and take spare parts.

Closer to Town

For good views, especially at sunset, climb **Mt Oxley**, 30 km south-east, off the Brewarrina road. At **Mt Gundabooka**, about 70 km south-west, off the Cobar road, there are more good views and abundant and atypical flora. The rock pools here almost always have water in them and the mountain is thought to have been of religious significance to Aborigines, whose cave-paintings can still be seen. Before heading to either mountain, visit the tourist office to pick up a key for Mt Oxley and to pay the Mt Gundabooka entry fee of $3 ($1.50 children) and the camping fee ($5).

About 60 km north-west on the road to Hungerford, **Fords Bridge** has a rare mudbrick hotel built in 1912, the *Warrego Hotel* (☎ (068) 74 7540). Meals and accommodation are available. Fords Bridge is apparently a top spot for yabbying.

On the highway 70-odd km south of Bourke is the hamlet of **Byrock**, with a pub, the *Mulga Creek Hotel-Motel* (☎ (068) 74 7311), which has accommodation and campsites. In early October, Byrock hosts the Outback Arts Festival and the Bog-Eye Races.

The **Cornerstone Community**, between Bourke and Wanaaring, is a sort of a Christian kibbutz on a cotton farm. This is the site of the Pera Bore, the first artesian water

supply in the area. Visitors are welcome; the tourist office and the backpacker hostel have more information.

Myandetta Station (☎ (068) 72 3029) is on the Darling River, but on the north bank and accessible from the Wanaaring road. Phone for detailed directions. There is accommodation in shearers' quarters here and at *Glenvilla*, owned by the same people and 16 km further downstream.

See the North-West chapter for information on Brewarrina.

Further Out

North along the Mitchell Highway, the hamlet of **Enngonia** is 95 km from Bourke and has accommodation at the *Oasis Hotel/Motel* (☎ (068) 74 7577). The sandhills around here are covered with flowers in spring, and when there is water in the swampland many species of birds can be seen. On the first weekend in September, up to 2000 people arrive for the annual races. West of Enngonia, *Cuttaburra Ridges* (☎ (068) 74 7604) offers basic accommodation or camping, with station activities.

Further north, almost on the Queensland border, **Barringun** is a hamlet with a pub (once frequented by Breaker Morant), a roadhouse and not much else.

Henry Lawson walked from Bourke to **Hungerford** in 1892, and he wasn't all that impressed with what he saw there. Read about it in his story *Hungerford*. The population today is about 10 people. The *Royal Mail Hotel* (☎ (067) 55 4093) is still there and has accommodation at about $20 per person for a double. The Hungerford Field Day in July attracts thousands of visitors, and the Sports Day in October is also popular. Hungerford straddles the Queensland border, and just over the border is the small **Currawinya National Park**, where large lakes offer habitats for many birds.

DOWN THE DARLING

The Darling River is first called that just north-east of Bourke, after the Barwon is joined by the Culgoa and the Bogan rivers. It flows south-west across northern NSW and meets the Murray at Wentworth. Although it passes through some of the driest country in the state, the Darling usually has at least some water in it and its banks are lined with river gums. With the Murray, the Darling forms one of the world's longest exotic rivers – that is, for much of its length it flows through country from which it receives no water.

The road that runs along the south bank of the Darling is the main route downstream from Bourke. It's possible to drive all the way down the Darling to Wentworth, although the road is unsealed and sections can be impassable after rain.

The tiny town of **Louth**, about 100 km from Bourke, hosts up to 4000 people during the annual race-meeting on the first or second Saturday in August. The landing strip is crowded with planes, racehorses outnumber the town's usual population and a score of bookmakers turn over hundreds of thousands of dollars.

Shindy's Inn, the local pub, doesn't have accommodation, but there are some *cabins* (☎ (068) 74 7416) available nearby for $25 a single (only). *Hollyanna* (☎ (068) 74 7443) is a houseboat based at Louth which sleeps four adults and costs $100 per day, including fuel. Even when the river is low you can cruise 30 km downstream.

Another 90-odd km further downstream is **Tilpa**, where the *Tilpa Hotel* (☎ (068) 37 3928) has meals, fuel, accommodation and, of course, beer. From Tilpa you could stay by the river and travel 125 km downstream to Wilcannia and on to Menindee, but the road deteriorates and you should check conditions.

Alternatively, you could head south to the Barrier Highway, 100 km away, or north on an outback track to Wanaaring. On the north bank, 12 km upstream from Tilpa, Kallara Station has a variety of accommodation at *Coolabah Lodge* (068) 37 3963). They prefer groups, but individuals are catered for at about $30/40.

From Tilpa, the Darling flows down to **Wilcannia**, then down to a system of lakes at **Menindee**, surrounded by **Kinchega National Park**. These places are accessible by sealed road from Broken Hill and are covered in the following Barrier Highway section. Another 125 km on dirt road brings you to **Pooncarie**, a pretty hamlet with a pleasant pub, the Telegraph Hotel, and a jumping-off point for Mungo National Park. From Pooncarie a sealed road runs to **Wentworth**, not far from the city of Mildura across the border in Victoria. See the Riverina chapter for information on Wentworth.

Bog-Eyes

Bog-eyes (shingleback lizards) are those slow-moving stumpy critters that love to lie on the road, and are so ugly that they're cute. When approached, a bog-eye will open that big mouth wide and show its blue tongue and crimson gullet. If you poke a finger too close to one, it might just chomp onto it. Bog-eyes aren't poisonous, but they have a very strong grip. Locals kill the lizards to get them off, but National Parks advises resting your hand on the ground and hoping that the lizard will eventually get bored and let go. It can take a while... ∎

BOURKE TO TIBOOBURRA

The lonely road running west from Bourke to Tibooburra is an adventurous drive.

About 190 km west of Bourke, **Wanaaring** is a tiny place but the largest for a long way. Fuel is available and there's accommodation at the *Outback Inn* (☎ (068) 74 7758) for around $20 per person, or you can camp at the petrol station. The Paroo Sports Day is held during the September/October school holidays.

About 35 km west from Wanaaring and two km south of the main road, you can see the remains of the old mudbrick **Urisino Post Office**. Next to the post office is *Urisino Homestead* (☎ (068) 74 7639), a large mudbrick homestead dating from the early 1900s, with even older date palms perhaps planted by the Afghan cameleers. The property was part of Sir Stanley Kidman's cattle empire and the homestead is surprisingly comfortable, with marble fireplaces. Urisino once covered 500,000 hectares but today is a mere 32,000 hectares.

The homestead is worth seeing and you can drop in for morning or arvo tea and a look around for $5. There is also accommodation, either in good rooms in the homestead ($35 per person, or $60 including all meals and activities) or in backpacker accommodation in old mudbrick cottages ($15 per person). Swags are available if you want to camp. There's a bar and there will be air-con at the homestead when mains electricity is connected.

The young couple running the homestead spent a couple of years travelling on camels, and they offer camel rides and longer treks at $60 a day. They're friendly people. Keep an eye out for leaflets advertising dances out at Urisino station. If you don't have transport it might be possible to arrange a lift on the mail run, or phone Urisino to see if someone is making a trip to Bourke.

West of Urisino the scrub thins and there are some large claypans which fill with birds after rain. I saw a pair of brolgas – tall, graceful cranes.

After you pass the turn-off to Milparinka the country changes and you drive past the small mesas of the eastern half of **Sturt National Park**. The mesas aren't very high but they look like mountain ranges after the flat country further east.

CORNER COUNTRY

There are no 'mountains' out west, only ridges on the floor of hell.

Henry Lawson
Some Popular Australian Mistakes, 1893

The far western corner of the state is a semi-desert of red plains, heat, dust and flies, but with interesting physical features and prolific wildlife. As well as kangaroos and emus, watch out for goannas and other lizards on the road, and even big wedge-tailed eagles, which take a long time to get airborne. Running along the Queensland border is the dingo-proof fence, patrolled every day by boundary riders who each look after a 40 km section.

Tibooburra

Tiny Tibooburra, 335 km north of Broken Hill and the hottest town in the state, boasts two fine sandstone pubs, a couple of petrol stations, a small shop or two, a police station, a bush hospital and even a tiny outdoor cinema. Tibooburra is the closest town to Sturt National Park and there's a large and helpful National Parks office (☎ (080) 91 3308) in town, open daily from 8.30 am to 5 pm.

Tibooburra used to be called The Granites, after the granite outcrops nearby, which are good to visit on a sunset walk. Although the town is so isolated, international flights bound for Sydney pass overhead.

Places to Stay & Eat There's a campsite just north of town at *Dead Horse Gully* ($5). In town, *The Granites Caravan Park* (☎ (080) 91 3305) has sites for $10, on-site vans for $24, cabins for $34 and motel units from $36/46.

Both the pubs, the *Family Hotel* (☎ (080) 91 3314) and the *Tibooburra Hotel* (☎ (080) 91 3310) (known as 'the two-storey'), have accommodation from $20/30. Both bars are worth a beer: the Family has a bacchanalian mural by Clifton Pugh, while the two-storey has more than 60 impressively well-worn hats on the wall, left behind when their owners bought new headgear at the pub.

The pubs have good counter meals and even have tables outside where you can sit and watch the occasional 4WD pass by.

Milparinka

Milparinka is very nearly a ghost town, with a pub and a few occupied houses. Not much remains of the gold town which once had a population of 3000, except the pub and the courthouse, a fine sandstone building with a very solid sandstone dunny out the back.

In 1845 members of Charles Sturt's expedition from Adelaide, searching for an inland sea, were forced to camp near here for six months. The temperatures were high, the conditions terrible and their supplies inadequate. Ask at the pub for directions to the grave of James Poole, Sturt's second-in-command, about 14 km north-west of the settlement. Poole died of scurvy!

The only fuel between Milparinka and Broken Hill is at the Packsaddle roadhouse, about halfway along the Silver City Highway, a largely unsealed road.

Sturt National Park

Taking in both gibber plains and the edge of the great Strzelecki Desert, this huge park (310,650 hectares) was once a pastoral lease. Feral animals such as goats and pigs have been cleared and regeneration of this marginal ecosystem is proceeding. It takes nine people to keep the park free of goats and pigs – which is not many when you consider the huge area, but more than the nearby pastoral leases can afford in bad times or can spare in good times.

The park has 300 km of driveable tracks, camping areas and walks, on the Jump Up Loop drive and to the top of Mt Wood. It is recommended that you inform the ranger at Tibooburra before venturing into the park. The entry fee is $7.50 per car and camping costs $5 for two people.

At **Camerons Corner** there's a post to mark the place where Queensland, South Australia and NSW meet. It's a favourite goal for visitors and a 4WD is not always necessary to get there. In the Queensland corner, the *Corner Store* (!) does good sandwiches, homemade pies and even ice cream. Everybody coming by the Corner stops here and they have good advice on road conditions. At the time of writing you could buy fuel here but that hasn't always been the case – check in Tibooburra.

The Barrier Highway

The Barrier Highway, running from Nyngan west through Cobar, Wilcannia and Broken Hill, is the far west's main road and is the main route to Adelaide. Several of the state's more remote places are some way south of the highway and are included in this section.

NYNGAN

Nyngan (population 2500) is at the junction of the Barrier and Mitchell highways and is also close to the centre of NSW; a cairn marks the exact spot 72 km south of the town. Tourist information is available from Burns Video & Gifts (☎ (068) 32 1155) on the main street.

Major Mitchell's party passed through in 1835, but the town didn't begin to grow until the 1880s. The great flood of 1990, when the Bogan River overwhelmed the town and the entire population was evacuated by helicopter, still looms large in local memory. Some photos of the flood are displayed at Arnold's Cafe on the main street.

Nyngan's dusty main street isn't very interesting, but on Cobar St, parallel and a block south, there are three public buildings in very different styles: the solid **courthouse**, the Corinthian **town hall** and the **post office**, closer in style to the town's modest domestic architecture.

Places to Stay & Eat

There are a couple of caravan parks, the *Nyngan* (☎ (068) 32 1705) east of town and

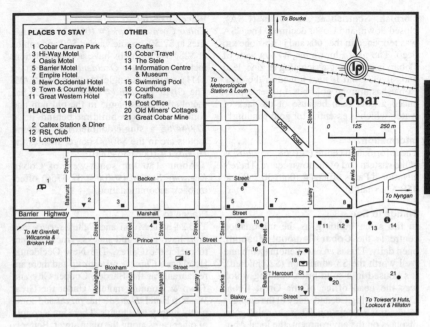

PLACES TO STAY
1 Cobar Caravan Park
3 Hi-Way Motel
4 Oasis Motel
5 Barrier Motel
7 Empire Hotel
8 New Occidental Hotel
9 Town & Country Motel
11 Great Western Hotel

PLACES TO EAT
2 Caltex Station & Diner
12 RSL Club
19 Longworth

OTHER
6 Crafts
10 Cobar Travel
13 The Stele
14 Information Centre
   & Museum
15 Swimming Pool
16 Courthouse
17 Crafts
18 Post Office
20 Old Miners' Cottages
21 Great Cobar Mine

Cobar

the *Riverside* (☎ (068) 32 1729) west of town.

Barrett's Hotel (☎ (068) 32 1028), a big old place across the railway line from the main street, has pub accommodation, as does the more modern *Canoba* (☎ (068) 32 1559) on the main street, which also has motel units. The *Alamo Motel* (☎ (068) 32 1324) is on the Cobar side of the town centre and is the cheapest of the motels at about $40/50.

Arnold's Cafe is a takeaway place on the main street with tables and a limited menu.

Getting There & Away
Bus Countrylink buses run to Dubbo, Broken Hill, Brewarrina and Bourke.

Car & Motorbike As well as the highways, an unsealed but fairly well-travelled road runs south through Tottenham to Bogan Gate, on the road between Parkes and Condoblin. See the North of Condoblin section

of the Central West chapter for more information on routes in this area.

COBAR
On the edge of the outback, beyond the fences but before the low bush tails off into saltbush, Cobar (population 5500) is at the start of the Barrier Highway, which runs west to Broken Hill, 455 km away. Semi-arid woodland is the main vegetation in the area, and there's a quiet beauty to the rolling sea of tough little trees. Sheep manage to eke out an existence on the clearer sections, in competition with destructive feral goats and pigs. After rain the flood plains of the usually dry creeks come alive with flowers.

History
Like Broken Hill, Cobar is a mining town, but here copper is the mainstay. Rich copper ore was discovered in 1871 and for the next 40 years the town grew steadily. In the 1920s the two biggest mines, Great Cobar and the

Cornish, Scottish & Australian (CSA), closed down, and Cobar declined. The CSA was reopened in the '60s and is now one km deep. The new Elura mine, 47 km west of Cobar, is exploiting a rich plug of zinc, lead and silver. Gold is also mined in the area. Cobar has alluvial gold but it never experienced a gold rush because of the lack of water, which is essential for gold panning!

Information

The information centre (☎ (068) 36 2448) is at the eastern end of the town centre. There's a National Parks office (☎ (068) 36 2692) at 45B Marshall St.

Things to See

In the same building as the information centre is the **Cobar Regional Museum**, open daily. This is an excellent museum and well worth the $3 admission ($2 children). It's housed in a solid brick building which was the head office of the Great Cobar Copper Mining Co, and many of the displays reflect this association. There are also good displays on the environment, the local Aborigines and the early Europeans. Don't miss it.

Off the road just west of the museum is the **Stele**, dedicated to the town and its mining past. Egyptian motifs are combined with the names of the three men who found copper here and the occupation (*bagal*, Cornish for someone who grades copper ore) of the woman who identified it.

Pick up a walking-tour map of the town from the information centre. There are a surprising number of interesting buildings, most fairly modest. An exception is the enormous **Great Western Hotel** (1898), which has perhaps the longest pub verandah in the state.

Weather balloons are released at 9 am and 3 pm from the meteorological station on the edge of town, off the Louth road.

There are currently no tours of the mines, but ask at the information centre as this might change. Mining skills are displayed at the national rock-drilling championships in September.

Places to Stay

Cobar Caravan Park (☎ (068) 36 2425) has sites at $7.50, on-site vans at $20 and cabins at $28. Several pubs have accommodation, including the *New Occidental* (☎ (068) 36 2111), which has singles/doubles for $15/25. The *Great Western* (☎ (068) 36 2053) has motel-style units, some in the old pub and some in the new building behind it, at $28/44/55 a single/double/triple. Several motels are in the $40/50 range, such as the *Hi-Way* (☎ (068) 36 2000).

About 130 km south-west of Cobar, *Keewong Station* (☎ (068) 37 3756) offers outback accommodation.

Places to Eat

The 24-hour Mobil and Caltex *service stations* have grills and snacks. Truckies seem to prefer the Caltex. The New Occidental Hotel has a *Chinese restaurant*, and there are restaurants at the Barrier, Copper City and Town & Country motels. Under the Great Western Hotel, *Dougo's* has pizzas and some pretty greasy takeaways. There are a couple of other cafes along the main street. Better is the *Country Kitchen* at 32 Linsley St, with coffee and light meals such as quiche and lasagna. This is also a craft and souvenir shop. The Golf Club and the Ex-Services Club have meals.

Probably the best place to eat in Cobar is *Longworth*, a licensed restaurant in a beautiful old house at 55 Linsley St. It's open for dinner from Tuesday to Saturday.

Getting There & Away

The Barrier Highway runs east to Nyngan and west to Wilcannia. The Kidman Way runs north to Bourke and south through Mt Hope to Hillston. It is largely unsealed (although it's due to be upgraded) but is a popular route for trucks.

AROUND COBAR

East of Cobar, the Barrier Highway passes the curiously named **Mt Boppy**, site of a huge gold mine. **Hermidale**, about 100 km east of Cobar, is a railway-side hamlet consisting of a few houses and a shop.

Top Left: West side of the Great Divide, north of Lithgow, central west (JM)
Top Right: Mungo National Park, far west (JM)
   Bottom: Sculpture Symposium, Broken Hill, far west (JM)

Top: Wheat harvesting, Riverina (PS)
Bottom Left: Grain silos, Deniliquin, Riverina (JM)
Bottom Right: Stooked haystacks near Ganmain, Riverina (JM)

'Wildcannia'

Wilcannia prohibits drinking in public places, and offences against this law account for the huge arrest rate in the Aboriginal community. Towns which have this law and enforce it strictly tend to be those with large Aboriginal populations. For a variety of cultural, historical and economic reasons, Aborigines are more likely to use public places for socialising than Whites. Aborigines drinking in public 'looks bad' – worse, it seems, than the sight of police rounding up and jailing people night after night.

Wilcannia achieved brief notoriety in 1994 when the town went on strike against the violence which was wrecking it. The national media turned up for the day, a town meeting was held and not a lot was resolved. It became apparent that Whites thought that the meeting had been called to do something about those drunken Blacks; Blacks thought the meeting had been called to do something about those racist Whites. Most people at the meeting were White, but 80% of the town's population is Black. All of the town's businesses are owned by Whites, and all of the town's police are White. ■

Mt Grenfell Historic Site

Taking in part of the Mt Grenfell station, this site protects Aboriginal rock art in several caves along a well-watered gully, an important place for the local Wongaibon people. Apart from the art, the site is worth visiting for the chance to walk through some pretty country on the five-km-long walking track.

You'll probably see feral goats and perhaps pigs in the area and there are also plenty of kangaroos and emus. From about July onwards you'll see father emus herding their broods of chicks. If a couple of males are travelling together they can have quite a kindergarten to look after.

To get here, travel west from Cobar on the Barrier Highway and turn off after 40 km. The site is another 32 km away on a good dirt road. There is water at the site but you can't camp here.

WILCANNIA

Wilcannia (population 900) is on the Darling River and in the days of paddle-steamers was an important river port. Apparently there's still a tunnel leading from the old wharf up into a shop in town.

There isn't much commerce here today but some of the old buildings remain, such as part of the old wharf, the impressive sandstone police station and courthouse on Reid St (turn left just after the bridge if you're coming from Cobar) and the Athenaeum Chambers, on Reid St but on the other side

of the highway, which house the local **museum**.

In its heyday Wilcannia was known as the Queen of the West, but today it has been dubbed 'Wildcannia' because of problems caused by alcohol abuse. Things can get ugly.

Places to Stay & Eat

There are two motels, *Grahams Motel* (☎ (080) 91 5040) and the slightly dearer *Wilcannia Hotel* (☎ (080) 91 5874) charging around $50/60. Across the bridge there's a *camping area* (☎ (080) 91 5874). For food try the basic cafe at the service station. You're not advised to visit the pubs here.

Getting There & Away

From Wilcannia you can take the Barrier Highway east to Cobar or west to Broken Hill. White Cliffs is 100-odd km north-west on a good but mainly unsealed road. Running south from Wilcannia is the partly unsealed Cobb Highway.

THE COBB HIGHWAY

The Cobb Highway runs south from Wilcannia through Ivanhoe, Hay and Deniliquin to Moama (Echuca) on the Victorian border. It's a handy route.

The 190 km of road between Wilcannia and Ivanhoe is mostly unsealed and passes through some of the emptiest country in the state, although there are a few stations off the road. *Yelta* (☎ (080) 91 9467) is a sheep station 11 km off the Cobb Highway about 70 km south of Wilcannia. They offer accommodation (homestead, camping or in shearers' quarters) and the chance to participate in station activities. They can collect you from Wilcannia or Ivanhoe (where the Indian Pacific train stops).

Tiny **Ivanhoe** is the largest town for a very long way. It is built on the railway line (there's even a 'suburb' called Railtown) rather than on a river, and it isn't an especially interesting place, but with a pub (with accommodation), a friendly club (with meals), a petrol station (an NRMA affiliate), a basic caravan park ($4 for a tent site), a bush hospital and a few shops, it can be very useful.

South of Ivanhoe the Cobb is sealed for the 50-km run to **Mossgiel**, just a pub on the corner of the road running east to Willandra National Park and Hillston – this road closes at a hint of rain. The Cobb is again unsealed from Mossgiel to **Booligal**, a tiny town on the Lachlan River with a pub and some basic services. The historic **One Tree Hotel**, on the highway 38 km north of Hay, is now a private home, but you might be able to get a glimpse of the old bar.

See the Riverina chapter for information on Hay.

WHITE CLIFFS

About 100 km north-west of Wilcannia is White Cliffs (population 150), an opal-mining settlement founded 100 years ago. For a taste of life in a small outback community, it's worth the drive on a dirt road.

Pick up a map and pamphlet from the store or one of the many opal showrooms. For a guided tour around the area, see Ross Jones (☎ (080) 91 6607). His house is further on from the pub, on the other side of the road.

The town centre, such as it is, is on flat land south of the main digging area. At the digging area, there are thousands of holes in the ground and miners' camps surrounded by car graveyards (an obligatory part of opal mining). The two bare hills, Turley's Hill (with the radio-telephone mast on top) and

Smith's Hill (south of the centre), are relatively densely populated and command the plains like diminutive city-states.

You can fossick for opals around the old diggings, but keep a close eye on kids around those unfenced, deep holes. There are a number of opal showrooms and underground homes open for inspection. **Jock's Place** on Turley's Hill is worth seeing – he has old relics that were collected in the area, and he can tell you about opal mining.

Right in the centre of town is the **solar power-station** (it drives a steam-turbine) where emus often graze out the front. The station is open for inspection daily at 2 pm and is worth a visit if only to see the guide in action. Bill Finney gets through a lot of shirts! Until recently the solar station supplied White Cliff's electricity needs, but when the town grew beyond its capacities a diesel generator was installed. Given that the solar dishes use two litres of distilled water a day while the generator chugs through who-knows-how-much diesel fuel, it seems a rotten idea. Also, as everyone gets billed for the generator, there isn't much incentive to keep the numerous wind-generators in action.

Places to Stay & Eat

The *White Cliffs Hotel* (☎ (080) 91 6606) has basic rooms, but they have air-con and are good value at $14 per person. The management is friendly, meals are available (although pricey) and there is a 4WD vehicle for guests' use – around town only. Near the post office, *Opal View* (☎ (080) 91 6756) is a self-contained flat that sleeps four or five and costs $50 a night. Across the road at the swimming pool there's a small *camping area* (☎ (080) 91 6627) where sites cost just $2 per person and showers are $1.

Up on Smiths Hill, *Rosavilla* (☎ (080) 91 6632) is a large dugout home which offers bed & breakfast for $26 per person, $10 extra for dinner.

Nearby, the *White Cliffs Underground Motel* (☎ (080) 91 6677; 1800 021 154 toll-free bookings) is an extraordinary place. It's quite a maze (you get a map when you check in), but it is surprisingly bright, comfortable and not at all claustrophobia-inducing. The rooms are simple, with no TV and separate bathrooms ('off-suites'), but they are well furnished and very quiet, with several metres of rock separating guests from their neighbours. Down here it's a constant 22°C, no matter whether there's a heatwave or a frost up on the surface. You can climb a staircase to emerge on top of Smith's Hill, from where the sunset is worth seeing. Singles/doubles/triples cost $34/68/84. The meals are reasonable but expensive – $6 for a continental breakfast, $12 for a cooked breakfast and $18 ($9 children) for a set-menu dinner.

The *golf club*, near the solar station, sometimes has filling roast lunches for $5 on Sunday.

Getting There & Away

White Cliffs is accessible on a 100-km unsealed road running north from Wilcannia, and from Broken Hill on a longer route which skirts the western side of Mootwingee National Park. Sections of the roads on the Broken Hill route tend to stay muddy after rain, and there are a number of creek crossings – these are usually dry but they fill quickly after rain and, even when the water has gone, deep drifts of mud remain.

MOOTWINGEE NATIONAL PARK

This park in the Bynguano Range, 131 km north-east of Broken Hill, teems with wildlife and is a place of exceptional rough beauty. In spring the roads can be like country lanes, flanked by 'hedges' of blue and white flowers. It is well worth the 1½ to two-hour drive from Broken Hill on an isolated dirt road. You can also get here from White Cliffs, but neither route should be attempted after rain. Entry to the park is $7.50 per car.

The reliable water-supply in the range was critically important to Aborigines in the area, and there are important **rock carvings** and **cave paintings**. Some cave paintings have been badly damaged by vandals, and the major site is now controlled by the Aboriginal community and is off-limits except on

ranger-escorted tours on Wednesday and Saturday morning ($4). The National Parks office in Broken Hill (☎ (080) 88 5933) has details.

There are walks through the crumbling sandstone hills to rock pools, which often have enough water for swimming, and rock paintings can be seen in the areas that are not off-limits.

There is a *campsite* ($10 for two people) at Homestead Creek, with gas barbecues, toilets and showers. Water for drinking might not be always available, and fuel and food are not available in the park. You should collect firewood from the signposted areas near the park entrance. Book sites, especially during school holidays.

Getting There & Away

Air You can arrange a charter flight from Broken Hill, and Splitters Creek Airlines (☎ (060) 21 1136) might soon have flights from Albury in historic DC3 aircraft.

Car & Motorbike The unsealed road to Broken Hill is very good. The road to White Cliffs is also good but tends to stay muddy longer after rain and has a number of creek crossings – these are usually dry but fill quickly after rain, and, even when the water has gone, deep drifts of mud remain.

BROKEN HILL

Out in the far west, Broken Hill (population 27,000) is an oasis in the wilderness. It's a fascinating town, not only for its comfortable existence in an extremely unwelcoming environment, but also for the fact that it was once a one-company town which spawned one equally strong union. Some of the state's best national parks are in the area, plus some interesting near-ghost towns.

Elements of traditional Australian culture that are disappearing in other cities can still be found in Broken Hill: hard work, hard drinking and the sensibilities which come with easy access to a huge, unpopulated landscape. The less attractive aspects of this culture (forcefully expressed in the novel and film *Wake in Fright)* have been considerably mellowed by the city becoming a major centre for naive artists, most of them local. This is a surprising but delightful development.

History

The Broken Hill Proprietary Company (BHP), after which the town was named, was formed in 1885 after a boundary rider, Charles Rasp, discovered a silver lode. Miners working on other finds in the area had failed to notice the real wealth. Other mining claims were staked, but BHP was always the 'big mine' and dominated the town. Charles Rasp went on to amass a personal fortune, and BHP, which later diversified into steel production, became Australia's largest company.

Early conditions in the mine were appalling. Hundreds of miners died and many more suffered from lead poisoning and lung disease. This gave rise to the other great force in Broken Hill, the unions. Many miners were immigrants – from Ireland, Germany, Italy and Malta – but all were united in their efforts to improve mining conditions.

The first 35 years of Broken Hill saw a militancy rarely matched in Australian industrial relations. Many campaigns were fought, police were called in to break strikes, and though there was a gradual improvement in conditions, the miners lost many confrontations. The turning-point was the Big Strike of 1919 and 1920, which lasted for over 18 months. The miners won a great victory, achieving a 35-hour week and the end of dry drilling, which was responsible for the dust that afflicted so many miners.

The concept of 'one big union', which had helped to win the strike, was formalised in 1923 with the formation of the Barrier Industrial Council, which still largely runs the town.

Today the richest silver/lead/zinc deposit in the world is still being worked, but lead and zinc have assumed a greater importance in the Silver City, as Broken Hill is known. There is enough ore left to ensure at least another 20 years of mining, but the new

technology has greatly reduced the number of jobs in the mines.

Orientation

The city is laid out in a straightforward grid pattern, and the central area is easy to get around on foot. Argent St is the main shopping street and the blocks between Bromide and Iodide Sts make up downtown Broken Hill.

Information

The big Tourist and Travellers Centre (☎ (080) 87 6077) on the corner of Blende and Bromide Sts is open daily from 8.30 am to 5 pm. This is where the buses arrive and there's a bus booking agency on the premises, as well as a cafeteria and a car rental desk (Hertz). Also here is the Broken Hill Interpretive Centre a good place to begin your visit – here there are displays on all aspects of Broken Hill and the area, and information on walks around the city. The Heritage Trails Map is a good buy at $2.

The National Parks office (☎ (080) 88 5933) is at 5 Oxide St. The Royal Automobile Association of South Australia (☎ (080) 88 4999) is at 261 Argent St and provides reciprocal service to members of other auto clubs. If you're venturing into the outback areas of South Australia you'll need a Desert Parks Pass, which is sold here.

The **swimming pool** is on the corner of Sulphide and Wolfram Sts.

There's a **laundromat** on Argent St just east of the West Darling Hotel.

If you find injured wildlife, contact Rescue & Rehabilitation of Australian Native Animals (RRANA) at the veterinary clinic on Rakow St (☎ (080) 87 7753).

Time Broken Hill operates on South Australian time (Central Standard), which is half an hour behind the time in the rest of the state. Towns near Broken Hill *don't* follow the Silver City's lead, keeping NSW time instead.

Mines

There are four working mines, controlled by

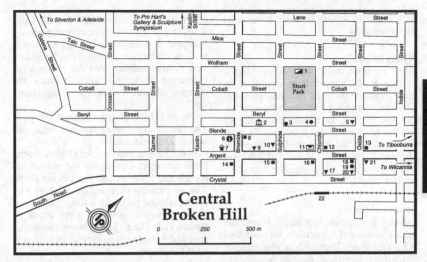

Central
Broken Hill

0   250   500 m

two companies. The deepest is the **North Mine**, 1600 metres down. At that depth it can reach 60°C and massive refrigeration plants are needed to control the temperature. You can't visit the working mines but there are tours of old mines.

Delprat's Mine (☎ (080) 88 1604) has an excellent underground tour daily except Sunday, where you don miners' gear and descend 130 metres for a tour lasting nearly two hours. It costs $18 (students $15). Nobody under eight years of age is allowed. To get there, go up Iodide St, cross the railway tracks and follow the signs – it's about a five-minute drive.

Day Dream Mine, established in 1881, is 33 km from Broken Hill, off the Silverton road. A one-hour tour costs $10 ($5 children, all ages allowed) and sturdy footwear is essential. Contact the Tourist Centre for bookings.

At **White's Mineral Art Gallery & Mining Museum**, 1 Allendale St, you can walk into a mining stope and see mining memorabilia and minerals. It has a craft shop and sells crushed mineral collages. Follow Galena St out to the north-west for two km or so. Whites now incorporates the Gladstone Mining Museum and is well worth visiting.

PLACES TO STAY

7	Tourist Lodge (YHA)
8	Black Lion Inn
12	Royal Exchange Hotel
13	West Darling Hotel
14	Silver Spade Motel
15	Mario's Palace Hotel
16	Grand Private Hotel
18	Astra House Backpackers

PLACES TO EAT

5	International Deli
9	Barrier Social Democratic Club
10	Champion Pizza & Chinese Takeaway
17	RSL Club
20	Silver City Chinese Restaurant
21	Papa Joe's Pizza

OTHER

1	Swimming Pool
2	Railway Museum
3	Trades Hall
4	Broken Hill City Art Gallery & Entertainment Centre
6	Tourist & Travellers Centre
11	Post Office
19	National Parks Office
22	Railway Station

It is open daily until at least 6 pm, and admission is $4.

Flying Doctor

You can visit the Royal Flying Doctor Service at the airport. Bookings must be made through the tourist information centre. The tour includes a film about the service, and you inspect the headquarters, aircraft and the radio room that handles calls from remote towns and stations. Tour times are Monday to Friday, 10.30 am and 3.30 pm, and weekends at 10.30 am. The cost is $2 (children free).

School of the Air

You can sit in on School of the Air broadcasts to kids in isolated homesteads, on weekdays at 8.30 am sharp. The one-hour session costs $2 (children free); book through the information centre. You can visit even when school is out, as a tape-recording is played for visitors during vacations.

Artists

Broken Hill seems to inspire artists and there is a plethora of galleries, including the Pro Hart Gallery at 108 Wyman St and Jack Absalom's Gallery at 638 Chapple St. Wyman and Chapple Sts run parallel to Mica St to the north-west of the town centre.

Pro Hart, a former miner, is Broken Hill's best-known artist and a local personality: there's even a Pro Hart gym! Apart from his own work, his gallery displays minor works

of major artists (such as Picasso, Dali, Roualt), but his collection of Australian art is superb. It's one of the largest private collections in the country and is displayed in a very relaxed manner. You can also see his collection of antique babies' rattles. He charges admission ($2), but many others don't.

The Ant Hill Gallery on Bromide St opposite the Tourist Centre features local and major Australian artists.

In the Broken Hill City Art Gallery (in the Entertainment Centre on the corner of Blende and Chloride Sts) you can see *Silver Tree*, an intricate silver sculpture which was commissioned by Charles Rasp. One room of the gallery is devoted to the artists of Broken Hill. The art gallery is open on weekdays and Saturday morning and admission is $2 ($1 children).

There are more galleries out at Silverton. Make sure you have a look inside the residential entrance of Mario's Palace Hotel on the corner of Argent and Sulphide Sts.

Other Attractions

The **Sulphide St Station Railway & Historical Museum** is in the Silverton Tramway Company's old station on Sulphide St. The tramway was a private railway running between Cockburn (South Australia) and Broken Hill via Silverton until 1970. Also in the complex is a mineral display and a hospital museum. It's open from 10 am to 3 pm daily and admission is $2.

The Flying Doctor

The flying doctor service was founded by John Flynn ('of the inland') in 1927. He envisioned a 'mantle of safety' for isolated properties in outback Australia, and with the development of simple, inexpensive short-wave radios – at first pedal-powered – much of the country suddenly had access to emergency health care in a matter of hours, instead of days of hard travelling.

Today, the service doesn't just respond to emergencies, it holds regular clinics, complete with specialists, in even the tiniest and remotest towns – and it's all free. That's why you should drop a few coins into a Royal Flying Doctor Service donation box.

One of the longest-running soap operas on Australian TV was *The Flying Doctors*; one of the shortest was its supposedly more realistic replacement, *RFDS*. It seems that audiences weren't ready for themes such as bitchiness, greed and racism sullying one of the few remaining icons of 'the real Australia'. ■

The Mint, on Beryl St near Chloride St, is open daily (only until 1 pm on weekends) and admission is free.

The **Sculpture Symposium** was a project by 12 sculptors from several countries who carved sandstone blocks on a hilltop outside town. After seeing all those paintings by local 'brushmen of the bush', it's interesting to see how foreign artists responded to this limitless landscape. They certainly don't see it full of cuddly marsupials and laconic stockmen! To get here drive north-west on Kaolin St and keep going on the unsealed road for a couple of km, until you get to the signposted turn-off on the right. From here it's another couple of km on a rough road, then a steep walk to the top of the hill. Bring water in summer.

Apart from the sculptures there are excellent views over the plains and this is a good place to watch one of Broken Hill's famous sunsets, as is the **Sundown Nature Trail** 10 km north-east of town off the Silver City Highway.

Historic Buildings

The **Afghani Mosque** is a simple old corrugated-iron building dating from 1891. Afghani cameleers helped to open up the outback, and the mosque was built on the site of a camel camp. It's on the corner of William and Buck Sts in North Broken Hill and is open on Sunday between 2.30 and 4.30 pm. It no longer functions as a mosque.

The **Trades Hall** on the corner of Sulphide and Blende Sts is a wedding-cake of a building, totally incongruous both in its setting and in relation to its function.

Even apart from the dreadful working conditions in the mines, the early settlers here lived tough lives. Miners' cottages were made of galvanised iron and must have literally been like ovens in the 40°C summers. Some corrugated-iron houses remain, especially in South Broken Hill.

Organised Tours

Plenty of companies offer tours of the town and nearby attractions, some going further out to White Cliffs, Mootwingee and other outback destinations. You'll pay about $20 for a tour of Broken Hill or Silverton and about $90 for a trip to White Cliffs. The Tourist Centre has information and takes bookings. Guided walks can be arranged here as well.

Several outfits have longer 4WD tours of the area. Goanna Safari (☎ (080) 91 2518) has 4WD outback tours which get good reports from travellers. Catherine Mould's family has worked the huge Westward Downs station, 180 km north of Broken Hill, for a century and she knows the country well. At $295 per person for three days/two nights, with a minimum of two people, visiting here is a good introduction to the outback. Shorter and longer tours can be arranged.

An interesting way to see some of the country beyond Broken Hill is to go along on an outback mail-run. Contact Crittenden Air (☎ (080) 88 5702), as far in advance as possible. The mail run departs at 6.30 am on Saturday and calls at about 14 outback stations, stopping in White Cliffs for a tour and lunch. The cost is $210. They also do various air tours, and if you are in a group of four these can work out cheaper than the mail run.

Festivals & Events

In early October a country music festival is held, with a rodeo and camel race.

Places to Stay

Caravan Parks *Broken Hill Caravan Park* (☎ (080) 87 3841) on Rakow St (the Barrier Highway) north-west of the centre has sites ($9), cabins (from $30) and on-site vans (about $25); *Lake View Caravan Park* (☎ (080) 88 2250) on Argent St (the Barrier Highway) to the east has sites ($8) and cabins (from $30). The small *Silverland Roadhouse Park* (☎ (080) 87 7389) north of here on Jabez St has sites ($8) and cabins (about $28).

Hostels *Astra House* (☎ (080) 87 7788), in the centre of town on the corner of Argent and Oxide Sts is a good backpacker hostel in a former pub. There's still a lot of renovating to be done, but it is a friendly place with huge verandahs and clean rooms. James, the manager, will drive you to local sights. There are bikes for hire ($5 a day) and twice a week there's a free meal for backpackers, which might be anything from kangaroo steaks to lentils. Dorm beds are $10, singles (when available) are $12 and doubles are $24.

The *Tourist Lodge* (☎ (080) 2086) at 100 Argent St, not far from the Tourist Centre, is an associate YHA hostel with dorms at $14 ($12 YHA members). Singles/twins cost from $20/32, with much cheaper weekly rates.

Hotels High ceilings, wide corridors and long verandahs come as standard equipment on pubs in this hot city. All the places mentioned here have air-con. As Broken Hill is the only large town for a very long way, its pubs are in the business of offering accommodation; their welcome isn't grudging.

The *Royal Exchange Hotel* (☎ (080) 87 2308) on the corner of Argent and Chloride Sts has singles/doubles for $24/40 or $34/50 with attached bathroom, fridge and TV. All rooms have tea & coffee-making facilities. The price drops by about 10% if you stay more than a couple of days. It's a definite alternative to motels. This nice old pub was built in 1898 and refurbished in 1941, when carpet reflecting the importance of agriculture was made especially for the hotel and its cockie patrons.

Diagonally opposite, the *Grand Private Hotel* (☎ (080) 87 5305) has clean rooms with TV but shared bathrooms for $40/48 a single/double.

Further west on Argent St, *Mario's Palace Hotel* (☎ (080) 88 1699) is an impressive old (1888) pub in its own right, but its coating of murals makes it extraordinary. All rooms have ceiling fans (as well as air-con), fridges, TVs and tea & coffee-making facilities. Some have phones. There's a lift (elevator). Singles/doubles cost $25/36 or $36/46 with attached bathroom. There are also some family rooms, one completely covered in murals – a truly weird place to sleep. You might want to check out your room before taking it, as some have very thin walls.

Offering more standard pub accommodation is the *West Darling Hotel* (☎ (080) 87 2691) on the corner of Argent and Oxide Sts. This is yet another fine old (1883) pub, but the rooms are in more original condition (perfectly reasonable, but you might want to check the bed). There's a variety of rooms, including some inter-connecting family rooms. A few rooms have attached bathrooms and go for $37 a single or double. There's also a family unit for $45. Rooms with shared bathroom (some have a shower attached but no toilet) are $23/36.

The *Black Lion Inn* (☎ (080) 87 4801), across from the Tourist Centre, isn't on the same scale but has reasonable rooms for $18/28 (no air-con in the single rooms).

Motels The *Sturt Motel* (☎ (080) 87 3558), on Rakow St (Barrier Highway) a few km north-west of the centre, charges from about $35/40. The *Silver Spade* (☎ (080) 87 7021), 77 Argent St, charges about $45/55; most of the other motels charge at least $55/65.

Cottages *Beryl Cottage* (☎ (080) 88 3288) at 350 Beryl St is a small house available by the night for $65 for four people plus $5 for each extra person up to six. Other six-person cottages are available for $60 a night or $320 a week – contact the owner (☎ (080) 87 8488) at 143 Knox St.

Places to Eat
The cafeteria in the information centre isn't bad value, with bacon & eggs for about $6 and other snacks and meals.

Broken Hill is a club town if ever there was one. They welcome visitors and in most cases you just sign the book at the front door and walk in. Most clubs have reasonably priced, reasonably good, very filling meals. The *Barrier Social Democratic Club* ('the Demo'), 218 Argent St, has meals including a breakfast (from 6 am, 7 am weekends) that will keep you going all day. The *Musician's Club* at 267 Crystal St, is slightly cheaper, while the *RSL* is a bit more upmarket.

There are lots of pubs too – this is a mining town – like the *Black Lion Inn* across from the Tourist Centre, which has a $5 counter lunch and main courses in the evening for around $10. Many other pubs also have counter meals.

Papa Joe's on Argent St has pasta and pizzas, plus steaks from around $9. Further east on Argent St are the *Oceania Chinese Restaurant* with $6 lunch specials and main courses from around $7.50, *Old Capri*, a small Italian place boasting home-made pasta, and the *Pussycat*, which has pasta for $6 and steaks from about $10. There's another Chinese place nearby on the corner of Oxide and Crystal Sts, the *Silver City Chinese Restaurant*, with most main courses at $8.60 and lunch specials.

Up on Sulphide St, *Champion Pizza & Chinese Takeaway* stays open late. Also good for late-night supplies is the *International Deli* on Oxide St near Beryl St, open until midnight all week. It has a good range of cheeses and smallgoods, plus takeaway salads. (The International *is* a deli, but you'll see shops calling themselves delis which aren't. This is a sign of how close to South Australia the city is: 'deli' is South Australian for 'milk bar'.)

If you're after a late-night pie, head for the *Camp Oven Pie Cart*, usually parked on Oxide St outside Papa Joe's.

At the Royal Exchange Hotel on the corner of Argent and Chloride Sts, the *Pepinella Room* is a better-than-average restaurant in a nice old pub dining-room. There's a two-course lunch special for $8 (weekdays only) and main courses from around $15 at dinner. The food is good and you might have to book on weekends (☎ (080) 87 2308). Further west on Argent St, across from the Demo Club, the *Paragon Restaurant* is also popular for a big night out and has steaks for about $12 and much more expensive seafood.

Entertainment

Maybe it's because this is a mining town that plays hard, or maybe it's because there are so many nights here when it's too hot to sleep, but Broken Hill stays up late. There isn't a great deal of formal entertainment, but

you can find pubs doing a roaring trade almost until dawn on Thursday, Friday and Saturday.

The Theatre Royale on Argent St has a disco. The Barrier Social & Democratic Club – the Demo – often has music and sometimes good bands. The Black Lion, across from the Tourist Centre, has been recommended as a good pub for a drink. They have a three-page cocktail list and two-for-one deals some nights. If you're after country music, try the Newtown Hotel on weekends. It's a small pub north-east of the centre on the corner of Buck and Lane Sts.

Two-up (gambling on the fall of two pennies, illegal until recently) is played at Burke Ward Hall on Wills St near the corner of Gypsum St, west of the centre, on Friday and Saturday nights. Broken Hill claims to have retained all the atmosphere of a real two-up 'school', unlike the sanitised versions played in casinos.

Getting There & Away

Air Standard one-way fares from Broken Hill include $160 to Adelaide with Kendell and Sunstate, $337 to Sydney with Hazelton ($250 advance-purchase), $98 to Mildura and $197 to Melbourne with Sunstate.

Train Broken Hill is on the Sydney to Perth railway line, so the Indian Pacific passes through. On Sunday and Wednesday it leaves Broken Hill at 3.05 pm and arrives in Sydney at 9.15 am the next day. The economy fare is $86. To Adelaide ($44) and Perth (from $214), it departs Broken Hill on Tuesday and Friday at 9 am.

There's a slightly faster and marginally cheaper daily service to Sydney called Laser. This is a Countrylink bus departing Broken Hill daily at 4 am (groan) and connecting with a train at Dubbo, arriving in Sydney at 9 pm.

The Countrylink booking office at the railway station (☎ 13 2232) is open on weekdays. Travel agents, such as Silver City Tours & Travel (☎ (080) 87 3310) on Argent St near the corner of Chloride St, make Countrylink bookings.

Bus Greyhound Pioneer Australia runs daily to Adelaide for $50, to Mildura for about $35 and to Sydney for $90 (sometimes less). Most buses depart from the Tourist Centre, where you can book seats.

A Victorian government V/Line bus runs to Mildura ($35) and Melbourne ($85) on Monday, Wednesday, Friday and Sunday. Book at the railway station.

Car & Motorbike The Barrier Highway runs east to Wilcannia and Cobar, a long, long drive. Westwards it heads into South Australia. The Silver City Highway runs south to Wentworth and, mostly unsealed, north to Tibooburra.

Getting Around

The Legion, Sturt, RSL and Musicians' clubs have a free bus to drive you home after a night's drinking. It leaves hourly between 6 pm and midnight. Phone (☎ (080) 88 0093) to arrange a pick-up.

Taxi Phone numbers which will get you a taxi include (☎ (080) 88 1144) and (☎ (080) 87 2222). There's a taxi office on Chloride St near Argent St.

Car Rental Hertz (☎ (080) 87 2719) has an office at the Tourist Centre, open daily. Other companies include Avis (☎ (080) 87 7532), 22 Bonanza St; Budget (☎ (080) 882160), 73 Oxide St; SCV (☎ (080) 87 3266), 320 Beryl St; Thrifty (☎ (080) 88 1928), 190 Argent St; and Broken Hill 4WD (☎ (080) 88 4265), 2 William St.

SILVERTON

Silverton, 25 km north-west of Broken Hill, is an old silver-mining town which peaked in 1885 when it had a population of 3000 and public buildings designed to last for centuries. In 1889 the mines closed and the population (and many of the houses) moved to the new boom-town at Broken Hill.

Today it's an interesting little ghost town, used as a setting in films such as *Mad Max II* and *A Town Like Alice*. A number of buildings still stand, including the old jail (now

the museum) and the Silverton Hotel. The hotel is still operating and displays photographs taken on the film sets. There are also a couple of art galleries. The information centre, in the old school, has a walking-tour map. Several artists, including Albert Woodroffe, have studios here.

Bill Canard (☎ (080) 88 5316) runs a variety of **camel tours** from Silverton. The camels are often hitched up near the hotel or the information centre. You can take a 15-minute tour of the town for $5, a one-hour ride for $20 or a two-hour sunset ride for $40 (children $20). There are also overnight treks ($150, children $75) and a five-day journey through the Barrier Ranges.

There's basic camping at *Penrose Park* (☎ (080) 88 5307), by a creek on the Broken Hill side of town. There's water for washing, but bring or boil drinking-water.

The road beyond Silverton becomes bleak and lonely almost immediately, but the **Umberumberka Reservoir**, 13 km from Silverton, is a popular picnic spot.

MENINDEE

This small town (population 500) on the Darling River is 112 km south-east of Broken Hill on a good sealed road. It is right by the big Menindee Lakes and Kinchega National Park, which surrounds one of the lakes.

Burke and Wills stayed at Maidens Hotel on their ill-fated trip north in 1860. The hotel was built in 1854 and has been with the same family for nearly 100 years. There's a courtyard which is a nice spot for a drink on a hot day.

There is a small but reasonably well-stocked supermarket in town, so you don't need to bring too many supplies.

The **Menindee Lakes** are natural lakes on the meandering Darling River, but they have been dammed to ensure year-round water. They offer the parched folk of Broken Hill a chance for watersports, and this area can be crowded on summer weekends. The Broken Hill Yacht Club is not far out of Menindee. Its pennant has a camel on it, appropriate for these ships (well, yachts) of the desert.

Places to Stay

In Menindee there is basic pub accommodation at the *Albermarle Hotel* (☎ (080) 91 4212) and at the historic *Maidens Hotel* (☎ (080) 91 4880). Just across from the Maidens, *Burke & Wills Motel* (☎ (080) 91 4313) charges $40/50.

There are caravan parks and cabins out of town by the lakes. There's also camping in Kinchega National Park.

Getting There & Away

Train Menindee is on the main railway line between Sydney and Adelaide, so you can catch the Indian Pacific here.

Car & Motorbike A good road runs to Broken Hill, and unsealed roads on both sides of the river run south to Pooncarie and Wentworth. The road on the east bank is usually a bit better than the west-bank road, but if there has been rain ask advice on the best route. Another unsealed road follows the river upstream to Wilcannia.

KINCHEGA NATIONAL PARK

Kinchega National Park is close to Menindee and includes the Darling River and several of the lakes in the Menindee system. These are a haven for bird life. The visitor centre is at the site of the old Kinchega homestead, about 16 km from the park entrance, and the shearing shed has been preserved. There is accommodation at the shearers' quarters (book at the Broken Hill National Parks office) for $15, and plenty of campsites ($5) along the river. Entry to the park costs $7.50.

MUNGO NATIONAL PARK

Mungo National Park (27,850 hectares), part of the Willandra Lakes World Heritage Area, is remote, beautiful and one of our species' most important places. The echoes of 400 centuries of continuous human habitation are almost tangible.

The story of both Australia and its oldest inhabitants is told in the dunes of Mungo. At least 40,000 years ago Aborigines settled on the banks of the fertile lakes, living on the plentiful fish, mussels, birds and animals.

Some of the animals were very much larger than their modern relatives. After 25,000 years the climate changed, the lakes dried up and the Aborigines adapted to life in a harsh semi-desert, with only periodic floods filling the lakes. The constant westerly wind drifted sand from the lake-bed up onto the dunes, gradually burying old campsites.

The people maintained their culture for another 15,000 years, but it was destroyed when Europeans arrived with their sheep just 150 years ago. Along with the remains of incredibly ancient animals and people, the dunes hold tracks of the Cobb & Co coaches which cut across the lake last century.

The park includes the dry lake-bed (it sometimes fills after heavy rain) and the spectacular 'lunette', a semi-circular range of sand dunes which line the eastern side. Some of the compressed sand has weathered into shimmering white cliffs known as the **Walls of China**. This weathering process began last century after sheep destabilised the dunes, which are now moving slowly eastwards under the constant west wind, leaving exposed immensely important archaeological evidence.

There's a visitor centre (not always staffed) where you can see some of the archaeological finds. Near the visitor centre is the old woolshed from the sheep station which was established here last century. During school holidays there are sometimes organised activities, such as walks and even bush dances. The National Parks office at Buronga (☎ (050) 23 1278), near Mildura, has information.

A 60 km drive circles the lunette, and there are various stopping places with informative noticeboards. There are a couple of short walks, the Grassland Nature Trail (one km), beginning near Main Camp, and the Mallee Walk (500 metres), off the road on the east side of the lunette. You can get onto the lunette from the Walls of China, and there are good dune walks from Vigars Wells on the north-east side of the lunette.

In summer, be sure to take the precaution of carrying water with you when you go walking on the dunes.

Mungo Dreaming

Under these dunes that sing to the perpetual west wind lie the bones and debris of a civilisation which is unlikely to be matched by the brief and sooty flicker of our materialist culture. The Mungo lunette is thick with spirits. Spirits from the 25,000 years of Eden, when the lakes were full and the land was fat. Spirits from the 15,000 years after the lakes dried up and new skills were perfected.

Mungo is a good place for dreaming.

Dream of our cultural ancestors, the Greeks, and their strange urge to build and to shape the world, and how this led to our failing experiment with industrialisation and urban life.

The Mungo people had already been here for 35,000 years when the Parthenon was new. Humanity's earliest known funerals were conducted here.

The dream becomes a guttering nightmare of syphilis, smallpox, guns and Christians, and this unimaginably old civilisation is wiped out in a generation.

Coincidentally, when I visited Mungo there were news reports of an alleged beating of an Aborigine by police in a nearby town. The media labelled it a 'Rodney King-style incident' but the story's main resemblance to the King beating was that it was taken seriously. Two centuries of brutality bordering on genocide is an entirely Australian phenomenon. ∎

Organised Tours

Mallee Outback Exploration (☎ (050) 21 1621) and Junction Tours (☎ (050) 21 4424) are two Mildura-based companies offering tours.

Splitters Creek Airlines (☎ (060) 21 1136) flies historic DC3 planes to Mungo from Albury, overnighting here and returning to Albury the next day. They prefer groups but individuals can sometimes go along, for about $300. This is a good deal.

Places to Stay

Accommodation fills up during school holidays. There are two campsites in the park: Main Camp is two km from the visitor centre and Belah Camp is in bushland on the eastern side of the lunette, a few km away from it. On this side of the lunette you're sheltered from the west wind, but you can hear it singing eerily along the dunes.

Camping costs $5 a night (plus the $7.50 entry fee). There is also shared accommodation in the old shearers' quarters, costing $15 per person or $25 for a room to yourself. There are cooking facilities. Accommodation in the shearers' quarters must be booked through the National Parks office in Buronga (☎ (050) 23 1278), near Mildura.

On the Mildura road about four km from the visitor centre is *Mungo Lodge* (☎ (050) 29 7297). Singles/doubles go for $55/65 and there are self-contained cottages sleeping five or six for $75. There's also a restaurant.

Getting There & Away

Air Mungo Lodge has an airstrip where charter flights can land.

Car & Motorbike No fuel is available in the park or along the roads leading to it. The unsealed roads into Mungo are well-maintained, but they can be closed by rain. Even after a light shower, sections are treacherous. Also, watch out for deep drifts of sand or soft dirt. These appear without warning and if you hit one at speed you'll have no control over the steering until you reach the end, hopefully still pointing in the right direction. Kangaroos and emus are another hazard – or, rather, you are a hazard for these locals.

Mungo is 110 km from Mildura and 150 km from Balranald. When you're adding up the km to make sure you have enough fuel to get to Mungo and back, don't forget the 60-odd km you'll probably drive within the park.

Coming from Balranald, you can take the signposted turn-off about 15 km north of town. This is Burke & Wills Rd; it's an interesting drive, but a little rough. If you want to travel on tar as far as possible, don't take this turn-off but keep heading north to another signposted turn-off, 53 km from Balranald.

FAR WEST

The Riverina

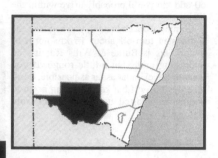

The Riverina takes in much of southern NSW, specifically the mighty Murray and Murrumbidgee rivers and the plains created by these waterways as they changed their courses over the millennia. Away from the rivers, which are popular for fishing holidays, much of this region sees few visitors. This is part of the Riverina's attraction – you can meet locals whose daily life is not geared to extracting dollars from your wallet.

History

The rivers of the Riverina provided an idyllic home for the Aborigines, and before Europeans arrived the area around Deniliquin was probably the most densely populated part of the continent. John Oxley, the first European to visit the area, was not impressed:

There is a uniformity in the barren desolation of this country which wearies one more than I am able to express...I am the first white man to see it and I think I will undoubtedly be the last.
John Oxley, expedition of 1817

A century later, after graziers had established sheep stations on the plains, Europeans were coming to terms with the environment:

The monotonous variety of this interminable scrub...so grave, subdued, self-centred...bespeaks an ungauged, unconfined potentiality...
Joseph Furphy, Such is Life, 1903

Not long after, the great irrigation schemes of the Murrumbidgee Irrigation Area (MIA) were begun and parts of the plains bloomed into fertile farmland.

Oddly, the name 'riverina' isn't the recent brainchild of a tourism committee but was widely used last century. The old-timers' Riverina was much larger than today's region. For them, the Riverina included the vast griddle of plains south of the Darling.

To get an idea of the terrain and the conditions of the Riverina, drive along the Cobb Highway from Wilcannia to Hay. This isn't a trip to take lightly, as much of the 400 km is unsealed and there are very few services along the road. Imagine how the trip would have been in a bullock wagon hauling eight tonnes of wool at a rate of less than 20 km a day!

Geography

To the east, the landscape is broken up by the last hills of the western slopes of the Great Divide, but much of the region is a huge, flat space, usually with a line of river red-gums straggling along a creek on the horizon, or native pines clustered on a sandy ridge, overlooking grazing country or, in the west and north, expanses of saltbush or mulga. Sleek hawks brood on the telephone wires or flutter above the roadside, hoping that your car will scare up some tucker.

Not only is the country flat, but it isn't far above sea level. The Murray has a fall of only 100 metres or so between Corowa and its mouth in South Australia. The inland rivers meander lazily, often changing their courses and often breaking their banks. This flooding was a vital part of the area's ecology. River red-gums need regular inundation to survive, but the big dams built for the irrigation schemes have limited the extent of the floods and the trees are suffering.

In the west the fences disappear and cattle grids on the road are the only signs that you are in worked country. Wedge-tailed eagles waft overhead or perch awkwardly on telegraph poles – there are no peaks or even tall trees for their eyries. The western grey kangaroos are dwarfed by the big reds.

Away from the serpentine rivers and their red-gum forests, the landscape can be monotonous, but if you're after a sense of distance and space, the Riverina is the place to come. Flat horizons of 360° are common, under a hot, blue sky – some Riverina towns have more hours of sunshine per year than the Gold Coast. The shimmering horizon blurs into mirages, and even in winter the light is blindingly strong. Autumn nights can be cold, with heavy frosts, but after the mists burn off, the days are beautiful.

Despite the landscape's apparent desolation, this is rich grazing and farming country. Irrigation schemes allow crops such as rice and grapes to flourish in several centres, while the small towns of the region are usually pleasant oases.

Warning River red-gums are notorious for dropping those huge, heavy branches without warning. Apparently, hot, still days in summer are the most dangerous times.

Getting There & Away
Air Major towns such as Deniliquin, Griffith and Wagga Wagga have regular passenger flights. Smaller operators also service the region, some connecting with flights to Sydney at Wagga Wagga.

Train The only railway line through this region is the main Sydney to Melbourne line, which runs through Junee, Wagga Wagga and Morgan Country.

Bus Major lines running along the Newell Highway between Melbourne and Brisbane service the Riverina, and some buses running between Sydney and Adelaide pass through. There are some useful smaller lines, such as MIA Intercity (Griffith to Melbourne) and Fearnes Coaches (various Hume Highway towns to Wagga Wagga).

Countrylink links most of the Riverina region's towns with the railway line at Wagga Wagga, Cootamundra or Albury. V/Line runs between Melbourne and the southern Riverina.

Car & Motorbike Several major highways cross the Riverina, and the Hume Highway skirts the eastern side.

The Newell Highway (Melbourne to Brisbane) runs from Tocumwal north to Narrandera, the Cobb Highway (Moama to Wilcannia) runs north from Moama to Hay, and the Olympic Highway (Albury to Bathurst) runs through Morgan Country, Wagga Wagga and Junee.

The Sturt Highway enters the Riverina at Wagga Wagga and runs west through Narrandera, Hay and Balranald and on into South Australia.

The Riverina Highway runs from Albury west to Deniliquin, but if you want to continue west from Deniliquin on a major road you'll have to head south and pick up Victoria's Murray Valley Highway at Echuca, or head north and pick up the Sturt Highway at Hay. Another route into the Riverina is the Mid-Western Highway, which runs west from Bathurst and enters the Riverina north of Griffith, meeting the Sturt Highway at Hay.

See the various sections in this chapter for some interesting smaller roads to and around the Riverina.

Down the Murrumbidgee

The Murrumbidgee rises in the Snowy Mountains and by the time it reaches Wagga Wagga, not far from the foothills, it's already a broad river. Further downstream its waters are used in the big MIA around Griffith, then it flows though harsher country and meets the Murray downstream from Balranald.

RIVERINA

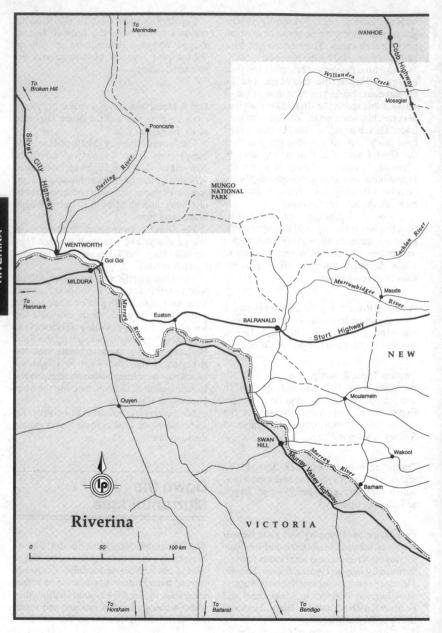

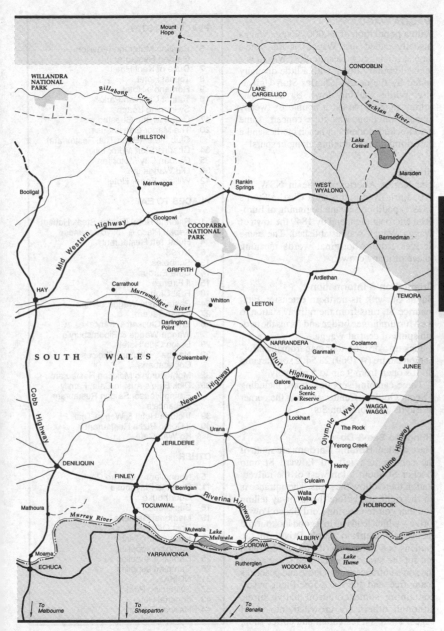

WAGGA WAGGA

With a population of 54,000, Wagga Wagga (usually called just Wagga) is the state's largest inland city. Despite this, Wagga is a relaxed country town, with a little diversity added by the nearby Charles Sturt University. While walking down Baylis St one Friday night I passed a couple of tweedy citizens on their way to a concert, some dreadlocked students in beach clothes and a half-drunk drover jingling along in spurs!

History

The largest Aboriginal tribe in NSW, the Wiradjuri, lived in this area. Charles Sturt's 1829 expedition saw the beginning of European encroachment and by 1849 the town of Wagga Wagga was established. The name derives from Aboriginal words meaning 'place of many crows'.

Orientation & Information

Baylis St, with its northern extension Fitzmaurice St, runs from the railway station to the Murrumbidgee bridge and forms the two-km spine of central Wagga.

Pick up a driving-tour map from the information centre (☎ (069) 23 5402) on Tarcutta St. It's open from 9 am to 5 pm daily.

Three camping supplies shops, including a Scout Outdoor Centre, are near the corner of Baylis and Tompson Sts.

Things to See & Do

The excellent **Botanic Gardens** are south of the centre; turn left off Edward St onto Docker St about a km west of the railway station then follow the signs. The entrance is on the right just before the archway telling you that you're entering Lord Baden Powell Drive – which leads up to a good lookout and the scenic **Captain Cook Drive**. In the gardens is a small **zoo** (if you're tall watch out for the strand of electrified fence above the zoo's entrance gate). Geese and peacocks roam free and there's a free-flight aviary containing some colourful native birds, although others are crowded into small cages. There's a restaurant and coffee shop,

PLACES TO STAY

3	Pavilion Motor Inn (Pavilion Garden Restaurant)
7	Duke of Kent Hotel
8	Tourist Hotel
9	Romano's Hotel
10	Tourist Caravan Park & Swimming Beach
17	Crepe Myrtle Guesthouse
20	The Manor Guesthouse
33	Club Motel (Baan Thai Restaurant)
34	Charles Sturt Motor Inn
35	Garden City Motor Inn
36	Old Wagga Inn
42	William Farrer Hotel

PLACES TO EAT

1	Riverina Hotel (Bridge Steak House)
2	Kebab Place & Tokyo Japanese
4	Huatt Tatt Restaurant
6	No 96
13	Scribbles
14	Cafe Europa
15	Il Firenze
18	RSL Club
24	Pasta Pasta Wagga Wagga
27	Indian Tavern
28	Emma Chissett's, Pancakes at Wagga Wagga & Bloomsbury's
29	Union Club Hotel
30	Nahiba's Kitchen, Choices & Copacabana
32	Montezuma's Mexican Restaurant
38	Dick Eyle's Aussie Cafe, Family Eating House, Saigon Restaurant & Bianca's
39	Victoria Hotel & Wagga Thai
40	Il Corso Pizza Restaurant
41	Ko Wah Cafe

OTHER

5	Ngungilanna Culture Centre
11	Riverina Playhouse
12	Courthouse
16	Bus Station
19	Memorial Gardens
21	Post Office
22	Information Centre
23	Camping supplies
25	Camping supplies
26	Camping supplies
31	NRMA
37	Swimming Pool
43	Imperial Hotel
44	Railway Station

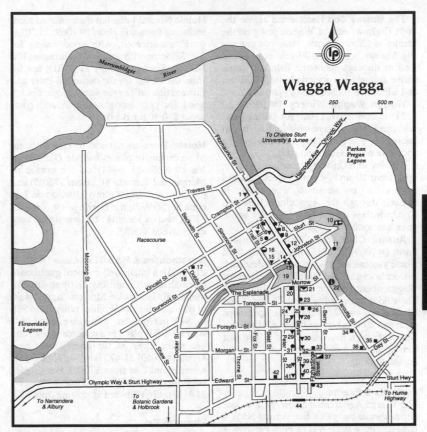

Wagga Wagga

0   250   500 m

To Charles Sturt
University & Junee

Parkan
Pregan
Lagoon

Murrumbidgee River

Travers St

Fitzmaurice St

Crampton St

Beckwith St

Simmons St

Racecourse

Kincaid St

Dobbs St

Gurwood St

Shaw St

Docker St

Flowerdale
Lagoon

The Esplanade

Tompson St

Forsyth St

Fox St

Best St

Morgan St

Thorne St

Edward St

Olympic Way & Sturt Highway

To Narrandera
& Albury

To
Botanic Gardens
& Holbrook

Sturt St

Johnston St

Morrow St

Peter St

Baylis St

Tarcutta St

Berry St

Dey St

Fitzhardinge Street

Sturt Hwy

To Hume
Highway

RIVERINA

and you can ride a model train on the first and third Sundays of the month.

Charles Sturt University is north of town, off the Olympic Way. The campus is huge, although there aren't yet many buildings. To get to the Student Union turn left at the roundabout at the entrance.

The **Riverina Galleries** on the Esplanade has a big programme of exhibitions by Australian artists, and the **Ngungilanna Culture Centre** on Gurwood St has a wide range of Koori items for sale, both traditional and modern.

The **Wiradjuri Walking Track** begins at

the information centre and eventually returns there after a 30 km tour of the area, including some good lookouts. There's a shorter 10 km loop past the Wollundry Lagoon. The walks can be done in stages and the information centre has maps.

There's a **swimming beach** near the Tourist Caravan Park with changing-rooms and a kiosk.

Wagga Wagga is a major centre for **live-stock sales**, although the computerised bidding and indoor ring don't have quite the same atmosphere as a smaller town's outdoor saleyards.

The **Murray Cod Hatcheries** are on the Sturt Highway east of Wagga, just past the hamlet of Gumly Gumly. Here you can see Big Murray, a 50 kg, 100-year-old cod, as well as displays about the fish, and some native animals. It's open daily from 9.30 am and admission is about $5 ($3 children).

Wagga Wagga Winery (☎ (069) 22 1221) is open from 11 am for tastings and sales, and meals are available for $10. It's an interesting place, midway between Wagga and Oura on the Gundagai road.

Charles Sturt University also has a winery, open from 10 am to 4 pm on weekdays and from 11 am on weekends. The winery is reached through the Agriculture Research Unit, which is off the Olympic Way about three km north of Wagga.

Aurora Clydesdale Stud & Pioneer Farm (☎ (069) 28 2215) is a working farm where you can see magnificent Clydesdales. Aurora is south of the Sturt Highway west of Wagga, about nine km west of Collingullie. The stud is open daily except Thursday and admission is just $2 ($1 children). For groups of about 20 at $3 a head they will put the horses through their paces, but if you just turn up there's a chance that you'll see the horses working.

Festivals & Events
The Wagga Agricultural Show, held in late September or early October, is rural NSW's largest. The Wagga Wagga Folk Festival is also a biggie, and is held in early October.

Places to Stay
Caravan Parks Of the several caravan parks in the area, the *Tourist Caravan Park* (☎ (069) 21 2540) has the best location. It's on the river right next to the swimming beach and a couple of blocks from the town centre. You could walk here from the railway station and the bus terminal. There are plenty of trees (and plenty of inquisitive possums in them) and a grassy camping area. Tent sites are $7 for two people, on-site vans cost from $22 and cabins range up to $40 with TV and bathroom. Add $4 for each extra person.

Hotels Several pubs have accommodation, including *Romano's Hotel* (☎ (069) 21 2013) on Fitzmaurice St, with good rooms for $30/38, some with attached bathrooms. The *William Farrer* (☎ (069) 21 3631), not far from the station on the corner of Peter and Edward Sts, isn't in the same league but it's good for pub accommodation and costs about $30/40 for B&B.

Motels There are 20-odd to choose from. More expensive places include *Old Wagga Inn* (☎ (069) 21 6444) on the corner of Morgan and Tarcutta Sts (from $75/85) and the *Charles Sturt* (☎ (069) 21 8088) on Tarcutta St ($60/70); the *Burringa* (☎ (069) 22 3100), also on Tarcutta St, is among the least expensive at $45/55.

Guesthouses & B&B The *Manor* (☎ (069) 21 5962) is a small, well-restored guesthouse (furnished with antiques) opposite the Memorial Gardens on Morrow St, just west of Baylis St. Singles/doubles range from $25 to $45 per person, including breakfast. Another B&B place in a restored house, this one much older, is the interesting *Crepe Myrtle* (☎ (069) 21 4757) at 102 Kinkaid St, where rooms cost from $70/80. For simpler B&B there's *Rose Maree Cottage* (☎ (069) 21 4117) at 163 Edward St, costing from $30.

Places to Eat
At the top end of Fitzmaurice St is one of the Colonel's outlets, and at the bottom end of Baylis St there is another. Between these unpromising gateways is a surprisingly diverse range of good places to eat. A culinary stroll beginning near the top of Fitzmaurice St might include the following places.

The Kebab Place, a Lebanese takeaway that has added a restaurant and gained good reviews from food writers. A few doors down is the *Tokyo Japanese Restaurant*, closed after a fire at the time of writing. A little further down is *No 96*, a trendy bar where you can eat and drink if you aren't wearing runners (sneakers). It's open from 6 pm to 3 am Monday to Saturday and for lunch on Friday.

Cafe Europa is on Johnston St just west of Baylis/Fitzmaurice St. It's open for lunch and dinner daily and has pasta ($8) and pizzas. There are tables on the footpath. Further west on Johnston St is *Il Firenze*. Wagga Wagga Writers Writers, a local literary group, sometimes holds readings here.

Back on Baylis/Fitzmaurice St, *Scribbles* is a light-hearted cafe serving focaccia, coffee and light meals during the day and into the evening from Thursday to Saturday. Nachos will set you back $7. *The Manor* guesthouse has a good restaurant open Monday to Saturday for dinner. The interesting menu has main courses for around $15 to $20 and there's a touch of elegance.

In D'Hudson arcade at 176 Baylis St, nearly opposite the Plaza Cinema, the *Indian Tavern* has a tandoori oven and is open for dinner daily and for lunch from Wednesday to Friday. There are set-menu lunch specials for around $10 and main courses range from $7 to $12. They also do takeaways.

Across the street from here is a cluster of places. *Emma Chissett's* ('emma chissett' is Strine for 'could you please tell me the price of this article?') serves coffee, snacks and light meals during the day. A little further along is *Pancakes at Wagga Wagga*, a nice place with a large menu of pancake permutations and other dishes including various pastas (around $8). They give 15% student discounts and if you buy your movie tickets here with a meal you get $2 off. It's open from Monday to Saturday for lunch and from Tuesday to Saturday for dinner.

Nearby but upstairs is *Bloomsbury's*, an airy cafe-style place with a small balcony overlooking the street. It has recently changed hands and the new menu hasn't settled down yet, but they serve some interesting, moderately-priced dishes. Currently it's open for lunch Tuesday to Saturday and dinner Thursday to Saturday.

In Neslo Arcade is *Nahiba's Kitchen*, a small Lebanese takeaway (with tables) where everything is cooked in front of you. The menu of simple, inexpensive dishes includes some Indian items, and vegetarians are catered for. Although the food lacks some of the piquancy of the Lebanese food served in more upmarket places, it's probably a lot closer to traditional village cooking. It's open Monday to Saturday and well worth checking out.

The *Union Club Hotel* has counter meals from $5.

For something completely unauthentic you could try *Montezuma's Mexican Restaurant*, where *comidas* (meals) cost around $10 and other main courses are about $13. It's open from 6 pm Tuesday to Sunday and for lunch from Wednesday to Friday.

The bistro at the *Victoria Hotel* has a good reputation, a large menu on which nothing costs over $10, and dress regulations – no thongs, singlets or work clothes. In the Baylis Centre next door is the popular *Wagga Thai Restaurant*, a large, plush place which has a $5 lunchtime buffet and main courses in the $9 to $12 range. There's another Thai restaurant, the *Bahn Thai*, at the Club Motel on Morgan St.

Dick Eyle's *Aussie Cafe* is about the only example of a main-street cafe on Baylis St, but it's a good one and is open for breakfast. Bacon & eggs are a bit pricey at $7.50, but they come with chips. A few doors down is the *Family Eating House*, a huge smorgasbord place where you can eat as much as you like for $7.80 at lunch (11 am to 2.30 pm) and $8.80 at dinner (5.30 to 9.30 pm). The menu is changed weekly but it's mainly Asian with some incongruous dishes such as shepherd's pie thrown in.

Further down is the small *Saigon Restaurant* with lunch specials for about $4. It stays open until at least 9.30 pm. *Bianca's Place* is a coffee-shop-style establishment serving breakfast, snacks and light meals. Across the road is *Il Corso Pizza Restaurant*, with pasta dishes for $8.50 and other main courses around $12. Finally, back across the street and next to the KFC is the large *Ko Wah Cafe* which has lunch specials and main courses around $7.50.

Whew. And that's just Baylis St and nearby. The *Leagues Club* on Gurwood St

RIVERINA

has $5 lunches and $10 smorgasbord dinners; the *Huatt Tatt Restaurant* at 51 Trail St has great Malaysian food; the *Pavilion Garden Restaurant* on Kinkaid St (in an extravagantly-designed motel) has seafood and a $25 table d'hote...

Entertainment
The Riverina Playhouse and the Civic Theatre often stage performances.

This is a student town, of sorts, and a few of the pubs have bands, including the Duke of Kent and the Tourist hotels on Fitzmaurice St. The Imperial Hotel, not far from the station on Edward St, has a student night on Wednesday. There are a couple of disco-type places with formidable dress requirements on Baylis St, Choices and Copacabana, both open until late most days of the week. Choices is probably the easier to get into. The various clubs sometimes have entertainment.

Other popular watering-holes are the Union Club Hotel, on Baylis St, and Romano's Hotel on Fitzmaurice St.

Getting There & Away
Air Ansett Express (☎ 13 1300), Kendell (☎ (069) 22 0100), Western (☎ (069) 22 7777) and Link (☎ (069) 22 7900) have services connecting Wagga with Sydney, Melbourne, Brisbane and a number of places in NSW.

Train Wagga is on the main line between Sydney and Melbourne. There's a Countrylink Rail Travel Centre (☎ (069) 22 0448) at the railway station.

Wedge-tailed eagle

Bus Countrylink buses meet some trains and run to Griffith via Narrandera and Leeton, to Echuca (Victoria) via Jerilderie, Finley, Deniliquin and Moama. Countrylink leaves from the railway station. All other long-distance services leave from the terminal at the corner of Gurwood and Trail Sts. You can make bookings here or at one of the travel agents along Baylis St. Fearnes Coaches runs to Sydney ($35) via the Hume Highway, stopping at most major towns, such as Gundagai, Goulburn and Mittagong.

Glass Buslines runs a local service to Junee on weekdays and picks up along Baylis St.

Car & Motorbike Wagga is at the junction of the Sturt Highway, which runs east to the Hume Highway and west to Narrandera, and the Olympic Way, which runs north-east to Cootamundra and south to Albury. Smaller roads, often interesting drives, link Wagga with the small towns of this well-populated area.

Car Rental Avis (☎ (069) 21 1077) is at the corner of Edward and Fitzhardinge Sts.

AROUND WAGGA WAGGA
The Rock
On the Olympic Way about 25 km south-west of Wagga, The Rock is a small village near a large, rocky hill rising out of the flat plain. The town was called Hanging Rock until the boulder balanced on top of the hill fell off late last century. But having *lost* their rock, why did the town decide on an even more emphatically stony name?

Heckenberg's is an interesting antique shop and auction room.

The hill is **The Rock Nature Reserve** and there's a walking trail to the summit which takes about three hours for the return journey. Near the top the going is steep and you have to be careful of falling rocks.

Near **Yerong Creek**, 15 km south of The Rock, *Hanericka Holiday Farm* (☎ (069) 20 3709) is a large complex geared to foreign tourists. Accommodation costs in the region of $90 per person, including all meals and farm activities. For something simpler you could try the impressive *Yerong Creek Hotel* (☎ (069) 20 3515).

Galore Scenic Reserve

Henry Osborne walked from Wollongong to Adelaide in 1840 and on the way he climbed this sudden hill, exclaiming at the top, 'There is land and galore'. Now a scenic reserve, Galore Hill is worth a visit if you're in the area, for its bush (and the plantings near the base of the hill) and for the 360° views from the platform at the top. There are toilets and fireplaces near the platform but you can't camp here. This reserve is refreshingly free of the ravages of beer parties and trail-bike vandals.

Galore Hill is 14 km south of the Sturt Highway, down a turn-off about 60 km west of Wagga, and it's also accessible from Lockhart.

Lockhart

This little town of 1000 people is known for its verandahs – both sides of the main street are lined with them. There's a small craft-shop/museum at the end of the street, open at various times on Wednesday and Friday to Sunday. The gates to the showground, where there's an old pavilion, are concrete wool bales.

Three pubs and a motel have accommodation and there's a small caravan park.

Ganmain

Ganmain is a sleepy little town on the interesting road between Junee and Narrandera, and is accessible from Wagga via Junee or more directly via **Coolamon**, a larger but also pretty little place. North of Coolamon, four km out on the Temora road, you can stay in an old railway carriage or in a self-contained cottage at *Avondale Farm* (☎ (069) 27 3055) for $30 per person. Also in the area is *Narua* (☎ (069) 22 9212), 26 km north of Wagga on the Coolamon road, a farmstay where you sleep in the family homestead.

Apart from its somnolent charm, Ganmain is notable for its hay industry. Last century the farms here gained a reputation for high-quality wheaten hay and chaff and they've been producing it ever since, currently 20,000 tonnes a year. What makes the area special is that the hay is still bound into sheaves which are stooked by hand and carted in horse-drawn wagons (sometimes) to be stacked into 'real' haystacks, which you can see sitting in the stubbled paddocks like so many enormous loaves of bread. There's a roadside information booth in Ganmain where you can see a video on the hay production and even activate one of the old binders. The hay-cutting season is October and November.

Ganmain's other claim to fame is its meat pies, which are highly regarded in the district.

MORGAN COUNTRY

The area known as Morgan Country is a rough circle of pretty country south of Wagga Wagga, west of Holbrook and north of Albury, containing some interesting little towns, including Henty, Culcairn and Jindera.

The area was once the stamping-ground of bushranger Mad Dog Morgan. Unlike Ned Kelly, Morgan was a bushranger no-one respected. He began his career in Victoria in the 1850s but was captured and spent six years on a prison hulk in Port Phillip Bay (probably enough to turn anyone into a mad dog). On receiving parole he escaped and moved into NSW where for two years he killed and looted in this small area. Declared an outlaw, he fled to Victoria (where he was still wanted) in 1865, resolving to 'take the flashness out of the Victorian people and police'. He didn't get very far. At Peechelba station, just south of the Murray near Corowa, he was shot dead. His head was cut off and it's said that his scrotum became a tobacco pouch.

Information

For tourist information on the area see the craft shop next to the hotel in Culcairn, or phone Gaynor McLeish (☎ (060) 29 6136).

RIVERINA

Culcairn

Culcairn was a major overnight stop for people travelling by train between Sydney and Melbourne, and the town's main feature, the **Culcairn Hotel** (1891), reflects this status. It's a grand old hotel, the largest between the two cities until the 1930s, with a beer garden that deserves a more lavish name – there's even a fountain! Next to the pub is Sholz's Building, a long terrace of shops, and these two form the bulk of the town.

Across the tracks from the pub, the old stationmaster's residence is being restored as a **museum**, and there are plans to locate some old carriages here. There are several other historic buildings in this little town, with half the main street classified by the National Trust. On Gordon St is the artesian pumping station, first used to supply Culcairn's water in 1926.

Not far out of Culcairn is **Round Hill Station**, with an enormous and very old woolshed. The functions held here are sometimes open to the public (bush dances, for example).

At **Premier Yabbies**, about six km south-west from Culcairn off the Walla Walla road, you can see an interesting display on yabbies and resist putting your fingers into the tanks that hold some large specimens. Admission is $4 ($2 children) and refreshments including yabbie sandwiches (very tasty) are available. You can also catch your own. The farm is closed on Tuesday and throughout August.

Places to Stay & Eat The very small *Culcairn Caravan Park* is by the creek.

The *Morgan Country Motel* (☎ (060) 29 8501) is good, but it's hard to resist a night at the *Culcairn Hotel* (☎ (060) 29 8501), at $25/35 including a serve-yourself breakfast. The rooms are standard pub accommodation with shared bathrooms, but the carpets and beds are new, the paint is fresh and French windows lead onto wonderful balconies. The decor steers an uneasy course between genuine antiques and gaudy kitsch, but the pub is big enough to take it. Tour groups stay here so it's advisable to book.

As well as a couple of simple cafes, there's a *bistro* at the hotel and a *Chinese restaurant* at the bowling club.

Morgan's Lookout

A low hill with a cluster of huge boulders on top, this would have made a superb lookout for any bushranger. You can climb up for great views and there are gas barbecues. The lookout is about 20 km south-west of Culcairn on the sealed road to Walla Walla, just past the Walbundrie turn-off. The pub in **Walbundrie** makes the modest claim of having 'the best and only beer in town'.

Walla Walla

This little town was settled in 1869 by Germans from South Australia's Barossa Valley. Today there's a large Lutheran Church and a boarding school. On the second Sunday of each month a **craft market** is held in the old blacksmith's shop on Main St; German food is available.

Just north of town there's a wetland area, **Walla Walla Tank Wildlife Refuge**, with a stand of river red-gum forest.

Walla Walla has motel and camping accommodation.

Henty

The Taylor Header, which revolutionised grain harvesting around the world, was invented in Henty in 1914. There's a display commemorating this in Henty Park.

Each year the **Henty Machinery Field Days** are held on Tuesday, Wednesday and Thursday of the third week in September. If you're interested in farm equipment (or are interested in the people who are) this is the place to come. About 50,000 people turn up for this event, perhaps the best of its type in Australia.

Doodle Cooma Swamp is a wetlands area, two km west of town on the Pleasant Hills road.

The *Doodle Cooma Arms* (☎ (069) 29 3013) and the more conservatively named *Central Hotel* (☎ (069) 29 3149) have meals and pub accommodation. The pub in Pleasant Hills, about 25 km west of Henty, apparently has good meals.

Jindera

Jindera was also settled by German immigrants, and the early days are remembered in the outstanding **Jindera Museum**. The museum centres around Wagners store, an old-style country store that was left as it was when it closed in 1958 – although it must have been a very old-fashioned store even then. The many exhibits include some buggies and wagons, including one which carried the area's first German settlers across from Adelaide. Check out the enormous builder's wagon, too. The museum is open daily from 10 am to 4.30 pm and admission is $3 (50c children).

Getting There & Away

Train Trains running between Sydney and Melbourne stop at Culcairn, Henty and The Rock.

Bus Greyhound Pioneer Australia stops in Culcairn, Henty and The Rock on the run between Melbourne and Brisbane.

Car & Motorbike The Olympic Way (Albury to Bathurst) runs through this area, which is also accessible from the Hume Highway at Holbrook.

JUNEE

Junee is a small country town with a disproportionate number of impressive buildings. It's a friendly place and well worth a stop.

Pubs

If you like pubs, downtown Junee is like a glimpse of heaven, with two magnificent old pubs, their massive verandahs dripping with iron lace, standing cheek by jowl. Turn around, and across the tracks looms yet another enormous old hotel. All three pubs deserve at least one beer, and there are another three in town if you want to make a day of it.

The **Commercial Hotel** has a busy bar

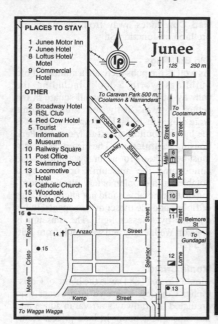

PLACES TO STAY
1 Junee Motor Inn
7 Junee Hotel
8 Loftus Hotel/Motel
9 Commercial Hotel

OTHER
2 Broadway Hotel
3 RSL Club
4 Red Cow Hotel
5 Tourist Information
6 Museum
10 Railway Square
11 Post Office
12 Swimming Pool
13 Locomotive Hotel
14 Catholic Church
15 Woodoak
16 Monte Cristo

crowded with after-work drinkers. The **Loftus** is the town's grandest hotel, with a frontage running for an entire block. The main bar has been refurbished but it's still a pleasant spot for a quiet drink. Check out the residential entrance and the staircase. The gaudy Chinese lantern hanging in the foyer seems entirely appropriate for the surroundings.

Across the tracks, the **Junee** is at least a big as the Loftus and was built by Christopher Crawley, owner of the Monte Cristo mansion on the hill behind. The pub hasn't had a lot done to it over the years and it's a little run-down, but that just means that the original fittings are still intact. The billiards room off the main bar is crying out for a couple of full-sized tables. On Broadway St, the **Broadway** is another fair-sized pub, a bit the worse for wear but with a green-tiled bar that deserves a look. The **Locomotive** on Hill St is just a country pub, a little out of its league in this company, and the single-storey

Red Cow hides away from its mammoth brethren on Junction St.

Old Buildings

As well as the pubs there are a number of old buildings worth a look, including the **railway buildings** on a small square in the centre of town. Sadly, refreshment rooms were closed in 1993. In complete contrast is the humble building next to Memorial Park housing the **museum**. The historical society must be sticklers for accuracy, as the plaque announcing the museum's opening by a notable has a supplementary plaque recording that the notable could not attend because of floods and the museum was opened in his absence by a lesser light. The museum is open on Wednesday and weekends from 2.30 to 5 pm.

Monte Cristo

Monte Cristo (1884) was the home of Christopher Crawley, a shrewd land-owner who predicted the railway's arrival in Junee and the subsequent boom in land prices. Actually, it's suspected that he was a little more than shrewd, as the railway was supposed to go through Old Junee, some way distant, but somehow ended up running through Crawley's land. The mansion sits on a hill on the west side of town, near the impressive Catholic church. Once these were the only buildings on this side of the tracks, because Crawley would not sell building blocks that would spoil his view.

Monte Cristo isn't an especially large mansion but it is crammed full of superb antiques collected by the owners during their 30-year restoration of the property. It had nearly been destroyed by weather and vandals, who weren't deterred by the house's reputation for supernatural goings-on.

The mansion is open from 10 am to 4 pm daily and the admission price of $5 ($2.50 children) includes an informative guided tour. You can also wander through the outbuildings which contain other exhibits, including a large display of old carriages and buggies. Car access to Monte Cristo is from the Wagga Wagga road, but you could find

your way up here on foot if you used the church as a landmark.

On the road to Monte Cristo is **Woodoak**, a house where you can see some enormous oak carvings brought out from England.

Places to Stay & Eat

Willows Caravan Park (☎ (069) 24 1316) is small but pleasant and charges just $6 for a tent site. It's at the northern end of Broadway St on the outskirts of town.

There's a motel, the *Junee* (☎ (069) 24 1266), but this is a town where you should try a pub, and there are three good options. The *Commercial* (☎ (069) 24 1023) is a friendly, popular place with good rooms for just $12/24. There's a large guests' lounge and kitchen facilities. The Commercial has a bistro where standard counter-meal dishes cost around $7. The pub also has *The Crossing* restaurant in a very nice dining room. The menu is a little more extensive than the bistro's but it's still mainly country favourites. The restaurant is open from Wednesday to Sunday and on other days if you book.

Next door, the *Loftus* (☎ (069) 24 1511) has some simple motel-style units which are good value at $20/42 including a light breakfast, but you should consider taking one of the hotel rooms ($20/32) which look out onto that fabulous verandah. Despite its more upmarket feel, counter meals at the Loftus are slightly cheaper than those at the Commercial. There's also a Chinese restaurant in the old dining room.

Across the railway lines, the *Junee* (☎ (069) 24 1124) has clean but more original rooms (complete with the old iron bedsteads) for about $15/26. The new owners might refurbish these rooms but they don't need much work.

Getting There & Away

Train Junee is on the main Sydney to Melbourne line.

Bus Greyhound Pioneer Australia runs through Junee on the run between Melbourne and Brisbane. Junee Travel (☎ (069) 24 2399) on Railway Square sells tickets.

Glass, a local company, runs weekday services to Wagga Wagga. Their depot is on Main St near the railway level-crossing.

Car & Motorbike The Olympic Way runs north to Young and south to Wagga Wagga. The road from Junee west to Narrandera is interesting (see the Around Wagga Wagga section) and there's a good drive south-east to the Hume Highway at Gundagai, some of it alongside the Murrumbidgee River.

TEMORA

On the edge of the Riverina, almost part of the central west, Temora (population 4700) is a pleasant place, with a classic country-town main street and an air of solidity. Late last century there were over 20,000 diggers here searching for gold, but today sheep and wheat keep the town going.

Tourist information is available from the White Rose Cafe on the main street and from the museum on the Junee-Wagga road.

A number of **old buildings** reflect the prosperity of the area and also its social distinctions. On one corner in the town centre is the stolid Anglican church, backed by banks and the post office and next to the courthouse and police residence. Diagonally opposite this display of the established powers of church and state is the large Catholic church, with a school behind, a gorgeous presbytery beside and a pretty little park next door to that. The small Presbyterian church across the street by the local council chambers seems to have pleaded no contest.

Ignoring this confrontation of ideologies and taking the most prominent corner in town is a life-size statue of **Paleface Adios**, a local horse which won 108 harness races. Temora is in harness-racing territory and there are several studs in the area.

The interesting **Rural Museum** displays implements and historical items relating to the district. Bagdad Hall, an old dance-hall, has been moved here and it still hosts functions. The museum is on the Junee-Wagga road, across the railway line and south of the town centre. It's open daily from 2 to 5 pm and on the second Saturday in March there

are live exhibitions. Ask here about the possibility of organising a visit to the **goldmine** at Gidginbung, 12 km north of Temora and the largest operating mine in the state.

Temora's airport is one of the most reliably fog-free in the state and there's quite a lot of activity here, including **skydiving**. Instruction and tandem dives are available with the Australian National Skydiving Centre (☎ (069) 77 4150).

If you haven't yet had your fill of small Riverina villages, drop into sleepy **Ariah Park**, 35 km west of Temora on the road to Griffith. There's nothing in particular to see or do here, it's just a hamlet in flat, red-soil country, but it has an atmosphere of times fast vanishing. Yarning on the bench outside the post office, beating the heat with a cold beer at the verandahed pub, smelling the peppercorn trees in the middle of the main street, watching an old dog cross the road – these are essential Aussie activities which the theme parks and tourist towns can't quite match. There's a basic but free *camping area* at the Recreation Ground.

Bardeman, with its huge mineral-water swimming pool, is 30 km north on the Wyalong road.

Festivals & Events

Temora might be a good place to experience 'the trots'. The Trotting Club holds harness races at the showgrounds track from October to April, with the prestigious Temora Pacers' Cup run at the first meeting in February.

The Temora Show is held in late September.

Places to Stay & Eat

The *Temora Caravan Park* (☎ (069) 77 1712) near the Rural Museum on the Junee-Wagga road has tent sites for about $10.

The *Terminus Hotel* (☎ (069) 77 1302) at the corner of Loftus and Crowley Sts has accommodation, although there are bands or a disco here on weekends. The *Shamrock Hotel* (☎ (069) 77 2016) on the main street has pub rooms and motel units.

The good *Goldtera Motel* (☎ (069) 77 2433) on Loftus St at the corner of Baker St charges \$55/60 and up. The other motels in town, the *Temora* (☎ (069) 77 1866) and the *Aromet* (☎ (069) 77 1877), are cheaper.

On the main street, opposite the Fossey's store (which is in an old building in incongruous Spanish style) is the *Waratah Cafe* with grills and snacks. Several other cafes offer much the same. In winter, the *Federal Hotel* on the main street bakes its famous Federal Pies. All the pubs have counter meals and there's an *Ex-Services Club* on Loftus St.

Getting There & Away

Bus Countrylink stops at Temora on the long journey between Balranald and Cootamundra, running via Griffith and Hay. Lynch's travel agency (☎ (069) 77 1296) at 194 Hoskins St sells tickets.

NARRANDERA

Charles Sturt passed through in his 1829 journey down the Murrumbidgee and many other people have done so since, as Narrandera (population 5100) straddles the Sturt and Newell Highways, with good connections to Sydney, Melbourne, Adelaide and Brisbane. Despite the amount of through traffic, Narrandera remains a friendly country town with good services and accommodation.

Orientation & Information

The Newell Highway runs through town; the Sturt passes just south of it. The information centre (☎ (069) 59 1766) is in Narrandera Park on the Newell Highway. It is open from 9 am to 5 pm on weekdays and from 10 am to 4 pm on weekends. Here there's 'the world's largest playable guitar', although the strings would need a lot of tensioning before you could get a tune out of it. If you have some time to spare, pick up a walking-tour map of the town which takes you past many old buildings.

Things to See & Do

Behind the information centre there's a lovely **cricket ground**, complete with a small wooden grandstand. In another corner of the park is the **Mini Zoo**, consisting mainly

of birds and some bored animals. There's also a **ceramic fountain**, Royal Doulton no less, perhaps one of only two in the world.

The **Parkside Cottage Museum** is across from the park on the corner of Twynan St. The extremely diverse collection, from '1000 years of monarchy' to skis from Scott's Antarctic expedition, is in the best tradition of small-town museums. Admission is \$2 (50c children) and the museum is open on Monday and Tuesday afternoons and from 11 am the rest of the week.

Lake Talbot is a watersports reserve, partly a long artificial lake and partly a swimming pool complex with some good waterslides. For just 30c you can ride a wooden toboggan down the slide, shooting out at the bottom and skimming across the pool like a skipped stone. A great way to relieve highway tensions!

Bush (including a koala regeneration area) surrounds the lake and a number of trails make up the **Bundidgerry Walking Track**, ranging from the Lake Talbot Short Loop (two km) to the Murrumbidgee Loop (11 km). The information centre has a map and brochure. The complex can be reached from the top end of Larmer St, where there's a good view down the Murrumbidgee before you take the steep road down to the lake. This is also the trackhead for the walks.

The **John Lake Centre** at the Inland Fisheries Research Station has guided tours (on which you can see a huge Murray cod) on weekdays at 10.30 am. Tours cost \$5 (\$2.50 children), but the centre is also open for casual inspection from 9 am to 4 pm. The turn-off to the centre is on the Sturt Highway four km south-east of Narrandera.

The **Old Pub Gallery** on the corner of East St and the Newell Highway has a large collection of old and new dolls.

Near Painters Siding, nine km north of Narrandera, is **Craigtop Deer Farm** with pet deer 'available for public interaction'. The farm is open most days (closed mid-December to mid-January) and admission is \$3. On the Leeton road just after the Painters Siding turn-off is a **Jumbuck Dairy** where you can sample cheese and yoghurt and see a rotary

1 Old Railway Station
2 Star Lodge (YHA)
3 Charles Sturt Hotel
4 New Criterion Hotel
5 Ex-Servicemen's Club
6 Information Centre
7 Mini Zoo
8 Pizzas
9 Museum
10 Post Office
11 Royal Mail Hotel
12 Town Hall
13 Gateway Motel
14 Murrumbidgee Hotel
15 Narrandera Hotel
16 Midtown Motel

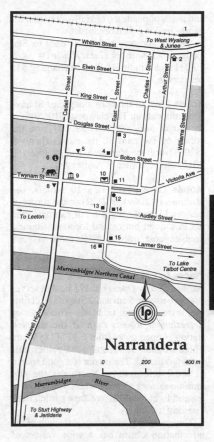

Narrandera

0   200   400 m

RIVERINA

dairy in action from 8 to 9 am and 4 to 5 pm daily for $3.

Festivals & Events

A rodeo is held in late January, when there are water-skiing championships on Lake Talbot. On the first Saturday in September there's the Agricultural Show. Other September events include Fly Kites For Peace. In October the Murrumbidgee Sheepdog Trials are held and the Tree-mendous Celebrations, centred around Narrandera's trees but including events such as a home-brewing competition and the National Guinea Pig Show. In November there's a Country Music Festival, which explains that guitar at the information centre.

Places to Stay

The information centre takes bookings for the various farmstays in the area.

Caravan Parks The *Lake Talbot Caravan Park* (☎ (069) 59 1302) is on a hill overlooking the Lake Talbot complex and dense red-gum forest stretching to the horizon. It's a nice park with a good tent area ($10 for a site) as well as on-site vans (from $25 a double) and self-contained units (from $35 a double). It's some way from the town centre at the east end of Larmer St. The *Narrandera Caravan Park* (☎ (069) 59 2955) is slightly cheaper, but it's across the river south of town.

Hostel Narrandera has one of the more impressive YHA hostels, *Star Lodge* (☎ (069) 59 1768), in a fine old hotel complete with verandahs and iron lace. Only YHA members can use the dorm accommodation ($12, $8 children), but there are also single and double rooms available to anyone for $15/28. One room has an attached bathroom (very narrow because it's built into the old chimney-niche!) and costs $20/35. This is a very clean, very pleasant place to stay and as it's opposite the old railway station it's handy for long-distance buses.

On the highway right next door to Star Lodge is *Kilmarnock Guest House* (☎ (069) 59 2119), a simple B&B place charging $15 per person.

Hotels Most of the pubs along East St have accommodation. The cheapest ($10/20) is at the *Royal Mail* (☎ (069) 59 2007) on the corner of Twynam St; the most expensive ($20/30) is at the *Murrumbidgee* (☎ (069) 59 2011) on the corner of Audley St.

Motels Of Narrandera's 10 motels, the *Midtown* (☎ (069) 59 2122) on the corner of East and Larmer Sts is a fair example, and it's in a quiet but central location. Singles/doubles cost from $35/50, more at peak times.

Places to Eat

Babbsy's Early Opener at 173 East St serves snacks between 5 am and 2.30 pm and claims the lowest prices in town. The *Railway Refreshment Rooms* cafe at the disused station is open daily from 6.30 am to 9 pm. There are snacks and some good-value meals from around $3. The owner is a good source of local information. Nearby is the *Old Stationmaster's Cottage* where you can have tea and light meals in a cottage garden from Tuesday to Sunday.

The unnamed *pizza place* just south of the information centre has a wide variety of dishes, including Sunday roast lunches for $6. There's a Chinese restaurant, the *Hing Wah*, at 96 East St, the *Ex-Servicemen's Club* on Bolton St has a bistro and a dining room and the Murrumbidgee Club at 43 Douglas St has the *Polo Dining Room*, open Friday and Saturday evenings. You have to book (☎ (069) 59 31148). The pubs have the usual counter meals.

Getting There & Away

Bus McCafferty's stops here on the Melbourne to Brisbane run, as does Greyhound Pioneer Australia, which also stops here en route between Sydney and Adelaide. Coun-

trylink runs to Wagga Wagga (where there are trains to Sydney and Melbourne) and Griffith.

Car & Motorbike As well as the highways linking Narrandera with four capital cities, smaller roads run north-west to Leeton and Griffith and east to the Olympic Way at Junee.

LEETON & AROUND

Leeton (population 7000) is the MIA's oldest town, and although it doesn't have the range of services of Griffith, it makes a pleasant base for exploring the area.

All those cypress trees that make the town such an attractive place might not be there much longer, as there are calls to axe them to get rid of the annoying grubs that live in them.

Leeton was founded as an MIA town in 1913; there was no settlement here before the water came. It was the first of the Burley Griffin-designed MIA towns, and it works better than nearby Griffith. That's partly because until recently there were limits placed on development. These have been lifted, and a highway sprawl is developing.

One early resident was Henry Lawson, who came to Leeton in 1916 in an attempt to break the cycle of poverty and drunkenness which dogged his later years. Things seemed promising: he had a grant from the NSW government, Leeton was 'dry', and he ran into an old mate he'd known in Bourke, when his star was on the rise. A new series of works was begun (the *Previous Convictions* stories), but Lawson returned to Sydney after a year and died a few years later.

Rice-growing began near Leeton in 1924, and today the Riverina's Ricegrowers' Co-op exports 750,000 tonnes a year.

Orientation & Information

The Visitors Centre (☎ (069) 53 2832) is next to the shire offices on Chelmsford Place. It's open on weekdays from 9 am to 5 pm and on weekend mornings. Pick up a copy of the walking-tour map for a one or two-hour orientation.

Things to See

Several of the area's food-processing plants have tours: the **Rice Mill** at 9.30 am and 2.45 pm on weekdays, the **Letona Cannery** at 10.30 am and 1.30 pm on weekdays from January to April (you can visit during the rest of the year), and the **Quelch Juice Factory** at 10.45 am on weekdays. You must wear shoes for these tours. The **Tavella Cheese Factory**, where cheese is made from sheep's milk, has tours and tastings after 2 pm on weekdays.

Lillypilly Estate and Toorak Wines are two **wineries** near Leeton, open daily except Sunday for tastings and for tours on weekdays; 11.30 am at Toorak and 4 pm at Lillypilly.

There are also daily tours of the restored **Historic Hydro Motor Inn**.

In **Yanco**, a village that has almost become part of Leeton's new development, see if the Powerhouse Museum is up and running yet. If it isn't, you might meet a couple of engaging old blokes and their dogs who seem to be caretaking. Yanco was the original railhead for the MIA and the powerhouse once supplied all the area's electricity.

A few km west of Yanco (the signposted turn-off is just south of the town) is **Yanco Agricultural High School**. Sited in the countryside and with extensive grounds, it must be a great place to go to school. Visitors are welcome to drive through and during school hours you can wander around the buildings. If you keep going down the road that leads to the school entrance, you'll come to an old bridge across the Murrumbidgee where there's a fireplace and a potential camping spot. This road leads on to Euroley and the Sturt Highway west of Narrandera.

Also just out of Yanco there's a turn-off to the east, leading to the **Yanco Agricultural College**, opened in 1908 as an experimental farm for the new irrigation scheme. Today the college has educational programmes and offers an advisory service to farmers in the area. You can drive through, but unless you have a specific interest in agriculture there isn't a lot to see.

Whitton, 25 km west of Leeton, was here before the MIA was begun, and there's a museum in the courthouse.

The north bank of the Murrumbidgee near Leeton has several beaches and picnic areas. Ask the information centre for a map.

Festivals & Events

The Sunwhite Rice Festival is held over Easter in even-numbered years; the Murrumbidgee Farm Fair is held at the Yanco Agricultural College in April; and the Leeton Agricultural Show is held on the second Friday and Saturday in October. The Leeton Eisteddfod is held over three weeks in August, culminating in a big concert.

Places to Stay

Several properties in the Leeton area offer farmstays. The Leeton Visitors Centre makes bookings.

Caravan Parks There are three caravan parks, south of town on Yanco Ave, north on Brobenah Rd (the continuation of Chelmsford Place) and east on Corbie Hill Rd (off Yanco Ave).

Hotels & Motels The *Leeton Hotel* (☎ (069) 53 2027) at 71 Pine Ave charges $20 per person for bed and breakfast and the nearby *Wade Hotel* (☎ (069) 53 3266) at 42 Pine Ave also has accommodation.

Probably the biggest building in town is the *Historic Hydro Motor Inn* (☎ (069) 53 2355), a huge old guesthouse with a National Trust listing. Motel-style units are $40/45 a single/double and $50 for a twin room, including a cooked breakfast. There are also rooms with shared bathroom. Despite its restoration the Hydro is a little faded, but it has wide verandahs, a large garden and is well-positioned. There are plenty of other motels if this doesn't appeal.

Places to Eat

Leeton doesn't have anywhere near the range of eating places that nearby Griffith has. On Pine Ave there are a couple of Chinese places, *Lee's* and *Chan's Hong Kong*, as well as a few cafes and coffee

RIVERINA

shops, such as *Penny's Pantry* at 117 Pine Ave. Other than that, there are counter meals and bistros in the hotels, in the motel dining rooms (the *Bygalorie* and the *Riverina* on Yanco Ave and the *Leeton Gardens* on Wade Ave) and in the *Soldier's Club* and the *All-Servicemen's Club*.

Getting There & Away
Countrylink buses stop here on the run between Griffith and Wagga Wagga.

GRIFFITH
Griffith (population 15,000) is a small but relatively sophisticated city and is the main centre of the MIA, although it's some way north of the river. The city styles itself the wine and food capital of the Riverina, and it certainly is that. There are vineyards which you can visit and Griffith's cafes and restaurants offer a variety and quality unmatched for a very long way. West of here you're definitely into 'steak-and-lots-of-it' country.

Griffith is at the edge of the last hills of the Great Divide's western slopes. West of here the country becomes very flat; due west is the beginning of the outback, to the southwest is the Riverina heartland.

Like nearby Leeton, Griffith was designed by Walter Burley Griffin, the American architect of Canberra. Griffith does have something of Canberra's openness about it, and Griffin had similar climate and country to work on. Leafy suburbs rise up the steep hills behind the flat town centre, and Banna Ave, beginning at the circular roads of the administrative centre, is a wide boulevard. It's also a very long boulevard – a country town's shopping street magnified several times and too long to conveniently walk. As the railway line interrupts the flow of cross-traffic on one side and the canal for part of the other side, Banna Ave can be slow driving.

Information
The information centre (☎ (069) 62 4145) is on the corner of Banna and Jondaryan Aves; out the front is a Fairy Firefly plane perched on a pole. The centre is open from 9 am to 5 pm on weekdays, until 3 pm on Saturday and from 10 am to 2 pm on Sunday.

Things to See
High on a hill to the north of the town centre, **Pioneer Park** is a re-creation of an early Riverina village which is worth seeing. There are about 40 displays, and unlike at some other village re-creations many of the old buildings are original, having been relocated here. A friendly wallaby might follow you around. Admission is $5 ($3 children) and the park is open daily from 8.30 am to 5 pm. To get there from Banna Ave take Crossing St or Ulong St then Beale Ave.

Not far from Pioneer Park is the **Rotary Lookout** with great views of the town and the surrounding farmland. Also up here on Scenic Hill are three **walking tracks**, Trates Loop (two km), Barinji Loop (five km) and Narinari Loop (6.5 km). There's another lookout at **Sir Dudley's Chair**, 1.5 km east of Pioneer Park. Just below this lookout is the **hermit's cave**, home of an Italian recluse for many years – until he was interned during WW II on suspicion of being a spy.

The **Griffith Regional Art Gallery** is on Banna Ave and is open from 10.30 am to 4.30 pm Wednesday to Saturday. Exhibitions change monthly and there's also a permanent collection of Australian jewellery.

The **Griffith Regional Theatre** has a huge, community-produced soft-sculpture curtain depicting the region and its activities. You can see it at 11 am and 2.30 pm on weekdays and on Saturday at 10 am, providing there are no productions under way. There's also a photographic exhibition in the foyer.

Lake Wyangan, north of the city, is home to a lot of noisy water transport – there's a jet sprint-boat course.

Every Sunday morning, a **market** is held in Verona Place on Banna Ave.

Wineries Although the Hunter Valley is the best-known wine-producing area in NSW, the Griffith area produces 80% of the state's wine and some of it is very good. If you want to sample some before you come, order the

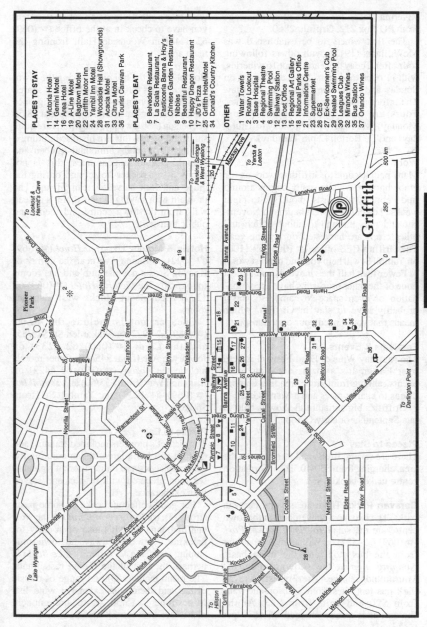

PLACES TO STAY

11 Victoria Hotel
14 Gemini Motel
16 Area Hotel
19 A-Line Motel
20 Bagtown Motel
22 Griffith Motor Inn
24 Yambil Inn Motel
28 Woodside Hall (Showgrounds)
31 Acacia Motel
33 Citrus Motel
36 Tourist Caravan Park

PLACES TO EAT

5 Belvedere Restaurant
7 La Scala Restaurant,
   Pasticceria Banna & Hoy's
   Chinese Garden Restaurant
8 Nibbles
9 Beautiful Restaurant
10 Happy Dragon Restaurant
17 JD's Pizza
25 Griffith Hotel/Motel
34 Donald's Country Kitchen

OTHER

1 Water Towers
2 Rotary Lookout
3 Base Hospital
4 Regional Theatre
6 Swimming Pool
12 Railway Station
13 Post Office
15 Regional Art Gallery
18 National Parks Office
21 Information Centre
23 Supermarket
26 CES
27 Ex-Servicemen's Club
29 Heated Swimming Pool
30 Leagues Club
32 Miranda Wines
35 Bus Station
37 Orlando Wines

Griffith

Riverina Dozen for about $72 plus postage from PO Box 212, Griffith, 2860.

The first winery to be established was McWilliams (1913), with others following soon after. Today there are about 16 wineries, with 11 open to visitors. Most don't open on Sunday and some don't open on Saturday. The information centre has the latest times. Tours are held at McWilliams (2 pm Monday), Miranda (2 pm Monday to Thursday) and De Bortoli (2 pm Tuesday).

Work
Many people come to Griffith to work on the grape harvest, which usually begins around mid-February and lasts about six to eight weeks. The citrus harvest begins in November and runs through to about March and other crops are harvested during the year. The Griffith CES office (☎ (069) 69 1100) on Yambil St will help you find harvest work.

Fewer than half the vineyards and almost none of the other properties have accommodation or even space to camp, so you'll probably have to stay in Griffith, which means that you'll need your own transport.

Festivals & Events
The four-day Wine & Food Festival is held over Easter. It's a major occasion, with events ranging from grape-treading competitions to chariot races and a Mardi Gras.

Griffith's big agricultural show is held in late September or early October.

Places to Stay
There are several B&Bs and farmstays in the area, charging from $30/40. The information centre makes bookings.

Caravan Parks There are several caravan parks. The two most convenient for the town centre are the small *Tourist Caravan Park* (☎ (069) 62 4537) on Willandra Ave, not far from the bus stop, and the more basic *camping area* at the showgrounds, off Murrumbidgee Ave. The Tourist Caravan Park has tent sites from $10, on-site vans from $20 and units from $33. At the showgrounds you're charged $5 ($30 per

week) for a site. Before you set up your tent you have to check in at the office (☎ (069) 62 3148) in Woodside Hall, fronting the main arena.

Hostel Up on the hill overlooking the town, *Pioneer Park* (☎ (069) 62 4196) has shared accommodation in an old tin building once used as shearers' quarters. It costs just $8.50 per person ($50 a week). The rooms are quite small and basic – this is a historic building – but there's a good communal kitchen and lounge. Despite appearances, this is not purely a backpacker hostel and during the grape and fruit harvest it can fill up. The problem with staying here is that it's a steep walk from the town centre and there's no public transport.

Hotels & Motels The *Area Hotel* (☎ (069) 62 1322) on Banna Ave near the corner of Kooyoo St is a popular pub and has rooms for $25/35. The *Victoria Hotel* (☎ (069) 62 1299) a couple of blocks west also has rooms.

Cheaper motels include the *A-Line* (☎ (069) 62 1922) on Wakarden St ($45/55) and the *Citrus* (☎ (069) 62 6233) on Jondaryan Ave (from $45/55). Other motels include the *Acacia* (☎ (069) 62 4422) on Irrigation Way (from $55/60) and *Yambil Inn* (☎ (069) 64 1233) on Yambil St (from $60/65).

Places to Eat
The district's pioneers included Italians, and Griffith still has a large Italian community. Several places serve Italian food; it's great to see food prepared with respect and served with exuberance.

For good coffee and cake or some pasta (from $5), try *Pasticceria Banna* at the west end of Banna Ave. It's also open daily for breakfast. A few doors away and down some sloping steps, the Vico family's *La Scala* is perhaps the best of the Italian restaurants. The menu includes a good range of classic dishes and there's an extensive wine list. Minestrone is $5.50, pasta and gnocchi dishes are between $8 and $10, and main courses range from about $16. La Scala is open from 6 pm Tuesday to Sunday.

Not far away, on the corner of Banna Ave and Kookora St, is the *Belvedere Restaurant*. This has more of a cafe atmosphere and it's also a busy takeaway pizzeria, but the food is good. The prices are a little lower than La Scala's and there's a delivery service (☎ (62 1488). For pizzas cooked in a wood oven, head out to *La Villa Bianca* at 40 Mackay Ave.

There are a few Chinese places in the same area. The *Beautiful Restaurant* on the corner of Banna Ave and Ulong St is a large, pleasant place with an extensive menu (including non-Asian dishes) and a bar. There's a buffet lunch special for $10, and at dinner most main courses are around $10. It's open from Tuesday to Sunday. Down an arcade just west of here is *Hoy's Chinese Garden*, with a similar menu and karaoke. Across the street, the *Happy Dragon* is smaller and has some good specials, down to about $4.

The Griffith Hotel/Motel on Yambil St has a *Thai restaurant*. The *Ex-Servicemen's Club* on Jondaryan Ave has a restaurant and a bistro, and meals are also available at many of Griffith's nine other clubs, often only on weekends.

If you just want a hamburger, go to *Nibbles* on Banna Ave, where good old-fashioned hamburgers can be taken away or eaten at old-fashioned partitioned tables.

At Koala Gourmet Foods, 4 Whybrow St, you can sample and buy a range of Italian preserves, such as sun-dried tomatoes and garlic olives. Next to the Victoria Hotel on Banna Ave, Pacific Island Foods sells a range of Fijian produce.

Entertainment

Most of the entertainment is in the clubs, such as the Ex-Servicemen's on Jondaryan Ave, the Leagues Club on the corner of Jondaryan and Banna Aves and, probably the most lively, the Yoogali Club on Leeton Rd.

Getting There & Away

Air Hazelton (☎ (063) 61 5888) flies between Griffith and Sydney daily.

Bus The long-distance bus stop is at the Griffith Travel & Transit Centre (☎ (069) 62 7199), in Donald's Country Kitchen on Jondaryan Ave. You can make bookings here daily.

Greyhound Pioneer Australia runs to Sydney ($60), to Melbourne ($55), to Adelaide ($100) and to Brisbane ($100).

Countrylink runs to Balranald via Hay, Wagga via Leeton and Narrandera, and Cootamundra via Temora.

A local company, MIA Intercity Coaches (☎ (069) 62 3419), runs to and from Melbourne on Monday, Wednesday and Friday for $50, taking about six hours. This service is a handy way of getting around the MIA, with stops including Tocumwal ($33 from Griffith) and Jerilderie ($29). The service also stops in Leeton, but the fare from Griffith is a hefty $21.

Getting Around

Bus You can ride along on one of the area's schoolbuses for a weekday tour of the district for just $1 – slow but interesting. The information centre has details.

Taxi Griffith has a taxi service (☎ (069) 64 1444).

Car Rental Avis (☎ (069) 62 6266) is at 83 Banna Ave, Budget (☎ (069) 62 7473) is at 7 Wyangan Ave and Hertz (☎ (069) 64 1233) is at the Yambil Inn Motel on Yambil St.

AROUND GRIFFITH
Cocoparra National Park

Cocoparra (8350 hectares) takes in one of the fingers of low ranges that make up the westernmost edge of the hills in the state. If you're heading west from here you're in for some very flat country. This whole area is pretty. **Rankins Springs**, on the Mid-Western Highway just north of the park, is a tiny town with a pub and a motel set in a beautiful horseshoe valley. See the Central West chapter for more information on towns north and east of Cocoparra.

Cocoparra is not a large park but its hills and gullies provide some contrasts and there is a fair amount of wildlife and birds. At Spring Hill picnic area, in the southern section of the park, there is a walking trail to Falcon Falls (dry unless there has been rain). From the **Binya State Forest**, adjoining the south-western end of the park, there's a walking track which leads you to the top of Mt Brogden.

The camping area is on Woolshed Flat in the north of the park, not far from Woolshed Falls. Day-use of the park costs $7.50 and camping is another $5. Bush camping is permitted away from the roads. Bring your own water.

Access is from the unsealed (and sometimes impassable) Whitton Stock Route, which runs along the park's western edge. The stock route meets the Yenda to Ardlethan road just east of Yenda. You can get here from the Western Highway via a turn-off to Griffith about 15 km west of Rankins Springs.

Darlington Point

Due south of Griffith and on the Murrumbidgee, Darlington Point (population 800) was an important river port last century. It has dwindled to a quiet, picturesque town with good swimming beaches and red-gum forest. There's a *caravan park* (☎ (069) 68 4237).

West of here, either via the Sturt Highway or along a dirt road that follows the north bank of the Murrumbidgee, **Carrathool** is another old port quietly dying in a pretty location. Each February a picnic race-meeting brings in a lot of visitors.

Coleambally

About 30 km south of Darlington Point and in a huge triangle of almost uninhabited plain between Narrandera, Jerilderie and Hay, Coleambally (population 600) is the centre of a new irrigation area. The town is also new and dates from 1968, in complete contrast to old Darlington Point. There are a couple of motels and a caravan park.

The Black Stump

Between Griffith and Hillston is **Merri-**

wagga, a roadside hamlet which claims to be the home of the Black Stump. The Black Stump is a useful Australian geographical indicator – places 'beyond the Black Stump' are a long way from anywhere. However, as a plaque in Merriwagga will tell you, there is no actual stump because the name is a grisly reference to the death by burning of a woman in the 1880s.

LAKE CARGELLIGO

Midway between Condoblin and Hillston, Lake Cargelligo (the first 'g' is soft, the second hard; the town is locally known as 'the Lake') is both a town (population 1300) and the adjacent lake.

Some tourist information is available from a craft shop at the lake end of the main street, or phone (☎ (068) 98 1501).

Next to the caravan park is a large collection of rusty old farm machinery, part of the **museum**.

Places to Stay

The council-run *caravan park* (☎ (068) 98 1077) is near the sports ground, which is by the lake. From the main street, turn right at the lake. Tent sites cost $8 for two people and cabins are $37.

The *Royal Mail Hotel* (☎ (068) 98 1006) is a solid pub with a big verandah, on the main street near the lake. Single/double rooms are $14/28, including breakfast. There are a couple of motels, the *Lake Cargelligo* (☎ (068) 98 1303) on Canada St and the more expensive *Lachlan Way* (☎ (068) 98 1201) on Foster St.

Getting There & Away

Bus Countrylink buses stop here on the run between Condoblin and Cootamundra via West Wyalong.

Car & Motorbike There are some interesting routes to and from the Lake, but as far as major roads go it's quite isolated. A sealed road runs south-east to West Wyalong and partly-sealed roads run east to Condoblin and west to Hillston. See the Hillston section for a route to Cobar.

HILLSTON

This is a pretty little town (population 1050) on the Lachlan River and the edge of nowhere. The local **museum**, open on Sunday, is a few blocks from the town centre, on the Lake Cargelligo road. Check out the Real Cafe on the main street, long past its glory days but still with high, pressed tin ceilings and leadlight windows. The Golden Gate milk bar, across the road, isn't as grand but is in better nick.

Places to Stay & Eat

There's a *caravan park* at the north end of the main street. Nearby is a new motel, the *Kidman Way* (☎ (069) 67 2151), and there's also the *Hillston Motel* (☎ (069) 67 2573) at the southern entrance to town. The club and the pubs have meals.

Getting There & Away

Hillston is on the Kidman Way, a semi-official name for the unsealed road (it's due to be sealed soon) running to Cobar and on to Bourke. The turn-off for the Kidman Way is on the Lake Cargelligo road 35 km east of Hillston; the road heading directly north from Hillston is not as good. See the North of Condoblin section in the Central West chapter for information on towns on and near this road.

An unsealed road heads west for 40-odd km to the Willandra National Park turn-off, and continues on, narrower and rougher, another 55 km to Mossgiel on the Cobb Highway. A largely-unsealed road runs east to Lake Cargelligo, a nice drive through well-treed country around the Lachlan River and past the Lachlan Range.

Except for the sealed road running south to the Mid-Western Highway, all the roads out of Hillston can be cut off by rain.

WILLANDRA NATIONAL PARK

Like Mungo National Park, Willandra is part of a huge sheep-station on a system of dry lakes. The lakes here tend to become temporary wetlands more often than Mungo's ancient basins, especially Hall's Lake, and birdlife is abundant. The plains in this area are home to many emus, and kangaroos are plentiful, even during the day. You'll see both western greys and big reds; the latter can grow taller than two metres.

The historical interest of Willandra centres around the wool industry, although there were certainly Aboriginal civilisations in the area, probably of the same antiquity as those at Lake Mungo. The Willandra area was first grazed in the 1840s, then in 1868 some enterprising Melbourne grocers acquired several runs and formed the sheep station **Big Willandra** – the national park (about 19,400 hectares) is less than 10% of Big Willandra.

The old shearing shed, with its latitude and longitude painted on the roof to assist pilots in this featureless landscape, is still occasionally used and you can watch the shearing if you're here at the right time. The park manager has details. The nearby old shearers' quarters are not used, partly because they don't meet current union standards (which must be higher than the standards in some hostels).

A discreet distance away from the shearers' quarters is the homestead, the third to be built on the increasingly busy station. This homestead was built in 1918, using a

Grey Kangaroo

then revolutionary material, fibro-cement. It's a large building, with rooms for visiting wool-buyers as well as the manager's family and staff, but it's by no means palatial. Life here, with gardens, tennis courts and a nearby weir on the creek for swimming, would have been pleasant but not easy. The homestead is currently being restored, with the family rooms and the manager's office now in the condition they would have been in during the 1920s.

The thatched ram shed, where the real kings of the station lived, is near the homestead.

There are several walking tracks in the park, none very long, and the Merton Motor Trail which takes you on a loop around the eastern half of the park. The western half, beyond the stock route, has no vehicular access but you can walk here – if you're *very* sure of what you are doing.

Places to Stay

You can camp at the site near the homestead ($4) or, with permission, anywhere else in the park. Shared accommodation is available in the old station's men's quarters for $8 a night. During school holidays all accommodation, including campsites, can be booked out.

Getting There & Away

The turn-off to Willandra is on the Hillston to Mossgiel road, 40-odd km west of Hillston. If you're coming from Mossgiel you can take the Trida turn-off, about 10 km west of the main turn-off. The unsealed Hillston to Mossgiel road is quite good between Hillston and the park turn-off, but deteriorates between the turn-off and Mossgiel. Slow down to cross cattle-grids on this section. The roads into Willandra are definitely dry-weather only; it takes less than 10 mm of rain to close them. You should phone the park manager (☎ (069) 67 8159) to check on conditions before you arrive, and bring in enough supplies to tide you over if you are stuck – there is no shop here. The National Parks office in Griffith (☎ (069) 62 7755) also has information on Willandra.

HAY

Hay is a substantial town (population 3000) for this part of the world, and its position at the junction of the Sturt and Cobb highways makes it an important transit point.

It's very much a rural service-centre and on Saturday morning the main street is full of utes, all with dogs in the back noisily catching up on the district's gossip. Station hands from the big merino properties in the area make good use of the half-dozen pubs on weekends and court reports in the local paper make interesting reading. Alcohol-related offences seem to take up half the magistrate's time, with marijuana-related offences figuring largely in the other half.

The information centre (☎ (069) 93 1003), open from 9 am to 5 pm on weekdays and until noon on weekends, is just off Lachlan St (the main street) on Moppett St. Here you can pick up a drive-tour map of the town, although if you have time it would be much nicer to walk around.

Things to See

There are several impressive old buildings in town, including the **Lands Department** on Lachlan St. Around the corner in Moppett St, the **courthouse** is impressive.

Bishop's Lodge, accessible from the highway just east of the roundabout at the entrance to Hay, is a mansion built entirely of corrugated iron as a residence for the Anglican Bishop. From the highway it doesn't look especially inviting, but the building faces the other way, towards the river, and there's a garden at the front. Bishop's Lodge is open for inspection on Saturday from 2 to 4 pm and admission is $2. The tourist office can arrange for it to be opened at other times. The old **railway station** on Murray St has been renovated and is now home to Hay's community radio station and a youth employment project.

The **Old Jail Museum**, on Church St east of Lachlan St, is well worth the $1 entry fee. The jail itself is a small place surrounded by a wall with almost toy guard towers. The museum is in the old cells and consists of a fairly random collection of the district's memorabilia and detritus. It's like a very, very good junk shop. Some of the more modern items are just as interesting as the old – check out the photos of the 1978 fire at Donahue's Building Supplies. This is all very pleasant until you get to the cell that's set up as it was when the jail was a detention centre for wayward girls, its last incarnation before it closed in 1973. Perhaps more appalling than the dim, spartan cell is the fact that the cells were called cabins! Still, the place was run by the Child *Welfare* Department, perhaps another inappropriate euphemism...

Ruberto's Cellars, on the highway near town, is open daily for tastings of the local product.

A short way north-west of the town, off Thelangerin Rd, is a **wetlands area** being developed as a bird sanctuary.

The **Sunset Viewing Area**, 16 km north of Hay on the Cobb Highway, is a good place to watch the sun go down over the flat horizon.

Darkness comes in. It doesn't seem to come *down*, but moves in from somewhere in the outer wilds; approaching sullenly, sulkily, furtively, unobserved...
Henry Lawson, *By the Banks of the Murrumbidgee*, 1916

Festivals & Events
On Australia Day, Hay holds a fun 'Surf Carnival' at Sandy Point beach on the Murrumbidgee (a good place for a swim at any time).

Places to Stay & Eat
There are several caravan parks, with *Riverina X-Roads* (☎ (069) 93 1875) on Nailor St being the closest to the town centre and the *Hay Caravan Park* (☎ (069) 93 1415) on the highway (and close to the river) not far east.

Most of the pubs advertise accommodation, but only the big *Commercial Hotel* (☎ (069) 93 1504) on the corner of Lachlan and Leonard Sts seems enthusiastic about providing it, with singles/doubles for $20/35. Of the town's six motels, *Bishop's Lodge* (☎ (069) 93 3003) on the Sturt

Highway is the most expensive at $60/65, while the *Hay Motel* (☎ (069) 93 1804), by the roundabout, and the *New Crown Hotel/Motel* (☎ (069) 93 1600) on Lachlan St vie for the title of least expensive, with rooms at about $35/45.

The *Inlander* and *Bishop's Lodge* motels have dining rooms, as do the *Bowling Club* and Ex-Services Club. The *Paragon Cafe* is a standard country-town cafe, and there's *Our Coffee Shop*, opposite the Commercial Hotel and open on weekdays. *Hay Fish Supply* on the main street is a takeaway with a big range, including some good salads. A quarter-chicken and two salads costs $4, which is good value.

Around Hay Off the Sturt Highway 11 km east of Hay, the *Bidgee Beach Primitive Camping Area* (☎ (069) 93 1180) is, as the name says, a simple camping-ground on the banks of the Murrumbidgee. Tent sites are $10. In the hamlet of Boorooban, on the Cobb Highway about 45 km south of Hay and 70 km north of Deniliquin, the historic *Royal Mail Hotel* (☎ (069) 93 0694) has single/double rooms for $20/35 or $45 for a double with attached bathroom. This place is worth a look even if you don't stay here.

At tiny Maude, 52 km west of Hay, there's a basic *camping reserve* by a weir on the Murrumbidgee and a *caravan park* next to the pub.

Kelsey Homestead (☎ (069) 93 2172), on a big sheep and cattle property on the edge of the outback, charges $30 per person ($10 children) with a minimum charge of $60, in a self-contained, air-conditioned homestead. There's a swimming pool, tennis courts and lots of wildlife to be seen. When you book you can ask for groceries to be bought for you, or meals can be prepared by prior arrangement. To get here, travel north-east on the Mid-Western Highway and take the Wongalea turn-off, 50 km from Hay. After five km you'll come to the Kelsey entrance and the homestead is three km from here.

Getting There & Away
Harvey World Travel (☎ (069) 93 1974) at

RIVERINA

181 Lachlan St handles bus and plane bookings.

Air Link Air flies to Wagga Wagga ($120), where you can connect with flights to Sydney ($239 from Hay).

Bus Long-distance buses stop outside the tourist information centre on Moppett St, near the old Cobb & Co coach, Sunbeam, which once made the tough run between Deniliquin and Wilcannia.

Greyhound Pioneer Australia and McCafferty's come through on the run between Adelaide and Brisbane or Sydney. Countrylink's Balranald to Cootamundra run also stops here. There are no direct services to Melbourne. The nearest town on the Melbourne run is Deniliquin.

Car & Motorbike The Sturt Highway runs west to Balranald and east to Narrandera. The Mid-Western Highway runs north-east to West Wyalong and the Cobb Highway runs south to Deniliquin. See the Far West chapter for information on the Cobb Highway north to Wilcannia.

BALRANALD

On the Sturt Highway west of Hay, Balranald is today a sleepy little town (population 1600) but it was once a bustling river port. Most of the town is new and not especially inspiring but there is a definite sense that you are on the brink of a vast emptiness. North of here the water dries up and the farms are vast, barely viable stations. Balranald makes a good jumping-off point for Mungo National Park.

The information centre (☎ (050) 20 1599) is on the main street. Check here for road conditions before venturing into Mungo, although the National Parks office (☎ (050) 23 1278) in Buronga (near Mildura) might have better information.

There's a swimming and picnic area on the bank of the Murrumbidgee at the end of the oddly named We St (turn off the highway at the fire station). Not far from here, at the corner of Court and Mayall Sts is a gem of an old house.

There are other picnic sites at Yanga Lake, eight km east along the Sturt Highway, and the Low Level Weir, six km west of town.

Places to Stay & Eat

The *Balranald Caravan Park* (☎ (050) 20 1321) is on a sharp bend in the Murrumbidgee, close to the bridge. Tent sites cost $7 and on-site vans from $25.

There are a few motels in town. The *Sturt* (☎ (050) 20 1309) on River St and the *Shamrock Hotel/Motel* (☎ (050) 20 1107) on Mayall St are far enough from the highway to avoid the rumble of semis running along the Sturt Highway.

The *Shamrock* has counter meals and a dining room, and *Rafferty's Cafe* nearby on the main street is open during the day for snacks and light meals. The *Ex-Servicemen's Club* on the main street has meals most days.

The Southern Riverina

Albury, the largest town on the Murray River, is covered in the South-East chapter.

If you plan to do some fishing for Murray cod, note that there's a closed season between 1 September and 30 November, and at other times you're only allowed to catch two a day and have in your possession a maximum of four. You'll also have to learn to distinguish between Murray cod and Murray trout, as the latter is totally protected.

COROWA

This sizeable river town (population 5100) is one of the few instances of a town on the NSW side of the border which is larger than its twin (Wahgunyah) across the river in Victoria. However, Rutherglen, the main town in Victoria's best-known wine region, is only 10 km further away.

History

The Bangerang people were living in this area when the first Europeans arrived in the

1830s. The first town to be established was Wahgunyah, then a private town on John Foord's Wahgunyah station. North Wahgunyah, today's Corowa, was also founded by Foord, but the influx of people on their way to the Beechworth goldfields and the trade and river traffic that followed saw Corowa become an official town.

As was the case in many towns, the proclamation of the Colony of Victoria in 1850 and the ensuing customs hassles across the Murray caused many people in the area to push for federation of the colonies. In 1893 a conference was held in Corowa which began the process of federation, achieved in 1901. There had been previous conferences but Corowa's was the first to capture the public's attention and was the first at which the vague democratic leanings of the federationists were put into practice. It's perhaps no coincidence that today's stirrings to abandon state government altogether are coming from riverside councils.

Another lasting product from Corowa is the famous Tom Roberts painting *Shearing the Rams*, which was researched in the woolshed of Brocklesby station. Less well-known but more significant are the sketches by Tommy McCrae, one of the Bangerang people at the time of first contact with Europeans. They are among the few concrete records of an indigenous people's reaction to European invasion. You can see some of the sketches at the Federation Museum.

Orientation & Information
The information centre (☎ (060) 33 3221) is in the old railway station on John St, it is open from 9.45 am to 4.30 pm, daily except Sunday. The main street, where you'll find most of the pubs and shops, is Sanger St. It leads down to the Foord Bridge across the Murray to the small town of Wahgunyah on the Victorian side. Federation Ave is a leafy street cutting through town to the Mulwala road.

Things to See
The **Federation Museum**, in an old Music Hall on Queen St, opposite the neat Ellerslie Gardens, is only open from 2 to 5 pm on weekends and some holidays, although you might find someone there at other times. Admission is $1. It's worth a look for the display on the history of federation and the large jumble of domestic items, including some fine women's clothing.

Murray Bank Yabby Farm, next to the Corowa Caravan Park on the road to Mulwala, charges $5 for a visit. You can catch your own yabbies and cook them there. The farm is open from 11 am to 4 pm daily.

At the other end of town, next to the Rivergums caravan park, is **Corowa Wine Cellars**, once the Lindemans cellars and over 120 years old. Sales and tastings are held daily. St Leonards vineyards, across the river and east of Wahgunyah, were established in 1860, although their current incarnation dates from the 1970s. You can buy their respected product daily and there's a restaurant here (☎ (060) 33 3146).

Apparently there's an arcade of shops beneath the Star Hotel, built there for summer coolness. Unfortunately there's no public access.

The statue of Mercury above the Free Press building on Sanger St wears the football jumper of the local team, the Corowa Kangaroos (it's the same jumper as worn by the AFL's North Melbourne Kangaroos, as Corowa was in their recruiting zone before deregulation). Mercury is missing his torch and looks uncannily like a footballer celebrating the kicking of a goal. Go Roos!

Activities
The riverboat *Elizabeth T* (☎ (060) 33 2846) has cruises on the Murray, some of which go to the St Leonards winery. There are about a dozen other wineries in the Rutherglen area which are open for tastings.

Corowa is a centre for gliding and hot-air ballooning. The information centre has details of balloon flights, and you can ask the Gliding Club (☎ (060) 33 1296) about possible joy-flights on Sundays.

Festivals & Events
Over the Australia Day weekend in January,

Corowa holds the Federation Festival, with parades, marching bands and general merriment. This is perhaps the largest Australia Day celebration in rural Australia, although that isn't saying much – Aussies are pretty low-key about patriotism.

The Rutherglen Winery Walkabout in June is the premier event on the Victorian wine-buff's calendar, and Corowa is a good base from which to take part in it.

Places to Stay

Caravan Parks There are several caravan parks in the area, including *Rivergums* (☎ (060) 33 1990) on the road in from Albury, *Corowa Caravan Park* (☎ (060) 33 1944) on the road out to Mulwala and *Ball Park* (☎ (060) 33 1426) on Bridge Rd. All three are by the river and all have sites and cabins. The Corowa has on-site vans as well.

Hotels & Motels Most of the pubs have accommodation, ranging upwards from $15 per person (including light breakfast) at the *Star Hotel* (☎ (060) 33 1145) on Sanger St.

There are more than a dozen motels. The cluster on the Mulwala road (Federation Ave) are in hot competition and you might find a double for $45 in the off-season, though prices rise in summer and around holidays.

Places to Eat

The pubs along Sanger St compete for your meal-time dollars and there are some counter-meal bargains, from about $5. Check the blackboards. A couple of delis on Sanger St have light meals during the day and the various clubs (including the Bowling Club, which has 54 rinks and claims to be the world's largest) have dining rooms.

In Howlong, a small town 25 km east of Corowa on the road to Albury, the *Peppercorn Cottage Restaurant* is open for lunch daily and dinner on weekends (☎ (060) 26 5282 for dinner bookings). It's in a restored Cobb & Co coaching station and serves both snacks and quite formal meals.

Getting There & Away

Bus Countrylink stops here on its run between Albury and Echuca (Victoria), via Cobram (Victoria), Tocumwal, Finley and Deniliquin.

Car & Motorbike The Riverina Highway runs east to Albury and north-west to Deniliquin. A smaller road runs down the river to Mulwala and Tocumwal.

Getting Around

There's a 24-hour taxi service (☎ (060) 33 1634).

MULWALA

This small town on Lake Mulwala was the base for several big rock concerts in the '70s, Australia's answer to Woodstock. Today it's a quiet place, completely overshadowed by Yarrawonga, a resort and retirement centre across the river in Victoria. Lake Mulwala, an irrigation dam on the river, is a popular spot for fishing and power-boating.

There are several caravan parks, many motels and the old *Royal Mail Hotel* (☎ (057) 44 3121) which charges $25/30 including breakfast.

TOCUMWAL

Tocumwal is a small, pleasant town on the Newell Highway and on a big bend in the Murray River. The nearest Victorian town is Cobram, but the towns don't have the usual Siamese-twin relationship of river towns because they are separated by a wide redgum forest growing on the meanderings and billabongs of the Murray.

There is an information centre (☎ (058) 74 2131) in the centre of town.

Things to See & Do

A huge statue of a Murray cod stands next to the information centre; if you have a look in the bar of Tattersalls Hotel across the road you'll see some stuffed Murray cod that are almost in the same league.

The **Murray River Heritage Centre** is about three km out of town on the road to Finley. It's still in the process of being built, and as it's a community undertaking it might take a while to be completed. So far, the main centre has been completed: a homestead-style building in local timber and mud-brick – perhaps the biggest mud-brick structure in Australia.

Across the river at the Time Out complex, there's a **horseriding** set-up, charging about $10 an hour for guided rides. They might need a minimum number of people.

Tocumwal is a centre for **gliding** and you can also get your ultra-light pilot's licence here. The Sportavia centre (☎ (058) 74 2989) at the aerodrome (a very large airbase during WW II) has package deals involving flights, tuition and accommodation. For $45 you can try a glider flight.

Just out of **Barooga**, a small town 20 km west of Tocumwal (and across the river from Victoria's Cobram), are Seppelts vineyards and the Kranmer Cellars, open daily and on weekend afternoons.

Places to Stay
Camping There are several basic campsites by the river, such as Mulberry and Pebbly beaches, but most are across the river from town and quite a distance away on winding tracks.

There are a couple of caravan parks in town. They're nice enough, but semis roll through Tocumwal at night and things can be bloody noisy. You might have a better night's sleep at *Bushlands on the Murray* (☎ (058) 74 2752), not far from town as the cod swims but about three km by road. Tent sites cost from $9 to $11, on-site vans $25 to $30 and units $36 to $42, all for two people.

Further out, in the red-gum forest (which is part of Tocumwal Regional Park, administered by the Victorian Department of Conservation & Natural Resources) and by the river, is *Time Out* (☎ (058) 74 2031), a large caravan park. Take the signposted turn-off just after the first bridge on the road to Victoria and it's about three km along a dirt road. Watch out for stray cattle. Tent sites cost $4 per person ($1 children) all year and on-site vans are $35 a double, rising to $45 in January and at Easter. There's a fairly

well-stocked shop out here. Free camping is allowed in the park, but you can't use Time Out's facilities unless you stay there.

Hotel & Motels The *Tocumwal Hotel* (☎ (058) 74 2025), a nice place with an air of importance out of proportion to the modest town, has motel-style units from $30/40. There are several other motels, all more expensive.

Places to Eat
The interesting antique shop near the information centre has *tea-rooms*, or there's the *Lime Tree Cafe* nearby on the main street. There's also the *River Garden* Chinese restaurant. The *Tokumwal Kafe* on the Melbourne side of the town centre is open for breakfast. The pubs have counter meals from about $9 for steaks. Both the *Bowling Club* and the *Golf Club* have restaurants.

The nice old *Terminus Hotel*, away from the centre on a cul de sac near the bridge, has a good beer-garden.

Getting There & Away
Bus Countrylink buses pass through Tocumwal on the run between Echuca and Albury. Victoria's V/Line runs to Tocumwal from Melbourne via Seymour and Barooga. MIA Intercity Coaches stop in Tocumwal on runs between Griffith and Melbourne.

Greyhound Pioneer Australia stops here on the run between Brisbane and Melbourne.

Car & Motorbike The Newell Highway runs north to Finley and Jerilderie and south to Melbourne. A smaller road runs east along the river to Corowa and Albury. Heading west, minor roads run to the Cobb Highway at Mathoura, passing through a state forest full of river red-gums, and indirectly to Deniliquin.

JERILDERIE
Jerilderie (population 1100) is a highway town on the Newell, a welcome oasis in this baking landscape.

The Kelly Gang held up Jerilderie for three days in 1879, earning themselves an

RIVERINA

Australia-wide reputation for brazenness. The speech Ned Kelly made to his captives in the Royal Hotel (still operating as a pub) and the letter he wrote complaining of his treatment at the hands of the authorities created the suspicion that young Ned might be a latent political activist. Holding up the town sealed Kelly's fate, for the NSW government declared him an outlaw (anyone could kill him without penalty) and the colony was no longer a safe haven – he was already outlawed in Victoria.

The Willows (1878), an old house by the Billabong Creek, is part museum and part souvenir shop, and they serve drinks and snacks daily. On the lawns of the house is a unique Jerilderie red tree, a cross between a kurrajong and an Illawarra flame tree. Nearby in Luke Park is **Steel Wings**, a massive windmill dating from 1910.

Places to Stay & Eat

The *caravan park* (☎ (058) 86 1366) is on the highway and backs onto the pretty Billabong Creek. All of the three pubs have accommodation and there are three or four motels, including the *Jerilderie Budget* (☎ (058) 86 1301) a couple of km south of the town centre.

The pubs have counter meals, not especially cheap, and there are dining rooms at the golf and bowling clubs.

A few km out of Jerilderie, *Pittfour Homestead Restaurant* (☎ (058) 86 1271) is a restaurant on a sheep station on Billabong Creek. There's also a cottage where you can stay. Bookings are essential.

Getting There & Away

Bus MIA Intercity Coaches stop here on the run between Griffith and Melbourne. Countrylink stops here on the run between Wagga Wagga and Echuca (Victoria). McCafferty's and Greyhound Pioneer Australia stop on their runs between Brisbane and Melbourne.

Car & Motorbike The Newell Highway runs north to Narrandera and south to Finley and Tocumwal. A smaller road runs west along the Billabong Creek to Conargo then south

to Deniliquin. West of Jerilderie a network of minor roads run to small villages.

DENILIQUIN

Deniliquin (population 8000) is a pretty, bustling town on a wide bend of the Edward River. It's big enough to offer most services but small enough to retain its easy-going rural feel. Summing up the sense of prosperity, continuity and conservatism is the local Holden-dealer's ad: 'Where did your father buy his first Holden? Probably the same place you did and your son will in years to come'.

History

Before the White invasion, the Deniliquin area was the most densely populated part of Australia. The flood plains and their networks of creeks and billabongs provided plenty of food, although stone for tools was hard to come by in this vast expanse of rich soil.

The Edward River was missed by Hume's 1838 expedition; a party sent by the enterprising Ben Boyd found the river in 1842 and established a station called Deniliquin ('sand hills'), along with a pub. Boyd's shaky empire fell apart soon after (see the South Coast chapter) but a town was growing and by 1849 it was officially recognised. It initially prospered because it was at the end of major droving routes leading down from Queensland, but later wool-growing and sheep-breeding became important.

Orientation & Information

Deniliquin is situated in the crook of a bend in the Edward River. Although the town covers quite a wide area, its centre, the blocks around Napier and Cressy Sts, is compact.

The information centre (☎ (058) 81 2878) is at the east end of Cressy St, near the entrance to the Island Sanctuary. It's open daily and the manager is a good source of information.

Things to See

Deniliquin is an interesting old town, and to

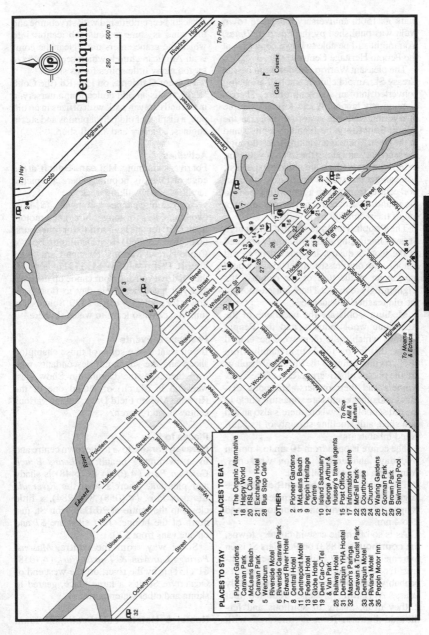

Deniliquin

RIVERINA

PLACES TO STAY

1 Pioneer Gardens
  Caravan Park
4 McLeans Beach
  Caravan Park
5 Wendburn
  Riverside Motel
6 Riverside Caravan Park
7 Edward River Hotel
8 Central Hotel
11 Centrepoint Motel
13 Federal Hotel
16 Globe Hotel
19 Deni Car-O-Tel
  & Van Park
25 Railway Hotel
31 Deniliquin YHA Hostel
32 Mason's Paringa
  Caravan & Tourist Park
33 Deniliquin Motel
34 Riviana Motel
35 Peppin Motor Inn

PLACES TO EAT

14 The Organic Alternative
18 Happy World
20 RSL Club
21 Exchange Hotel
28 Bus Stop Cafe

OTHER

2 Pioneer Gardens
3 McLeans Beach
9 Peppin Heritage
  Centre
10 Island Sanctuary
12 George Arthur &
  Hussey's travel agents
15 Post Office
17 Information Centre
22 McFall Park
23 Courthouse
24 Church
26 Waring Gardens
27 Gorman Park
29 Brown Park
30 Swimming Pool

mark its 150th anniversary a detailed **town walk** was published by the *Pastoral Times*. You might still be able to buy a copy ($1) at the Peppin Heritage Centre.

The pleasant **Waring Gardens** run beside Cressy St. An old church and hall are being converted into an arts centre here. There's also a pretty lagoon. A less formal example of riverine wetlands is not far away, in the **Island Sanctuary**, bushland on a big island in the river. There is a walking track through the sanctuary and along the river. If you want to feed the birds (there are about 80 species), you can get birdseed at the nearby information centre, from where a footbridge leads to the island. The over-friendly emus are kept out of the picnic hut by iron bars!

The **Peppin Heritage Centre** on George St is an interesting museum largely devoted to the wool industry. It's housed in an old school, with one classroom set up as it would have been at the turn of the century. It's frighteningly realistic! There is a tea-room in the old teacher's residence.

Medium wools are the backbone of the Australian wool industry and the Peppin merinos which grow them were developed in the district by the Peppin family from 1862. As interesting as the historical displays are the photos of 'Riverina Ram of the Year' winners and their owners. Sheepdog displays and other events are sometimes held in the old schoolyard, where there's also an old ram shed, still smelling strongly of its pampered inhabitants.

The centre is open from 10 am to 4 pm on weekdays and until 2 pm on weekends. Admission is $3 ($1 children).

The visitor centre at **SunRice Mill**, the largest rice mill in the southern hemisphere, is open on weekdays from 10 am to noon and 2 to 4 pm.

As is so often the case in country towns, the **courthouse** (1883) on Poictiers St is an extremely imposing building. Cases resulting from pioneering drinking habits probably formed the bulk of its work in early years. A visiting preacher reported that '...they drink madly of spiritous and fermented liquors. Rum is tinctured with tobacco, beer embittered with strychnine and the wine is some odious fabrication into which the grape enters not'. Near the court is an Anglican church which seems to have far too many little spires for its size.

Pioneer Gardens, on Hay Rd (the Cobb Highway), is an odd collection: a nursery, a motel and caravan park with offices in an old pub, a display of old petrol pumps and steam engines, a gallery and a craft shop.

Activities

For river swimming, **McLeans Beach**, at the edge of town, is popular. There are picnic facilities and a walking track.

You can hire canoes and kayaks ($14 for two hours, less for longer hires) and motorboats ($20 for one hour to $40 for four hours, no license required) from Deniliquin Boat & Canoe Hire at Masons' Paringa Caravan & Tourist Park (☎ (058) 81 1131). For $60 they'll drive you and your canoe up the river and you have the whole day to float back down; for a half-day trip it's $30. Sounds like fun. You can also learn to water-ski here.

Festivals & Events

If you want to see some of those champion sheep and the squatters' descendants who own them, try the Deniliquin Show (last weekend in March) or attend one of the Riverina Merino Field Days, held in various centres in mid-March.

Places to Stay

Caravan Parks Close to the town centre and by a swimming beach, *McLeans Beach Caravan Park* (☎ (058) 81 2448) is shady and pleasant. There's also the *Riverside Caravan Park* (☎ (058) 81 1284), a little closer to the centre at 20 Davidson St, just north of the bridge. Tent sites are $7 and on-site vans from $20.

Some way from the centre, *Masons' Paringa Caravan & Tourist Park* (☎ (058) 81 1131) is by the river, off the west end of Ochtertyre St. It's a large place, geared to skiing and other watersports.

Hostel & Hotels The *Deniliquin Youth*

Hostel (☎ (058) 81 5025) is on the corner of Wood and Macauley Sts south-west of the town centre. It's pretty basic but clean. YHA members (only) can stay here for $7 a night ($3.50 children). The manager lives around the corner in Macauley St.

The hotels have accommodation. The *Globe* (☎ (058) 81 2030) on Cressy St is good value, with rooms at $18 per person including a cooked breakfast. At the other pubs you're left to make your own. The *Federal Hotel* (☎ (058) 81 1260) on the corner of Cressy and Napier Sts has clean, newly-painted rooms for $20/35 a single/double and $40 for a twin. The *Railway Hotel* (☎ (058) 81 1498), on Napier St a few blocks south-west of the centre, has some rooms with attached bathroom for just $16/30.

Motels Among Deniliquin's many motels, the *Wendburn* (☎ (058) 81 2311) at the top end of Charlotte St probably has the best position, overlooking the river and some blocks from the highway and all those midnight semis. Rooms start at $50. The *Deniliquin* (☎ (058) 81 1820) on the corner of Crispe and Wick Sts is a little cheaper; the *Peppin* (☎ (058) 81 2722) and the *Riviana* (☎ (058) 81 2033) on Crispe St are dearer.

B&B West of Deniliquin the *Riverina Homestead* (☎ (085) 84 1625) offers B&B at $45 per person. To get there take the road to Wakool and turn off onto the Coloma road after about 10 km.

Places to Eat

The Organic Alternative on Cressy St sells health food and takeaways. Next door to the Federal Hotel on Napier St is *Brontes' Cafe*, with light meals and coffees during the day. Further along Napier St there's another coffee shop, and around the corner is the *Bus Stop Cafe*. The *George St Restaurant & Coffee Lounge* at 369 George St serves home-made meals and snacks in a courtyard.

The *Federal Hotel* on the corner of Napier and Cressy Sts has $5 counter-meal specials, and the other pubs can usually match or beat

it. The *Central Hotel*, further north-east on Napier St, has a comfortable bistro.

For takeaways and basic sit-down meals, *Happy World* is right next to the information centre and is open daily. There are some Asian dishes on the menu, such as Chinese sausage and rice for $3.50. There's a much larger Chinese restaurant, *Ho's*, nearby on the corner of Wellington and End Sts, open for lunch and dinner from Tuesday to Sunday.

The *RSL Club* has a bistro as well as a more upmarket dining room and there's *PJ's Bistro* at the bowling club.

Entertainment

The Railway Hotel and the RSL Club sometimes have bands. The Central Hotel is your best bet for events such as horizontal bungee-jumping or mock-Sumo wrestling.

Getting There & Away

Air Western Airlines (☎ 1800 804 775 toll-free) has a daily air service to Sydney's Bankstown airport via Wagga Wagga. MacKnights (☎ (058) 81 2504) is a local company offering air charters, which might soon offer passenger services.

Bus Long-distances buses stop at the Bus Stop Cafe, on Whitelock St near the corner of Napier St. If you walk through the arcade near here you'll emerge on Cressy St near the two travel agents, George Arthur Travel (☎ (058) 81 1744) and Hussey's Travel (☎ (058) 81 1544).

Countrylink stops here on the run between Wagga Wagga and Echuca (Victoria). McCafferty's stops here on the run between Melbourne and Brisbane. Victoria's V/Line runs to Melbourne via several other Riverina towns.

On the second Tuesday of the month, a community bus runs to Shepparton in Victoria ($12 return) via Finley ($10 return) and Tocumwal ($8 return), departing Deniliquin at 8 am.

Car & Motorbike The Cobb Highway runs south to Echuca (Victoria) and north to Hay.

RIVERINA

The Riverina Highway runs south-east to Albury. Smaller roads run south-west to Barham and north-west to Balranald.

Getting Around

Taxi There are two taxi companies, Black & White (☎ (058) 81 2129) and Taits (☎ (058) 81 1373).

AROUND DENILIQUIN

Outside **Wanganella station**, on the Newell Highway 40 km north of Deniliquin, there's a memorial to the Peppin family's merino breeding.

Finley

On the Riverina Highway 50 km east of Deniliquin, Finley is a quiet rural town. The Mary Lawson Rest Centre is a roadside stop on the southern end of the main street with a small log-cabin museum and craft shop, where you can buy tea and coffee. There's a *caravan park* at the other end of town, near the artificial lake. A Japanese company is establishing the world's first liquorice farm in the Finley area (liquorice is usually harvested from wild plants, but the supply is dwindling).

Berrigan, 22 km east of Finley, is even smaller and quieter. The caravan park is basic but in a nice park and the pubs have accommodation.

Mathoura

On the road south to Moama and Echuca, Mathoura is a tidy hamlet with a couple of small *caravan parks*. There's also a railway siding piled high with newly-cut red-gum sleepers, which help explain why there are so few red-gum giants left in the nearby state forest. Still, the forest is the largest remaining stand of river red-gum anywhere, even if it is largely regrowth. You can drive through all the way to Tocumwal (partly on dirt roads) or take one of the scenic drives.

At **Picnic Point**, in the forest about 11 km east of Mathoura, there is a swimming beach on the banks of the Murray and several accommodation options, including the *Picnic Point Caravan Park* (☎ (058) 84 3375), where a tent site costs $10 and on-site vans from $20 a double. They hire canoes for $6 an hour and some fairly ordinary bikes for $3 an hour, both less for longer hires. Nearby is *Tarragon Lodge* (☎ (058) 3387) where you can join in canoe trips and horseriding. They mainly cater to groups so you have to phone first to see if there's a free place. Picnic Point is a popular holiday spot and the sound of power boats could make it less than idyllic at peak times. A courtesy bus takes people between Picnic Point and Mathoura's clubs in the holiday period, so you might be able to get a lift.

Moama

The poor relation of the big Victorian town of Echuca, Moama lures gamblers across the bridge into NSW, but Victoria's legalisation of poker machines might make a dent in their tourist trade. Over the river in Echuca there is a lot to do and see, including the restored Port of Echuca, and plenty of accommodation, including a *YHA Hostel* (☎ (054) 80 6522) on Mitchell St.

Plenty of transport passes through Echuca/Moama, with Countrylink running to Albury and V/Line to Adelaide, Albury and Melbourne. Book on (☎ (054) 82 5308). Dyson's (☎ (054) 82 2576) also runs from Melbourne to Moama.

BARHAM

Barham is a small town without many attractions of its own to offer, but it's on the river and is popular for fishing holidays. The Services Club here has regular entertainment (Chubby Checker had been here the week before I arrived) and movies. There are dress restrictions. There is plenty of accommodation in and near the town, most of it fairly expensive at weekends.

Barham is the last sizeable settlement on the NSW side of the Murray River until Wentworth. The skeins of creeks and rivers downstream from here also mean that the roads are indirect, so if you want to keep following the Murray you will be better off crossing over to Victoria and taking the Murray Valley Highway through Swan Hill to Euston/Robinvale, where you meet the Sturt Highway.

AROUND BARHAM
Wakool
Wakool is just a hamlet with a pub, a club and a store in a Nissen-hut-style building, but the well-watered lawns and trees are a welcome sight after a hot drive across the shimmering plain. Just north of here on the road to Moulamein is a big red sandhill planted with rows of European trees. Both the hill and the trees are incongruous in this landscape.

Moulamein
Moulamein feels much larger than Wakool, although its population is only 500. The town is on the Edward River and has a couple of pubs. There is accommodation (motel-style) at *Tattersalls Hotel* (☎ (058) 87 5017) for $32/48 with breakfast, and a club with Chinese meals. The *caravan park* is by the lake on the edge of town. It's an inviting place but home to power boats.

North of Moulamein the country rises a little and the plains give way to red soil, mulga and native pines.

Getting There & Away
The road from Barham east to Moama runs parallel to the Murray and there are several access points to the state forests along the river. It's a reasonable road, although narrow, but there's a 25 km unsealed section which is very slippery after rain and also has some patches of sand. The various other roads through this river-riddled part of the world are similar. The unsealed section between Moulamein and Balranald is a little rocky but should be OK in the wet.

WENTWORTH
This old riverport (population 1300) is overshadowed by nearby Mildura in Victoria, but it is a quiet and pleasant place to contemplate the impressive merging of the Murray and Darling rivers. Information is available at Apphara Arts & Crafts (☎ (050) 27 3714) on Adams St.

You can see some local history in the **Old Gaol** (admission $3.50, $2 students, $1 children) and across the road in the **Pioneer Museum** (admission $2.50, $1), which has a large collection of photos of the paddle steamers which once made this a major port. The jail closed in the 1930s but reopened briefly in 1962 to accommodate rioting fruit-pickers. The old paddle-steamer *Ruby* is on display near the Darling River bridge in **Fotherby Park**, where there's a statue of Possum, one of the river's last swaggies.

The **confluence** of the Murray and Darling is an impressive sight. The two rivers are often different colours, depending on whether one has had rain somewhere upstream. Six km out of town, off the road to Broken Hill, the **Perry Dunes**, big, startlingly orange sand-dunes, present the drier side of the outback picture.

The MV *Loyalty* (☎ (050) 27 3330), built in 1914, has two-hour cruises to the confluence and Lock 10 on Tuesday and Thursday, leaving the Wentworth Services Club at 1.45 pm. The fare is $12 ($4 children).

An attraction that should be open by now is the **Outback Dunny Farm**. I haven't seen it myself, but the ad sounds intriguing: 'set on 200 exciting acres...a mighty contribution to the outback way of life'.

Places to Stay
Caravan Parks *Willow Bend Caravan Park* (☎ (050) 27 3213) has sites, on-site vans and cabins.

Motels There are motels in town and some more out on the road to Broken Hill. Most cost in the region of $45/55. The *Royal Hotel/Motel* (☎ (050) 27 3005) on Darling St is a bit cheaper.

Houseboats *Sunshine River Houseboats* (☎ (050) 27 3237) has a couple of boats and charges the array of rates somehow peculiar to houseboats. Basically you'll pay from about $50 per day (minimum three days) for a four-berth boat, more in peak times. *Drifter Houseboats* (☎ (050) 27 3325) has a boat sleeping up to eight people from around

RIVERINA

$400 for three nights in the off-season. There's also *Riverside Houseboats* (☎ (050) 27 3633) charging from around $600 for three nights in the off-season.

Farmstay *Avoca Station* (☎ (050) 27 3020), a grand homestead on the Darling dating from 1868, has accommodation in self-contained cabins from $250 a week for two people. It's about 25 km north-east of Wentworth – get detailed directions when you book (essential).

Getting There & Away

Many more long-distance buses run through Mildura than through Wentworth. Greyhound Pioneer Australia has a run between Mildura and Broken Hill which stops in Wentworth, and the Victorian V/Line bus running between Melbourne and Broken Hill also stops here.

A local service runs to Mildura on weekdays, about three times a day. Contact Coomealla Bus Lines (☎ (050) 27 4704) for times.

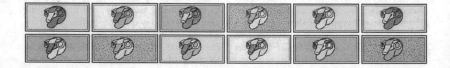

The South-East

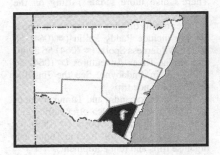

This chapter covers the rugged south-eastern corner of NSW – the high country bounded on the north and west by the Hume Highway. There are three main sections: the Monaro Tableland, including the Snowy Mountains and Kosciusko National Park; west of the Snowies, the area between Kosciusko National Park and the Hume Highway; and the Hume itself, from Goulburn to Albury.

The south coast and the ACT have their own chapters, and the chain of national parks in the Great Dividing Range, stretching from Nowra down to the Victorian border, is covered in the South Coast chapter.

The Monaro Tableland

The tableland is just that – undulating but largely flat (cyclists might not agree), and in places totally bare of trees. It can be a bit lunar at times. Monaro is pronounced 'mon-*air*-ro' (although Holden's popular muscle-car of the '70s is pronounced 'mon-*ah*-ro').

History
The Ngarigo people lived on the high plains at the time of the first White encroachment. Other people came up here during the annual bogong moth harvest, a big event for people from a wide area.

Explorer John Ovens came through the area in 1823 and graziers soon followed. In the 1860s there was a gold rush at Kiandra and, despite the inhospitable climate, thousands of diggers flocked to the area. Bushrangers, who had earlier preyed on the graziers and their herds, now became endemic – and extremely hard to catch, as they knew the area well and were superb riders.

After the gold fizzled out, the area settled back into its pastoral activities, to be again disturbed when the ACT was carved from the Monaro in 1908 and when the huge Snowy Mountains Hydro-Electric Scheme was constructed in the 1950s and '60s – and every winter when skiers flock to the mountains.

Although the Monaro is rich in history, little of it is obvious. The goldminers established no large towns, the graziers were too few to leave much of a mark (although their cattle certainly left their mark on the ecology) and the towns that grew around their industry mainly did so on the lower slopes of the winter pastures. Several of the small towns that were established up on the Monaro were drowned in the dams of the Snowy Mountains Hydro-Electric Scheme.

Geography
The Monaro is one of the string of tablelands along the Great Dividing Range, running south from around Goulburn to the Victorian border. On the south-western side, the Snowy Mountains rise above the tablelands; on the eastern side the range drops to the coastal strip.

Activities
Although snow sports are the obvious and most popular activities in this area, it is also well worth visiting in seasons other than winter.

A couple of major operators hire equipment and organise activities. Talk to these people to get an idea of what's available. In

467

Jindabyne see Paddy Pallin (☎ (064) 56 2922) at the Thredbo turn-off and in Tumut see Adventure Sports (☎ (069) 47 2478, 1800 020 631 toll-free). There are plenty of other operators as well – see the various sections in this chapter. Thredbo Village has an extensive activities programme in summer.

Snow Sports See the following Skiing & Resorts section for details. Ski hire is available on the slopes and in many of the towns in the nearby area. Outfits such as Paddy Pallin in Jindabyne can arrange cross-country skiing.

Bushwalking Summer bushwalking is popular in Kosciusko National Park and other areas. Remember that conditions can change rapidly and snow can fall at any time of year. Be prepared and don't walk alone. See if you can find a copy of *Snowy Mountains Bushwalks*, which is published by the Geehi Bushwalking Club (about $15). On the west side of the mountains, the Hume & Hovell Walking Track runs from near Yass to near Albury, and trackheads include those near Wee Jasper, Tumut, Holbrook and Tumbarumba.

Horseriding When the weather warms up the Monaro is a popular place for horseriding and there are many outfits offering day rides and longer treks.

Watersports Because of all those big dams, watersports are popular. It's strange to be in an area where some cars have ski-racks and others are towing power boats. Jindabyne, on the doorstep of the ski-fields, even has sailing boats and seagulls!

There's also the Murray River, which rises at the Pilot, a peak in the Pilot Wilderness Area of Kosciusko National Park. Upper Murray White-Water Rafting (☎ (060) 76 9566) has trips from near Tom Groggin Station, off the Alpine Way, to near Khancoban. Parts of the ride offer genuine whitewater excitement, but in other stretches you get a chance to take in some excellent scenery. A day-trip costs $90 and a two-day trip is $210. There are also packages which include a day's horseriding at Tom Groggin. There's also more sedate rafting on the Swampy Plains River near Khancoban.

Other outfits offering rafting on the upper Murray include Paddy Pallin (☎ (064) 56 2922), Wilderness Sports (☎ (064) 56 2966) and Alpine River Adventures (☎ (064) 56 1199), all in Jindabyne. See the Jingellic section for canoe trips.

The Goobarragandra and Tumut rivers to the north of this area also offer rafting and canoeing. Adventure Sports (☎ (069) 47 2478, 1800 020 631 toll-free) in Tumut can organise trips and rent equipment.

Canoeing is also popular and in summer you'll find many outfits offering day trips and longer trips.

Cycling Summer cycling in this area can be superb, if hilly. The summit of Mt Kosciusko was first conquered by bicycle last century! Carrying your bike on the Skitube up to Perisher cuts out some of the uphill. You can hire mountain bikes at the Bullocks Flat Skitube terminal for $45 a day, including a Skitube ticket.

Getting There & Away
Air There are flights from Sydney and Melbourne to Cooma.

Bus The ski-fields are well served by buses in winter, with fewer in summer. Cooma is the main transport hub and buses from Melbourne, Sydney and Canberra run there.

Car & Motorbike The Monaro is easily accessible from Canberra, Sydney and the south coast, and by some interesting routes from the south and west.

From Canberra, the Monaro Highway runs down to Cooma. It's a good road, although not especially wide for the amount of traffic it carries.

The quickest route from Sydney is to take the Hume Highway to Goulburn and the Federal Highway to Canberra. A longer alternative is to take the Princes Highway then

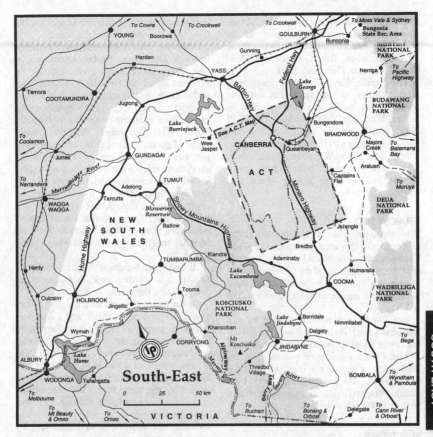

climb up onto the tableland from Wollongong, Batemans Bay or Bega.

The Snowy Mountains Highway runs from Bega to Cooma (the road between Cooma and Bombala is both the Monaro Highway and the Snowy Mountains Highway), then north-west through the Kosciusko National Park to Tumut, meeting the Hume Highway at Gundagai.

From Cooma, the Monaro Highway heads south to Bombala and the Victorian border, where it becomes the Cann Valley Highway and meets the Princes Highway in Cann River. From the small town of Delegate, near

Bombala, the unsealed Bonang Highway runs south to meet the Princes Highway in Orbost (Victoria).

The Barry Way is a largely unsealed, narrow and winding mountain road running from near Jindabyne to Buchan in Victoria. It's a spectacular drive through national parks, but it can be a difficult route when wet. Caravans can't use this route but logging trucks do, so be careful. Fuel is not available anywhere along this road.

The Alpine Way, a spectacular mountain road, runs from Khancoban around the southern end of the ski-fields, passing close to Mt Kosciusko, Thredbo and Jindabyne. Caravans aren't permitted on parts of the Alpine Way, which climbs 1000 metres in the 18 km between Tom Groggin and Dead Horse Gap near Thredbo Village.

The Alpine Way is the most direct route from Albury to the ski-fields and the Monaro, but it can be closed by snow in winter. If so, you'll have to take the Elliott Way from Tooma or Tumbarumba to the Snowy Mountains Highway near Kiandra, although the Elliott Way sometimes closes in winter and you might have to head up to Tumut and take the Snowy Mountains Highway.

BRAIDWOOD

Braidwood (population 1100) is in the north-east corner of this area, on the road between Canberra and Batemans Bay. The town is near the eastern edge of the tableland and is a centre for visiting the spectacular national parks in the ranges tumbling down to the south coast.

Braidwood has been classified by the National Trust. Not only is it well preserved, but it was a well-planned town to start with.

There's an alternative power shop on Wallace St, a sign of the interesting people who live in and around Braidwood. Poet Judith Wright is one of many artists and writers living in the area.

Information

The information centre (☎ (048) 42 2310) is in the museum on Wallace St, the main street, just north of the courthouse and park. It has a good range of information on Braidwood and the local area, including a walking-tour map of the town (20c) and maps and books on bushwalks in the area.

Like many businesses in Braidwood, the visitor information centre is closed on Tuesday and Wednesday, the weekend for this visitor-oriented town.

Things to See

Just strolling down Wallace St is an experience, especially if you've arrived from the rough-and-ready towns of the Monaro or the ugly strip-development of the coast.

There are quite a few galleries and studios in town. Don't miss **Studio Altenburg**, in one of the more impressive buildings on Wallace St, an old bank built in 1888. The architecture is Italianate style, but with a proportion and dignity complementing rather than clashing with that potentially florid style. The gallery displays a wide range of goods by local artists and craftspeople, and some from further afield. There's everything from home-made chutney to fine jewellery to sculpture and etchings, all well displayed in the fine old rooms. There is a courtyard cafe, Cafe Altenburg, which is a relaxing place for a coffee or a meal. Studio Altenburg is open from 10 am to 5 pm on Monday to Thursday and until 9 pm Friday to Sunday.

Across from Studio Altenburg, Antiques & Kitsch is worth a look, as much for its design as for the stock.

St Andrews Church on Elrington St has a restored pipe organ inside and a fine collection of gargoyles leering from the tower.

Bedervale, an impressive homestead reached from Monkittee St, was built in 1836 to the design of John Verge, architect of Elizabeth Bay House in Sydney. It was owned by the same family for generations and their accumulated furnishings and knick-knacks provide a good overview of the taste of more affluent Australians over 130 years. It is still a working farm, but is open to the public on the first Sunday of the month from September to April ($5, $1.50 children) or by appointment at other times.

The **Old Rectory** on Wilson St is a nursery which has a cottage garden worth seeing. Several private **gardens** are open to the public at certain times of the year. The information centre has the dates.

Festivals & Events

The Braidwood Show, an annual event since 1872, is held in late February or early March. There are several horse-racing meetings each year, including the Braidwood Cup in early February.

Places to Stay

The impressive *Royal Mail Hotel* (☎ (048) 42 2488), used in the *Ned Kelly* film starring Mick Jagger, has rooms for $25/45 a single/double, including breakfast. The pub was once called the Royal Hotel – the 'Mail' was added for the film and has stuck.

Torpy's Motel (☎ (048) 42 2395) is a block beyond the information centre at 202 Wallace St and is a nice place to stay, with a good restaurant. The motel units are well-designed and don't make the usual attempt at glitz, and they look out onto a shady lawn. During the week singles/doubles go for $45/55 with a light breakfast or $75 per person for dinner, bed and breakfast (on Saturday nights they'd prefer you to take the dinner option). There's also a restored house (once the postmaster's residence) where you can stay in very pleasant rooms for $85 per person including dinner, breakfast and butler service.

There are a couple of other motels, *Cedar Lodge* (☎ (048) 42 2244), back from the main street on Duncan St, and the *Braidwood Colonial Motel* (☎ (048) 42 2027), at the north end of Wallace St, both charging about $40/50.

The *Dorchester Inn* guesthouse (☎ (048) 42 2356) has an impressive garden, restored rooms and a French chef. It's a large building (once a pub and a convent) across the park from the courthouse. Dinner, bed and breakfast costs about $70/120; B&B is $50/80.

Places to Eat

A pleasant place for a snack or a meal is *Cafe Altenburg*, in the courtyard at Studio Altenburg, which has healthy food and reasonable prices. Main courses cost between $6 and $9 and the servings are large.

Diagonally opposite Studio Altenburg is *Cafe Cornucopia*, a whole-food store selling takeaways and some food to eat there. It's the place with the giant carrot hanging over the footpath. The *Bakers Paddle*, not far away on Wallace St, is a pleasant restaurant with main courses between about $10 and $13.

Torpy's Dining Room, a good restaurant, is in an old house at Torpy's Motel. The

Ex-Servicemen's Club on Victory St (at the west end of Wilson or Duncan St) has meals. There's an unobtrusive *Chinese restaurant* in the white building on the corner of Wallace and Duncan Sts.

Getting There & Away

Bus Murrays stops here on the run between Canberra and Batemans Bay. Ask at the information centre about schoolbus routes which will take you (eventually) to some of the smaller places in the area.

Car & Motorbike Braidwood is on the road between Canberra and Batemans Bay. About 20 km east of Braidwood the road enters thick forest then drops over the edge of an escarpment to begin the winding drive to the coast. The first few km is extremely steep and winding; the rest of the way is less steep, but this is one of those roads where you should take the speed recommendations on the corners seriously!

An alternative route to the south coast at Moruya runs through Araluen and some beautiful country on the northern edge of Deua National Park. The road is sealed as far as Araluen, but after that it is not suitable for caravans. Another unsealed route heads north-east to the coast near Nowra, via Nerriga, passing through the southern end of Morton National Park.

If you're heading to Cooma, consider taking the scenic partly-sealed road running via Numeralla. It follows the Shoalhaven River up to its source, Big Badja Hill (also called Badja Mountain). A couple of sections of this road can be cut by floods, so if it has been raining be prepared to change your plans. There are also a couple of unexpected one-lane bridges on the sealed section. This route is quite a bit shorter (although maybe not any faster) than following the main road to and taking the Monaro Highway from there.

Via Goulburn and the Hume Highway to Sydney it's about 95 km north on a good road.

A Small Triumph for Innocence

On the road between Braidwood and Batemans Bay, just after you begin the steep descent, there's a sharp corner signposted Pooh Corner. In the apex of the corner is a tiny cave with the nameboard Mr Sanders. Inside, people leave notes, flowers and 'hunny' – messages and gifts for Pooh. Despite the slick (and recent) sign-writing and the Disney-Pooh figure, this is a spontaneous and touching place, a rarity on Australia's commercialised and vandalised roadsides.

In India, journeys are often broken by *puja* stops at roadside shrines. Perhaps here you should stop for *pu*. ∎

AROUND BRAIDWOOD

Nearby **Budawang National Park** and the southern end of **Morton National Park** are accessible from Braidwood, and the information centre sells maps and books. There are also state forests nearby, with interesting walks and drives. The alternative routes to both Cooma and the coast at Moruya described in the Braidwood Getting There & Away section skirt **Deua National Park**.

In **Majors Creek**, reached via a detour on the Braidwood to Moruya scenic road, the *Elrington Hotel* (☎ (048) 46 1145) charges $20/35 a single/double for rooms and serves meals every day. There's a basic camping area nearby. There are several old buildings in the town.

Araluen, in the pretty Araluen Valley, has the *Araluen Valley Hotel* (☎ (048) 46 4023) and the *Old Court House* (☎ (048) 46 4053), a small, friendly guesthouse in the old court and jail, a very interesting place charging $125 per person for dinner, bed and breakfast.

Captains Flat, on a partly-sealed southern route to Canberra, straggles along the bottom of a steep, narrow valley. There's a Dogpatch air about it.

LAKE EUCUMBENE AREA

Lake Eucumbene is a massive dam, built as part of the Snowy Mountains Hydro-Electric Scheme, and is adjacent to the central section of Kosciusko National Park. Some of the lake's forested arms and inlets are scenic, although much of the area has been cleared of trees. The lake is popular for fishing in summer and there are several small communities on the shores with camping and other accommodation.

Adaminaby

Adaminaby is a tiny town (population 400) on the Snowy Mountains Highway, built to replace the old town now lying beneath Lake Eucumbene 10 km away. Still, it's the largest town for some way and there is a good range of services. The town might be small, but the trout in front of it is big.

Adaminaby is the closest town to the **Mt Selwyn ski-fields** (a day-use resort), and the Adaminaby Bus Service (☎ (064) 54 2318) runs there and to Cooma. You can hire ski gear at Adaminaby Ski Hire (☎ (064) 54 2455) in the Bullwheel complex. Those in need of bullwhips to liven up the apres-ski could try the leather shop.

Places to Stay & Eat The *Alpine Tourist Park* (☎ (064) 54 2438) has sites ($10), on-site vans (from $30) and a range of cabins (from $30). *Tandarra Lodge* (☎ (064) 54 2470) charges from $20/36, the *Snow Goose Hotel/Motel* (☎ (064) 54 2202) has rooms from $40/50, and the *Adaminaby Country Club* (☎ (064) 54 2462) charges from $60/70. All these places charge more in winter and might be booked out by groups on ski packages.

There are counter and bistro meals at the Snow Goose and several cafes on the main street. The *Bullwheel Steakhouse* has been recommended.

Around the Lake

The area's brief gold-rush of the 1860s saw the construction of 14 pubs in Adaminaby, all of which closed soon after as the diggers rushed on to the richer Lambing Flat. The town all but disappeared beneath Lake Eucumbene, but there's a sizeable replacement growing on the lake's shores – **Old Adaminaby** is probably newer than 'new' Adaminaby. A few buildings escaped the flood, including the school (now the office of the caravan park) and a small church nearby, once on a hill above the town but now on the lake's shore.

Anglers Reach is a new development on a pretty, forested arm of Lake Eucumbene, about 18 km from Adaminaby. Both the caravan park and the Lakeside Village (see Places to Stay below) will rent you a boat to explore the lake for $45 a day. They also have ski hire.

Other settlements by the lake are **Buck-enderra**, where there's horseriding (☎ (064) 53 7242), **Eucumbene**, **Braemar Bay** and **Frying Pan Creek**.

Places to Stay The only accommodation at Old Adaminaby is the rather pleasant *Old Adaminaby Caravan Park* (☎ (064) 54 2317), with sites from $6 and basic on-site vans from $30 a double.

At Anglers Reach, *Anglers Reach Caravan Park* (☎ (064) 54 2223) has tent sites from $5.50 per person and on-site vans from $22/32 a single/double.

The nearby *Lakeside Village* (☎ (064) 54 2276) has cabins starting from $45 (much more in winter).

Farmstays

Reynella (☎ (064) 54 2386) is a working sheep and cattle property which also offers accommodation. You can stay in two- to six-person cabins for $100 for adults, $65 for those aged 15 to 18 and $54 for children under 15. The cost of accommodation includes all meals and horseriding. In the ski season there are cheaper rates ($75 for adults) that don't include riding, and they also have skiing packages. Reynella specialises in horseriding holidays, and day rides are available, as well as treks of up to five days through the north of Kosciusko National Park. A five-day ride costs about $800 per person and a three-day ride is about $450. The Reynella turn-off from the Snowy Mountains Highway is about eight km south of Adaminaby.

San Michel (☎ (064) 54 2229) is a resort on an old farm, off the highway between Adaminaby and Cooma. Trail rides and other activities are offered and full board costs from $70 per person.

Old Yaouk (☎ (064) 54 2421) is 21 km north of Adaminaby, near the ACT border. It's a working sheep-property, and they offer a variety of accommodation options, ranging from fully catered in the homestead, to self-catering in a cottage, to bunkrooms and camping.

SOUTH-EAST

The Snowy Mountains Hydro-Electric Scheme

In 1946 the government decided to embark on one of the largest and most challenging engineering projects the world had seen. Work began in 1949, in mountainous country that had barely been explored, much less settled. Workers from around the world flocked to the project, 17 large dams were built (Lake Eucumbene alone could hold the water of eight Sydney Harbours), rivers were diverted and all sorts of tunnelling and building records were smashed.

The project took 25 years to complete and today provides electricity to Canberra, NSW and Victoria. Water from the diverted rivers irrigates the inland. It is estimated that if the electricity produced by the scheme had been produced by coal-fired turbines, five million tonnes of carbon dioxide would be released into the atmosphere each year!

An unexpected benefit of the project has been its social impact. Australia in the '50s was a pretty parochial island, and the postwar turmoil in Europe and Asia didn't do much to change that. With workers from 30 countries vital to a project that was a source of immense national pride, attitudes to 'reffos' (refugees) changed and Australia's multiculturalism began.

Also, the sheer size of the project meant a government commitment previously unheard of in this country and perhaps indirectly led to acceptance of later 'socialist' programmes such as the universal health care scheme. ■

COOMA

Cooma is the largest town on the Monaro, although its present population of 8000 is just half the 16,000 who crowded in during the construction of the Snowy Mountains Hydro-Electric Scheme, for which it was the headquarters.

Orientation & Information

The Monaro and the Snowy Mountains highways meet in central Cooma. The main shopping street is Sharp St, which is the Snowy Mountains Highway west of Bombala St (the Monaro Highway) and the Monaro Highway east of Bombala St.

The visitor centre, on Sharp St next to Centennial Park and near the corner of Bombala St, is open daily from 9 am to 5 pm and has a lot of information on the area. They make accommodation bookings and may know of special deals.

The Snowstop centre is on Sharp St a few blocks north-east of the main shopping centre. Most buses stop here, there's a restaurant or two and you can hire ski gear.

For film and camera equipment go to Schoo's Studio on Bombala St (the Monaro Highway) near the corner of Sharp St (Snowy Mountains Highway). The supermarket in the Hain Centre, on Sharp St about one km south-west of the visitor centre, is open daily from 7 am to 9 pm. There's a laundromat at 63 Sharp St, and Snowy Disposals at 98 Sharp St sells outdoor gear.

Things to See & Do

The best way to become acquainted with Cooma is to take the five km, 2½-hour **Lambie Town Walk**, which leads you past some historic buildings and a little way into the countryside. The visitor centre has brochures detailing the walk. If you haven't time for this, make sure you at least see **Lambie St**, where there are a number of historic buildings (you can have coffee on the verandah of the Lord Raglan Inn, now a gallery), and the imposing granite **courthouse** and the nearby **jail** on Vale St.

Next to the visitor centre in **Centennial Park** is a series of mosaic scenes from the

history of the Monaro. In the park are the flags of the 27 nations represented in the Snowy Mountains Scheme workforce and there's a relief map of the mountains cast in metal, handy for orienting yourself to the ups and downs of the area.

The **Snowy Mountains Information Centre** (☎ (064) 53 2003) is concerned with the hydro-electric scheme and has models of the tunnels and power stations, a large 3D map and a video about the project. The centre is open on weekdays from 8 am to 4.30 pm. The centre is in the Snowy Mountains Hydro-Electric Authority headquarters, off the Monaro Highway a couple of km north of the town centre. Two **power stations** are open to visitors, neither very close to Cooma: the Murray 1 station near Khancoban (tours at 10 am, noon, 1.30 and 2.30 pm) and the Tumut 3 station near Talbingo (tours at 10 and 11 am, noon, 1 and 2 pm).

The **Aviation Pioneers Memorial** incorporates some of the wreckage of the *Southern Cloud*, an aircraft which crashed in the Snowies in 1931 but wasn't discovered until 1958.

The **Old Gaol Museum** on Vale St is open from 1 to 3 pm on weekdays. Entry is free. The name is a little misleading – the museum is in a new house near the old jail and while the jail *is* old, it is still a jail (all right, 'correctional facility'). Inmates' work is sold at the museum.

Across Sharp St from Centennial Park is the **Clog Maker**, a Dutch craftsperson who makes clogs and sells souvenirs. The **Loegoss Gallery** in the Mystic Munchies cafe on Sharp St has works by local artists in a variety of media. Other local work is shown in the **Little Gallery** in the Hain Centre, open Tuesday to Friday, Monday afternoon and Saturday morning.

The **Llama Farm** (☎ (064) 52 4593), off the Snowy Mountains Highway 19 km west of Cooma, is the place to visit if you want to buy a llama. Even if you don't feel the need to own one, you can meet the animals, tour the farm, see a video and perhaps buy llama wool and products made from it. You can also go on a half-day (or longer) walk with a

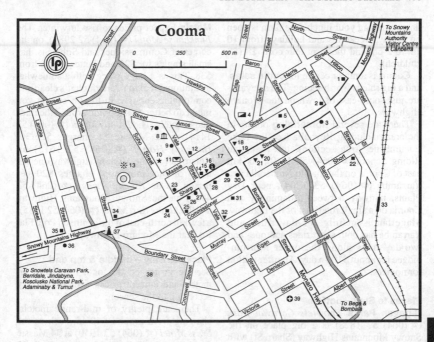

Cooma

PLACES TO STAY

1 Kinross Inn Motel
2 Summit Motel
5 Swiss & Family Motels
12 Cooma Hotel
14 Australian Hotel
22 Coffey's Hotel
24 Hawaii Motel
25 Bunkhouse Motel/Backpackers
26 Alpine Hotel
28 Monaro Hotel
31 Dodds Hotel
34 Alkira Motel
35 Royal Hotel

PLACES TO EAT

3 Grand Court Chinese Restaurant
6 Shell Diner
15 Pizza House & Cafe Upstairs
18 Cooma Chinatown Restaurant
19 Alpine Cafe
20 Real Thing Cafe
21 Double Luck Chinese Restaurant

32 RSL Club
35 Buckinghams Restaurant

OTHER

3 Snowstop
4 Swimming Pool
7 Jail
8 Old Gaol Museum
9 Courthouse
10 Police Station
11 Post Office
13 Lookout
16 Cooma Visitor Centre
17 Centennial Park
23 Wool Store Antiques
27 Laundromat
29 Snowliner Travel
30 Schoo's Studio
33 Railway Station
36 Hain Centre
37 Aviation Pioneers Memorial
38 Showground
39 Hospital

llama carrying your lunch. The farm is open on Friday, weekends and holidays from 10 am to 2 pm and the farm tour costs $8 ($3 children).

Cooma is a major centre for **cattle sales**, and a big sale is worth seeing. The saleyards are just south-east of town on the Monaro Highway.

There are several **horseriding** outfits in the area, including Reynella (see the Lake Eucumbene Area section), the Magellan Riding School (☎ (064) 52 1110), six km east of Cooma on the road to Numeralla and Yarramba (☎ (064) 53 7204), near Dry Plains, midway between Adaminaby and Cooma on a small road east of the highway. Magellan is mainly for day rides and Yarramba has both short rides and one- and two-day treks along the upper Murrumbidgee for about $100 a day. All offer tuition for novices.

Places to Stay – bottom

Caravan Parks *Snowtels Caravan Park* (☎ (064) 52 1828) is a big place on the Snowy Mountains Highway (Sharp St) with sites from $11, on-site vans about $30 (you can hire doonas and linen) and self-contained flats sleeping six from $50 a double.

Hostels Both the *Bunkhouse Motel* (☎ (064) 52 2983) on the corner of Commissioner and Soho Sts and the *Family Motel* (☎ (064) 52 1414) at 32 Massie St have shared rooms for about $15 per person. The Bunkhouse has been dealing with backpackers longer.

Pubs Cooma's six pubs all have accommodation, and they all charge around $20/30 a single/double. At *Coffey's Hotel* (☎ (064) 52 2064) on Short St singles are only $15. The big *Alpine Hotel* (☎ (064) 52 1466) on Sharp St also has ensuite rooms for $50 and the *Australian Hotel* (☎ (064) 52 1844) has ensuite singles/doubles for $30/50. At the beautiful old *Royal Hotel* (☎ (064) 52 2132) at the corner of Sharp and Lambie Sts you might get a room leading onto that wonderful verandah.

Motels Expect prices to rise in winter. The *Bunkhouse Motel* (☎ (064) 52 2983), on the corner of Commissioner and Soho Sts, has small singles for $25 and better rooms from $38. This is a large place with a somewhat institutional feel to it, although it's clean and comfortable enough. In the off-season you might do better by shopping around the mid-range motels. The *Family Motel* (☎ (064) 52 1414) at 32 Massie St charges $25/30, *Harmony Hostel* (☎ (064) 52 1613) on Bolaro St (off the Monaro Highway one km north of the Snowstop) charges $20 per person, as do *Pinehill Lodge* (☎ (064) 52 4467) on the Snowy Mountains Highway and the *Alpine Rest Motel* (☎ (064) 52 1085), a few km north-east of the centre on Polo Flat Rd near the Monaro Highway.

Places to Stay – middle & top end

See the visitor centre for a full listing of motels and current prices, which can vary according to the season.

There are plenty of mid-range motels, charging from around $40/45, such as the *Swiss Motel* (☎ (064) 52 1950) at 34 Massie St, the *High Country Motel* (☎ (064) 52 1277) at 12 Chapman St and the *Hawaii Motel* (☎ (064) 52 1211) at 192 Sharp St. A notch higher up the scale are the *White Manor Motel* (☎ (064) 52 1152) at 252 Sharp St and the *Summit Motel* (☎ (064) 52 1366) at 35 Sharp St.

The *Alkira* (☎ (064) 52 3633) at 213 Sharp St is one of the better of Cooma's 20-odd motels. Other highly-rated places include *Kinross Inn* (☎ (064) 52 4133) at 15 Sharp St, the *Marlborough Motel* (☎ (064) 52 1133) on the highway a km or so north of the centre, and the *Nebula Motel* (☎ (064) 52 4133) at 42 Bombala St. The Nebula is the cheapest of the three, with singles/doubles from around $50/55.

Places to Eat

Sharp St has a lot of places to eat, mainly cafes. There's a cluster around the corner of Bombala and Sharp Sts. Right on the corner, the *Alpine Cafe* has breakfasts from $6 and steaks from $8.50. Across the road in Sharp

St, the *Double Luck* Chinese restaurant has lunchtime specials for $5.50 and a $10 all-you-can eat deal on Friday, Saturday and Sunday nights. Around the corner on the continuation of Bombala St and opposite Centennial Park is another Chinese place, *Cooma Chinatown*, which is bigger and more upmarket. It's open for lunch and dinner daily and has main courses for between $9 and $14.

Back on Sharp St and near the Double Luck, the *Real Thing* is a BYO cafe which gives discounts to Motorcycle Riders Association members. Its menu is a little more sophisticated than those of the other cafes in the area. Also near here is the *East End Cafe*, open for breakfast from 6.30 am and 5.30 am in the ski season. A few blocks south-east in an old bank, *Mystic Munchies* has coffee, snacks and meals.

The *Grand Court* Chinese restaurant is on the Snowstop centre on Sharp St. Across the road and a bit closer to the town centre, the Shell service station has a *steakhouse/diner*.

The Australian Hotel on Sharp St has a bistro and, from Thursday to Sunday, the *Mahafif A Sham* Indian restaurant, open for dinner and with main courses under $10. The nearby *Monaro Hotel* has a bistro with pastas for about $8.50 and steaks from $11. There are much cheaper bar meals, featuring good old rissoles, sausages and the like. Most of the other pubs also do counter meals and the *Cooma Hotel*, an impressive old structure, has a steakhouse.

On Sharp St, upstairs in the arcade next to the visitor centre, the *Cafe Upstairs* is open from noon to around 2 am. You can get cocktails (and fruit 'mocktails'), and there's a big menu, with hamburgers from $3.80, kebabs with all the trimmings for $12, and many other dishes.

The big *RSL Club* on Vale St has both a bistro and a restaurant (Friday to Sunday) and claims to have the cheapest beer in the mountains. Several of the motels have restaurants, including *Gables Restaurant* at the Cooma Motor Lodge, on the Snowy Mountains Highway about a km north of the centre.

Probably the best restaurant in town is *Buckinghams* (☎ (064) 52 5033 or 52 2132), part of the Royal Hotel on the corner of Sharp and Lambie Sts. It's open for dinner from Wednesday to Saturday and the small but interesting menu offers two courses for $20 and three for $25, plus coffee. Bookings are essential.

Getting There & Away

Air Eastern Airlines flies from Sydney ($162), and Kendell flies from Melbourne ($160).

Bus Snowliner Travel (☎ (064) 52 1422), on Sharp St opposite the visitor centre, handles bus bookings. All buses except V/Line (which stops near Centennial Park) stop at the Snowstop.

Cooma is about 6½ hours from Sydney and under two hours from Canberra.

Greyhound Pioneer Australia runs to Cooma from Sydney ($36) and Canberra ($14). In winter most of their services continue to the Skitube terminal and the resorts, or connect with the resort shuttle service at Jindabyne. Outside the ski season there's at least one service a day from Sydney and Canberra to Cooma.

Countrylink runs between Canberra and Eden on the far south coast, via Cooma, Bombala and Merimbula.

Victoria's V/Line runs twice weekly between Melbourne and Canberra via Cooma on a service taking you by train to Sale and connecting with a bus running up the Cann Valley/Monaro Highway to Cooma and Canberra. Going the other way the entire trip is by bus. Melbourne to Cooma takes 9½ hours. This would be an interesting trip.

Adaminaby Bus Service (☎ (064) 54 2318) runs between Cooma and Mt Selwyn.

Greyhound Pioneer Australia began a winter route to Thredbo and Cooma from Albury, via the Alpine Way, but discontinued it. It might start up again, so ask around.

Car & Motorbike The Snowy Mountains Highway runs north-west to Tumut and south-east to Bega; the Monaro Highway runs north to Canberra and south to Bombala. Other roads run west to Jindabyne and the Snowy Mountains.

From Cooma to Batemans Bay you can travel via Numeralla to Braidwood on a partly-sealed road skirting Deua National Park. At Braidwood you can continue down to Batemans Bay on a major road or take another beautiful road through Araluen to Moruya. This section, largely unsealed, is not suitable for caravans.

Getting Around

Taxi Cooma Radio Taxis (☎ (064) 52 1188) will get you around Cooma and even up to the ski resorts.

Car Rental Thrifty Car Rental has an agent (☎ (064) 52 5300) at 1/30 Baron St.

NUMERALLA

This hamlet is 22 km east of Cooma, at the end of the sealed road and the starting-point for partly-sealed routes to Braidwood to the north and Nimmitabel in the south.

Big Badja Studio (☎ (064) 53 3221) sells pottery and other art, and there's also a tiny observatory which you can arrange to visit at night ($4). Other craftspeople in the area include Annette Kalnins, whose tiger-striped mailbox is on the left as you drive from Cooma. Phone (☎ (064) 53 3259) to arrange a visit to see her glass engraving and other works.

NIMMITABEL

Nimmitabel is a pretty little place (population 250) on the highway 35 km south of Cooma, with flowers in the gardens and a slow pace to life. It's a good place to break your trip although its only real 'attraction' is the impressive old windmill. A German immigrant spent seven years building the mill last century, but when it was finished he was told he couldn't use it because the spinning sails would frighten horses! There are several antique shops along the main street and one junk shop where you could find anything.

Places to Stay & Eat

The council *caravan park* (☎ (064) 454 6225) is small but very neat and clean. There are hot showers. It's in the recreation area near the northern edge of town. Tent sites cost from $5.

The *Royal Arms* (☎ (064) 54 6422) is a handsome restored hotel, now a guesthouse and restaurant. Rooms cost $50/75 for a single/double, and there's a small room with an external bathroom costing $20 per person. There's also a restaurant, open daily from 8 am to 8 pm, with main courses around $9 to $12.

The *Tudor Inn* (☎ (064) 54 6204) is a cosy pub with accommodation ($20/40), and there's also the small *Nimmitabel Motel* (☎ (064) 54 6387) with rooms for $40/50.

The *bakery* across the road from the Royal Arms has breakfast and other meals and a good range of breads and cakes. The Nimmitybele Emporium claims to have the largest range of lollies in NSW.

BOMBALA

The sign at the outskirts announces that Bombala (population 1300) is a timber town, but it's also the centre of a prime cattle district. There are also some good state forests and national parks in the area.

Maybe St is the tentatively named main street. To the left as you come in on the road from Cooma are a couple of antique/junk shops and the *Good Food Store*, with a wide range of health foods and organic produce.

There's a small, irregularly open **Folk Museum** on the highway just north of town centre. Nearby, the impressive **courthouse** commands the town from high on a hill. On Caveat St, off Maybe St, is the surprisingly large Bombala Literary Institute, now defunct, and next door is the **Masonic Lodge**, which has a shingled upper storey. **Endeavour Reserve**, on a hill overlooking the town, is a good place for picnics.

You can arrange **fly-fishing** trips with Mandi and Grant Stevenson (☎ (064) 58 7226).

The Bombala Agricultural Show, which

has been an annual event since 1878, is held in late March.

Places to Stay

The small *Apex Caravan Park* (☎ (064) 58 3270) is pleasantly situated by the river on the northern edge of town. They have a few on-site vans for $28 plus $4 per person.

All three pubs, the *Globe* (☎ (064) 58 3077), the *Imperial* (☎ (064) 58 3211) and the *Bombala* (☎ (064) 58 3155), have accommodation for around $20/30 a single/double. They're all on Maybe St.

The *Mail Coach Inn* (☎ (064) 58 3721) on the corner of Maybe and Young Sts is a good guesthouse in the newly-renovated old post office. Bed and breakfast costs $45/49 in the two rooms with ensuite bathrooms, or $24 per person in the room which uses a nice old bathroom across the hall. This is good value.

The *Maneroo Motel* (☎ (064) 58 3878) on Maybe St is fairly spartan, but it has recently been taken over by the couple who run the guesthouse, so it will probably improve. Single/double rooms go for $40/48.

Places to Eat

Cafes and takeaways along Maybe St include the *Top Cafe*, open until at least 9 pm, and *Magic Munchies*. The pubs offer inexpensive counter meals, from $4 at the Globe. The big *Ex-Servicemens Club*, in an old building on the corner of Maybe and Caveat Sts, has Chinese meals from Tuesday to Sunday. The *Mail Coach Inn* has good lunches and dinners every day except Sunday, with main courses for about $14.

Getting There & Away

Bus Countrylink runs to Cooma, where you can connect with a bus to Canberra. V/Line stops here on the run between Cooma and Melbourne.

Car & Motorbike The Monaro Highway runs north to Cooma and south to the Victorian Border, where it becomes the Cann Valley Highway and meets the Princes Highway at Cann River. The road running south-west from Bombala through the hamlet of Delegate crosses the border and becomes the Bonang Highway, running through Bonang and meeting the Princes Highway at Orbost.

A road runs east from Bombala to the Princes Highway near Merimbula, and a road off the Monaro Highway south of Bombala runs east past national parks to the Princes Highway near Eden.

NUNGATTA NATIONAL PARK

The Monaro/Cann River Highway runs down the western side of Nungatta National Park (6100 hectares) just north of the state border, but there is no vehicle access and you have to ford the Genoa River to get into the park. There's good walking in the Genoa River Gorge, but you should notify the National Parks office in Eden (☎ (064) 96 1434) before setting out. Take your own water.

JINDABYNE

Jindabyne (population 1800) is the closest town to the major ski-resorts and it's a sizeable place, swelling to enormous when those scores of apartments and motels fill up in winter – the town can sleep more than 12,000 visitors!

Orientation & Information

As with so many other towns on the Monaro, today's Jindabyne is a new incarnation of an original settlement which is now below the surface of a hydro-electric dam, in this case Lake Jindabyne.

The Snowy River Information Centre (☎ (064) 56 2444) is in Petamin Plaza, on the main road in from Cooma, on the left as the road begins its sweeping left-hand turn around the lake. Nugget's Crossing, on your left after the road curves around from the information centre, is a handy shopping centre, with a supermarket, banks and places to eat. The shopping centre is named after a local pioneer and horseman, and on the walls there are some old pieces of horse tack which are worth a look.

Summer Activities

Strangely, people come to this town at the foot of Australia's largest ski-fields to sail, on Lake Jindabyne. Alpine Sailing at the Snowline Caravan Park (☎ (064) 56 7195) rents Hobie cats, sailboards and canoes. Also at Snowline you can book trout-fishing tuition and tours (from $60). You can go for a cruise on the lake on MV *Kalinga*; book at the information centre.

Ski 'n' Save (☎ (064) 56 2687), next to the post office in the town centre, rents mountain bikes for $35 a day. They're also available from Paddy Pallin at the Thredbo turn-off, and from Wilderness Sports in the Nugget's Crossing centre.

Snowy Mountain Trail Rides (book through Paddy Pallin) has half-day horse-rides, and there's riding at Eagles Range (see Places to Stay). Snowy River Trail Rides (☎ (064) 56 2922) is another outfit.

Paddy Pallin (☎ (064) 56 2922) out at the Thredbo turn-off rents tents and other walking equipment. A sleeping bag costs about $15 for one day's hire (lower rates for longer hires). They also package two- and four-day walks. Wilderness Sports (☎ (064) 56 2966) in Nugget's Crossing also has organised walks for about $220 per person for a two-day walk and $400 for a four-day. Groups of four or more can arrange their own departure date, otherwise they are pre-determined. They also have canoeing and kayaking.

Places to Stay

Winter sees a huge influx of visitors to Jindabyne. Prices soar, overnight accommodation all but disappears and many places book out months ahead. If you're coming to ski, plan well ahead and check out the various packages offered by the resorts and lodges. Travel agents throughout Australia have information on these, and they can be good value. If you can get a group of at least four people together (six is best), costs come down to a more realistic level.

Overnight Accommodation *Lake Jinda-byne Caravan Park* (☎ (064) 56 2249) is in town by the lake. Sites cost $12 and on-site vans cost from $35 (two-berth) to $75 (eight-berth) in winter, from $30 to $50 at other times. In winter only there are basic rooms for $30 a double plus $5 for each extra person up to six.

Snowline Caravan Park (☎ (064) 52 2099) is better equipped, with a restaurant, a heated amenities block (with games room and lounge, even a masseuse) and a bar. You can hire boats and fishing tackle. Tent sites cost about $12 plus $3 per person and cabins cost from $35 a double plus $3 per extra person. Prices rise in winter. Snowline is east of town, at the intersection of the Alpine Way and the Kosciusko road. *Pat's Patch* caravan park (☎ (064) 56 2354) is out of town on the road to Dalgety.

There's a fair range of motel-style places, some of them converting to long-term accommodation in winter. *Aspen Chalet* (☎ (064) 56 2372) at 1 Kosciusko Rd has doubles from $50 in summer and $130 in the peak season, which is pretty cheap for this town. *Lakeview Plaza Lodge* (☎ (064) 56 2134) on Snowy River Ave (behind Nugget's Crossing) charges $50 a double in summer and up to $160 in winter. A couple of guest-houses with moderate summer prices are *Sonnblick Lodge* (☎ (064) 56 2472) at 49 Gippsland St and the *Ski Inn* (☎ (064) 56 2918) at 9 Nettin Circuit. The *Lake Jin-dabyne Hotel/Motel* (☎ (064) 56 2203), a big place by the lake in the centre of town, has conference facilities and a gym. Singles/doubles can cost as little as $45/70 in summer but rocket up to $170/210 in winter.

Flats, Apartments & Lodges There are many, many places offering accommodation to skiers, but they can fill up. If possible you should book months in advance (some places don't refund your hefty deposit if you give less than 60 days notice of cancellation). There are many letting agents, some of which have glossy brochures showing the properties on their books, including Jindabyne Real Estate (☎ (064) 56 2216; 1800 020 657 toll-free).

There can be as many as five pricing

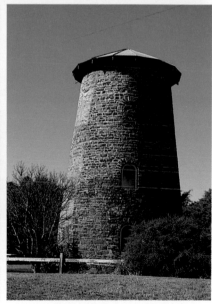

Top: Cloudy day on the Alpine Way, south-east (JM)
Bottom Left: Misty morning at Cooma courthouse, south-east (JM)
Bottom Right: Old windmill, Nimmitabel, south-east (JM)

Top: Th' Ettamogah Pub, north of Albury, south-east (JM)
Bottom Left: Pooh's Cave, Braidwood to Bateman's Bay road, south-east (JM)
Bottom Right: 'Moozeum', Lightning Ridge, north-west (JM)

seasons to deal with: low winter (late May to early July and mid-September to mid-October), high winter (early July to early September), shoulder (early to mid September), low summer (mid-September to mid-December and early February to late May) and high summer (mid-December to early February, plus Easter and the April school holidays). Very approximately, the cheapest fully-equipped apartments sleeping six cost from about $300 a week in the low summer season to $900 a week in the high winter season. You can pay a hell of a lot more.

Farmstay *Eagles Range* (☎ (064) 56 2728), 12 km south-east of Jindabyne off the road to Dalgety, has purpose-built accommodation from about $40/70 in summer and various packages in winter.

Places to Eat
There are several cafes and takeaway places on Petamin Plaza, but the best place to read through the brochures you've just picked up from the information centre is *Walita's Coffee Shop*, which has good coffee and a range of cakes and pastries.

In Nugget's Crossing there are a couple of Italian places, *Angie's* and *Bacco's*. The *Lake Jindabyne Hotel* has a Thai restaurant and several of the lodges have restaurants, including the *Mineshaft Restaurant* at the Lakeview Plaza.

Getting There & Away
Air Cooma is currently the nearest airport for passenger flights, but Snowy Mountains Airlines, a local charter company, might soon offer passenger flights into Jindabyne. See Snowy River Travel (☎ (064) 56 2184) on Snowy River Ave, behind Nugget's Crossing.

Car & Motorbike Just west of Jindabyne is an intersection where you can head south on the Alpine Way to Bullocks Flat, Thredbo and, eventually, Khancoban. The right-hand road is Kosciusko Rd which runs to Sawpit

Creek (the visitor centre for Kosciusko National Park) and on to Perisher and Charlotte Pass. You have to carry chains if you're venturing into the ski-fields in winter – there's a big fine if you don't.

The Barry Way (unsealed and unsuitable for caravans) runs south into Victoria, and other roads run north-east to Berridale and Cooma, and south-east to Dalgety and the Monaro Highway near Bombala.

Bus Snowy River Travel (☎ (064) 56 2184) on Snowy River Ave, behind Nugget's Crossing, handles bus bookings.

Greyhound Pioneer Australia runs from Sydney ($45) and Canberra ($27) to Jindabyne and the ski-fields, as well as shuttle services from Jindabyne to the resorts in winter. It's about 7½ hours from Sydney to Jindabyne and under three hours from Canberra.

To the Ski-Fields The Skitube terminal at Bullock Flat is less than half an hour from Jindabyne by car.

Greyhound Pioneer Australia's shuttle service operates in winter only and makes about six runs a day to/from the Crackenback Resort, Bullocks Flat and Thredbo, and at least three runs a day to/from Sawpit Creek, Smiggin Holes and Perisher. It costs $11 one way, $18 return (including the National Parks entry fee) from Jindabyne to Smiggin Holes, Perisher or Thredbo, and $6 one-way or $11 return to Bullocks Flat. The trip to Perisher takes 45 minutes, and to Thredbo it's about an hour.

The Snowy Mountains Taxi Service (☎ (064) 56 2644) will drive up to five people to the ski-fields from Jindabyne. The one-way fare to Thredbo or Perisher is $50 and to Bullocks Flat (the Skitube terminal) it's $30. You can buy a return ticket for $115 which includes a week's car-parking in Jindabyne. These prices don't include the National Parks entry fee. Taxis run all night on Fridays in the ski season, when you're advised to book ahead.

AROUND JINDABYNE
Berridale

You'll know you're approaching the ski-fields when you get to Berridale (population 400), north-east of Jindabyne. It's a small village with a lot of accommodation and ski-hire places. In the off-season the accommodation can be great value, but you'd be advised to book in winter as they get a lot of coach tours.

The Snowy River Winery (☎ (064) 56 5041) is south of Berridale, off the road to Dalgety. You can visit between 10 am and 5 pm daily. There's a restaurant here.

Places to Stay & Eat Motels include the *Snowy Mountains Coach & Motor Inn* (☎ (064) 56 3283), which is a quiet place charging $30/50 from October to May, becoming lively in winter with a disco and games room. Winter prices are triple the summer rates. All year round there's a heated indoor pool.

The motels have dining rooms, and the cosy *Old Berridale Inn* has counter meals. On the main street, *Poplars* restaurant has meals and reasonable pizzas; next door is the *Dragon Gate* Chinese restaurant.

Getting There & Away Greyhound Pioneer Australia services on the run between Sydney/Canberra and Thredbo stop here, so it's a feasible base for skiing if you don't have transport. Berridale to Sydney costs $41 and takes seven hours; to Canberra it's $24 and takes two hours. The half-hour trip to Jindabyne costs $7; to Thredbo it's $23.

Dalgety

Dalgety is a hamlet practically in the shadow of Mt Kosciusko, but it's definitely a rural centre rather than a ski-resort town. A few km west of Dalgety is the **Ag Barn** (☎ (064) 56 5102), where you can see hour-long demonstrations of sheep and goat shearing, milking, etc. It's a working angora stud, but has moved into tourism in a big way. The demonstrations are held at 2 pm daily and cost $8 ($6 children).

South-east of Dalgety, the **Bungarby**

Berry Farm has teas and samplings of berry wine. You can pick your own berries.

KOSCIUSKO NATIONAL PARK

The state's largest national park (647,100 hectares) includes caves, glacial lakes, forest and all of the state's ski-resorts, as well as the highest mountain in Australia. Mt Kosciusko (pronounced 'kozzyosko' and named after a Polish hero of the American War of Independence) is 2228 metres high.

Most famous for its snow, the national park is also popular in summer when there are excellent bushwalks and marvellous alpine wildflowers. Outside the snow season you can drive to within eight km of the top of Mt Kosciusko, up the Kosciusko Rd from Jindabyne to Charlotte Pass.

Orientation & Information

Mt Kosciusko and the main ski resorts are in the south-central area of the park. From Jindabyne, Kosciusko Rd leads to the National Parks visitor centre (☎ (064) 56 2102) about 15 km north-west at Sawpit Creek, then on to the resorts of Smiggin Holes, Perisher Valley (33 km) and Charlotte Pass, with a turn-off before Perisher Valley to Guthega and Mt Blue Cow. The Alpine Way also runs from Jindabyne, to Bullocks Flat and Thredbo (35 km from Jindabyne) and on to Khancoban on the south-west side of the mountains.

The Mt Selwyn resort is in the north of the park, off the Snowy Mountains Highway west of Kiandra.

There's another National Parks visitor centre at the Yarrangobilly Caves (☎ (064) 54 9597) in the north of the park, and there are park-ranger stations at Perisher (☎ (064) 57 5214) and Thredbo (☎ (064) 57 6255).

Entry to the national park (and that includes all the ski resorts) costs $12 per car, *per day*. Motorbikes pay $3.50 and bus passengers $4 ($2 children; this is usually included in the bus fare). A car parked anywhere in the park without a permit is liable for a $75 fine. There are toll booths on the Alpine Way and the road up to Charlotte Pass and you can also buy permits at Sawpit Creek

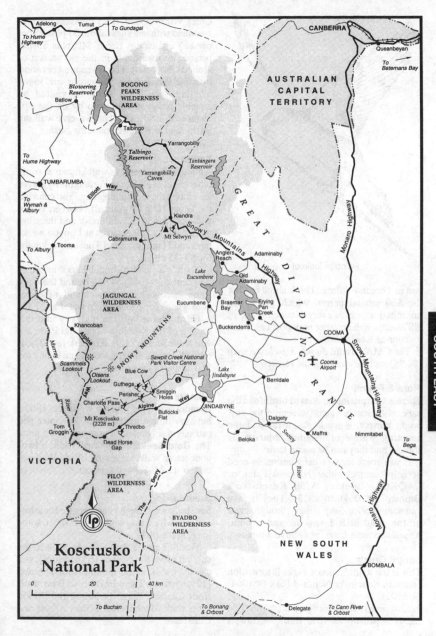

Adelong
Tumut
To Gundagai
CANBERRA
To Hume Highway
Queanbeyan
To Batemans Bay
Blowering Reservoir
BOGONG PEAKS WILDERNESS AREA
Batlow
AUSTRALIAN CAPITAL TERRITORY
Talbingo
Yarrangobilly
To Hume Highway
Talbingo Reservoir
Tantangara Reservoir
Yarrangobilly Caves
TUMBARUMBA
Elliott Way
To Wymah & Albury
Kiandra
G R E A T
To Albury
Tooma
Cabramurra
Mt Selwyn
Snowy Mountains Highway
Anglers Reach
Adaminaby
Lake Eucumbene
Old Adaminaby
D I V I D I N G
JAGUNGAL WILDERNESS AREA
Eucumbene
Braemar Bay
Frying Pan Creek
Khancoban
Buckenderra
COOMA
Alpine Way
Murray
SNOWY MOUNTAINS
Sawpit Creek National Park Visitor Centre
Lake Jindabyne
Cooma Airport
R A N G E
Scammels Lookout
Blue Cow
Berridale
Snowy Mountains Highway
Olsens Lookout
Guthega
River
Perisher
Smiggin Holes
Charlotte Pass
Alpine Way
Bullocks Flat
JINDABYNE
Tom Groggin
Mt Kosciusko (2228 m)
Thredbo
Dalgety
Beloka
Snowy
Maffra
Nimmitabel
To Bega
Dead Horse Gap
River
VICTORIA
PILOT WILDERNESS AREA
The Barry Way
Monaro Highway
Kosciusko National Park
BYADBO WILDERNESS AREA
NEW SOUTH WALES
BOMBALA
0   20   40 km
To Buchan
To Bonang & Orbost
To Cann River & Orbost
Delegate

Rainbow lorikeet

and in Thredbo Village. Think about buying the $60 annual permit which gives you unlimited access to every National Park in NSW, although no other park costs as much to enter as Kosciusko.

The CMA's useful *Snowy Kosciusko* map ($4.95) includes maps of the resorts.

Flora & Fauna
There's a surprising amount of birdlife in the park, with stately eagles sweeping the sky, bright parrots, noisy kookaburras and the haunting warble of magpies. Marsupials abound and they can be pretty tame.

If you come across a baby animal in need of help, contact either National Parks or LAOKO – Looking After Kosciusko's Orphans (☎ (064) 56 1313). They'll give you some advice. Surprisingly, though, most of the road-kills I saw in and around Kosciusko were foxes, not native animals.

Sawpit Creek
This is the main National Parks information centre in Kosciusko National Park (☎ (064) 56 2102).

Kosciusko Mountain Retreat (☎ (064) 56 2224) is just up the road from the Sawpit Creek visitor centre. It's a pleasant place in bushland with tent sites (about $7 plus $5 per person) and cabins (from $40 plus $5 per person, no overnights in the ski season or around Christmas). The lawns are kept short by some very friendly kangaroos, and in the evenings you'll probably be visited by amiable possums who drop by on the off-chance of a bit of tucker. Several walking tracks lead into the surrounding bush.

Yarrangobilly Caves
Although they aren't as well known as some other caves in NSW, the Yarrangobilly Caves are among the most interesting. You can visit the Glory Hole by yourself between 10 am and 4 pm for $4 ($2 children), and there are guided tours of other caves at 1 pm on weekdays and 11 am, 1 pm and 3 pm on weekends, for $8 ($5 children).

There's a good National Parks information centre (☎ (064) 54 9597), and there are some short walks in the area and a thermal pool where you can swim in water at 27°C.

Having turned off the highway into this section of the Kosciusko National Park, are you liable for the $12-a-day park fee? Theoretically yes – another good reason to buy the $60 all-parks pass.

Kiandra
Kiandra was a gold-rush town in the 1860s, but very little remains today. In winter you can pay the National Parks entry fee here. The **Gold Seekers Walking Track**, a two-hour return walk, leaves the Elliott Way just east of the Mt Selwyn turn-off.

Bushwalking
See the Sawpit Creek visitor centre for information on the many walks, some short, some long, in the park.

From Charlotte Pass you can walk to the summit of Mt Kosciusko (16 km return); you can also walk to the summit from Thredbo (12 km return). There are other walking trails from Charlotte Pass, including the 20-km lakes walk which includes Blue, Albina and Club lakes.

Skiing & Resorts

The first people to ski in Australia were the fur hunters of Tasmania in the 1830s, using three-foot boards. Norwegians at the Kiandra goldfields introduced skiing in the 1860s, and the world's first ski races were held there. The skis in those days were home-made, crude objects; the method of braking was a pole held between the two skis. Early this century the development of the sport began, with lodges like the one at Charlotte Pass and the importing of European skis.

Snow skiing in Australia can be a marginal activity. The season is short (July, August and early September is really all there is) and good snow is by no means a safe bet, although the increased use of snow-making machines is making it more so. Nor are the mountains ideal for downhill skiing – their gently rounded shapes mean that most long runs are relatively easy and the harder runs tend to be short and sharp. Worse, the short seasons mean the operators have to get their returns quickly, so costs can be high.

Having told you the bad, here's the good: when the snow's there and the sun's shining, the skiing can be just fine. You will find all the fun (not to mention heart-in-mouth fear) you could ask for.

Further, the open slopes are a ski-tourer's paradise – nordic (cross-country or langlauf) skiing is becoming increasingly popular and most resorts now offer lessons and hire equipment. The national park includes some of the most famous trails – Kiandra to Kosciusko, the Grey Mare Range, Thredbo or Charlotte Pass to Kosciusko's summit and the Jagungal wilderness. The possibilities for nordic touring are endless, and often old cattle-herders' huts are the only form of accommodation apart from your own tent.

In addition to touring, there is ample scope for cross-country racing (classic or skating) in the Perisher Valley. On the steep slopes of the Main Range near Twynam and Carruthers the cross-country downhill (XCD) fanatics get their adrenalin rushes. In winter, the cliffs near Blue Lake become a practice ground for alpine climbers.

Lift charges vary – see the following infor-mation on the various resorts. Group lessons cost from $25 or can be included in a package with lift tickets from about $50 a day, much less per day for five days. Boots, skis and stocks can be hired for around $30 a day, less for longer and less off the mountain. It's a trade-off whether to hire in the city and risk adjustment problems or at the resort and possibly pay more. There are hire places in towns close to the resorts and many garages hire ski equipment as well as chains. Snow chains must be carried in the mountains during winter even if there is no snow – there are heavy penalties if you haven't got them.

Australian ski resorts are short of the frenetic nightlife of many European resorts, but compensate with lots of partying between the lodges. Nor is there a great variety of alternative activities apart from toboggan runs. Weekends are crowded because the resorts are so convenient, particularly to Canberra.

For snow and road reports ring the various visitor centres. In Sydney there's a recorded service (☎ 11 539). Thredbo has its own number (☎ 0055 34320).

Bullocks Flat

Bullocks Flat, on the Alpine Way between Jindabyne and Thredbo, is the site of the Skitube terminal.

Near Bullocks Flat there's a pretty but basic free campsite near the Skitube, called *Thredbo Diggings*. Not far away but at the other end of the price-scale is *Lake Crackenback Resort* (☎ (064) 56 2960), a superb new complex below the main snowline but within walking distance of the Bullocks Flat Skitube terminal. Drop in for a look at the architecture even if you don't plan to stay. There are four pricing seasons, the highest being from early July to early September and the lowest the months either side of this. Costs range from about $250 a double to $400 a double, with lower rates for longer stays or with up to four people sharing a room. There are also five-day winter packages which include accommodation and some meals and lift tickets. In summer activities are run from here, including guided canoe and mountain-bike trips.

Thredbo (1370 metres) Thredbo has the longest runs (the longest is over three km through 670 metres of vertical drop) and the best and most expensive skiing in Australia. A day ticket costs $52, a five-day pass $240 and a five-day lift and lesson package costs $295. In summer Thredbo is still a good place to visit, unlike the other resorts which become ghost towns. It's a popular bushwalking centre with all sorts of excellent and scenic tracks.

Although Thredbo Village covers only a small area, it's tightly packed with lodges and small streets wind around the steep valley side. There are two turn-offs for Thredbo from the Alpine Way, one directing you to the lodges and the other to the commercial centre. Both will get you to the village but if you take the lodges turn-off it would be a good idea to know where you're going. Pick up a map of the village at the Thredbo Centre in Jindabyne's Nuggets Crossing shopping-centre before you arrive. If you've arrived by bus, there's a map in the bus-shelter showing the location of the lodges, and there's an information centre in the Valley Terminal – walk there on the wooden footbridge near the bus shelter.

There are 15 bars and 20 restaurants in Thredbo. Perhaps the most interesting place to eat is the *Eagles Nest Restaurant* on top of Mt Crackenback and accessible by ski-lift.

The chairlift to the top of Mt Crackenback runs right through the summer ($11 one-way, $5 children; $13 return, $7 children). From the top of the chairlift it's a two-km walk or cross-country ski to a good lookout point over Mt Kosciusko, or seven km to the top of the mountain itself. Other walks, longer and shorter, leave from the top of the lift. Maps are available at the Sports Centre. Remember to carry adequate clothing and be prepared for all conditions, even in summer.

The Sports Centre at the Valley Terminal hires mountain bikes for $20 a half-day and $30 a day. You'll have to have a credit card to hire one, as they take an imprint as a deposit.

The Thredbo Jazz Festival is held towards the end of April.

Places to Stay Accommodation at Thredbo is in commercial lodges or privately-owned apartments, with some private club lodges.

The *YHA Thredbo Lodge* (☎ (064) 57 6376) costs just $13 a night ($16 per person twin-share) outside the ski season and $30 a night ($39 Saturday night) and $175 a week in the ski season. This is astounding value, and not surprisingly there's stiff competition for beds in winter. A ballot is held for winter places and you have to enter by April. Most people get the nights they want and even if you aren't in the ballot it's worth checking to see if there are cancellations. In June and the end of September, when snow might be scanty, there is less pressure on places at the lodge. There's plenty of room in the off-season. The YHA Travel Centre in Sydney (☎ (02) 261 1111) is the best place to start making enquiries about Thredbo Lodge.

Several Thredbo lodges, such as the *Snow Goose* (☎ (064) 57 6222) and the *House of Ullr* (☎ (064) 57 6210), have very good deals outside the ski season, from around $14 sharing in a twin room and $25 a double.

Perisher Valley & Smiggin Holes (1680 metres) Perisher Valley has a good selection of intermediate runs. Smiggin Holes is just down the road from Perisher and is run by the same management, so a combined ski/tow ticket is available. A shuttle bus runs between the two resorts and they are also joined by a lift system so it is possible to ski from one resort to the other. Together they have over 100 km of runs and 30 lifts. A day ticket costs $52, a five-day pass costs $218, and a five-day lesson-and-lift package costs $276 ($218 for beginners). The Smiggin Holes ski school (☎ (064) 57 5303) has information. Peak winter rates at *The Lodge* (☎ (064) 57 5012) at Smiggin Holes are around $130/160 including ski hire, dinner and light breakfast.

Mt Blue Cow (1640 metres) The Mt Blue Cow resort (☎ (064) 56 2890), between Perisher Valley and Guthega in the Perisher Range, has beginners' to intermediate skiing.

Mt Blue Cow is a day resort (no accommodation) accessible by the Skitube, but there are accommodation packages which include shuttles and Skitube tickets (☎ 1800 251 354 toll-free, (02) 580 6555 in Sydney). Combined lift and Skitube tickets cost $50 ($25 children), less for more than one day; Skitube, lifts and lessons cost $69 ($49 children), or $55 for beginners ($42 children). There are various deals available if you take more days.

Guthega (1630 metres) This is mainly a day resort, best suited to intermediate and, to a lesser extent, beginner skiers. *Guthega Lodge* (☎ (064) 57 5383) is the only commercial accommodation. Guthega is smaller and less crowded than other places. From here, cross-country skiers head out for the Main Range or Rolling Ground.

Charlotte Pass (1780 metres) At the base of Mt Kosciusko, this is the highest and one of the oldest and most isolated resorts in Australia. In winter you have to snowcat the last eight km from Perisher Valley (about $25, although this is often included in the price of a package). Five lifts service rather short but uncrowded runs, and this is good ski-touring country.

There are a number of lodges, including *Kosciusko Chalet* (☎ (064) 57 5245; 1800 026 369 toll-free), a grand old place dating from the 1930s. In summer, packages including dinner, bed & breakfast cost $110/160 with a $10 surcharge on Saturday night. Other lodges at Charlotte Pass include *Stillwell Lodge* (☎ (064) 57 5073) which is also open in summer.

Mt Selwyn (1492 metres) This is the only ski resort in the northern end of the national park, halfway between Tumut and Cooma. It has 13 lifts and is ideal for beginners. One-day lift tickets are $38 ($20 children), and packages including five days plus lessons are $220 ($140 children). It's another day resort – most accommodation is in the Adaminaby

area. The booking centre (☎ 1800 020 777 toll-free) books accommodation, some of which is relatively cheap – self-catering units from $40 a double, plus $12 for each extra adult, and caravan-park units sleeping four from $50. Adaminaby Bus Service (☎ (064) 54 2318) runs between Cooma and Mt Selwyn.

To commemorate the early skiers on the Kiandra goldfields, Mt Selwyn hosts the Kiandra Goldrush in July, a race in period costume and equipment.

Places to Stay

Bush camping is permitted in most of the national park, but not in ecologically fragile areas. Some picnic areas, where you can camp, have fireplaces and pit toilets. The only formal camping area is near Sawpit Creek. Many of the resorts have good deals on accommodation in summer.

Winter Accommodation In winter, the cheapest (and by far the most fun) way to get out on the slopes is to gather a bunch of friends and rent an apartment. If your budget is tight you might find yourself staying in Jindabyne or further afield, although there's a YHA hostel at Thredbo. Bring as much food and drink as you can, as supplies in the resorts are expensive.

For accommodation during the ski season you're advised to begin making enquiries as early as February. Costs vary enormously but can be within the bounds of reason. As very rough examples, a two-bedroom apartment in Thredbo costs from about $2500 for a week during the peak ski season (roughly early July to early September) and a double room in a lodge costs at least $1000, including some meals. There are midweek and weekend deals, but it's unlikely that you'll find overnight accommodation on the mountain in season.

If you have a group of at least four people and you investigate the various packages on offer there's a good chance that you'll pay considerably less. Many agents (including most travel agents) book accommodation and packages on the ski-fields. Specialists include the Jindabyne Reservation Centre (☎ 1800 026 356 toll-free), the Perisher Reservation Centre (☎ 1800 020 700 toll-free), Thredbo Accommodation Services (☎ (064) 57 6387, 1800 801 982 toll free) and the Thredbo Resort Centre (☎ (064) 57 6360, (02) 438 3122 in Sydney). Travel agents, including the NSW Travel Centres in Sydney (☎ (02) 231 4444) and other capital cities, also make bookings.

See the Thredbo section for more information on winter accommodation.

Getting There & Around

Bus Greyhound Pioneer Australia (☎ 13 2323) is the main carrier in this area. There are plenty of services from Sydney and Canberra to Cooma and Jindabyne, from where shuttles run to the resorts in winter. It costs $11 ($18 return) from Jindabyne to Smiggin Holes, Perisher (45 minutes) or Thredbo (one hour). In summer buses run to Thredbo ($32 from Canberra), but not always daily.

Car & Motorbike In winter you can normally drive as far as Perisher Valley, but snow chains must be carried and fitted where directed. There are sometimes parking restrictions in the park in winter. The simplest and safest way to get to Perisher and Smiggin Holes in winter is to take the Skitube, a tunnel railway up to Perisher Valley and Blue Cow from below the snowline at Bullocks Flat on the Alpine Way. A return trip from Bullocks Flat to either Blue Cow or Perisher costs $16, and there are deals on combined Skitube and lift tickets. You can hire skis and equipment at Bullocks Flat, and luggage lockers and overnight parking are available. The Skitube runs to a reduced timetable in summer.

See the West of the Snowies section for western routes into the national park.

Taxi The Snowy Mountains Taxi Service (☎ (064) 56 2644) will drive up to five people to the ski-fields from Jindabyne. See the Jindabyne section for more information.

West of the Snowies

The western slopes of the Snowy Mountains are steeper than those on the east, and the area is more intensively farmed, although there's still plenty of bush and, south of Khancoban on the Alpine Way, some of the most spectacular scenery in the whole region. The farms and small towns in the area blaze with colour in the autumn when poplars and fruit trees are preparing to shed their leaves. This is a rural area, totally different in atmosphere from the resort-minded Monaro.

Getting There & Around

Bus A Countrylink bus runs from Cootamundra and Gundagai to Tumut, Adelong, Batlow and Tumbarumba.

Car & Motorbike There are several approaches to the Snowies from the west, all accessible from the Hume Highway. The main route, the Snowy Mountains Highway, leaves the Hume about 30 km south of Gundagai and takes you first to Tumut. Smaller roads also lead to Tumut from the Hume Highway near Gundagai.

From Albury you can travel on Victoria's Murray Valley Highway to Corryong, then head across the river to Khancoban for the Alpine Way or north to other roads crossing the mountains. The Murray Valley Highway exit from the Hume Highway is about 10 km south of Albury.

Another road in Victoria parallels the Murray Valley Highway, but follows closely the south bank of the Murray. This road leaves the Hume Highway just north of Albury and crosses back into Victoria at the big Hume Weir. This route is longer but perhaps more interesting than the Murray Valley Highway, and offers a choice of places to cross the Murray. You can drive all the way around to Towong, the crossing near Corryong and Khancoban, or cross near Jingellic and take the partly unsealed road to Tumbarumba, or cross on the vehicle ferry near Wymah and take the dirt road following the north bank of the Murray to Jingellic. The Wymah ferry runs on demand between 6 am and 9 pm from September to April and between 7 am and 8 pm from May to August, with breaks for the crew's breakfast (7.15 to 8 am), lunch (11.45 am to 1 pm) and dinner (5.15 to 6.30 pm).

In Victoria, not far from Wymah, there's a good place to stay, the *Herb & Horse* (☎ (060) 72 9553), which offers B&B from $40 per person and both horseriding and bushwalking. To get here from Wymah, follow the road south-east, ignore the Granya/Tallangatta turn-off and keep going for five km. It's the white house on the hill. You can get here more simply from Albury via the Bethanga Bridge on the Hume Weir.

The dirt road along the north bank of the Murray, narrow and winding but in good condition, is also accessible from the Hume Highway north of Albury, at Bowna (a boomerang factory and not much else) and Woomargama.

From Holbrook on the Hume Highway, a sealed road runs all the way to Jingellic, and other sealed roads run from the Hume to Tumbarumba.

The road running down the western side of the range, from Tumut to Khancoban and the Alpine Way, passes through Batlow and Tumbarumba. It's a hilly, scenic drive. From Tumbarumba you can cross the mountains on the Elliott Way, to Mt Selwyn and the Snowy Mountains Highway at Kiandra. This crossing is also accessible via several roads near Towong if you're coming from Corryong. It sometimes closes in winter.

There's another crossing to Mt Selwyn and Kiandra just north of Khancoban, but snow ploughs don't clear sections of it in winter, and you're advised to leave the area as soon as snow begins to fall. Caravans can't use this road.

TUMUT

A mountain town in the pretty Tumut Valley, Tumut (population 6300) is the closest centre to the northern end of Kosciusko National Park and there is other mountainous country north-east of Tumut. In the area there are many pine plantations (second only to the great swathe of pines in South Australia's south-east) and orchards, mainly growing apples.

History
The explorers Hume and Hovell were the first Europeans to see the Tumut Valley. Farmers and graziers followed, but development of the town was slow. One of the area's most famous early residents was author Miles Franklin (her most famous book is *My Brilliant Career*), who was born at Talbingo.

Information
The information centre (☎ (069) 47 1849) on Fitzroy St is open daily from 9 am to 5 pm.

Things to See
The **Rotary Lookout**, at the end of Wynyard St, gives a good view of the town and the Tumut Valley.

The **Whip Works** is a saddlery, selling other local crafts as well, in the old butter factory on the Adelong road (the Snowy Mountains Highway), just before the dilapidated old railway station. Across the road from the butter factory is the **broom factory**, where brooms are still made from millet. You can see more local craft at the **Swaledale Gallery**, near the roundabout at the corner of Capper and Wynyard Sts. The rather small **museum** is at the corner of Capper and Merivale Sts and is open on Wednesday, Saturday and school holidays from 2 to 4 pm. There is a room devoted to Miles Franklin.

Activities
Adventure Sports (☎ (069) 47 2478, 1800 020 631 toll-free) is in a building just behind the old butter factory on the Adelong road. This is a friendly and knowledgeable outfit which can organise just about any outdoor activity – canoeing, rafting, abseiling, mountain biking, bushwalking – for groups or individuals. They also hire skis in winter.

You can take a short flight over the Tumut Valley for just $25 per person (minimum two people). Contact the information centre, or phone the airport (☎ (069) 47 1148).

Festivals & Events

The Tumut Agricultural Show and rodeo is held in early March, and the Festival of the Falling Leaf is held in late April and early May.

Places to Stay

There are a couple of caravan parks in the vicinity, the closest to town being the *Riverglade Caravan Park* (☎ (069) 47 2528) on the highway a few blocks from the centre. It's a shady place on the Tumut River. Sites cost $11, on-site vans about $30 and cabins $40. You'll need to book ahead at Christmas and Easter.

The *Oriental Hotel* (☎ (069) 47 1174) on the corner of Fitzroy and Wynyard Sts has rooms for $20/30. It's a nice old pub and the rooms look onto that big balcony, but you might want to see if you prefer the rooms across the street at the *Woolpack Hotel* (☎ (069) 47 1027).

The *Royal Hotel* (☎ (069) 47 1129) and the *Commercial Hotel* (☎ (069) 47 1040) have motel-style units, and there are several motels including the *Creel* (☎ (069) 47 2311) on Fitzroy St and the *Ashton* (☎ (069) 47 1999) on Wynyard St.

Places to Eat

There are several bakeries and cake shops. The one opposite the RSL Club (which defiantly flies the Union Jack) on Russell St has tables on the footpath. For coffee and snacks, *Chit Chat* in the Wynyard Centre on Wynyard St is open during the day. The pubs have counter meals, from $6 at the *Royal Hotel* on Wynyard St. Behind the Royal, off Fuller St, the *Tirami Su* has Italian food, pricey at about $11 for a main-course pasta.

There are several Chinese places, including the BYO *Happy Billy's* on Fitzroy St. It's open daily for lunch and dinner and the food is MSG-free.

In The Hub, a small complex on Wynyard St near the corner of Fitzroy St, *Panache* is

---

PLACES TO STAY

4	Riverglade Caravan Park
6	Creel Motel
7	Oriental Hotel
9	Woolpack Hotel
13	Commercial Hotel/Motel
15	Ashton Motel
16	Tumut Hotel
17	Royal Hotel/Motel

PLACES TO EAT

5	Brooklyn on Fitzroy
8	Happy Billy's
18	RSL Club

OTHER

1	Railway Station
2	Old Butter Factory (Whip Works)
3	Broom Factory
10	The Hub
11	Supermarket
12	Museum
14	Wynyard Centre
19	Swimming Pool
20	Information Centre
21	Rotary Lookout
22	Hospital

---

a pleasant licensed restaurant and cocktail bar with main courses around $14.

Bernie's Family Restaurant is upstairs on Wynyard St near the Wynyard Centre. It's fully licensed and doesn't feel especially 'family'. A steak will set you back about $11.

The best restaurant in town is *Brooklyn on Fitzroy* at 10 Fitzroy St, in an impressive renovated house. It's open for dinner only, from Tuesday to Saturday.

The *Tuckertorium*, eight km from town on the road to Adelong and Wagga Wagga, serves locally-grown trout.

Getting There & Away

Bus Countrylink buses stop outside the National Bank on the corner of Russell and Wynyard Sts. Harvey World Travel (☎ (069) 47 3055) in The Hub centre on Wynyard St sells tickets.

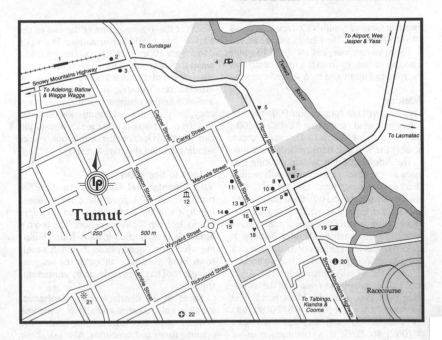

Tumut

Car & Motorbike

The Snowy Mountains Highway runs north-west to the Hume Highway and south-east through Kosciusko National Park to Adaminaby and Cooma. Another smaller road runs to the Hume near Gundagai. From the Snowy Mountains Highway at Adelong, 22 km west of Tumut, you can drive south to Batlow, Tumbarumba and Khancoban.

The interesting road from Tumut north to Wee Jasper, from where you can get to Yass, is reasonable but in wet weather you might need 4WD.

AROUND TUMUT

The Thomas Boyd trackhead of the **Hume & Hovell Walking Track** is 23 km from Tumut, and there are camping facilities there. The Tumut information centre sells route maps. On the way here, 19 km from Tumut on the Lacmalac road, you could catch your dinner at the **Triton Trout Farm**. It's open daily except Tuesday. You can hire fishing tackle here for $2, and you pay by the kg for the fish that you catch.

Lake Blowering is a large dam, nearly 20 km long, and is part of the Snowy Mountains Hydro-Electric Scheme. There are walks along the forested shores and the lake is popular for watersports. The small town of **Talbingo** is nearby. The Tumut 3 Power Station near Talbingo has free tours between 10 am and 2.30 pm daily.

Batlow

Batlow (population 1200) clusters around one side of a bowl-shaped valley, in the middle of the apple orchards which are the town's main reason for existing. The orchards blossom in October and the harvest starts around mid-March. Picking work is usually available. There's a part-time CES office in Tumut (☎ (069) 47 2077) which can help with enquiries, or contact the Wagga Wagga CES (☎ (069) 38 3444).

Tourist information for the area can be

found at Granny Smith's Cottage tea-rooms (☎ (069) 49 1447), and buses stop nearby.

There's a *caravan park* (☎ (069) 49 1444) a couple of blocks from the town centre, on the road to Tumut and by a shaded creek.

Adelong

This neat village (population 900) was the centre of a gold rush in the 1850s and '60s, and several buildings in the main street, notably the Westpac Bank, reflect this status.

The **Adelong Falls**, within walking distance of the town centre, are worth seeing. Head up the main street, take the right turn towards Gundagai and take the turn-off to the falls on the right just after the stockyards. Much more interesting are the extensive remains of the ingenious **Reefer Battery**. It looks like the foundations of an ancient city and was entirely powered by waterwheels.

The *Golden Gully Caravan Park* (☎ (069) 46 2282) is across the river near the swimming pool (you can hire bikes here). The *Adelong Hotel* (☎ (069) 46 2009) has accommodation, and the *Old Pharmacy* (☎ (069) 46 2263) is a combination of an antique shop, tea-rooms and a guesthouse, charging $55 a single or double. The *Services & Citizens' Club* on the main street has a restaurant.

TUMBARUMBA

Tumbarumba (usually called just Tumba) is a large town for this part of the world (population 2000), and there are some nice old buildings, such as the courthouse and the council chambers opposite. The area was first settled by graziers who wintered their cattle here when the snows came to the high plains, and a small gold-rush in the 1860s boosted the population. Today, forestry is the major industry, along with orchards growing cool-climate fruits, as well as some vineyards. Sheep and cattle are farmed on the lower hills to the west.

Orientation & Information

The main street through town is Tumbarumba Pde, usually just called the Parade.

The Wool & Craft Centre (☎ (069) 48

4805) at the T-intersection at the end of the Parade has tourist information. It's open daily from 10 am to 4.30 pm. There's also a small museum here. The interesting antiques shop on the main street also has some tourist information. Topographic maps of the area are sold at the pharmacy and the newsagency, and the Forestry Commission office on Winton St has details of the area's forests and can give advice on the numerous tracks winding around the state forests.

Things to See & Do

The **Bicentennial Gardens** on Tumbarumba Creek is a good place for a picnic lunch; it's on the Khancoban road, a couple of blocks from the town centre. The town's **library** is here, housed in an A-frame building which was once a prison chapel. It's built from local materials, although the original shingle roof has been replaced by aluminium sheeting.

Some of the district's many **orchards**, growing nuts, cherries and apples, welcome visitors. Ask the information centre for opening times and directions. Also ask about the several small **wineries and vineyards**.

The Tumba rodeo is held in early January and the show is the fortnight before Easter. A polocrosse carnival takes place around April/May, and there's even a mountain bike festival in March.

Places to Stay & Eat

The small *Captain Cook Caravan Park* (☎ (069) 48 2097) is just off the Parade near the showground, and there are apparently trout in the stream running through it. Sites cost $6. Check in (you'll need a key for the showers and toilets) at the antiques shop in the main street. You can also camp at the small *Tumbarumba Motel* (☎ (069) 48 2494) on Albury St which has single/double rooms for $40/50.

The *Tumbarumba Hotel* (☎ (069) 48 2562) on the Parade charges $25/45, and the *Union Hotel* (☎ (069) 48 2013) also has rooms.

The pubs serve counter meals and the Tumbarumba also has a restaurant and sells

takeaway pizzas. There's also a coffee shop nearby. The golf club, on the northern edge of town, has a *Chinese restaurant*, and the *bowling club* on Winton St serves meals.

The antiques shop sells 'fruit leather'; parchment-like rolls of pressed dried fruit. It's good and chewy, a bit like beef jerky for fruitarians. A roll costs $3.50 and lasts a long time.

Getting There & Away
From Tumbarumba, roads run west to the Hume Highway, north to Tumut, east to Mt Selwyn and the Snowy Mountains Highway, and south to Khancoban and the Alpine Way, and to Corryong in Victoria.

The ski slopes at Mt Selwyn are about an hour away on the Elliott Way. You'll need chains in winter.

AROUND TUMBARUMBA
The **Pioneer Women's Hut** is in the **Glenroy Heritage Reserve**, eight km west of Tumbarumba on the road to Rosedale (known as the Wagga road). As well as craft and historical displays there's a tea-room. The reserve is open from 11 am to 4 pm on Wednesday and 10 am to 5 pm on weekends and holidays.

The Henry Angel trackhead of the **Hume & Hovell Walking Track** is about 10 km south of Tumbarumba on the Khancoban road. The information office in Tumba sells tracknotes. Another five km further on there's a turn-off for **Paddy's River Falls**, two km down a steep but sealed road. There are toilets, water, picnic tables and a walking trail to the base of the falls.

There are a couple of places near Tumbarumba that are popular for **fossicking** for gold and sapphires. The information centre has maps but you'll need to buy a fossicking licence from the courthouse or the sports shop on the Parade. Licences cost $2.50 or $5 for a family.

The hamlet of **Tooma**, 35 km south of Tumba on the Khancoban road, is in a pretty, cleared valley and has an old hotel, tearooms and a restaurant. The *Tooma Hotel*

(☎ (069) 48 4466) might again be offering accommodation.

Jingellic is a pretty hamlet with a store, a petrol station and a pub – and lots of big deciduous trees. This would be a pleasant place to break the journey into the Snowies. You can camp for no charge in the camping ground by the creek on the eastern edge of the town, next to the pub. It's basic but attractive.

Just across the border from Jingellic, Upper Murray Experience (☎ (060) 37 1226) runs canoe and mountain-bike tours. All equipment and accommodation are provided and you can paddle for up to four days ($600 for two people). A half-day paddle costs $30. You can rent one of their self-catering cottages without taking part in a tour. Prices start at $90 and you'll need to bring or hire ($7) linen. There are also cheaper units without cooking facilities (there are barbecues, and the pubs in nearby Jingellic and Walwa have meals) for about $55 a double, including linen. Rates drop with longer stays.

The road from Jingellic to Tumbarumba is not all sealed and is a little bumpy. Watch out for logging trucks.

KHANCOBAN
Khancoban (pronounced can-*co*-bn) is a small town (population 500) built by the Snowy Mountains Authority. Towns built by public authorities are often bureaucratic monstrosities, but Khancoban is a beautiful exception. With Kosciusko National Park beginning a couple of km away and good road connections to Victoria and Albury, it's an ideal base for exploring the Snowies and the upper Murray River. At an altitude of 300 metres, Khancoban's climate is relatively mild, but just 70 km on you're crossing the 1580-metre Dead Horse Gap.

There's a National Parks office (☎ (060) 76 9393) where you must buy your park visitor's permit ($12 per car per day or a $60 pass that gets you into every park in NSW for a year) if you're heading down the Alpine Way. There's a good range of information and publications available here. The Khan-

coban Roadhouse (☎ (060) 76 9400) has some tourist information.

Activities

Upper Murray White Water Rafting (☎ (060) 76 9566) has trips from near Tom Groggin Station, off the Alpine Way, to near Khancoban. See the Activities section at the start of this chapter.

Khancoban Trail Rides (☎ (060) 76 9566) offer horseborne adventures, only between October and April, from a half-day to a week.

The caravan park and the Alpine Inn hire boats and fishing tackle and the Alpine Hideaway hires canoes.

Mike Spry (☎ (060) 76 9496) runs fly-fishing tours and offers tuition.

Places to Stay & Eat

Murray Gates Caravan Park (☎ (060) 76 9488), by the Khancoban Dam, has tent sites for $9 and on-site vans from $20 for two people. *Khancoban Backpackers & Fisherman's Lodge* has share accommodation for $11 and single/double rooms for $15/22. Each extra person (up to six) costs $5. You need to supply your own bedding and cooking utensils. Book and check in at the nearby *Khancoban Alpine Inn* (☎ (060) 76 9471). The Inn is a pleasant hotel/motel with rooms from about $40, rising to about $75 during the ski season. Here there's the *Pickled Parrot Restaurant*, which is open for

breakfast, lunch and dinner every day. The *Country Club* has a Chinese restaurant.

The *Alpine Hideaway* (☎ (060) 76 9498) is across the valley from the town – the road crosses the dam's spillway. There are great views of the Snowies from here. This is a nice place, offering good accommodation in fully-equipped, self-catering lodges. There's also an excellent restaurant. There is a variety of packages, with overnight rates at about $55 per person or about $75 with all meals. A whole lodge, sleeping six, costs from around $150. Canoeing and mountain-biking is offered and many other activities can be arranged, ranging from fly-fishing to ultra-light flying. The Hideaway closes during June and July.

Just up the hill from the Hideaway is *Lyrebird Lodge* (☎ (060) 76 9566), a smaller place offering B&B for just $30/40 a single/double, and dinner, bed and breakfast for $40/60. This is a base for Khancoban Trail Rides which operates from Tom Groggin Station, and they can arrange other activities.

Getting There & Away

The Alpine Inn hires Mini Mokes for very reasonable rates, around $40 for the first day and $25 a day after that – Mokes are pretty cold to drive in the winter but fun in summer.

Over the border in Corryong, R S Wilkinson (☎ (060) 76 1418) runs both taxis and taxi-minibuses into Kosciusko National Park.

THE ALPINE WAY

This spectacular route runs through dense forest from Khancoban, around the bottom end of Kosciusko National Park to Thredbo Village and on to Jindabyne. Sections can be closed during winter, and caravans and trailers aren't permitted on the section between Tom Groggin and the Pilot Lookout at any time. There's no fuel available between Khancoban and Thredbo.

The **Murray 1 Power Station** (☎ (060) 76 9463), off the Alpine Way eight km south of Khancoban, has free daily tours at 11 am, noon, 1 and 2 pm. Even from the road above the power station you can hear the new-born

Sulphur-crested cockatoo

electricity sizzling through the wires at the speed of light.

Another seven km further south is **Scammel's Lookout**, offering superb views. There are toilets and picnic tables here. You can camp at **Geehi**, a National Parks rest area, and the facilities are currently being upgraded.

At **Tom Groggin**, home of the original Man From Snowy River, the road skirts the Murray River, good for a swim on a hot day. You can camp here and there's another site about 10 km further on. Also near Tom Groggin is *Tom Groggin Station* (☎ (060) 76 9455), from where there are two- to seven-day horserides and accommodation for about $40/55. After Tom Groggin there's an unsealed section as the road climbs 800 metres to the **Pilot Lookout** (1300 metres), with views across a wilderness area to the Pilot (1830 metres), the source of the Murray River. There's another climb to **Dead Horse Gap** (1580 metres), named after some brumbies which froze here, then a descent to Thredbo Village (1400 metres), the Skitube terminal at Bullocks Flat, and Jindabyne.

The Hume Highway

The Hume is the busiest road in Australia, running nearly 900 km from Sydney down to Melbourne, Australia's second-largest city. See the Around Sydney chapter for towns between Sydney and Goulburn.

From Sydney to beyond Goulburn the Hume is now a freeway, but it will be a long time before the whole road is upgraded. There are long stretches of narrow, two-lane road carrying a lot of traffic with tired drivers behind the wheel. Drive carefully!

The highway is named after Hamilton Hume, who followed roughly this route when he walked from Parramatta to Port Phillip, later the site of Melbourne, with William Hovell in 1824. Hume was a native-born Australian while Hovell was an upper-crust Englishman, and their association was not entirely happy. Their return journey became a race to be the first in Sydney with news of new lands. Despite chicanery on Hovell's part, they both arrived at the same time.

GOULBURN & AROUND

Goulburn is a big, old town (population 22,000) and makes a good break en route between Sydney and Melbourne.

History

John Oxley was the first European to visit the site of Goulburn, in 1820. The town developed to serve the grazing communities on the region's high pastures, and was proclaimed in 1833.

Orientation & Information

Goulburn is discovering that being bypassed by the Hume Highway doesn't mean the death-knell for retail activity, and the interesting old city centre is recovering from the traffic. The town's main shopping street is Auburn St.

The visitor centre (☎ (048) 21 5343) is on Montague St, off Auburn St and across from Belmore Park. Pick up a walking-tour map.

Things to See

The **museum** is housed in St Clair, an old house (1843) at 318 Sloane St. It's open daily. Of all the impressive country courthouses in NSW, Goulburn's **courthouse** (1887), on Montague St, must be the most imposing. The **old courthouse**, which did a lot of business in sentencing the bushrangers who plagued the highlands, is around the corner on Sloane St. Other interesting old buildings in the town centre include the **post office** (1881) on the corner of Auburn and Montague Sts, the **Catholic cathedral** (1880) on the corner of Bourke and Verner Sts and the **Anglican cathedral** nearby on the corner of Montague and Bourke Sts.

Goulburn is surrounded by sheep country and there's a three-storey-high **Big Merino**, on the corner of Cowper St (the old highway) and Mary St. It looks truly diabolical with its green eyes glowing at night. By day you can climb up inside and check out the view

through those eyes, passing through an interesting display on the Australian wool industry on the way up. A visit to the display is free – the big souvenir shop no doubt provides the profits.

The **Old Goulburn Brewery** (1836) is a large complex down on the riverflats, off Bungonia Rd. It's run by Father O'Hallouran. The brewery dates from 1836 and, as well as the brewery, you can see a cooper in action, the maltings, tobacco curing and a steam-powered flour mill. And, of course, you can try the ale. There is a restaurant (sometimes a theatre restaurant) and accommodation here. The complex is open daily from 11 am and there are tours on Sunday.

Gulsons Craft Village, about three km north of the town centre on Common St, has various craft shops and tea-rooms, most of them open daily. The complex is in the Potteries, an old brickworks, and covers a large area.

Riverdale began its career in 1840 as a coaching inn and is now a National Trust property with very fine gardens. It's open for inspection on Friday, Saturday and Sunday. It's on Maude St at the north side of town, by the Wollondilly River.

About 40 km south-east of Goulburn and abutting Morton National Park is **Bungonia State Recreation Area** (☎ (048) 48 4277), with a dramatic forested gorge and some deep caves. There are camping facilities near the main entrance. Bungonia itself, 13 km before the park entrance, is a tiny collection of buildings, some of them stone, with no shops or even a pub.

Just off the highway between Goulburn and Yass, **Gunning** is a small town with an antique shop or two.

Activities

Pelican Sheep Station (☎ (048) 21 4668) is a working property that is heavily into tourism. There are various **tours**, mainly for groups, but individuals can be catered for. The basic tour of the station takes 1¼ hours and on Tuesday and Wednesday you can go along to the cattle and sheep auctions.

This area has its share of **horseriding**

outfits, one being the Wattle Riding School at Kangaroobie (☎ (048) 48 1261), 16 km from Goulburn on the Crookwell road. The rates are about $15 an hour or $25 for two hours, less for children.

Festivals & Events

The Lilac Festival is held over the Labour Day long weekend in early October.

Places to Stay

Caravan parks *Governors Hill Carapark* (☎ (048) 21 7373) is on the old highway north of town, and *Goulburn South Caravan Park* (☎ (048) 21 3233) is on the old highway south of town.

Hotels & Motels A number of pubs on Sloane St (the street running parallel to the railway line) have accommodation, including the *Carlton* (☎ (048) 21 3820), with rooms for $30/40, and the *Coolavin* (☎ (048) 21 2498), with rooms for $20/30. The *Exchange Hotel* (☎ (048) 21 1566) at 9 Bradley St charges $23/34/45 for a single/double/triple.

There are plenty of motels. Some close to the city centre include the *Alpine Motor Lodge* (☎ (048) 21 2930) on Sloane St not far from the railway station and the information centre (from $40/45), and *Goulburn Central* (☎ (048) 21 1655) on the corner of Auburn and Verner Sts (from $40/50).

Other Accommodation The *Old Goulburn Brewery* (☎ (048) 21 6071) has good accommodation in the renovated mews for $35 per person.

The *Yurt Farm* is 20 km north of Goulburn on the Grabben Gullen road (the continuation of Clinton St). It includes an activities camp for school children, with the emphasis on learning to live simply. There are a great many signs and notices around the 'yurt village', but almost none of them say 'Do Not...'. Like-minded travellers are welcome to stay in the yurt village for $10 a night if there's room; if not, you can stay in the farmhouse for $10 and do a few hours' work in exchange for meals. You'll need to have a

sleeping-bag. It's interesting, friendly and a great place to stay. Phone first (☎ (048) 29 2114) to see if there's room. If you ring a few days in advance they might be able to arrange a lift out from Goulburn or even from Sydney.

Ask at the information centre about farmstays in the area.

Places to Eat

The Big Merino is at a service station complex called, incongruously, Life Australia. This complex includes the bland but good (for a truck-stop cafe) *Viennaworld Restaurant*, where main courses are around $7.50.

As a legacy of the days when the Hume Highway ran through town, there are several cafes on Auburn St. The *Paragon Cafe* opposite the post office is the most impressive. It's licensed and has a large menu, including seafood and pasta dishes from around $6. Less grand and less expensive is the *Radnor*.

On Sloane St, near the railway station, the *Coolavin Hotel* is a newly-renovated bar and bistro.

Broadbent's Restaurant (☎ (048) 21 4833) is on the ground floor of the Goulburn Club, across Belmore Park from the courthouse at 19 Market St. The small menu changes often and emphasises fresh local produce, and it's licensed. Two courses costs $25; for three it's $30.

Out at the *Old Goulburn Brewery* you can have a three-course meal for about $30.

Getting There & Away

Train Trains running between Sydney and Melbourne stop here.

Bus Buses running on the Hume between Sydney and Melbourne stop here. Some stop at the Big Merino, about 1.5 km south-east of the information centre. The information centre takes bus bookings.

Car & Motorbike The Hume Highway runs north-east to Mittagong and west to Yass. The Federal Highway to Canberra branches off the Hume about 10 km west of Goulburn.

Smaller roads run south to Braidwood, south-east to Bungonia State Recreation Area and north into the country around Crookwell (see the Central West chapter). The Wombeyan Caves (see the Around Sydney chapter) are 60 km north of Goulburn, via Taralga.

YASS

The Ngunawal people owned the area when Europeans arrived in the 1820s. Among the first to pass through were the explorers Hume and Hovell. Graziers soon followed, and by the time Hume returned to settle in the area in 1830 a town was growing on the banks of the Yass River. Yass was considered as a site for the national capital but was passed over and remains a busy rural centre. Some of the finest wool in the world is grown on the sheep in the surrounding paddocks.

With the town about to be bypassed by the highway there's a great deal of sprucing-up being done, with shops replacing their long-lost verandahs and applying liberal coats of paint in 'heritage' colours. You can almost hear the community's sigh of relief that their historic main street is soon to be free of impatient cars and trucks.

Yass has a fearsome reputation as a place for stranding hitch-hikers midway between Sydney and Melbourne. It always seems to be cold, wet and dark when you're dropped here.

The information centre (☎ (06) 226 2557) is on Comur St, the main street, on the Sydney side of the shopping centre. Another information centre is due to open at the service centre on the highway bypass.

The **railway museum** off Comur St is open on Sunday. **The Sheep's Back** is an art & craft gallery in an impressive old bank building on Comur St. It's open daily.

The **Hamilton Hume Museum** on Comur St is open daily except Tuesday and Thursday. Hume's house, **Cooma Cottage**, is off the highway, across from the Barton Highway turn-off on the Sydney side of Yass. The original timber cottage was built in the 1830s and other buildings here date from later in the 19th century. The National

Trust has restored the buildings and you can visit daily except Tuesday.

Places to Stay
Caravan Park *Yass Caravan Park* (☎ (06) 226 1173) takes up one corner of pretty Victoria Park, on the Gundagai (and Melbourne) side of town. There are sites, on-site vans and cabins.

Hotels & Motels Most of the motels are pricey, but that might change when the highway bypass is completed. They include the *Hamilton Hume* (☎ (06) 226 1722) on the old highway south of the centre (from $45/50) and the *Thunderbird* (☎ (06) 226 1158) on the main street (from $60/65).

Getting There & Away
Train Trains running between Sydney and Melbourne stop at Yass Junction, a few km from the town.

Bus Long-distance buses heading to Melbourne stop near the information centre; heading to Sydney they stop at the NRMA garage across the road. V/Line buses stop at the Liberty Cafe on the main street. These arrangements might change when the bypass is completed.

Transborder Buses (☎ (06) 226 1378) has several daily services between Yass and Canberra ($8). They leave from Rossi St, the first cross street on the town side of the river.

Car & Motorbike The Hume Highway runs east to Goulburn and south-west to Gundagai. The Barton Highway, branching off the Hume four km on the Sydney side of Yass, runs to Canberra. Smaller roads run south to Wee Jasper and on to Tumut (after rain, ask advice before attempting this section). Other small roads run north-east into the country around Crookwell – see the Central West chapter.

AROUND YASS
The only settlement of any size on the highway between Yass and Gundagai is **Jugiong**.

Wineries
Around Murrumbateman, on the Barton Highway to Canberra, you'll find a growing number of cool-climate wineries. Most are open for sales and tastings on weekends and some during the week. The Yass information centre can give directions.

Burrinjuck State Recreation Area
Burrinjuck Dam, south of Yass, supplies water to the Murrumbidgee Irrigation Area and its long arms wind among steep valleys. It's popular for watersports and there is wildlife in the surrounding bush. There are cruises on the dam (☎ (06) 227 7270), which would be around 100 km long if you straightened out the arms. Several well-equipped caravan parks are by the lake, including *Lake Burrinjuck Leisure Resort* (☎ (06) 227 7271) where you can hire boats. The Hume & Hovell Walking Trail passes the south-eastern end of the dam and offers simpler camping at Careys Reserve (☎ (06) 227 9626).

Wee Jasper
About 60 km south-west of Yass, Wee Jasper is a small village in a beautiful valley. You can join the **Hume & Hovell Walking Track** here, and there are limestone caves to visit on weekend afternoons. There's a store and a pub, and fuel is available.

Valley Horse Treks (☎ (06) 227 9627) is based near Wee Jasper and has one to four-day treks through the wild Brindabella Ranges for $60 a day plus $25 per night. There is no minimum group size – a real boon to solo travellers.

Somerset Tourist Camp (☎ (06) 227 9653) has sites and cabins. *Wee Jasper Station* (☎ (06) 227 9642) has shared accommodation geared to groups, but they might have room for individuals.

The road from Yass has an unsealed section and you should check conditions after rain. Continuing south-west to Tumut the road deteriorates for the climb out of the valley, but it's OK when dry.

GUNDAGAI

Gundagai, 386 km from Sydney, is one of the more interesting small towns (population 2100) along the Hume.

Information

The tourist office (☎ (069) 44 1341) is on Sheridan St, the main street, a little before the shopping centre. It's open daily from at least 9 am to 5 pm, but closes between noon and 1 pm on weekends.

Things to See

The long wooden **Prince Alfred Bridge** (now closed to traffic, but you can walk it) crosses the flood plain of the Murrumbidgee River, a reminder that in 1852 Gundagai suffered Australia's worst flood disaster when 89 people were drowned.

Gold rushes and bushrangers were part of Gundagai's colourful early history, and the notorious Captain Moonlight was tried in Gundagai's 1859 courthouse.

The **museum** on Homer St is in a new building with an impressive old sandstone portico. Admission is $1 (40c children). Other places of interest include the **Gabriel Gallery** of historic photos and, at the visitor information centre, the **Marble Marvel**, a 20,000-piece cathedral model. Is it art? Is it lunacy? Is it worth the $1 entry fee? Probably. You at least get to hear a snatch of *Along the Road to Gundagai.*

Places to Stay

Caravan Parks *Gundagai River Caravan Park* (☎ (069) 44 1702) is by the river near the south end of the Prince Alfred Bridge (take Homer St from town), with sites from $8 a double. In town, *Gundagai Caravan Village* (☎ (069) 44 1057) has sites from $14 and on-site vans from $28.

The Dog on the Tuckerbox

Gundagai features in a number of famous songs, including *Along the Road to Gundagai, My Mabel Waits for Me* and *When a Boy from Alabama Meets a Girl from Gundagai.* Its most famous monument is eight km east of town just off the highway. There, still sitting on his tuckerbox, is the Dog on the Tuckerbox memorial, a sculpture of the dog who in a 19th-century bush ballad (and a more recent, perhaps even better known, poem by Jack Moses) refused to help its master get his bullock team out of a bog. The original poem goes:

As I was coming down Conroys Gap
I heard a maiden cry,
'There goes Bill the bullocky,
He's bound for Gundagai.
A better poor old bastard
Never earned an honest crust,
A better poor old bugger
Never drug a whip through dust'.

His team got bogged at Five Mile Creek,
Bill lashed and swore and cried,
'If Nobby don't get me out of this
I'll tattoo his bloody hide'.

But Nobby strained and broke his yoke
And poked out the leader's eye,
Then the dog sat on the tuckerbox
Five miles from Gundagai.

A popular tale has it that the dog was even less helpful because in the original version it apparently shat on the tuckerbox. ■

Holbrook & Submarines
The town, founded in 1858, was called Germantown until WW I, when it was thought politic to display some patriotism. British Captain Holbrook earned himself the first VC of the war by commanding a submarine that sank a Turkish ship near the Dardanelles, and Germantown decided to adopt his name. A nine-metre model of Holbrook's vessel was acquired (it's displayed in town, along with a sculpture of a submariner at his periscope) and the town forged enduring links with the Australian Navy's submarine corps. Occasional visits by official parties of sailors have seen some riotous times in the pubs, and the navy is donating a conning tower to Holbrook, which will be displayed in a new park. All this in a town more than 250 km from the sea! ■

Hotels & Motels On Sheridan St the *Criterion Hotel* (☎ (069) 44 1048) and the *Royal Hotel* (☎ (069) 44 1024) have accommodation. Motels include the *Gundagai* (☎ (069) 44 1066) on Sheridan St (from $40/50) and the *Poets Recall* (☎ (069) 44 1777) on the corner of Punch and West Sts (from $45/55).

Places to Eat

The *Niagara Cafe* has an illustrious history (prime minister John Curtin once visited) and is something of a gem among country-town cafes. The menu doesn't differ much from the standard snacks and grills, but it is licensed and it's good to see a country-town cafe taking itself seriously.

There are one or two Chinese places on Sheridan St, and the pubs have counter meals.

Getting There & Away

The tourist office sells bus tickets, and buses stop nearby. Countrylink runs north to Cootamundra and south to Tumut and Tumbarumba. Buses running on the Hume Highway between Sydney and Melbourne stop here.

The only highway town of any size between Gundagai and Holbrook is Tarcutta, where there are a couple of cafes and a motel (☎ (069) 28 7294).

HOLBROOK

This small town (population 1400) is worth a look around, and it's the best place to turn off the highway for a drive through Morgan Country to the west (see the Riverina chapter). To the east a road runs through the pretty Wontagong Valley and past a track-

head of the **Hume & Hovell Walking Track** at Lankey's Creek (a nice picnic spot), to Jingellic and then on to Tumbarumba or Khancoban, gateway towns for the mountains.

Holbrook has a good **museum** in the old Woolpack Inn on the highway. It's open daily from 10 am and admission is $3 ($1.50 students, $1 children). There's an impressive dining room which seats 16, and five-course meals served by people in period costume can be arranged. If there are 16 of you it will cost about $30 a head. The museum is also the information centre for the area (☎ (060) 36 2131).

Near the museum is a short walking track along the banks of Ten Mile Creek, a nice break from the rigours of the Hume.

Places to Stay & Eat

In Holbrook There are four motels and a couple of pubs, including the *Holbrook Hotel* (☎ (060) 36 2099) with single/double rooms for $20/30, as well as a caravan park. In the area are several farms with accommodation. The pubs have counter meals from $5 and there's also the *Jolly Swagman Bistro* and meals at the Returned Servicemen's Club.

Surrounding Area Glenfalloch (☎ (060) 36 7203), a long-established sheep station, is a beautiful place, with big elms and 500 acres of bush, through which there are walking trails. The accommodation is in bunkrooms (about $10 per person) and there's a good kitchen and common room. You can use the pool and tennis courts at the 130-year-old homestead at certain times. They get quite a

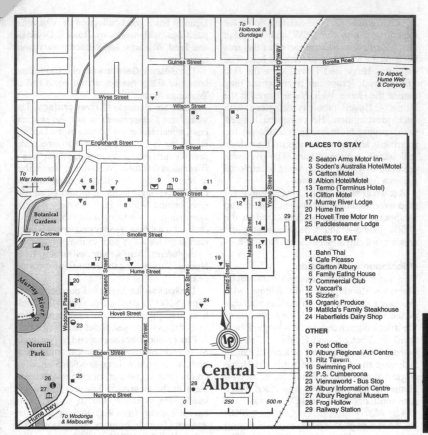

PLACES TO STAY

2 Seaton Arms Motor Inn
3 Soden's Australia Hotel/Motel
5 Carlton Motel
8 Albion Hotel/Motel
13 Termo (Terminus Hotel)
14 Clifton Motel
17 Murray River Lodge
20 Hume Inn
21 Hovell Tree Motor Inn
25 Paddlesteamer Lodge

PLACES TO EAT

1 Bahn Thai
4 Cafe Picasso
5 Carlton Albury
6 Family Eating House
7 Commercial Club
12 Vaccari's
15 Sizzler
18 Organic Produce
19 Matilda's Family Steakhouse
24 Haberfields Dairy Shop

OTHER

9 Post Office
10 Albury Regional Art Centre
11 Ritz Tavern
16 Swimming Pool
22 P.S. Cumberoona
23 Viennaworld - Bus Stop
26 Albury Information Centre
27 Albury Regional Museum
28 Frog Hollow
29 Railway Station

few groups here, so you're advised to book ahead. Glenfalloch is about nine km east of the Hume, down a signposted turn-off 20 km north of Holbrook.

Other rural accommodation in the area includes *Ardrossan* (☎ (060) 36 9222), *Giles Creek* (☎ (060) 36 8140) and *Oxton* (☎ (060) 36 4125).

Getting There & Away

If you're heading to Jingellic you might be able to get a lift in the mail car, which runs on Monday, Wednesday and Friday. Ask at the Post Office.

ALBURY

Albury (population 40,000) is on the Murray River, just below the big Hume Weir. The city makes a good base for trips into a wide variety of country: downstream to the Riverina and the Victorian wineries around Rutherglen; upstream to the Snowy Mountains and across to the Victorian high country.

History

Aboriginal tribes once gathered near Albury, to plan their annual expeditions up into the mountains to gather Bogong moths (and

Albury remains a good starting-point for expeditions into the NSW and Victorian alps). Europeans were attracted to the area because the Murray was fordable here. The explorers Hume and Hovell were the first Europeans to cross the river, which they named the Hume. Well, *Hume* named it the Hume – Hovell probably disagreed with such presumption. He contented himself with carving his name into a tree on the riverbank, and a plaque marks his tree which still stands in Noreuil Park. The river was renamed by Charles Sturt when he explored the area further downstream.

A town grew up and became an important stop-over on the route between Sydney and Melbourne (which it remains), and in the 1850s paddle-steamers began carrying the area's wool clip down to South Australia.

Orientation & Information
The long Lincoln Causeway over the Murray's flood plain links Albury with Wodonga, its large twin on the Victorian side of the river. Downtown Albury consists of the blocks bounded by Wodonga Place, Swift St, Young St and Hume St. Dean St, where you'll find the post office, is the main shopping street. From the north, the Hume Highway runs down Young St, turns onto Hume St then onto Wodonga Place which runs south onto the Lincoln Causeway.

The Albury Information Centre (☎ (060) 21 2655) is on Wodonga Place (the highway) as you enter Albury from Wodonga. The larger Gateway Information Centre (☎ (060) 41 3875), with information on both NSW and Victoria, is on the highway in Wodonga. Tourist information is broadcast on 88 FM.

Work Some seasonal fruit-picking is available in the area; see the CES (☎ (060) 21 3400) at 488 Swift St. The backpacker hostel might also know of work.

Things to See & Do
The **Albury Regional Museum** is in an old pub in Noreuil Park, near the information centre.

The **Albury Regional Art Centre** at 546 Dean St has a good collection of Australian paintings, with works by Russell Drysdale and Fred Williams, and contemporary photography.

The **Botanic Gardens** are old, formal and beautiful. They run beside the north end of Wodonga Place.

There are a couple of **river cruises**. The steamboat *Cumberoona* is not the original boat, which lies at the bottom of the Darling River, but is a close replica built as a community project to celebrate Australia's Bicentenary. It runs from around September to March, when its relatively deep draught can find enough water. It's moored on the river behind Noreuil Park. There's also the *Discovery*, a modern vessel but with a draught enabling year-round trips, which start at $9 for a 1½-hour cruise.

In summer there's **river swimming** from Noreuil Park behind the Albury information centre.

The backpacker hostel has popular **canoe trips** ($20/15 a day/half-day) and you don't have to stay there to join in. They can arrange longer trips – and just about anything else.

Frog Hollow, at the east end of Nurigong St, is a sort of a non-mechanical amusement park, with a maze, lawn snooker (based on croquet), mini golf and sometimes entertainment in the Courtyard Theatre. Meals and snacks are available, too. It's open daily except Tuesday from 9 am to 6 pm in winter and until 9 pm in summer. Admission is $3.

The **Nail Can Hill Walking Track** rambles over the steep, bush-covered ridges on the eastern side of town. There are sometimes views across to the Victorian alps. You can start from Noreuil Park or head up Dean St to the war memorial and pick up the trail there. The information centre has a map.

You can take a **scenic flight** in a biplane (☎ (060) 21 3950) from $45 for 10 minutes. In 1934 the citizens of Albury turned out to light the runway with their car headlights so a lost plane taking part in an air race from London to Sydney could land.

Organised Tours
Mylon Motorways (☎ (060) 56 3100) has a

number of day tours from Albury, most down into the historic areas of the Victorian high country. They cost around $35 per person, and there's also a Sunday afternoon tour of Albury/Wodonga for $24.

Places to Stay
Accommodation Albury Wodonga (1800 806 939 toll-free) books most places to stay.

Caravan Parks *Albury Central Caravan Park* (☎ (060) 21 8420) is a couple of km north of the centre on North St and has tent sites from $10 and cabins from $30. There are a few other caravan parks on the highway further north.

Hostel *Murray River Lodge* (☎ (060) 41 1822) is a good backpacker hostel with dorm beds at $13 and a double room for $32. It's on Hume St not far from the bus stop and Noreuil Park. You can hire bikes for $3 a day. This is a friendly place which takes care of its guests. They'll help you get involved in adventure activities or find a farm where you can work for your board. The owners are opening a hostel at Tawonga in Victoria's high country and can arrange transport there.

Hotels *Soden's Australia Hotel* (☎ (060) 21 2400) on the corner of Wilson and David Sts has some interesting leadlighting on its verandah. Pub rooms go for around $20 and claustrophobia-inducing motel-style units cost from $30. The *Termo* (☎ (060) 24 1777), the Terminus Hotel on the corner of Young and Dean Sts, has rooms from $25/35. The *Albion Hotel/Motel* (☎ (060) 21 3377) at 593 Dean St has pub rooms for $25/40.

Motels With 40 motels, Albury isn't short of rooms. Finding one which costs less than $60/70 is not easy and you might have to head out to the northern suburb of Lavington, where there's a string of them along the highway. There are other motels across the border in Wodonga. When things are slow, the more expensive places might be open to a little negotiation – ask about standby rates.

Some cheaper central motels include the *Clifton* (☎ (060) 21 7126) at 424 Smollett St, near the railway station (from $45/55), the *Albion Hotel/Motel* (☎ (060) 21 3377) at 593 Dean St (from $45/55) and the *Hume Inn* (☎ (060) 21 2733) at 406 Wodonga Place (from $55/65).

The *Seaton Arms* (☎ (060) 21 5999) on the corner of Olive and Wilson Sts has very good ground-floor rooms and more average upper-storey rooms, from $60/70.

Top places to stay include the *Carlton Motel* (☎ (060) 21 5366), the tall semicircular landmark on the corner of Dean and Elizabeth Sts, from $70 a single or double. *Paddlesteamer Lodge* (☎ (060) 41 1711) (from $80/90) and *Hovell Tree Motor Inn* (☎ (060) 41 2666) (from $90/100) are both on Wodonga Place near the information centre.

Places to Eat
Matilda's Family Steakhouse, a member of a fledgling chain, is at the corner of David and Hume Sts and has lunch specials from $8 (all you can eat) and other meals for around $12. Children's meals cost about $5. The *Family Eating House* at 639 Dean St has all-you-can-eat smorgasbords daily, with roasts at weekends. *Sizzler*, another 'family restaurant' chain, has an outlet on the corner of Young and Smollett Sts.

There's a weekday lunch buffet for $9.50 at the *Carlton Motel* on the corner of Dean and Elizabeth Sts. On Dean St next to the Carlton, *Cafe Picasso* is a Spanish restaurant with main courses around $13.

Bahn Thai, a good Thai restaurant, is open nightly in a Victorian house at 592 Kiewa St.

The *Commercial Club* on Dean St has fairly stiff dress regulations (ties – for men only, presumably – are required in the dining room; jeans and runners aren't allowed anywhere) but also a reputation for very good food. As well as the dining room, which has a $15 lunch deal, there's a bistro with $7 main course specials and a more expensive pasta bar and a grill.

Many pubs have counter meals and Dean St is a long strip of cafes and takeaways.

Vaccari's, on the corner of Dean and Macauley Sts, is a simple Italian place with lunch specials from $6.50.

Haberfields is a large dairy which manufactures an interesting range of cheeses. You can buy them at *Haberfields Dairy Shop* on Hovell St between David and Olive Sts. You might encounter some oddities there, as the shop is used to test customer reaction to new products. Organic produce is sold from a shop next door to the big Barbecues Galore store on Hume St.

Entertainment

Albury's reputation as a great place to see cars doing wheelies on Saturday night is fading, and there's some nightlife, mainly in pubs and clubs. Check the local paper for details. The Termo (the Terminus Hotel) on the corner of Young and Dean Sts has bands, sometimes quite big acts, mainly on weekends. The Ritz Tavern at 480 Dean St has a nightclub on weekends.

If you have a chance to see the **Flying Fruit-Fly Circus**, take it. Flying Fruit-Fly is a wonderful project teaching circus skills to local kids. Despite the constant turnover of performers (members hand in their leotards when they leave school), the circus is excellent and performs around the country and overseas.

Getting There & Away

Air Ansett, Eastern, Hazelton and Kendell all fly from Albury to Sydney, Melbourne and Wagga Wagga.

Ring-tailed possum

Splitters Creek Airlines (☎ (060) 21 1136) flies historic DC3 aircraft on tours to Mungo National Park. They prefer groups, but individuals can sometimes tag along for about $300. This is a good deal. They have various other tours and might be offering flights to Mootwingee National Park.

Train XPTs running between Sydney and Melbourne stop here. If you're travelling between the two capital cities it's much cheaper to stop over in Albury on a through ticket to buy two separate tickets.

Although railway lines have connected Albury with Sydney and Melbourne since last century, it's only since 1962 that you didn't have to change trains here because the colonies of NSW and Victoria used different rail gauges!

Bus Most of the long-distance lines running on the Hume between Sydney and Melbourne stop at Viennaworld (a service station/diner) on the highway on the corner of Hovell St, across from Noreuil Park.

Mylon Motorways (☎ (060) 56 3100) has a daylight service to Adelaide, which goes via Bendigo and western Victoria. Pyles Coaches (☎ (057) 57 2024) runs to the Victorian high country. Countrylink runs to Echuca, on the Murray River in Victoria, via several towns in the southern Riverina. V/Line runs to Mildura along the Murray.

AROUND ALBURY

See the Riverina chapter for the interesting towns in Morgan Country, not far north of Albury.

The **Ettamogah Wildlife Sanctuary**, 11 km north on the Hume Highway and open daily ($5, children $2), has a collection of Aussie fauna, most of which arrived sick or injured, so this is a genuine sanctuary. A few km north, the grotesque **Ettamogah Pub** looms up near the highway – a real-life recreation of a famous Aussie cartoon pub, and proof that life (of a sort) follows art, not vice versa. **Cooper's Winery**, 100 years old but overshadowed by its lager-lout of a neighbour, is also here.

About 15 km further north is **Bowna**, a town that has shrunk to just a couple of buildings, including the boomerang-maker's shop. Old Yarakila is quite a character and his boomerangs fly well. At Bowna there's a turn-off to the *Great Aussie Camping Resort* (☎ (060) 20 3236) on the banks of the Hume Reservoir. This is a very well-equipped place with fairly pricey sites, on-site vans, on-site tents and rather elaborate cabins. This road leads further on to **Wymah**, which is also accessible by vehicle ferry from the Murray Valley Highway on the other side of the river. See the West of the Snowies section earlier in this chapter for information on this route to the snowfields.

The South Coast

Although it doesn't attract anywhere near as much attention as the north coast, the south coast is well worth visiting – partly for that reason, as well as for the excellent beaches.

The Princes Highway runs along the south coast from Sydney to the Victorian border. Although this is a longer and slower route between Sydney and Melbourne than the Hume Highway, it's infinitely more interesting.

This chapter covers the coast from Kiama down to the Victorian border. The coast between Sydney and Wollongong is covered in the Around Sydney chapter.

Geography & Climate

Like the north coast, this area is a coastal strip of good beaches, backed by the mountains of the Great Dividing Range. South of Nowra the sandstone of the Sydney area gives way to granite and good soils, and the forests start to soar.

The south coast's climate is pretty good for most of the year – Batemans Bay is on the same latitude as the French Riviera. You're unlikely to want to swim in winter, but summers are as hot they are on the north coast and even winter has its share of pleasant days.

Getting There & Around

Bus Greyhound Pioneer Australia travels the Princes Highway between Sydney and Melbourne. Typical fares from Sydney include Bega $44, Narooma $38 and Batemans Bay $30. A local company, Pioneer Motor Service, offers better services between Eden and Sydney and its sector fares are cheaper. Pioneer Motor Service's head office is in Nowra (☎ (044) 21 7722) and most towns along the south coast have ticket agents.

Various companies have services running inland to Mittagong, Canberra, Cooma and Bombala.

Car & Motorbike The Princes Highway follows the coast, all the way from Sydney's George St to Melbourne's St Kilda Rd. It's known as the coastal route, but don't expect too many ocean views (although there are some beauties). Most of the way the highway runs a little way inland. All the way there are turn-offs for some interesting places to visit, both on the coast and up in the Great Divide where there's an almost unbroken chain of superb national parks and state forests.

For more information on routes from the coast up to the Snowy Mountains and the Monaro tablelands, see the South-East chapter.

Kiama to Ulladulla

Shoalhaven is a large municipality stretching from north of Nowra almost as far south as Batemans Bay, and taking in some great beaches, state forests and, in the ranges to the west, the big Morton National Park (see the Around Sydney chapter). It is named for the Shoalhaven River which winds through the area. The river was named by explorer George Bass in 1797 when his boat encountered shoals at the river-mouth.

This is a popular family holiday destination. In fact, in terms of beds and caravan park sites occupied, it's the most popular

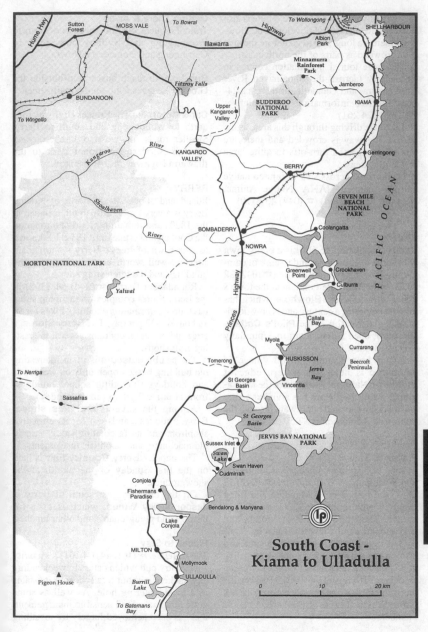

South Coast -
Kiama to Ulladulla

municipality in the whole state. There is also a lot of new residential development. However, there's a long way to go before the area is as crowded as parts of the north coast.

There are tourist information centres in Bomaderry (across the Shoalhaven River from Nowra) and Ulladulla, or there's a 24-hour toll-free information phone number (☎ 1800 024 261).

Take care driving through this area, as the narrow highway is crowded and there are lots of unexpected turn-offs to quite large residential areas.

If you come across sick or injured native animals, contact NANA (Native Animal Network Association) (☎ (044) 43 5110).

KIAMA

Kiama (population 16,500) is a pretty town with some old buildings and a sense of community. The information centre (☎ (042) 32 3322) is on Blowhole Point, near the town's major attraction, the **Blowhole**, which has drawn visitors for a century and is now flood-lit at night. Nearby is the **Pilot's Cottage Museum**, open from 11 am to 3 pm daily except Tuesday.

Inland from Kiama the old village of **Jamberoo** is near the eastern edge of **Budderoo National Park** where the **Minnamurra Rainforest Park** has a visitor centre and a 1.5 km elevated boardwalk through the rainforest. Admission is $7.50 per car.

Places to Stay

Several of Kiama's pubs have accommodation, including the *Grand Hotel* (☎ (042) 32 1037) on the corner of Manning and Bong Bong Sts with rooms for $20/35 and less in winter. There are plenty of motels and caravan parks and a few B&B places.

Gerringong, 10 km south of Kiama and also on the railway line, is not as attractive as Kiama but it does have *Chittick Lodge*, an associate YHA hostel (☎ (042) 34 1249). It's on Bridges Rd, a five-minute walk up the hill from Werri Beach. Beds are $11 for members.

Getting There & Away

Train Frequent electric trains run north to Wollongong and Sydney and south to Gerringong and Bomaderry/Nowra.

Bus Long-distance buses stop outside the Group 7 Leagues Club on the main street.

Car & Motorbike The Princes Highway runs north to Wollongong and south to Berry. Smaller roads run west to Jamberoo and through Budderoo National Park to the Illawarra Highway near Roberston.

BERRY

Inland and about 20 km north of Nowra, Berry is a very pretty little town, founded in the 1820s and remaining a private town on the Coolangatta estate until 1912. It's known as 'the town of trees'. Berry's short main street is well worth a stroll, both for the buildings and the interesting shops.

Roundabout Berry (☎ (044) 64 2102) in the Berry Stores complex on the main street has tourist information and hires bikes for $8 an hour or $22 per day. The **Berry Stores**, a large old building, contains several interesting craft shops.

The nearby **museum** is in an interesting old building but it's open only on weekends and holidays (including school holidays) from 11 am to 2 pm (3 pm on Sunday).

Among the several **antiques shops**, Berry Antiques stands out for its attractive shopfront and its fascinating stock: largely old machinery and scientific instruments.

The popular **Berry Country Fair** is held on the first Sunday of the month at the showgrounds.

Off the highway just south of Berry is **Jasper Valley Wines**, which is open for tastings and ploughman's and other lunches.

Places to Stay

The *Hotel Berry* (☎ (044) 64 1011) is a rarity – a country pub which caters to weekending city-slickers without totally losing its status as a local watering hole. As well as some good renovation and sensible management, this has been achieved largely by installing

a coffee shop, which gives an alternative to the bar-room atmosphere. Accommodation costs $30/40/50 a single/double/triple, with weekend packages available. You'll probably have to book on weekends as it's a popular place. The rooms are standard pub bedrooms, but large and well renovated. Why can't more pubs be like this?

Next door to the hotel and in one of the town's more impressive buildings, an old bank, is the excellent *Bunyip Inn Guesthouse* (☎ (044) 64 2064), with 10 rooms from $90 a double. Only some of the rooms have attached bathrooms.

The *Great Southern Hotel* (☎ (044) 64 1009), a new place built in an old style, has motel units from $25/50.

Places to Eat

On the main street, next door to Berry Antiques, *For Love of Country* is a simply-decorated restaurant serving interesting Italian-inspired and other dishes, including game, from around $10 to $15. It's open for dinner from Tuesday to Sunday, and on Sunday there's a three-course roast lunch for $20.

There are several cafes, including the *Postmasters Coffee Shop*, which has an outdoor seating area. It's next to the museum. On the other side of the museum, behind the Berry Community Activities Centre, is a *wholefood cafe*. The coffee shop at the *Hotel Berry* serves light meals, and for $12 you can get a huge breakfast.

The *Chinese restaurant* at the Great Southern Hotel has lunch specials for about $5.

Getting There & Away

The Princes Highway runs north-east to Kiama and south-east to Bomaderry/Nowra. The main road to Kangaroo Valley and up to Mittagong leaves the highway just south of Berry, but there's also a very scenic route to Kangaroo Valley which runs from Berry and travels via the hamlets of Woodhill and Wattamolla.

NOWRA

The largest town in the Shoalhaven area (population 22,000), Nowra is a centre for the area's dairy farms and its increasing tourism and retirement development.

Orientation & Information

Central Nowra is south of the Shoalhaven River and west of the highway. The main shopping streets are Kinghorne and Junction Sts. Junction St continues west up the hill to the showgrounds, which are entered through impressive memorial gates.

The area's good information centre (☎ (044) 21 0778; 1800 024 261 toll-free) is in Bomaderry, on the highway north of the bridge and about four km from central Nowra.

There's a National Parks office (☎ (044) 23 9800) at 24 Berry St, on the corner of Junction St.

Things to See & Do

The **Nowra Animal Park**, on the north bank of the Shoalhaven upstream from Nowra, is a pleasant place to meet some Australian animals. It's on 6.5 hectares and is much nicer than the depressing little zoos you sometimes come across. It's open daily and costs $5 ($2 children). To get here from Nowra, cross the bridge and immediately turn left, then branch left onto McMahons Rd and turn left again at Rockhill Rd. The park is about four km from the bridge.

Shoalhaven Historic Museum at the corner of Kinghorne and Plunkett Sts is open on weekends. **Meroogal**, on the corner of West and Worrigee Sts, is a historic house containing the artefacts accumulated by its generations of owners. It's open on Saturday from 1 to 4.30 pm and Sunday from 10 am to 4.30 pm; admission is $5.

Walks The information centre produces a handy compilation of walks in the area. The Lands Department's **Bomaderry Creek Walking Track** runs for 5.5 km through the sandstone gorges of the creek, from a trackhead at the end of Narang Rd, off the highway about 500 metres on the Sydney

side of the information centre. This walk can connect with **Bens Walk**, which runs along the south bank of the Shoalhaven in Nowra, starting at the bridge and running up Nowra Creek.

Cruises Shoalhaven River Cruises (☎ (044) 23 1844) will take you up the beautiful river. The office is at 1 Scenic Drive, on the river west of the bridge.

Horseriding The Valhalla Appaloosa Stud near Falls Creek, 13 km south of Nowra, charges $15 for an hour of horse-riding and less for longer rides. Groups of six experienced riders can take part in two-day rides for $150 each.

Swimming Nowra is a handy centre for this part of the world but it isn't on the sea. The nearest beach is at Shoalhaven Heads and just north of the heads is **Seven Mile Beach National Park**. If you don't have transport the easiest way to get to the beach is to take a train from Bomaderry to Kiama, 20 minutes away. There are frequent services and it costs only about $3 for a day return. This is especially handy if you're staying at the Barracks Hostel at Bomaderry, near the station.

Canoeing Coolendel Canoe Tours (☎ (044) 21 4586) organises canoe trips on the Shoalhaven River.

Organised Tours
The managers of the Barracks Hostel in Bomaderry also run the Bushmobile, a big purpose-built vehicle with 6WD – it can get just about anywhere. As well as day trips (on which YHA members get discounts), the Bushmobile makes some long trips, including an annual journey up to Cape York in July.

Places to Stay
Caravan Parks There's a small *Easts* caravan park off the highway close to the bridge (and thus noisy) and the *Shoalhaven Caravan Village* (☎ (044) 23 0770) on the

river a km or so east of the town. There are a lot of permanents here, but there's a good camping area. There's no shop out here, so buy your supplies before you come. The *Nowra Animal Park* (☎ (044) 21 3949) has tent sites in bushland for $9, rising to $14 at peak times.

Hostel The *Barracks* (☎ (044) 23 0495) is a good associate YHA hostel across the river in Bomaderry, near the railway station. It's a well-run place in a solid building that once housed railway workers. Dorm beds cost $12 and there are plenty of twin rooms for $16 per person. They can pick you up from the Nowra bus stop.

Nowra might be your first stop after Sydney, and the Barracks is a good place to pick up information about travel down the coast – it's also a good place to get tips on Sydney for those heading the other way. If you're having car trouble, the managers have contacts with local mechanics who don't charge an arm and a leg.

Guesthouses, Hotels & Motels The *White House* (☎ (044) 21 2084) on Junction St no longer has backpacker accommodation but it's still reasonably priced at $25/35. The *Empire Hotel* (☎ (044) 21 2433) is an outstandingly ugly cream-brick building at the corner of Kinghorne and Moss Sts, with single/double rooms for $25/30.

The *City Centre Motel* (☎ (044) 21 3455) at 16 Kinghorne St is beginning to show its age but it's quiet, central and a good deal at $40/45 (more in summer). The *George Bass Motor Inn* (☎ (044) 21 6388) is on leafy Bridge Rd, the northern continuation of Berry St. Rooms cost from $50/55. There are plenty of more expensive motels.

Places to Eat
The *Wholemeal Tea & Coffee Inn* is a cosy place in an alley running into Stewart Place from Junction St near the corner of Berry St. It's open during the day on weekdays and sometimes on Thursday, Friday and Saturday evenings. You can buy snacks, salads and bean dishes, as well as cakes and

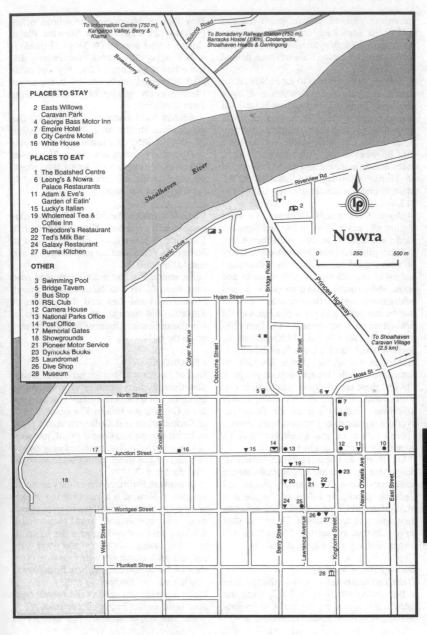

PLACES TO STAY

2 Easts Willows
   Caravan Park
4 George Bass Motor Inn
7 Empire Hotel
8 City Centre Motel
16 White House

PLACES TO EAT

1 The Boatshed Centre
6 Leong's & Nowra
   Palace Restaurants
11 Adam & Eve's
    Garden of Eatin'
15 Lucky's Italian
19 Wholemeal Tea &
    Coffee Inn
20 Theodore's Restaurant
22 Ted's Milk Bar
24 Galaxy Restaurant
27 Burma Kitchen

OTHER

3 Swimming Pool
5 Bridge Tavern
9 Bus Stop
10 RSL Club
12 Camera House
13 National Parks Office
14 Post Office
17 Memorial Gates
18 Showgrounds
21 Pioneer Motor Service
23 Dymocks Books
25 Laundromat
26 Dive Shop
28 Museum

To Information Centre (750 m),
Kangaroo Valley, Berry &
Kiama

To Bomaderry Railway Station (750 m),
Barracks Hostel (1 km), Coolangatta,
Shoalhaven Heads & Gerringong

Bolong Road

Bomaderry Creek

Shoalhaven River

Riverview Rd

Nowra

0   250   500 m

Scenic Drive

Bridge Road

Princes Highway

Hyam Street

Colyer Avenue

Osbourne Street

Graham Street

To Shoalhaven
Caravan Village
(2.5 km)

Moss St

North Street

Shoalhaven Street

Nowra O'Keefe Ave

East Street

Junction Street

West Street

Berry Street

Lawrence Avenue

Kinghorne Street

Worrigee Street

Plunkett Street

SOUTH COAST

smoothies and, of course, good tea and coffee. For something completely different go to *Ted's Milk Bar*, an old-style grills and hamburger cafe facing Stewart Place, behind Kinghorne St.

One of the best places to eat in Nowra, for snacks or meals, is the new *Adam & Eve's Garden of Eatin'* on the Junction St mall just east of Kinghorne St. The food, which is as interesting as it is healthy, emphasises vegetarian dishes, but meat is also served. It's a cafe on week days, with focaccia, salads, cakes and light meals; and a BYO restaurant on Thursday, Friday and Saturday nights. Main courses at dinner cost around $10 to $12.

Burma Kitchen at 90 Worrigee St is open nightly and serves Thai, Indian and Burmese food for around $7 to $9 a main course.

Other places include *Theodore's* on Berry St, with a good Italian menu including such dishes as veal shanks as well as pasta and pizza. Main-course pasta is around $9.50 and other main courses in the area of $13. *Lucky's Italian* is a pasta and pizza place in the old fire station on Junction St west of Berry St.

The Flounder Grill at 242 Kinghorne St, opposite the Pizza Hut, is a licensed restaurant open for dinner from Tuesday to Saturday. A whole flounder will set you back $14 and there are plenty of other fish to eat.

For meals with a view, try the upmarket *Riverfront Seafood Bar* at the Boatshed, overlooking the river just next to the bridge. There's also a bar and a cafe here and it's open daily from 11 am to 1 am.

On North St, near the intersection of Kinghorne St, there are a couple of Chinese restaurants. *Leong's* has an Australian and Chinese menu, and *Nowra Palace* has Malaysian and Chinese food. Both are open daily and both are licensed. There's another large Chinese place, the *Galaxy*, on the corner of Berry and Worrigee Sts.

Getting There & Away

Train The nearest station is across the river at Bomaderry (☎ (044) 21 2022). Frequent electric trains run up the coast to Sydney taking 2½ to three hours and costing $14.

Bus Pioneer Motor Service's head office (☎ (044) 21 7722) is in Stewart Place. Boag's Travel Service (☎ (044) 23 0276) is at 21 Kinghorne St, across from the long-distance bus stop. They're friendly and often give advice to newly-arrived backpackers (despite rarely getting any business from them in return).

Several local companies run to various destinations in the area. Nowra Coaches (☎ (044) 21 2855), for instance, meets trains in Bomaderry and runs down to Huskisson and other destinations on Jervis Bay, weekdays only, with one service on Saturday in the Christmas holidays.

Car & Motorbike The Princes Highway runs north to Berry and on to Kiama, and south to Ulladulla. Smaller roads run north-west to Kangaroo Valley and up to Mittagong, and east to the coast.

An interesting and mainly unsealed road runs from Nowra to Braidwood, through Morton National Park and the hamlets of Sassafras and Nerriga. At the south end of Kinghorne St take Albatross Rd, which veers off to the right.

AROUND NOWRA

East of Nowra the Shoalhaven River meanders through dairy country in a system of estuaries and wetlands, finally reaching the sea at Crookhaven Heads. The nearby towns of **Crookhaven** and **Culburra** aren't especially interesting and **Orient Point**, just west of Crookhaven, is distinguished only by the fact that all the street names seem to begin with the letter O.

Greenwell Point, on the estuary about 15 km east of Nowra, is a quiet fishing village and a pretty place. The village boasts a champion oyster-opener and 'world famous' fish & chips, sold at the shop near the wharf. It has a huge range of seafood and good daily specials such as snapper with chips and coleslaw for $6.50. On the way here from Nowra you'll pass the **Jindyandy Mill**, a convict-built flour-mill and now a craft centre. Next door is the Butter Factory Restaurant.

On the north side of the estuary is

Top: The Big Merino, Goulburn, south-east (RN)
Bottom Left: Kangaroos at Murramurang National Park, south coast (JM)
Bottom Right: Cattle sales, Cooma, south-east (JM)

Top: War Memorial & Parliament Houses from Mt Ainslie, Canberra, ACT (RI)
Bottom Left: Parliament House & mosaic, Canberra, ACT (RI)
Bottom Right: Lake Burley Griffin & Telecom Tower, Canberra, ACT (RI)

Shoalhaven Heads, where the river once reached the sea but is now blocked by sandbars.

Just before you get to the town of Shoalhaven Heads, which is partly a dormitory suburb of Nowra and partly a holiday resort, you pass through **Coolangatta**, the site of the earliest European settlement on the south coast. The **Coolangatta Historic Village Resort** (☎ (044) 48 7131) has craft shops, expensive accommodation in convict-built buildings and, on Saturday nights, Mr Berry's Banquet with bush-dancing and entertainment. There are a couple of other places to eat and you can sample the wines from Coolangatta Estate on weekends. The wine is made from grapes grown here but vintaged at Tyrrells in the Hunter Valley.

Coolangatta is also the home of **Bigfoot**, a strange vehicle which will carry you to the top of Mt Coolangatta for $10 ($5 children) on weekends and school holidays.

JERVIS BAY

This large, sheltered bay has been considered as the site for many projects, everything from a huge naval base to a nuclear reactor. None of these has come to pass and despite extensive housing development it retains its clean, very white beaches and crystal-clear water (no large rivers flow into the bay). There are dolphins, and whales sometimes drop in when swimming past on their annual migrations from June to October.

The bay's original inhabitants lived a good life here until the coming of Europeans. The Aboriginal community has made a small start at reclaiming its property, winning a land claim in the Wreck Bay area.

Most of the development around Jervis Bay is on the south-west shore, around the towns of Huskisson and Vincentia. The north shore is much less developed and state forest backs the beaches at **Callala Bay**. There are caravan parks near here. **Beecroft Peninsula** forms the north-eastern side of Jervis Bay. Most of the peninsula is navy land which is off-limits to civilians, but **Currarong**, at the end of the peninsula near Beecroft Head, is a small town with a caravan park. This area is largely cleared.

Huskisson

With much of this area turning into a vast urban sprawl, it's surprising that Huskisson, the oldest town on Jervis Bay, remains a small fishing port (population 1000) with a sense of community.

Lady Denman, a ferry dating from 1912, is the centrepiece of the **Museum of Jervis Bay, Science & the Sea**, by the bay on the Nowra side of Huskisson. Also here is Timbey's Aboriginal Arts & Crafts which has work produced by the local Aboriginal community. There's also a boardwalk through wetlands. The museum is open Tuesday to Friday from 1 to 4 pm and on weekends and holidays from 10 am to 4 pm, and admission is $2 ($1 children); the rest of the complex is open daily.

Cruises Dolphin Watch Cruises (☎ (044) 41 6311) has several cruises on offer, starting at about $20 ($15 children).

Diving Jervis Bay is popular with divers and at least two places in Huskisson offer diving and courses. The Jervis Bay Dive Centre (☎ (044) 41 5255) on Owen St (the main street) charges about $30 for a boat dive or $45 for two dives, plus equipment hire (about $25 for a full set), and they also hire snorkelling gear for $10 a day. Sea Sports (☎ (044) 41 5598), also on Owen St, has similar rates and also runs cruises.

Places to Stay One of the Shoalhaven council's good *Holiday Haven* caravan parks (☎ (044) 41 5142) is a little way out of Huskisson, on the road to Vincentia, and there are other caravan parks in the area. *The Lodge* (☎ (044) 41 5019) on Owen St, opposite the Husky pub, is a simple guesthouse where dorm beds cost $15 and there are also private rooms. Huskisson has several motels.

Shoalhaven Realty (☎ (044) 41 5014) at 52 Owen St handles holiday letting.

Jervis Bay National Park

The national park takes up the south-eastern spit of land on Jervis Bay. It's an interesting park offering good swimming, surfing and diving on bay and ocean beaches. Much of it is heathland, with some forest and small pockets of rainforest. It's administered by the federal government (it is in federal territory) so you won't read about it in NSW National Parks brochures.

There's a good visitor centre (☎ (044) 43 0977) at the park entrance. Inside the park is the **Jervis Bay Botanic Gardens**, which are open daily except Saturday, the **Royal Australian Naval College**, which has a museum which is sometimes open to the public.

Be careful on the clifftops as apparently people fall off regularly. Cliff bottoms on the ocean side can be dangerous too – watch out for waves. After walking in the park check for ticks, which are common.

Entry to the park costs $5 per car and is valid for a week. There are campsites at Green Patch and Bristol Point and a more basic camping area at Caves Beach ($8 to $10). You have to book and sites might not be available at peak times.

Australian pelican

JERVIS BAY TO ULLADULLA

A large body of water encircled by Jervis Bay's southern peninsula, **St Georges Basin** has access to the sea through narrow Sussex Inlet. The north shore of the basin has succumbed to housing developments, reminiscent of the suburban sprawl on the central coast.

On the southern side of **Sussex Inlet** is a fair-sized town of the same name, in an area a little less developed than that on the northern side of the basin. You can hire houseboats at Danbar Pleasure Hire (☎ (044) 41 2074) in South Sussex Inlet.

Further south is **Swan Lake**, yet another lake connecting to the ocean via a narrow inlet. The small towns of **Swan Haven**, **Berrara** and **Cudmirrah** lie between the lake and the sea beaches. Swan Lake Caravan Park in Cudmirrah hires canoes for $5 an hour. The beach south of Berrara is backed by the **Conjola State Forest.**

South of the state forest are **North Bendalong** and **Bendalong**, small towns with caravan parks on nice beaches, and further south is **Manyana**. These places are about 15 km east of the highway and are quieter than the towns further north. There's also a fair amount of bush in the area.

The next inlet and lake is pretty **Lake Conjola**, with a quiet town of holiday shacks and a couple of caravan parks; the *Holiday Haven* (☎ (044) 56 1141) is closest to the ocean. Lake Conjola township is not far south of Manyana but it's across the inlet, so travelling by road between the two involves a trip back to the highway and over 30 km. Lake Conjola (the lake, not the township) extends west almost to the highway and near this end there's the holiday hamlet of **Fishermans Paradise**.

Milton, on the highway six km north of Ulladulla, is this area's original town, built to serve the nearby farming communities. Like so many early towns along the coast, Milton is several km inland – tastes have changed. *Annabel's Settlement Cafe* has healthy lunches and coffee.

ULLADULLA

Ulladulla (population 10,000) isn't an especially attractive town but it has excellent beaches and is close to the Pigeon House mountain in the far south of Morton National Park, and to Budawang National Park. It's

also the largest town on the highway between Nowra and Batemans Bay and has a good range of services and accommodation.

The town's sonorous name is perhaps a corruption of 'holey dollar', the punched-out coin that was an early Australian currency. 'Holy dollar' would not be an appropriate substitute; this is still a fishing port and surfies' hangout rather than a tacky sprawl of housing estates.

Orientation & Information

Ulladulla itself is on rocky Warden Head, but a short walk north of Ulladulla harbour is Mollymook, a suburb on a lovely surf beach. A little further north is Narrawallee, another residential area with surf beaches and a quieter inlet.

Burrill Lake, a few km south of Ulladulla, is a small town on the inlet to Burrill Lake. Kings Point is a residential area inland, on the lake's north shore. The lake is pretty, but there are few facilities for visitors and lots of power-boating.

Ulladulla's information centre (☎ (044) 55 1269; 1800 024 261 toll-free for the Nowra office) is in the Civic Centre, at the bottom of the main-street hill.

Activities

Around Ulladulla, **watersports** are popular, and Totally Board on Mollymook beach hires boards and bikes. Ulladulla Watersports Hire (on the south side of the Burrill Lake Bridge, a few km south of Ulladulla) has windsurfers, surf-skis and canoes. Nearby, Burrill Lake Cat Hire (☎ (044) 55 5883) rents catamarans between October and the end of April and during school holidays.

Budawang Walkabout (☎ (044) 55 3729; 54 0274 AH) organises **walks** in the Budawangs from two to five days, and also day walks. They can supply all the equipment but it's cheaper if you have your own. The same people run the Budawang Wilderness Store, in Rowen's Arcade (underneath Funland on the main street), where you can buy hiking gear.

Monolith Mountain Bikes (☎ (044) 54 0274) hires **bikes** for $10 a half-day and $35

for the whole day, including lunch. The dive shop (☎ (044) 55 5303) is on Wason St, the street leading to the fishing wharf.

Climbing the **Pigeon House** (1400 metres) in the far south of Morton National Park is a popular activity. A road runs close to the summit, from where it's a walk of four hours to the top and back. The first hour's walk from the car park is a steady climb, but after that it levels out a little. The main access road to the Pigeon House leaves the highway about eight km south of Ulladulla, and you can also get there from Milton and Termeil.

Festivals & Events

At Easter the Blessing of the Fleet ceremony is held and other non-marine celebrations take place, such as a rodeo. In nearby Milton, the Settlers Fair is held in early October.

Places to Stay

Caravan Parks There are plenty of caravan parks in the area. The *Holiday Haven* (☎ (044) 55 2457), one of Shoalhaven Council's well-run chain, is on the headland a few blocks from the town centre (at the end of South St) but a bit of a walk from the beach. There are more caravan parks off the highway south of town.

Hostel *South Coast Backpackers* (☎ (044) 54 0500) is at 67 Princes Highway. It's towards the top of the hill to the north of the shopping centre. Coming from the north, look for it on your right as you come around a corner just before descending the hill. It's a small, clean place with spacious five-bed dorms and all the usual facilities. Beds cost $12.50 a night and if you're staying here they'll take you to Murramarang National Park or the Pigeon House for $10.

Motels Ulladulla has plenty of motels but Mollymook is a nicer place to stay. Most motels here are pricey during holiday periods but reasonable at other times. Less expensive places include *Surfside* (☎ (044) 55 1966) on Golf Ave (the beachfront road), costing from $45/50, and *Mollymook Beach*

(☎ (044) 55 2221) at 44 Ocean St, costing from $40/55.

Following the beachfront road north through Mollymook, you rise up onto the headland and come to *Bannister Lodge* (☎ (044) 55 3044) at 191 Mitchell Pde, a motel with superb views of the coast and ocean. Rates start at $50/60. There's a licensed restaurant here.

Places to Eat

There are plenty of coffee shops and pasta places on Ulladulla's main street and in the arcades running off it. *Just Good Food*, in the arcade towards the bottom of the hill, opposite the Westpac bank, has snacks, quiche and felafel. *Rudolph's Pasta & Pizza*, across from the Marlin Hotel, has all-you-can-eat nights, as do several other places at various times.

At the south end of the main street, up the hill, *Raja's Restaurant* is open daily and has curries for about $9.50. On the last Sunday of the month they hold an Indian Bazaar here.

AGee's Restaurant & Brasserie on Green St is open for lunch on weekdays and for dinner Monday to Saturday. They serve Cajun and contemporary Australian food, with $8 lunch specials.

The best views are at the *Harbourside Terrace*, where there's a restaurant selling the catch of the day for about $16 and other steak and seafood dishes, and a cheaper cafe. Breakfast costs about $8.

At the fishing wharf on Wason St you can buy fresh fish; across the road is *Tony's Seafood Restaurant*. It's licensed and there are good views. Downstairs is a takeaway section selling fresh fish & chips.

Getting There & Away

Bus Fares with Pioneer Motor Service include Sydney, $12; Nowra, $11.40; Merry Beach (at the north end of Murramarang National Park), $5.50; the North Durras turn-off (about 10 km to Pebbly Beach in Murramarang National Park), $6.50; Batemans Bay, $8.80; and Eden, $29.20. Ticket agents are Ulladulla Travel Service (☎ (044)

55 1630) in the Plaza shopping centre and Tollgate Travel (☎ (044) 55 5122) in the Pacific Terrace centre.

Car & Motorbike The Princes Highway runs north to Nowra and south to Batemans Bay, passing Murramarang National Park. The small towns at the north end of the park are reached from Termeil, on the highway 20 km south of Ulladulla.

Getting Around

Bus Ulladulla Bus Lines (☎ (044) 55 1674) services the local area, mainly between Milton, Mollymook, Ulladulla and Burrill Lake. There are about three services a day.

BUDAWANG NATIONAL PARK

South of Morton National Park, Budawang is not large (16,100 hectares) but it offers rugged scenery and wilderness walking. There are no roads through the park nor any facilities in it. Easiest access is from the hamlet of Mongalowe, 14 km east of Braidwood.

For more information see the National Parks office in Nowra (☎ (044) 23 9800).

The Far South Coast

The far south coast is the least developed stretch of coast in the state and it has some of the best beaches and forests. Even so, the population triples during holiday times, especially in the Eurobodalla area (from Batemans Bay to Narooma), and prices rise accordingly.

Activities

As well as the beaches and inlets, with swimming, surfing and fishing, there are good walks in the national parks.

The visitor centres in Batemans Bay and Narooma sell topographic maps and copies of Graham Barrow's book *Walking on the South Coast*, which details mainly short walks between Nowra and Eden.

Mimosa Kayaks (☎ (064) 52 3826 or 93

5035) offers sea kayaking on weekends (fortnightly in winter), either by the day or on overnight trips. The minimum group size is three, but they might be able to fit in solo kayakers. They charge $30 a day for kayak hire plus $30 a day for instruction/guides.

MURRAMARANG NATIONAL PARK
This beautiful coastal park begins about 20 km south of Ulladulla and stretches almost all the way south to Batemans Bay. The park is in two sections, with a break in the middle around Durras Lake.

The park includes some thick forest with big old trees – there are state forests west of the park and you can see how logging has deprived them of the age and diversity of trees that the national park enjoys.

Depot, Pebbly and Merry beaches are all popular with surfies, as is Wasp Head south of Durras.

Places to Stay
In the Park The National Parks campsite (☎ (044) 78 6006) is at lovely Pebbly Beach and costs $10 a double, plus the $7.50 per car park-entry fee. A kiosk operates during school holidays – when tent sites are scarce. You should book in summer. The kangaroos are incredibly friendly here. Don't feed them bread (it's bad for them), but unless you keep your food locked away they'll probably find it anyway. To get here, turn off the highway at East Lynne. Caravans can't use the last section of the road to Pebbly Beach.

Nearby Settlements There are small towns on the borders of the park, and one or two on old leases within the park itself. If campsites in the park are booked out you could try these places.

Turn off from the highway at Termeil to get to **Bawley Point** and **Kioloa**, near the north end of the park. There are caravan parks in these small towns and just south of Kioloa are caravan parks at **Merry Beach** and **Pretty Beach**, both privately run but within the boundary of the national park. They are reasonable places and the beaches are, as usual, excellent, but they lack the

Far South Coast - Ulladulla to Narooma

steep and forested slopes behind the beaches that you'll find further south. There's a shopping centre on the road between Bawley Point and Kioloa.

The East Lynne turn-off from the highway will get you to the National Parks camping area at Pebbly Beach and to **Depot Beach** and **North Durras**. Any of these places is worth spending time in because of the great beaches and beautiful bushland.

At Depot Beach there's the basic *Moore's Caravan Park* (☎ (044) 78 6010), with tent sites for $4 plus $3 per person and a range of on-site vans, cabins and flats from about

$400 per week in summer or from $45 a night in the off-season. There's no shop at Depot Beach but a truck selling essentials calls in most days.

North Durras has a small shop and several large caravan parks but not much else. As well as the superb beach, North Durras is on the inlet to Durras Lake. *Durras Lake North Caravan Park* (☎ (044) 78 6072) has a cabin or an on-site van set aside for backpackers, and charges $8 a bed. Ask at the shop. The tent sites here are good, too, as you can camp in the bush, maybe meeting some bandicoots.

At the south end of the park (turn off the highway at Bendanderah), **Durras** is a quiet village of substantial holiday houses. The great beaches are backed by thick bush. At the south end of the town is the resort-style *Murramarang Caravan & Camping Resort* (☎ (044) 78 6355). It's a big place with sites (from $11), on-site vans (from $30) and cabins (from $50). There are more elaborate cabins (with spas!) from $100. Prices rise considerably during holidays. They also have lots of activities and even 'floor-show' entertainment! That a complex like this, on the edge of one of the world's more beautiful national parks, should win tourism awards says something about Australian taste.

One or two km north of Durras is South Durras (yes – it's south of North Durras on the other side of Durras Lake), on a spit of land between the ocean and the lake. This is a fibro-cement town and the two caravan parks don't aspire to the heights of their competitor.

Getting There & Away
The Princes Highway runs parallel to Murramarang but it's about 10 km from the highway to the beach or the small settlements in and near the park. Pioneer Motor Service runs to Merry Beach and will drop you on the highway at the North Durras turn-off. The backpacker hostel in Ulladulla drives guests to Pebbly Beach for $10.

BATEMANS BAY
Batemans Bay (population 8500) is a fishing port which has boomed to become one of the south coast's largest holiday centres, partly because of its good beaches and beautiful estuary, partly because it's the closest coastal town to land-locked Canberra.

Orientation & Information
Batemans Bay is on the neck of the beautiful Clyde River estuary. The estuary winds up to near Nelligen, about 10 km inland on the road to Canberra. The actual bay is the flaring of the estuary as it enters the sea. Small islands, including Tollgate Island, dot the estuary mouth.

Batemans Bay township is a small, pleasant place with a mixture of tourism and commercial fishing activity. There's a long strip of tourist development shading into housing estates as you follow Beach Rd (which becomes George Bass Drive) south from the town centre, through the suburbs of Batehaven, Denhams Beach and Surf Beach. South of here the development dwindles and the forest takes over, but there are plenty of For Sale signs tacked to trees. The small satellite suburb of Broulee marks the southern end of Batemans Bay's sphere of influence.

The large visitor centre (☎ (044) 72 6900, 1800 802 528 toll-free) is on the Princes Highway near the town centre. It's open daily.

Things to See & Do
Corrigans Beach is the closest beach to the town centre. South of Corrigans is a series of small beaches nibbled into the rocky shore. There are longer beaches along the coast north of the bridge, leading into Murramarang National Park.

Surfies flock to Surf Beach, Malua Bay, the small McKenzies Beach (just south of Malua) and Broulee, which has a small wave when everywhere else is flat. For the experienced, the best surfing in the area is at Pink Rocks (near Broulee) when a north swell is running, sometimes producing six-metre waves.

On the north side of the estuary just across the bridge (but if you're driving you'll have

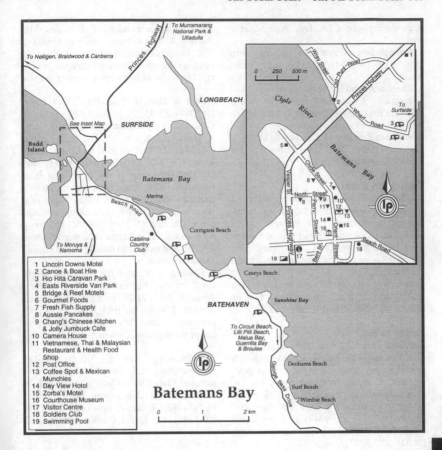

1 Lincoln Downs Motel
2 Canoe & Boat Hire
3 Hio Hita Caravan Park
4 Easts Riverside Van Park
5 Bridge & Reef Motels
6 Gourmet Foods
7 Fresh Fish Supply
8 Aussie Pancakes
9 Chang's Chinese Kitchen
  & Jolly Jumbuck Cafe
10 Camera House
11 Vietnamese, Thai & Malaysian
   Restaurant & Health Food
   Shop
12 Post Office
13 Coffee Spot & Mexican
   Munchies
14 Bay View Hotel
15 Zorba's Motel
16 Courthouse Museum
17 Visitor Centre
18 Soldiers Club
19 Swimming Pool

Batemans Bay

0   1   2 km

to keep going to the Canberra turn-off and take the first left) you can hire **canoes and paddleboats** for a pricey $10 for half an hour and outboards for $30 for two hours. **Sailing boats** are hired out on Corrigans beach in summer.

Several outfits offer **cruises** up the Clyde estuary; the visitor centre has details. Some cruises can be combined with 4WD expeditions into the bush with Tangletours. Some of these are good value. Tangletours (☎ (044) 78 1007), which is run, of course, by Tangles, offers other interesting day trips. There are also sea cruises, during which you

might see penguins on the islands of the Tollgate Nature Reserve. The information centre has details.

The small **Courthouse Museum**, on the corner of Orient and Beach Sts, has displays relating to local history. It's open Tuesday, Thursday and Saturday, more often during school holidays, and admission is $1 (20c children).

Birdland Animal Park on Beach Rd near Batehaven is open daily. Admission is $7 ($5 children). Would a seaside holiday be complete without a visit to a **shell museum**? Batemans Bay's is at 142 Beach Rd and is

open during school holidays. Admission is free.

Paragliding is available all year with Drag'n'Fly (☎ (044) 76 7255), at the main wharf.

The **Corn Trail** in the Buckenbowra State Forest is a 13-km trail down the Buckenbowra River from Clyde Mountain, which is the cause of that steep section on the road down from Braidwood. Contact the Forestry Office (☎ (044) 72 6211) on Crown St for more information.

Festivals & Events

The Neptune Festival is held over the second weekend in November and there's a game-fishing tournament in February. Up in Nelligen, a Country Music Festival twangs over the first weekend in January. The Moruya Rodeo is held on Easter Sunday and Eurobodalla Shire's agricultural show is held there in late January. Moruya used to have a Mardi Gras in April, and there is talk of reinstating it. Blues and Texas music feature.

Places to Stay

Caravan Parks As with other accommodation, you might have to book for a minimum period or pay a surcharge for sites at peak periods. Coming from the north on the Princes Highway, turn left just before the bridge to get to the big *Easts Van Park Riverside* (☎ (044) 72 4048) and the much smaller and simpler *Rio Rita Caravan Park* (☎ (044) 72 5741).

Other caravan parks include the pricey *Coachhouse Tourist Van Park* (☎ (044) 72 4392), off Beach Rd at the beginning of Corrigans Beach. Sites cost $15 and on-site vans from $25 a double. Cabins with ensuites start at $40 a double. There's a kitchen for campers.

Hostel Across the river at Longbeach (turn off the highway five km north of the bridge) there's a quiet suburb and the *YMCA Camp* (☎ (044) 72 4695) where you can stay if it isn't booked out by school groups. They might be able to pick you up from town, 12 km away. The camp is not far from the beach

and is on a nice wooded hill. Beds cost $10, B&B is $14 and dinner, bed and breakfast $20. To get here just keep following the main road into Longbeach and the camp is on your right as the road turns down to meet the sea.

Hotel & Motels The *Bay View Hotel* (☎ (044) 72 4522), in the town centre on Orient St, has pub rooms for $20/30.

There are many motels. The *Bridge Motel* (☎ (044) 72 6344) is a good mid-range place. It's on Clyde St; turn right immediately after crossing the bridge if you're coming from the north. Off-season rates are about $40/45, rising to $90/100 in peak times. Right next door is a good example of an upper-range place, the *Reef* (☎ 1800 024 902 toll-free), with a range of accommodation from about $70/80, and more than double that at Christmas and Easter.

Off-season prices at the resorts are worth checking out. For example, *Tyrolia Bluegrass* (☎ (044) 71 1671), a little way inland from Surf Beach, has B&B deals for $35 per person in winter. It's a well-equipped but rather incongruous Bavarian-style place.

Self-Catering There are many holiday apartments which do good business in summer. Out of season you might be able to rent one for less than a week. Letting agents include Real Estate Professionals (☎ (044) 72 4444) and David Burdett (☎ (044) 72 5722).

Other Accommodation *Bay River Houseboats* (☎ (044) 72 5649) on Wray St, west along on the estuary on the north side, hires eight- and ten-berth houseboats. From May to August an eight-berth boat costs about $500 for four nights (Monday to Friday) hire and $550 for the weekend. This doubles in peak times and there are further surcharges for school and other holidays. Still, between a few people this could be good value and a great way to get around. Clyde River Boat Hire (☎ (044) 72 6369) also on Wray St, hires houseboats for about the same rates.

In Nelligen, 10 km west on the road to Canberra, the *Old Post Office Guesthouse*

(☎ (044) 78 1179) is close to the river and charges $95 a double for B&B.

Places to Eat

The *Fresh Fish Supply* is on the foreshore by the fishing wharf and sells seafood straight off the boats. They'll also cook you sit-down or takeaway meals, such as tuna, chips and coleslaw for $7. The menu depends on the catch. Across the road, *Gourmet Foods* is a good takeaway, with fish & chips for $4.50, a range of salads (from $2.80 for a generous serving) and various pasta dishes for $3.50.

Mexican Munchies, upstairs in the building south of the post office, is licensed, opens at 6 pm and has main courses at about $13. At the back of this building, on the foreshore walk, the *Coffee Spot* has outdoor tables and serves breakfast, meals (main courses around $11) and snacks. The breakfasts are a little pricey at $8 for bacon and eggs, but as a dolphin swam past while I was eating mine, I didn't mind. Just north of here, also on the foreshore walk, is *Bayview Pizza*, with pasta for $8 and veal dishes from $9.50, as well as pizzas.

Across from the post office, the *Batemans Bay Vietnamese, Thai & Malaysian Restaurant*, a small place with a long name, has lunchtime specials at $4.50 and main courses for $7.50. It's a neat, spartan place which would look right at home on Melbourne's Victoria St strip of Vietnamese restaurants. In the shopping centre behind the BBVTMR is the *Bay Centre Deli* which has a big range of health food as well as deli items, and takeaways.

On North St, near the corner of Orient St, the *Jolly Jumbuck Cafe* is a little more upmarket than the name would suggest. Main courses are about $12. Next door, *Chang's Chinese Kitchen* sells takeaway food for around $8 for main courses. There are a couple of tables where you can eat in. Further along North St is *Aussie Pancakes* with a huge menu based on pancakes and crepes ranging from $3 to $7. They have smoothies for $2.50.

The *Taliva* (☎ (044) 72 4278) at 236 Beach Rd in Batehaven is a highly-rated French restaurant with game and seafood featuring on the menu. In the off-season they have some special deals, such as three courses for $25. Also in Batehaven, the licensed *Stockyard* is a family-oriented place with steak and salad dinners from $10, Wednesday to Monday.

Many of the motels have restaurants, including the *Reef* at the Reef Motel, with main courses approaching $20 and a seafood platter for $52 per person. *Briars Restaurant*, at the upmarket Lincoln Downs resort north of the bridge, has a menu featuring game and terrines.

Entertainment

Beachies Nightspot on Beach Rd in Batehaven stays open late most nights in the summer, but you have to arrive by 11.45 pm, in neat clothes. The Bowling Club, the Soldiers Club and the Catalina Country Club have music of some sort on weekends. Check the local paper for details.

Getting There & Away

Bus Harvey World Travel (☎ (044) 72 5086) on Orient St handles bus bookings and has timetables in the window.

Greyhound Pioneer Australia stops here on the run between Sydney ($30) and Melbourne ($58).

Pioneer Motor Service (☎ (044) 21 7722 in Nowra) runs between Eden ($25 from Batemans Bay) and Sydney ($29) via Batemans Bay at least daily. Some services connect with trains at Bomaderry.

Murrays (☎ (06) 295 3611 in Canberra) runs between Narooma ($11.20 from Batemans Bay) and Canberra ($21.75) at least daily. The Sapphire Coast Express (☎ (044) 73 5517) runs between Batemans Bay and Melbourne ($57) twice a week

Car & Motorbike The Princes Highway runs north to Ulladulla and south to Moruya and Narooma. You can follow the beachfront road south as far as the north shore of the Duea (Moruya) River and rejoin the highway at Moruya. A scenic road runs inland to Nelligen, Braidwood and Canberra.

SOUTH COAST

Getting Around

Priors Bus Service (☎ (044) 72 4040) runs regular but infrequent services to Moruya via Batehaven and Broulee. There are even fewer services north of the bridge, to Surfside, Longbeach and Maloney's Beach.

There's a taxi service (☎ (044) 71 1444).

DEUA NATIONAL PARK

Inland from Moruya, Deua National Park (81,800 hectares) is a mountainous wilderness area with swift-running rivers (good for canoeing) and some challenging walking. There are also many caves. There are simple camping areas off the scenic road running between Araluen and Moruya and off the road between Braidwood and Numeralla, plus a couple more on tracks within the park.

See the National Parks office in Narooma (☎ (044) 76 2888) for more information.

BATEMANS BAY TO NAROOMA

This stretch of coast is known as the Eurobodalla Coast, a reference to the many lakes, bays and inlets along it. Eurobodalla is an Aboriginal word meaning 'place of many waters'.

Mogo

This strip of old wooden shops and houses is almost entirely devoted to Devonshire teas, crafts and antiques. Some of those 'old' buildings are still under construction. Half a km back from the highway is **Old Mogo Town**, a re-creation of a small pioneer village, open Friday, Saturday, Sunday and holidays. Admission is $6 or $12 for a family. Two km east off the highway from Mogo is the Somerset Sanctuary & Zoo, open 10 am to 5 pm daily. Admission is $5 ($2 children). There is a fair range of animals here but some of the more exotic ones are stuffed. Further down this road, about halfway between Mogo and the sea, is **Mogo Goldfields**, another small historic park. There's a caravan park here.

Broulee

Almost an outer suburb of Batemans Bay, Broulee (pronounced *brow*-lee) is on a good beach and there are holiday houses as well as the *Broulee Beach Van Park* (☎ (044) 71 62 47) with sites from $13 and cabins from $45 a double. There are several other large resort-style parks between here and Batemans Bay.

Priors Buses run as far south as Broulee. See the Batemans Bay Getting Around section.

Moruya

Moruya, 25 km south of Batemans Bay and about five km inland, is on the estuary of the Deua River (also called the Moruya). This small town is more a rural service centre than a tourist haven and it's the administrative centre of Eurobodalla Shire. The river's banks turn into wetlands as it sprawls down to the sea at **Moruya Heads**, the hamlet on the south head, where there's a good surf beach and views from Taragy Point.

In town there are a couple of motels and a caravan park by the river, but you're better off going to Moruya Heads, seven km east. The large and pleasant *Dolphin Beach Caravan Park* (☎ (044) 74 2728) charges about $12 for tent sites and from $30 a double in on-site vans. Prices jump during the Christmas week and at Easter. Priors Buses run from Batemans Bay to Moruya and you might be able to get a lift to Moruya Heads on a school bus. Over on the north head (you have to return to Moruya to get there) is a big council camping area costing from $8 a site.

Congo

South from Moruya Heads, Congo is a small cluster of houses on an estuary and a long surf beach, very pretty and peaceful. Volunteers are helping to repair damage to the dunes here and they welcome assistance. There's a basic camping area (due to be upgraded) where sites cost $8 or $10 in summer. You might have to bring in all your food and bring or boil drinking water.

A dirt road to Congo runs off the road between Moruya and Moruya Heads, and another dirt road (currently being sealed) to Congo leaves the highway about 10 km

south of Moruya. The latter road also leads to **Meringo**, another tiny place on the coast.

Tuross Head
This big development of suburban houses is at the end of a peninsula that separates Coila Lake and Tuross Lake, both large inlets. Tuross Head describes itself as 'the most talked-about town on the south coast', but I can't imagine why. **Tuross Lake** is attractive, although most of the country around it has been cleared, but the town could be part of any suburb in the country.

There's a small caravan park on the good ocean beach and another on Tuross Lake, several km away from the town and the sea. The pub in town has motel units (☎ (044) 73 8112).

South of Tuross Head, on the other side of Tuross lake, is **Potato Point**, where there's another good beach.

NAROOMA
Narooma (population 3500) is becoming a seaside holiday town but is nowhere near as developed as Batemans Bay to the north or Merimbula to the south. The town is on a strip of land between the ocean and beautiful Wagonga Inlet.

The town should be called Noorooma, an Aboriginal word meaning 'clear blue water', but a clerical error produced today's spelling. Late last century the town was a timber-milling and ship-building centre, as well as a service centre for the dairy farms in the district.

Part of the town is on a point between two sections of the inlet, but many of the facilities and residential streets are south of here, up a steep hill. To get to the surf beach turn off the highway down Fuller St, near the information centre, and follow it around.

The good information centre (☎ (044) 76 2881) on the beachfront is open daily from 9 am to 5 pm. Here there's also the small **Lighthouse Museum**. You can buy CMA maps and Forestry Commission maps which detail walking trails in the nearby state forests. Narooma is also an access point for both Deua and Wadbilliga national parks,

Fairy penguins

and there's a National Parks office (☎ (044) 76 2888), one shop back from the highway at the corner of Field St, just north of the information centre.

Things to See & Do
About 10 km offshore from Narooma is **Montague Island**. This island, once an important source of food for local Aborigines (who called it Barunguba) is now a nature reserve. Fairy penguins nest here, and although you'll see some all year, there are many thousands in late winter and spring. Many other seabirds, along with hundreds of seals, make their homes on the island. There's also a historic lighthouse. A boat trip to Montague Island and a tour conducted by a National Parks ranger costs $40 ($25 children) and can be booked at the information centre. The boat leaves at 3.30 pm on Monday, Wednesday and Friday (in time to see the penguins waddle up the beach at dusk), with extra trips in summer. The clear waters around the island are good for diving.

You can **cruise** up the Wagonga River on the *Wagonga Princess*, a nice old boat. A three-hour cruise, including a stop for a walk through the bush and some billy tea, costs $15 ($10 children). Book at the information centre. There are several boat-hire places along Riverside Drive, running off the highway near the bridge, so you can get out on Wagonga Inlet under your own steam.

Austwild Tours (☎ (044) 76 2845) runs evening **wildlife-spotting tours** into the

mountains for $45 ($25 children). They say there's a good chance of seeing a platypus.

A good rainy-day activity is to see a film at the **Narooma Kinema**, a picture palace that began showing flicks in 1928 and hasn't changed much since.

Paragliding is sometimes available; the information centre has details.

The Bowling Club often has music, sometimes big touring bands in summer.

For **surfing**, Mystery Bay between Cape Dromedary and Corunna Point is rocky but good, as is Handkerchief Beach, especially at the north end. Narooma's Bar Beach is best when a south-easterly is blowing. Potato Point is another popular hang-out for surfies.

Festivals & Events

The Lighthouse Festival and the Surfboat Marathon are held in November.

Places to Stay

There's a range of accommodation, although the hostel on Wagonga Inlet has closed. Narooma Real Estate (☎ (044) 76 2169) handles holiday letting.

Caravan Parks There are several caravan parks, with two members of the Easts chain (☎ (044) 76 2161 and 76 2046) on the highway near the information centre and the smaller, cheaper and quieter *Surf Beach* (☎ (044) 76 2275) around by the surf beach.

Hotel & Motels *Lynch's Hotel* (☎ (044) 76 2001) is on the highway, up on the hill at the south end of town. Basic rooms cost $20/30 a single/double.

There are plenty of motels, most of which charge around $45 a single in the off-season but more in summer. Cheaper places include the *Tree* (☎ (044) 76 2233) and the *Vintage* (☎ (044) 76 2256).

Places to Eat

Gypsy Gourmet on the highway has wholefood snacks, kebabs and seafood. The *Narooma Marine Centre* on Riverside Drive has a bistro overlooking the lake and fresh takeaway seafood. The *Ex-Servicemen's*

Club has snacks at lunchtime and meals from 6 pm. The *Bowling Club* also has a restaurant. *Tatlers on Campbell*, 107 Campbell St, is a licensed restaurant featuring local wines. There are many other places, including *LaSallian Centre Restaurant* on the highway, with three-course dinners for $20.

Getting There & Away

Bus Bus bookings are handled by Harvey World Travel (☎ (044) 76 2688), in the St George Building Society office on the hill. All buses stop nearby.

Greyhound Pioneer Australia stops here on the run between Sydney and Melbourne; Murrays stops on the run between Narooma and Canberra via Batemans Bay; and Sapphire Coast Express stops on its run between Batemans Bay and Melbourne.

Car & Motorbike The Princes Highway runs north to Batemans Bay and south to Bega. Just south of Narooma a scenic route loops inland to Central Tilba, rejoining the highway near Tilba Tilba. The northern turn-off for Wallaga Lake and Bermagui is also near Tilba Tilba.

AROUND NAROOMA
Dalmeny

Now a suburb of Narooma, five km south, Dalmeny is a quiet residential area on Mummaga Lake, yet another of the Eurobodalla Coast's pretty inlets. There's a council camping area.

Mystery Bay

Near Dromedary Head, about 12 km south of Narooma, this little settlement of new houses has a fine rocky beach (and sandy ones nearby) and a big but basic camping area in a forest of spotted gums. Sites cost $7 and $9 in summer. Mystery Bay is so named because the boat of a surveying party which vanished in 1880 was found here.

Central Tilba & Around

Central Tilba is a tiny wooden town almost unchanged since it was built last century – except that now the main street is jammed

with visitors' cars. It would be worth staying here just to see what happens when all the visitors leave. You can get a good guide to the town from the store at the start of the main street. There are several working craft shops and a cheese factory. You can even have a massage or have your aura read.

Not far from Central Tilba there's a **winery**, Tilba Valley Wines, and Brooklands **deer farm**.

The **Tilba Festival**, with lots of music and entertainment, is held at Easter, although it's hard to imagine how the 8000-plus visitors fit.

Central Tilba perches on the side of **Mt Dromedary**, the highest mountain on the south coast (800 metres) and renamed by Captain Cook in 1770 (the original name is Gulaga). He judged it to be 'a pretty high mountain'. There is lush forest on the mountain, which is a flora reserve, and from the top there are great views. You can walk to the top, beginning at the **Tilba Tilba** store (where you can buy lunch for the walk) and following an old pack-horse trail. The return walk of 11 km takes about five hours. There is often rain and mist on the mountain, so come prepared. You could also ride up with Mt Dromedary Trail Rides (☎ (044) 76 3376).

From Tilba Tilba the highway swings inland to **Cobargo**, another small town that has changed little since it was built, and where there are craft shops, a pub and motels. There's also a tantalisingly named antique shop, No Wife, No Horse, No Moustache.

Places to Stay & Eat The *Dromedary Hotel* (☎ (044) 73 7223) in Central Tilba has a couple of basic rooms for $25/50 including a cooked breakfast. If you've come to stay in an original town it perhaps makes sense to stay in an original pub, but you won't pay much more for considerably more comfort at *Wirrina Guesthouse* (☎ (044) 73 7279), which charges $58 a double for B&B. A few km away near Tilba Tilba is *Green Gables* guesthouse (☎ (044) 73 7435) with B&B doubles from $65.

The *Tilba Teapot* has snacks and meals. A

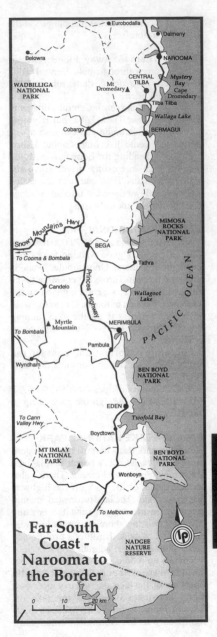

Far South Coast – Narooma to the Border

SOUTH COAST

traveller recommends the hamburgers at the Tilba Tilba store.

Getting There & Away Pioneer Motor Service comes through both Central Tilba and Tilba Tilba on its daily run between Sydney and Eden.

By car, you can reach Central Tilba from the turn-off near Tilba Tilba, but if you're coming from Narooma you can also take a signposted scenic diversion of about 15 km.

If you're heading for Bermagui or if you just want an interesting drive, leave the highway at Tilba Tilba and take the sealed road that follows the coast through Wallaga Lake National Park to Bermagui.

WADBILLIGA NATIONAL PARK

A rugged wilderness area of 79,000 hectares, Wadbilliga offers good walking for experienced bushwalkers. One popular walk is along the five-km Tuross River Gorge to the Tuross Falls. There's a camping area on the north-western side of the park, near the walk to the falls. Access is off the road running from Countegany (east of Numeralla) south to Tuross.

For more information, contact the National Parks office in Narooma (☎ (044) 76 2888).

Wadbilliga Trail Rides (☎ (064) 93 6737 AH) offers rides through the park of up to four days.

WALLAGA LAKE NATIONAL PARK

This small park takes in most of the western shore of Wallaga Lake, a beautiful tidal lake at the mouth of several creeks. There's also another chunk of the park off the highway just west of here. The lake is forested (mainly regeneration after logging) and its many tiny bays and twisting shoreline invite leisurely exploration by boat. Birdlife is prolific and you'll probably meet animals in the bush.

There's no road access into the park, but the little towns of **Beauty Point** and **Regatta Point** are on the lake and you can hire boats there. Merriman Island, in the lake off Regatta Point, is off-limits because of its significance to the Aboriginal community.

Similarly, sites (such as middens, the remains of shellfish feasts) and relics you might come across in the park are protected.

Umbarra Cultural Tours (☎ (044) 73 7232, 73 7414 AH), run by people from the Wallaga Aboriginal community, has tours of the lake and other places of historical and cultural importance. This operation is just starting out so details are a bit hazy, but tours will probably cost about $15 per person for a half-day and $30 for a day. The minimum group size is six.

Places to Stay

There are several caravan parks in and near Regatta Point and Beauty Point, small, neighbouring towns on a peninsula separating the lake from the ocean. The lake is a popular place in summer – prices can double and there might be minimum stays around Christmas and Easter.

Perhaps the nicest caravan park is the big *Ocean Lakes Caravan park* (☎ (064) 93 4055) with sites for $10 and on-site vans from $25 a double. Nearby *Uncle Tom's Tourist Park* (☎ (064) 93 4253) is a bit cheaper and also has self-contained units costing from $30 a double. Both these places are on the lake and are a bit of a walk to the ocean beach. The closest caravan park to the ocean is *Wallaga Lake Park* (☎ (064) 93 4655), off the main road between Bermagui and Narooma, just south of Beauty Point. Sites cost from $10 and vans from $25.

BERMAGUI

Bermagui is a small fishing community (population 1000) centred on pretty Horseshoe Bay. Many visitors come here, mainly to fish, and there are six big-game tournaments a year. It's a handy base for visits to both Wallaga Lake and Mimosa Rocks national parks, and for Wadbilliga National Park, inland in the ranges.

American cowboy-novelist Zane Grey once visited Bermagui and included his experiences in a book.

The information centre (☎ (064) 93 4174) is on Coluga St, the continuation of the main road north of the bridge.

Bermagui has a taxi service (☎ (064) 93 4686).

Places to Stay & Eat

Zane Grey Park (☎ (064) 93 4382) is right in the town centre, overlooking Horseshoe Bay, and has sites from $12 and on-site vans from $35 a double. Prices rise considerably at peak times.

Blue Pacific Flats (☎ (064) 93 4921) at 77 Murrah St has backpacker accommodation for $12 a bed and a double room for $30. Cooked breakfast costs $6. Blue Pacific is a friendly place, and worth considering for non-hostel accommodation as well. Their self-contained flats sleep six and cost $450 a week around January and Easter, dropping to $250 in winter, when they also offer doubles for $180 a week. Overnight stays cost $40 a double all year, although there's unlikely to be a vacancy in the peak season. Blue Pacific is up a hill off the road running along the beach north of the town centre. The turn-off is signposted, just north of the fishing-boat wharf (where you can buy very fresh fish & chips).

There are many other holiday houses and apartments. Letting agents include Town & Country (☎ (064) 93 4124).

The *Horseshoe Bay Hotel/Motel* (☎ (064) 93 4206) has units from about $30/45. The other motels are more expensive, very much so in summer.

Roly's Wharf Restaurant serves seafood and some innovative dishes. During the day, *Love at First Bite*, just north of the bridge, has a good range of cafe-style salads, antipasto and meals.

Getting There & Away

Bus Bermagui is off the highway, so transport can be a little complicated. Bega Valley Coaches (☎ (064) 92 2418) has a weekday service between Bermagui and Bega ($9.90) and a feeder service connects with Pioneer Motor Service's bus north to Nowra.

Car & Motorbike Heading north, the quickest way back to the highway is to go north past Wallaga Lake National Park, and this is

also a pretty drive. Heading south, the quickest way is to go west and join the highway at Cobargo, but if you have time you could drive south on the unsealed road that runs alongside Mimosa Rocks National Park to Tathra, from where you can rejoin the highway at Bega. Watch out for lyrebirds.

MIMOSA ROCKS NATIONAL PARK

Running along 17 km of beautiful coastline, Mimosa Rocks (5180 hectares) is a wonderful coastal park, with dense and varied bush and great beaches. There are basic campsites at Aragunnu Beach, Picnic Point and Middle Beach, and a camping area with no facilities at Gillards Beach. Camping costs $5 plus the $7.50 park entry fee. All these camping areas and the picnic areas are accessible from the road running between Bermagui and Tathra.

Contact the National Parks office in Narooma (☎ (064) 76 2888) for more information.

TATHRA

This small town is popular with people from the Bega area in summer. The town is on a long beach and continues up on the headland. Here, up the very steep road, you'll find the post office and the pub, as well as access to the historic wharf.

There is tourist information at the Beach House Gallery, across from the Surf Club.

Tathra wharf is the last remaining coastal steamship wharf in the state and a popular place for fishing. The wharf storehouse now houses a small **Maritime Museum** (admission $1.50) as well as a tackle and takeaway shop.

Cliff Place, a narrow street that runs off the headland road next to the road down to the wharf, has great views. You can walk up on a path that begins near the surf club.

At Mongaeeka Inlet, three km north of Tathra, Bega River Cruises (☎ (064) 94 1523) runs cruises and rents boats, catamarans, sailboards and canoes.

Places to Stay

Prices for accommodation in Tathra rise considerably in summer.

There are three caravan parks. *Tathra Beach Tourist Park* (☎ (064) 94 1302) is right on the beach in the centre of town. There could be a bit of road-noise here. There are sites (from $10) and on-site vans (from $30). The *Seabreeze* (☎ (064) 94 1350) is across the road and has sites (from $15), on-site vans (from $30) and cabins (from $40). *Tathra Beach Motor Village* (☎ (064) 94 1577) is just north of the centre and is less cramped than the other two. It has sites (from $12), on-site vans (from $30) and cabins (from $30).

The *Tathra Hotel/Motel* (☎ (064) 94 1101) is a popular eating, drinking and dancing place up on the headland. There's motel accommodation in adequate but not especially nice units for $35/55, rising to $45/75 in summer. The pub has entertainment on weekends (which means noise for the motel units) and in summer they host big touring acts. There's also a *guesthouse* (☎ (064) 94 2133) at 5 Cliff Place, the small road that heads off to the left next to the road down to the old wharf. B&B costs about $40 per person.

L J Hooker (☎ (064) 94 1077) is one of the real estate agents handling holiday letting.

Places to Eat

The pub has counter meals and a bistro. Also on the headland, next to the road going down to the beach, *Harbourmaster Bar & Grill* is a pleasant place in an old house, with main courses around $20. Down on the beachfront street, the *Greatest Crepe* is a licensed cafe with a big menu of crepes and other meals. Main courses are around $12. The *Bowling Club* has a Chinese restaurant. On the beach next to the surf lifesaving club, the *Tathra Beach Kiosk* is actually a good BYO restaurant that's open most days for dinner and for other meals on weekends. It closes for winter.

Getting There & Away

Bus Buses to Bega depart at 8.20 am (schooldays only), 10.20 am and 2.30 pm on weekdays. See the Bega Getting There & Away section for more details.

Car & Motorbike Tathra is 18 winding km from the Princes Highway at Bega. If you're heading north, consider the unsealed road through to Bermagui which runs through forest and by Mimosa Rocks National Park. Heading south to Merimbula you can turn off the road to Bega five km out of Tathra onto Sapphire Coast Drive, which runs past Bournda National Park.

BEGA

Bega (population 6000) is a centre for the rich dairy and cattle country of the southern Monaro. Most of Canberra's milk comes from the valleys around here.

Orientation & Information

The information centre (☎ (064) 92 2045) is in Gipps St (Princes Highway) near the corner of Carp St (both the Princes Highway and the Snowy Mountains Highway), in a craft shop, the Cumquat Gallery. It's open from 10 am to 5 pm on weekdays and 10 am to 2 pm on Saturday. It sometimes opens on Sunday as well in the summer.

In Church St, running north off Carp St, the Environmental Network has information about environment-related events and campaigns in the area. You can buy health food here and more in the shop next door. Also on Church St is a disposals shop selling some camping gear, and the Candelo Bookshop is next door.

There's a laundromat on Auckland St just north of Carp St.

The Forestry Commission office is upstairs in the building next to the post office, on Carp St near the corner of Gipps St.

Things to See & Do

There are a number of mildly interesting old buildings. The information centre has a walking-tour map.

The **Family Museum** on Bega St near Auckland St is open on weekdays from 10.30 am to 4 pm and on Saturday morning. Admission is $2 (20c children). You can visit the **Bega Cheese Factory**, across the river, between 9 am and 5 pm on weekdays and from 10 am to 4 pm on weekends. **Grevillea**

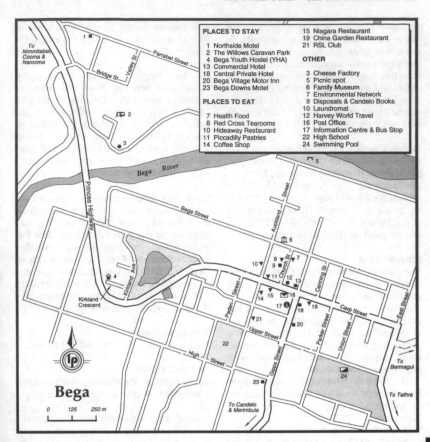

PLACES TO STAY

1 Northside Motel
2 The Willows Caravan Park
4 Bega Youth Hostel (YHA)
13 Commercial Hotel
18 Central Private Hotel
20 Bega Village Motor Inn
23 Bega Downs Motel

PLACES TO EAT

7 Health Food
8 Red Cross Tearooms
10 Hideaway Restaurant
11 Piccadilly Pastries
14 Coffee Shop

15 Niagara Restaurant
19 China Garden Restaurant
21 RSL Club

OTHER

3 Cheese Factory
5 Picnic spot
6 Family Museum
7 Environmental Network
9 Disposals & Candelo Books
10 Laundromat
12 Harvey World Travel
16 Post Office
17 Information Centre & Bus Stop
22 High School
24 Swimming Pool

Bega

0   125   250 m

Estate Winery is open to visitors daily and has a restaurant. It's about two km from the town centre. Follow the highway across the river and take the first left after the bridge.

The Bega Riding School (☎ (064) 92 3351) has **trail rides** in the area.

Places to Stay

Caravan Parks The *Bega Caravan Park* (☎ (064) 92 2303) is on the Princes Highway south of the centre and *The Willows* caravan park (☎ (064) 92 2106) is just north of the bridge near the cheese factory. The Willows is marginally more expensive for sites but a

little cheaper for on-site vans. The Bega also has self-contained units costing from $40 a double, much more in summer.

Hostel The *Bega YHA Hostel* (☎ (064) 92 3103) is a modern YHA hostel, made of mud-brick, on Kirkland Crescent. It costs $12 a night, and it's a friendly place.

Hotels The *Commercial Hotel* (☎ (064) 92 1011) at the corner of Gipps and Carp Sts has pub rooms for $20/40, or $30/50 with ensuite bathroom. On Gipps St across from the information office, the *Central Private Hotel*

SOUTH COAST

(☎ (064) 92 1263) is a big, slightly musty place with some permanent residents. A room with shared bathroom costs $25/45, and there's a motel section costing $35/60. A traveller has written to recommend this place, and its breakfast. Several other pubs also have accommodation, including the *Grand Hotel* (☎ (064) 92 1122) on Carp St with ensuite rooms from just $20/30,

Motels Cheapest of the half-dozen motels is the *Northside* (☎ (064) 92 1911), a couple of km north of the centre on the old highway, where rooms cost from $35/45. Others include the *Bega Village Motor Inn* (☎ (064) 92 2466) on Gipps St (from $55/65) and *Bega Downs Motel* (☎ (064) 922 2944) further south on Gipps St (from $60/70).

Places to Eat

The *Niagara Restaurant* on Carp St is your standard large country-town cafe, selling meals and takeaways. *Piccadilly Pastries* on Carp St near the corner of Auckland St has cakes and pastries and coffee. Nearby on Auckland St, south of Carp St, there's a *coffee shop*. On Carp St just east of Gipps St, *China Garden* has MSG-free meals with main courses about $6.50.

The *Hideaway* licensed restaurant is right at the back of Auckland Plaza, on Auckland St just north of Carp St. They sometimes have music.

If it's Tuesday and you're strapped for cash you could have lunch at the *Red Cross Tearooms*, in a nice old building on Church St. It's open between 11 am and 2 pm and lunch costs $3.50.

The recreation reserve by the river at the north end of Auckland St is a good place for a picnic.

Getting There & Away

Bus Harvey World Travel (☎ (064) 92 3599) at 163 Carp St handles bus bookings. Buses leave from near the information office.

Greyhound Pioneer Australia stops here on the run between Sydney and Melbourne. Sapphire Coast Express also runs to Melbourne but only as far north as Batemans

Bay. Pioneer Motor Service runs north to Sydney and south to Eden. Countrylink's Eden to Canberra service passes through Bega.

A local service, Edwards (☎ (064) 96 1422), runs between Bega and Eden on weekdays. Bega Valley Coaches (☎ (064) 92 2418) has a weekday service between Bermagui and Bega ($9.90). On weekdays buses to Tathra leave from the post office at 9.30 am, from Church St at 2 pm and from the High School (schooldays only) at 3.30 pm.

Car & Motorbike The Princes Highway runs north to Narooma and south to Merimbula and Eden. The Snowy Mountains Highway branches off the Princes Highway five km north of Bega, and runs to Cooma. Smaller roads run east to Tathra and south-east to Candelo and on to other small towns, eventually reaching Bombala. A more direct route to Bombala is via the Snowy Mountains Highway and the Monaro Highway.

Getting Around

There's a taxi service (☎ (064) 92 2156).

AROUND BEGA

Off the highway about five km north of Bega is **Mumballa Falls**, where there's a picnic area.

Candelo is a pleasant old village southeast of Bega, straggling along both sides of a steep valley and split by the large, sandy Candelo Creek. The nearby country is cleared, but it's still pretty. There are several craft galleries, including the Old Hospital Gallery on the hillside high above town. To get there follow the road on the Bega side of the creek and turn left near the end. Just west of Candelo is **Kameruka Estate**, a National Trust homestead open daily and further on is the **Bimbaya Moozeum** in an old butter factory. Tantawangalo Trail Rides (☎ (064) 93 2350) offers horse-riding in the area.

The *Candelo Hotel* (☎ (064) 93 2214) has some accommodation.

From Candelo you can drive back to the Princes Highway via Toothdale, or continue

south to the Bombala road. This route takes you over **Myrtle Mountain** where there's a picnic area with good views, and drives in the state forest. The Bombala road leads you west to **Wyndham**, a small village just after the intersection with the Candelo road, or east to Pambula and Merimbula.

MERIMBULA
Merimbula is a holiday and retirement mecca, and motels and apartments have mushroomed on the hillsides surrounding the impressive lake, actually an inlet. If this sounds like a recipe for tackiness you're partly right, but there is still some charm about the town's beautiful setting and the lake is big enough to dwarf the development. Nearby Pambula Beach is much quieter but is close enough to take advantage of Merimbula's services.

Orientation & Information
The highway enters Merimbula from the west, runs south through the town centre and crosses Merimbula Lake to the spit of land that forms the southern head of the lake's sea entrance. It then runs south to Pambula. There are lakeside beaches and surf beaches on the ocean sides of the peninsulas that form the north and south sides of the lake entrance.

The information centre (☎ (064) 95 1129) is on the waterfront at the bottom of Market St, the main shopping street. It's open daily.

There's a camping equipment shop next to the post office on Market St and another nearby on Alice St.

Things to See & Do
Around at the wharf on the eastern point there's a small **aquarium** (admission $5, children $3) and a coffee shop. There are good views across the lake from near here.

Diving is popular, with plenty of fish and several wrecks in the area, including two tugs sunk in 1987. One of the places offering dives and certificate courses is Merimbula Divers Lodge (☎ (064) 95 3611). If you want to try diving without signing up for a course, the Divers Lodge offers basic instruction and one shallow dive for $60. They charge $360

for a certificate course, which includes five days' accommodation in the off-season.

Various outfits offer **cruises**. Book at the information centre.

There are a couple of **boat-hire places**, Bottom Lake on the jetty near the information centre and Top Lake, on the north shore west of the bridge, at the end of Lakewood Drive. They have various types of power boats, little trimaran yachts, canoes and rowing boats. Cycle 'n' Surf on Marine Pde (near the caravan park south of the bridge) hires bikes, body boards and surf-skis as well as fishing tackle. Sapphire Coast Canoes (book at the information centre) has day-trips on various inland waterways in the area.

Magic Mountain on Sapphire Coast Drive is an amusement park with water-slides, go-karts and the like.

Places to Stay
Caravan Parks *South Haven Caravan Park* (☎ (064) 95 1304) and the smaller *Tween Lakes* (☎ (064) 95 1530) are south of the bridge, with access to surf and lake beaches. Both have sites from about $15 and cabins from around $30. East of the town centre but right on the surf beach on the north side of the lake entrance, *Merimbula Caravan Park* (☎ (064) 95 1269) has sites from $12, on-site vans from $30 and cabins from $35. Access is from Cliff St, which branches off the road running around the north side of the lake.

Other Accommodation A new YHA hostel, *Wandarrah Lodge*, is being built at 18 Marine Pde.

Merimbula Divers Lodge (☎ (064) 95 3611) offers backpackers shared accommodation in a self-contained unit for $20 per person – a bargain. Whole units are also available. The lodge is at 15 Park St, an easy walk from the information centre. To get here from Market St cut through the Centrepoint Mall (really an arcade) then head across the car park. Park St is on your right and the lodge is only a few doors away.

In quiet times you can find motel rooms from around $45/50, but in summer prices go through the roof. Your best chance of

finding an affordable room is at one of the motels on the highway west of the town centre.

Letting agents for the area include Fisk & Nagle (☎ (064) 95 3222), in Centrepoint near the information centre, and L J Hooker (☎ (064) 95 1026) nearby at 35 Market St. One of the many apartment places deserves a special mention: *Gracelands* (☎ (064) 95 2005) at the corner of Cameron St and Munn Sts is in the style of that well-known monument to excess and has a guitar-shaped swimming pool with a portrait of you-know-who on the bottom!

Places to Eat
The *Waterfront Cafe*, right next to the information centre, is a good place to have a coffee while looking out over the busy Merimbula Lake. There are also snacks and relatively expensive meals. Next door, without the views but with tables outside, is the *Panda Chinese Restaurant*. Diagonally across from these, on the corner of Alice St, *Poppy's Courtyard Cafe* has breakfasts for around $6.50 and a wide range of sandwiches and snacks.

Alley Catz in the Centrepoint Mall has snacks, pasta from $4.50 and pizzas. On Market St, across from the post office, *Fed Up* has a good menu, with main courses around $12, and a little further along is *Monty's* bar and restaurant where main courses are around $14.

The *Retreat Restaurant* in Pambula is a pleasant place in an old house, with a cocktail bar, an interesting menu and free transport to and from Merimbula (☎ (064) 95 6674) for two or more diners. Also in Pambula, *McKell's* has roast dinners every night for $8.50.

There are many other places, and all the clubs, including the *Bowling Cub* and the *RSL*, have bistros and restaurants.

Getting There & Away
Air Kendell flies to and from Melbourne ($175) and Hazelton flies to and from Sydney.

Bus Bus bookings can be made at Harvey World Travel (☎ (064) 95 1205) in Princes Arcade or Summerland Travel (☎ (064) 95 1008) in Merimbula Plaza.

Greyhound Pioneer Australia stops here on the run between Sydney and Melbourne. Pioneer Motor Service runs up the coast between Eden and Sydney. Countrylink stops here on the run between Eden and Canberra.

Edwards (☎ (064) 96 1422) is a local company running between Bega and Eden.

Car & Motorbike The Princes Highway runs north to Bega and south to Eden. Ten km south of Merimbula, just south of Pambula, a small road runs west to Bombala.

Getting Around
There's a taxi service (☎ (064) 95 2103).

AROUND MERIMBULA
Bournda National Park
Taking in most of the coast from Merimbula north to Tathra, Bournda (2350 hectares) has some good beaches and several walking trails, although they can get pretty crowded at peak times. Camping is permitted at Hobart Beach, on the southern shore of the big Wallagoot Lagoon, where there are toilets and hot showers. During the Christmas and Easter holidays sites are usually booked out. Contact the National Parks office (☎ (064) 94 1209) for more information.

Woodbine Park (☎ (064) 95 9333) borders Bournda and is a one km walk from the beach. It's a friendly place with six-person self-contained cabins costing from $180 a week for a double in the lowest season (May to September, other than school holidays) up to $640 in January. Head north from Merimbula on Sapphire Coast Drive and take the signposted turn-off after about seven km.

Pambula
Just south of Merimbula, Pambula is a small town that has largely avoided the development of its glitzy neighbour. There's a

Sunday morning **craft market** at the Retreat Restaurant. At Pambula Beach, four km east, there's a *caravan park* (☎ (064) 95 6363) with some very friendly wildlife. Keep your food hidden!

The northern section of Ben Boyd National Park begins just south of Pambula Beach, across the inlet.

NALBAUGH NATIONAL PARK

This small park (4100 hectares) is a rugged wilderness area with no facilities. Access is difficult, with just a 4WD track running off the Cann River Highway south of Bombala. Contact the National Parks office in Eden (☎ (064) 96 1434) for more information.

EDEN

Eden (population 4000) remains very much a fishing port, with one of the largest fleets in the state. It's also a timber town. The town's population doubled when a woodchip mill opened in the '70s, so you won't meet many people voicing anti-woodchipping sentiments.

The information centre (☎ (064) 96 1953) on Imlay St (the Princes Highway) is open from 9 am to 4 pm on weekdays and from 9 am to noon on weekends. There's a National Parks office (☎ (064) 96 1434) in Twofold Arcade on Imlay St.

For walks south into Victoria, buy a copy of the book *Walking the Wild Coast*, published by Wildcoast Publications.

Things to See

The **Killer Whale Museum**, at the bottom end of Imlay St, was established in 1931, mainly to preserve the skeleton of Old Tom, a killer whale (orca). Old Tom led a pack of killer whales which rounded up other whales so they could be killed by Eden's whalers. The killer whales ate only the tongues of their prey, so it was a good working relationship. After Old Tom died, the pack lost interest in the hunt and this contributed to the demise of whaling here. The museum has recently been expanded, and it's an interesting little place. If you've ever read *Moby Dick*, this is your chance to see a real whale

boat, with all those arcane pieces of equipment described by Melville. The museum is open from 10.15 am to 3.45 pm on weekdays and 11.15 am to 3.45 pm on weekends. Admission is $3 ($1 children).

Whales still swim along the coast in October and November, no doubt singing dark songs about the terrible days of Old Tom, and Cat Balou Cruises has **whale-spotting cruises** and other cruises costing from $15. These and other boat and canoe day-trips can be booked at the information centre.

The **Seamen's Memorial Wall**, near the lighthouse on Lookout Point, commemorates local sailors and fishers lost at sea.

Boydtown, off the highway 10 km south of Eden, has relics of Ben Boyd's still-born empire. The ruins of a church can be seen, and the impressive Seahorse Inn still operates (see Places to Stay & Eat, below).

Places to Stay & Eat

There are a couple of caravan parks by the highway on the north side of town, and on Aslings Beach is *Eden Tourist Park* (☎ (064) 96 1139) with sites from $10 and on-site vans from $25. From the information centre head north-east on Mitchell St, which becomes Aslings Beach Rd. The caravan park is on a spit separating Aslings beach from Lake Curalo.

The *Australasia Hotel* (☎ (064) 96 1600) on Imlay St has backpacker beds for $11 and singles/doubles for $20/25 in the hotel. There are also some motel-style units. The *Great Southern Inn* (☎ (064) 96 1515) is also on Imlay St and also has accommodation and meals.

Motels include the *Centre Town* (☎ (064) 96 1475) on Imlay St between Mitchell and Bass Sts (from $40/45), the *Halfway* (☎ (064) 96 1178) on the corner of Imlay and Mitchell Sts (from $45/50) and the *Twofold Bay* (☎ (064) 96 3111) on Imlay St between Chandos and Cocora Sts (from $55/60). Prices rise in summer.

The *Seahorse Inn* (☎ (064) 96 1361) at Boydtown is a solid old building, built by Ben Boyd as a guesthouse in 1843. This

SOUTH COAST

The Rise & Fall of Benjamin Boyd

Benjamin Boyd was a strange person, part empire-builder, part capitalist and part adventurer, mixed with a large dash of incompetence. He never really completed anything he set out to do, but he was unsuccessful in a very big way.

Boyd was a stockbroker in London who decided that the colony of New South Wales offered scope for the large amounts of money he could raise. His plans were vague, and included a half-baked idea for a private colony in the South Pacific.

He founded the Royal Bank, which quickly attracted £1,000,000 in investments, then set out for Sydney in his racing yacht *Wanderer*, arriving in 1842. Boyd, who had accomplished precisely nothing except the acquisition of a great deal of other people's money, was greeted with much official and public enthusiasm in Sydney.

He began a coastal steamship service, but the boat was damaged and withdrawn from service in its first year of operations. Boyd nevertheless convinced the governor that he was a fit person to be granted vast landholdings, second only in size to the Crown's.

Boyd decided to set up headquarters at Twofold Bay and an extensive building programme began. Money ran short, although the investors were assured that their golden reward was just around the corner, and Boyd issued his own banknotes.

Things went from bad to worse and the Royal Bank (nominally the owner of Boyd's empire) sacked him. By 1849 the bank decided that it was easier to simply collapse than to untangle Boyd's complex financial wheelings and dealings.

Ben Boyd, in the classic mould of the entrepeneur smiling amidst the ruins of his speculations, decided that New South Wales hadn't really been the right place for his ventures and set sail in *Wanderer* for the Californian goldfields.

Things didn't quite work out there either, and in 1851 he sailed back into the Pacific. One morning while moored at Guadalcanal he left his yacht to go shooting and disappeared without trace. ■

would be an interesting place to stay, and doubles cost about $90 (not all have bathrooms). You could just visit for a meal at *Benjamin's Restaurant*. There's also a *camping ground* here, with sites for $10.

Down at Snug Cove, Eden's fishing harbour, *Neptune's Kitchen* has seafood to take away or eat there. Next door there's a fruit and vegetable shop, strangely sited on a fishing wharf. For more upmarket seafood try the *Eden Fishermen's Club* on Imlay St, where there are a couple of places to eat. The *Lamplighter Restaurant* at the Coachmans Inn Motel on the highway has an interesting menu and is open for dinner nightly.

Getting There & Away
Bus Bus bookings can be made at Harvey World Travel (☎ (064) 96 1314) at 44 Bass St.

Car & Motorbike If you have time, there's the five-hour Wallagaraugh Forest Drive through the Nadgee State Forest (not to be

confused with the better-preserved Nadgee Nature Reserve east of here) that leaves the highway 27 km south of Eden and rejoins it near the Victorian border. There are great views from Mallacoota Lookout.

BEN BOYD NATIONAL PARK
Protecting some relics of Ben Boyd's operations, this national park (9450 hectares) has dramatic coastline, bush and some walks. The main access road to the park is the sealed Edrom Rd, which leaves the Princes Highway about 25 km south of Eden. Edrom Rd runs to the big woodchip mill on the south shore of Twofold Bay (and along the road you can see the dense but regimented and unvaried plantings that have replaced the bush – which has been turned into paper).

Before the mill is a turn-off to the left which leads to the old **Davidson Whaling Station** on **Twofold Bay**, now a historic site. Further along Edrom Rd is the turn-off for **Boyd's Tower**, an impressive structure built with sandstone brought from Sydney. It was

intended to be a lighthouse but the government wouldn't give Boyd permission to operate it.

Off Edrom Rd closer to the highway is Green Cape Rd, running down to Green Cape, from where there are good views. Off Green Cape Rd smaller roads lead to **Saltwater Creek** and **Bittangabee Bay**. There are campsites at both places and a nine km walk runs between the two. You should book sites at Christmas and Easter, at the National Parks office in Eden.

The northern section of Ben Boyd National Park runs up the coast from Eden, although access is from the Princes Highway north of the town. From Haycock Point, where there are good views, a walking trail leads to a headland overlooking the Pambula River.

NADGEE NATURE RESERVE

Nadgee continues down the coast from Ben Boyd National Park but it's much less accessible. At least part of this pristine reserve is due to be proclaimed a Wilderness Area, which will stop vehicle access altogether.

Places to Stay

Wonboyn, a small settlement on Wonboyn Lake at the north end of the reserve, has a store selling petrol and basic supplies. There's also *Wonboyn Cabins & Caravan Park* (☎ (064) 96 9131), where you'll meet

some friendly rainbow lorikeets. Tent sites cost from $12 and on-site vans start at $30 a double, with a minimum of a week ($220) at Christmas and Easter. There are also cabins. Wonboyn is near access roads into Nadgee but to get to the beach at Disaster Bay you'll need a 4WD or a boat (available from the caravan park) – or legs.

Across the lake from Wonboyn, but with access from Green Cape Rd in Ben Boyd National Park, is the *Wonboyn Lake Resort* (☎ (064) 96 9162), which has self-contained cabins from around $55 for four people. As usual, in-season prices are higher. Canoes and boats can be hired.

MT IMLAY NATIONAL PARK

This small national park (3800 hectares) surrounds **Mt Imlay** (886 metres) and you can walk to the top. The track from the end of the road to the summit is only three km long, but it's steep and the last 500 metres follows a narrow ridge. There are no facilities in the park.

The road to the **Mt Imlay Walking Track** runs west from the Princes Highway just south of the turn-off into Ben Boyd National Park. A little further south, just past the turn-off to Wonboyn, Imlay Rd leads west to meet the Monaro-Cann River Highway near the Victorian border. It passes to the south of Mt Imlay National Park and there's a picnic area beside the Imlay River.

Australian Capital Territory

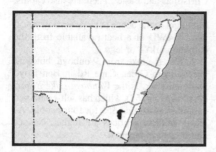

When the separate colonies of Australia were federated in 1901 and became states, the decision to build a national capital was part of the constitution. The site was selected in 1908, diplomatically situated between arch rivals Sydney and Melbourne, and an international competition to design the city was won by the American architect Walter Burley Griffin. In 1911 the Commonwealth government bought land for the Australian Capital Territory (ACT) and in 1913 decided to call the capital Canberra, believed to be an Aboriginal term for 'meeting place'.

Development of the site was slow and it was not until 1927 that parliament was first convened in the capital. From 1901 until then, Melbourne was the seat of the national government. The Depression virtually halted development and things really only got under way after WW II. In 1960 the population topped 50,000, reaching 100,000 by 1967. Today the ACT has almost 300,000 people.

Canberra

Don't let people in other states put you off visiting Canberra (population 285,000). Those who were dragged around the capital on school excursions probably remember it as a cold place full of nothing but buildings about which they had to write assignments, and for those who have done time in the Commonwealth Public Service, Canberra looms as the mecca of all that bureaucratic lunacy. But for visitors without whip-cracking teachers or memories of pen-pushing, it's well worth seeing.

Some of the best architecture and exhibitions in Australia are here and the whole city is fascinating because it is totally planned and orderly, although if you don't have a car you'll appreciate that living here might not be such fun. If you do have wheels you'll enjoy some of the best urban driving or cycling conditions anywhere.

The city also has a beautiful setting, surrounded by hills, and close to good skiing and bushwalking country.

Canberra is a place of government with few local industries and it has that unique, stimulating atmosphere that's only to be found in national capitals. It is also acquiring the furnishings of a true centre of national life – like the exciting National Gallery, the new and splendid Parliament House and the excellent National Botanic Gardens. What's more, Canberra has quite a young population, including a lot of students, and entertainment is livelier than we're usually led to expect. Finally, this is the only city in Australia that's really *Australian* – as opposed to South Australian, Victorian, Western Australian or whatever.

Orientation

The city is arranged around the natural-looking, but artificial, Lake Burley Griffin. On the north side is Canberra's city centre, known as Civic. Nearby is most of the short-term accommodation, the university, and a number of the neighbourhoods which are the basic unit of Canberra's urban structure. Neighbourhoods surrounding Civic include Reid, Braddon, Turner and Acton.

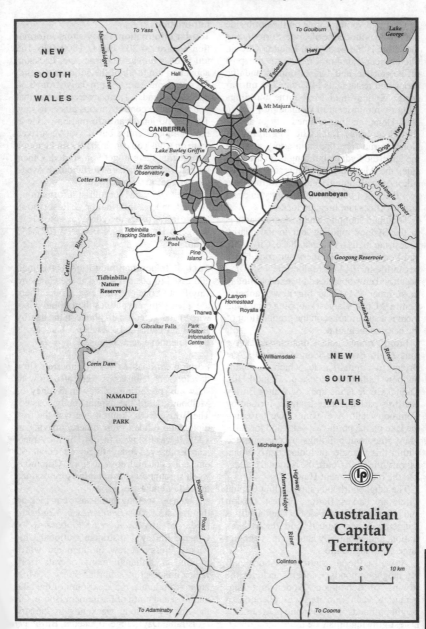

Australian
Capital
Territory

0   5   10 km

The huge Vernon Circle on the north side of the lake is the centre of Civic. Surrounding the circle is the hexagonal London Circuit. On or near London Circuit are the post office, airline and bus terminals and the shops and restaurants of Civic. The mirror-image Sydney and Melbourne buildings (slightly reminiscent of Connaught Place in New Delhi, another planned city in an ex-British colony) flank the beginning of Northbourne Ave, the main artery north of the lake (the Sydney building is on the west side, the Melbourne building on the east side). At the Jolimont Centre in Northbourne Ave there is a bus station, Countrylink and airline offices and luggage lockers.

The main shopping and restaurant area is in the Sydney building and in the nearby pedestrian malls – Garema Place, City Walk and Petrie Plaza. The merry-go-round here began life in 1914 on Melbourne's St Kilda beach and now operates daily except Sunday in summer ($1). The big new Canberra Centre is Civic's largest shopping centre and there is a supermarket on the ground floor of the car park behind it.

From Vernon Circle, Commonwealth Ave runs south over the Commonwealth Ave Bridge to Capital Circle, which surrounds the new Parliament House on Capital Hill. Capital Circle is the apex of Walter Burley Griffin's parliamentary triangle, formed by Commonwealth Ave, Kings Ave (crossing the lake on the north-east side) and the lake. Many important buildings are concentrated within this triangle, including the National Library, the High Court, the National Gallery and the old Parliament House.

The neighbourhoods surrounding Capital Circle are Parkes, Barton, Forrest, Deakin and Yarralumla. South-east of Capital Hill is Kingston, where you'll find the railway station, and Manuka, where there is another large shopping centre.

As well as the city centre and its surrounding neighbourhoods, Canberra includes the 'towns' of Belconnen, Woden and Tuggeranong, each with its own collection of neighbourhoods. Tuggeranong is Australia's fastest-growing urban area.

Information

Tourist Information The Visitors Information Centre (☎ 205 0044, 1800 026 166 toll-free) is on Northbourne Ave, Dickson, about two km north of the Jolimont Centre. It's open from 9 am to 5 pm daily (from 8.30 am on weekends). There are free phones that you can use to contact various places to stay. There is no longer an information office at the Jolimont Centre, but if you've arrived there on a bus you can probably find enough information there to get you started. Otherwise, it's a long walk up Northbourne Ave to the main information centre.

Tune to 98.9 FM for tourist information.

The Canberra Information & Reservation Centre has an office in Sydney, at suite 611A, Wingello House, Angel Place (☎ (02) 233 3666).

Post & Telecommunications Have mail addressed to poste restante at the Canberra City Post Office on Alinga St, Civic. There are plenty of payphones here (and elsewhere) and a credit-card phone in the nearby Jolimont Centre (and elsewhere). Canberra's STD telephone area code is 06.

Foreign Embassies With Canberra's slow development, embassies were also slow to show up, preferring to stay in Sydney or Melbourne until the capital really existed. The British High Commission was the first diplomatic office to move here, arriving in 1936. It was followed in 1940 by the American Embassy. Today there are about 60 embassies and high commissions (Commonwealth countries have high commissions instead of embassies).

Embassy-spotting enthusiasts can pick up the tourist office's *Embassies in Canberra* folder or buy *Canberra's Embassies* by Graeme Barrow (Australian National University Press). A few of them are worth looking at, although many operate from rather nondescript suburban houses. Most are in Yarralumla, the area south of the lake and west and north of Parliament House. On the Sunday of long weekends in January (Australia Day), June (Queen's Birthday)

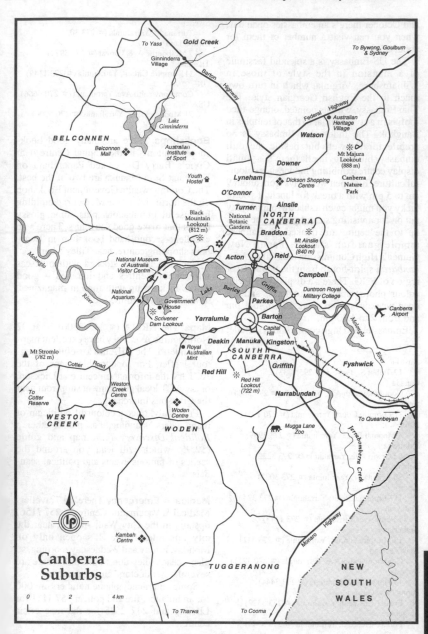

Canberra
Suburbs

and October there's an embassies open day, when you can visit a number of them for about $5.

The US Embassy is a splendid facsimile of a mansion in the style of those in Williamsburg, Virginia, which in turn owe much to the English Georgian style. The Thai Embassy, with its pointed, orange-tiled roof, is in a style similar to that of temples in Bangkok. The Indonesian Embassy is no architectural jewel, but beside the dull embassy building itself there's a small display centre exhibiting Indonesia's colourful culture. It's open weekdays from about 9 am to 5 pm with a break for lunch; if you're lucky you might catch a shadow-puppet play put on for a visiting school group. The steps up to the centre are flanked by Balinese temple-guardian statues. Papua New Guinea's High Commission looks like a *haus tambaran* spirit-house from the Sepik River region of PNG. There's a display room with colour photographs and artefacts, and it's open weekdays from about 10 am to 1 pm and from 2 to 4.30 pm.

Embassies and high commissions include:

Austria
    12 Talbot St, Forrest (☎ 295 1533)
Canada
    Commonwealth Ave, Yarralumla (☎ 273 3844)
Germany
    119 Empire Court, Yarralumla (☎ 270 1911)
India
    3 Moonah Place, Yarralumla (☎ 273 3999)
Indonesia
    8 Darwin Ave, Yarralumla (☎ 273 3222)
Ireland
    20 Arkana St, Yarralumla (☎ 273 3022)
Japan
    112 Empire Circuit, Yarralumla (☎ 273 3244)
Malaysia
    7 Perth Ave, Yarralumla (☎ 273 1543)
Netherlands
    120 Empire Circuit, Yarralumla (☎ 273 3111)
New Zealand
    Commonwealth Ave, Yarralumla (☎ 270 4211)
Norway
    17 Hunter St, Yarralumla (☎ 273 3444)
Papua New Guinea
    Forster Crescent, Yarralumla (☎ 273 3322)
Singapore
    Forster Crescent, Yarralumla (☎ 273 3944)

Sweden
    Turrana St, Yarralumla (☎ 273 3033)
Switzerland
    7 Melbourne Ave, Forrest (☎ 273 3977)
Thailand
    111 Empire Circuit, Yarralumla (☎ 273 1149)
UK
    Commonwealth Ave, Yarralumla (☎ 270 6666)
USA
    21 Moonah Place, Yarralumla (☎ 270 5000)

Bookshops There are many good bookshops. Dalton's in the Capital Centre near Civic's Barry Drive, and Paperchain on Furneaux St in Manuka are two of the best. The Commonwealth Government Bookshop on the north side of the Melbourne building has useful publications plus some glossy books that make good souvenirs. There's an excellent second-hand bookshop in Lyneham shopping centre, near Tilley's bar.

Canberra is well stocked with overseas information centres and libraries – good places to keep up with foreign magazines, newspapers and films.

Maps The NRMA (☎ 243 8800) is at 92 Northbourne Ave. They have excellent maps of Canberra. The YHA has a useful walking-tour leaflet. For topographic maps of the ACT try the information centre at Dickson, or the ACT local government shopfront near the Civic bus interchange.

Fred Daly, once a colourful politician of many years' standing, has put together a *Political Discovery Tour* map and guide ($2.95) which will lead you around the scenes of famous events and political scandals.

Medical & Emergency There's a Travellers Medical & Vaccination Centre (☎ 257 7156) upstairs in the City Walk Arcade, near the city bus interchange. It's open only on Monday, Friday and Wednesday morning, so plan ahead. They don't bulk-bill. There are several other doctors' clinics nearby.

Some emergency phone numbers are 000 for ambulance, fire and police; 257 1111 for Lifeline and 247 2525 for the rape crisis centre.

There is a toilet block that's open 24 hours, behind the Civic bus interchange near the Jolimont Centre.

Lookouts & Views

Canberra's main axis, for views and symbolism, not transport, is Kings Ave. From one end you can look down the avenue and across the lake to the old Parliament House, with the new Parliament House towering over it; from the other end you see Anzac Pde leading up to the **War Memorial** with Mt Ainslie rising up behind.

There are fine views of the lake and the city from the surrounding hills. Immediately west of Civic, Black Mountain rises to 812 metres and is topped by the 195-metre **Telecom Telecommunications Tower**, complete with a revolving restaurant. There is also a display on telecommunications history. The view from the tower can be taken in daily from 9 am to 10 pm for $3 ($1 children). There are also splendid vistas from nearby lookouts and from the approach road. Bus No 904 runs to the tower or you can walk up on a two-km trail through the bush, starting on Frith Rd. There are other good bushwalks round the back of the mountain, accessible from Belconnen Way and Caswell Drive. The information centre has a brochure with a map.

Other mountain lookouts, all with roads to them, are the 722-metre Red Hill, the 840-metre Mt Ainslie and the 665-metre Mt Pleasant. **Mt Ainslie** is close to the city on the north-east side and has particularly fine views across the city and out over the airport. From the top you'll also appreciate how green and full of parks Canberra is. The view is excellent at night.

There are also foot trails up Mt Ainslie from behind the War Memorial, and out behind Mt Ainslie to 888-metre Mt Majura four km away. You may see a kangaroo or two on the hike up.

Lake Burley Griffin

The lake was named after Canberra's designer, but was not finally created until the Molonglo River was dammed in 1963. The lake is not recommended for swimming, but you can go boating (beware of strong winds which can blow up suddenly from nowhere) or cycle around it – see the Activities and Getting Around sections.

There are a number of places of interest around the 35 km shore. The most visible is the **Captain Cook Memorial Water Jet** which flings a six-tonne column of water 140 metres into the air, and will give you a free shower if the wind is blowing from the right direction (despite an automatic switch-off which is supposed to operate if the wind speed gets too high.) The jet, built in 1970 to commemorate the bicentenary of Captain Cook's visit to Australia, operates from 10 am to noon and 2 to 4 pm daily, and also from 7 to 9 pm during daylight-savings time. At **Regatta Point**, nearby on the northern shore, is a skeleton globe with Cook's three great voyages traced on it.

The **National Capital Exhibition**, also at Regatta Point, is open daily from 9 am to 6 pm and has displays on the growth of the capital. It's free and interesting. Further round the lake, to the east, is **Blundell's Farmhouse** (1858). The simple stone and slab cottage is a reminder of the area's early farming history and is open daily from 10 am to 4 pm ($1).

A little further around the lake, at the far end of Commonwealth Park which stretches east from the Commonwealth Ave Bridge, is the **Carillon**, on Aspen Island. The 53-bell tower was a gift from Britain in 1963, Canberra's 50th anniversary. The Carillon was completed in 1970, and the bells weigh from seven kg to six tonnes. There are recitals on Wednesday from 12.45 to 1.30 pm and on weekends and public holidays from 2.45 to 3.30 pm.

West of the bridge, still on the north side of the lake, are Acton and Black Mountain peninsulas. The south shore of the lake, along which the impressive National Gallery and High Court are situated, forms the base of the parliamentary triangle.

Parliament House

South of the lake, the four-legged flagmast

on top of Capital Hill marks Parliament House, at the end of Commonwealth Ave. This, the most recent aspect of Walter Burley Griffin's vision to become a reality, sits at the apex of the parliamentary triangle. Opened by the Queen in 1988, it cost $1.1 billion, took eight years to build and replaces the 'temporary' old Parliament House lower down the hill on King George Terrace, which served for 11 years longer than its intended 50-year life. The new Parliament House was designed by the US-based Italian Romaldo Giurgola, who won a competition entered by more than 300 architects.

It's built into the top of the hill and the roof has been grassed over so that it resembles the original hilltop. Part of the building is subterranean, which has provoked jibes about MPs being buried in a 'sci-fi mausoleum', but the interior design and decoration is splendid. Seventy new art and craft works were commissioned from Australian artists, and a further 3000 were bought for the building. A different combination of Australian timbers is used in each of its principal sections.

The main axis of the building runs northeast to south-west, in a direct line from the old Parliament House, the War Memorial across the lake, and Mt Ainslie. On either side of this axis two high, granite-faced walls curve out from the centre to the corners of the site – on a plan these walls look like back-to-back boomerangs. The House of Representatives is to the east of the walls, the Senate to the west. They're linked to the centre by covered walkways.

Extensive areas of Parliament House are open to the public from 9 am to 5 pm every day. You enter through the white marble **Great Verandah** at the north-east end of the main axis, where Nelson Tjakamarra's *Meeting Place* mosaic, within the pool, represents a gathering of Aboriginal tribes. Inside, the grey-green marble columns of the foyer symbolise a forest, while marquetry panels on the walls depict Australian flora. From the 1st floor you look down on the **Reception Hall**, with its 20-metre-long Arthur Boyd tapestry. A public gallery above

PLACES TO STAY

| 1 | Downtown Speros Motel |
| 40 | Lakeside Hotel |

PLACES TO EAT

2	Fringe Benefits
7	Gus'
8	Sammy's Kitchen & Asian Noodle House
9	Noshes
10	Dorettes Bistro & Happy's
11	Mama's Trattoria
14	Club Asmara & Red Sea Restaurant
15	Clarry's Restaurant
17	Zorba's Char-Grill & Charcoal Restaurant
19	Waffles Piano Bar
20	Thai Lotus & Canberra Vietnamese
22	Tosolini's, Australian Pizza Kitchen & Bailey's Corner
23	Antigo Cafe
32	Anarkali Restaurant
34	Capital Parkroyal
35	Glebe Park Food Hall

OTHER

3	Dalton's Bookshop
4	University Students Union
5	Post Office
6	Jolimont Centre(Countrylink, Airlines & Bus Station)
9	Wilderness Society & Heaven Nightclub
12	Travellers' Medical & Vaccination Centre
13	Bus Interchange & Information
15	Gorman House Arts Centre
16	Commonwealth Government Bookshop
18	Commonwealth Bank
19	Private Bin Nightclub
21	Moosehead's Bar
24	ANZ Bank
25	Merry-go-round
26	Supermarket
27	Westpac Bank
28	Canberra Centre (shopping centre)
29	Police Station
30	Canberra Theatre Centre
31	Westpac Bank
33	Electric Shadows Cinemas
36	Casino/Convention Centre
37	Swimming Pool
38	National Film & Sound Archive
39	Academy of Science

ACT

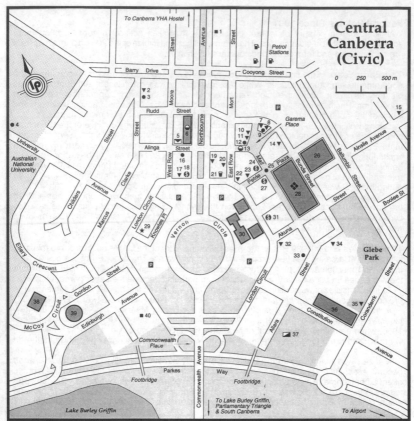

Central
Canberra
(Civic)

0   250   500 m

To Canberra YHA Hostel

Petrol
Stations

Barry   Drive

Cooyong   Street

Garema
Place

Rudd   Street

Alinga   Street

University

Australian
National
University

Plaza

Penfe

Akuna

Glebe
Park

Commonwealth
Place

Lake Burley Griffin

Parkes   Way

Footbridge   Footbridge

To Lake Burley Griffin,
Parliamentary Triangle
& South Canberra

To Airport

the Reception Hall has a 16-metre-long embroidery, worked on by 1000 people.

Beyond the Reception Hall you reach the gallery above the Members' Hall, the central 'crossroads' of the building, with the flag-mast above it and passages to the debating chambers on each side. One of only four known originals of the **Magna Carta** is on display here. South of the Members' Hall are the committee rooms and ministers' offices. The public can view the committee rooms and attend some of their proceedings.

Other visitor facilities include a cafeteria, a terrace with city views, and a small theatre

where you can watch a film that tells the story of Australian democracy. You can also wander over the grassy top of the building.

If you want to make sure of a place in the **House of Representatives** gallery, book by phone (☎ 277 4890) or write to the Principal Attendant, House of Representatives, Parliament House, Canberra. Some seats are left unbooked, but on sitting days you'd have to queue early to get one. Seats in the Senate gallery are almost always available. Senate debates are much tamer affairs than those in the House, where the Prime Minister and the Leader of the Opposition slug it out.

ACT

Federal Politics Since 1901

With less than a century of federal government, Australian political history is much more accessible than that of older nations. The virtues, failings and foibles of the 20-odd prime ministers are remembered and form part of the country's folk history.

The Early Years In the first decade or so, questions of trade (free or protected) dominated the governments, and the notorious White Australia policy was established. Although this was blatantly racist, the alternative might have been worse, as the policy stopped the importing of people from Pacific islands to work the Queensland canefields. This was practically slavery and many of the labourers had been tricked into coming to Australia; some were kidnapped.

During WW I the Labor Party won office and in 1915 Billy Hughes ('the little digger') became prime minister. Hughes decided that conscription was necessary to bolster Australia's contribution to the European war, but his party disagreed, as did the Australian people, who narrowly rejected conscription in an acrimonious referendum. Hughes was sacked as leader of the Labor Party, but he joined with conservatives to form a new government and remained prime minister. Another referendum on conscription was lost in 1917, but Hughes established himself as a world figure during the post-war peace conferences at Versailles and remained prime minister until 1923.

Stanley Bruce, the epitome of a conservative prime minister, took over from Hughes and led the government until 1929 when Labor won the general election. Internal squabbling saw Joe Lyons leave the party and join the conservatives to form the United Australia Party (UAP), which won government in 1931.

The Menzies Era In 1939 Robert Menzies became leader of the UAP, and thus prime minister. Like Stanley Bruce, he was very proper and very conservative. The Labor Party ousted Menzies in the 1941 election and John Curtin steered the country through WW II. Curtin died just before the war ended and Joe Chifley, a train-driver from Bathurst, became the Labor prime minister.

Chifley's policies of welcoming refugees from Europe, building universities and instituting large projects such as the Snowy Mountains Hydro-Electric Scheme shaped postwar Australia.

In 1949 the conservatives won office, again under Robert Menzies, now leader of the new Liberal Party (which is *not* a liberal party, except in the economic sense). He was to rule until 1966, when he retired. After a bout of McCarthy-style repression of Communists, the Menzies years passed like a long, long dream where old values comfortably enveloped and smothered new ideas.

Menzies was besotted with the British royal family but saw that alliance with the USA had become essential and he led the country into the Vietnam disaster. After his retirement, subsequent Liberal prime ministers continued conscripting 18-year-olds (who were too young to vote) to fight in Vietnam. 'All the way with LBJ', simpered Prime Minister Harold Holt. Massive protests against the war helped the Labor Party under Gough Whitlam to win power in the 1972 elections.

Whitlam & the Dismissal The Whitlam government irrevocably changed Australia. In the government's three hectic years many things now taken for granted were instituted: free health care, free tertiary education (now being whittled away), land rights for Aborigines, equal pay for women, no-fault divorce, legal aid and much more.

However, the pace of change stirred up strong opposition and the government became embroiled in a series of scandals. On 11 November 1975 Governor General John Kerr dismissed the government. (Coincidentally, 11 November is also the date of the WW I armistice and the day Ned Kelly was hung – the Armistice Day minute of silence has varied meanings in this country.)

On non-sitting days there are free **guided tours** every half-hour; on sitting days there's a talk on the building in the Great Hall Gallery every half-hour. For $3/5 a single/double you can hire an audio-cassette and player for a self-guided tour (there are seven languages available).

Bus Nos 901, 234 and 352 run from the city to Parliament House.

Old Parliament House

On King George Terrace, halfway between the new Parliament House and the lake, this building was the seat of Australia's federal

The proclamation dismissing Whitlam and installing Liberal leader Malcolm Fraser as prime minister ended, 'God save the Queen'. Whitlam's fiery response concluded 'Well may you say God save the Queen, because *nothing* will save the Governor General'. Until then most Australians had considered the governor general as a quaint piece of decoration, a hangover from the days when the country was a British colony. To find that the Queen, via the governor general, could dismiss an elected government came as a rude shock, but Whitlam nevertheless lost the subsequent elections.

Fraser presided over six years of dismantling Whitlam's reforms. It seemed that another Menzies era was beginning, but Bob Hawke, leader of the powerful Council of Trade Unions, was hurried into parliament and manoeuvred into leadership of the Labor Party in time to win the 1983 elections. After the Whitlam debacle the Labor Party decided not to rock the boat, with the result that Hawke's years at the helm seemed pretty bland.

Politics in the '90s In 1991 Hawke was ousted as party leader by his treasurer, Paul Keating, who thus became prime minister. Keating earned his spurs by winning the apparently unwinnable elections of 1993 and, despite a penchant for Italian suits and antique clocks, his rough-house debating style has earned him a reputation as a tough Labor leader of the old school.

Keating is also an extremely astute politician. So much so that you have to suspect that the 'putting an arm around the Queen' incident was calculated. Keating did nothing more than courteously guide the Queen though a crowd, but the British tabloids claimed that it was a salacious attack. They dubbed his wife, the urbane and intelligent Annita Keating, 'the Witch of Oz' because she failed to curtsey to the Queen. These responses mystified and angered many Australians and gave a boost to the Keating agenda of making Australia a republic.

The current governor general is Bill Hayden. Hayden was a Queensland policeman who became a minister in the Whitlam government and he was the Labor Party leader who was forced to make way for Bob Hawke in 1983. That Bill Hayden, a left-wing leader, should become governor general is one of the oddest things to have happened in Canberra. ■

government from 1927 to 1988. Its parliamentary days were ended in style: as the corridors of power echoed to the Defence Minister's favourite Rolling Stones records, the Prime Minister and Leader of the Opposition sang together arm-in-arm, and bodies were seen dragging themselves away well after dawn the next morning – and that's just what got into print!

The views from the grounds are good, and there are tours of the building and displays from the collections of the National Museum and the Australian Archives.

The old Parliament House is also home to

the new **National Portrait Gallery** (☎ 262 1156). It's open daily from 9 am to 4 pm (admission $2 adults, $1 children, $5 families).

National Gallery of Australia

At the bottom of the parliamentary triangle, on Parkes Place, beside the High Court and Lake Burley Griffin, is the excellent art gallery, which was opened in 1982.

The Australian collection ranges from traditional Aboriginal art through to 20th century works by Arthur Boyd, Sidney Nolan and Albert Tucker. Aboriginal works include bark paintings from Arnhemland, burial poles from the Tiwi people of Melville and Bathurst Islands off Darwin, printed fabrics by the women of Utopia and Ernabella in central Australia, and paintings from Yuendumu, also in central Australia. There are often temporary exhibitions from the Kimberley and other areas where Aboriginal art is flourishing.

In addition to works from the early decades of European settlement and the 19th-century romantics, there are examples of the early nationalistic statements of Charles Conder, Arthur Streeton and Tom Roberts. The collection is not confined to paintings: sculptures, prints, drawings, photographs, furniture, ceramics, fashion, textiles and silverware are all on display. The Sculpture Garden has a variety of striking sculptures.

There are two *restaurants* at the gallery.

The gallery is open from 10 am to 5 pm daily and there are tours at 11 am and 2 pm. Admission is $3, or free if you have a student card. Free lectures are given on Tuesday, Wednesday and Thursday at 12.45 pm. On the last Thursday night of each month there's a free session beginning with a guided tour, followed by informal discussion groups, a film and then a guest lecture. Phone the gallery for details (☎ 271 2502).

High Court

The High Court building (☎ 270 6811), by the lake next to the National Gallery, is open daily from 9.45 am to 4.30 pm (free admis-sion). The High Court was opened in 1980, and the building's grandiose magnificence caused it to be dubbed 'Gar's Mahal', a reference to Sir Garfield Barwick, Chief Justice during the construction of the building. To tell the truth, there is a touch of Indian Mogul palace about the ornamental watercourse burbling alongside the entrance path to this grand building.

Questacon – National Science & Technology Centre

This is a 'hands on' science museum (☎ 270 2800) in the snappy white building between the High Court and the National Library. It's open daily from 10 am to 5 pm and entry is $6 ($3 students with ID). There are 200 'devices' in the centre's five galleries and outdoor areas where you can use 'props' to get a feeling for a scientific concept, and then see its application to an everyday situation. There are lots of helpful attendants.

My favourite displays include the earthquake experience, the 'thongaphone' and the exhibit which gives you the chance to be a judge of Olympic diving, a process which had been one of life's little mysteries for me.

If you're totally broke, there are a few exhibits in the entry foyer which you can see without going through the turnstiles.

National Library

Also on Parkes Place, beside the lake, is the National Library (☎ 262 1111), one of the most elegant buildings in Canberra. It has more than 4.5 million books, and displays include rare books, paintings, early manuscripts and maps, a cannon from Cook's ship the *Endeavour*, a fine model of the ship itself and special exhibitions. The library is open from 9 am to 9 pm Monday to Thursday, 9 am to 4.45 pm Friday and Saturday, and 1.30 to 4.45 pm on Sunday. There are guided tours (☎ 269 1699), and free films on Tuesday lunchtime and Thursday night – phone for programmes (☎ 262 1475). There's also a restaurant and a cafe.

Royal Australian Mint

The mint (☎ 202 6999), on Denison St,

Deakin, south of the lake, produces all of Australia's coins. Through the plate-glass windows (to keep you at arm's length from the readies) you can see the whole process, from raw materials to finished coins. There's a collection of rare coins in the foyer. The mint is open from 9 am to 4 pm on weekdays and 10 am to 3 pm on weekends, and admission is free. Bus Nos 230 and 231 run past on weekdays; on weekends take No 267.

Australian War Memorial

The massive war memorial, north of the lake and at the foot of Mt Ainslie, looks directly along Anzac Parade to the old Parliament House across the lake. It was conceived in 1925 and finally opened in 1941, not long after WW II broke out in the Pacific. It houses an amazing collection of pictures, dioramas, relics and exhibitions, including a fine collection of old aircraft. For anyone with an interest in toy soldiers, the miniature battle scenes are absorbing.

For the less military-minded, the memorial has an excellent **art collection**.

The **Hall of Memory** is the focus of the memorial. It features a quite beautiful interior, some superb stained-glass windows and a dome made of six million Italian mosaic pieces. Entombed here is the Unknown Australian Soldier, whose remains were brought from a WW I battlefield in 1993. Leading to the hall is the reflecting pool. Note the gargoyles on the walls around the pool – they are very nasty versions of cuddly Australian animals and an Aborigine.

The War Memorial is open from 10 am to 5 pm daily, and admission is free. Several free tours are held each day, some focusing on the artworks. Phone (☎ 243 4211) for times. Bus Nos 901 and 302 run from the city; No 303 runs nearby.

Several specific conflicts and campaigns also have memorials along Anzac Ave, including the impressive **Crete memorial** and the new **Vietnam memorial** further down towards the lake.

Australian National University

The ANU's attractive grounds take up most of the area between Civic and Black Mountain, and it's a pleasant place to wander around. There's an information centre (☎ 249 0794) on Balmain Crescent which is open on weekdays. The **University Union** on University Ave offers a variety of cheap eats and entertainment. On the corner of Kingsley St and Barry Drive is the **Drill Hall Gallery**, an offshoot of the National Gallery with changing exhibitions of contemporary art. It's open from noon to 5 pm from Wednesday to Sunday. Admission is free.

National Film & Sound Archive

The archive is on McCoy Circuit, at the south-eastern edge of the university area, and is open from 9.30 am to 4 pm daily. Admission is free. Interesting exhibitions from the archive's collections are shown. Over the road is the **Australian Academy of Science** (not open to the public), known locally as the Martian Embassy – it looks like a misplaced flying saucer.

National Botanic Gardens

Yes, a botanic garden was part of Walter Burley Griffin's plan too – one dedicated to Australia's unique native flora. Like so much of Canberra it has taken a long time for this vision to become a reality – planting only started in 1950 and the gardens were officially opened in 1970.

On the lower slopes of Black Mountain, behind the ANU, the beautiful 50-hectare gardens are devoted to Australian flora. There are educational walks, including one amongst plants used by Aborigines. A highlight is the **rainforest area**, achieved in this dry climate by a 'misting' system. The **eucalypt lawn** has 600 species of this ubiquitous Australian tree, while the **Mallee section** displays the typical vegetation of semi-desert country. The **herbarium** (collection of pressed and dried plant specimens used for research) and nursery are closed to the public, but if you're a botanist you may be able to talk your way in.

The gardens are reached from Clunies Ross St and are open from 9 am to 5 pm daily. There are **guided tours** at 11 am on Wednes-

day, Friday and Sunday, with a 2 pm tour on Saturday and Sunday. The information centre, open from 9.30 am to 4.30 pm daily, has an introductory video about the gardens and the **Botanical Bookshop** has an excellent range of books, cards and posters. Near where the walks start and finish is a *cafe* with a pleasant outdoor section.

Bus No 904 runs past the gardens.

National Museum of Australia
A site for the long-awaited museum might have finally been found on Acton Peninsula, west of the Commonwealth Ave Bridge. Meanwhile, the visitor centre (☎ 256 1126) on Lady Denman Drive north of Yarralumla is open from 10 am to 4 pm weekdays and from 1 to 4 pm weekends and displays items from the museum's collection. One item is the heart of Phar Lap, Australia's wonder racehorse of the 1930s, who died in suspicious circumstances in California. The rest of him is in the National Museum of Victoria in Melbourne.

Australian Institute of Sport
Founded in 1981 as part of an effort to improve Australia's performance at events like the Olympics, the AIS is on Leverrier Crescent, in the northern suburb of Bruce, not far from the YHA hostel. It provides training facilities for the country's top sportspeople, who lead hour-long **tours** of the institute ($2; children $1) daily at 2 pm. The tennis courts and swimming pools are open to visitors; phone (☎ 252 1257) for information on times.

Bus No 431 will take you to the AIS from the city centre.

National Aquarium
On Lady Denman Drive near Scrivener Dam, the west end of the lake, the impressive aquarium (☎ 287 1211) now includes a **wildlife sanctuary**. It's open daily from 9 am to 5.30 pm and admission is $10 ($5 students).

Mugga Lane Zoo
About seven km south of the city centre, the zoo has about 80 species of native and exotic

PLACES TO STAY

1	Kythera Motel
2	Acacia Motor Lodge
3	Olim's Canberra Hotel
25	Macquarie Private Hotel
27	Victor Lodge
30	Kingston Hotel

OTHER

4	War Memorial
5	University Information Centre
6	Ferry Terminal, Bike & Boat Hire
7	Church of St John the Baptist
8	National Capital Exhibition
9	Captain Cook Memorial Water Jet
10	Blundell's Farmhouse
11	National Library
12	National Science & Technology Centre
13	High Court
14	National Gallery
15	Carillon
16	Australian-American Memorial
17	UK High Commission
18	PNG High Commission
19	Old Parliament House
20	Indonesian Embassy
21	US Embassy
22	Thai Embassy
23	The Lodge
24	Parliament House (on Capital Hill)
26	Kingston Shopping Centre
28	Railway Station
29	Manuka Shopping Centre

animals and is open daily ($6.50). Bus No 352 runs nearby.

Other Sights
You can do no more than drive by and peek through the gates of the prime minister's official Canberra residence, **The Lodge**, on Adelaide Ave, Deakin – Australia's version of 10 Downing St. The same is true of **Government House**, the residence of the governor general, which is on the south-west corner of Lake Burley Griffin, but there's a lookout beside Scrivener Dam at the end of the lake, giving a good view of the building. The governor general is the representative of the Australian monarch – who lives in

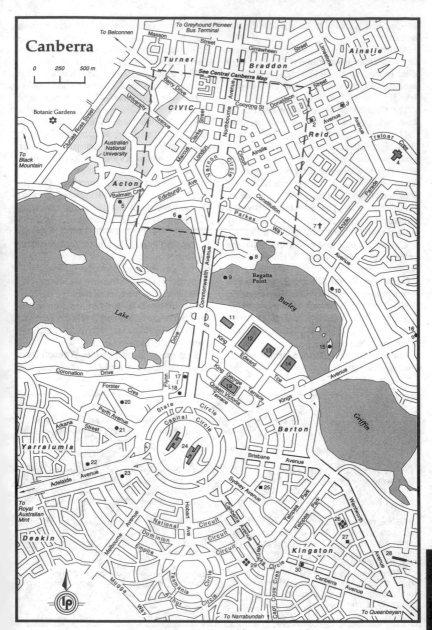

Canberra

0   250   500 m

To Belconnen

To Greyhound Pioneer
Bus Terminal

Masson Street

Girrawheen Street

Limestone

Ainslie

Turner

Braddon

See Central Canberra Map

Barry Drive

Cooyong St

Donaldson

CIVIC

University Avenue

Northbourne Avenue

Marcus Clarke Street

London

Vernon Circuit

Ainslie Avenue

Avenue

Reid

Treloar Cres

Botanic Gardens

To
Black
Mountain

Australian
National
University

Acton

Balmain Cres

Edinburgh Ave

Constitution

Parkes Way

Anzac Parade

Clunies Ross Street

Lake

Commonwealth Avenue

Regatta
Point

Burley

Avenue

Drive

King Edward Tce

Coronation Drive

Flynn

Forster Cres

King George Terrace

Queen Victoria Terrace

Kings Avenue

Griffin

Perth Avenue

State Circle

Capital Circle

Barton

Arkana Street

Adelaide Avenue

Yarralumla

Brisbane Avenue

Sydney Avenue

Telopea Park

Wentworth

To
Royal
Australian
Mint

Melbourne Avenue

National Ave

Hobart Circuit

Canberra Avenue

Wentworth Avenue

Deakin

Dominion Circuit

Empire Circuit

Capt Cook Cres

Kingston

Circle

Canberra Avenue

Mugga Way

Tasmania Circle

State Circle

To
Narrabundah

To Queanbeyan

ACT

London and happens to be also the British monarch.

At the east end of Kings Ave, the **Australian-American Memorial** is a 79-metre-high pillar topped by an eagle which commemorates American support of Australia during WW II.

The **Church of St John the Baptist**, in Reid, just east of Civic, was built between 1841 and 1845 and thus predates the capital. The stained-glass windows show pioneering families of the region. There is an adjoining schoolhouse with some early relics, open on Wednesday from 10 am to noon and on weekends from 2 to 4 pm, more often during school holidays. The **Serbian Orthodox Church** in Forrest has its walls and ceiling painted with a series of biblical murals.

Canberra's **mosque** is in Yarralumla, the embassy area, on the corner of Hunter St and Empire Circuit.

Duntroon Royal Military College was once a homestead, with parts dating from the 1830s. Tours of the grounds start at the sign in Starkey Park, Jubilee Ave, at 2.30 pm on weekdays (except public holidays) from February to November.

The enterprising **Tradesmen's Union Club** in Badham St, Dickson, off Antill St,

has a large collection of 'old and unusual bicycles'. It's good for kids and there's a BMX track next door which hires out bikes. There are also a gym and squash courts.

The club also runs the Downer Club nearby on Hawdon St, home to 'the world's largest beer collection'. If that doesn't grab you, they also have an Antarctic igloo on display. Not interested? Well, what about an observatory with an astronomer on duty from nightfall (or 7 pm, whichever is later) until midnight every day? Admission to all this is free.

Near the railway station on Geijera Place (off Cunningham St) in Kingston, there's a **Railway Museum** that's open on weekends. Admission is $4 ($2 children).

North of the centre on the corner of Anthill St and the Federal Highway, the **Australian Heritage Village** is a collection of craft shops, galleries and tea-rooms housed in some substantial old-style buildings. It's actually quite a pleasant place.

The **Brickworks Market**, held on weekends between 11 am and 5 pm, on Denman St in Yarralumla, has antiques, junk and everything in between.

Kids might enjoy a visit to **Weston Park** in Yarralumla, open on weekends and during

---

Life in Canberra

Thus did people live who had such an income; and in a land where each man's pay, age and position are printed in a book, that all may read, it is hardly worth while to play at pretences in word or deed.

Rudyard Kipling, 1898

Kipling's observation about the British Raj in India is less applicable to Canberra than it once was, as private enterprise is booming. However, the various strata of public service jobs are still the major social indicators in the city. Add to that the fact that the average wage in Canberra is $100 a week higher than in the rest of the country and you have a city very different from the Australian mainstream.

Rules and regulations spill over from the public service into other areas of life, and the city has strict planning regulations. Just finding a corner store can mean a major trek through the curving streets of the neighbourhoods, and you won't find petrol stations on prime sites. (Neon-light junkies can get a hit on Lonsdale St, where there are several service stations and a junkfood outlet in full regalia.)

Not surprisingly, there's a bit of a 'barrack-room lawyer' tendency. People lodge appeals about neighbours building houses a centimetre or so higher than the rules allow, and one group of home-owners demanded compensation from the government because a public housing estate was to built in their suburb! ∎

school holidays. There's a maze, a miniature railway, treehouses and other entertainments.

Activities

Watersports Dobel Boat Hire (☎ 249 6861) at the Acton Park Ferry Terminal on Lake Burley Griffin rents out canoes at $10 an hour and catamarans at $20 an hour, plus paddle boats and surf skis. However, private power boats aren't permitted on the lake. Canoeing in the Murrumbidgee River is also popular.

It's 150 km to the nearest surf beaches at Batemans Bay – Murrays buses run down daily. Swimming pools around the city include the Olympic Pool on Allara St, Civic. Swimming in Lake Burley Griffin is not recommended. There's river and lake swimming outside the city – see the Around Canberra section.

River Runners (☎ 288 5610) has rafting on the Shoalhaven River, 1½ hours from Canberra, for about $110, less if you have your own transport.

Cycling Canberra has a great series of bicycle tracks – probably the best in Australia. *Canberra Cycleways* ($2.50) is a widely available map. One popular track is a circuit of the lake; there are also peaceful stretches of bushland along some suburban routes. See the Getting Around section for bike rental information.

In-Line Skating Several places hire rollerblades, including Mr Spokes Bike Hire near the Acton Ferry Terminal ($15 for the first hour, $5 for subsequent hours) and Canberra Blades Centre on Allara St in the city, opposite the Parkroyal Hotel ($15 for the first *two* hours, $5 for subsequent *half* hours). The latter doesn't rent helmets.

Skiing There is sometimes enough snow for cross-country skiing in Namadgi National Park. The NSW snowfields are within four hours' drive of Canberra and the information centre can supply the latest news on conditions. There are plenty of equipment hire

places, and Deanes Buslines (☎ 299 3722) offer day-trip ski packages for around $60 for beginners, $70 for experienced skiers.

Bushwalking Tidbinbilla Fauna Reserve has marked trails. For other places see the Around Canberra section. Contact the Canberra Bushwalking Club through the Environment Centre (☎ 247 3064) on Kingsley St in the city. Here you can buy *Above the Cotter* ($13.70), which details walks and drives in the area. Graeme Barrow's *Twenty-five Family Bushwalks In & Around Canberra* is also useful. There are also some good rockclimbing areas.

Flights Taking a flight might be a good way of seeing the grand scale of the city's plan. Several outfits offer aeroplane flights, such as Aerial Adventure (☎ 247 4777) which charges from $35 (minimum two people). Balloon Aloft (☎ 285 1540) offers flights over Canberra for $130 midweek, $185 for a champagne-breakfast flight on weekends. Children under 12 get discounts. The best time is winter, although flights operate all year.

Organised Tours

The information centre in Dickson has details of the many tours of the city and the ACT. Half-day city tours start at around $25 and there is a variety of day trips to places like the Snowy Mountains, nature reserves, the satellite tracking station, sheep stations, horse studs and fossicking areas around the ACT.

Canberra Cruises (☎ 295 3544) has cruises on Lake Burley Griffin from $10.

For details of Murray's Canberra Explorer bus sightseeing tours and other sightseeing buses, see the Getting Around section (Bus – Special Services) later in this chapter.

Festivals

The Canberra Festival takes place over 10 days each March and celebrates the city's birthday with music, food, Mardi Gras, displays, an exciting raft race, a birdman and birdwoman rally, and a big parade. Many of

ACT

the events are held in Commonwealth Park, which is the site of a carnival. A very popular event is the Royal Military College band playing the *1812 Overture*, complete with cannon!

After the sort of winter they get up here on the Monaro, spring is something to celebrate and Canberra does it with verve, with the Floriade Festival. Just seeing those groves of European trees come into leaf is an unusual experience for Australians, and there are many events and activities.

Out of character with Canberra's image as a somewhat staid centre of government, the Street Machine Summer Nats (basically a big hot-rod show) are held here in December.

Places to Stay

Because of the large numbers of public servants arriving in Canberra before residential areas were developed, the government established hostels to house them. Many of these are now privately run as guesthouses, private hotels and even motels. They can be perfectly all right, but some retain a rather institutional feel. When you book, you might be asked which government department will be picking up the tab!

Caravan Parks *Canberra Motor Village* (☎ 247 5466), three km north-west of the centre on Kunzea St, O'Connor, has a bush setting and charges $18 for sites, $39 a double for on-site vans and from $60 a double in cabins. There's a restaurant, kitchen, tennis court and swimming pool. *Canberra Carotel* (☎ 241 1377) off the Federal Highway in Watson, six km north of the centre, has sites from $10, on-site vans from $40 for four people and more expensive motel-style cabins. *Southside Motor Park* (☎ 280 6176) is eight km south of the city in Fyshwick, on the main road to Queanbeyan. For two people it costs $12 for a site, from $35 for an on-site van and from $45 for a cabin.

More rural camping – cheaper too – can be found out of the city at places like Cotter Dam. See the Around Canberra section.

Hostels 'The best YHA I've ever seen' is how one traveller described the *Canberra YHA Hostel* (☎ 248 9155). It's purpose-built and well-designed and equipped. There is now a travel desk (☎ 248 0177) at the hostel which handles domestic and international travel. Nightly charges are $15, plus $3 if you need a sleeping-sheet and there are twin rooms with attached bathrooms for $20 a person, or $18 with shared bathroom. (Add $5 if you aren't a YHA member.) The office is open from 7 am to 10.30 pm but you can check in up until midnight if you give advance warning. The hostel is on Dryandra St, O'Connor, about six km north-west of Civic. Bus No 380 runs from the city twice an hour on weekdays and hourly on weekends to the Scrivener St stop on Miller St, O'Connor. From there, follow the signs. From the Greyhound/Pioneer Australia terminal on Northbourne Ave, take bus No 381 to the corner of Scrivener and Brigalow St, head north-east up Scrivener St to Dryandra St and turn right. Driving, turn west off Northbourne Ave onto Macarthur Ave and after about two km turn right onto Dryandra. You can hire bicycles at the hostel.

On the other side of town in Manuka, a couple of km from Parliament House, the *Kingston Hotel* (☎ 295 0123) on the corner of Canberra Ave and Giles St offers shared accommodation for $12 per person with non-compulsory linen hire at $4. There are cooking facilities and counter meals are available. Bus No 352 from the city runs past. The Kingston is a large and popular pub. See the following section for Victor Lodge, which is popular with backpackers.

Guesthouses & Private Hotels *Victor Lodge* (☎ 295 7777) is a clean and friendly place at 29 Dawes St Kingston, 500 metres from the railway station and a couple of km south-east of Parliament House. Rooms with shared bathrooms are $35/40 a single/double or you can share a twin room for $19 or a four-bunk room for $15. There are no cooking facilities but a barbecue is planned and a light breakfast is included in the tariff. The beds are new and you get doonas and

free linen. Several travellers have reported that they enjoyed their stay here. To get here from the city take bus No 352 to the nearby Kingston shops, or phone to ask if they can pick you up (this isn't always possible). They rent bikes.

Also south of the lake, *Macquarie Private Hotel* (☎ 273 2325), on National Circuit at the corner of Bourke St, is a very large and fairly modern place with zero atmosphere. The 500 rooms all share bathrooms. Singles/doubles are $35/60 or $112/167 per week, including cooked breakfast. Bus No 350 from the city stops at the front door.

As you enter Canberra from the Hume Highway you pass a clutch of guesthouses on the left (east) side of Northbourne Ave in Downer, just south of where the Barton Highway from Yass and the Federal Highway from Goulburn meet. All are plain and straightforward but clean and quite comfortable. It's worth having a look at all of them and asking if there are any special deals. From here it's four km or so into town, but buses run along Northbourne Ave, and Dickson shopping centre is not far away.

At No 524, *Blue & White Lodge* (☎ 248 0498) has shared rooms from $24 a person and singles between $36 and $40. Prices include a cooked breakfast, and all rooms have TV and a fridge, but bathrooms are shared. Rooms with attached bathroom go for $60 a single or double. They can probably pick you up from the bus station. *Blue Sky* at No 528 is run by the same people. *Chelsea Lodge* (☎ 248 0655) at No 526 also does pick-ups and charges $38/48 a single/double including breakfast, or $48/58 with private bathroom. *Northbourne Lodge* (☎ 257 2599) at No 522 is similar.

Colleges The Australian National University, in Acton just west of Civic, has a selection of residential colleges which may have empty rooms during the Easter (one week), June or July and September (two weeks) and late-November to late-February uni vacations. The uni campus is a very pleasant place to stay. Most of the colleges are along Clunies Ross St. Try *Toad Hall* (!)

(☎ 267 4999), $15 per night, $90 per week; *Ursula College* (☎ 279 4300), students/non-students $35/45 per night, $210/270 per week (rates include breakfast, and other meals are available); or *Burgmann College* (☎ 267 5222), students/nonstudents $30/40 with breakfast or $38/48 for full board.

Motels, Hotels & Apartments Most motels are quite expensive. You might do better than the prices listed here if you book at the tourist office, as they often have special rates.

Acacia Motor Lodge (☎ 249 6955) at 65 Ainslie Ave charges from $65/70 including light breakfast and it's only 500 metres from the centre of Civic. As usual for Canberra, this doesn't much resemble the popular idea of a motel and the rooms are fairly small. *Downtown Speros* (☎ 249 1388) at 82 Northbourne Ave and *Kythera* (☎ 248 7611) nearby at No 98 charge about the same. In Kingston next door to Victor Lodge at No 27 Dawes St, *Motel Monaro* (☎ 295 2111) has special offers, such as doubles from $50 or $60.

Other places are scattered through the suburbs, with a concentration of mid-range motels about eight km south of the city in Narrabundah, such as *Crestwood Garden* (☎ 295 0174) at 39 Jerrabomberra Ave (from ($50/60) and *Sundown Village* (☎ 239 0333) on Jerrabomberra Ave near Hindmarsh Drive, which is quite attractive, with self-contained 'villas' (with kitchenettes) costing $70 a double plus $10 for an extra person, and two-bedroom villas at $80 a double plus $10 per extra person.

Some caravan parks also have motel-type accommodation: *Canberra Lakes Carotel* (☎ 241 1377), just off the Federal Highway at Watson, six km north of the centre, has 'chalets' which sleep up to 12 people, with cooking facilities, TVs and bathrooms, from $45 a double. Bedding is provided and there's a pool and a cafeteria. *Red Cedars Motel* (☎ 241 3222), on the corner of Stirling Ave and Aspinall St, Watson, has units from $49/56/63 a single/double/triple, $5 per person for a unit with a kitchen. There's a pool and TVs. *Southside Motor Park* (☎ 280

6176), on Canberra Ave, Fyshwick, about eight km south-east of the centre, charges $43/50 for motel-style units.

Canberra-Wide Budget Apartments (☎ 257 7637) have a range of apartments around the city, usually let by the week (from $300 for a one-bedroom apartment and $550 for a two-bedroom apartment), but they can sometimes offer overnight stays (from $60 and $70).

Top End Top-end places to stay include *Olim's Canberra Hotel* (☎ 248 5511) at the corner of Ainslie and Limestone Aves in Braddon. Rooms cost from $95 a single or double and it's a pleasant old place. Other places in roughly the same price-range include the *Travelodge* (☎ 248 5311) at 150 Northbourne Ave (this used to be the Rex), the *Capital Parkroyal* (☎ 247 8999) on Binara Ave and the *Country Comfort* (☎ 249 1411) at 102 Northbourne Ave. The rates at these and the other more expensive places can vary quite a lot, so you should ring around or ask at the information centre.

Capital Apartments (☎ 295 1111) at 102 Northbourne Ave has studio apartments from $106 and larger single bedroom apartments from $130. *Capital Tower* (☎ 276 3444) at 2 Marcus Clarke St has serviced apartments from around $150.

Canberra's only five-star hotel is the *Hyatt Hotel Canberra* (☎ 270 1234) on Commonwealth Ave in Yarralumla. This is the old Hotel Canberra, a venerable institution. Rooms start at around $300.

Places to Eat

Canberra's eating scene has improved out of sight over the past few years. Most places are still around Civic, with an upmarket outpost in Manuka and other options scattered around the suburbs.

City Centre There's a *food hall* in the lower section of the Canberra Centre. The range of places isn't great and main courses are in the $6.50 area. There's another food hall in Glebe Park, behind the Casino/Convention Centre. The range is a little wider but prices aren't rock-bottom.

One of the best places to eat is the *Thai Lotus* in the Sydney Building on East Row, open nightly for dinner and for lunch from Tuesday to Friday. The food is excellent and prices are reasonable, mostly around $10 to $13. Also excellent but up several notches in price and be-seen points is *Fringe Benefits*, a brasserie at 54 Marcus Clarke St which wins national food awards and has main courses around $18.

On East Row near Thai Lotus, the *Canberra Vietnamese Restaurant*, upstairs at No 21 East Row, has main courses for less than $10.

Bailey's Corner, the building at the south end of East Row on the corner of London Circuit has a couple of places with outdoor tables. *Tosolini's* is an Italian-based bistro, good for a drink or a meal, with lunchtime specials around $10 and an evening menu with main courses under $14. It stays open late and opens early for breakfast. Downstairs, the *Australian Pizza Kitchen* is cheaper and has wood-fired ovens. Around the corner in Petrie Plaza, *Antigo* is a cafe and bar open daily until late. The menu is interesting and main courses are around $10.

Waffles Piano Bar on the Northbourne Ave side of the Sydney Building offers food of the steak, pasta, burger and pizza variety at around $10 for a main meal. Around the corner on Alinga St is *Waffles Patisserie & Bakery*, and a few doors east is the *Pancake Parlour*, open late every day and 24 hours from Thursday to Sunday. It has pancakes for around $5 at lunch on weekdays.

On the south end of the Melbourne building, *Zorba's Char-Grill* and the *Charcoal Restaurant* are side-by-side competitors offering good steaks and seafood. Zorba's is slightly cheaper, with steaks around $18. In the Wales Centre on the corner of London Circuit and Akuna St, the *Anarkali* Pakistani restaurant has lunch specials (around $12) on weekdays and is open for dinner as well. *Chinese Inn*, upstairs at 116 Alinga St, has good-value lunch specials.

The *Capital Parkroyal* on Binara St has

several restaurants and an all-you-can eat buffet for $22 at breakfast, lunch and dinner.

Garema Place Garema Place, just northeast of London Circuit, is full of restaurants and cafes. *Happy's* is a reasonably-priced Chinese restaurant with lunchtime specials. Upstairs is the long-running *Dorettes Bistro* with main courses around $15 and good jazz or folk music most nights. Nearby, *Mama's Trattoria* does home-made pasta for about $9 and other meals for about $12.

Around the corner on Bunda St is *Gus'*, which has outdoor tables. It serves quite good cafe food with soup about $4 and pastas and goulashes around $7.50. It is open until midnight and later on weekends. Not far away, *Sammy's Kitchen* is a Chinese and Malaysian place with a good reputation and many dishes between $7 and $9; and the nearby *Asian Noodle House* has many dishes under $7. *Ali Baba*, on the corner of Bunda St and Garema Place's southern arm, does Lebanese take-aways, with shwarmas and felafels for around $4 and meals around $9.

The *Red Sea Restaurant* at Club Asmara on Bunda St has interesting decor and main courses, some African, from $12 to $16. Just south of Club Asmara, the *fruit shop* does takeaway fruit salads, fresh juices and healthy sandwiches.

Manuka South of the lake, not far from Capital Hill, is the Manuka shopping centre which services the diplomatic corps and well-heeled bureaucrats from surrounding neighbourhoods. There's a cinema centre here and several bars and cafes which stay open late, such as *Metropole* on the corner of Furneaux and Franklin Sts and the stylish *La Grange* bar and brasserie further south on Franklin St, with main courses between $10 and $16.

Across Franklin St is *My Cafe*, with a bagel-based menu and main courses between $6 and $9. Upstairs in nearby Style Arcade, *Alanya* is a good Turkish restaurant with main courses between $10 and $15. Also up here is *Chez Daniel*, one of Canberra's better restaurants, with main courses around $20.

Timmy's Kitchen on Furneaux St is a very popular Malaysian/Chinese place with main courses under $10 and many under $8. There are plenty of other cafes and restaurants.

Elsewhere *Clarry's* in the Gorman House Arts Centre on Ainslie Ave (but go around the back to Batman St for Clarry's), a few minutes' walk from Civic, is a good cafe that's open Monday to Saturday for lunch and Thursday to Saturday for dinner, with main courses from $8.

In Lyneham at 96 Wattle St is well-known *Tilley's*, a cafe, bar and art gallery. The food is healthy (if you don't count the great cakes) and the clientele is diverse. There is often entertainment here. *Parakeet Cafe* at Wakefields Gardens (the Ainslie shopping centre) has good vegetarian food and a good atmosphere. The menu changes regularly, but main courses are always $12, salads cost from $7 and desserts are $4. They also have great pizzas. It's open from Tuesday to Sunday for dinner, and for lunch on weekdays except Monday. The Malaysian *Rasa Sayang* at 43 Woolley St in Dickson is quite good and reasonably priced. There are other inexpensive Asian places in Dickson.

A popular place for Sunday breakfast is the *Cornucopia Bakery* at 40 Mort St in Braddon, just north of the city centre.

Cheap food can be found at the student union *Refectory* at the ANU.

Entertainment

Canberra is more lively than its reputation suggests. For one thing, liberal licensing laws allow hotels unlimited opening hours and there are some 24-hour bars. The Good Times section in the Thursday *Canberra Times* has full entertainment listings, and the free monthly *BMA* magazine lists bands and other events.

The Canberra Theatre Centre, on Civic Square, has several theatres with a varied range of events from rock bands and drama to ballet, opera and classical concerts. Also check with the foreign cultural organisations like Maison de France and the Goethe Centre to find out what's on. Gorman House Arts

Centre on Ainslie Ave, Braddon, sometimes has theatre or dance performances or exhibitions. An interesting market is held here on weekends.

If you're tired of Oz club culture, phone one of the clubs catering to Australians of foreign descent, to see whether visitors are welcome – see the Yellow Pages under 'Clubs, Social'.

Casino The new Casino Canberra (☎ 1800 806 833 toll-free) at the Convention Centre on Constitution Ave in Civic is open from 10 am on Friday all the way through to 4 am on Monday, and from 10 am to 4 am for the rest of the week. It regards itself as being 'stylishly elegant yet friendly' – that is, punters wearing denim, T-shirts, sports shoes etc don't make it through the door. Men have to wear jackets and ties after 7 pm.

Dancing & Drinking There's live music two or three nights a week during term at the ANU union bar, a reasonable place for a drink even when there's no entertainment. Big touring acts often play the Refectory here.

In Civic, Moosehead's Bar on the south side of the Sydney Building is popular. Around the corner on Northbourne Ave, the Private Bin is a big place that's popular with younger dancers. Not far away, Pandora's on the corner of Alinga and Mort Sts has a bar downstairs and a dance club upstairs. Asylum, upstairs at 23 East Row (near London Circuit) has live music most nights, mainly young bands. Entry costs between $3 and $8, depending on who's playing. The Terrace Bar near the Electric Shadows cinemas on Akuna St has bands several nights.

Heaven, on Garema Place, is a venue popular with gays. Nearby and upstairs from Happy's restaurant, Dorettes Bistro is a relaxed and pleasant wine-bar with live acoustic music; you can have a meal or just a drink. There's music every night, with a cover charge from Thursday to Saturday. Club Asmara, at 128 Bunda St near Garema Place, is home to a fairly pricey African

restaurant (the Red Sea), but if you turn up after about 9 pm you can listen to the music, sometimes live, without ordering a meal. There's a $4 cover charge on Friday and Saturday.

Olim's Canberra Hotel on the corner of Ainslie and Limestone Aves in Braddon has a piano/jazz bar and a popular beer-garden. Tilley's in Lyneham often has live music, usually a cut above pub bands, on Friday, Saturday and Sunday nights. The Southern Cross Club in Woden sometimes has good jazz. Bobby McGee's at the Lakeside Hotel south-west of Vernon Circle is a popular dining/drinking/dancing complex.

Other places that sometimes have bands include the Canberra Workers' Club, on Childers St, and the Canberra Labor Club, on Chandler St, Belconnen. The Southern Cross Club in Phillip has local bands on Friday night.

Cinemas There are several cinemas in the Civic Square and London Circuit area. The Boulevard Twin Cinemas, on Akuna St, are collectively known as Electric Shadows and show repertory-type films. Manuka has another cinema centre.

The National Library shows free films on Tuesday lunchtimes and Thursday evenings – phone for details (☎ 262 1475). The National Gallery has concerts and films on Saturday and Sunday afternoons at around 2.30 pm.

Getting There & Away

Air Canberra is not an international airport (yet). Sydney is normally just half an hour away; the standard fare with the two major airlines is $138; Melbourne is about an hour's flight and costs $193. Direct flights to Adelaide cost $309 and to Brisbane it's $281. There are always advance purchase and other special offers which are considerably cheaper. Ansett offers a night flight to Sydney for $59. You can't fly *from* Sydney with this deal (except back to Canberra on a return ticket, $118). Qantas (☎ 13 1313) and Ansett (☎ 13 1300) are both in the Jolimont Centre on Northbourne Ave.

ACT

Fares on Eastern Australian and Ansett Express are the same as the regular flights, although they fly more frequently. Other smaller airlines fly to NSW country destinations.

Bus Most bus-lines have booking offices at the Jolimont Centre, which is also the terminal for many lines. The Greyhound Pioneer Australia (☎ 13 2030) terminal is on the corner of Northbourne Ave and Ipima Ave, a few blocks north of the centre (at the Canberra Travelodge, the old Rex Hotel). They also have a booking office in the Jolimont Centre.

Murrays (☎ 295 3611) at the Jolimont Centre, is a local company with three daily express (under four hours) buses to Sydney for $28 or around $20 if you pay in advance. They also run to the coast at Batemans Bay ($21.75) and connect with buses to Nowra ($39).

Greyhound Pioneer Australia (☎ 13 2030) has the most frequent Sydney service ($28) including one direct from Sydney Airport ($32). It takes four to five hours. They also run to Adelaide (about $99) and Melbourne ($52). They run to Cooma ($14) and the NSW snowfields ($32, including park entry fees). Services are frequent in winter, less so at other times. Deanes Buslines (☎ 299 3722) has day-trip ski packages.

Transborder Express (☎ 226 1378) runs to Yass ($8). Capital Coachlines (book through Greyhound Pioneer Australia) runs to Bathurst ($36), Orange ($36) and Dubbo ($50), as does Rendell's (☎ 1800 023 328 toll-free). Sid Fogg's (☎ 1800 045 952 toll-free) runs to Newcastle ($43) four times a week, daily in school holidays.

The Countrylink Travel Centre (☎ 257 1576 or 13 2232) is in the Jolimont Centre. Countrylink buses run to Sydney three times a day and cost $35. There's a daily service to Adelaide via Albury which involves two buses and a train and costs about $90; it's quicker and no more expensive to go by bus via Melbourne.

Train The railway station (☎ 239 0133, 6 am

to 6 pm daily) is south of Lake Burley Griffin, on Wentworth Ave, Kingston. You can make bookings for trains and connecting buses at the Countrylink Travel Centre in the Jolimont Centre. To Sydney there are two trains daily, taking about 4½ hours and costing $35/48 in economy/1st class. There's a possibility that the Speedrail project will go ahead and travel time will be cut to 75 minutes. This is a few years away, though.

There is no direct train to Melbourne. The daily V/Line Canberra Link service involves a train between Melbourne and Wodonga and a connecting bus to Canberra. This costs $45 in economy and takes about 10 hours. A longer but much more interesting train/bus service to Melbourne is the V/Line Capital Link which runs via Cooma and Bombala and the superb mountain forests of Victoria's East Gippsland, then down the Princes Highway to Sale where you catch a train. This takes over 11 hours and costs $45.

Car & Motorbike The Federal Highway runs north to the Hume Highway near Yass and the Barton Highway meets the Hume near Goulburn. (People in Canberra refer to the Hume as Sesame Street – no-one could tell me why.)

Car Rental Avis (☎ 249 6088), Hertz (☎ 257 4877), Budget (☎ 13 2727) and Thrifty (☎ 247 7422), have offices at the airport and in town.

Cheaper outfits include Rumbles (☎ 280 7444) at the corner of Kembla and Wollongong Sts in Fyshwick, and Rent a Dent (☎ 257 5947), who will pick you up from the Jolimont Centre. Expect to pay $35 to $40 a day with 100 free km, with better deals on longer rentals.

Getting Around

To/From the Airport The airport is seven km from the city centre. Note all the government cars lined up outside waiting to pick up 'pollies' and public servants. Hertz, Budget, Avis and Thrifty have desks at the airport. The only airport bus service is ACT Mini Buses (☎ 295 6999) which charges $4.50

ACT

and picks up from the Jolimont Centre, various hotels and the YHA. You have to book. The taxi fare from the airport to Civic is around $9.

Bus Action is the public transport bus system, and buses run fairly frequently around Canberra. Phone (☎ 207 7611) for information from 7 am to 11 pm Monday to Saturday and from 8.30 am to 6 pm Sunday. The main interchange is on the corner of Alinga St and East Row in Civic, not far from the Jolimont Centre. The information kiosk here is open daily until about 11 pm. If you plan to use a lot of buses it's worth spending $2 on *The Bus Book*, available at the information kiosk. Unfortunately it's not exactly pocket-sized.

The flat 'one route' fare is $2 and if you pay cash you should have the exact change. Some express buses (700 series) cost twice the normal fare. You can save money with pre-purchase tickets, available from newsagents and elsewhere but not on buses. A book of 10 Fare Go tickets costs $10.60 and a weekly ticket is $18. Daily Tickets are great value as they offer unlimited travel for $4.80.

(Acronym enthusiasts will have already discovered that Action stands for Australian Capital Territory Internal Omnibus Network!)

Special Services The free Downtowner service is a bus disguised as a tram which runs around the Civic shopping centre, stopping at specially designated stops.

Sightseeing Bus No 901 runs to the War Memorial, Regatta Point, Questacon, the National Gallery, Parliament House and several embassies in Yarralumla. No 904 goes to the Botanic Gardens, the aquarium and to Telecom Tower atop Black Mountain. Both services depart hourly from the Civic interchange, No 901 between 9 am and 3 pm and No 904 between 10.25 am and 3.25 pm. You'll need a Daily Ticket ($4.80) to ride these services.

Murray's Canberra Explorer (☎ 295 3611) runs a 25-km route around 19 points of interest and you can get on and off wherever you like. It departs hourly from the Jolimont Centre between 10.15 am and 4.15 pm daily, and tickets ($15, $8 children) are sold on the bus. If you just want to make one circuit without getting off, a good way to orient yourself, buy a one-hour tour ticket, $7 (children $5).

Car & Motorbike Canberra's wide and relatively uncluttered main roads make driving a joy, although once you enter the maze of curving roads in the residential areas things become much more difficult. Take a map. Note that speeding on the main roads is common (if illegal, and dangerous for the newcomer because of unexpected roundabouts and exits), but *everyone* observes the 40 km/h limit in school areas.

Taxi Call Aerial Taxis (☎ 285 9222).

Bicycle Canberra is a cyclist's paradise, with bike paths making it possible to ride around the city hardly touching a road. One popular track is a circuit of the lake; there are also peaceful stretches of bushland along some suburban routes. Get a copy of the *Canberra Cycleways* map from bookshops or the information centre ($2.50). Mr Spokes Bike Hire (☎ 257 1188), near the Acton Park Ferry Terminal, charges $6 an hour or $20 a day, plus $1 for a helmet. The rates are similar at Glebe Park, on Coranderrk St, a few blocks west of Vernon Circle. Another company is Dial a Bicycle (☎ 286 5463) which will deliver the bike. They hire 10-speed mountain bikes by the day, from $20 for one day up to $60 for a week, including helmet.

Pedicab In Garema Place you'll probably see pedicabs (sort of upmarket rickshaws) which can carry you around the city centre and across to the parliamentary triangle, (although the steep hill up to the new Parliament House might be too much for your rider). The pedicabs charge $8 for 15 minutes, $15 for half an hour and $25 for an hour. You can make phone bookings (☎ 259 2396, 018 621 056).

Around Canberra

The ACT is 80 km from north to south and about 30 km wide. There's plenty of unspoiled bush just outside the urban area and a network of paved roads into it. Both the NRMA's *Canberra & District* map and the tourist bureau's *Canberra Sightseeing Guide with Tourist Drives* are helpful.

The plains and isolated hills of the ACT's north, where Canberra lies, rise to rugged ranges in the south and west of the territory. The Murrumbidgee River flows across the territory from south-east to north-west. Namadgi National Park in the south covers 40% of the ACT and adjoins the Kosciusko National Park.

Picnic & Walking Areas

Picnic and barbecue spots, many with gas barbecues, are scattered through and around Canberra. **Black Mountain**, just west of the city, is a convenient place for picnics. There are good swimming spots along the Murrumbidgee and Cotter rivers. Other riverside areas include **Uriarra Crossing**, 24 km north-west of Civic, on the Murrumbidgee near its meeting with the Molonglo River; **Casuarina Sands**, 19 km west, at the meeting of the Cotter and Murrumbidgee; **Kambah Pool**, 21 km further upstream (south) on the Murrumbidgee; the **Cotter Dam**, 23 km west, on the Cotter, which also has a camping area ($9); **Pine Island** and **Point Hut Crossing**, on the Murrumbidgee, upstream of Kambah Pool; and **Gibraltar Falls**, 48 km south-west, which also has a camping area.

There are good walking tracks along the Murrumbidgee from Kambah Pool to Pine Island (seven km), or to Casuarina Sands (about 21 km).

The spectacular **Ginninderra Falls** are at Parkwood, north-west of Canberra, just across the NSW border. The area is open daily and includes a nature trail, gorge scenery, canoeing and camping. There's a $3 admission charge.

The **Tidbinbilla Nature Reserve** (☎ 237 5120), south-west of the city in the hills beyond the Tidbinbilla tracking station, has bushwalking tracks, some leading to interesting rock formations. There are also enclosed areas where you'll probably see koalas. The reserve is open from 9 am to 6 pm (later during daylight-savings time); the visitor centre is open from 11 am to 5 pm. South-west of here in the Corin Forest, there's a one-km-long metal 'bobsled' run on weekends and during school holidays; rides are $4.

Other good walking areas include Mt Ainslie, on the north-east side of the city, and Mt Majura behind it (the combined area is called **Canberra Nature Park**), and Molonglo Gorge near Queanbeyan.

Namadgi National Park, occupying the whole south-west of the ACT and partly bordering mountainous Kosciusko National Park in NSW's Snowy Mountains, has seven peaks over 1600 metres and offers challenging bushwalking. Sections have been described as being 'like Scotland with kangaroos'.

Boboyan Rd crosses the park, going south from Tharwa in the ACT to Adaminaby on the eastern edge of the Snowy Mountains in NSW. The park visitor information centre (☎ 237 5222) is on this road, two km south of Tharwa, but you can also pick up brochures and maps at the Canberra information centre. There are several picnic areas, but the only formal campsites are at the Orroral River crossing and Mt Clear, both accessible from Boboyan Rd. Mudmap Tours (you can book through the travel agency at the YHA) have tours running into the park.

Observatories & Tracking Stations

The ANU's **Mt Stromlo Observatory** is 16 km west of Canberra and has a 188-cm telescope plus a visitors' annexe open from 9 am to 4 pm daily. The Canberra Deep Space Communication Complex (usually called the **Tidbinbilla Tracking Station**), 40 km south-west of Canberra, is a joint US-Australian deep space tracking station. The visitor centre has displays of spacecraft and

tracking technology. It's free, and open from 9 am to 5 pm daily. The area is popular for bushwalks and barbecues.

Gold Creek

Near the Barton Highway about 15 km north of the city, Gold Creek has a number of attractions. Hard to resist is the **National Dinosaur Museum** (despite the name, this is a private collection) with replica skeletons of 10 dinosaurs and many bones and fossils. Admission is $7.50 ($5 children), and it's open daily from 10 am to 5 pm. **Ginninderra Village** is a collection of craft workshops and galleries. Next door is **Cockington Green**, a miniature replica of an English village, open daily (admission $6).

Other Attractions

There are native animals at **Rehwinkel's Animal Park**, on Macks Reef Rd, off the Federal Highway 24 km north of Canberra, in NSW. It's open daily and admission is $6.

Bywong Mining Town is a re-creation of a mining settlement, about 30 km north of Canberra. It's open daily between 10 am and 4 pm and there are tours at 11 am, 1 pm and 3 pm. Admission is $7.

The beautifully restored **Lanyon Homestead** is about 20 km south of the city centre, on the river near Tharwa. The early stone cottage on the site was built by convicts and the grand homestead was completed in 1859. This National Trust homestead, which now documents the life of the region before Canberra existed, is open from 10 am to 4 pm from Tuesday to Sunday. A major attraction is a gallery of Sidney Nolan paintings.

Cuppacumbalong, also near Tharwa, is another old homestead, although neither as grand nor of such importance as Lanyon. It is now a craft studio and gallery and is open from 11 am to 5 pm Wednesday to Sunday.

Day Trips

A popular drive is east into NSW, past Bungendore, to **Braidwood** (an hour or so) with its many antique shops, craft stores and restaurants. **Bungendore** is a small country town which has craft galleries such as the Bungendore Wood Works and some old buildings. On Anzac Day there's a display by the Light Horse cavalry.

Another good route takes in **Tharwa** and the nearby old homesteads (see the Other Attractions section) in hilly grazing lands. From here, the route goes north-west to Gibraltar Falls and Tidbinbilla Nature Reserve (see the Picnic & Walking Areas section). The Tidbinbilla Space Tracking Station (see the Observatories & Tracking Stations section) is on the way back into town along a slow, winding, scenic road.

QUEANBEYAN

Just across the NSW border south-east of Canberra is Queanbeyan (population 27,000), now virtually a suburb of the capital it predates. It's strikingly obvious that Canberra's planning regulations don't apply here. Until 1838 it was known as 'Queen Bean'. There's a history museum in the town, and good lookouts on Jerrabomberra Hill (five km west of the town centre) and Bungendore Hill (four km east).

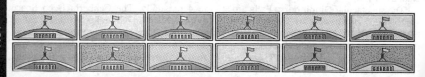

Index

562 Index

Guides to the Pacific

Australia – a travel survival kit
The complete low-down on Down Under – home of Ayers Rock, the Great Barrier Reef, extraordinary animals, cosmopolitan cities, rainforests, beaches ... and Lonely Planet!

Bushwalking in Australia
Two experienced and respected walkers give details of the best walks in every state, covering many different terrains and climates.

Bushwalking in Papua New Guinea
The best way to get to know Papua New Guinea is from the ground up – and bushwalking is the best way to travel around the rugged and varied landscape of this island.

Islands of Australia's Great Barrier Reef – Australia guide
The Great Barrier Reef is one of the wonders of the world – and one of the great travel destinations! Whether you're looking for the best snorkelling, the liveliest nightlife or a secluded island hideaway, this guide has all the facts you'll need.

Melbourne – city guide
From historic houses to fascinating churches and from glorious parks to tapas bars, cafés and bistros, Melbourne is a dream for gourmets and a paradise for sightseers.

Sydney – city guide
From the Opera House to the surf; all you need to know in a handy pocket-sized format.

Outback Australia
The outback conjures up images of endless stretches of dead straight roads, the rich red of the desert, and the resourcefulness and resilience of the inhabitants. A visit to Australia would not be complete without visiting the outback to see the beauty and vastness of this ancient country.

Victoria – Australia guide
From old gold rush towns to cosmopolitan Melbourne and from remote mountains to the most popular surf beaches, Victoria is packed with attractions and activities for everyone.

Fiji – a travel survival kit
Whether you prefer to stay in camping grounds, international hotels, or something in-between, this comprehensive guide will help you to enjoy the beautiful Fijian archipelago.

Hawaii – a travel survival kit
Share in the delights of this island paradise – and avoid some of its high prices – with this practical guide. It covers all of Hawaii's well-known attractions, plus plenty of uncrowded sights and activities.

Micronesia – a travel survival kit
The glorious beaches, lagoons and reefs of these 2100 islands would

dazzle even the most jaded traveller. This guide has all the details on island-hopping across the Micronesian archipelago.

New Caledonia – a travel survival kit

This guide shows how to discover all that the idyllic islands of New Caledonia have to offer – from French colonial culture to traditional Melanesian life.

New Zealand – a travel survival kit

This practical guide will help you discover the very best New Zealand has to offer: Maori dances and feasts, some of the most spectacular scenery in the world, and every outdoor activity imaginable.

Tramping in New Zealand

Call it tramping, hiking, walking, bushwalking or trekking – travelling by foot is the best way to explore New Zealand's natural beauty. Detailed descriptions of over 40 walks of varying length and difficulty.

Papua New Guinea – a travel survival kit

With its coastal cities, villages perched beside mighty rivers, palm-fringed beaches and rushing mountain streams, Papua New Guinea promises memorable travel.

Rarotonga & the Cook Islands – a travel survival kit

Rarotonga and the Cook Islands have history, beauty and magic to rival the better-known islands of Hawaii and Tahiti, but the world has virtually passed them by.

Samoa – a travel survival kit

Two remarkably different countries, Western Samoa and American Samoa offer some wonderful island escapes, and Polynesian culture at its best.

Solomon Islands – a travel survival kit

The Solomon Islands are the best-kept secret of the Pacific. Discover remote tropical islands, jungle-covered volcanoes and traditional Melanesian villages with this detailed guide.

Tahiti & French Polynesia – a travel survival kit

Tahiti's idyllic beauty has seduced sailors, artists and travellers for generations. The latest edition of this book provides full details on the main island of Tahiti, the Tuamotos, Marquesas and other island groups. Invaluable information for independent travellers and package tourists alike.

Tonga – a travel survival kit

The only South Pacific country never to be colonised by Europeans, Tonga has also been ignored by tourists. The people of this far-flung island group offer some of the most sincere and unconditional hospitality in the world.

Vanuatu – a travel survival kit

Discover superb beaches, lush rainforests, dazzling coral reefs and traditional Melanesian customs in this glorious Pacific Ocean archipelago.

Also available:

Pidgin phrasebook.

Lonely Planet Guidebooks

Lonely Planet guidebooks cover every accessible part of Asia as well as Australia, the Pacific, South America, Africa, the Middle East, Europe and parts of North America. There are five series: *travel survival kits*, covering a country for a range of budgets; *shoestring guides* with compact information for low-budget travel in a major region; *walking guides*; *city guides* and *phrasebooks*.

Jon Murray

Jon Murray took a year off uni a long time ago and, after various adventures, ended up working in the Lonely Planet office. He left to go cycling in Asia, but found himself updating guidebooks instead. He has updated Lonely Planet's *Bangladesh – a travel survival kit*, *Papua New Guinea – a travel survival kit* and *Sydney city guide*, contributed to *Australia – a travel survival kit* and *Africa on a shoestring* and co-authored *South Africa, Lesotho & Swaziland – a travel survival kit*.

From the Author

Thanks to Naomi Richards for tolerant support, to Mary Neighbour and David Kemp at Lonely Planet for diligent editing and mapping, and to Colin Bransgrove and Andrea Lawless from Tourism Albury-Wodonga, who introduced me to Morgan Country, an area I might otherwise have passed through too quickly. Many other people in the travel industry, especially hostel managers, provided invaluable information, and travellers were, as usual, good company and a source of reliable tips.

This Book

Although this is a new book, some sections of it have been expanded from the NSW and ACT chapters of Lonely Planet's *Australia – a travel survival kit*. Jon Murray updated those chapters for the last two editions of *Australia*, but some work by the original author, Tony Wheeler, and subsequent updaters is found in this book. Lonely Planet's *Sydney city guide*, originally written by Barbara Whiter and recently revised by Jon, was the foundation of the Sydney chapter of this book.

From the Publisher

This first edition of *New South Wales & the ACT* was edited by Mary Neighbour at Lonely Planet's Melbourne office. Jenny Missen did additional editing and proofreading, and Ian Ward also helped with the proofreading. Thanks also to Caroline Williamson for editorial guidance.

David Kemp was responsible for design and cartography, with additional cartography by Chris Love, Tamsin Wilson, Indra Kilfoyle, Louise Keppie and Jacqui Saunders. The cover was designed by Tamsin and David, and the illustrations are by David and other artists. Thanks also to Dan Levin for the climate charts, to Peter Morris for the cartoons and to Ann Jeffree for indexing.

Warning & Request

Things change – prices go up, schedules change, good places go bad and bad places go bankrupt – nothing stays the same. So if you find things better or worse, recently opened or long since closed, please write and tell us and help make the next edition better.

Your letters will be used to help update future editions and, where possible, important changes will also be included in a Stop Press section in reprints.

We greatly appreciate all information that is sent to us by travellers. Back at Lonely Planet we employ a hard-working readers' letters team to sort through the many letters we receive. The best ones will be rewarded with a free copy of the next edition or another Lonely Planet guide if you prefer. We give away lots of books, but, unfortunately, not every letter/postcard receives one.

Contents

Map Legend

BOUNDARIES

- ...International Boundary
- ...Internal Boundary

ROUTES

- ...Freeway
- ...Highway
- ...Major Road
- ...Unsealed Road or Track
- ...City Road
- ...City Street
- ...Railway
- ...Monorail
- ...Tram
- ...Walking Track
- ...Walking Tour
- ...Ferry Route
- ...Cable Car or Chairlift

AREA FEATURES

- ...Park, Gardens
- ...National Park
- ...Forest
- ...Built-Up Area
- ...Pedestrian Mall
- ...Cemetery
- ...Reef
- ...Beach or Desert
- ...Rocks

HYDROGRAPHIC FEATURES

- ...Coastline
- ...River, Creek
- ...Intermittent River or Creek
- ...Lake, Intermittent Lake
- ...Canal
- ...Swamp

SYMBOLS

✪ CAPITAL	...National Capital	
◉ Capital	...State Capital	
⬤ CITY	...Major City	
● City	...City	
● Town	...Town	
● Village	...Village	
■	...Place to Stay	
▼	...Place to Eat	
⊌	...Pub, Bar	
✉ ☎	...Post Office, Telephone	
❶ ❸	...Tourist Information, Bank	
⊖ 🅿	...Transport, Parking	
🏛 ⛺	...Museum, Youth Hostel	
🏕 ⚠	Caravan Park, Camping Ground	
† ⛪ †	...Church, Cathedral	
☪ ✡	...Mosque, Synagogue	
⊥ 卐	Buddhist Temple, Hindu Temple	

⊕ ★	...Hospital, Police Station	
✈ ✝	...Airport, Airfield	
◪ ✿	...Swimming Pool, Gardens	
❖ 🐘	...Shopping Centre, Zoo	
☙ 🏕	...Winery or Vineyard, Picnic Site	
← 33	One Way Street, Route Number	
⁂	...Archaeological Site or Ruins	
🏛 ⚲	...Stately Home, Monument	
🏯 ⚑	...Castle, Golf Course	
⌒ ⌂	...Cave, Hut or Chalet	
▲ ✳	...Mountain or Hill, Lookout	
🏮 ⚡	...Lighthouse, Ski field	
Ⓤ	...Underground Railway Station	
	...Ancient or City Wall	
	...Rapids, Waterfalls	
	...Cliff or Escarpment, Tunnel	
	...Railway Station	

Note: not all symbols displayed above appear in this book

Introduction

The site of the first European settlement in Australia and still the country's largest and liveliest metropolis, Sydney is one of the world's great cities. The city's cosmopolitan population, beautiful setting and easy-going lifestyle make it an essential destination, and it will be a superb venue for the 2000 Olympics. Within easy reach of Sydney there are many beautiful beaches and forests, the spectacular Blue Mountains and the wineries of the Hunter Valley.

The well-beaten route up the north coast from Sydney to Queensland is deservedly popular, passing through resort towns such as Coffs Harbour and Byron Bay, as well as an endless string of superb and often quite deserted surf beaches, and offering easy access to the national parks of the coast-hugging Great Dividing Range. Australia's largest ski-fields are in the Snowy Mountains, in the south-east of NSW, and nearby is the Australian Capital Territory, a city-state containing Canberra, the fascinating national capital.

However, there's a lot more to NSW than these well-known attractions.

For a start, the south coast is at least as scenic as the north coast and is a lot less developed. On top of the Great Dividing Range is a series of high tablelands, including New England, with its spectacular gorges and waterfalls, and west of the range you'll meet rural Australia. There are some fine old towns in the rich farmlands of the western slopes, and another winery area around Mudgee. Further west are the vast land-

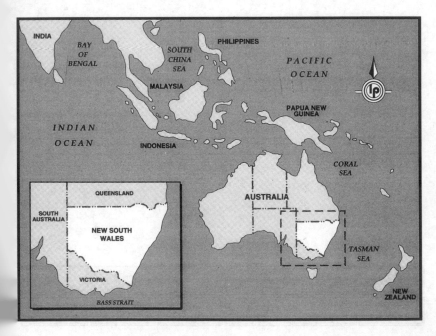

9

scapes and huge skies of the great plains, merging into the red soil of the baking outback in the state's north-west. South of the plains is the Riverina with its lazy rivers and redgum forests.

Many of the state's national parks have World Heritage status, and some are wilderness areas where possibilities for adventure activities abound. The climate ranges from winter blizzards in the Snowy Mountains to scorching summers in the outback; the landscape ranges from steamy subtropical rainforest to neat vineyards and orchards.

Practically everything that is considered 'typically Australian' – ancient Aboriginal sites, pristine surf beaches, kangaroos bounding across desert dunes, lyre-birds dancing in rainforest, picturesque country pubs, weather-beaten drovers and friendly small-town people – can be found in NSW.

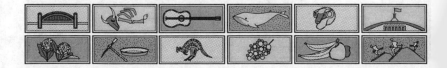

Facts about the Region

HISTORY
The Aborigines

The ancestors of the Aborigines journeyed from South-East Asia to the Australian mainland at least 40,000 years ago, possibly much earlier. They probably came overland across the now submerged Sahul Shelf or travelled by rafts or canoes where there were no land connections. Archaeological evidence suggests that the descendants of these first settlers colonised the entire continent within a few thousand years. They were the first people in the world to manufacture polished edge-ground stone tools, cremate their dead and engrave and paint representations of themselves and the animals they hunted.

When Europeans arrived in New South Wales just over 200 years ago, there were some 750,000 Aborigines in Australia and more than 200 regional languages – many of these languages as distinct from each other as English is from Chinese.

Around what is now Sydney, there were approximately 3000 Aborigines using three main languages, although there were several dialects and groups. Ku-Ring-Gai was spoken on the north shore, Dharawal along the coast south of Botany Bay, and Dharug and its dialects were spoken across the plains into the lower Blue Mountains.

Aboriginal society, based on family groups rather than large political units, could not present a united front to the European colonisers, and in the crude realpolitik of the late 18th century, the British assumed that a people which didn't defend its land had no right to that land. (In other colonies such as New Zealand and India, widespread organised resistance to colonisation lead to treaties with the indigenous peoples.)

At a local level, individuals resisted the encroachment of settlers. Warriors including Pemulwy, Yagan, Dundalli, Pigeon and Nemarluk were, for a time, feared by the colonists in their areas. But although some settlements had to be abandoned, the effect of such resistance only temporarily postponed the inevitable.

Without any legal right to the lands they once lived on, Aborigines became dispossessed. Some were driven away by force and thousands succumbed to exotic diseases (everything from measles to syphilis was new to Australia). Others voluntarily left their tribal lands to travel to the fringes of settled areas to obtain new commodities such as steel and cloth, and, once there, experienced hitherto unknown substances such as tea, tobacco, alcohol and opium.

By the early 1900s, legislation designed to segregate and 'protect' Aboriginal people imposed restrictions on Aborigines' rights to own property and to seek employment; and the Aboriginals Ordinance of 1918 even allowed the state to remove children from Aboriginal mothers if it was suspected that the father was non-Aboriginal. Many Aborigines are still bitter about having been

Aboriginal woman

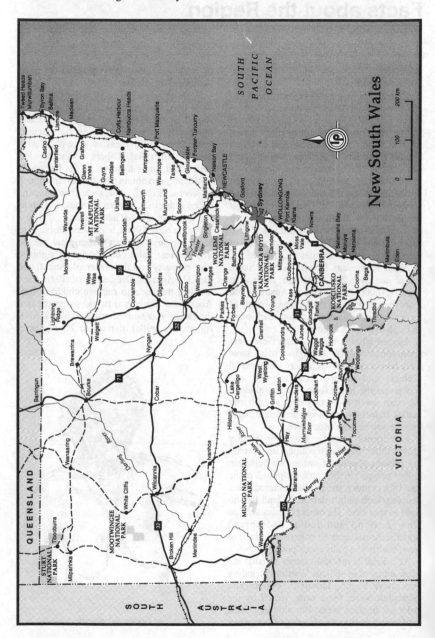

separated from their families and forced to grow up apart from their people. Archie Roach's recent song *Took the Children Away* tells of this time – the song made it onto the charts and you might see the good video on TV music-video shows.

After WW II 'assimilation' was tried, but this just meant that Aborigines' rights were reduced even further. The government had control over everything from where Aborigines could live to whom they could marry. Many people were forcibly moved to townships, the idea being that they would adapt to the European culture, which would in turn aid their economic development. This was a dismal failure.

In the 1960s the assimilation policy came under a great deal of scrutiny, and non-Aboriginal Australians became increasingly aware of the inequity of their treatment of Aborigines. In 1967 non-Aboriginal Australians voted to give Aborigines and Torres Strait Islanders the status of citizens, and gave the federal government power to legislate for them in all states, a great step forward as federal governments are usually electorally able to make more enlightened decisions than state governments.

The assimilation policy was finally dumped in 1972, to be replaced by the government's policy of self-determination, which for the first time brought Aborigines into the decision-making processes.

In 1976 the Aboriginal Land Rights Act gave Aborigines in the Northern Territory indisputable title to all Aboriginal reserves and a means for claiming other crown land. It also provided for mineral royalties to be paid to Aboriginal communities. This legislation was supposed to be extended to cover all of Australia, but the removal of the reformist Labor government in 1975 (see later) put paid to that prospect.

Today Many Aborigines in south-eastern Australia now identify themselves as Kooris.

Only in the past few years has the non-Aboriginal community come to grips with the fact that a meaningful conciliation between indigenous and non-indigenous Australia was vital to the psychological well-being of all Australians. In 1992 the High Court handed down what became known as its Mabo ruling. It was the result of a claim by a Torres Strait Islander, Eddy Mabo, challenging the established concept of *terra nullius* – the idea that Australia belonged to no-one when Europeans first arrived. The court ruled that Aborigines did once own Australia and that where there was continuous association with the land they had the right to claim it back.

The ruling resulted in some fairly hysterical responses, with non-Aborigines fearing their precious backyard was suddenly going to be subject to an Aboriginal land claim.

In 1993 the Federal government introduced its Native Title legislation, which formalised the High Court's Mabo ruling. The content of the bill had, somewhat surprisingly, been agreed upon by all the major players involved – the miners, the farmers, the government and of course the Aborigines (although some states are now challenging the legislation). While the legislation can do nothing to solve the injustices of the past, it does go a long way towards creating, for the first time in the country's history, the conditions for just land dealings between Aborigines and non-Aborigines.

Many Aborigines still live in appalling conditions. They are 26 times more likely to be jailed than non-Aborigines, and substance abuse is a big problem. This is not really surprising. Imagine that Cold War nightmares had come true and the USSR had invaded the USA, killing a large proportion of the population, putting all the children into 're-education centres', dispossessing all landowners and banning Christianity and baseball. Any resistance is met with massacres. I reckon there might be more than a few Yanks who found it difficult to be very enthusiastic about the future, and after 200 years of this treatment it would be very tempting to do whatever was necessary to forget that their culture had ever existed.

The Founding of New South Wales

In the late 18th century, Britain was a mess.

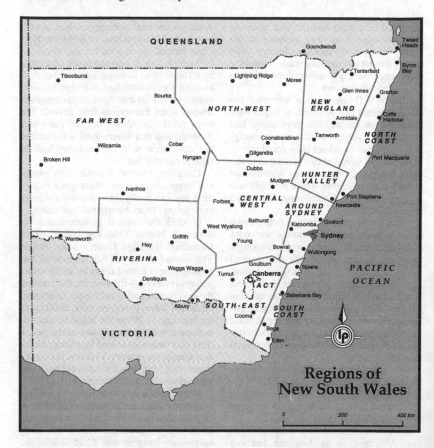

QUEENSLAND

Goondiwindi

Tweed Heads

Byron Bay

Tenterfield

Tibooburra

Lightning Ridge

Moree

Glen Innes

Grafton

Bourke

NORTH-WEST

NEW ENGLAND

Armidale

Coffs Harbour

FAR WEST

Coonabarabran

Tamworth

NORTH COAST

Wilcannia

Cobar

Gilgandra

Port Macquarie

Broken Hill

Nyngan

Dubbo

Ivanhoe

Mudgee

HUNTER VALLEY

Forbes

CENTRAL WEST

AROUND SYDNEY

Port Stephens

Newcastle

West Wyalong

Bathurst

Katoomba

Gosford

Wentworth

Griffith

Young

Bowral

Sydney

Hay

Wollongong

RIVERINA

Wagga Wagga

Tumut

Goulburn

Nowra

PACIFIC OCEAN

Deniliquin

Canberra

ACT

Albury

SOUTH-EAST

Batemans Bay

Cooma

SOUTH COAST

VICTORIA

Bega

Eden

Regions of New South Wales

0   200   400 km

Most of the American colonies had been lost in 1776, and at home the new cities that had sprung up were proving to be a dangerous shambles. Poor people from all over the country drifted into London and anarchy threatened. Even in the counties law and order was a headache, and Ireland was in turmoil.

There were far too many criminals, and even hanging them for crimes such as stealing handkerchiefs didn't reduce the numbers much. There seemed to be a certain logic in the idea that if you got rid of the criminals

there would be no more crime. America could no longer be a dumping-ground for the poor and the rebellious, so the government began to consider other options.

The inhospitable north and west coasts of Australia had been charted in the 1640s by Dutch explorer Abel Tasman and he had named the continent New Holland. It wasn't until 1770 that Captain James Cook, the famous British explorer, sailed up the fertile east coast, landing at Botany Bay (among other places) and naming the area New South Wales. Although Cook charted the east coast,

no-one had much idea of how his maps fitted together with other pieces of the continent that had been seen by Europeans.

In 1779 Joseph Banks, who had sailed with Cook as a botanist, suggested New South Wales as a fine site for a colony of thieves, and in 1786 Lord Sydney announced that the King had decided upon Botany Bay as a place to send convicts under sentence of transportation.

Less than two years later, in January 1788, the First Fleet sailed into Botany Bay under the command of Captain Arthur Phillip, who was to be the colony's first governor. Phillip was disappointed with the landscape and sent a small boat north to find a more suitable landfall. The crew soon returned with the news that in Port Jackson they had found the finest harbour in the world and a good sheltered cove.

The fleet, comprised of 11 ships carrying about 750 male and female convicts, 400 sailors, four companies of marines and enough livestock and supplies for two years, weighed anchor again and headed for Sydney Cove to begin establishing a settlement. The British flag was raised (the site is possibly somewhere near the obelisk in Macquarie Place), and New South Wales was defined as everything east of longitude 135° East (roughly where Coober Pedy is today) and claimed for the British Crown.

The early settlement did it hard. The soils around Sydney Cove proved to be poor and the tools were worse, so the settlers were dependent on their stores and supply ships from England. None came for 2½ years.

Shortly after a supply ship relieved the famine in 1790, the Second Fleet struggled into Sydney Cove, bringing few supplies but another 740 convicts. Conditions on the Second Fleet had been hellish, with more than one in four convicts dying on the voyage and most of the survivors too weak to walk.

For the convicts, New South Wales was a harsh and horrible place. The reasons for transportation were often minor, and the sentences, of no less than seven years with hard labour, were tantamount to life sentences as

there was little hope of returning home. Whippings were common and were designed to break the spirit.

Hunger to the point of weakness afflicted most of the convicts, while the need for strong labourers to grow food remained urgent. A farm was established at Parramatta (today's Parramatta Rd basically follows the old cart track) where the soil was more fertile, and gradually the situation improved. However, it was more than a decade until enough food was grown in the colony for the threat of famine to disappear completely.

Right from the start, the British government had no fixed idea about the future of New South Wales. What was to happen to the free-born children of the convicts; who should own the land; and should the colony should aim to be self-supporting or even an asset to the British Empire? Answers to these questions changed with changing governments in Britain, but events in New South Wales usually ended up dictating government policy rather than the other way around.

The Early Colony

As crops began to yield, New South Wales became less dependent on Britain for food. There were still, however, huge social gulfs in the fledgling colony: officers and their families were in control and clinging desperately to a modicum of civilised British living; soldiers, free settlers and even emancipated convicts were beginning to eke out a living; yet the majority of the population were still in chains, regarded as the dregs of humanity and living in squalid conditions.

Little of the country was explored during those first years, and few people ventured further than Sydney Cove.

Phillip believed New South Wales would not progress if the colony continued to rely solely on the labour of convicts, who were already busy constructing government roads and buildings. He believed prosperity depended on attracting free settlers, to whom convicts could be assigned as labourers, and on granting land to officers, soldiers and

worthy emancipists (convicts who had served their time).

Phillip returned to England in 1792 and his second-in-command, Major Grose, took over. In a classic case of 'jobs for the boys', Grose tipped the balance of power further in favour of the military by granting land to officers of the New South Wales Corps. With money, land and cheap labour at their disposal, the officers became exploitative, making huge profits at the expense of the small farmers.

To encourage convicts to work, the officers were given permission to pay them in rum. The officers quickly prospered and were soon able to buy whole shiploads of goods and resell them at huge profits. The colony was becoming an important port on trade routes, and whaling and sealing were increasing. The officers, who became known as the Rum Corps, met little resistance and continued to do virtually as they pleased, all the while getting richer and more arrogant.

A new governor, William Bligh, was appointed to restore order, but the bad temper which had already caused him to suffer a mutiny on the *Bounty* again caused his downfall, and he suffered another rebellion and was arrested by the Rum Corps. This rebellion, known as the Rum Rebellion, was the final straw for the British government, which in 1809 dispatched Lieutenant-Colonel Lachlan Macquarie with his own

Convict cuffs and leg fetters

regiment and orders for the return to London of the New South Wales Corps.

John Macarthur, one of the officers involved in the Rum Rebellion, was already a successful farmer and was to have far-reaching effects on the colony's first staple industry. He saw the country's wool-growing potential and set about breeding a strain of merino sheep that could prosper here. His wife, Elizabeth, did much of the work, as John remained in England for nearly a decade for his part in the rebellion.

Governor Macquarie, having broken the stranglehold of the Rum Corps, set about putting the colony to rights. Arthur Phillip had had plans for Sydney's development, with wide, straight streets, but of course public works were not high on the Rum Corps' agenda, and by now Sydney was a chaotic town of 6000 people. It was too late to lay grand plans without pulling the whole place down and starting again, but Macquarie was able to rectify some things and today's central city layout is basically his work.

He also instituted a building programme, employing talented convict architect Francis Greenway, several of whose buildings remain today (see the Sydney and Around Sydney chapters). Because hamlets along the riverflats of the Hawkesbury were repeatedly flooded, Macquarie established five well-planned towns on higher ground around Windsor – the Macquarie towns (see the Around Sydney chapter). He encouraged explorers to find a route across the Blue Mountains and, when they did, had a road across completed in just six months, then established the town of Bathurst on the plains beyond.

So far, so good.

However, Macquarie also had the strange idea that convicts who had served their time should be allowed rights as citizens, and he began appointing emancipists to public positions. Worse, he even sat down to dinner with some of them.

The gentry of Sydney Cove wanted nothing to do with ex-cons or their children. Anti-emancipists, including the irascible

John Macarthur, were outraged at what they saw as a social perversion and began carping about Macquarie's expensive public works programmes and creating the impression that the colony was ungovernable. Apart from any philosophical stand about being 'polluted' by ex-convicts, many of the wealthier colonists were simply annoyed that Macquarie's building programmes were using all the available convicts, leaving them no free labour for their farms.

Macquarie, generally agreed to have been be the best of the early governors, returned to England under a cloud in 1821. His reign had been a watershed for the colony. When he arrived it was a struggling penal settlement; when he left there was little doubt that a permanent and potentially wealthy colony had been established.

For both the Aborigines and the continent's ecology, disaster loomed.

No-one thought of conserving anything... When jellied, fly-blown human backs had the sanction of society, there was no tenderness towards animals, no artistic or scientific realisation that in Australia's living unique flora, fauna and avifauna were masterpieces beyond anything she can ever contribute to museums and galleries.
Miles Franklin, *All that Swagger*, 1936

A New People
From the earliest days of New South Wales, Australian-born colonials saw themselves as different from the upper-crust British officers who ran the colony, who they regarded as effete. Anyway, with an increasing number of Irish political prisoners and their descendants, it wasn't likely that an affection for the Old Dart would burn brightly.

Before long, the free-born children of the convicts became a sizeable proportion of the population. They were called Currency Lads and Lasses. Little is known about these first White Australians and it's unlikely that anyone but they themselves considered them to be Australians. The power and money in the colony rested with people who had their sights set on making their name or their fortune and returning home. For the free-born, Australia *was* home.

Astoundingly, the lowest crime-rate in the early colony was among the free-born, lower even than that among the free settlers. Commissioner Bigge wrote in 1823:

The class of inhabitants that have been born in the colony affords a remarkable exception to the moral and physical character of their parents: they are generally tall in person, and slender in the limbs... They are capable of undergoing more fatigue, and are less exhausted by labour than native Europeans; they are active in their habits but remarkably awkward in their movements. In their tempers they are quick and irascible but not vindictive...

Exploration & Expansion
By 1800 there were only two small settlements in Australia – at Sydney and on Norfolk Island. While unknown areas on world maps were shrinking, most of Australia was still one big blank. It was even suspected that it might be two large, separate islands, and it was hoped that there might be a vast sea in the centre.

George Bass charted the coast south of Sydney almost down to the present location of Melbourne during 1797-98, and in the following year, with Matthew Flinders, he sailed around Van Diemen's Land (Tasmania), establishing that it was an island. Flinders went on in 1802 to sail right around Australia – he suggested that the continent should be called Australia rather than New Holland.

The Blue Mountains at first proved an impenetrable barrier, limiting the size of the colony, but in 1813 a path was finally forced through and the western plains were reached by the explorers Blaxland, Wentworth and Lawson. Soon after, George Evans led two expeditions across the mountains and found the Macquarie and Lachlan rivers.

In 1817, John Oxley's party set out from the newly-founded town of Bathurst down the Lachlan River in search of more good land and perhaps an inland sea. The river petered out into swamps so they headed south-west across arid plains then turned north, crossing the Lachlan and reaching the Macquarie River, which they followed upstream to Bathurst. Oxley was extremely

unenthusiastic about the country he had found, but he had been unlucky. If he had persisted through the swamps on the Lachlan, he would have soon reached the Murrumbidgee River, and if he had continued south he would also have reached it.

The following year, Oxley was sent to find the mouth of the Macquarie River, only to find that it too flowed through poor country and ended in great marshes. The party headed east to the coast, crossing the Liverpool Plains (which were to prove to be some of the best grazing land in the world), found a way across the Great Divide and followed the fertile Hastings Valley to the rivermouth, which Oxley named Port Macquarie. This country was much more promising.

In 1819 a route to Bathurst from Cow Pastures (around Camden) was found by Charles Throsby, thereby opening up the southern highlands to graziers, and James Meehan explored a route from the southern highlands to the coast near Jervis Bay, finding still more fertile land.

In 1824 the explorers Hume and Hovell, starting from near present-day Canberra, made the first overland journey southwards, reaching the western shores of Port Phillip Bay. On the way they discovered a large river and named it after Hume, although it was later renamed the Murray by another great explorer, Charles Sturt. By 1830, Sturt had established that the Murrumbidgee and Darling River systems tied in with the Murray, and had followed the Murray to its mouth, finally dispelling the inland sea theory.

From 1831 to 1836 the colony's surveyor-general, Major Mitchell, conducted some extensive explorations of the Murray, Murrumbidgee and Darling rivers.

By now the general layout of present-day New South Wales was understood, and by the 1830s settlers with their herds and flocks eagerly followed the explorers' routes. The settlers often pushed into territory that was outside the defined 'limits of settlement', but the government inevitably expanded those limits in reaction to the new settlements.

Thanks to the Macarthurs' sheep-breeding experiments and the discovery of vast tracts of land beyond the Blue Mountains, the colony was increasingly seen as a promising place to make money. The British government and the wealthier colonials began to envisage a rich pastoral colony to which English society could be transplanted.

The increasing number of large landholders began to debate whether convicts (cheap but unreliable) or the free-born (good workers but uppity and expensive) made better farm labourers. Some demanded that more convicts should be sent, but a growing minority wanted an end to transportation altogether. This view eventually prevailed and the last ship bringing convicts to New South Wales arrived in 1848.

When Arthur Phillip arrived in 1788, New South Wales comprised about half of the continent and Tasmania. The western half of the continent (which became Western Australia after some shifting of borders) was claimed by Britain in 1829 and Tasmania became a separate colony in 1825. The mainland colonies were progressively carved from New South Wales – South Australia (1834), Victoria (1850) and Queensland (1859). From *being* Australia, New South Wales became one of several Australian colonies.

New South Wales was granted responsible government in 1855 and a couple of years later all males in the colony were given the vote. Women had to wait until 1902 before they were allowed to vote, but both men and women were given the vote here much earlier than in many other countries.

Gold!
The discovery of gold in the 1850s brought about the most significant changes in the social and economic structure of the colony.

The large quantities of gold found at Ophir (near Orange) in 1851 caused a rush of hopeful miners from Sydney, and for the rest of the century there were rushes throughout New South Wales and much of Australia. The influx of miners from around the world and the independence of life on the diggings swept away any hope of the Australian col-

onies remaining strictly controlled pastoral societies.

Besides the population and economic growth that came with the gold rushes, they also contributed greatly to the development of a distinctive Australian folklore. The music brought by the English and Irish, for instance, reflected life on the diggings, while poets, singers and writers began telling stories of the people, the roaring gold towns and the boisterous hotels, the squatters and their sheep and cattle stations, the swagmen, and the derring-do of the notorious bushrangers, many of whom became folk heroes.

Although few people actually made their fortunes on the goldfields, many stayed to settle the country, as farmers, workers and shopkeepers. At the same time, the Industrial Revolution in England produced a strong demand for raw materials. With the agricultural and mineral resources of such a vast country, Australia's economic base became secure.

The 20th Century

During the 1890s, calls for the separate colonies to federate became increasingly strident. Supporters argued that it would improve the economy (which was undergoing a severe depression – more than half of Sydney's banks folded in 1893) by removing intercolonial tariffs. Also, a sense of an Australian identity, spurred by painters and writers, had grown. Sydney was by now a vigorous city of nearly 500,000 people and a great port.

With Federation, which came about on 1 January 1901, New South Wales became a state of the new Australian nation. But Australia's loyalties and many of its legal ties to Britain remained. When WW I broke out in Europe, Australian troops were sent to fight in the trenches of France, the Gallipoli fiasco and the Middle East.

The site for Canberra, the new national capital, was chosen in 1908 (after much bickering between Sydney and Melbourne), and the Australian Capital Territory (ACT) was created in 1911. See the ACT chapter for the story of Canberra's development.

There was great economic expansion in the 1920s, but all this came to a halt with the Great Depression, which hit Australia hard. In 1931 almost a third of breadwinners were unemployed and poverty was widespread.

Sydney's population was approaching one million and conditions in the crowded inner suburbs were desperate. NSW premier Jack Lang ('the Big Fella') attempted to raise money to alleviate the suffering by defaulting on the state's loans from Britain. This made him enormously popular, but he was soon sacked as premier and expelled from the Labor party.

By 1932, however, the economy was starting to recover as a result of rises in wool prices and a rapid revival of manufacturing. With the opening of the Harbour Bridge in that same year, Sydney's building industry picked up again.

When WW II broke out, Australian troops again fought beside the British in Europe, but after the Japanese bombed Pearl Harbour Australia's own national security finally began to take priority. In May 1942, four midget Japanese submarines were destroyed in Sydney Harbour, and week later a Japanese submarine surfaced off the coast and lobbed shells into the suburbs of Bondi and Rose Bay. Australia's location in Asia, a long, long way from Europe, suddenly became frighteningly relevant. The Japanese advance was stopped by Australian and US forces in Papua New Guinea and ultimately it was the USA, not Britain, that helped protect Australia from the Japanese.

In the postwar years, construction boomed again in Sydney and the city spread west rapidly. The new immigration programmes brought growth and prosperity to Australia and living conditions improved.

Australia came to accept the US view that it was not so much Asia but *communism* in Asia that threatened the increasingly Americanised Australian way of life, so it was no surprise that in 1965 the conservative government committed troops to serve in the Vietnam War. As Prime Minister Holt said, it was 'all the way with LBJ'.

During the Vietnam War years, Sydney's

face changed as American GIs flooded the city for their R&R (rest and recreation) leave. Kings Cross flaunted its sleaziness – and the hippie and peace movements became established in Australia.

Support for involvement in Vietnam was far from absolute, and conscripting 18-year-olds to fight a foreign war troubled many Australians. Even during the two world wars Australians had voted to reject sending conscripts to foreign battlefields. Civil unrest eventually contributed to the rise to national power, in 1972, of the Australian Labor Party for the first time in 20 years. The Whitlam government withdrew Australian troops from Vietnam and instituted many reforms, such as free tertiary education and free universal health care.

Labor, however, was hampered by a hostile Senate and talk of mismanagement. On 11 November 1975, the governor general dismissed Parliament and installed a caretaker government led by the leader of the Opposition, Malcolm Fraser. Such action was unprecedented in the history of the Commonwealth of Australia, and the powers that the governor general had been able to invoke had long been regarded by many as an anachronistic vestige of Australia's now remote British past, the office itself as that of an impotent figurehead.

See the Politics Since Federation section in the ACT chapter for more on the Federal political scene.

In NSW, long years of conservative rule ended in 1976 with the election of Labor under Neville Wran. While conservative Prime Minister Malcolm Fraser was telling Australians that 'life wasn't meant to be easy', Wran was instituting reforms and presiding over the clean-up of a state that had been slipping into corruption. Wran left politics in 1986 and, without his charismatic presence, Labor lost the next election. Liberal premiers Nick Greiner and the current incumbent John Fahey have proved to be a lot less colourful than 'Nifty Nev' Wran, concentrating on balancing the budget. (John Fahey is, however, proving to be a dab hand at leaping – into the air when

Sydney was awarded the 2000 Olympics, and onto a man who fired a toy gun at Prince Charles in 1994.)

After the '80s boom, which saw a lot of development in Sydney, Australia found itself in recession again in the early '90s – which left some big holes in the ground in Sydney after construction projects folded. Unemployment was the highest it had been since the early 1930s, hundreds of farmers were being forced off the land because they couldn't keep up mortgage payments, there was a four-million-bale wool stockpile that no-one seemed to know how to shift, the building and manufacturing areas faced a huge slump and there was a general air of doom and gloom. The recession is now over, according to the government, but recovery will take some time.

An Australian Republic? One of the current issues being hotly debated is whether or not Australia should become a republic. Republican murmurings have always been a part of the political scene, but it was the Governor General's dismissal of the Whitlam government in 1975 which caused many people to take the idea seriously. In recent years the desire for change has become widespread.

It came as a shock to realise that the British monarch was the person who should open the Olympic Games in Sydney in the year 2000, as the British monarch is technically Australia's head of state. Many feel it would be fitting that the games be opened by the constitutional head of the new republic of Australia, especially as the games will be held just months before the country celebrates the centenary of its nationhood. The issue is far from decided but change seems inevitable.

Even if (or when) Australia becomes a republic, the country could and almost certainly would remain a member of the British Commonwealth, as is the case with the republic of India.

GEOGRAPHY
Australia is an island continent whose land-

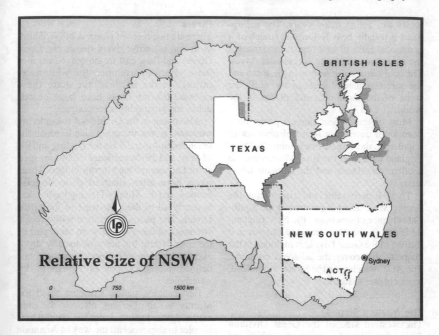

BRITISH ISLES

TEXAS

NEW SOUTH WALES

Sydney

ACT

Relative Size of NSW

0   750   1500 km

scape is the result of gradual changes wrought over millions of years. Although there is still seismic activity in the eastern and western highland areas, Australia is one of the most stable land masses and for about 100 million years has been free of the mountain-building forces that have given rise to huge ranges elsewhere.

There are four main areas of NSW, handily falling into an east-to-west pattern: the coastal strip, the Great Dividing Range, the western slopes and the western plains.

The Coast

The strip of land between the sea and the Great Divide runs from Tweed Heads on the Queensland border to Cape Howe on the Victorian border. The entire coast is lined with superb surf beaches and Australians' unflagging love-affair with The Beach has plenty of opportunity for consummation.

Right along the coast but especially in the southern half, there are many bays, lakes and meandering estuaries backing the beaches, offering more sedate swimming.

The coast and the eastern slopes of the Great Divide from Kiama to the Victorian border are covered in the South Coast chapter of this book; from Wollongong to Lake Macquarie in the Around Sydney chapter (Sydney's many fine beaches are covered in the Sydney chapter); and from Port Stephens to the Queensland border in the North Coast chapter.

The Great Dividing Range

This great mountain-range runs the length of Australia's east coast. In the south of NSW the range rears up to form the Snowy Mountains, with Australia's highest peak, Mt Kosciusko (2228 metres). The enormous Kosciusko National Park protects much of the Snowies.

The eastern side of the range tends to form an escarpment, such as the one which prevented the early colony from expanding

westwards for so many years. The escarpment is usually heavily forested (much of it is national parks or state forests) and most of the roads crossing it are spectacular drives. The cool-climate rainforests in the south and the subtropical rainforests in the north are some of the most beautiful places in the world.

Most of the ancient range's peaks have been worn down to a series of plateaux or tablelands, the largest ones being the New England tableland, the Blue Mountains, the southern highlands and the Monaro tableland.

The Monaro tableland (including the Snowy Mountains) is covered in the South-East chapter of this book, the New England tableland in the New England chapter and the rest of the Great Divide is included in the chapters that cover the adjacent coastline. The ACT, which is on the Monaro tableland, has a chapter to itself.

The Western Slopes

The western side of the Great Dividing Range dwindles into a series of foothills and valleys which provide some of the most fertile farmland in the country.

The South-East chapter of this book covers the slopes to the west of the alps; the Central West, New England and North-West chapters cover the rest of the western slopes.

The Western Plains

The western slopes of the Great Divide peter out about 300 km inland from the coast, and from here west the state is almost entirely flat, with only the odd undulation and hill (generally honoured with the title of 'mountain') to break the huge horizon. Right on the western edge of NSW, Broken Hill sits at the end of a long, low range which juts into the state from South Australia and is rich with minerals.

North of the Darling River, which cuts diagonally across the plains, the country takes on the red soil of the outback.

The Far West and Riverina chapters of this book cover the western plains.

Rivers

There are two types of rivers in NSW. Short, swift and bountiful rivers rise in the Great Divide and flow east to the sea. Several of these offer opportunities for whitewater rafting. In the north of the state these eastward-flowing rivers have large coastal deltas and are mighty watercourses.

Also rising in the Divide but meandering westward across the dry plains to reach the sea in South Australia are the Darling and the Murray, and their significant tributaries such as the Lachlan and the Murrumbidgee. These rivers have often changed their sluggish courses, and the Murray-Darling basin takes in nearly all of the state west of the Great Divide. The plains are riddled with creeks, swamps and lakes which were once part of the river system but are now usually dry – except when they are in flood. Someone once defined an outback river as 'a chain of dry waterholes'.

Last century, paddle-steamers plied the Murray and the Darling, offering the only easy access to the interior of the state. It was simpler to ship wool all the way to Adelaide than to haul it across the Great Divide to ports in NSW.

Many early European explorers set out on expeditions to find where the inland rivers entered the sea. Their westward tendency led to the theory that the centre of the continent was a vast inland sea. The reality, a huge, harsh desert, seems to mock these hopes, but in prehistoric times much of Australia was at least a wetland, if not a sea. In the west of NSW people lived in a lush Eden of lakes and rivers. These slowly dried with the changing climate, but the evidence of 40,000 years of continuous occupation by an incredibly adaptive civilisation can be seen at Mungo and other places.

Land Use

Most of the state is farmland, much of it pretty marginal. By the mid-19th century sheep-farming had been at least attempted throughout the entire state, with ponderous bullock wagons hauling the wool clip across hundreds of km of tough country to river

ports such as Bourke, Wilcannia and Hay. Today there are still sheep stations in the most unlikely terrain.

There has been a lot of diversification since then, with wheat, rice, cotton and beef becoming important export products. The wide range of climates means that just about every fruit and vegetable imaginable is grown here.

Despite the wholesale clearing of forests (until recently, 'improved land' was land where all the trees had been cut down), the economic importance of native timber was recognised fairly early and the Forestry Commission was allocated vast tracts of forest. Many state forests have since become national parks.

Most of the dense forest is in the Great Divide, partly because there was less incentive to clear such steep country for sheep stations, and partly because that's where much of the forest was in the first place.

CLIMATE

As Australia is in the southern hemisphere, its seasons are the antithesis of those in Europe and North America. It's hot in December and many people spend Christmas at the beach, while in July and August it's midwinter. Summer starts in December, autumn in March, winter in June and spring in September.

The climate in NSW varies depending on where you are, but the rule of thumb is that the further north you go the warmer it will be. Geographical factors tend to make it hotter (and drier) the further west you are.

Although there's more likelihood of cloudy weather in midwinter, rainfall is generally sparse and unpredictable.

Finally there was a few spots of rain, so we thought 'bugger it' and we harrowed and sowed. We was sending dust up to 30,000 feet. We might get a crop and we might be just feeding the bloody galahs. Who knows?

Riverina farmer in a dry autumn

Sydney is blessed with a temperate climate. The temperature rarely falls below 10°C except overnight in the middle of winter and,

although temperatures can hit 40°C during summer, the average summer maximum is a pleasant 25°C. Average monthly rainfall ranges from 75 mm to 130 mm. However, torrential downpours are not uncommon, especially from October to March. When it's hot and the humidity skyrockets, the climate can become quite oppressive, day and night.

Canberra suffers the more extreme climate of the high country, with deep frosts and some snow in winter, and baking days in summer. Spring and autumn are the best times to visit the national capital.

Summer

The whole state is hot, with temperatures rising above 40°C in the north-west corner, and not much less on the rest of the baking plains. The air quivers and shakes above the boiling horizon, and mirages are common. Bourke holds the record for the state's highest recorded temperature, a blistering 51.7°C in the shade (that's 125° F) and shares an old record of 37 consecutive days over 100°F (38°C). Tibooburra, in the north-western corner, is regarded as the state's hottest town. Of course, there are a lot of empty spaces in the far west, and who knows how hot it gets out there?

Luckily, the places with extreme temperatures are also very dry, and the heat can be bearable if you drink lots of water – without water, the heat quickly becomes life-threatening. If you're travelling in remote regions you *must* carry water.

In the Great Divide, the days can be hot but the nights are often pleasantly cool. Summer on the south coast is as hot as you could want for a seaside holiday, but when a cool change arrives the temperature drops lower than it would on the north coast. Sydney and the north coast can be humid, with spectacular thunderstorms. Although you get the odd very hot day, coastal temperatures are usually below the mid-30s.

Autumn

In the Great Divide and the southern parts of the western slopes, the days become cool, deciduous trees turn red and gold, and the

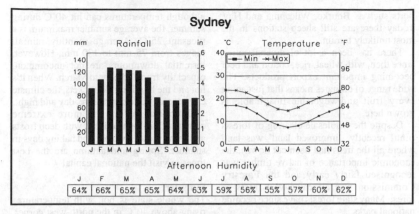

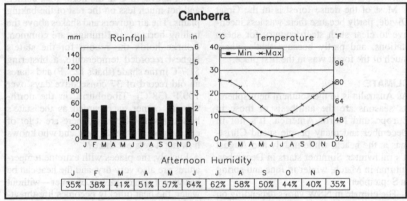

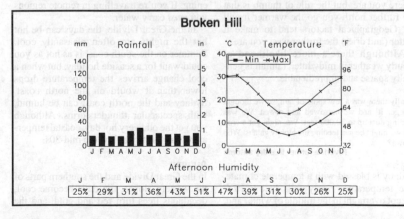

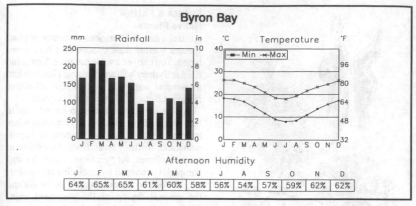

Byron Bay

Rainfall (mm / in)

Temperature (°C / °F) — Min / Max

Afternoon Humidity

J	F	M	A	M	J	J	A	S	O	N	D
64%	65%	65%	61%	60%	58%	56%	54%	57%	59%	62%	62%

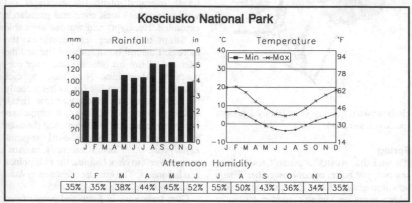

Kosciusko National Park

Rainfall (mm / in)

Temperature (°C / °F) — Min / Max

Afternoon Humidity

J	F	M	A	M	J	J	A	S	O	N	D
35%	35%	38%	44%	45%	52%	55%	50%	43%	36%	34%	35%

clear nights often bring frosts. In Sydney the humidity recedes and the warm, clear days make this an ideal time to visit. Fewer swimmers each day venture into the water along the south coast, but in the north it's only the locals who find that the beach is becoming too cool. The water temperature stays quite warm until the beginning of winter.

Winter

Temperatures in the far west drop to a comfortable level and the skies are often blue and clear. There can be frosts at night out on the plains, but this is the best time to visit the outback.

Up on the Great Divide it's becoming decidedly chilly, with heavy frosts and occasional snowfalls, but it's only in the Snowy Mountains that the snow accumulates and offers skiing.

Sydney slips into winter gradually, with sometimes gloomy weather in June and July but nothing like a dismal European (or Melbourne) winter. Most Sydneysiders muffle themselves in scarves, gloves and overcoats and complain about the cold, but there are a few hardy souls who wear shorts all year round. Unless you come from a hot climate you might want to emulate them. Still, if you've arrived with nothing else but beach

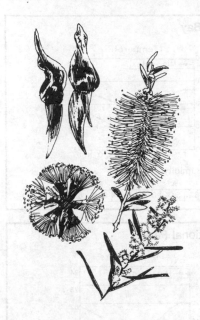

clothes you'll quickly want to buy a jumper (pullover, sweater).

Spring

It's said that Australia doesn't really have seasons, just hotter or cooler weather. That's how it might seem to a European sensibility which relies on spring's sudden bloom to wipe out the memory of a miserable winter, but you don't have to look hard to be aware of the year's turning in NSW. After the warm spring rains on the plains, carpets of flowers emerge among the tall grasses, and on the north coast the frangipani blooms. Animals, birds and insects burst into frenetic activity – and snakes sun themselves after their winter hibernation. The wattle blooms, and in the old towns of the Great Divide and the Central West, deciduous trees put on their new leaves.

In the north, spring is well underway by September, and by the end of October the far west is becoming uncomfortably hot. On the ranges the cool nights linger and pockets of snow remain in the Snowy Mountains.

FLORA & FAUNA
Native Plants

Australia has an enormous diversity of plant species – more than Europe and Asia combined. You can see a wide range of Australian flora at Sydney's Royal Botanic Gardens and its several outposts, and at the all-native National Botanic Gardens in Canberra.

Australia's distinctive vegetation began to take shape about 55 million years ago when it broke from the supercontinent of Gondwanaland, drifting away from Antarctica to warmer climes. At this time, Australia was completely covered by cool-climate rainforest, but due to its geographic isolation and the gradual drying of the continent, rainforests retreated, plants like eucalypts and wattles (acacias) took over and grasslands expanded. Eucalypts and wattles were able to adapt to warmer temperatures, the increased natural occurrence of fire and the later use of fire for hunting and other purposes by Aborigines. Now many species actually benefit from fire (or, as has recently been discovered, from the smoke from fires).

The gum tree, or eucalypt, is ubiquitous except in the deepest rainforests and the most arid regions. Of the 700 species of the genus *Eucalyptus*, 95% occur naturally in Australia, the rest in New Guinea, the Philippines and Indonesia. The gum tree features in Australian folklore, art and literature.

Gum trees vary in form and height from the tall, straight hardwoods such as mountain ash *(Eucalyptus regnans)* and river red-gum *(E. camaldulensis)* to the stunted, twisted snow gum *(E. pauciflora)* with its colourful trunk striations. Other distinctive gums are the spotted gum *(E. maculata)* of NSW's coast; the scribbly gum *(E. haemastoma)*, which has scribbly insect tracks on its bark; and the ghost gum *(E. papuana)*, with its distinctive white trunk. Many varieties flower, the wood is prized and its oil is used for pharmaceutical and perfumed products.

Fast-growing but short-lived wattles occur in many warm countries, but around 600 species are found in Australia. Many wattles have deep green leaves and bright yellow to orange flowers. Most species

flower during late winter and spring. Then, the country is ablaze with wattle and the reason for the choice of green and gold as our national colours is obvious. Wattle is Australia's floral emblem.

Other common natives include grevilleas, hakeas, banksias, waratahs (telopeas), bottlebrushes (callistemons), paperbarks (melaleucas), tea-trees (leptospermums), boronias, and native pines (casuarinas).

Animals

The native animals you're most likely to see in the wild are wallabies and kangaroos, possums and koalas. However, that doesn't mean that there isn't a huge range of small, mainly nocturnal animals going about their business unobserved. Part of the reason for Australia's appalling record of animal extinction is that many species died out before anyone (anyone European, that is) knew that they were there. This process continues today.

Australia's most distinctive fauna are the marsupials and monotremes. Marsupials such as kangaroos and koalas give birth to partially developed young which they suckle in a pouch. Monotremes – platypuses and

Wallaby

echidnas – lay eggs but also suckle their young.

If you find an injured native animal, there are usually people nearby who can take care of it – see the Useful Organisations section of the Facts for the Visitor chapter.

Kangaroos The extraordinary breeding cycle of the kangaroo is well adapted to Australia's harsh, often unpredictable environment.

The young kangaroo, or joey, just millimetres long at birth, claws its way unaided to the mother's pouch where it attaches itself to a nipple that expands inside its mouth. A day or two later the mother mates again, but the new embryo does not begin to develop until the first joey has left the pouch permanently.

At this point the mother produces two types of milk – one formula to feed the joey at heel, the other for the baby in her pouch. If environmental conditions are right, the mother will then mate again. If food or water is scarce, however, the breeding cycle will be interrupted until conditions improve.

As well as many species of wallabies (some endangered), there are two main species of kangaroos in NSW, the western grey and the majestic red kangaroo, which is common in the far west and can stand two metres tall. Unlike most cute kangaroos, the red has a facial expression which suggests that it don't take no aggravation. Reds have been known to disembowel or drown dogs that are bothering them.

Possums There is a wide range of possums – they seem to have been able to adapt to all sorts of conditions, including those of the city, where you'll find them in parks, sometimes tame enough to eat from your hand. Look for them at dusk. Some large species are found in suburban roofs and will eat cultivated plants and food scraps. If you're camping, the weird noises that squabbling possums make can be spooky.

Wombats Wombats are slow, solid, powerfully built marsupials with broad heads and

Wombat

short, stumpy legs. These fairly placid and easily tamed creatures are legally killed by farmers, who object to the damage done to paddocks by wombats digging large burrows and tunnelling under fences.

Koalas The koala is distantly related to the wombat, and koalas are found along the eastern seaboard. Their cuddly appearance belies an irritable nature, and they will scratch and bite if sufficiently provoked.

Koalas initially carry their babies in pouches, but later the larger young cling to their mothers' backs. They feed only on the leaves of certain types of eucalypt (found mainly in the forests of the Great Dividing Range) and are particularly sensitive to changes to their habitat.

Platypuses & Echidnas The platypus and the echidna are the only living representatives of the monotremes, the most primitive group of mammals. Both lay eggs, as reptiles do, but suckle their young on milk secreted directly through the skin from mammary glands.

The amphibious platypus has a duck-like bill, webbed feet and a beaver-like body. Males have poisonous spurs on their hind feet. The platypus is able to sense electric currents in the water and uses this ability to track its prey. Platypuses are very shy creatures, but they occur in many rivers.

The echidna is a spiny anteater that hides from predators by digging vertically into the ground and covering itself with dirt, or by rolling itself into a ball and raising its sharp quills.

Dingoes Australia's native dog is the dingo, domesticated by the Aborigines and a stable breed for at least 3000 years, possibly much longer. Its ancestor is the Indian wolf. After the Europeans arrived and Aborigines could no longer hunt freely, dingoes again became 'wild', and by preying on sheep they earned the wrath of graziers. These sensitive, intelligent dogs are legally considered to be vermin. Some are still found in the high country.

Birds

Emus The only bird larger than the emu is the African ostrich, also flightless. The emu is a shaggy-feathered bird with an often curious nature. After the female emu lays the eggs, the male hatches them and raises the young. Emus are common in the Riverina and the far west.

Parrots & Cockatoos There is an amazing variety of these birds. The noisy pink and grey galahs are among the most common, although the sulphur-crested cockatoos have to be the noisiest. Rainbow lorikeets have one of the most brilliant colour schemes and in some parks they're not at all backward about taking a free feed from visitors.

Kookaburras A member of the kingfisher family, the kookaburra is heard as much as it is seen – you can't miss its loud, cackling laugh, usually at dawn and sunset. Kookaburras can become quite tame and pay regular visits to friendly households.

Lyrebirds The lyrebird, found in moist forest areas, is famous for both its vocal abilities and its beauty. Lyrebirds are highly skilled mimics which copy segments of other birds' songs to create unique hybrid compositions. During the courting season, with his colourful fern-like tailfeathers spread like a fan, the male puts on a sensational song-and-dance routine to impress potential partners.

Mail Order

Lonely Planet guidebooks are distributed worldwide. They are also available by mail order from Lonely Planet, so if you have difficulty finding a title please write to us. US and Canadian residents should write to Embarcadero West, 155 Filbert St, Suite 251, Oakland CA 94607, USA; European residents should write to 10 Barley Mow Passage, Chiswick, London W4 4PH; and residents of other countries to PO Box 617, Hawthorn, Victoria 3122, Australia.

Indian Subcontinent
Bangladesh
India
Hindi/Urdu phrasebook
Trekking in the Indian Himalaya
Karakoram Highway
Kashmir, Ladakh & Zanskar
Nepal
Trekking in the Nepal Himalaya
Nepali phrasebook
Pakistan
Sri Lanka
Sri Lanka phrasebook

Africa
Africa on a shoestring
Central Africa
East Africa
Trekking in East Africa
Kenya
Swahili phrasebook
Morocco, Algeria & Tunisia
Arabic (Moroccan) phrasebook
South Africa, Lesotho & Swaziland
Zimbabwe, Botswana & Namibia
West Africa

Central America & the Caribbean
Baja California
Central America on a shoestring
Costa Rica
Eastern Caribbean
Guatemala, Belize & Yucatán: La Ruta Maya
Mexico

North America
Alaska
Canada
Hawaii

Europe
Baltic States & Kaliningrad
Dublin city guide
Eastern Europe on a shoestring
Eastern Europe phrasebook
Finland
France
Greece
Hungary
Iceland, Greenland & the Faroe Islands
Ireland
Italy
Mediterranean Europe on a shoestring
Mediterranean Europe phrasebook
Poland
Scandinavian & Baltic Europe on a shoestring
Scandinavian Europe phrasebook
Switzerland
Trekking in Spain
Trekking in Greece
USSR
Russian phrasebook
Western Europe on a shoestring
Western Europe phrasebook

South America
Argentina, Uruguay & Paraguay
Bolivia
Brazil
Brazilian phrasebook
Chile & Easter Island
Colombia
Ecuador & the Galápagos Islands
Latin American Spanish phrasebook
Peru
Quechua phrasebook
South America on a shoestring
Trekking in the Patagonian Andes
Venezuela

The Lonely Planet Story

Lonely Planet published its first book in 1973 in response to the numerous 'How did you do it?' questions Maureen and Tony Wheeler were asked after driving, bussing, hitching, sailing and railing their way from England to Australia.

Written at a kitchen table and hand collated, trimmed and stapled, *Across Asia on the Cheap* became an instant local bestseller, inspiring thoughts of another book.

Eighteen months in South-East Asia resulted in their second guide, *South-East Asia on a shoestring*, which they put together in a backstreet Chinese hotel in Singapore in 1975. The 'yellow bible' as it quickly became known to backpackers around the world, soon became *the* guide to the region. It has sold well over half a million copies and is now in its 8th edition, still retaining its familiar yellow cover.

Today there are over 140 Lonely Planet titles in print – books that have that same adventurous approach to travel as those early guides; books that 'assume you know how to get your luggage off the carousel' as one reviewer put it.

Although Lonely Planet initially specialised in guides to Asia, they now cover most regions of the world, including the Pacific, South America, Africa, the Middle East and Europe. The list of *walking guides* and *phrasebooks* (for 'unusual' languages such as Quechua, Swahili, Nepali and Egyptian Arabic) is also growing rapidly.

The emphasis continues to be on travel for independent travellers. Tony and Maureen still travel for several months of each year and play an active part in the writing, updating and quality control of Lonely Planet's guides.

They have been joined by over 50 authors, 90 staff – mainly editors, cartographers & designers – at our office in Melbourne, Australia, at our US office in Oakland, California and at our European office in Paris; another five at our office in London handle sales for Britain, Europe and Africa. Travellers themselves also make a valuable contribution to the guides through the feedback we receive in thousands of letters each year.

The people at Lonely Planet strongly believe that travellers can make a positive contribution to the countries they visit, both through their appreciation of the countries' culture, wildlife and natural features, and through the money they spend. In addition, the company makes a direct contribution to the countries and regions it covers. Since 1986 a percentage of the income from each book has been donated to ventures such as famine relief in Africa; aid projects in India; agricultural projects in Central America; Greenpeace's efforts to halt French nuclear testing in the Pacific and Amnesty International. In 1993 $100,000 was donated to such causes.

Lonely Planet's basic travel philosophy is summed up in Tony Wheeler's comment, 'Don't worry about whether your trip will work out. Just go!'.